CHEVROLET | CHEVY/OLDS/PONTIAC APVs 1990-91 REPAIR MANUAL

CHILTON'S

President	Gary R. Ingersoll
Senior Vice President	Ronald A. Hoxter
Publisher	Kerry A. Freeman, S.A.E.
Editor-In-Chief	Dean F. Morgantini, S.A.E.
Managing Editor	David H. Lee, A.S.E., S.A.E.
Manager of Manufacturing	John J. Cantwell
Production Manager	W. Calvin Settle, Jr., S.A.E.
Senior Editor	Richard J. Rivele, S.A.E.
Senior Editor	Nick D'Andrea
Senior Editor	Ron Webb
Editor	Martin J. Gunther

CHILTON BOOK COMPANY

ONE OF THE **ABC PUBLISHING COMPANIES,**
A PART OF **CAPITAL CITIES/ABC, INC.**

Manufactured in USA
© 1991 Chilton Book Company
Chilton Way, Radnor, PA 19089
ISBN 0–8019–8134–4
Library of Congress Catalog Card No. 90–056125
1234567890   0987654321

Contents

Contents

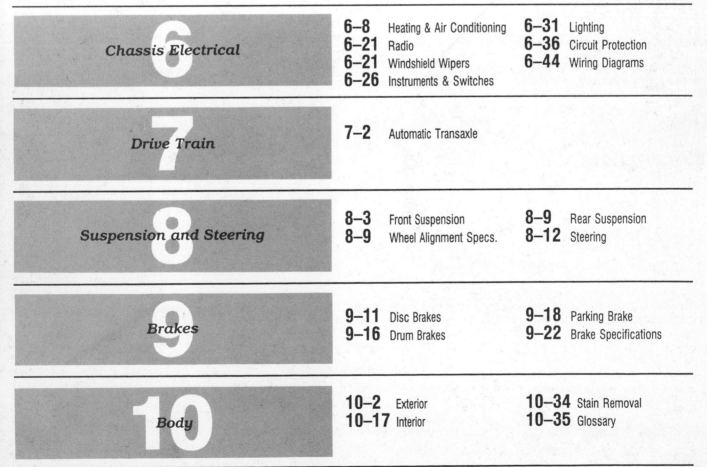

SAFETY NOTICE

Proper service and repair procedures are vital to the safe, reliable operation of all motor vehicles, as well as the personal safety of those performing repairs. This manual outlines procedures for servicing and repairing vehicles using safe, effective methods. The procedures contain many NOTES, CAUTIONS and WARNINGS which should be followed along with standard safety procedures to eliminate the possibility of personal injury or improper service which could damage the vehicle or compromise its safety.

It is important to note that the repair procedures and techniques, tools and parts for servicing motor vehicles, as well as the skill and experience of the individual performing the work vary widely. It is not possible to anticipate all of the conceivable ways or conditions under which vehicles may be serviced, or to provide cautions as to all of the possible hazards that may result. Standard and accepted safety precautions and equipment should be used when handling toxic or flammable fluids, and safety goggles or other protection should be used during cutting, grinding, chiseling, prying, or any other process that can cause material removal or projectiles.

Some procedures require the use of tools specially designed for a specific purpose. Before substituting another tool or procedure, you must be completely satisfied that neither your personal safety, nor the performance of the vehicle will be endangered

Although information in this manual is based on industry sources and is complete as possible at the time of publication, the possibility exists that some car manufacturers made later changes which could not be included here. While striving for total accuracy, Chilton Book Company cannot assume responsibility for any errors, changes or omissions that may occur in the compilation of this data.

PART NUMBERS

Part numbers listed in this reference are not recommendations by Chilton for any product by brand name. They are references that can be used with interchange manuals and aftermarket supplier catalogs to locate each brand supplier's discrete part number.

SPECIAL TOOLS

Special tools are recommended by the vehicle manufacturer to perform their specific job. Use has been kept to a minimum, but where absolutely necessary, they are referred to in the text by the part number of the tool manufacturer. These tools can be purchased under the appropriate part number, from your Chevrolet, Oldsmobile or Pontiac dealer or regional distributor or an equivalent tool can be purchased locally from a tool supplier or parts outlet. Before substituting any tool for the recommended one, read the SAFETY NOTICE at the top of this page.

ACKNOWLEDGMENTS

The Chilton Book Company expresses its appreciation to General Motors Corporation, Detroit, Michigan for their generous assistance.

General Information and Maintenance

1

QUICK REFERENCE INDEX

GENERAL INDEX

HOW TO USE THIS BOOK

Chilton's Total Car Care Manual for 1990–91 Chevrolet Lumina APV, Oldsmobile Silhouette and Pontiac Trans Sport is intended to help you learn more about the inner workings of your vehicle and save you money on its upkeep and operation.

The first two sections will be the most used, since they contain maintenance and tune-up information and procedures. Studies have shown that a properly tuned and maintained van can get at least 10% better gas mileage (which translates into lower operating costs) and periodic maintenance will catch minor problems before they turn into major repair bills. The other sections deal with the more complex systems of your van. Operating systems from engine through brakes are covered. It will give you the detailed instructions to help you change your own brake pads and shoes, tune-up the engine, replace spark plugs and filters, and do many more jobs that will save you money, give you personal satisfaction and help you avoid expensive problems.

A secondary purpose of this book is a reference guide for owners who want to understand their van and/or their mechanics better. In this case, no tools at all are required. Knowing just what a particular repair job requires in parts and labor time will allow you to evaluate whether or not you're getting a fair price quote and help decipher itemized bills from a repair shop.

Before attempting any repairs or service on your van, read through the entire procedure outlined in the appropriate chapter. This will give you the overall view of what tools and supplies will be required. There is nothing more frustrating than having to walk to the bus stop on Monday morning because you were short one gasket on Sunday afternoon. So read ahead and plan ahead. Each operation should be approached logically and all procedures thoroughly understood before attempting any work. Some special tools that may be required can often be rented from local automotive jobbers or places specializing in renting tools and equipment. Check the yellow pages of your phone book.

All sections contain adjustments, maintenance, removal and installation procedures, and overhaul procedures. When overhaul is not considered practical, we tell you how to remove the failed part and then how to install the new or rebuilt replacement. In this way, you at least save the labor costs. Backyard overhaul of some components (such as the alternator or water pump) is just not practical, but the removal and installation procedure is often simple and well within the capabilities of the average van owner.

Two basic mechanic's rules should be mentioned here. First, whenever the LEFT side of the van or engine is referred to, it is meant to specify the DRIVER'S side of the van. Conversely, the RIGHT side of the van means the PASSENGER'S side. Second, all screws and bolts are removed by turning counterclockwise, and tightened by turning clockwise, unless otherwise noted.

Safety is always the most important rule. Constantly be aware of the dangers involved in working on or around an automobile and take proper precautions to avoid the risk of personal injury or damage to the vehicle. See the section in this section, Servicing Your Vehicle Safely, and the SAFETY NOTICE on the acknowledgment page before attempting any service procedures and pay attention to the instructions provided. There are 3 common mistakes in mechanical work:

1. Incorrect order of assembly, disassembly or adjustment. When taking something apart or putting it together, doing things in the wrong order usually just costs you extra time; however it CAN break something. Read the entire procedure before beginning disassembly. Do everything in the order in which the instructions say you should do it, even if you can't immediately see a reason for it. When you're taking apart something that is very intricate (for example, a throttle body), you might want to draw a picture of how it looks when assembled at one point in order to make sure you get everything back in its proper position. We will supply exploded views whenever possible, but sometimes the job requires more attention to detail than an illustration provides. When making adjustments (especially tune-up adjustments), do them in order. One adjustment often affects another and you cannot expect satisfactory results unless each adjustment is made only when it cannot be changed by any other.

2. Overtorquing (or undertorquing) nuts and bolts. While it is more common for overtorquing to cause damage, undertorquing can cause a fastener to vibrate loose and cause serious damage, especially when dealing with aluminum parts. Pay attention to torque specifications and utilize a torque wrench in assembly. If a torque figure is not available remember that, if you are using the right tool to do the job, you will probably not have to strain yourself to get a fastener tight enough. The pitch of most threads is so slight that the tension you put on the wrench will be multiplied many times in actual force on what you are tightening. A good example of how critical torque is can be seen in the case of spark plug installation, especially where you are putting the plug into an aluminum cylinder head. Too little torque can fail to crush the gasket, causing leakage of combustion gases and consequent overheating of the plug and engine parts. Too much torque can damage the threads or distort the plug, which changes the spark gap at the electrode. Since more and more manufacturers are using aluminum in their engine and chassis parts to save weight, a torque wrench should be in any serious do-it-yourselfer's tool box.

There are many commercial chemical products available for ensuring that fasteners won't come loose, even if they are not torqued just right (a very common brand is Loctite®). If you're worried about getting something together tight enough to hold, but loose enough to avoid mechanical damage during assembly, one of these products might offer substantial insurance. Read the label on the package and make sure the product is compatible with the materials, fluids, etc. involved before choosing one.

3. Crossthreading. This occurs when a part such as a bolt is screwed into a nut or casting at the wrong angle and forced, causing the threads to become damaged. Crossthreading is more likely to occur if access is difficult. It helps to clean and lubricate fasteners, and to start threading with the part to be installed going straight in, using your fingers. If you encounter resistance, unscrew the part and start over again at a different angle until it can be inserted and turned several times without much effort. Keep in mind that many parts, especially spark plugs, use tapered threads so that gentle turning will automatically bring the part you're threading to the proper angle if you don't force it or resist a change in angle. Don't put a wrench on the part until it's been turned in a couple of times by hand. If you suddenly encounter resistance and the part has not seated fully, don't force it. Pull it back out and make sure it's clean and threading properly.

Always take your time and be patient; once you have some experience, working on your van will become an enjoyable hobby.

TOOLS AND EQUIPMENT

Naturally, without the proper tools and equipment it is impossible to properly service your vehicle. It would be impossible to catalog each tool that you would need to perform each or every operation in this book. It would also be unwise for the amateur to rush out and buy an expensive set of tools an the theory that he may need one or more of them at sometime.

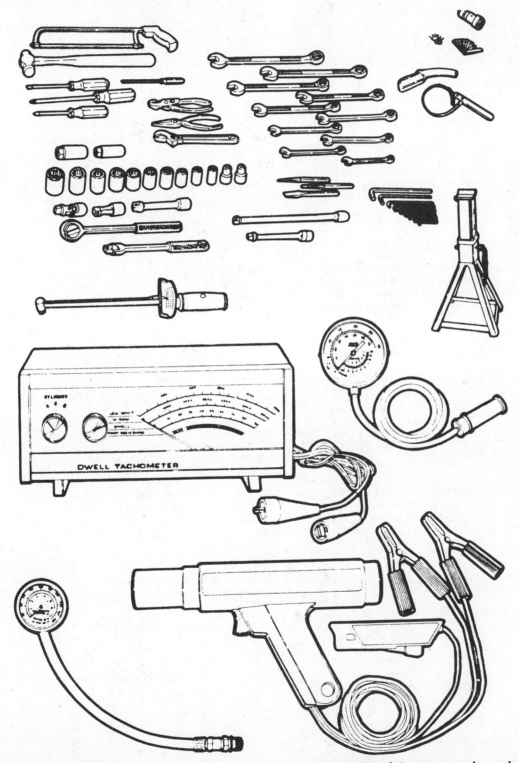

You need only a basic assortment of hand tools for most maintenance and repair jobs

The best approach is to proceed slowly, gathering together a good quality set of those tools that are used most frequently. Don't be misled by the low cost of bargain tools. It is far better to spend a little more for better quality. Forged wrenches, 6- or 12-point sockets and fine tooth ratchets are by far preferable to their less expensive counterparts. As any good mechanic can tell you, there are few worse experiences than trying to work on a van with bad tools. Your monetary savings will be far outweighed by frustration and mangled knuckles.

Certain tools, plus a basic ability to handle tools, are required to get started. A basic mechanics tool set, a torque wrench, and, a Torx® bits set. Torx® bits are hexagon drivers which fit both inside and outside on special Torx® head fasteners used in various places.

Begin accumulating those tools that are used most frequently; those associated with routine maintenance and tune-up.

In addition to the normal assortment of screwdrivers and pliers you should have the following tools for routine maintenance jobs (your van uses metric fasteners):

1. Metric wrenches, sockets and combination open end/box end wrenches in sizes from 3mm to 19mm, and a spark plug socket ($^{13}/_{16}$ in.) If possible, buy various length socket drive extensions. One break in this department is that the metric sockets available in the U.S. will all fit the ratchet handles and extensions you may already have (¼ in., ⅜ in., and ½ in. drive).

2. One set of metric combination (one end open and one end box) wrenches.

3. Wire-type spark plug feeler gauge.

4. Blade-type feeler gauges.

5. Slot and Phillips head screwdrivers in various sizes.

6. Oil filter strap wrench, necessary for removing oil filters (never used, though, for installing the filters).

7. Funnel, for pouring fresh oil or automatic transaxle fluid from quart oil bottles.

8. Pair of slip-lock pliers.

9. Pair of vise-type pliers.

10. Adjustable wrench.

11. A hydraulic floor jack of at least 1½ ton capacity. If you are serious about maintaining your own van, then a floor jack is as necessary as a spark plug socket. The greatly increased utility, strength, and safety of a hydraulic floor jack makes it pay for itself many times over through the years.

12. At least 4 sturdy jackstands for working underneath the van. Any other type of support (bricks, wood and especially cinderblocks) is just plain dangerous.

13. An inductive timing light.

In addition to the above items there are several others that are not absolutely necessary, but handy to have around. These include oil-dry (cat box litter works just as well and may be cheaper), a transaxle funnel and the usual supply of lubricants, antifreeze and fluids, although these can be purchased as needed. This is a basic list for routine maintenance, but only your personal needs and desires can accurately determine your list of necessary tools.

This is an adequate set of tools, and the more work you do yourself on your van, the larger you'll find the set growing — a pair of pliers here, a wrench or two there. It makes more sense to have a comprehensive set of basic tools as listed above, and then to acquire more along the line as you need them, than to go out and plunk down big money for a professional size set you may never use. In addition to these basic tools, there are several other tools and gauges you may find useful.

1. A compression gauge. The screw-in type is slower to use but it eliminates the possibility of a faulty reading due to escaping pressure.

2. A manifold vacuum gauge, very useful in troubleshooting ignition and emissions problems.

3. A drop light, to light up the work area (make sure yours is UL approved, and has a shielded bulb).

4. A volt/ohm meter (multi-tester). These are handy for use if a wire is broken somewhere and are especially necessary for working on today's electronics-laden vehicles.

As a final note, you will probably find a torque wrench necessary for all but the most basic work. The beam type models are perfectly adequate, although the newer click (breakaway) type are more precise, and you don't have to crane your neck to see a torque reading in awkward situations. The breakaway torque wrenches are more expensive and should be recalibrated periodically.

Torque specification for each fastener will be given in the procedure in any case that a specific torque value is required. If no torque specifications are given, use the following values as a guide, based upon fastener size:

Bolts marked 6T
6mm bolt/nut — 5–7 ft. lbs. (9–10 Nm)
8mm bolt/nut — 12–17 ft. lbs. (15–22 Nm)
10mm bolt/nut — 23–34 ft. lbs. (26–47 Nm)
12mm bolt/nut — 41–59 ft. lbs. (54–81 Nm)
14mm bolt/nut — 56–76 ft. lbs. (74–102 Nm)

Bolts marked 8T
6mm bolt/nut — 6–9 ft. lbs. (8–13 Nm)

Special Tools

Normally, the use of special factory tools is avoided for repair procedures, since these are not readily available for the do-it-yourself mechanic. When it is possible to perform the job with more commonly available tools, it will be pointed out, but occasionally, a special tool was designed to perform a specific function and should be used. Before substituting another tool, you should be convinced that neither your safety nor the performance of the vehicle will be compromised.

Some special tools are available commercially from major tool manufacturers such as:
Kent-Moore
Service Tool Division
29784 Little Mack
Roseville, MI 48066–2298
Others can be purchased through your GM dealer.

SERVICING YOUR VAN SAFELY

It is virtually impossible to anticipate all of the hazards involved with automotive maintenance and service but care and common sense will prevent most accidents.

The rules of safety for mechanics range from "don't smoke around gasoline," to "use the proper tool for the job." The trick to avoiding injuries is to develop safe work habits and take every possible precaution.

Do's

● Do keep a fire extinguisher and first aid kit within easy reach.

● Do wear safety glasses or goggles when cutting, drilling, grinding or prying.

● Do shield your eyes whenever you work around the battery. Batteries contain sulphuric acid. In case of contact with the eyes or skin, flush the area with water or a mixture of water and baking soda and get medical attention immediately.

● Do use safety stands for any undervan service. Jacks are for raising vehicles; safety stands are for making sure the vehicle stays raised until you want it to come down. Whenever the vehicle is raised, block the wheels remaining on the ground and set the parking brake.

● Do disconnect the negative battery cable when working on the electrical system. The primary ignition system can contain up to 40,000 volts.

● Do properly maintain your tools. Loose hammerheads, mushroomed punches and chisels, frayed or poorly grounded electrical cords, excessively worn screwdrivers, spread wrenches (open end), cracked sockets, slipping ratchets, or faulty droplight sockets can cause accidents and injuries.

● Do use the proper size and type of tool for the job being done.

● Do, when possible, pull on a wrench handle rather than push on it, and adjust your stance to prevent a fall.

● Do be sure that adjustable wrenches are tightly adjusted on the nut or bolt and pulled so that the face is on the side of the fixed jaw.

● Do select a wrench or socket that fits the nut or bolt. The wrench or socket should sit straight, not cocked.

● Do strike squarely with a hammer—avoid glancing blows.

● Do set the parking brake and block the drive wheels if the work requires that the engine be running.

Don'ts

● Don't run an engine in a garage or anywhere else without

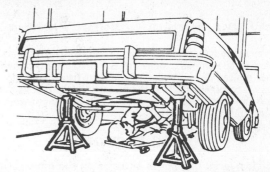

Always support the car securely with jackstands; never use cinder blocks or tire changing jacks

proper ventilation—EVER! Carbon monoxide is poisonous. It takes a long time to leave the human body and you can build up a deadly supply of it in your system by simply breathing in a little every day. Always use power vents, windows, fans or open the garage doors.

● Don't work around moving parts while wearing a necktie or other loose clothing. Short sleeves are much safer than long, loose sleeves and hard toed shoes with neoprene soles protect your toes and give a better grip on slippery surfaces. Jewelry is not safe when working around a car. Long hair should be hidden under a hat or cap.

● Don't use pockets for toolboxes. A fall or bump can drive a screwdriver deep into your body. Even a wiping cloth hanging from the back pocket can wrap around a spinning shaft or fan.

● Don't smoke when working around gasoline, cleaning solvent or other flammable material.

● Don't smoke when working around the battery. When the battery is being charged, it gives off explosive hydrogen gas.

● Don't use gasoline to wash your hands. There are excellent soaps available. Gasoline may contain lead, and lead can enter the body through a cut, accumulating in the body until you are very ill. Gasoline also removes all the natural oils from the skin so that bone dry hands will absorb oil and grease.

● Don't service the air conditioning system unless you are equipped with the necessary tools and training. The refrigerant, R-12, is extremely cold and when exposed to the air, will instantly freeze any surface it comes in contact with, including your eyes. Although the refrigerant is normally non-toxic, R-12 becomes a deadly poisonous gas in the presence of an open flame. One good whiff of the vapors from burning refrigerant can be fatal.

HISTORY

The Lumina APV, Silhouette and Trans Sport belong to the carline U, an all-purpose mid-size van. The vehicle began in the 1990 model year. The van is constructed from a welded steel space frame covered with damage resistant composite panels.

SERIAL NUMBER IDENTIFICATION

Vehicle Identification Plate

The vehicle identification number is embossed on a plate, that is attached to the top left corner of the instrument panel. The number is visible through the windshield from the outside of the vehicle. The eighth digit of the number, indicates the engine model and the tenth digit represents the model year (example is **L** for 1990 and **M** for 1991).

Engine Number

The engine serial number is stamped on the top right front corner of the engine.

Transaxle Number

The transaxle number is stamped into the top of the case next to the valve body oil pan.

1. VIN location
2. Engine code location

EXAMPLE

K	05	15	XXX
ENGINE SOURCE	MONTH	DAY	ENGINE CODE

K - GM CANADA

3.1L engine number location

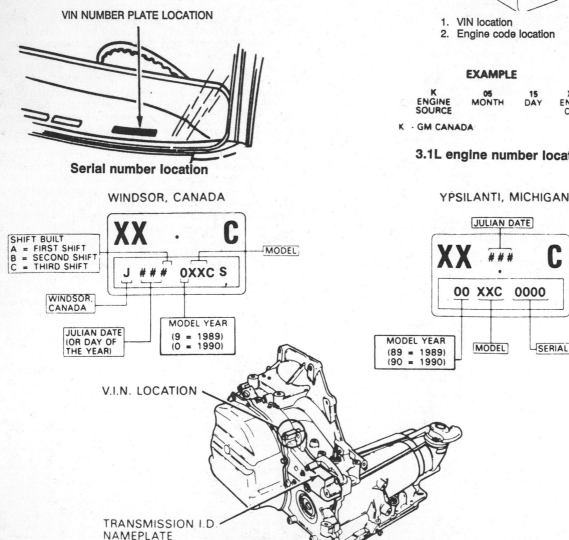

Serial number location

125C (3T40) automatic transaxle number location

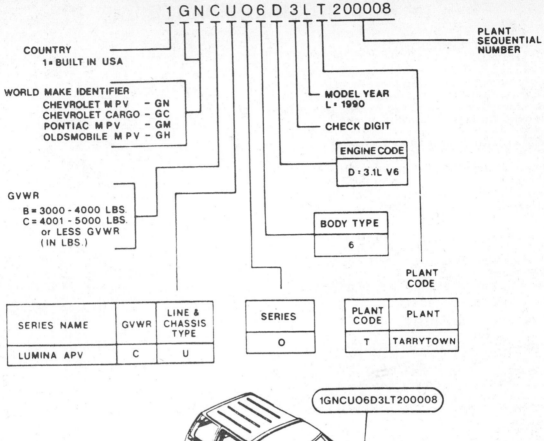

1 G N C U O 6 D 3 L T 200008

COUNTRY
1 = BUILT IN USA

WORLD MAKE IDENTIFIER
CHEVROLET M P V — GN
CHEVROLET CARGO — GC
PONTIAC M P V — GM
OLDSMOBILE M P V — GH

GVWR
B = 3000 - 4000 LBS.
C = 4001 - 5000 LBS.
or LESS GVWR
(IN LBS.)

PLANT
SEQUENTIAL
NUMBER

MODEL YEAR
L = 1990

CHECK DIGIT

ENGINE CODE

D = 3.1L V6

BODY TYPE

6

PLANT
CODE

SERIES NAME	GVWR	LINE & CHASSIS TYPE
LUMINA APV	C	U

SERIES
O

PLANT CODE	PLANT
T	TARRYTOWN

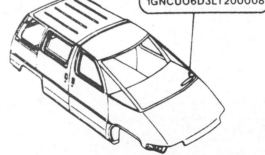

1GNCUO6D3LT200008

VIN (serial) number identification

ENGINE IDENTIFICATION CHART

Years	No. of Cylinders and Cu. In. Displacement	Actual Displacement			Fuel System	Type	Built by	Engine Code
		Cu. In.	CC	Liters				
1990	6-191	190.88	3128	3.1	TBI	OHV	Chevrolet	D
1991	6-191	190.88	3128	3.1	TBI	OHV	Chevrolet	D

AUTOMATIC TRANSMISSION APPLICATION CHART

Transmission	Years	Models
Hydra-Matic 3T40	**1990–91**	All

ROUTINE MAINTENANCE

Air Cleaner

The air cleaner has a dual purpose. It not only filters the inducted air going to the engine, but also acts as a flame arrester if the engine should backfire. If an engine maintenance procedure requires the temporary removal of the air cleaner, remove it; otherwise, never run the engine without it.

REMOVAL AND INSTALLATION

NOTE: The air cleaner assembly on vans with throttle body injection are mounted directly over the throttle body near the radiator. It is connected to the intake manifold by flexible air intake ducting. The air cleaner element may be replace easily.

1. Remove the wingnut at the top of the air cleaner.
2. Remove the cover and air cleaner assembly.
3. To install, replace gasket and position air cleaner.
4. Install the air cleaner cover.
5. Install the air cleaner wingnut and tighten finger tight.

Fuel Filter

The fuel filter used on the van is an inline filter located in the engine compartment.

The in-tank fuel filter is located on the lower end of the fuel pickup tube in the fuel tank. The filter is made of woven plastic and prevents dirt from entering the fuel line and also stops water unless the filter becomes completely submerged in water. This filter is self-cleaning and normally requires no maintenance.

REMOVAL AND INSTALLATION

— CAUTION —

Never smoke when working around gasoline! Avoid all sources of sparks or ignition. Gasoline vapors are EXTREMELY volatile!

1. Disconnect the negative battery cable.
2. Remove the fuel filler cap to aid in fuel system pressure relief.

NOTE: The internal constant bleed feature of the throttle body on these vehicles relieves the fuel system pressure when the engine is turned OFF.

3. Remove the filter bracket plastic body clips.
4. Grasp the filter and one fuel line fitting. Twist the quick connect fitting ¼ turn in each direction to loosen any dirt within the fitting. Repeat for the other fuel line fitting.
5. Squeeze the plastic tabs of the male end connector and pull the connection apart. Repeat for the other fitting.
6. Remove the protective caps from the new filter and apply a few drops of clean engine oil to both tube ends of the filter and O-rings. Install the fuel filter so that the flow arrow faces towards the throttle body.
7. Install the new plastic connector retainers on the filter inlet and outlet tubes.
8. Push the connectors together to cause the retaining tabs to snap into place. Once installed pull on both ends of each connection to make sure they are secure.
9. Position the fuel return line and fuel level meter electrical connector under the in line filter bracket.
10. Install the fuel filter and bracket on the frame with new plastic body clips.

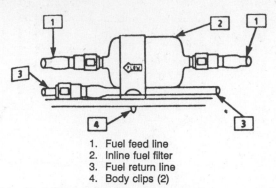

1. Fuel feed line
2. Inline fuel filter
3. Fuel return line
4. Body clips (2)

Inline fuel filter located in the engine compartment

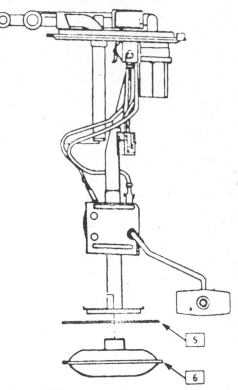

Intank fuel filter—5. deflector, 6. filter

11. Install the fuel filler cap and connect the negative battery cable.
12. Start the engine and check for leaks.

Positive Crankcase Ventilation (PCV)

The crankcase ventilation system (PCV) must be operating correctly to provide complete scavenging of the crankcase vapors. Fresh air is supplied to the crankcase from the air filter, mixed with the internal exhaust gases, passed through the PCV valve and into the intake manifold.

The PCV valve meters the flow at a rate depending upon the manifold vacuum. If the manifold vacuum is high, the PCV restricts the flow to the intake manifold. If abnormal, operating conditions occur, excessive amounts of internal exhaust gases

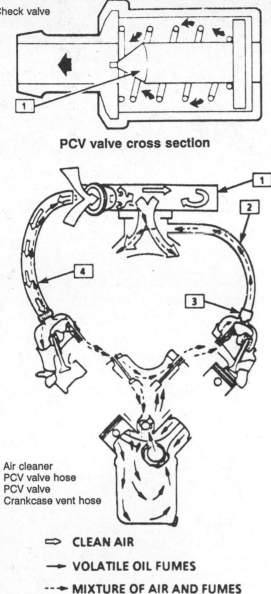

1. Check valve

PCV valve cross section

1. Air cleaner
2. PCV valve hose
3. PCV valve
4. Crankcase vent hose

⇨ **CLEAN AIR**

➤ **VOLATILE OIL FUMES**

--➤ **MIXTURE OF AIR AND FUMES**

PCV valve flow

back flow through the crankcase vent tube into the air filter to be burned by normal combustion.

If the engine is idling roughly, a quick check of the PCV valve can be made. While the engine is idling, pull the PCV valve from the valve cover, place your thumb over the end of the PCV valve and check for vacuum. If no vacuum exists, check for a plugged PCV valve, manifold port, hoses or deteriorated hoses. Turn the engine **OFF**, remove the PCV valve and shake it. Listen for the rattle of the check needle inside the valve. If it does not rattle, replace the valve.

The PCV system should be checked at every oil change and serviced every 30,000 miles.

NOTE: Never operate an engine without a PCV valve or a ventilation system, for it can become damaged.

Evaporative Canister

To limit gasoline vapor discharge into the air this system is

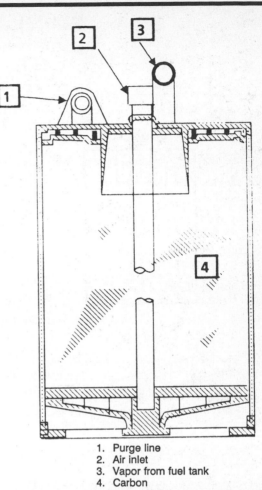

1. Purge line
2. Air inlet
3. Vapor from fuel tank
4. Carbon

Fuel vapor canister (Evaporative Emission Control System)

designed to trap fuel vapors, which normally escape from the fuel tank. Vapor arrest is accomplished through the use of the charcoal canister. This canister absorbs fuel vapors and stores them until they can be removed to be burned in the engine. The canister is purged progressively with throttle opening when the engine is running. Ambient air is allowed into the canister through the air tube in the top. The air mixes with the vapor and the mixture is drawn into the intake manifold.

REPLACEMENT

1. Tag and disconnect all hoses connected to the charcoal canister.
2. Loosen the retaining clamps and then lift out the canister.
3. Grasp the filter in the bottom of the canister with your fingers and pull it out. Replace it with a new one.
4. Install canister and tighten retaining clamps.
5. Install all hoses to canister.

NOTE: Some models do not have replaceable filters.

Battery

All General Motors vehicles have a "maintenance free" battery as standard equipment, eliminating the need for fluid level checks and the possibility of specific gravity tests. Nevertheless, the battery does require some attention.

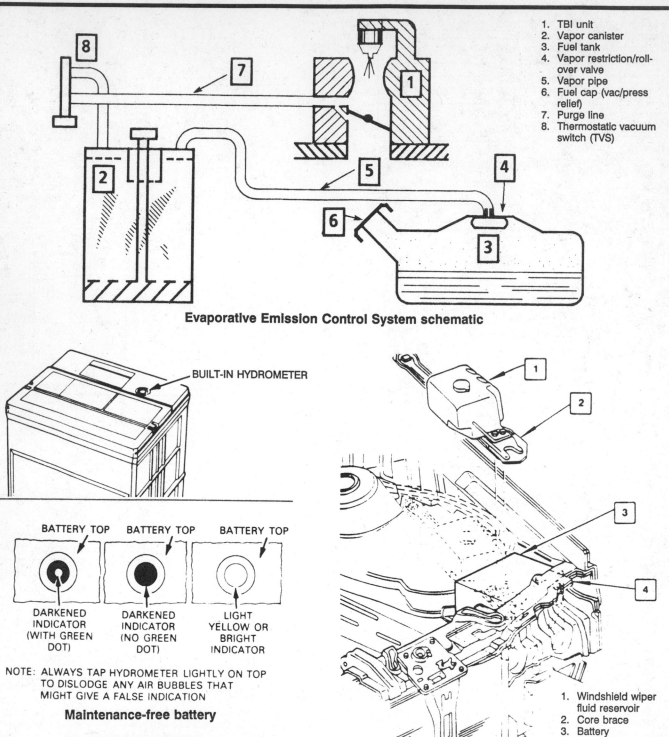

1. TBI unit
2. Vapor canister
3. Fuel tank
4. Vapor restriction/roll-over valve
5. Vapor pipe
6. Fuel cap (vac/press relief)
7. Purge line
8. Thermostatic vacuum switch (TVS)

Evaporative Emission Control System schematic

BUILT-IN HYDROMETER

BATTERY TOP

BATTERY TOP

BATTERY TOP

DARKENED INDICATOR (WITH GREEN DOT)

DARKENED INDICATOR (NO GREEN DOT)

LIGHT YELLOW OR BRIGHT INDICATOR

NOTE: ALWAYS TAP HYDROMETER LIGHTLY ON TOP TO DISLODGE ANY AIR BUBBLES THAT MIGHT GIVE A FALSE INDICATION

Maintenance-free battery

1. Windshield wiper fluid reservoir
2. Core brace
3. Battery
4. Upper tie bar

Battery Installation

Once a year, the battery terminals and the cable clamps should be cleaned. Remove the side terminal bolts and the cables, negative cable first. Clean the cable clamps and the battery terminals with a wire brush until all corrosion, grease, etc. is removed and the metal is shiny. It is especially important to clean the inside of the clamp thoroughly, since a small deposit of foreign material or oxidation there will prevent a sound electrical connection and inhibit either starting or charging. Special tools are available for cleaning the side terminal clamps and terminals.

Before installing the cables, loosen the battery holddown

clamp, remove the battery, and check the battery tray. Clear it of any debris and check it for corrosion. Rust should be wire-brushed away, and the metal given a coat of anti-rust paint. Install the battery and tighten the holddown clamp securely, but be careful not to overtighten, which will crack the battery case.

After the clamps and terminals are clean, reinstall the cables, negative cable last. Give the clamps and terminals a thin external coat of grease after installation, to retard corrosion.

Check the cables at the same time that the terminals are cleaned. If the cable insulation is cracked or broken, or if the ends are frayed, the cable should be replaced with a new cable of the same length and gauge.

CAUTION

Keep flames or sparks away from the battery; it gives off explosive hydrogen gas! Battery electrolyte contains sulphuric acid. If you should get any on your skin or in your eyes, flush the affected areas with plenty of clear water; if it lands in your eyes, get medical help immediately!

TESTING THE MAINTENANCE FREE BATTERY

Maintenance free batteries do not require normal attention as far as fluid level checks are concerned. However, the terminals require periodic cleaning, which should be performed at least once a year.

The sealed top battery cannot be checked for charge in the

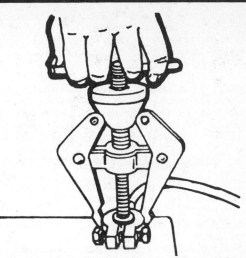

Use a puller to remove the battery cable

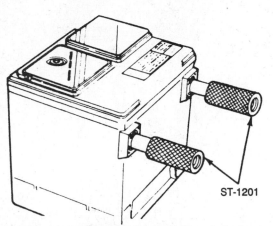

ST-1201

Use battery removing tools to prevent damage

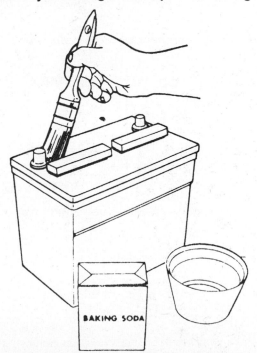

BAKING SODA

Cleaning the battery with baking soda and water

Clean the battery cable clamps with a wire brush

normal manner, since there is no provision for access to the electrolyte. To check the condition of the battery:
1. Check the built in hydrometer on top of the battery:
   a. If a green dot appears in the middle of the indicator eye on top of the battery , the battery is sufficiently charged.
   b. If the indicator eye is clear or light yellow, the electrolyte fluid is too low and the battery must be replaced.
   c. If the indicator eye is dark, the battery has a low charge and should be charged.
2. Load test the battery:
   a. Connect a battery load tester and a voltmeter across the battery terminals (the battery cables should be disconnected from the battery).
   b. Apply a 300 ampere load to the battery for 15 seconds to remove the surface charge. Remove the load.

c. Wait 15 seconds to allow the battery to recover. Apply the appropriate test load, as specified:

- 70–315 Battery — Test load: 150 amperes
- 70–355 Battery — Test load: 170 amperes
- 75–500 Battery — Test load: 250 amperes
- 75–630 Battery — Test load: 310 amperes

Read voltage after loaded for 15 seconds. Disconnect the load.

d. Check the results against the following chart. If the battery voltage is at or above the specified voltage for the temperature listed, the battery is good. If the voltage falls below what's listed, the battery should be replaced.

CHARGING THE BATTERY

NOTE: Do not charge a battery if the indicator eye is clear or light yellow. The battery should be replaced. If the battery feels hot (125°F) or if violent gassing or spewing of the electrolyte through the vent hole(s) occurs, discontinue charging or reduce the charging rate. Always follow the battery charger manufacturer's information for charging the battery.

1. To charge a sealed terminal battery out of the vehicle, install adapter kit ST-1201 or 1846855 or equivalent.
2. Make sure that all charger connections are clean and tight.

NOTE: For best results, the battery should be charged while the battery electrolyte and plates are at room temperature. A battery that is extremely cold may not accept the charging current for several hours after starting the charger.

3. Charge the battery until the indicator eye shows a green dot. (It may be necessary to tip the battery from side to side to get the green dot to appear after charging.) The battery should be checked every half hour while charging.

Belts

INSPECTION

The belts which drive the engine accessories such as the alternator, the air pump, power steering pump, air conditioning compressor and water pump are of serpentine belt design. Older belts show wear and damage readily, since their basic design was a belt with a rubber casing. As the casing wore, cracks and fibers were readily apparent. Newer design, caseless belts do not show wear as readily, and many untrained people cannot distinguish between a good, serviceable belt and one that is worn to the point of failure.

It is a good idea, therefore, to visually inspect the belt regularly and replace it, routinely, every two to three years.

ADJUSTING

Serpentine Belt

A single belt is used to drive all of the engine accessories formerly driven by multiple drive belts. The single belt is referred to a serpentine belt. All the belt driven accessories are ridgedly mounted with belt tension maintained by a spring loaded tensioner. Because of the belt tensioner, no adjustment is necessary.

REMOVAL AND INSTALLATION

To remove the drive belt, use a ⅜ in ratchet or breaker bar to unload the tensioner and remove the belt.

NOTE: Take care as not to bend the tensioner when applying torque. Damage to the tensioner may occur. Maximum torque to load belt should not exceed 30 ft. lbs.

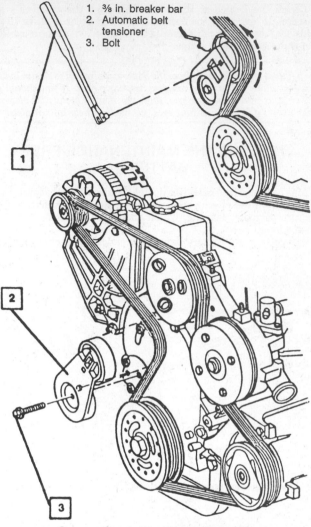

1. ⅜ in. breaker bar
2. Automatic belt tensioner
3. Bolt

Serpentine belt routing diagram

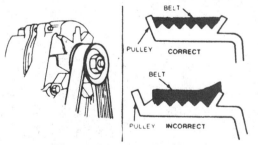

Proper serpentine belt alignment

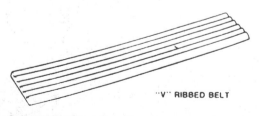

6-rib "V" belt

Serpentine belt configuration

HOW TO SPOT WORN V-BELTS

V–Belts are vital to efficient engine operation—they drive the fan, water pump and other accessories. They require little maintenance (occasional tightening) but they will not last forever. Slipping or failure of the V–belt will lead to overheating. If your V–belt looks like any of these, it should be replaced.

Cracking or Weathering

This belt has deep cracks, which cause it to flex. Too much flexing leads to heat build–up and premature failure. These cracks can be caused by using the belt on a pulley that is too small. Notched belts are available for small diameter pulleys.

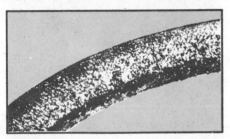

Softening (Grease and Oil)

Oil and grease on a belt can cause the belt's rubber compounds to soften and separate from the reinforcing cords that hold the belt together. The belt will first slip, then finally fail altogether.

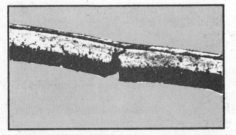

Glazing

Glazing is caused by a belt that is slipping. A slipping belt can cause a run-down battery, erratic power steering, overheating or poor accessory performance. The more the belt slips, the more glazing will be built up on the surface of the belt. The more the belt is glazed, the more it will slip. If the glazing is light, tighten the belt.

Worn Cover

The cover of this belt is worn off and is peeling away. The reinforcing cords will begin to wear and the belt will shortly break. When the belt cover wears in spots or has a rough jagged appearance, check the pulley grooves for roughness.

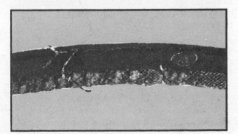

Separation

This belt is on the verge of breaking and leaving you stranded. The layers of the belt are separating and the reinforcing cords are exposed. It's just a matter of time before it breaks completely.

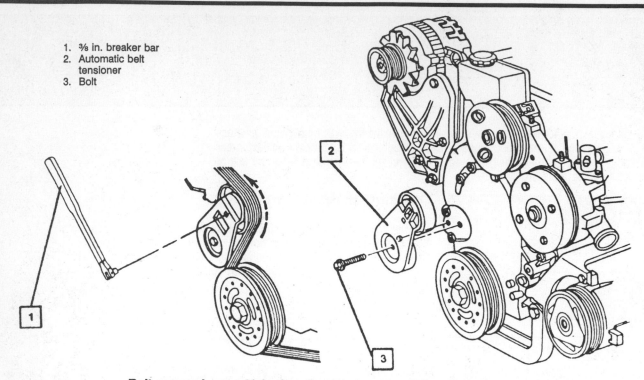

1. ⅜ in. breaker bar
2. Automatic belt tensioner
3. Bolt

Belt removal—use ⅜ in. breaker bar to unload the tensioner

Hoses

REMOVAL AND INSTALLATION

—————— CAUTION ——————

When draining the coolant, keep in mind that cats and dogs are attracted by the ethylene glycol antifreeze, and are quite likely to drink any that is left in an uncovered container or in puddles on the ground. This will prove fatal in sufficient quantity. Always drain the coolant into a sealable container. Coolant should be reused unless it is contaminated or several years old.

Radiator hoses are generally of two constructions, the pre-formed (molded) type, which is custom made for a particular application, and the spring-loaded type, which is made to fit several different applications. Heater hoses are all of the same general construction.

Hoses are retained by clamps. To replace a hose, loosen the clamp and slide it down the hose, away from the attaching point. Twist the hose from side to side until it is free, then pull it off. Before installing the new hose, make sure that the outlet fitting is as clean as possible. Coat the fitting with non-hardening sealer and slip the hose into place. Install the clamp and tighten it.

Air Conditioning System

Regular maintenance of the air conditioning system includes periodic checks of the drive belt and tension. In addition, the system should be operated for at least 5 minutes every month. This ensures an adequate supply of lubricant to the bearings and also helps to prevent the seals and hoses from drying out. To do this comfortably in the winter months, turn the air conditioning "ON", place the temperature control lever on "WARM" or "HI" position and turn the blower fan to its highest setting. This will engage the compressor, circulating the lubricating oils

within the system, but prevents the discharge of cold air. The system should be checked for proper refrigerant charge using the procedure given below.

GENERAL SERVICING PROCEDURES

The most important aspect of air conditioning service is the maintenance of pure and adequate charge of refrigerant in the system. A refrigeration system cannot function properly if a significant percentage of the charge is lost. Leaks are common because the severe vibration encountered in an automobile can easily cause a sufficient cracking or loosening of the air conditioning fittings. As a result, the extreme operating pressures of the system force refrigerant out.

The problem can be understood by considering what happens to the system as it is operated with a continuous leak. Because the fixed orifice (expansion) tube regulates the flow of refrigerant to the evaporator, the level of refrigerant there is fairly constant. The accumulator stores any excess of refrigerant, and so a loss will first appear there as a reduction in the level of liquid. As this level nears the bottom of the vessel, some refrigerant vapor bubbles will begin to appear in the stream of liquid supplied to the fixed orifice. This vapor decreases the capacity of the orifice tube very little. As the quantity of liquid in the condenser decreases, the operating pressure will drop there and throughout the high side of the system. As the R-12 continues to be expelled, the pressure available to force the liquid through the orifice tube will continue to decrease, and, eventually, the orifice will prove to be too much of a restriction for adequate flow.

At this point, low side pressure will start to drop, and severe reduction in cooling capacity, marked by freeze-up of the evaporator coil, will result. Eventually, the operating pressure of the evaporator will be lower than the pressure of the atmosphere surrounding it, and air will be drawn into the system wherever there are leaks in the low side.

Because all atmospheric air contains at least some moisture,

HOW TO SPOT BAD HOSES

Both the upper and lower radiator hoses are called upon to perform difficult jobs in an inhospitable environment. They are subject to nearly 18 psi at under hood temperatures often over 280°F, and must circulate nearly 7500 gallons of coolant an hour—3 good reasons to have good hoses.

Swollen Hose

A good test for any hose is to feel it for soft or spongy spots. Frequently these will appear as swollen areas of the hose. The most likely cause is oil soaking. This hose could burst at any time, when hot or under pressure.

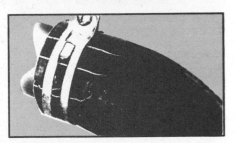

Cracked Hose

Cracked hoses can usually be seen but feel the hoses to be sure they have not hardened; a prime cause of cracking. This hose has cracked down to the reinforcing cords and could split at any of the cracks.

Frayed Hose End (Due to Weak Clamp)

Weakened clamps frequently are the cause of hose and cooling system failure. The connection between the pipe and hose has deteriorated enough to allow coolant to escape when the engine is hot.

Debris In Cooling System

Debris, rust and scale in the cooling system can cause the inside of a hose to weaken. This can usually be felt on the outside of the hose as soft or thinner areas.

1 GENERAL INFORMATION AND MAINTENANCE

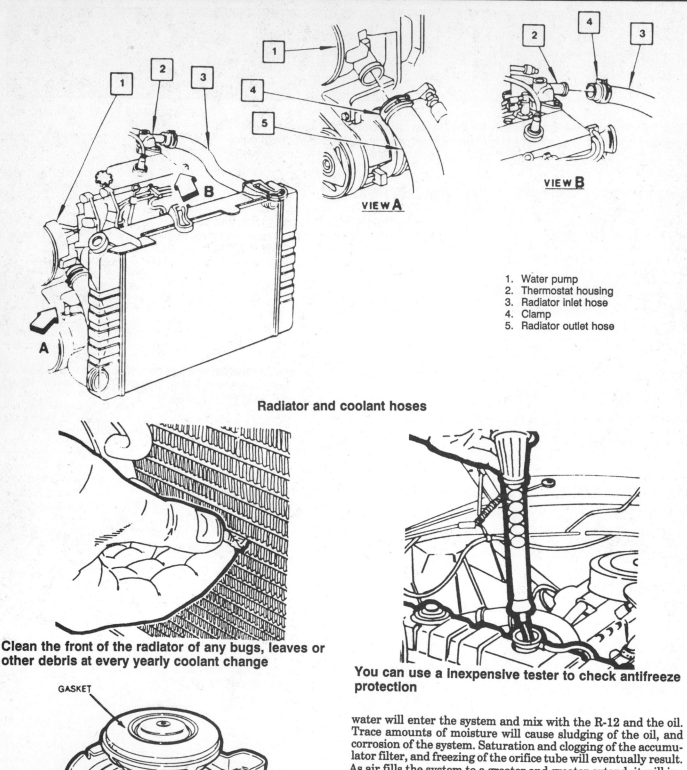

1. Water pump
2. Thermostat housing
3. Radiator inlet hose
4. Clamp
5. Radiator outlet hose

VIEW A

VIEW B

Radiator and coolant hoses

Clean the front of the radiator of any bugs, leaves or other debris at every yearly coolant change

You can use a inexpensive tester to check antifreeze protection

GASKET

Check the condition of the radiator cap gasket

water will enter the system and mix with the R-12 and the oil. Trace amounts of moisture will cause sludging of the oil, and corrosion of the system. Saturation and clogging of the accumulator filter, and freezing of the orifice tube will eventually result. As air fills the system to a greater and greater extend, it will interfere more and more with the normal flows of refrigerant and heat.

A list of general precautions that should be observed while doing this follows:

1. Keep all tools as clean and dry as possible.
2. Thoroughly purge the service gauges and hoses of air and moisture before connecting them to the system. Keep them capped when not in use.

1-16

3. Thoroughly clean any refrigerant fitting before disconnecting it, in order to minimize the entrance of dirt into the system.

4. Plan any operation that requires opening the system beforehand in order to minimize the length of time it will be exposed to open air. Cap or seal the open ends to minimize the entrance of foreign material.

5. When adding oil, pour it through an extremely clean and dry tube or funnel. Keep the oil capped whenever possible. Do not use oil that has not been kept tightly sealed.

6. Use only refrigerant 12. Purchase refrigerant intended for use in only automotive air conditioning system. Avoid the use of refrigerant 12 that may be packaged for another use, such as cleaning, or powering a horn, as it is impure.

7. Completely evacuate any system that has been opened to replace a component, other than when isolating the compressor, or that has leaked sufficiently to draw in moisture and air. This requires evacuating air and moisture with a good vacuum pump for at least one hour.

If a system has been open for a considerable length of time it may be advisable to evacuate the system for up to 12 hours (overnight).

8. Use a wrench on both halves of a fitting that is to be disconnected, so as to avoid placing torque on any of the refrigerant lines.

ADDITIONAL PREVENTIVE MAINTENANCE CHECKS

Antifreeze

In order to prevent heater core freeze-up during air conditioner operation, it is necessary to maintain permanent type antifreeze protection of $+15°F$ ($-9°C$) or lower. A reading of $-15°F$ ($-26°C$) is ideal since this protection also supplies sufficient corrosion inhibitors for the protection of the engine cooling system.

WARNING: Do not use antifreeze longer than specified by the manufacturer.

Radiator Cap

For efficient operation of an air conditioned vehicle's cooling system, the radiator cap should have a holding pressure which meets manufacturer's specifications. A cap which fails to hold these pressure should be replaced.

Condenser

Any obstruction of or damage to the condenser configuration will restrict the air flow which is essential to its efficient operation. It is therefore, a good rule to keep this unit clean and in proper physical shape.

NOTE: Bug screens are regarded as obstructions.

Condensation Drain Tube

This single molded drain tube expels the condensation, which accumulates on the bottom of the evaporator housing, into the engine compartment.

If this tube is obstructed, the air conditioning performance can be restricted and condensation buildup can spill over onto the vehicle's floor.

SAFETY PRECAUTIONS

Because of the importance of the necessary safety precautions that must be exercised when working with air conditioning systems and R-12 refrigerant, a recap of the safety precautions are outlined.

1. Avoid contact with a charged refrigeration system, even when working on another part of the air conditioning system or vehicle. If a heavy tool comes into contact with a section of copper tubing or a heat exchanger, it can easily cause the relatively soft material to rupture.

2. When it is necessary to apply force to a fitting which contains refrigerant, as when checking that all system couplings are securely tightened, use a wrench on both parts of the fitting involved, if possible. This will avoid putting torque on the refrigerant tubing. (It is advisable, when possible, to use tube or line wrenches when tightening these flare nut fittings.)

3. Do not attempt to discharge the system by merely loosening a fitting, or removing the service valve caps and cracking these valves. Precise control is possibly only when using the service gauges. Place a rag under the open end of the center charging hose while discharging the system to catch any drops of liquid that might escape. Wear protective gloves when connecting or disconnecting service gauge hoses.

4. Discharge the system only in a well ventilated area, as high concentrations of the gas can exclude oxygen and act as an anesthetic. When leak testing or soldering this is particularly important, as toxic gas is formed when R-12 contacts any flame.

5. Never start a system without first verifying that both service valves are backseated, if equipped, and that all fittings throughout the system are snugly connected.

6. Avoid applying heat to any refrigerant line or storage vessel. Charging may be aided by using water heated to less than 125°F (52°C) to warm the refrigerant container. Never allow a refrigerant storage container to sit out in the sun, or near any other source of heat, such as a radiator.

7. Always wear goggles when working on a system to protect the eyes. If refrigerant contacts the eye, it is advisable in all cases to see a physician as soon as possible.

8. Frostbite from liquid refrigerant should be treated by first gradually warming the area with cool water, and then gently applying petroleum jelly. A physician should be consulted.

9. Always keep refrigerant can fittings capped when not in use. Avoid sudden shock to the can which might occur from dropping it, or from banging a heavy tool against it. Never carry a refrigerant can in the passenger compartment of a vehicle.

10. Always completely discharge the system before painting the vehicle (if the paint is to be baked on), or before welding anywhere near the refrigerant lines.

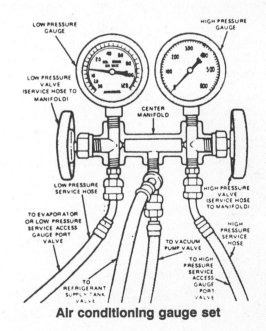

Air conditioning gauge set

TEST GAUGES

Most of the service work performed in air conditioning requires the use of a set of two gauges, one for the high (head) pressure side of the system, the other for the low (suction) side.

The low side gauge records both pressure and vacuum. Vacuum readings are calibrated from 0 to 30 inches Hg and the pressure graduations read from 0 to no less than 60 psi.

The high side gauge measures pressure from 0 to at last 600 psi.

Both gauges are threaded into a manifold that contains two hand shut-off valves. Proper manipulation of these valves and the use of the attached test hoses allow the user to perform the following services:

1. Test high and low side pressures.
2. Remove air, moisture, and contaminated refrigerant.
3. Purge the system (of refrigerant).
4. Charge the system (with refrigerant).

The manifold valves are designed so that they have no direct effect on gauge readings, but serve only to provide for, or cut off, flow of refrigerant through the manifold. During all testing and hook-up operations, the valves are kept in a close position to avoid disturbing the refrigeration system. The valves are opened only to purge the system or refrigerant or to charge it.

INSPECTION

----- CAUTION -----

The compressed refrigerant used in the air conditioning system expands into the atmosphere at a temperature of −21.7°F (−30°C) or lower. This will freeze any surface, including your eyes, that it contacts. In addition, the refrigerant decomposes into a poisonous gas in the presence of a flame. Do not open or disconnect any part of the air conditioning system.

Sight Glass Check

NOTE: Most late model vehicles are not equipped with a sight glass. The only way to find out if the system has enough refrigerant is to install a set of test gauges.

You can safely make a few simple checks to determine if your air conditioning system needs service. The tests work best if the temperature is warm (about 70°F [21.1°C]).

NOTE: If your vehicle is equipped with an aftermarket air conditioner, the following system check may not apply. You should contact the manufacturer of the unit for instructions on systems checks.

1. Operation of the air conditioning blower at all four speeds with the mode button in any position except OFF and engagement of the compressor clutch would indicate that the electrical circuit are functioning properly. (The blower will not operate in any speed with the mode button in the OFF position.)
2. The same hand felt temperature of the evaporator inlet pipe and the accumulator surface of an operating system would indicate a properly charged system.
3. Operation of the air conditioning control selector (mode) button to distribute air from designed outlets would indicate proper functioning.

NOTE: If it is determined that the system has a leak, it should be corrected as soon as possible. Leaks may allow moisture to enter and cause a very expensive rust problem. Exercise the air conditioner for a few minutes, every two weeks or so, during the cold months. This avoids the possibility of the compressor seals drying out from lack of lubrication.

Troubleshooting Basic Air Conditioning Problems

Problem	Cause	Solution
There's little or no air coming from the vents (and you're sure it's on)	• The A/C fuse is blown • Broken or loose wires or connections • The on/off switch is defective	• Check and/or replace fuse • Check and/or repair connections • Replace switch
The air coming from the vents is not cool enough	• Windows and air vent wings open • The compressor belt is slipping • Heater is on • Condenser is clogged with debris • Refrigerant has escaped through a leak in the system • Receiver/drier is plugged	• Close windows and vent wings • Tighten or replace compressor belt • Shut heater off • Clean the condenser • Check system • Service system
The air has an odor	• Vacuum system is disrupted • Odor producing substances on the evaporator case • Condensation has collected in the bottom of the evaporator housing	• Have the system checked/repaired • Clean the evaporator case • Clean the evaporator housing drains
System is noisy or vibrating	• Compressor belt or mountings loose • Air in the system	• Tighten or replace belt; tighten mounting bolts • Have the system serviced

Troubleshooting Basic Air Conditioning Problems (cont.)

Problem	Cause	Solution
Sight glass condition		
Constant bubbles, foam or oil streaks	• Undercharged system	• Charge the system
Clear sight glass, but no cold air	• No refrigerant at all	• Check and charge the system
Clear sight glass, but air is cold	• System is OK	
Clouded with milky fluid	• Receiver drier is leaking dessicant	• Have system checked
Large difference in temperature of lines	• System undercharged	• Charge and leak test the system
Compressor noise	• Broken valves	• Replace the valve plate
	• Overcharged	• Discharge, evacuate and install the correct charge
	• Incorrect oil level	• Isolate the compressor and check the oil level. Correct as necessary.
	• Piston slap	• Replace the compressor
	• Broken rings	• Replace the compressor
	• Drive belt pulley bolts are loose	• Tighten with the correct torque specification
Excessive vibration	• Incorrect belt tension	• Adjust the belt tension
	• Clutch loose	• Tighten the clutch
	• Overcharged	• Discharge, evacuate and install the correct charge
	• Pulley is misaligned	• Align the pulley
Condensation dripping in the passenger compartment	• Drain hose plugged or improperly positioned	• Clean the drain hose and check for proper installation
	• Insulation removed or improperly installed	• Replace the insulation on the expansion valve and hoses
Frozen evaporator coil	• Faulty thermostat	• Replace the thermostat
	• Thermostat capillary tube improperly installed	• Install the capillary tube correctly
	• Thermostat not adjusted properly	• Adjust the thermostat
Low side low—high side low	• System refrigerant is low	• Evacuate, leak test and charge the system
	• Expansion valve is restricted	• Replace the expansion valve
Low side high—high side low	• Internal leak in the compressor—worn	• Remove the compressor cylinder head and inspect the compressor. Replace the valve plate assembly if necessary. If the compressor pistons, rings or
Low side high—high side low (cont.)		cylinders are excessively worn or scored replace the compressor
	• Cylinder head gasket is leaking	• Install a replacement cylinder head gasket
	• Expansion valve is defective	• Replace the expansion valve
	• Drive belt slipping	• Adjust the belt tension

Troubleshooting Basic Air Conditioning Problems (cont.)

Problem	Cause	Solution
Low side high—high side high	• Condenser fins obstructed • Air in the system • Expansion valve is defective • Loose or worn fan belts	• Clean the condenser fins • Evacuate, leak test and charge the system • Replace the expansion valve • Adjust or replace the belts as necessary
Low side low—high side high	• Expansion valve is defective • Restriction in the refrigerant hose	• Replace the expansion valve • Check the hose for kinks—replace if necessary
Low side low—high side high	• Restriction in the receiver/drier • Restriction in the condenser	• Replace the receiver/drier • Replace the condenser
Low side and high normal (inadequate cooling)	• Air in the system • Moisture in the system	• Evacuate, leak test and charge the system • Evacuate, leak test and charge the system

TESTING THE SYSTEM

1. Connect a gauge set. Connect the low side gauge hose to the accumulator (aluminum can) and the high side hose to the discharge hose between the compressor and condenser.
2. Close (clockwise) both gauge set valves.
3. Mid-position both service valves.
4. Park the vehicle in the shade. Start the engine, set the parking brake, place the transaxle in **N** and establish an idle of 1,500 rpm.
5. Run the air conditioning system for full cooling, but NOT in the **MAX** or **COLD** mode.
6. Insert a thermometer into the center air outlet.
7. Use the accompanying performance chart for a specifications reference. If pressures are abnormal, refer to the air conditioner performance chart in this section.

WARNING: These pressures are the norm for an ambient temperature of 70–80°F (21–27°C). Higher air temperatures along with high humidity will cause higher system pressures. At idle speed and an ambient temperature of 110°F (43°F), the high pressure reading can exceed 300 psi.

Under these extreme conditions, you can keep the pressures down by directing a large electric floor fan through the condenser.

DISCHARGING THE SYSTEM

1. Remove the caps from the high and low pressure charging valves in the high and low pressure lines.
2. Turn both manifold gauge set hand valves to the fully closed (clockwise) position.
3. Connect the manifold gauge set.
4. If the gauge set hoses do not have the gauge port actuating pins, install fitting adapters on the manifold gauge set hoses. If the vehicle does not have a service access gauge port valve, connect the gauge set low pressure hose to the accumulator service access gauge port valve. A special adapter may be required to attach the manifold gauge set to the high pressure service access gauge port valve at the discharge hose between the compressor and condenser.

5. Place the end of the center hose away from you and the vehicle.
6. Open the low pressure gauge valve slightly and allow the system pressure to bleed off.
7. When the system is just about empty, open the high pressure valve very slowly to avoid losing an excessive amount of refrigerant oil. Allow any remaining refrigerant to escape.

EVACUATING THE SYSTEM

NOTE: This procedure requires the use of a vacuum pump.

1. Connect a gauge set. Connect the low side gauge hose to the accumulator (aluminum can) and the high side hose to the discharge hose between the compressor and condenser.
2. Discharge the system.
3. Make sure that the low pressure gauge set hose is connected to the low pressure service gauge port on the top center of the accumulator/drier assembly and the high pressure hose connected to the high pressure service gauge port on the compressor discharge line.
4. Connect the center service hose to the inlet fitting of the vacuum pump.
5. Turn both gauge set valves to the wide open position.
6. Start the pump and note the low side gauge reading.
7. Operate the pump until the low pressure gauge reads 25–30 inch Hg. Continue running the vacuum pump for 10 minutes more. If you have replaced some component in the system, run the pump for an additional 20–30 minutes.
8. Leak test the system. Close both gauge set valves. Turn off the pump. The needle should remain stationary at the point at which the pump was turned off. If the needle drops to zero rapidly, there is a leak in the system which must be repaired.

LEAK TESTING

Some leak tests can be performed with a soapy water solution. There must be at least a ½ lb. charge in the system for a leak to be detected. The most extensive leak tests are performed with either a Halide flame type leak tester or the more preferable electronic leak tester.

RELATIVE HUMIDITY (%)	AMBIENT AIR TEMP		LOW SIDE		ENGINE SPEED (rpm)	CENTER DUCT AIR TEMPERATURE		HIGH SIDE	
	°F	°C	kPa	PSIG		°F	°C	kPa	PSIG
20	70	21	200	29	2000	40	4	1034	150
	80	27	200	29		44	7	1310	190
	90	32	207	30		48	9	1689	245
	100	38	214	31		57	14	2103	305
30	70	21	200	29	2000	42	6	1034	150
	80	27	207	30		47	8	1413	205
	90	32	214	31		51	11	1827	265
	100	38	221	32		61	16	2241	325
40	70	21	200	29	2000	45	7	1138	165
	80	27	207	30		49	9	1482	215
	90	32	221	32		55	13	1931	280
	100	38	269	39		65	18	2379	345
50	70	21	207	30	2000	47	8	1241	180
	80	27	221	32		53	12	1620	235
	90	32	234	34		59	15	2034	295
	100	38	276	40		69	21	2413	350
60	70	21	207	30	2000	48	9	1241	180
	80	27	228	33		56	13	1655	240
	90	32	249	36		63	17	2069	300
	100	38	296	43		73	23	2482	360
70	70	21	207	30	2000	50	10	1276	185
	80	27	234	34		58	14	1689	245
	90	32	262	38		65	18	2103	305
	100	38	303	44		75	24	2517	365
80	70	21	207	30	2000	50	10	1310	190
	80	27	234	34		59	15	1724	250
	90	32	269	39		67	19	2137	310
90	70	21	207	30	2000	50	10	1379	200
	80	27	249	36		62	17	1827	265
	90	32	290	42		71	22	2275	330

Air conditioning performance chart

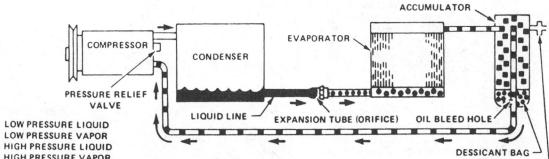

LOW PRESSURE LIQUID
LOW PRESSURE VAPOR
HIGH PRESSURE LIQUID
HIGH PRESSURE VAPOR

COMPRESSOR

CONDENSER

EVAPORATOR

ACCUMULATOR

PRESSURE RELIEF VALVE

LIQUID LINE

EXPANSION TUBE (ORIFICE)

OIL BLEED HOLE

DESSICANT BAG

PRESSURE CYCLING SWITCH

Air conditioning system

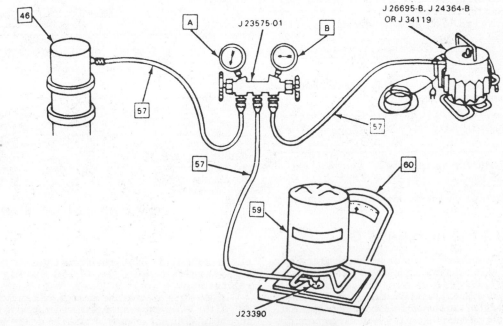

Air conditioning service points

In either case, the equipment is expensive, and, the use of a Halide detector can be **extremely** hazardous!

CHARGING THE SYSTEM

------ CAUTION ------

NEVER OPEN THE HIGH PRESSURE SIDE WITH A CAN OF RE-FRIGERANT CONNECTED TO THE SYSTEM! OPENING THE HIGH PRESSURE SIDE WILL OVERPRESSURIZE THE CAN, CAUSING IT TO EXPLODE!

1. Connect a gauge set. Connect the low side gauge hose to the accumulator (aluminum can) and the high side hose to the discharge hose between the compressor and condenser.
2. Start and run the engine until it reaches operating temperature. Then set the air conditioning mode control button on **OFF**.
3. With the R-12 cans inverted, open the R-12 source valve(s) and allow one 14 oz. can of liquid R-12 to flow into the system through the low side service fitting.
4. As soon as one can of R-12 has been added to the system, immediately engage the compressor by setting the air conditioning control button to **NORM** and the blower speed on **HI**, to draw in the remainder of the R-12 charge.

NOTE: The charging operation can be speeded up by using a large volume fan to pass air over the condenser. If the condenser temperature is maintained below the charging cylinder temperature, R-12 will enter the system more rapidly.

5. Turn off the R-12 source valve and run engine for 30 seconds to clear the lines and gauges.
6. With the engine not running, remove the charging low side hose adapter from the accumulator service fitting. Unscrew rapidly to avoid excess R-12 escape from the system.

------ CAUTION ------

Never remove a gauge line from its adapter when the line is connected to the air conditioning system. Always remove the line adapter from the service fitting to disconnect a line. Do not remove charging hose at the gauge set while attached to the accumulator. This will result in complete discharge of the system due to the depressed Schrader valve in service low side fitting, and may cause personal injury due to escaping R-12.

6. Replace protective cap on accumulator fitting.
7. Turn engine off.
8. Leak check system with electronic leak detector J-29547 or equivalent.
9. Start engine.
10. With the system fully charged and leak checked, continue to operate the system performance.

------ CAUTION ------

NEVER ALLOW THE HIGH PRESSURE SIDE READING TO EXCEED 240 psi.

The maximum charge for systems is:
44 oz (2.75 lbs.) [1.25 kg].

NOTE: Remember that the disposable cans are only 14 oz., not 16 oz.

ADDING REFRIGERANT OIL

Refrigerant oil can be purchased in raw or pressurized cans. The raw oil can be added when the system is discharged and has no pressure or forced in under pressure using a oil injection pump. The can is pressurized with R-12 and has 4 oz. of refrigerant oil per can. The oil is added in the same manner as the refrigerant.

Refrigerant oil must be added after the system has been discharged. The air conditioner system requires a total of **8 fluid** onces (240ml) of 525 viscosity refrigerant oil ONLY. **New oil quantities must be added during component replacement.**

With no signs of excessive leakage, add as follows:

1. If the V-5 compressor is removed, the oil in the compressor should be drained, measured and recorded. Added the same amount plus 1 oz. (30ml) to the new compressor.

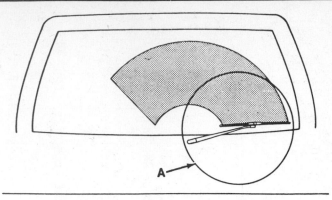

VIEW A WIPER ARM REPLACEMENT

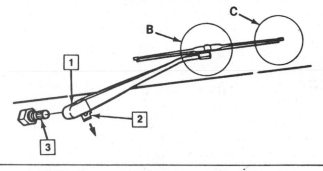

VIEW B BLADE ASSEMBLY REPLACEMENT

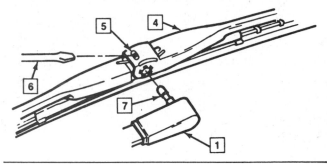

VIEW C REFILL REMOVAL

1. Wiper arm
2. Wiper arm retaining latch
3. Wiper pivot shaft
4. Wiper blade assembly
5. Blade retaining spring
6. Suitable prybar
7. Wiper arm pin
8. Wiper blade refill
9. Refill retainer

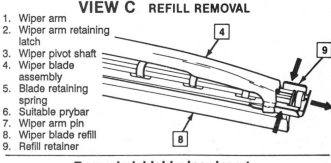

Rear windshield wiper insert

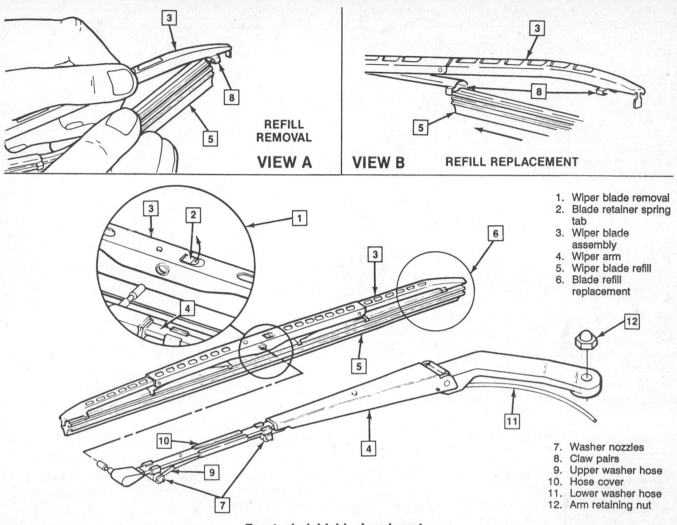

REFILL REMOVAL

VIEW A

VIEW B   REFILL REPLACEMENT

1. Wiper blade removal
2. Blade retainer spring tab
3. Wiper blade assembly
4. Wiper arm
5. Wiper blade refill
6. Blade refill replacement
7. Washer nozzles
8. Claw pairs
9. Upper washer hose
10. Hose cover
11. Lower washer hose
12. Arm retaining nut

Front windshield wiper insert

NOTE: When installing a new compressor, drain the new compressor and add the amount of oil in step 1. Do not add the amount in step 1 without draining the compressor first because the system will be overfilled.

2. If the evaporator is removed, add 3 oz. (90ml) of oil.
3. If the condenser is removed, add 1 oz. (30ml) of oil.
4. If the accumulator is removed, the oil in it must be drained, measured and recorded. The same amount of new oil must be replaced. If installing a new accumulator, add an extra 3.5 oz. (105ml) plus the original recording.

With signs of excessive leakage, add oil as follows:

1. If less than 3 oz. (90ml) is drained out of the accumulator, 3 oz. (90ml) of oil should be installed.
2. If more than 3 oz. (90ml) of oil was drained, add that amount.

Windshield Wipers

For maximum effectiveness and longest element life, the windshield and wiper blades should be kept clean. Dirt, tree sap, road tar and so on will cause streaking, smearing and blade deterioration if left on the glass. It is advisable to wash the windshield carefully with a commercial glass cleaner at least once a month. Wipe off the rubber blades with the wet rag afterwards.

If the blades are found to be cracked, broken or torn, they should be replaced immediately. Replacement intervals will vary with usage, although ozone deterioration usually limits blade life to about one year. If the wiper pattern is smeared or streaked, or if the blade chatters across the glass, the elements should be replaced. It is easiest and most sensible to replace the elements in pairs.

WIPER REFILL REPLACEMENT

The element of the wiper blade uses a spring type retainer on the end of the element. To remove the element, insert and rotate a screwdriver. Slide the element upward out of the housing retaining tabs.

To install the new element, slide it into the housing retaining tabs, lining up the slot in the element with the housing tab and snap the element into place.

Tires and Wheels

TIRE ROTATION

Tire rotation is recommended the first 7,500 miles, and every 15,000 miles thereafter to obtain maximum tire wear. The pattern you use depends on whether or not your van has a usable spare. Radial tires should not be cross-switched (from one side

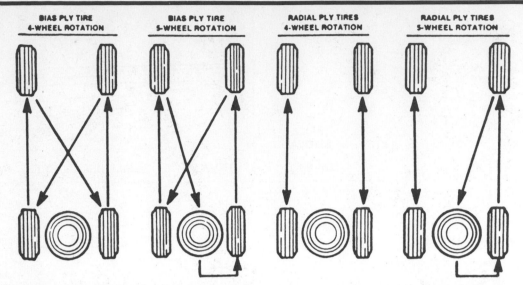

| BIAS PLY TIRE 4-WHEEL ROTATION | BIAS PLY TIRE 5-WHEEL ROTATION | RADIAL PLY TIRES 4-WHEEL ROTATION | RADIAL PLY TIRES 5-WHEEL ROTATION |

Tire rotation diagram, note that radials should NOT be cross-switched

of the vehicle to the other); they last longer if their direction of rotation is not changed. Snow tires sometimes have directional arrows molded into the side of the carcass; the arrow shows the direction of rotation. They will wear very rapidly if the rotation is reversed.

NOTE: Mark the wheel position or direction of rotation on radial tires or studded snow tires before removing them.

TIRE DESIGN

For maximum satisfaction, tires should be used in sets of five. Mixing or different types (radial, bias-belted, fiberglass belted) should be avoided. Conventional bias tires are constructed so that the cords run bead-to-bead at an angle. Alternate plies run at an opposite angle. This type of construction gives rigidity to both tread and sidewall. Bias-belted tires are similar in construction to conventional bias ply tires. Belts run at an angle and also at a 90° angle to the bead, as in the radial tire. Tread life is improved considerably over the conventional bias tire. The radial tire differs in construction, but instead of the carcass plies running at an angle of 90° to each other, they run at an angle of 90° to the bead. This gives the tread a great deal of rigidity and the sidewall a great deal of flexibility and accounts for the characteristic bulge associated with radial tires.

Radial tire are recommended for use on all models. If they are used, tire sizes and wheel diameters should be selected to maintain ground clearance and tire load capacity equivalent to the minimum specified tire. Radial tires should always be used in sets of five, but in an emergency radial tires can be used with caution on the rear axle only. If this is done, both tires on the rear should be of radial design.

NOTE: Radial tires should never be used on only the front axle.

TIRE INFLATION

Tires should be checked weekly for proper air pressure. A chart, located either in the glove compartment or on the driver's or passenger's door, gives the recommended inflation pressures. Maximum fuel economy and tire life will result if the pressure is maintained at the highest figure given on the chart. Pressures should be checked before driving since pressure can increase as much as 6 pounds per square inch (psi) due to heat buildup. It is

A penny works as well as anything for checking the tire depth; when you can see the top of Lincoln's head, it is time for a new tire

Tread depth can be checked with an inexpensive gauge

a good idea to have your own accurate pressure gauge, because not all gauges on service station air pumps can be trusted. When checking pressures, do not neglect the spare tire. Note that some spare tires require pressures considerably higher than those used in the other tires.

While you are about the task of checking air pressure, inspect the tire treads for cuts, bruises and other damage. Check the air valves to be sure that they are tight. Replace any missing valve caps.

Check the tires for uneven wear that might indicate the need for front end alignment or tire rotation. Tires should be replaced when a tread wear indicator appears as a solid band across the tread.

When buying new tires, give some thought to the following

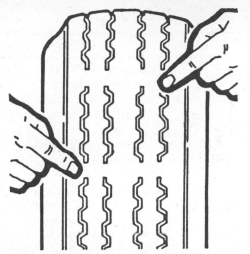

Tread wear indicators will appear when the tires is worn out

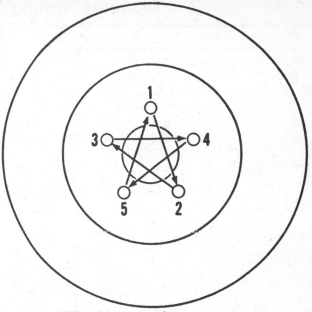

Wheel nut torquing sequence

points, especially if you are considering a switch to larger tires or a different profile series:

1. All 4 tires must be of the same construction type. This rule cannot be violated. Radial, bias, and bias-belted tires must not be mixed.

2. The wheels should be the correct width for the tire. Tire dealers have charts of tire and rim compatibility. A mismatch will cause sloppy handling and rapid tire wear. The tread width should match the rim width (inside bead to inside bead) within 25mm (1 inch). For radial tires, the rim width should be 80% or less of the tire (not tread) width.

3. The height (mounted diameter) of the new tires can change speedometer accuracy, engine speed at a given road speed, fuel mileage, acceleration, and ground clearance. Tire manufacturers furnish full measurement specifications.

4. The spare tire should be usable, at least for short distance and low speed operation, with the new tires.

5. There shouldn't be any body interference when loaded, on bumps, or in turns.

NOTE: The tires will perform well at all normal loads when inflated as recommended on the Tire Placard (located on the driver's door of your van).

STORAGE

Store the tires at the proper inflation pressure if they are mounted on wheels. Keep them in a cool dry place, laid on their sides. If the tires are stored in the garage or basement, do not let them stand on a concrete floor; set them on strips of wood.

The spare tire is mounted under the rear floor behind the rear axle. Raise or lower the spare by opening the liftgate and insert the lug wrench and ratchet into the slot and turn counterclockwise to lower the spare. Turn the cable retainer to remove from the center of the rim.

CARE OF SPECIAL WHEELS

An aluminum wheel may become porous and leak air. Locate the leak by inflating the assembly to 40 psi and dipping the assembly into water. Mark the leak areas. Remove the tire from the wheel and scuff the inside rim surface with 80 grit sandpaper. Apply a thick layer of adhesive/sealant part number 1052366 or equivalent to the leak area and allow six hours to dry.

Clean special wheels with a special mag wheel cleaner or mild soap and water. Do not use harsh detergents or solvents because the protective coating may be damaged.

Troubleshooting Basic Wheel Problems

Problem	Cause	Solution
The car's front end vibrates at high speed	• The wheels are out of balance • Wheels are out of alignment	• Have wheels balanced • Have wheel alignment checked/adjusted
Car pulls to either side	• Wheels are out of alignment • Unequal tire pressure • Different size tires or wheels	• Have wheel alignment checked/adjusted • Check/adjust tire pressure • Change tires or wheels to same size

Troubleshooting Basic Wheel Problems

Problem	Cause	Solution
The car's wheel(s) wobbles	• Loose wheel lug nuts • Wheels out of balance • Damaged wheel • Wheels are out of alignment • Worn or damaged ball joint • Excessive play in the steering linkage (usually due to worn parts) • Defective shock absorber	• Tighten wheel lug nuts • Have tires balanced • Raise car and spin the wheel. If the wheel is bent, it should be replaced • Have wheel alignment checked/adjusted • Check ball joints • Check steering linkage • Check shock absorbers
Tires wear unevenly or prematurely	• Incorrect wheel size • Wheels are out of balance • Wheels are out of alignment	• Check if wheel and tire size are compatible • Have wheels balanced • Have wheel alignment checked/adjusted

Troubleshooting Basic Tire Problems

Problem	Cause	Solution
The car's front end vibrates at high speeds and the steering wheel shakes	• Wheels out of balance • Front end needs aligning	• Have wheels balanced. • Have front end alignment checked
The car pulls to one side while cruising	• Unequal tire pressure (car will usually pull to the low side) • Mismatched tires • Front end needs aligning	• Check/adjust tire pressure • Be sure tires are of the same type and size • Have front end alignment checked
Abnormal, excessive or uneven tire wear See "How to Read Tire Wear"	• Infrequent tire rotation • Improper tire pressure • Sudden stops/starts or high speed on curves	• Rotate tires more frequently to equalize wear • Check/adjust pressure • Correct driving habits
Tire squeals	• Improper tire pressure • Front end needs aligning	• Check/adjust tire pressure • Have front end alignment checked

Tire Size Comparison Chart

| "Letter" sizes | | | Inch Sizes | Metric-inch Sizes | | |
"60 Series"	"70 Series"	"78 Series"	1965–77	"60 Series"	"70 Series"	"80 Series"
			5.50-12, 5.60-12	165/60-12	165/70-12	155-12
		Y78-12	6.00-12			
		W78-13	5.20-13	165/60-13	145/70-13	135-13
		Y78-13	5.60-13	175/60-13	155/70-13	145-13
			6.15-13	185/60-13	165/70-13	155-13, P155/80-13
A60-13	A70-13	A78-13	6.40-13	195/60-13	175/70-13	165-13
B60-13	B70-13	B78-13	6.70-13	205/60-13	185/70-13	175-13
			6.90-13			
C60-13	C70-13	C78-13	7.00-13	215/60-13	195/70-13	185-13
D60-13	D70-13	D78-13	7.25-13			
E60-13	E70-13	E78-13	7.75-13			195-13
			5.20-14	165/60-14	145/70-14	135-14
			5.60-14	175/60-14	155/70-14	145-14
			5.90-14			
A60-14	A70-14	A78-14	6.15-14	185/60-14	165/70-14	155-14
	B70-14	B78-14	6.45-14	195/60-14	175/70-14	165-14
	C70-14	C78-14	6.95-14	205/60-14	185/70-14	175-14
D60-14	D70-14	D78-14				
E60-14	E70-14	E78-14	7.35-14	215/60-14	195/70-14	185-14
F60-14	F70-14	F78-14, F83-14	7.75-14	225/60-14	200/70-14	195-14
G60-14	G70-14	G77-14, G78-14	8.25-14	235/60-14	205/70-14	205-14
H60-14	H70-14	H78-14	8.55-14	245/60-14	215/70-14	215-14
J60-14	J70-14	J78-14	8.85-14	255/60-14	225/70-14	225-14
L60-14	L70-14		9.15-14	265/60-14	235/70-14	
	A70-15	A78-15	5.60-15	185/60-15	165/70-15	155-15
B60-15	B70-15	B78-15	6.35-15	195/60-15	175/70-15	165-15
C60-15	C70-15	C78-15	6.85-15	205/60-15	185/70-15	175-15
	D70-15	D78-15				
E60-15	E70-15	E78-15	7.35-15	215/60-15	195/70-15	185-15
F60-15	F70-15	F78-15	7.75-15	225/60-15	205/70-15	195-15
G60-15	G70-15	G78-15	8.15-15/8.25-15	235/60-15	215/70-15	205-15
H60-15	H70-15	H78-15	8.45-15/8.55-15	245/60-15	225/70-15	215-15
J60-15	J70-15	J78-15	8.85-15/8.90-15	255/60-15	235/70-15	225-15
	K70-15		9.00-15	265/60-15	245/70-15	230-15
L60-15	L70-15	L78-15, L84-15	9.15-15			235-15
	M70-15	M78-15				255-15
		N78-15				

NOTE: Every size tire is not listed and many size comaprisons are approximate, based on load ratings. Wider tires than those supplied new with the vehicle should always be checked for clearance

FLUIDS AND LUBRICANTS

Fuel Recommendations

The engine is designed to operate on unleaded gasoline ONLY and is essential for the proper operation of the emission control system. The use of unleaded fuel will reduce spark plug fouling, exhaust system corrosion and engine oil deterioration.

In most parts of the United States, fuel with an octane rating of 87 should be used; in high altitude areas, fuel with an octane rating as low as 85 may be used. Using fuels with a lower octane may decrease engine performance, increase emissions and engine wear.

In some areas, fuel consisting of a blend of alcohol may be used; this blend of gasoline and alcohol is known as gasohol. When using gasohol, never use blends exceeding 10% ethanol or 5% methanol.

NOTE: The use of fuel with excessive amounts of alcohol may jeopardize the new car warranties.

Oil Recommendations

Use only oil which has the API (American Petroleum Institute) designation "SG", "SG/CC" or "SG/CD".

Since fuel economy is effected by the viscosity (thickness) of the engine oil, it is recommended to select an oil with reference to the outside temperature. For satisfactory lubrication, use a lower viscosity oil for colder temperatures and a higher viscosity oil for warmer temperatures.

OIL LEVEL CHECK

Every time you stop for fuel, check the engine oil as follows:
1. Make sure the van is parked on level ground.
2. When checking the oil level it is best for the engine to be at normal operating temperature, although checking the oil immediately after stopping will lead to a false reading. Wait a few minutes after turning off the engine to allow the oil to drain back into the crankcase.
3. Open the hood and locate the dipstick which will be on either the right or left side depending upon your particular engine. Pull the dipstick from its tube, wipe it clean and then reinsert it.
4. Pull the dipstick out again and, holding it horizontally, read the oil level. The oil should be between the "FULL" and "ADD" marks on the dipstick. If the oil is below the "ADD"

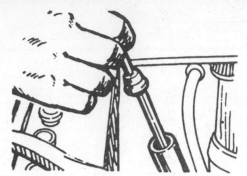
The oil level is checked with the dipstick

The oil level should be between the "ADD" and "FULL" marks on the dipstick

mark, add oil of the proper viscosity through the capped opening in the top of the cylinder head cover.
5. Replace the dipstick and check the oil level again after adding any oil. Be careful not to overfill the crankcase. Approximately 1 quart of oil will raise the level from the "ADD" mark to the "FULL" mark. Excess oil will generally be consumed at an accelerated rate.

CHANGING OIL AND FILTER

The oil is to be changed every 7,500 miles or 12 months, which ever occurs first. Under normal conditions, change the filter at first oil change and then at every other oil change, unless 12 months pass between changes. We recommend that the oil filter be changed every time the oil is changed. About a quart of dirty oil remains in the old filter. For a few dollars, it is a small expense for extended engine life.

If driving under such conditions, such as : dusty areas, trailer towing, idling for long periods of time, low speed operation, or when operating with temperatures below freezing and driving short distances (under 4 miles), change the oil and filter every 3,000 miles or 3 months.

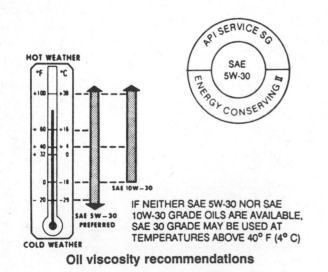

IF NEITHER SAE 5W-30 NOR SAE 10W-30 GRADE OILS ARE AVAILABLE, SAE 30 GRADE MAY BE USED AT TEMPERATURES ABOVE 40° F (4° C)

Oil viscosity recommendations

By keeping inward pressure on the plug as you unscrew it, oil will not escape past the thread

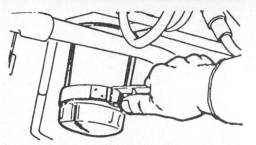

Remove the oil filter with a strap wrench

Coat the new oil filter gasket with clean oil

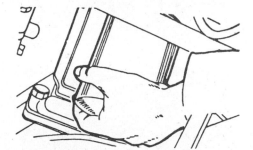

Install the new oil filter by hand

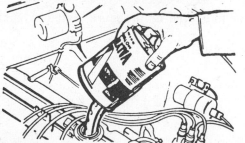

Add oil through the capped opening in the cylinder head cover

REMOVAL AND INSTALLATION

1. Raise the van and support on jack stands. Remove the oil pan plug and drain oil into a catch pan.
2. Using an oil filter wrench, remove the oil filter and place it in the oil catch pan. Using a clean rag, wipe oil filter mounting surface.

To install:

3. When installing the oil filter, place a small amount of oil on the sealing gasket and tighten the filter only hand tight. Install the oil pan plug and torque to 20 ft. lbs. (27 Nm).

4. Make sure the plug is tight in the pan, but do not overtighten. Using a funnel, add oil through the valve cover cap. Lower the van, start the engine and inspect for oil leaks.

Transaxle

FLUID RECOMMENDATION

Use only DEXRON®II Automatic transaxle Fluid.

FLUID LEVEL CHECK

Check the automatic transaxle fluid level at least every 15,000 miles or 12 months. The dipstick can be found on the left (driver) side of the engine compartment. The fluid level should be checked only when the transaxle is hot (normal operating temperature). The transaxle is considered hot after about 20 miles of highway driving.

1. Park the van on a level surface with the engine idling. Shift the transaxle into Neutral and set the parking brake.
2. Remove the dipstick, wipe it clean and then reinsert it firmly. Be sure that it has been pushed all the way in. Remove the dipstick again and check the fluid level while holding it horizontally. With the engine running, the fluid level should be between the second notch and the "FULL HOT" line. If the fluid must be checked when it is cool, the level should be between the first and second notches.
3. If the fluid level is below the second notch (engine hot) or the first notch (engine cold), add DEXRON®II automatic transaxle fluid through the dipstick tube. This is easily done with the aid of a funnel. Check the level often as you are filling the transaxle. Be extremely careful not to overfill it. Overfilling will cause slippage, seal damage and overheating. Approximately 1 pint of ATF will raise the fluid level from one notch/line to the other.

NOTE: Use only DEXRON®II ATF. The use of any other fluid will cause severe damage to the transaxle.

The fluid on the dipstick should always be a bright red color. If it is discolored (brown or black), or smells burnt, serious transaxle troubles, probably due to overheating, should be suspected. The transaxle should be inspected by a qualified technician to locate the cause of the burnt fluid.

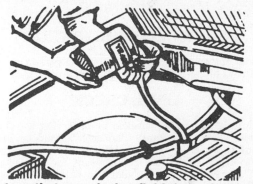

Add automatic transmission fluid through the dipstick tube

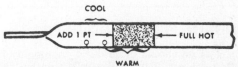

Automatic transaxle dipstick marks; the proper level is within the shaded area

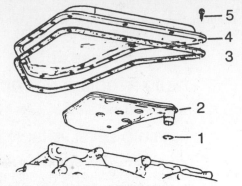

1. O-ring seal
2. Filter
3. Pan gasket
4. Oil pan
5. Oil pan bolt

Automatic transaxle pan and filter

DRAIN AND REFILL

1. Raise and support the van on jack stands. Place an oil catch pan under the transaxle.
2. Remove the oil pan bolts from the front and side only.
3. Loosen the rear oil pan bolts approximately 4 turns.
4. Using a rubber mallet, lightly tap the oil pan and allow the fluid to drain.
5. Remove the remaining oil pan bolts and remove the pan and gasket. Remove the filter and the O-ring.
6. Clean the oil pan and transaxle surfaces with a scraper. Wash the mating surfaces with solvent to remove the oil film.
7. Install the new filter and O-ring (coat the O-ring with petroleum jelly).
8. Raise the oil pan into position with the new gasket and install the bolts. Torque the bolts to 15 ft. lbs. (20.3 Nm) and lower the vehicle.
9. Add new transaxle fluid through the dipstick tube. Operate the engine and transaxle and check for leaks.

Differential

The front drive differential is part of the automatic transaxle. The assembly is lubricated by the transaxle fluid.

Coolant

FLUID RECOMMENDATION

When adding or changing the fluid in the system, create a 50/50 mixture of high quality ethylene glycol antifreeze and water.

LEVEL CHECK

The fluid level may be checked by observing the fluid level marks of the recovery tank. The level should be below the "ADD" mark when the system is cold. At normal operating temperatures, the level should be between the "ADD" and the "FULL" marks. Only add coolant to bring the level to the "FULL" mark.

—— CAUTION ——
Should it be necessary to remove the radiator cap, make sure that the system has had time to cool, reducing the internal pressure.

DRAIN, FLUSH AND REFILL

The cooling system should be drained, thoroughly flushed and refilled at least every 30,000 miles or 24 months. These operations should be done with the engine cold.
1. Remove the radiator and recovery tank caps. Run the en-

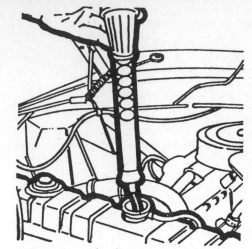

Coolant protection can be checked with a single float-type tester

The system should be pressure tested at least once a year

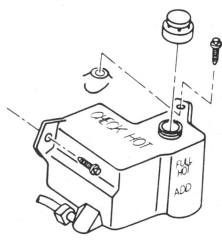

Coolant recovery tank

gine until the upper radiator hose gets hot. This means that the thermostat is open and the coolant is flowing through the system.

2. Turn the engine "OFF" and place a large container under the radiator. Open the drain valve at the bottom of the radiator. Open the block drain plugs to speed up the draining process, if so equipped.

3. Close the drain valves and add water until the system is full. Repeat the draining and filling process several times, until the liquid is nearly colorless.

4. After the last draining, fill the system with a 50/50 mixture of ethylene glycol and water. Run the engine until the system is hot and add coolant, if necessary. Replace the caps and check for any leaks.

Master Cylinder

FLUID RECOMMENDATION

When adding or replacing the brake fluid, always use a top quality fluid, such as Delco Supreme II or DOT-3. DO NOT allow the brake fluid container or master cylinder reservoir to remain open for long periods of time; brake fluid absorbs moisture from the air, reducing its effectiveness and causing corrosion in the lines. General Motors recommends that silicone brake should not be used in the brake system. Damage to the rubber parts may result.

FLUID LEVEL

The master cylinder — located in the left rear section of the engine compartment — consists of an aluminum body and a translucent nylon reservoir with minimum fill indicators. The fluid level of the reservoirs should be kept near the top of the observation windows.

NOTE: Be careful not to spill any brake fluid on painted surfaces, for it eats the paint.

Any sudden decrease in the fluid level indicates a possible leak in the system and should be checked out immediately.

Power Steering Pump

FLUID RECOMMENDATION

When filling or replacing the fluid of the power steering pump reservoir, use GM part #1050017 power steering fluid only. Automatic transmission fluid may cause damage to the internal power steering components.

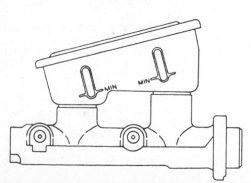

The fluid should be level with the top of the observation windows

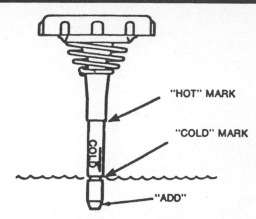

Use the dipstick to check the power steering fluid

LEVEL CHECK

Power steering fluid level should be checked at least once every 12 months or 7,500 miles. To prevent possible overfilling, check the fluid level only when the fluid has warmed to operating temperatures and the wheels are turned straight ahead. If the level is low, fill the pump reservoir until the fluid level measures "full" on the reservoir dipstick. Low fluid level usually produces a moaning sound as the wheels are turned (especially when standing still or parking) and increases steering wheel effort.

NOTE: GM recommends that you use power steering fluid, GM part #1050017 or its equal. DEXRON®II is not an acceptable substitute.

Chassis Greasing

Chassis greasing can be performed with a pressurized grease gun or it can be performed at home by using a hand-operated grease gun. Wipe the grease fittings clean before greasing in order to prevent the possibility of forcing any dirt into the component. Do not over grease the components because damage may occur to the grease seals.

Body Lubrication

HOOD LATCH AND HINGES

Clean the latch surfaces and apply clean engine oil or all purpose lithium grease to the latch pilot bolts, spring anchor and hood hinges as well. Use a chassis grease to lubricate all the pivot points in the latch release mechanism.

DOOR HINGES

The gas tank filler door, front door rear tailgate hinges and sliding door rollers should be wiped clean and lubricated with clean engine oil. Silicone spray also works well on these parts, but must be applied more often. Use engine oil to lubricate the tailgate lock mechanism and the lock bolt and striker. The door lock cylinders can be lubricated easily with a shot silicone spray or one of the many dry penetrating lubricants commercially available.

PARKING BRAKE LINKAGE

Use chassis grease on the parking brake cable where it con-

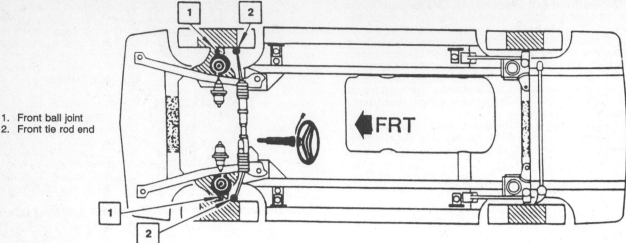

1. Front ball joint
2. Front tie rod end

Chassis lubrication points

tacts the guides, links, levers, and pulleys. The grease should be a water resistant one for durability under the van.

ACCELERATOR LINKAGE

Lubricate the throttle body and the accelerator pedal lever at

the support inside the van with clean engine oil or silicone spray.

TRANSMISSION SHIFT LINKAGE

Lubricate with clean engine oil or silicone spray.

TRAILER TOWING

Your General Motors van was designed and intended primarily to carry people. Towing a trailer may affect some characteristic of the vehicle, like handling, durability and economy. Proper use of the correct equipment is highly recommended for your safety and satisfaction. The trailer should never weigh more than 1,400 lbs. with up to 6 occupants or more than 2,000 lbs. with up to 2 occupants. Even that can be too heavy, depending on the speed, temperature, altitude and road grades.

Factory trailer towing packages are available on most vehicles. However, if you are installing a trailer hitch and wiring on your vehicle, there are a few thing that you ought to know.

Trailer Weight

Trailer weight is the first, and most important, factor in determining whether or not your vehicle is suitable for towing the trailer you have in mind. The horsepower-to-weight ratio should be calculated. The basic standard is a ratio of 35:1. That is, 35 pounds of GVW for every horsepower.

To calculate this ratio, multiply you engine's rated horsepower by 35, then subtract the weight of the vehicle, including passengers and luggage. The resulting figure is the ideal maximum trailer weight that you can tow. One point to consider: a numeri-

cally higher axle ratio can offset what appears to be a low trailer weight. If the weight of the trailer that you have in mind is somewhat higher than the weight you just calculated, you might consider changing your rear axle ratio to compensate.

Hitch Weight

There are three kinds of hitches: bumper mounted, frame mounted, and load equalizing.

Bumper mounted hitches are those which attach solely to the vehicle's bumper. Many states prohibit towing with this type of hitch, when it attaches to the vehicle's stock bumper, since it subjects the bumper to stresses for which it was not designed. Aftermarket rear step bumpers, designed for trailer towing, are acceptable for use with bumper mounted hitches.

Frame mounted hitches can be of the type which bolts to two or more points on the frame, plus the bumper, or just to several points on the frame. Frame mounted hitches can also be of the tongue type, for Class I towing, or, of the receiver type, for Classes II and III.

Load equalizing hitches are usually used for large trailers. Most equalizing hitches are welded in place and use equalizing bars and chains to level the vehicle after the trailer is hooked up.

The bolt-on hitches are the most common, since they are relatively easy to install.

Check the gross weight rating of your trailer. Tongue weight is usually figured as 10% of gross trailer weight. Therefore, a trailer with a maximum gross weight of 2,000 lb. will have a maximum tongue weight of 200 lb. Class I trailers fall into this category. Class II trailers are those with a gross weight rating of 2,000–3,500 lb., while Class III trailers fall into the 3,500–6,000 lb. category. Class IV trailers are those over 6,000 lb. and are for use with fifth wheel trucks, only.

When you have determined the hitch that you'll need, follow the manufacturer's installation instructions, exactly, especially when it comes to fastener torques. The hitch will subjected to a lot of stress and good hitches come with hardened bolts. Never substitute an inferior bolt for a hardened bolt.

Wiring

Wiring the vehicle for towing is fairly easy. There are a number of good wiring kits available and these should be used, rather than trying to design your own. All trailers will need brake lights and turn signals as well as tail lights and side marker lights. Most states require extra marker lights for overly wide trailers. Also, most states have recently required back-up lights for trailers, and most trailer manufacturers have been building trailers with back-up lights for several years.

Additionally, some Class I, most Class II and just about all Class III trailers will have electric brakes.

Add to this number an accessories wire, to operate trailer internal equipment or to charge the trailer's battery, and you can have as many as seven wires in the harness.

Determine the equipment on your trailer and buy the wiring kit necessary. The kit will contain all the wires needed, plus a plug adapter set which included the female plug, mounted on the bumper or hitch, and the male plug, wired into, or plugged into the trailer harness.

When installing the kit, follow the manufacturer's instructions. The color coding of the wires is standard throughout the industry.

One point to note, some domestic vehicles, and most imported vehicles, have separate turn signals. On most domestic vehicles, the brake lights and rear turn signals operate with the same bulb. For those vehicles with separate turn signals, you can purchase an isolation unit so that the brake lights won't blink whenever the turn signals are operated, or, you can go to your local electronics supply house and buy four diodes to wire in series with the brake and turn signal bulbs. Diodes will isolate the brake and turn signals. The choice is yours. The isolation units are simple and quick to install, but far more expensive than the diodes. The diodes, however, require more work to install properly, since they require the cutting of each bulb's wire and soldering in place of the diode.

One final point, the best kits are those with a spring loaded cover on the vehicle mounted socket. This cover prevents dirt and moisture from corroding the terminals. Never let the vehicle socket hang loosely. Always mount it securely to the bumper or hitch.

Cooling

ENGINE

One of the most common, if not THE most common, problem associated with trailer towing is engine overheating.

With factory installed trailer towing packages, a heavy duty cooling system is usually included. Heavy duty cooling systems are available as optional equipment on most vehicles, with or without a trailer package. If you have one of these extra-capacity systems, you shouldn't have any overheating problems.

If you have a standard cooling system, without an expansion tank, you'll definitely need to get an aftermarket expansion tank kit, preferably one with at least a 2 quart capacity. These kits are easily installed on the radiator's overflow hose, and come with a pressure cap designed for expansion tanks.

Another helpful accessory is a Flex Fan. These fan are large diameter units are designed to provide more airflow at low speeds, with blades that have deeply cupped surfaces. The blades then flex, or flatten out, at high speed, when less cooling air is needed. These fans are far lighter in weight than stock fans, requiring less horsepower to drive them. Also, they are far quieter than stock fans.

If you do decide to replace your stock fan with a flex fan, note that if your van has a fan clutch, a spacer between the flex fan and water pump hub will be needed.

Aftermarket engine oil coolers are helpful for prolonging engine oil life and reducing overall engine temperatures. Both of these factors increase engine life.

While not absolutely necessary in towing Class I and some Class II trailers, they are recommended for heavier Class II and all Class III towing.

Engine oil cooler systems consist of an adapter, screwed on in place of the oil filter, a remote filter mounting and a multi-tube, finned heat exchanger, which is mounted in front of the radiator or air conditioning condenser.

TRANSAXLE

Modern automatics have proven reliable and, of course, easy to operate, in trailer towing.

The increased load of a trailer, however, causes an increase in the temperature of the automatic transaxle fluid. Heat is the worst enemy of an automatic transaxle. As the temperature of the fluid increases, the life of the fluid decreases.

It is essential, therefore, that you install an automatic transaxle cooler.

The cooler, which consists of a multi-tube, finned heat exchanger, is usually installed in front of the radiator or air conditioning compressor, and hooked inline with the transaxle cooler tank inlet line. Follow the cooler manufacturer's installation instructions.

Select a cooler of at least adequate capacity, based upon the combined gross weights of the vehicle and trailer.

Cooler manufacturers recommend that you use an aftermarket cooler in addition to, and not instead of, the present cooling tank in your vehicle's radiator. If you do want to use it in place of the radiator cooling tank, get a cooler at least two sizes larger than normally necessary.

NOTE: A transaxle cooler can, sometimes, cause slow or harsh shifting in the transaxle during cold weather, until the fluid has a chance to come up to normal operating temperature. Some coolers can be purchased with or retrofitted with a temperature bypass valve which will allow fluid flow through the cooler only when the fluid has reached operating temperature, or above.

PUSHING AND TOWING

Push Starting

Push starting is not possible on vehicles equipped automatic transaxles.

Towing

This vehicle should not be towed on the front wheels unless absolutely necessary.

When towing the car on its front wheels, the steering wheel must be secured in a straight-ahead position and the steering column unlocked. The transaxle should be in Neutral and the brake released. Never exceed speeds of 35 mph or tow for more than 50 miles.

JUMP STARTING

The chemical reaction in a battery produces explosive hydrogen gas. This is the safe way to jump start a dead battery, reducing the chances of an accidental spark that could cause an explosion.

Precautions

1. Be sure both batteries are of the same voltage.
2. Be sure both batteries are of the same polarity (have the same grounded terminal).
3. Be sure the vehicles are not touching.
4. Be sure the vent cap holes are not obstructed.
5. Do not smoke or allow sparks around the battery.
6. In cold weather, check for frozen electrolyte in the battery.
7. Do not allow electrolyte on your skin or clothing.

Procedure

1. Bring the starting vehicle close (they must not touch) so that the batteries can be reached easily.
2. Turn the ignition OFF and all accessories must be off (except for hazard light, if required).
3. Put both cars in **P** or **N** and set the parking brake.
4. If the terminals on the run down battery are heavily corroded, clean them.
5. Identify the positive and negative posts on both batteries and connect the cables in the order shown.
6. Start the engine of the starting vehicle and run it at fast idle. Try to start the car with the dead battery. Crank it for no more than 10 seconds at a time and let it cool off for 20 seconds in between tries.
7. If it doesn't start in 3 tries, there is something else wrong.
8. Disconnect the cables in the reverse order.

Alternator bracket location for final battery jumper cable connection

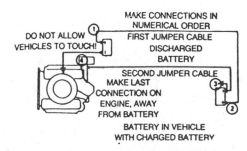

Recommended battery jumper connection sequence

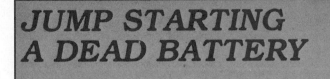

JUMP STARTING A DEAD BATTERY

The chemical reaction in a battery produces explosive hydrogen gas. This is the safe way to jump start a dead battery, reducing the chances of an accidental spark that could cause an explosion.

Jump Starting Precautions

1. Be sure both batteries are of the same voltage.
2. Be sure both batteries are of the same polarity (have the same grounded terminal).
3. Be sure the vehicles are not touching.
4. Be sure the vent cap holes are not obstructed.
5. Do not smoke or allow sparks around the battery.
6. In cold weather, check for frozen electrolyte in the battery. Do not jump start a frozen battery.
7. Do not allow electrolyte on your skin or clothing.
8. Be sure the electrolyte is not frozen.

CAUTION: Make certin that the ignition key, in the vehicle with the dead battery, is in the OFF position. Connecting cables to vehicles with on-board computers will result in computer destruction if the key is not in the OFF position.

Jump Starting Procedure

1. Determine voltages of the two batteries; they must be the same.
2. Bring the starting vehicle close (they must not touch) so that the batteries can be reached easily.
3. Turn off all accessories and both engines. Put both vehicles in Neutral or Park and set the handbrake.
4. Cover the cell caps with a rag—do not cover terminals.
5. If the terminals on the run-down battery are heavily corroded, clean them.
6. Identify the positive and negative posts on both batteries and connect the cables in the order shown.
7. Start the engine of the starting vehicle and run it at fast idle. Try to start the car with the dead battery. Crank it for no more than 10 seconds at a time and let it cool for 20 seconds in between tries.
8. If it doesn't start in 3 tries, there is something else wrong.
9. Disconnect the cables in the reverse order.
10. Replace the cell covers and dispose of the rags.

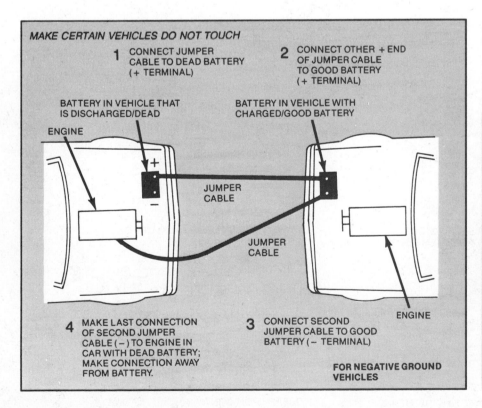

Side terminal batteries occasionally pose a problem when connecting jumper cables. There frequently isn't enough room to clamp the cables without touching sheet metal. Side terminal adaptors are available to alleviate this problem and should be removed after use

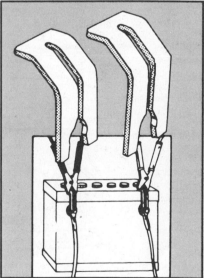

JACKING

The standard jack utilizes slots in the rocker panels to raise and lower the vehicle. The jack supplied with the car should never be used for any service operation other than tire changing. Never get under the car while it is supported by only a jack. Always block the wheels when changing tires.

The service operations in this book often require that one end or the other, or both, of the car be raised and safely supported. The ideal method, of course, would be a hydraulic hoist. Since this is beyond both the resource and requirement of the do-it-yourselfer, a small hydraulic, screw or scissors jack will suffice for the procedures in this guide. Two sturdy jackstands should be acquired if you intend to work under the car at any time. An

alternate method of raising the car would be drive-on ramps. These are available commercially or can be fabricated from heavy boards or steel. Be sure to block the wheels when using ramps. Never use concrete blocks to support the car. They may break if the load is not evenly distributed.

Regardless of the method of jacking or hoisting the car, there are only certain areas of the undercarriage and suspension you can safely use to support it. See the illustration and make sure that only the shaded areas are used. In addition, be especially careful that you do not damage the catalytic converter. Remember that various cross braces and supports on a lift can sometimes contact low hanging parts of the car.

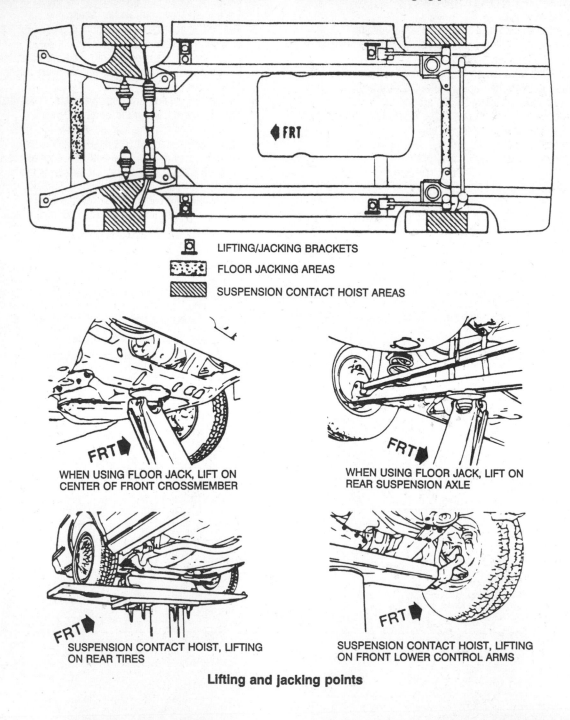

🔲 LIFTING/JACKING BRACKETS

▓▓▓ FLOOR JACKING AREAS

▨▨▨ SUSPENSION CONTACT HOIST AREAS

WHEN USING FLOOR JACK, LIFT ON CENTER OF FRONT CROSSMEMBER

WHEN USING FLOOR JACK, LIFT ON REAR SUSPENSION AXLE

SUSPENSION CONTACT HOIST, LIFTING ON REAR TIRES

SUSPENSION CONTACT HOIST, LIFTING ON FRONT LOWER CONTROL ARMS

Lifting and jacking points

MAINTENANCE INTERVALS CHART

Maintenance	Service Interval
Air cleaner element (Replace)	3,000 miles
Cooling system (Check)	Weekly
(Flush and refill)	30,000 miles (24 months)
Chassis lubrication	7,500 (12 months)
Automatic Transaxle (Check)	Weekly
(Fluid and filter change)	100,000 miles (Heavy duty service—15,000 miles)
Fuel filter (Replacement)	30,000 miles
PCV valve and filter (Replacement)	30,000 miles
Spark plug (Replacement)	30,000 miles
Spark plug wire (Inspection)	60,000 miles
Engine oil (Check)	Weekly
Engine oil and filter (Replacement)	7,500 miles
Throttle body mounting torque (Check—18 ft. lbs.)	After the 1st 7,500 miles
Tire pressure (Check)	Every month
Tire and wheel (rotation)	1st 7,500 miles and every 15,000 miles thereafter

CAPACITIES CHART

Years	Engine No. Cyl. Liters	Crankcase Includes Filter (qt.)	Transmission (pts.)	Fuel Tank (gal.)	Cooling System (qt.) w/AC	wo/AC
1990	6–3.1L	4.5	8.0	18.0	13.4	13.0
1991	6–3.1L	4.5	8.0	18.0	13.4	13.0

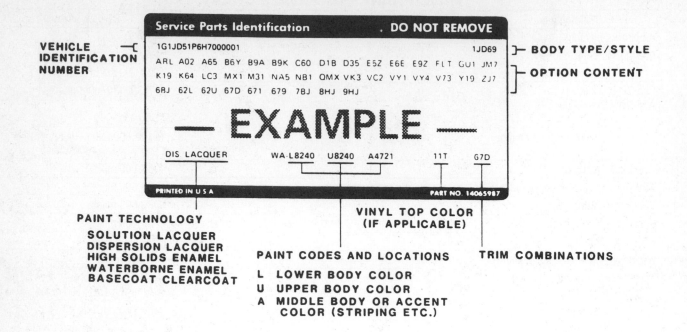

VEHICLE IDENTIFICATION NUMBER

BODY TYPE/STYLE

OPTION CONTENT

Service Parts Identification · **DO NOT REMOVE**

1G1JD51P6H7000001   1JD69

ARL A02 A65 B6Y B9A B9K C60 D1B D35 E5Z E6E E9Z FLT GU1 JM7
K19 K64 LC3 MX1 M31 NA5 NB1 QMX VK3 VC2 VY1 VY4 V73 Y19 ZJ7
6BJ 62L 62U 67D 671 679 7BJ 8HJ 9HJ

— EXAMPLE —

DIS LACQUER   WA·L8240 U8240 A4721   11T   G7D

PRINTED IN U S A   PART NO. 14065987

PAINT TECHNOLOGY

SOLUTION LACQUER
DISPERSION LACQUER
HIGH SOLIDS ENAMEL
WATERBORNE ENAMEL
BASECOAT CLEARCOAT

VINYL TOP COLOR (IF APPLICABLE)

PAINT CODES AND LOCATIONS

L LOWER BODY COLOR
U UPPER BODY COLOR
A MIDDLE BODY OR ACCENT
   COLOR (STRIPING ETC.)

TRIM COMBINATIONS

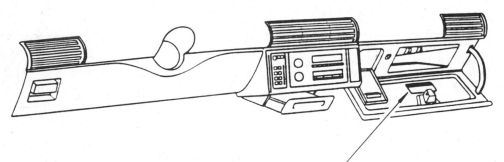

SERVICE PARTS IDENTIFICATION LABEL

Engine Performance and Tune-Up

2

QUICK REFERENCE INDEX

GENERAL INDEX

TUNE-UP SPECIFICATIONS

| Years | Engine No. Cyl. Liters | Spark Plugs | | Ignition Timing (deg.) | Idle Speed | Valve Clearance (in.) | |
		Type	Gap (in.)			In.	Exh.
1990	6-3.1L	R43TS	0.045	①	①	Hyd.	Hyd.
1991	6-3.1L	R43TS	0.045	①	①	Hyd.	Hyd.

① See underhood sticker

Diagnosis of Spark Plugs

Problem	Possible Cause	Correction
Brown to grayish-tan deposits and slight electrode wear.	• Normal wear.	• Clean, regap, reinstall.
Dry, fluffy black carbon deposits.	• Poor ignition output.	• Check distributor to coil connections.
Wet, oily deposits with very little electrode wear.	• "Break-in" of new or recently overhauled engine. • Excessive valve stem guide clearances. • Worn intake valve seals.	• Degrease, clean and reinstall the plugs. • Refer to Section 3. • Replace the seals.
Red, brown, yellow and white colored coatings on the insulator. Engine misses intermittently under severe operating conditions.	• By-products of combustion.	• Clean, regap, and reinstall. If heavily coated, replace.
Colored coatings heavily deposited on the portion of the plug projecting into the chamber and on the side facing the intake valve.	• Leaking seals if condition is found in only one or two cylinders.	• Check the seals. Replace if necessary. Clean, regap, and reinstall the plugs.
Shiny yellow glaze coating on the insulator.	• Melted by-products of combustion.	• Avoid sudden acceleration with wide-open throttle after long periods of low speed driving. Replace the plugs.
Burned or blistered insulator tips and badly eroded electrodes.	• Overheating.	• Check the cooling system. • Check for sticking heat riser valves. Refer to Section 1. • Lean air-fuel mixture. • Check the heat range of the plugs. May be too hot. • Check ignition timing. May be over-advanced. • Check the torque value of the plugs to ensure good plug-engine seat contact.
Broken or cracked insulator tips.	• Heat shock from sudden rise in tip temperature under severe operating conditions. Improper gapping of plugs.	• Replace the plugs. Gap correctly.

TUNE-UP PROCEDURES

In order to extract the full measure of performance and economy from your engine it is essential that it is properly tuned at regular intervals. A regular tune-up will keep your Van's engine running smoothly and will prevent the annoying breakdowns and poor performance associated with an untuned engine.

A complete tune-up should be performed every 30,000 miles (48,000km). This interval should be halved if the vehicle is operated under severe conditions such as trailer towing, prolonged idling, start-and-stop driving, or if starting or running problems are noticed. It is assumed that the routine maintenance described in Section 1 has been kept up, as this will have a decided effect on the results of a tune-up. All of the applicable steps of a tune-up should be followed in order, as the result is a cumulative one.

If the specifications on the underhood tune-up sticker in the engine compartment disagree with the Tune-Up Specifications chart in this Section, the figures on the sticker must be used. The sticker often reflects changes made during the production run.

Spark Plugs

Normally, a set of spark plugs requires replacement about every 20,000–30,000 miles (32,000–48,000km) on vehicles equipped with an High Energy Ignition (HEI) system. Any vehicle which is subjected to severe conditions will need more frequent plug replacement.

Under normal operation, the plug gap increases about 0.025mm (0.001 in.) for every 1,000–2,000 miles (1600–3200km). As the gap increases, the plug's voltage requirement also increases. It requires a greater voltage to jump the wider gap and about 2–3 times as much voltage to fire a plug at high speeds than at idle.

When you are removing the spark plugs, work on one at a time. Don't start by removing the plug wires all at once, for unless you number them, they may become mixed up. Take a minute before you begin and number the wires with tape. The best location for numbering the wires is near the distributor cap.

REMOVAL

When removing the spark plugs, work on one at a time. Don't start by removing the plug wire all at once because unless you number them, they're going to get mixed up. On some models though, it will be more convenient for you to remove all of the wires before you start to work on the plugs. If this is necessary, take a minute before you begin and number the wires with tape before you take them off. The time you spend here will pay off later on.

NOTE: The air cleaner will have to be removed to gain access to the rear spark plugs.

1. Remove the wing nut from the air cleaner attaching rod.
2. Disconnect the vacuum lines attached from the throttle body to the air cleaner.
3. Disconnect the breather hose from the air cleaner.
4. Remove the air cleaner and filter assembly.
5. Disconnect the attaching rod to the throttle body.
6. Remove the plug using the proper size socket, extensions and universals as necessary.
7. Twist the spark plug boot ½ turn and remove the boot from the plug. You may also use a plug wire removal tool designed especially for this purpose. *DO NOT pull on the wire itself.* When the wire has been removed, take a wire brush and clean the area around the plug. Make sure that all the grime is removed so that none will enter the cylinder after the plug has been removed.

8. If removing the plug is difficult, drip some penetrating oil (Liquid Wrench®, WD-40® or etc.) on the plug threads, allow it to work, then remove the plug. Also, be sure that the socket is straight on the plug, especially on those hard to reach plugs.

INSPECTION

Check the plugs for deposits and wear. If they are not going to be replaced, clean the plugs thoroughly. Remember that any kind of deposit will decrease the efficiency of the plug. Plugs can be cleaned on a spark plug cleaning machine, which can sometimes be found in service stations or you can do an acceptable job of cleaning with a stiff brush. If the plugs are cleaned, the electrodes must be filed flat. Use an ignition points file, not an emery board or the like, which will leave deposits. The electrodes must be filed perfectly flat with sharp edges; rounded edges reduce the spark plug voltage by as much as 50%.

Check the spark plug gap before installation. The ground electrode (the L-shaped one connected to the body of the plug) must be parallel to the center electrode and the specified size wire gauge (see Tune-Up Specifications) should pass through the gap with a slight drag. Always check the gap on the new plugs, they are not always set correctly at the factory. DO NOT use a flat feeler gauge when measuring the gap, because the reading will be inaccurate.

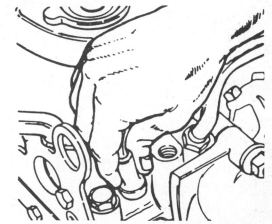

Twist and pull the boot to remove a spark plug wire

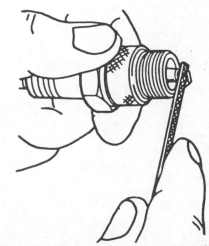

Filing the electrodes on a used plug

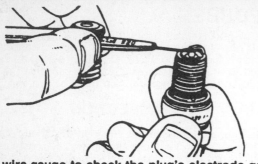

Use a wire gauge to check the plug's electrode gap

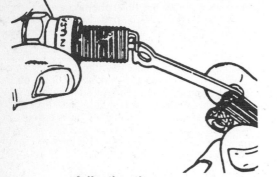

Adjusting the gap

PREFIX AND SUFFIX
LETTERS IDENTIFY
A SPECIFIC TYPE
SPARK PLUG. NUMBERS
RELATE TO THREAD
SIZE AND HEAT RANGE
AS FOLLOWS:

R = Resistor
4 = 14 mm Thread
6 = Heat Range
T = Taper Seat
S = Extended Tip

TAPERED SEAT
NO GASKET

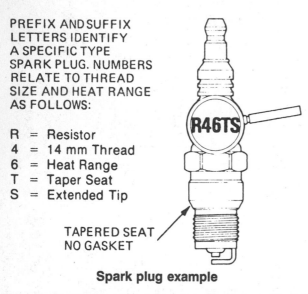

Spark plug example

Wire gapping tools usually have a bending tool attached. Use that to adjust the side electrode until the proper distance is obtained. **Absolutely, never bend the center electrode.** Also, be careful not to bend the side electrode too far or too often; it may weaken and break off within the engine, requiring removal of the cylinder head to retrieve it.

1st number denotes THREAD SIZE

4	= 14 mm	2	= ½-inch taper
8	= 18 mm	5	= ½-inch
10	= 10 mm	6	= ¾-inch
12	= 12 mm	7	= ⅞-inch

2nd number denotes HEAT RANGE

0-1-2-3-4-5-6-7-8-9
COLD ———— HOT

Spark plug coding

INSTALLATION

1. Lubricate the threads of the spark plugs with a drop of oil. Install the plugs and tighten them hand tight. Take care not to crossthread them.

2. Tighten the spark plugs with the socket. DO NOT apply the same amount of force you would use for a bolt; just snug them in. If a torque wrench is available, tighten to 20 ft. lbs. (27 Nm).

3. Install the wire on their respective plugs. Make sure the wires are firmly connected, you will be able to feel them click into place.

4. Replace the air cleaner and components, if removed.

Spark Plug Wires

Every 15,000 miles (24,000km), visually inspect the spark plug cables for burns, cuts or breaks in the insulation. Check the spark plug boots and the nipples on the distributor cap and coil. Replace any damaged wiring.

Every 30,000 miles (48,000km) or so, the resistance of the wires should be checked with an ohmmeter. Wires with excessive resistance will cause misfiring and may make the engine difficult to start in damp weather. Generally, the useful life of the cables is 30,000–45,000 miles (48,000–72,500km).

To check the resistance, remove the distributor cap, leaving the wires in place. Connect one lead of an ohmmeter to an electrode within the cap; connect the other lead to the corresponding spark plug terminal (remove it from the spark plug for this test). Replace any wire which shows a resistance over 30,000Ω. Generally speaking, however, resistance should not be over 25,000Ω, and 30,000Ω must be considered the outer limit of acceptability.

It should be remembered that resistance is also a function of length; the longer the wire the greater the resistance. Thus, if the wires on your van are longer than the factory originals, resistance will be higher, quite possibly outside these limits.

When installing a new set of spark plug wires, replace the wires one at a time so there will be no mixup. Start by replacing the longest cable first. Install the boot firmly over the spark plug. Route the wire exactly the same as the original. Insert the distributor end of the wire firmly into the distributor cap tower, then seat the boot over the tower. Repeat the process for each wire.

FIRING ORDERS

NOTE: To avoid confusion, remove and tag the wires one at a time, for replacement.

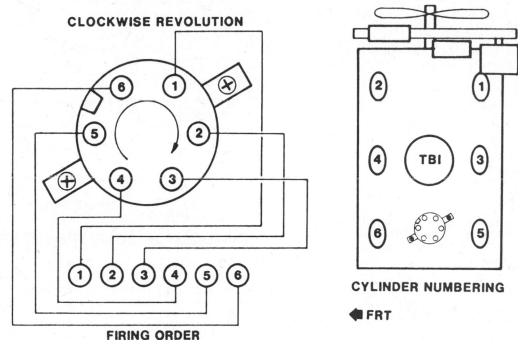

Firing order and cylinder numbering on the 3.1L engine

GM DELCO-REMY HIGH ENERGY IGNITION (HEI)

General Information

The ignition circuit consists of the battery, distributor, ignition coil, ignition switch, spark plugs and primary and secondary wiring

The High Energy Ignition (HEI) system uses an externally mounted ignition coil, having a secondary circuit high tension wire connecting the coil to the distributor cap and interconnecting primary wiring as part of the engine harness.

The High Energy Ignition HEI/EST distributor is equipped to aid in spark timing changes, necessary for Emissions, Economy and performance. This system is called the Electronic Spark Timing Control (EST). The HEI/EST distributor has an internal magnetic pick-up assembly, located inside the distributor containing a permanent magnet, a pole piece with internal teeth and a pick-up coil. When the teeth of the rotating timer core and pole piece align, an induced voltage in the pick-up coil signals the electronic module to open the coil primary circuit. As the

primary current decreases, a high voltage is induced in the secondary windings of the ignition coil, directing a spark through the rotor and high voltage leads to fire the spark plugs.

All spark timing changes in the HEI (EST) distributors are done electronically by the Electronic Control Module (ECM), which monitors information from the various engine sensors, computes the desired spark timing and signals the distributor to change the timing accordingly. With this distributor, no vacuum or centrifugal advances are used.

HEI SYSTEM PRECAUTIONS

Before going on to troubleshooting, it might be a good idea to take note of the following precautions:

Timing Light Use

Inductive pick-up timing lights are the best kind to use if your van is equipped with HEI. Timing lights which connect between the spark plug and the spark plug wire occasionally (not always) give false readings.

Spark Plug Wires

The plug wires used with HEI systems are of a different construction than conventional wires. When replacing them, make sure you get the correct wires, since conventional wires won't carry the voltage. Also, handle them carefully to avoid cracking or splitting them and never pierce them.

Tachometer Use

Not all tachometers will operate or indicate correctly when used on a HEI system. While some tachometers may give a reading, this does not necessarily mean the reading is correct. In addition, some tachometers hook up differently from others. If you can't figure out whether or not your tachometer will work on your van, check with the tachometer manufacturer. Dwell readings, of course, have no significance at all.

HEI Systems Testers

Instruments designed specifically for testing HEI systems are available from several tool manufacturers. Some of these will even test the module itself. However, the tests given in the following section will require only a ohmmeter and a voltmeter.

TROUBLESHOOTING THE HEI SYSTEM

The symptoms of a defective component within the HEI system are exactly the same as those you would encounter in a conventional system.
Some of these symptoms are:
- Hard or no Starting
- Rough Idle
- Fuel Poor Economy
- Engine misses under load or while accelerating

If you suspect a problem in the ignition system, there are certain preliminary checks which you should carry out before you begin to check the electronic portions of the system. First, it is extremely important to make sure the vehicle battery is in a good state of charge. A defective or poorly charged battery will cause the various components of the ignition system to read incorrectly when they are being tested. Second, make sure all wiring connections are clean and tight, not only at the battery, but also at the distributor cap, ignition coil, and at the electronic control module.

Since the only change between electronic and conventional ignition systems is in the distributor component area, it is imperative to check the secondary ignition circuit first. If the secondary circuit checks out properly, then the engine condition is probably not the fault of the ignition system. To check the secondary ignition system, perform a simple spark test. Remove one of the plug wires and insert some sort of extension in the plug socket. An old spark plug with the ground electrode removed makes a good extension. Hold the wire and extension about ¼" away from the block and crank the engine. If a normal spark occurs, then the problem is most likely not in the ignition system. Check for fuel system problems, or fouled spark plugs.

If, however, there is no spark or a weak spark, then further ignition system testing will have to be done. Troubleshooting techniques fall into two categories, depending on the nature of the problem. The categories are (1) Engine cranks, but won't start or (2) Engine runs, but runs rough or cuts out.

Engine Fails to Start

If the engine won't start, perform a spark test as described earlier. If no spark occurs, check for the presence of normal battery voltage at the battery (BAT) terminal in the distributor cap. The ignition switch must be in the **on** position for this test. Either a voltmeter or a test light may be used for this test. Connect the test light wire to ground and the probe end to the BAT terminal at the distributor. If the light comes on, you have voltage to the distributor. If the light fails to come on, this indicates an open circuit in the ignition primary wiring leading to the distributor. In this case, you will have to check wiring continuity back to the ignition switch using a test light. If there is battery voltage at the BAT terminal, but no spark at the plugs, then the problem lies within the distributor assembly. Go on to the ignition system check flow chart.

Engine Runs, but Runs Rough or Cuts Out

1. Make sure the plug wires are in good shape first. There should be no obvious cracks or breaks. You can check the plug wires with an ohmmeter, but do not pierce the wires with a probe. Check the chart for the correct plug wire resistance.
2. If the plug wires are OK, remove the cap assembly, and check for moisture, cracks, chips, or carbon tracks, or any other high voltage leaks or failures. Replace the cap if you find any defects. Make sure the timer wheel rotates when the engine is cranked. If everything is all right so far, go on to the Ignition System Check flow chart.

DISTRIBUTOR COMPONENTS TESTING

If the trouble has been narrowed down to the units within the distributor, the following tests can help pinpoint the defective component. An ohmmeter with both high and low ranges should be used. These tests are made with the cap assembly removed and the battery wire disconnected.

Remote Ignition Coil

Check the ignition coil with an ohmmeter for opens and ground.
1. Connect the negative lead of the ohmmeter, set at high scale, to a good metal ground and the positive lead to the B+ terminal of the ignition coil. The reading should be very high (infinite). If not, replace the coil.

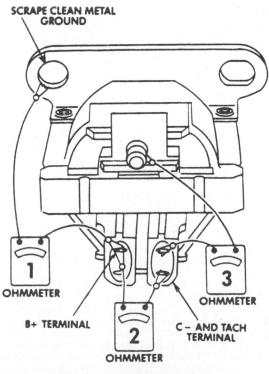

Remote coil electrical test

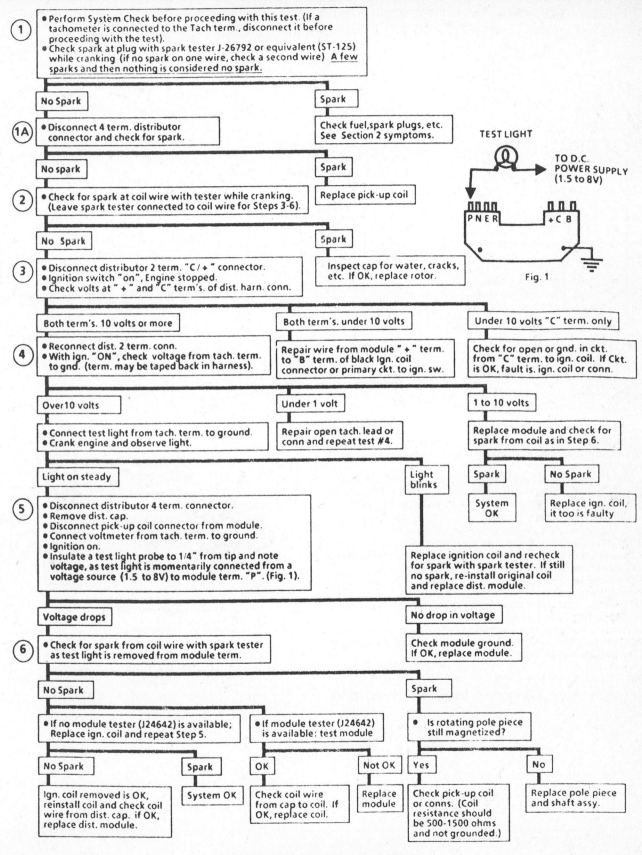

1
- Perform System Check before proceeding with this test. (If a tachometer is connected to the Tach term., disconnect it before proceeding with the test).
- Check spark at plug with spark tester J-26792 or equivalent (ST-125) while cranking (if no spark on one wire, check a second wire) A few sparks and then nothing is considered no spark.

No Spark → Spark

Spark → Check fuel, spark plugs, etc. See Section 2 symptoms.

1A
- Disconnect 4 term. distributor connector and check for spark.

TEST LIGHT

TO D.C. POWER SUPPLY (1.5 to 8V)

P N E R   + C B

Fig. 1

No spark → Spark

Spark → Replace pick-up coil

2
- Check for spark at coil wire with tester while cranking. (Leave spark tester connected to coil wire for Steps 3-6).

No Spark → Spark

Spark → Inspect cap for water, cracks, etc. If OK, replace rotor.

3
- Disconnect distributor 2 term. "C/+" connector.
- Ignition switch "on", Engine stopped.
- Check volts at "+" and "C" term's. of dist. harn. conn.

Both term's. 10 volts or more | Both term's. under 10 volts | Under 10 volts "C" term. only

4
- Reconnect dist. 2 term. conn.
- With ign. "ON", check voltage from tach. term. to gnd. (term. may be taped back in harness).

| Repair wire from module "+" term. to "B" term. of black Ign. coil connector or primary ckt. to ign. sw. | Check for open or gnd. in ckt. from "C" term. to ign. coil. If Ckt. is OK, fault is. ign. coil or conn.

Over10 volts | Under 1 volt | 1 to 10 volts

- Connect test light from tach. term. to ground.
- Crank engine and observe light.

Repair open tach. lead or conn and repeat test #4.

Replace module and check for spark from coil as in Step 6.

Light on steady

Light blinks

Spark | No Spark

System OK | Replace ign. coil, it too is faulty

5
- Disconnect distributor 4 term. connector.
- Remove dist. cap.
- Disconnect pick-up coil connector from module.
- Connect voltmeter from tach. term. to ground.
- Ignition on.
- Insulate a test light probe to 1/4" from tip and note voltage, as test light is momentarily connected from a voltage source (1.5 to 8V) to module term. "P". (Fig. 1).

Replace ignition coil and recheck for spark with spark tester. If still no spark, re-install original coil and replace dist. module.

Voltage drops | No drop in voltage

6
- Check for spark from coil wire with spark tester as test light is removed from module term.

Check module ground. If OK, replace module.

No Spark | Spark

- If no module tester (J24642) is available; Replace ign. coil and repeat Step 5.
- If module tester (J24642) is available: test module
- Is rotating pole piece still magnetized?

No Spark | Spark | OK | Not OK | Yes | No

Ign. coil removed is OK, reinstall coil and check coil wire from dist. cap. if OK, replace dist. module. | System OK | Check coil wire from cap to coil. If OK, replace coil. | Replace module | Check pick-up coil or conns. (Coil resistance should be 500-1500 ohms and not grounded.) | Replace pole piece and shaft assy.

Ignition system check flow chart

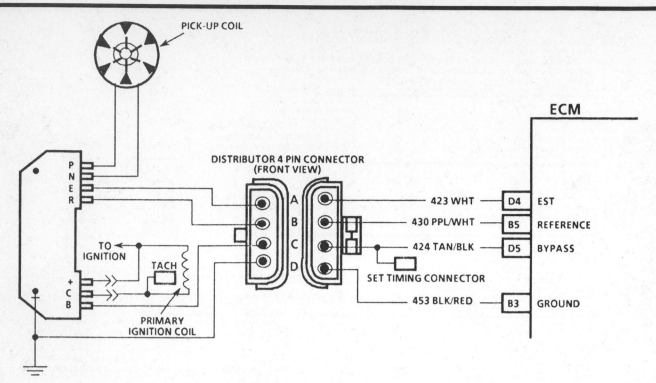

PICK-UP COIL

ECM

DISTRIBUTOR 4 PIN CONNECTOR
(FRONT VIEW)

423 WHT — D4 — EST
430 PPL/WHT — B5 — REFERENCE
424 TAN/BLK — D5 — BYPASS

SET TIMING CONNECTOR

453 BLK/RED — B3 — GROUND

TO IGNITION

TACH

PRIMARY IGNITION COIL

Ignition system check circuit

2. Use the low scale and connect the negative lead of the ohmmeter to the B- terminal of the coil and the positive lead to the C- (tach) terminal. The reading should be very low or zero. If not, replace the coil.

3. Use the high scale and connect the negative lead of the ohmmeter to the C+ terminal of the coil and the positive lead to the coil tower. The reading should not be infinite. If it does, replace the coil.

Pickup Coil

1. Remove the rotor and pickup coil leads from the module.
2. Connect an ohmmeter as illustrated.
3. Observe the ohmmeter and flex the leads by hand to check for intermittent opens.
4. The No. 1 ohmmeter connection should read infinite at all times. If not the pickup is defective.
5. The No. 2 ohmmeter connection should read one steady value between 500–1500 ohms as leads are flexed by hand. If not, the pickup coil is defective.

Module

For module testing please refer to the Ignition System Check flow chart.

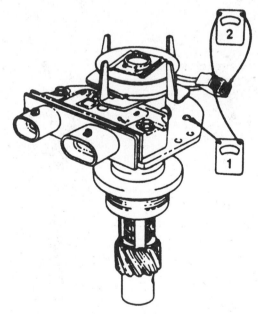

Pickup coil test

ELECTRONIC SPARK TIMING SYSTEM
(EST)

General Description

The High Energy Ignition (HEI) system controls fuel combustion by providing the spark to ignite the compressed air/fuel mixture, in the combustion chamber, at the correct time. To provide improved engine performance, fuel economy and control of the exhaust emissions, the ECM controls distributor spark advance (timing) with the Electronic Spark Timing (EST) system.

The standard High Energy Ignition (HEI) system has a modified distributor module which is used in conjunction with the EST system. The module has eight terminals instead of the four used without EST.

To properly control ignition/combustion timing, the ECM needs to know the following information:

1. Crankshaft position via the pickup coil.
2. Engine speed (rpm).
3. Engine load (manifold pressure or vacuum).
4. Atmospheric (barometric) pressure.
5. Engine temperature.
6. EGR

The EST system consists of the distributor module, ECM and its connecting wires. The distributor has four wires from the HEI module connected to a four terminal connector, which mates with a four wire connector from the ECM.

These circuits perform the following functions:

1. Distributor reference at terminal B – This provides the ECM with rpm and crankshaft position information.

2. Reference ground at terminal D – This wire is grounded in the distributor and makes sure the ground circuit has no voltage drop, which could affect performance. If this circuit is open, it could cause poor performance.

3. By-pass at terminal C – At approximately 500 rpm, the ECM applies 5 volts to this circuit to switch the spark timing control from the HEI module to the ECM. An open or grounded bypass circuit will set a Code 42 and the engine will run at base timing, plus a small amount of advance built into the HEI module.

4. EST at terminal A – This triggers the HEI module. The ECM does not know what the actual timing is, but it does know when it gets its reference signal. It then advances or retards the

spark timing from that point. Therefore, if the base timing is set incorrectly, the entire spark curve will be incorrect.

An open circuit in the EST circuit will set a Code 42 and cause the engine to run on the HEI module timing. This will cause poor performance and poor fuel economy. A ground may set a Code 42, but the engine will not run.

The ECM uses information from the MAP and coolant sensors, in addition to rpm, in order to calculate spark advance as follows:

1. Low MAP output voltage-more spark advance.
2. Cold engine would require more spark advance.
3. High MAP output voltage would require less spark advance.
4. Hot engine would require less spark advance.

RESULTS OF INCORRECT EST OPERATION

Detonation could be caused by low MAP output or high resistance in the coolant sensor circuit.

Poor performance could be caused by high MAP output or low resistance in the coolant sensor circuit.

HOW CODE 42 IS DETERMINED

When the systems is operating on the HEI module with no voltage in the by-pass line, the HEI module grounds the EST signal. The ECM expects to sense no voltage on the EST line during this condition. If it senses voltage, it sets Code 42 and will not go into the EST mode.

When the rpm for EST is reached (approximately 500 rpm), the ECM applies 5 volts to the by-pass line and the EST should no longer be grounded in the HEI module, so the EST voltage should be varying.

If the by-pass line is open, the HEI module will not switch to the EST mode, so the EST voltage will be low and Code 42 will be set.

If the EST line is grounded, the HEI module will switch to the EST, but because the line is grounded, there will be no EST signal and the engine will not operate. A Code 42 may or may not be set.

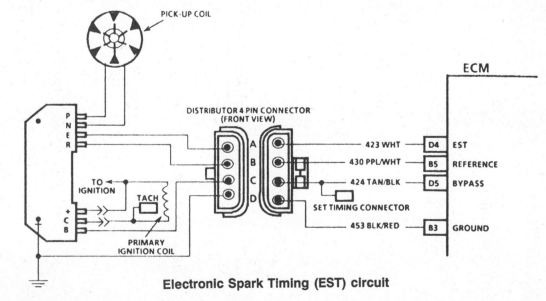

Electronic Spark Timing (EST) circuit

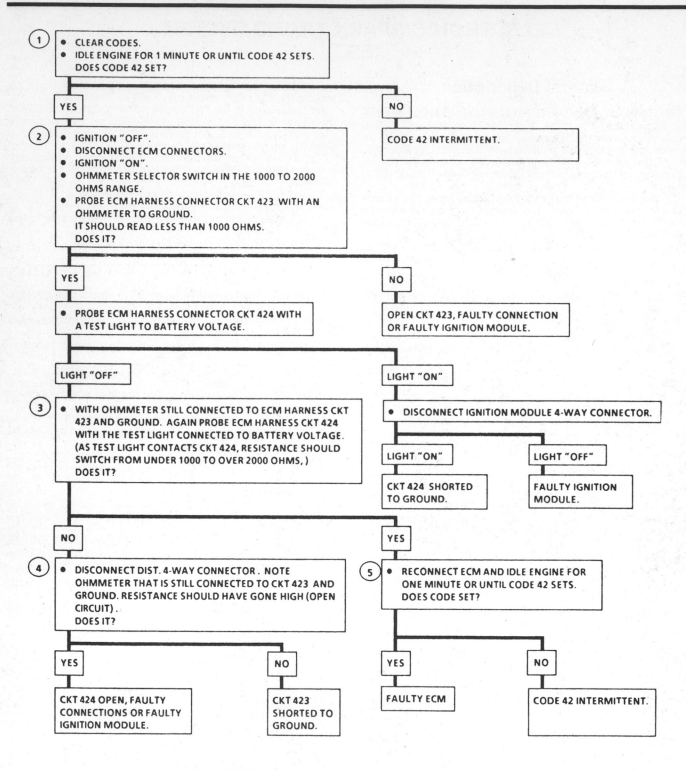

① • CLEAR CODES.
• IDLE ENGINE FOR 1 MINUTE OR UNTIL CODE 42 SETS.
DOES CODE 42 SET?

YES

NO

CODE 42 INTERMITTENT.

② • IGNITION "OFF".
• DISCONNECT ECM CONNECTORS.
• IGNITION "ON".
• OHMMETER SELECTOR SWITCH IN THE 1000 TO 2000 OHMS RANGE.
• PROBE ECM HARNESS CONNECTOR CKT 423 WITH AN OHMMETER TO GROUND.
IT SHOULD READ LESS THAN 1000 OHMS.
DOES IT?

YES

NO

• PROBE ECM HARNESS CONNECTOR CKT 424 WITH A TEST LIGHT TO BATTERY VOLTAGE.

OPEN CKT 423, FAULTY CONNECTION OR FAULTY IGNITION MODULE.

LIGHT "OFF"

LIGHT "ON"

③ • WITH OHMMETER STILL CONNECTED TO ECM HARNESS CKT 423 AND GROUND. AGAIN PROBE ECM HARNESS CKT 424 WITH THE TEST LIGHT CONNECTED TO BATTERY VOLTAGE. (AS TEST LIGHT CONTACTS CKT 424, RESISTANCE SHOULD SWITCH FROM UNDER 1000 TO OVER 2000 OHMS,)
DOES IT?

• DISCONNECT IGNITION MODULE 4-WAY CONNECTOR.

LIGHT "ON"

LIGHT "OFF"

CKT 424 SHORTED TO GROUND.

FAULTY IGNITION MODULE.

NO

YES

④ • DISCONNECT DIST. 4-WAY CONNECTOR. NOTE OHMMETER THAT IS STILL CONNECTED TO CKT 423 AND GROUND. RESISTANCE SHOULD HAVE GONE HIGH (OPEN CIRCUIT).
DOES IT?

⑤ • RECONNECT ECM AND IDLE ENGINE FOR ONE MINUTE OR UNTIL CODE 42 SETS.
DOES CODE SET?

YES

NO

YES

NO

CKT 424 OPEN, FAULTY CONNECTIONS OR FAULTY IGNITION MODULE.

CKT 423 SHORTED TO GROUND.

FAULTY ECM

CODE 42 INTERMITTENT.

CLEAR CODES AND CONFIRM "CLOSED LOOP" OPERATION AND NO "SERVICE ENGINE SOON" LIGHT.

Electronic Spark Timing (EST) Code 42 diagnostic chart

ELECTRONIC SPARK CONTROL SYSTEM
(ESC)

General Description

To control spark knock, an Electronic Spark Control (ESC) syatem has been added. This system is designed to retard spark timing up to 8°, to reduce spark knock to the engine. This allows the engine to use maximum spark advance to improve driveability and fuel economy

Varying octane levels in gasoline can cause detonation in engines. Detonation is called spark knock.

There are 2 basic components of the Electronic Spark Control (ESC) system, the ESC knock sensor and the ESC knock module.

The sensor is mounted in the engine block below the right bank of cylinders. When the ESC knock sensor detects abnormal vibration (spark knocking) in the engine, it produces a voltage that is received by the ESC module. As long as the ESC module sees no voltage from the knock sensor (knock not present), it sends a signal voltage (8–10 volts to the ECM and the ECM provides normal spark advance.

When the module detects voltage from the knock sensor (knock present), it turns OFF the signal to the ECM and the voltage at terminal B7 goes to 0 volts. The ECM then retards EST to reduce spark knock.

RESULTS OF INCORRECT ESC OPERATION

Loss of the ESC knock sensor signal or loss of the ground at the ESC module would cause the signal to the ECM to remain high. This condition would cause the ECM to control EST, as if no spark knocking were happening. No retard would occur, and spark knocking could become severe under heavy engine load conditions.

HOW CODE 43 IS DETERMINED

Loss of the ESC signal to the ECM would cause the ECM to constantly retard EST. This could result in sluggish performance and could cause a Code 43 to set. Scan tool are available that will indicate knock being present or no knock being present. If code 43 is present, refer to the code 43 chart in Section 4. If no code is present and the ESC system is suspected refer to the Electronic Spark Control (ESC) System Check flow chart which follows.

COMPONENT REPLACEMENT

Cap and Rotor

1. Disconnect the negative battery cable.
2. Remove the air cleaner assembly.

3. Remove the distributor cap by removing the 2 holddown screws and turning the cap counterclockwise until released.
4. Lift the rotor from the shaft.
5. Installation is the reverse of removal.

Remote Ignition Coil

1. Disconnect the negative battery cable.
2. Disconnect the secondary lead by pulling on the boot with a twisting motion.
3. Disconnect the primary connectors.
4. Remove the ignition coil mounting screws and remove the coil.
5. Installation is the reverse of removal.

Ignition Module

1. Disconnect the negative battery cable.
2. Remove the air cleaner assembly.
3. Remove the distributor cap and rotor
4. Remove the 2 module attaching screws and lift the module up.
5. Observe the color codes and disconnect the leads from the module.

To install:

6. Spread silicone grease on the metal face of the module and on the distributor base where the module seats.

NOTE: The grease is necessary for module cooling.

7. Reposition the module, attach the color coded leads and install the retaining screws.
8. Install the rotor and cap.
9. Install the air cleaner and negative battery cable.

ESC Knock Sensor

1. Disconnect the negative battery cable.
2. Raise and support the vehicle safely.
3. Disconnect the ESC wiring harness connector from the ESC sensor.
4. Remove the ESC sensor from the engine block.

To install:

5. Install the ESC sensor to the engine block and tighten to 14 ft. lbs. (19 Nm).
6. Connect the ESC wiring harness connector to the ESC sensor.
7. Lower the vehicle and connect the negative battery cable.

ESC Module

1. Disconnect the negative battery cable.
2. Remove the glove compartment assembly.
3. Disconnect the ESC module connector.
4. Remove the attaching screws and remove the ESC module.
5. Installation is the reverse of removal.

THIS CHART SHOULD BE USED AFTER ALL OTHER CAUSES OF SPARK KNOCK HAVE BEEN CHECKED. I.E., TIMING, EGR, ENGINE TEMPERATURE OR EXCESSIVE ENGINE NOISE, ETC. IF CODE 43 IS SET, USE THAT CHART FIRST.

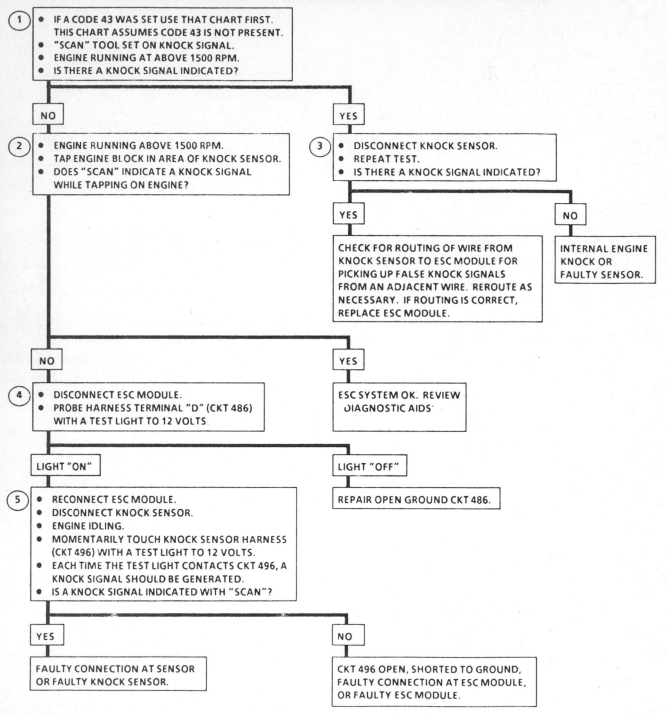

1
- IF A CODE 43 WAS SET USE THAT CHART FIRST. THIS CHART ASSUMES CODE 43 IS NOT PRESENT.
- "SCAN" TOOL SET ON KNOCK SIGNAL.
- ENGINE RUNNING AT ABOVE 1500 RPM.
- IS THERE A KNOCK SIGNAL INDICATED?

NO

YES

2
- ENGINE RUNNING ABOVE 1500 RPM.
- TAP ENGINE BLOCK IN AREA OF KNOCK SENSOR.
- DOES "SCAN" INDICATE A KNOCK SIGNAL WHILE TAPPING ON ENGINE?

3
- DISCONNECT KNOCK SENSOR.
- REPEAT TEST.
- IS THERE A KNOCK SIGNAL INDICATED?

YES

NO

CHECK FOR ROUTING OF WIRE FROM KNOCK SENSOR TO ESC MODULE FOR PICKING UP FALSE KNOCK SIGNALS FROM AN ADJACENT WIRE. REROUTE AS NECESSARY. IF ROUTING IS CORRECT, REPLACE ESC MODULE.

INTERNAL ENGINE KNOCK OR FAULTY SENSOR.

NO

YES

4
- DISCONNECT ESC MODULE.
- PROBE HARNESS TERMINAL "D" (CKT 486) WITH A TEST LIGHT TO 12 VOLTS.

ESC SYSTEM OK. REVIEW DIAGNOSTIC AIDS

LIGHT "ON"

LIGHT "OFF"

5
- RECONNECT ESC MODULE.
- DISCONNECT KNOCK SENSOR.
- ENGINE IDLING.
- MOMENTARILY TOUCH KNOCK SENSOR HARNESS (CKT 496) WITH A TEST LIGHT TO 12 VOLTS.
- EACH TIME THE TEST LIGHT CONTACTS CKT 496, A KNOCK SIGNAL SHOULD BE GENERATED.
- IS A KNOCK SIGNAL INDICATED WITH "SCAN"?

REPAIR OPEN GROUND CKT 486.

YES

NO

FAULTY CONNECTION AT SENSOR OR FAULTY KNOCK SENSOR.

CKT 496 OPEN, SHORTED TO GROUND, FAULTY CONNECTION AT ESC MODULE, OR FAULTY ESC MODULE.

Electronic Spark Control (ESC) system diagnostic chart

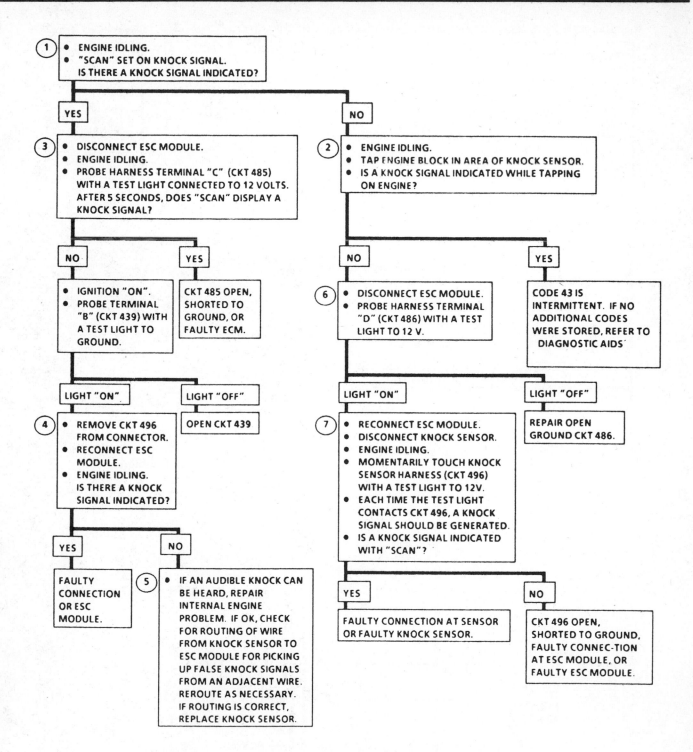

Electronic Spark Control (ESC) Code 43 diagnostic chart

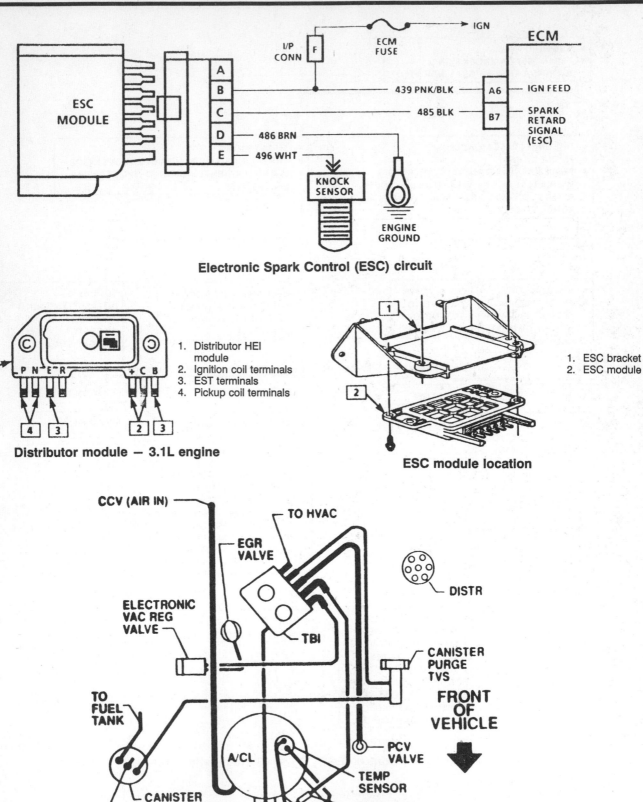

Electronic Spark Control (ESC) circuit

1. Distributor HEI module
2. Ignition coil terminals
3. EST terminals
4. Pickup coil terminals

Distributor module — 3.1L engine

1. ESC bracket
2. ESC module

ESC module location

Emission hose routing — 3.1L engine

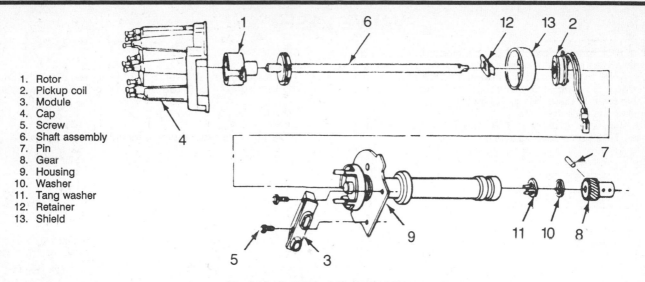

1. Rotor
2. Pickup coil
3. Module
4. Cap
5. Screw
6. Shaft assembly
7. Pin
8. Gear
9. Housing
10. Washer
11. Tang washer
12. Retainer
13. Shield

Exploded view of the HEI/EST distributor

IGNITION TIMING

Follow the instructions on the tune-up label attached to the front right side shock tower. If the label is missing or defaced, making the instructions unreadable, use the following procedure.
1. Run the engine to normal operating temperature.
2. If equipped with air conditioning, turn the system off.
3. Set the parking brake and block the drive wheels.
4. Check the **SERVICE ENGINE SOON** light. It should not be lit.
5. Set the EST (Electric Spark Timing) in the bypass mode by grounding the bypass circuit.

NOTE: The EST bypass circuit is a single tan wire with a black stripe and a connector that breaks out from the engine harness located in front of the shock tower.

6. Turn the engine off and connect the pick-up lead of an inductive type timing light to the number 1 spark plug wire.

WARNING: Do not pierce the wire or attempt to insert a wire between the boot and the wire.

7. Connect the timing light power leads according to the manufacturers instructions.
8. Start the engine, and aim the timing light at the timing mark. The line of the balancer or pulley will line up with the timing mark. If a change is necessary, loosen the distributor hold-down clamp bolt at the base of the distributor. While ob-

Timing mark pointer–3.1L engine

serving the mark with the timing light, slightly rotate the distributor until the line indicates the correct timing. Tighten the hold-down bolt and recheck the timing to specifications.
9. Turn off the engine and remove the timing light. Reconnect the No. 1 spark plug wire, if removed.
10. Disconnect the EST bypass wire from the ground and clear any trouble codes from the Electronic Control Module. Please refer to Section 4 for a further explanation of trouble codes.

VALVE LASH

The The 3.1L engine described in this manual utilizes a hydraulic valve lifter system to obtain zero lash. No adjustment is necessary. Refer to Section 3 for additional information. An initial adjustment is required anytime that the lifters are removed or the valve train is disturbed as follows:

1. Remove the rocker covers.
2. With the No. 1 cylinder at TDC the following valves may be adjusted 1–½ turns past zero lash:

- Exhaust — 1, 2, 3
- Intake — 1, 5, 6

3. Crank the engine 1 revolution to bring the No. 4 cylinder to TDC and adjust the following valves 1–½ turns past zero lash:

- Exhaust — 4, 5, 6
- Intake — 2, 3, 4

4. After all valves are adjusted, install the valve covers.

IDLE SPEED AND MIXTURE ADJUSTMENTS

The idle air speed screw is preset and sealed at the factory. Provision for adjustment during tune up is not provided. Do not attempt adjustment. Idle speeds are automatically controlled.

QUICK REFERENCE INDEX

GENERAL INDEX

UNDERSTANDING BASIC ELECTRICITY

Understanding the basic theory of electricity makes electrical troubleshooting much easier. Several gauges are used in electrical troubleshooting to see inside the circuit being tested. Without a basic understanding, it will be difficult to understand testing procedures.

Electricity is the flow of electrons, hypothetical particles thought to constitute the basic "stuff" of electricity. In a comparison with water flowing in a pipe, the electrons would be the water. As the flow of water can be measured, the flow of electricity can be measured. The unit of measurement is amperes, frequently abbreviated "amps". An ammeter will measure the actual amount of current flowing in the circuit.

Just as the water pressure is measured in units such as pounds per square inch, electrical pressure is measured in volts. When a voltmeter's two probes are placed on two "live" portions of an electrical circuit with different electrical pressures, current will flow through the voltmeter and produce a reading which indicates the difference in electrical pressure between the two parts of the circuit.

While increasing the voltage in a circuit will increase the flow of current, the actual flow depends not only on voltage, but on the resistance of the circuit. The standard unit for measuring circuit resistance is an ohm, measured by an ohmmeter. The ohmmeter is somewhat similar to an ammeter, but incorporates its own source of power so that a standard voltage is always present.

An actual electric circuit consists of four basic parts. These are: the power source such as a generator or battery; a hot wire, which conducts the electricity under a relatively high voltage to the component supplied by the circuit; the load, such as a lamp, motor, resistor, or relay coil; and the ground wire, which carries the current back to the source under very low voltage. In such a circuit the bulk of the resistance exists between the point where the hot wire is connected to the load, and the point where the load is grounded. In an automobile, the vehicle's frame, which is made of steel, is used as a part of the ground circuit for many of the electrical devices.

Remember that, in electrical testing, the voltmeter is connected in parallel with the circuit being tested (without disconnecting any wires) and measures the difference in voltage between the locations of the two probes; that the ammeter is connected in series with the load (the circuit is separated at one point and the ammeter inserted so it becomes a part of the circuit); and the ohmmeter is self-powered, so that all the power in the circuit should be off and the portion of the circuit to be measured contacted at either end by one of the probes of the meter.

For any electrical system to operate, it must make a complete circuit. This simply means that the power flow from the battery must make a complete circle. When an electrical component is operating, power flows from the battery to the component, passes through the component causing it to perform its function (lighting a light bulb) and then returns to the battery through the ground of the circuit. This ground is usually (but not always) the metal part of the van on which the electrical component is mounted.

Perhaps the easiest way to visualize this is to think of connecting a light bulb with two wires attached to it to your battery. The battery in your van has two posts (negative and positive). If one of the two wires attached to the light bulb was attached to the negative post of the battery and the other wire was attached to the positive post of the battery, you would have a complete circuit. Current from the battery would flow out one post, through the wire attached to it and then to the light bulb, where it would pass through causing it to light. It would then leave the light bulb, travel through the other wire, and return to the other post of the battery.

The normal automotive circuit differs from this simple example in two ways. First, instead of having a return wire from the bulb to the battery, the light bulb returns the current to the battery through the chassis of the vehicle. Since the negative battery cable is attached to the chassis and the chassis is made of electrically conductive metal, the chassis of the vehicle can serve as a ground wire to complete the circuit. Secondly, most automotive circuits contain switches to turn components on and off.

Some electrical components which require a large amount of current to operate also have a relay in their circuit. Since these circuits carry a large amount of current, the thickness of the wire in the circuit (gauge size) is also greater. If this large wire were connected from the component to the control switch on the instrument panel, and then back to the component, a voltage drop would occur in the circuit. To prevent this potential drop in voltage, an electromagnetic switch (relay) is used. The large wires in the circuit are connected from the battery to one side of the relay, and from the opposite side of the relay to the component. The relay is normally open, preventing current from passing through the circuit. An additional, smaller, wire is connected from the relay to the control switch for the circuit. When the control switch is turned on, it grounds the smaller wire from the relay and completes the circuit. When the control switch is turned on, it grounds the smaller wire from the relay. If you were to disconnect the light bulb (from the previous example of a light bulb being connected to the battery by two wires) from the wires and touch the two wires together (please take our word for this; don't try it), the result will be a shower of sparks. A similar thing happens (on a smaller scale) when the power supply wire to a component or the electrical component itself becomes grounded before the normal ground connection for the circuit. To prevent damage to the system, the fuse for the circuit blows to interrupt the circuit, protecting the components from damage. Because grounding a wire from a power source makes a complete circuit, less the required component to see the power, the phenomenon is called a short circuit. The most common causes of short circuits are: the rubber insulation on the wire breaking or rubbing through to expose the current carrying core of the wire to a metal part of the van, or a shorted switch.

Some electrical systems on the van are protected by a circuit breaker which is, basically, a self-repairing fuse. When either of the above described events takes place in a system which is protected by a circuit breaker, the circuit breaker opens the circuit the same way a fuse does. However, when either the short is removed from the circuit or the surge subsides, the circuit breaker resets itself and does not have to be replaced as a fuse does.

The final protective device in the chassis electrical system is a fuse link. A fuse link is a wire that acts as a fuse. It is connected between the starter relay and the main wiring harness for the van. This connection is under the hood, very near a similar fuse link which protects the engine electrical system. Since the fuse link protects all the chassis electrical components, it is the probably cause of trouble when none of the electrical components function, unless the battery is disconnected or dead.

Electrical problems generally fall into one of three areas:

1. The component that is not functioning is not receiving current.

2. The component itself is not functioning.

3. The component is not properly grounded.

Problems that fall into the first category are by far the most complicated. It is the current supply system to the component which contains all the switches, relays, fuses., etc.

The electrical system can be checked with a test light and a jumper wire. A test light is a device that looks like a pointed screwdriver with a wire attached to it. It has a light bulb in its handle. A jumper wire is a piece of insulated wire with an alligator clip attached to each end.

If a light bulb is not working, you must follow a systematic plan to determine which of the three causes is the villain.

1. Turn on the switch that controls the inoperable bulb.

2. Disconnect the power supply wire from the bulb. ·

3. Attach the ground wire on the test light to a good metal ground.

4. Touch the probe end of the test light to the end of the power supply wire that was disconnected form the bulb. If the bulb is receiving current, the test light will go on.

NOTE: If the bulb is one which works only when the ignition key is turned on (turn signal), make sure the key is turned on.

If the test light does not go on, then the problem is in the circuit between the battery and the bulb. As mentioned before, this includes all the switches, fuses, and relays in the system. Turn to the wiring diagram and find the bulb on the diagram. Follow the wire that runs back to the battery. The problem is an open circuit between the battery and the bulb. If the fuse is blown and, when replaced, immediately blows again, there is a short circuit in the system which must be located and repaired. If there is a switch in the system, bypass it with a jumper wire. This is done by connecting one end of the jumper wire to the power supply wire into the switch and the other end of the jumper wire to the wire coming out of the switch. Again, consult the wiring diagram. If the test light lights with the jumper wire installed, the switch or whatever was bypassed is defective.

NOTE: Never substitute the jumper wire for the bulb, as the bulb is the component required to use the power from the power source.

5. If the bulb in the test light goes on, then the current is getting to the bulb that is not working in the van. This eliminates the first of the three possible causes. Connect the power supply wire and connect a jumper wire from the bulb to a good metal ground. Do this with the switch which controls the bulb turned on, and also the ignition switch turned on if it is required for the light to work. If the bulb works with jumper wire installed, then it has a bad ground. This is usually caused by the metal area on which the bulb mounts to the van being coated with some type of foreign matter.

6. If neither test located the source of the trouble, then the light bulb itself is defective.

The above test procedure can be applied to any of the components of the chassis electrical system by substituting the component that is not working for the light bulb. Remember that for any electrical system to work, all connections must be clean and tight.

UNDERSTANDING THE ENGINE ELECTRICAL SYSTEM

The engine electrical system can be broken down into three separate and distinct systems:

1. The starting system.
2. The charging system.
3. The ignition system.

Battery and Starting System

The battery is the first link in the chain of mechanisms which work together to provide cranking of the automobile engine. In most modern vans, the battery is a lead/acid electro-chemical device consisting of six two-volt (2V) subsections connected in series so the unit is capable of producing approximately 12V of electrical pressure. Each subsection, or cell, consists of a series of positive and negative plates held a short distance apart in a solution of sulfuric acid and water. The two types of plates are of dissimilar metals. This causes a chemical reaction to be set up, and it is this reaction which produces current flow from the battery when its positive and negative terminals are connected to an electrical appliance such as a lamp or a motor. The continued

transfer of electrons would eventually convert sulfuric acid in the electrolyte to water, and make the two plates identical in chemical composition. As electrical energy is removed from the battery, its voltage output tends to drop. Thus, measuring battery voltage and battery electrolyte composition are two ways of checking the ability of the unit to supply power. During the starting of the engine, electrical energy is removed from the battery. However, if the charging circuit is in good condition and the operating conditions are normal, the power removed from the battery will be replaced by the generator (or alternator) which will force electrons back through the battery, reversing the normal flow, and restoring the battery to its original chemical state.

The battery and starting motor are linked by very heavy electrical cables designed to minimize resistant to the flow of current. Generally, the major power supply cable that leaves the battery goes directly to the starter, while other electrical needs are supplied by a smaller cable. During the starter operation, power flows from the battery to the starter and is grounded through the van's frame and the battery's negative ground strap.

The starting motor is a specially designed, direct current electric motor capable of producing a very great amount of power for its size. One thing that allows the motor to produce a great deal of power is its tremendous rotating speed. It drives the engine through a tiny pinion gear (attached to the starter's armature), which drives the very large flywheel ring gear at a greatly reduced speed. Another factor allowing it to produce so much power is that only intermittent operation is required of it. Thus, little allowance for air circulation is required, and the windings can be built into a very small space.

The starter solenoid is a magnetic device which employs the small current supplied by the starting switch circuit of the ignition switch. The magnetic action moves a plunger which mechanically engages the starter and electrically closes the heavy switch which connects it to the battery. The starting switch circuit consists of the starting switch contained within the ignition switch, a transmission neutral safety switch or clutch pedal switch, and the wiring necessary to connect these with the starter solenoid or relay.

A pinion, which is a small gear, is mounted to a one-way drive clutch. This clutch is splined to the starter armature shaft. When the ignition switch is moved to the **Start** position, the solenoid plunger slides the pinion toward the flywheel ring gear via a collar and spring. If the teeth on the pinion and flywheel match properly, the pinion will engage the flywheel immediately. If the gear teeth butt one another, the spring will be compressed and will force the gears to mesh as soon as the starter turns far enough to allow them to do so. As the solenoid plunger reaches the end of its travel, it closes the contacts that connect the battery and starter and then the engine is cranked.

As soon as the engine starts, the flywheel ring gear begins turning fast enough to drive the pinion at an extremely high rate of speed. At this point, the one-way clutch begins allowing the pinion to spin faster than the starter shaft so that the starter will not operate at excessive speed. When the ignition switch is released from the starter position, the solenoid is de-energized, and a spring contained within the solenoid assembly pulls the gear out of mesh and interrupts the current flow to the starter.

Some starters employ a separate relay, mounted away from the starter, to switch the motor and solenoid current on and off. The relay thus replaces the solenoid electrical switch, but does not eliminate the need for a solenoid mounted on the starter used to mechanically engage the starter drive gears. The relay is used to reduce the amount of current the starting switch must carry.

The Charging System

The automobile charging system provides electrical power for operation of the vehicle's ignition and starting systems and all the electrical accessories. The battery serves as an electrical surge or storage tank, storing (in chemical form) the energy originally produced by the engine-driven generator. The system also provides a means of regulating generator output to protect the battery from being overcharged and to avoid excessive voltage to the accessories.

The storage battery is chemical device incorporating parallel lead plates in a tank containing a sulfuric acid/water solution. Adjacent plates are slightly dissimilar, and the chemical reaction of the two dissimilar plates produces electrical energy when the battery is connected to a load such as the starter motor. The chemical reaction is reversible, so that when the generator is producing a voltage (electrical pressure) greater than that produced by the battery, electricity is forced into the battery, and the battery is returned to its fully charged state.

The vehicle's generator is driven mechanically, through V-belts, by the engine crankshaft. It consists of two coils of fine wire, one stationary (the "stator"), and one moveable (the "rotor"). The rotor may also be known as the "armature," and consists of fine wire wrapped around an iron core which is mounted on the shaft. The electricity which flows through the two coils of wire (provided initially be the battery in some cases) creates an intense magnetic field around both the rotor and stator, and the interaction between the two fields creates voltage, allowing the generator to power the accessories and charge the battery.

There are two types of generators; the earlier is the direct current (DC) type. The current produced by the DC generator is generated in the armature and carried off the spinning armature by stationary brushes contacting the commutator. The commutator plates, which are separated by a very short gap, are connected to the armature circuits so that the current will flow in one direction only in the wires carrying the generator output. The generator stator consists of two stationary coils of wire which draw some of the output current of the generator to form a powerful magnetic field and create the interaction of fields which generates the voltage. The generator field is wired in series with the regulator.

Newer automobiles use alternating current generators because they are more efficient, can be rotated at higher speeds, and have fewer brush problems. In an alternator, the field rotates while all the current produced passes only through the stator windings. The brushes bear against continuous slip rings rather than a commutator. This causes the current produced to periodically reverse the direction of its flow. Diodes (electrical one-way switches) block the flow of current from traveling in the wrong direction. A series of diodes is wired together to permit the alternating flow of the stator to be converted to a pulsating, but unidirectional flow at the alternator output. The alternator's field is wired in series with the voltage regulator.

The regulator consists of several circuits. Each circuit has a core, or magnetic coil of wire, which operates a switch. Each switch to ground through one or more resistors. The coil of wire responds directly to system voltage. When the voltage reaches the required level, the magnetic field created by the winding of wire closes the switch and inserts a resistance into the generator field circuit, thus reducing the output. The contacts of the switch cycle open and close many times each second to precisely control voltage.

While alternators are self-limiting as far as maximum current is concerned, DC generators employ a current regulating circuit which responds directly to the total amount of current flowing through the generator circuit rather than to the output voltage. The current regulator is similar to the voltage regulator except that all system current must flow through the energizing coil on its way to the various accessories.

SAFETY PRECAUTIONS

Observing these precautions will ensure safe handling of the

electrical systems components and will avoid damage to the vehicle's electrical system:

a. Be absolutely sure of the polarity of a booster battery before making connections. Connect the cables positive to positive, and negative to negative. Connect positive cables first and then make the last connection to a ground on the body of the booster vehicle so that arcing cannot ignite hydrogen gas that may have accumulated near the battery. Even momentary connection of a booster battery with the polarity reversed will damage alternator diodes.

b. Disconnect both vehicle battery cables before attempting to charge a battery.

c. Never ground the alternator or generator output or battery terminal. Be cautious when using metal tools around a battery to avoid creating a short circuit between the terminals.

d. Never ground the field circuit between the alternator and regulator.

e. Never run an alternator or generator without load unless the field circuit is disconnected.

f. Never attempt to polarize an alternator.

g. Keep the regulator cover in place when taking voltage and current limiter readings.

h. Use insulated tools when adjusting the regulator.

i. Whenever DC generator-to-generator wires have been disconnected, the generator *must* be re-polarized. To do this with an externally grounded, light duty generator, momentarily place a jumper wire between the battery terminal and the generator terminal of the regulator. With an internally grounded heavy duty unit, disconnect the wire to the regulator field terminal and touch the regulator battery terminal with it.

Ignition Coil

REMOVAL AND INSTALLATION

1. Disconnect the negative battery cable.
2. Disconnect the secondary lead by pulling on the boot with a twisting motion.
3. Disconnect the primary connectors.
4. Remove the ignition coil mounting screws and remove the coil.
5. Installation is the reverse of removal.

TESTING

Check the ignition coil with an ohmmeter for opens and ground.

1. Connect the negative lead of the ohmmeter, set at high scale, to a good metal ground and the positive lead to the B+ terminal of the ignition coil. The reading should be very high (infinite). If not, replace the coil.
2. Use the low scale and connect the negative lead of the ohmmeter to the B- terminal of the coil and the positive lead to the C- (tach) terminal. The reading should be very low or zero. If not, replace the coil.
3. Use the high scale and connect the negative lead of the ohmmeter to the C+ terminal of the coil and the positive lead to the coil tower. The reading should not be infinite. If it does, replace the coil.

Ignition Module

REMOVAL AND INSTALLATION

1. Disconnect the negative battery cable.
2. Remove the air cleaner assembly.
3. Remove the distributor cap and rotor

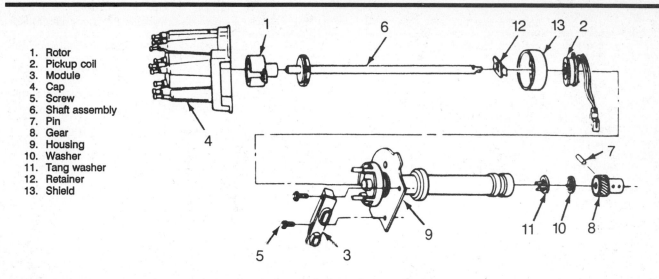

1. Rotor
2. Pickup coil
3. Module
4. Cap
5. Screw
6. Shaft assembly
7. Pin
8. Gear
9. Housing
10. Washer
11. Tang washer
12. Retainer
13. Shield

Exploded view of the distributor

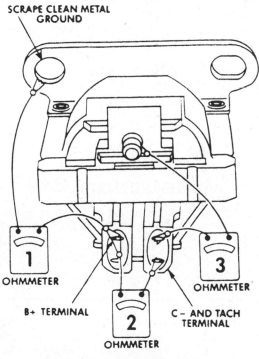

Separate coil electrical test

4. Remove the 2 module attaching screws and lift the module up.
5. Observe the color codes and disconnect the leads from the module.

To install:

6. Spread silicone grease on the metal face of the module and on the distributor base where the module seats.

NOTE: The grease is necessary for module cooling.

7. Reposition the module, attach the color coded leads and install the retaining screws.
8. Install the rotor and cap.
9. Install the air cleaner and negative battery cable.

Distributor

REMOVAL

1. Disconnect the negative battery cable.
2. Remove the air cleaner assembly.
3. Disconnect the 2 electrical connectors from the side of the distributor.
4. Turn the 2 screws counterclockwise to remove the distributor cap and move out of the way.
5. If necessary, remove the secondary wires from the cap, release the wiring harness latches and remove the wiring harness retainer. The spark plug wire numbers are indicated on the retainer.
6. Remove the screw and distributor hold down clamp.
7. Note the position of the rotor, then pull the distributor up until the rotor just stops turning counterclockwise and again note the position of the rotor.

INSTALLATION ENGINE DISTURBED

If the engine was accidentally cranked after the engine was removed, use the following procedure to install the distributor.

1. Remove the No 1 spark plug.
2. Place a finger over the No. 1 spark plug hole and crank the engine slowly until compression is felt.
3. Align the timing mark on the pulley to **0** on the engine timing indicator.
4. Turn the rotor to point between No. 1 and No. 6 spark plug towers on the distributor cap.
5. Install the distributor and tighten the hold down clamp screw and install the electrical connectors.
6. Install the distributor cap and spark plug wires.
7. Check the engine timing.
8. Install the air cleaner assembly and connect the negative battery cable.

INSTALLATION ENGINE NOT DISTURBED

1. Insert the distributor, positioning the rotor as removed.
2. Install the distributor hold down clamp and screw.
3. Install the wiring harness retainer and the secondary wires, if removed.
4. Install the distributor cap.
5. Connect the connectors to the side of the distributor.

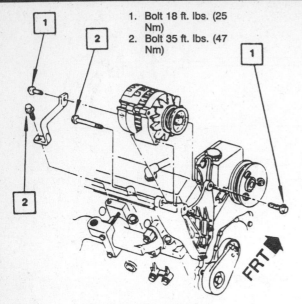

1. Bolt 18 ft. lbs. (25 Nm)
2. Bolt 35 ft. lbs. (47 Nm)

Alternator installation

6. Install the air cleaner assembly and connect the negative battery cable.

Alternator

ALTERNATOR PRECAUTIONS

Some precautions should be taken when working on this, or any other, AC charging system.
1. Never switch battery polarity.
2. When installing a battery, always connect the grounded terminal first.
3. Never disconnect the battery while the engine is running.
4. If the molded connector is disconnected from the alternator, never ground the hot wire.
5. Never run the alternator with the main output cable disconnected.

6. Never electric weld around the vehicle without disconnecting the alternator.
7. Never apply any voltage in excess of battery voltage while testing.
8. Never jump a battery for starting purposes with more than 12V.
9. Never Leave the ignition switch on when connecting or disconnecting battery cables or battery chargers

REMOVAL AND INSTALLATION

1. Disconnect the negative battery cable.
2. Remove the air cleaner assembly.
3. Remove the serpentine belt.
4. Disconnect the electrical connectors at the alternator.
5. Disconnect the alternator at the rear brace and manifold.
6. Remove the alternator mounting bolts and remove the alternator.
To install:

NOTE: If the alternator brace is removed, the studs must be retightened before installation or damage to the brace may result.

7. Place the alternator into position and install the brace bolt to the alternator but do not tighten.
8. Install the retaining bolts to the alternator and tighten the long bolts to 37 ft. lbs. (50 Nm) and the short bolts to 18 ft. lbs. (25 Nm).

NOTE: Make sure that the tightening brace bolt does not bind alternator.

9. Install the serpentine drive belt.
10. Connect the electrical connector to the alternator.
11. Connect the negative battery cable.

Regulator

REMOVAL AND INSTALLATION

The Model CS–130 alternator uses an internal regulator. The alternator is serviced as a complete unit and cannot be overhauled.

Troubleshooting Basic Charging System Problems

Problem	Cause	Solution
Noisy alternator	• Loose mountings • Loose drive pulley • Worn bearings • Brush noise • Internal circuits shorted (High pitched whine)	• Tighten mounting bolts • Tighten pulley • Replace alternator • Replace alternator • Replace alternator
Squeal when starting engine or accelerating	• Glazed or loose belt	• Replace or adjust belt
Indicator light remains on or ammeter indicates discharge (engine running)	• Broken fan belt • Broken or disconnected wires • Internal alternator problems • Defective voltage regulator	• Install belt • Repair or connect wiring • Replace alternator • Replace voltage regulator
Car light bulbs continually burn out—battery needs water continually	• Alternator/regulator overcharging	• Replace voltage regulator/alternator

Troubleshooting Basic Charging System Problems

Problem	Cause	Solution
Car lights flare on acceleration	• Battery low • Internal alternator/regulator problems	• Charge or replace battery • Replace alternator/regulator
Low voltage output (alternator light flickers continually or ammeter needle wanders)	• Loose or worn belt • Dirty or corroded connections • Internal alternator/regulator problems	• Replace or adjust belt • Clean or replace connections • Replace alternator or regulator

Battery

REMOVAL AND INSTALLATION

NOTE: Always turn off the ignition switch when connecting or disconnecting battery cables or battery chargers. Failing to do so could damage to the ECM or other electronic components.

Disconnecting the battery cable may interfere with the functions of the on board computer systems and may require the computer to undergo a relearning process, once the negative battery cable is disconnected.

1. Disconnect the negative and positive battery cables.
2. Disconnect the electrical connection at the washer reservoir.
3. Disconnect the left side headlamp bracket at the tie bar.
4. Disconnect the left cross brace with the washer reservoir attached.
5. Remove the battery hold down bolt and retainer and remove the battery.

To install:

6. Reposition the battery and install the retainer and hold down bolt and tighten to 13 ft. lbs. (18 Nm).
7. Install the positive and negative battery cable and tighten to 13 ft. lbs. (18 Nm).
8. Install the left cross brace and washer reservoir and tighten the bolts to 52 ft. lbs. (70 Nm).
9. Install the left headlamp bracket and bolts at the tiebar.
10. Connect the electrical connection at the washer reservoir.

Starter

REMOVAL AND INSTALLATION

1. Disconnect the negative cable.
2. Raise and support the vehicle safely.
3. Remove the nut from the brace at the air conditioner compressor.
4. Remove the nut at the engine and brace.
5. Place a drain pan under the engine oil pan.
6. Disconnect the electrical connector at the oil pressure sending unit and remove the oil pressure sending unit.
7. Remove the oil filter.
8. Disconnect the starter motor wiring.
9. Remove the starter motor bolts and remove the starter and shims, if used.

To install:

10. Install the starter motor and shims to the engine and tighten the bolts to 32 ft. lbs. (43 Nm).
11. Install the oil filter.
12. Connect the starter motor wiring.

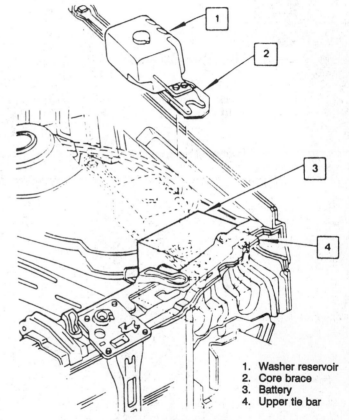

1. Washer reservoir
2. Core brace
3. Battery
4. Upper tie bar

Battery installation

13. Install the oil pressure sending unit and tighten to 115 inch lbs. (13 Nm).
14. Connect the electrical connector at the oil pressure sending unit.
15. Install the brace and nut to the engine.
16. Install the nut to the brace at the air conditioner compressor and tighten to 23 ft. lbs. (31 Nm).
17. Lower the vehicle and connect the negative battery cable.

OVERHAUL

1. Remove the field lead nut from the solenoid terminal.
2. Remove the through bolts, identification tag and commutator end frame from the motor assembly.

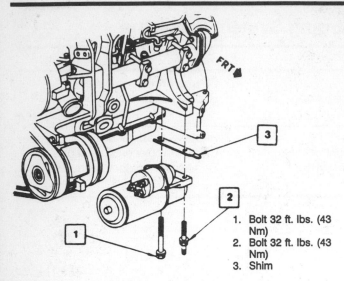

1. Bolt 32 ft. lbs. (43 Nm)
2. Bolt 32 ft. lbs. (43 Nm)
3. Shim

Starter Installation

NOTE: If the through bolt heads are different, note the location relative to the field lead for later reassembly.

3. Remove the brake washer from the armature shaft.
4. Remove the frame and field assembly from the drive end housing and armature.
5. Remove the heat shield attaching nuts, if used, from the solenoid attaching screws.
6. Remove the solenoid attaching screws, clamp and solenoid from the drive end housing.
7. Remove the plug from the slot in the drive end housing.
8. Remove the armature with drive, shift lever and plunger with spring, as an assembly from the drive end housing.

9. Remove the plunger and spring from the lever, then the lever from the drive by spreading the plastic arms just enough to disengage from the buttons on the drive collar.
10. Remove the thrust collar from the armature shaft, then snap the pinion stop collar off of the retainer ring. The collar will remain on the shaft next to the drive pinion.
11. Remove the retainer ring from the groove in the armature shaft. The ring is not resused. Bend the ring enough to avoid scratching the armature shaft surface as the ring is removed.
12. Remove the pinion stop collar and drive from the shaft.
To install:
13. Clean all parts, but do not use any grease dissolving solvents for cleaning, as this will remove the grease packed in the clutch and damage armature and field coil insulation.
14. Install the drive assembly onto the armature shaft as follows:
    a. Lubricate lightly the area on the armature shaft that will be under the drive assembly, using lubricant 1960954 or equivalent.
    b. Install the drive assembly onto the armature shaft with the pinion away from the armature.
    c. Install the pinion stop collar onto the armature shaft.
    d. Install a new pinion stop retainer ring into the groove on the shaft. Do not reuse the old ring.
    e. Install the thrust collar to the end of the shaft with flange toward the retainer ring. Use pliers to snap the pinion stop collar over the retainer ring.
15. Inspect the bushing in the drive end housing and replace the drive end housing as necessary.
16. Install the shift lever yoke to the collar on the drive, then the armature drive/lever assembly into the drive end housing.
17. Install the plug to the slot on the drive end housing.
18. Install the plunger with the spring onto the lever.
19. Install the solenoid over the plunger by compressing the spring, aligning the solenoid motor terminal with the slot in the motor housing. Attach a clamp to the solenoid and align to drive end housing. Install the attaching screws.
20. Install the frame and field assembly as follows:
    a. Push the brushes into the field holders and hold.

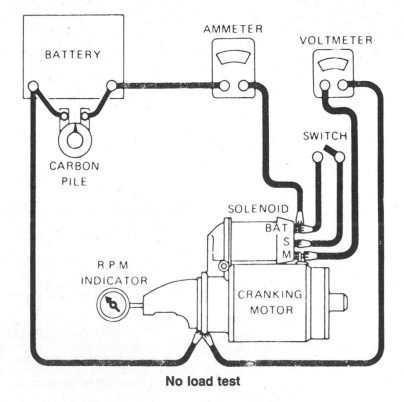

No load test

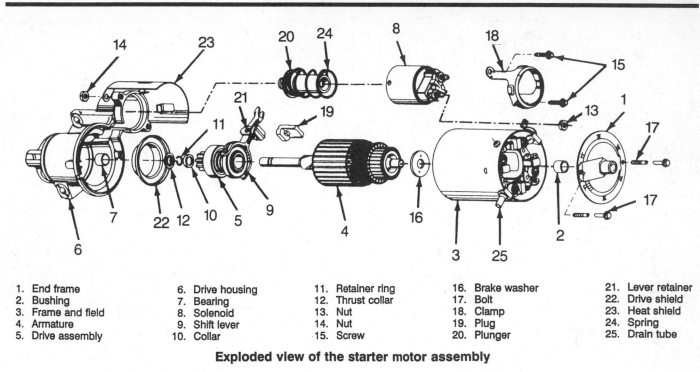

1. End frame
2. Bushing
3. Frame and field
4. Armature
5. Drive assembly
6. Drive housing
7. Bearing
8. Solenoid
9. Shift lever
10. Collar
11. Retainer ring
12. Thrust collar
13. Nut
14. Nut
15. Screw
16. Brake washer
17. Bolt
18. Clamp
19. Plug
20. Plunger
21. Lever retainer
22. Drive shield
23. Heat shield
24. Spring
25. Drain tube

Exploded view of the starter motor assembly

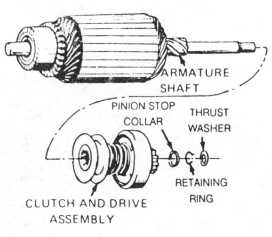

Armature shaft and drive installation

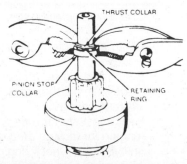

Installing the pinion stop collar

NOTE: Long life brushes are attached to the brush rigging. If the brushes are damaged, replace the frame and field assembly.

 b. Install the frame and field assembly over the armature, aligning properly to the drive end housing.

 c. Release the brushes onto the commutator. Make sure all 4 brushes are moving freely in the holders and contacting the commutator.

21. Install the brake washer onto the armature shaft.

22. Install the commutator end frame onto the armature shaft, aligning with the frame and field assembly.

23. Install the identification tag onto one through bolt, then install the 2 through bolts to the motor. If the through bolts have different heads, position as noted during disassembly.

24. Measure the pinion clearance as follows:

———— **CAUTION** ————

Keep fingers, tools and other objects away from the opening in the drive end housing while making electrical connections during this procedure.

 a. Secure the starter motor in a vise so that the opening in the drive end housing is accessible.

 b. Assure that the field lead is disconnected and insulated from the solenoid terminal.

 c. Connect a positive lead from a 12 volt battery to the solenoid **S** terminal. Connect the negative lead from the battery to a clean ground on the motor housing. This energizes the hold-in coil.

 d. Momentarily ground solenoid **M** terminal to motor housing. This energizes the pull-in coil in the solenoid and causes the drive pinion to move into the cranking position. the drive pinion will stay in this position when momentary ground is removed.

 e. Press on the drive just enough to take up any free movement of the pinion on the shaft. Use feeler gauges to check the clearance between the end of the pinion and the pinion stop retainer. The clearance should be 0.010–0.160 in. (0.25–4.06 mm).

 f. Disconnect the negative lead from the motor housing.

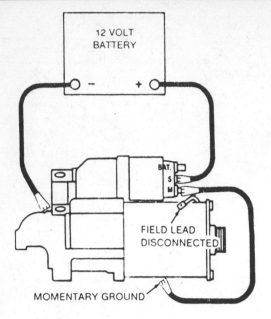

ELECTRICAL CONNECTIONS

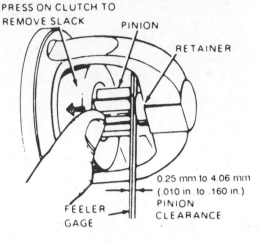

CHECKING CLEARANCE

Checking the pinion clearance

The drive pinion will retract into the drive end housing. Disconnect the positive lead from the **S** terminal.

g. If the clearance is outside specifications, recheck the motor for proper assembly. Assure that the plug is properly installed in the opening in the drive end housing under the solenoid. If the plug is OK, check for worn or damaged parts in the shift mechanism and drive assembly and replace if necessary.

25. Install the field lead to the solenoid terminal.
26. Install the heat shield, if equipped.

Starter Solenoid
REPLACEMENT

1. Disconnect the negative battery cable.
2. Remove the heat shield, if equipped.
3. Disconnect the field lead from the solenoid.
4. Remove the attaching screws and remove the solenoid.
5. Installation is the reverse of removal.

STARTER SPECIFICATIONS

| Years | Engine No. Cyl. Liters | No-Load Test | | |
		Amps	Volts	RPM
1990	6-3.1L	50–75	10	6,000–11,900
1991	6-3.1L	45–75	10	6,000–11,000

Troubleshooting Basic Starting System Problems

Problem	Cause	Solution
Starter motor rotates engine slowly	• Battery charge low or battery defective	• Charge or replace battery
	• Defective circuit between battery and starter motor	• Clean and tighten, or replace cables
	• Low load current	• Bench-test starter motor. Inspect for worn brushes and weak brush springs.
	• High load current	• Bench-test starter motor. Check engine for friction, drag or coolant in cylinders. Check ring gear-to-pinion gear clearance.

Troubleshooting Basic Starting System Problems

Problem	Cause	Solution
Starter motor will not rotate engine	• Battery charge low or battery defective	• Charge or replace battery
	• Faulty solenoid	• Check solenoid ground. Repair or replace as necessary.
	• Damage drive pinion gear or ring gear	• Replace damaged gear(s)
	• Starter motor engagement weak	• Bench-test starter motor
	• Starter motor rotates slowly with high load current	• Inspect drive yoke pull-down and point gap, check for worn end bushings, check ring gear clearance
	• Engine seized	• Repair engine
Starter motor drive will not engage (solenoid known to be good)	• Defective contact point assembly	• Repair or replace contact point assembly
	• Inadequate contact point assembly ground	• Repair connection at ground screw
	• Defective hold-in coil	• Replace field winding assembly
Starter motor drive will not disengage	• Starter motor loose on flywheel housing	• Tighten mounting bolts
	• Worn drive end busing	• Replace bushing
	• Damaged ring gear teeth	• Replace ring gear or driveplate
	• Drive yoke return spring broken or missing	• Replace spring
Starter motor drive disengages prematurely	• Weak drive assembly thrust spring	• Replace drive mechanism
	• Hold-in coil defective	• Replace field winding assembly
Low load current	• Worn brushes	• Replace brushes
	• Weak brush springs	• Replace springs

ENGINE MECHANICAL

Engine Overhaul Tips

Most engine overhaul procedures are fairly standard. In addition to specific parts replacement procedures and complete specifications for your individual engine, this section also is a guide to accept rebuilding procedures. Examples of standard rebuilding practice are shown and should be used along with specific details concerning your particular engine.

Competent and accurate machine shop services will ensure maximum performance, reliability and engine life. Procedures marked with the symbol shown above should be performed by a competent machine shop, and are provided so that you will be familiar with the procedures necessary to a successful overhaul.

In most instances it is more profitable for the do-it-yourself mechanic to remove, clean and inspect the component, buy the necessary parts and deliver these to a shop for actual machine work.

On the other hand, much of the rebuilding work (crankshaft, block, bearings, piston rods, and other components) is well within the scope of the do-it-yourself mechanic.

TOOLS

The tools required for an engine overhaul or parts replacement will depend on the depth of your involvement. With a few exceptions, they will be the tools found in a mechanic's tool kit (see Section 1). More in-depth work will require any or all of the following:

- a dial indicator (reading in thousandths) mounted on a universal base
- micrometers and telescope gauges
- jaw and screw type pullers
- scraper
- valve spring compressor
- ring groove cleaner
- piston ring expander and compressor
- ridge reamer
- cylinder hone or glaze breaker
- Plastigage®
- engine stand

Use of most of these tools is illustrated in this section. Many can be rented for a one-time use from a local parts jobber or tool supply house specializing in automotive work.

Occasionally, the use of special tools is called for. See the information on Special Tools and Safety Notice in the front of this book before substituting another tool.

INSPECTION TECHNIQUES

Procedures and specifications are given in this section for inspecting, cleaning and assessing the wear limits of most major components. Other procedures such as Magnaflux® and Zyglo® can be used to locate material flaws and stress cracks. Magnaflux® is a magnetic process applicable only to ferrous materials. The Zyglo® process coats the material with a flourescent dye penetrant and can be used on any material Check for suspected surface cracks can be more readily made using spot check dye. The dye is sprayed onto the suspected area, wiped off and the area sprayed with a developer. Cracks will show up brightly.

OVERHAUL TIPS

Aluminum has become extremely popular for use in engines, due to its low weight. Observe the following precautions when handling aluminum parts:

- Never hot tank aluminum parts (the caustic hot-tank solution will eat the aluminum.
- Remove all aluminum parts (identification tag, etc.) from engine parts prior to the tanking.
- Always coat threads lightly with engine oil or antiseize compounds before installation, to prevent seizure.
- Never overtorque bolts or spark plugs especially in aluminum threads.

Stripped threads in any component can be repaired using any of several commercial repair kits (Heli-Coil®, Microdot®, Keenserts®, etc.).

When assembling the engine, any parts that will be frictional contact must be prelubed to provide lubrication at initial start up. Any product specifically formulated for this purpose can be used, but engine oil is not recommended as a prelube.

When semipermanent (locked, but removable) installation of bolts or nuts is desired, threads should be cleaned and coated with Loctite® or other similar, commercial nonhardening sealant.

REPAIRING DAMAGED THREADS

Several methods of repairing damaged threads are available. Heli-Coil® (shown here), Keenserts® and Microdot® are among the most widely used. All involve basically the same principle, drilling out stripped threads, tapping the hole and installing a prewound insert, making welding, plugging and oversize fasteners unnecessary.

Two types of thread repair inserts are usually supplied: a standard type for most Inch Coarse, Inch Fine, Metric Course and Metric Fine thread sizes and a spark lug type to fit most spark plug port sizes. Consult the individual manufacturer's catalog to determine exact applications. Typical thread repair kits will contain a selection of prewound threaded inserts, a tap (corresponding to the outside diameter threads of the insert)

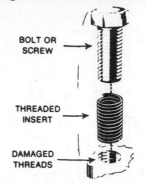

Damaged bolt holes can be repaired with thread repair inserts

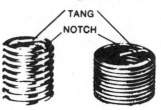

Standard thread repair insert (left) and spark plug thread insert (right)

Drill out the damaged threads with specified drill. Drill completely through the hole or to the bottom of the blind hole

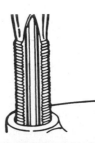

With the tap supplied, tap the hole to receive the thread insert. Keep the tap well oiled and back it out frequently to avoid clogging the threads

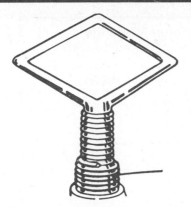

Screw the threaded insert onto the installation tool until the tang engages the slot. Screw the insert into the tapped hole until it is ¼-½ turn below the top surface. After installation break off the tang with a hammer and punch

and an installation tool. Spark plug inserts usually differ because they require a tap equipped with pilot threads and a combined reamer/tap section. Most manufacturers also supply blister packed thread repair inserts separately in addition to a master kit containing a variety of taps and inserts plus installation tools.

Before effecting a repair to a threaded hole, remove any snapped, broken or damaged bolts or studs. Penetrating oil can be used to free frozen threads; the offending item can be removed with locking pliers or with a screw or stud extractor. After the hole is clear, the thread can be repaired, as follows:

Checking Engine Compression

A noticeable lack of engine power, excessive oil consumption and/or poor fuel mileage measured over an extended period are all indicators of internal engine war. Worn piston rings, scored or worn cylinder bores, blown head gaskets, sticking or burnt valves and worn valve seats are all possible culprits here. A check of each cylinder's compression will help you locate the problems.

As mentioned in the Tools and Equipment section of Section 1, a screw-in type compression gauge is more accurate that the type you simply hold against the spark plug hole, although it takes slightly longer to use. It's worth it to obtain a more accurate reading. Follow the procedures below.

The screw-in type compression gauge is more accurate

1. Warm up the engine to normal operating temperature.
2. Remove all spark plugs.
3. Disconnect the high tension lead from the ignition coil.
4. On fuel injected vehicles, disconnect the cold start valve and all injector connections.
5. Screw the compression gauge into the No. 1 spark plug hole until the fitting is snug.

NOTE: Be careful not to crossthread the plug hole. On aluminum cylinder heads use extra care, as the threads in these heads are easily ruined.

6. Ask an assistant to depress the accelerator pedal fully. Then, while you read the compression gauge, ask the assistant to crank the engine two or three times in short bursts using the ignition switch.
7. Read the compression gauge at the end of each series of cranks, and record the highest of these readings. Repeat this procedure for each of the engine's cylinders. Compare the highest reading of each cylinder to the compression pressure specification in the Tune-Up Specifications chart in Section 2. The specs in this chart are maximum values.

A cylinders compression pressure is usually acceptable if it is not less than 80% of maximum. The difference between each cylinder should be no more than 12–14 lbs.
8. If a cylinder is unusually low, pour a tablespoon of clean engine oil into the cylinder through the spark plug hole and repeat the compression test. If the compression comes up after adding the oil, it appears that the cylinder's piston rings or bore are damaged or worn. If the pressure remains low, the valves may not be seating properly (a valve job is needed), or the head gasket may be blown near that cylinder. If compression in any two adjacent cylinders is low, and if the addition of oil doesn't help the compression, there is leakage past the head gasket. Oil and coolant water in the combustion chamber can result from this problem. There may be evidence of water droplets on the engine dipstick when a had gasket has blown.

Standard Torque Specifications and Fastener Markings

In the absence of specific torques, the following chart can be used as a guide to the maximum safe torque of a particular size/grade of fastener.

- There is no torque difference for fine or coarse threads.
- Torque values are based on clean, dry threads. Reduce the value by 10% if threads are oiled prior to assembly.
- The torque required for aluminum components or fasteners is considerably less.

U.S. Bolts

SAE Grade Number	1 or 2			5			6 or 7		
Number of lines always 2 less than the grade number.									
Bolt Size (Inches)—(Thread)	Ft./Lbs.	Kgm	Nm	Ft./Lbs.	Kgm	Nm	Ft./Lbs.	Kgm	Nm
¼ —20	5	0.7	6.8	8	1.1	10.8	10	1.4	13.5
—28	6	0.8	8.1	10	1.4	13.6			
⁵/₁₆ —18	11	1.5	14.9	17	2.3	23.0	19	2.6	25.8
—24	13	1.8	17.6	19	2.6	25.7			
⅜ —16	18	2.5	24.4	31	4.3	42.0	34	4.7	46.0
—24	20	2.75	27.1	35	4.8	47.5			
⁷/₁₆ —14	28	3.8	37.0	49	6.8	66.4	55	7.6	74.5
—20	30	4.2	40.7	55	7.6	74.5			
½ —13	39	5.4	52.8	75	10.4	101.7	85	11.75	115.2
—20	41	5.7	55.6	85	11.7	115.2			
⁹/₁₆ —12	51	7.0	69.2	110	15.2	149.1	120	16.6	162.7
—18	55	7.6	74.5	120	16.6	162.7			
⅝ —11	83	11.5	112.5	150	20.7	203.3	167	23.0	226.5
—18	95	13.1	128.8	170	23.5	230.5			
¾ —10	105	14.5	142.3	270	37.3	366.0	280	38.7	379.6
—16	115	15.9	155.9	295	40.8	400.0			
⅞ — 9	160	22.1	216.9	395	54.6	535.5	440	60.9	596.5
—14	175	24.2	237.2	435	60.1	589.7			
1 — 8	236	32.5	318.6	590	81.6	799.9	660	91.3	894.8
—14	250	34.6	338.9	660	91.3	849.8			

Metric Bolts

Relative Strength Marking	4.6, 4.8			8.8		
Bolt Markings						
Bolt Size Thread Size x Pitch (mm)	Ft./Lbs.	Kgm	Nm	Ft./Lbs.	Kgm	Nm
6 x 1.0	2–3	.2–.4	3–4	3–6	.4–.8	5–8
8 x 1.25	6–8	.8–1	8–12	9–14	1.2–1.9	13–19
10 x 1.25	12–17	1.5–2.3	16–23	20–29	2.7–4.0	27–39
12 x 1.25	21–32	2.9–4.4	29–43	35–53	4.8–7.3	47–72
14 x 1.5	35–52	4.8–7.1	48–70	57–85	7.8–11.7	77–110
16 x 1.5	51–77	7.0–10.6	67–100	90–120	12.4–16.5	130–160
18 x 1.5	74–110	10.2–15.1	100–150	130–170	17.9–23.4	180–230
20 x 1.5	110–140	15.1–19.3	150–190	190–240	26.2–46.9	160–320
22 x 1.5	150–190	22.0–26.2	200–260	250–320	34.5–44.1	340–430
24 x 1.5	190–240	26.2–46.9	260–320	310–410	42.7–56.5	420–550

Standard Torque Specifications and Fastener Markings

Troubleshooting Engine Mechanical Problems

Problem	Cause	Solution
External oil leaks	• Fuel pump gasket broken or improperly seated	• Replace gasket
	• Cylinder head cover RTV sealant broken or improperly seated	• Replace sealant; inspect cylinder head cover sealant flange and cylinder head sealant surface for distortion and cracks
	• Oil filler cap leaking or missing	• Replace cap
External oil leaks	• Oil filter gasket broken or improperly seated	• Replace oil filter
	• Oil pan side gasket broken, improperly seated or opening in RTV sealant	• Replace gasket or repair opening in sealant; inspect oil pan gasket flange for distortion
	• Oil pan front oil seal broken or improperly seated	• Replace seal; inspect timing case cover and oil pan seal flange for distortion
	• Oil pan rear oil seal broken or improperly seated	• Replace seal; inspect oil pan rear oil seal flange; inspect rear main bearing cap for cracks, plugged oil return channels, or distortion in seal groove
	• Timing case cover oil seal broken or improperly seated	• Replace seal
	• Excess oil pressure because of restricted PCV valve	• Replace PCV valve
	• Oil pan drain plug loose or has stripped threads	• Repair as necessary and tighten
	• Rear oil gallery plug loose	• Use appropriate sealant on gallery plug and tighten
	• Rear camshaft plug loose or improperly seated	• Seat camshaft plug or replace and seal, as necessary
	• Distributor base gasket damaged	• Replace gasket
Excessive oil consumption	• Oil level too high	• Drain oil to specified level
	• Oil with wrong viscosity being used	• Replace with specified oil
	• PCV valve stuck closed	• Replace PCV valve
	• Valve stem oil deflectors (or seals) are damaged, missing, or incorrect type	• Replace valve stem oil deflectors
	• Valve stems or valve guides worn	• Measure stem-to-guide clearance and repair as necessary
	• Poorly fitted or missing valve cover baffles	• Replace valve cover
	• Piston rings broken or missing	• Replace broken or missing rings
	• Scuffed piston	• Replace piston
	• Incorrect piston ring gap	• Measure ring gap, repair as necessary
	• Piston rings sticking or excessively loose in grooves	• Measure ring side clearance, repair as necessary
	• Compression rings installed upside down	• Repair as necessary
	• Cylinder walls worn, scored, or glazed	• Repair as necessary

Troubleshooting Engine Mechanical Problems (cont.)

Problem	Cause	Solution
	• Piston ring gaps not properly staggered	• Repair as necessary
	• Excessive main or connecting rod bearing clearance	• Measure bearing clearance, repair as necessary
No oil pressure	• Low oil level	• Add oil to correct level
	• Oil pressure gauge, warning lamp or sending unit inaccurate	• Replace oil pressure gauge or warning lamp
	• Oil pump malfunction	• Replace oil pump
	• Oil pressure relief valve sticking	• Remove and inspect oil pressure relief valve assembly
	• Oil passages on pressure side of pump obstructed	• Inspect oil passages for obstruction
	• Oil pickup screen or tube obstructed	• Inspect oil pickup for obstruction
	• Loose oil inlet tube	• Tighten or seal inlet tube
Low oil pressure	• Low oil level	• Add oil to correct level
	• Inaccurate gauge, warning lamp or sending unit	• Replace oil pressure gauge or warning lamp
	• Oil excessively thin because of dilution, poor quality, or improper grade	• Drain and refill crankcase with recommended oil
	• Excessive oil temperature	• Correct cause of overheating engine
	• Oil pressure relief spring weak or sticking	• Remove and inspect oil pressure relief valve assembly
	• Oil inlet tube and screen assembly has restriction or air leak	• Remove and inspect oil inlet tube and screen assembly. (Fill inlet tube with lacquer thinner to locate leaks.)
	• Excessive oil pump clearance	• Measure clearances
	• Excessive main, rod, or camshaft bearing clearance	• Measure bearing clearances, repair as necessary
High oil pressure	• Improper oil viscosity	• Drain and refill crankcase with correct viscosity oil
	• Oil pressure gauge or sending unit inaccurate	• Replace oil pressure gauge
	• Oil pressure relief valve sticking closed	• Remove and inspect oil pressure relief valve assembly
Main bearing noise	• Insufficient oil supply	• Inspect for low oil level and low oil pressure
	• Main bearing clearance excessive	• Measure main bearing clearance, repair as necessary
	• Bearing insert missing	• Replace missing insert
	• Crankshaft end play excessive	• Measure end play, repair as necessary
	• Improperly tightened main bearing cap bolts	• Tighten bolts with specified torque
	• Loose flywheel or drive plate	• Tighten flywheel or drive plate attaching bolts
	• Loose or damaged vibration damper	• Repair as necessary

Troubleshooting Engine Mechanical Problems (cont.)

Problem	Cause	Solution
Connecting rod bearing noise	• Insufficient oil supply	• Inspect for low oil level and low oil pressure
	• Carbon build-up on piston	• Remove carbon from piston crown
	• Bearing clearance excessive or bearing missing	• Measure clearance, repair as necessary
	• Crankshaft connecting rod journal out-of-round	• Measure journal dimensions, repair or replace as necessary
	• Misaligned connecting rod or cap	• Repair as necessary
	• Connecting rod bolts tightened improperly	• Tighten bolts with specified torque
Piston noise	• Piston-to-cylinder wall clearance excessive (scuffed piston)	• Measure clearance and examine piston
	• Cylinder walls excessively tapered or out-of-round	• Measure cylinder wall dimensions, rebore cylinder
	• Piston ring broken	• Replace all rings on piston
	• Loose or seized piston pin	• Measure piston-to-pin clearance, repair as necessary
	• Connecting rods misaligned	• Measure rod alignment, straighten or replace
	• Piston ring side clearance excessively loose or tight	• Measure ring side clearance, repair as necessary
	• Carbon build-up on piston is excessive	• Remove carbon from piston
Valve actuating component noise	• Insufficient oil supply	• Check for: (a) Low oil level (b) Low oil pressure (c) Plugged push rods (d) Wrong hydraulic tappets (e) Restricted oil gallery (f) Excessive tappet to bore clearance
	• Push rods worn or bent	• Replace worn or bent push rods
	• Rocker arms or pivots worn	• Replace worn rocker arms or pivots
	• Foreign objects or chips in hydraulic tappets	• Clean tappets
	• Excessive tappet leak-down	• Replace valve tappet
	• Tappet face worn	• Replace tappet; inspect corresponding cam lobe for wear
	• Broken or cocked valve springs	• Properly seat cocked springs; replace broken springs
	• Stem-to-guide clearance excessive	• Measure stem-to-guide clearance, repair as required
	• Valve bent	• Replace valve
	• Loose rocker arms	• Tighten bolts with specified torque
	• Valve seat runout excessive	• Regrind valve seat/valves
	• Missing valve lock	• Install valve lock
	• Push rod rubbing or contacting cylinder head	• Remove cylinder head and remove obstruction in head
	• Excessive engine oil (four-cylinder engine)	• Correct oil level

Troubleshooting the Cooling System

Problem	Cause	Solution
High temperature gauge indication— overheating	• Coolant level low	• Replenish coolant
	• Fan belt loose	• Adjust fan belt tension
	• Radiator hose(s) collapsed	• Replace hose(s)
	• Radiator airflow blocked	• Remove restriction (bug screen, fog lamps, etc.)
	• Faulty radiator cap	• Replace radiator cap
	• Ignition timing incorrect	• Adjust ignition timing
	• Idle speed low	• Adjust idle speed
	• Air trapped in cooling system	• Purge air
	• Heavy traffic driving	• Operate at fast idle in neutral intermittently to cool engine
	• Incorrect cooling system component(s) installed	• Install proper component(s)
	• Faulty thermostat	• Replace thermostat
	• Water pump shaft broken or impeller loose	• Replace water pump
	• Radiator tubes clogged	• Flush radiator
	• Cooling system clogged	• Flush system
	• Casting flash in cooling passages	• Repair or replace as necessary. Flash may be visible by removing cooling system components or removing core plugs.
	• Brakes dragging	• Repair brakes
	• Excessive engine friction	• Repair engine
	• Antifreeze concentration over 68%	• Lower antifreeze concentration percentage
	• Missing air seals	• Replace air seals
	• Faulty gauge or sending unit	• Repair or replace faulty component
	• Loss of coolant flow caused by leakage or foaming	• Repair or replace leaking component, replace coolant
	• Viscous fan drive failed	• Replace unit
Low temperature indication— undercooling	• Thermostat stuck open	• Replace thermostat
	• Faulty gauge or sending unit	• Repair or replace faulty component
Coolant loss—boilover	• Overfilled cooling system	• Reduce coolant level to proper specification
	• Quick shutdown after hard (hot) run	• Allow engine to run at fast idle prior to shutdown
	• Air in system resulting in occasional "burping" of coolant	• Purge system
	• Insufficient antifreeze allowing coolant boiling point to be too low	• Add antifreeze to raise boiling point
	• Antifreeze deteriorated because of age or contamination	• Replace coolant
	• Leaks due to loose hose clamps, loose nuts, bolts, drain plugs, faulty hoses, or defective radiator	• Pressure test system to locate source of leak(s) then repair as necessary

Troubleshooting the Cooling System (cont.)

Problem	Cause	Solution
Coolant loss—boilover	• Faulty head gasket • Cracked head, manifold, or block • Faulty radiator cap	• Replace head gasket • Replace as necessary • Replace cap
Coolant entry into crankcase or cylinder(s)	• Faulty head gasket • Crack in head, manifold or block	• Replace head gasket • Replace as necessary
Coolant recovery system inoperative	• Coolant level low • Leak in system • Pressure cap not tight or seal missing, or leaking • Pressure cap defective • Overflow tube clogged or leaking • Recovery bottle vent restricted	• Replenish coolant to FULL mark • Pressure test to isolate leak and repair as necessary • Repair as necessary • Replace cap • Repair as necessary • Remove restriction
Noise	• Fan contacting shroud • Loose water pump impeller • Glazed fan belt • Loose fan belt • Rough surface on drive pulley • Water pump bearing worn • Belt alignment	• Reposition shroud and inspect engine mounts • Replace pump • Apply silicone or replace belt • Adjust fan belt tension • Replace pulley • Remove belt to isolate. Replace pump. • Check pulley alignment. Repair as necessary.
No coolant flow through heater core	• Restricted return inlet in water pump • Heater hose collapsed or restricted • Restricted heater core • Restricted outlet in thermostat housing • Intake manifold bypass hole in cylinder head restricted • Faulty heater control valve • Intake manifold coolant passage restricted	• Remove restriction • Remove restriction or replace hose • Remove restriction or replace core • Remove flash or restriction • Remove restriction • Replace valve • Remove restriction or replace intake manifold

NOTE: *Immediately after shutdown, the engine enters a condition known as heat soak. This is caused by the cooling system being inoperative while engine temperature is still high. If coolant temperature rises above boiling point, expansion and pressure may push some coolant out of the radiator overflow tube. If this does not occur frequently it is considered normal.*

Troubleshooting the Serpentine Drive Belt

Problem	Cause	Solution
Tension sheeting fabric failure (woven fabric on outside circumference of belt has cracked or separated from body of belt)	• Grooved or backside idler pulley diameters are less than minimum recommended • Tension sheeting contacting (rubbing) stationary object • Excessive heat causing woven fabric to age • Tension sheeting splice has fractured	• Replace pulley(s) not conforming to specification • Correct rubbing condition • Replace belt • Replace belt
Noise (objectional squeal, squeak, or rumble is heard or felt while drive belt is in operation)	• Belt slippage • Bearing noise • Belt misalignment • Belt-to-pulley mismatch • Driven component inducing vibration • System resonant frequency inducing vibration	• Adjust belt • Locate and repair • Align belt/pulley(s) • Install correct belt • Locate defective driven component and repair • Vary belt tension within specifications. Replace belt.
Rib chunking (one or more ribs has separated from belt body)	• Foreign objects imbedded in pulley grooves • Installation damage • Drive loads in excess of design specifications • Insufficient internal belt adhesion	• Remove foreign objects from pulley grooves • Replace belt • Adjust belt tension • Replace belt
Rib or belt wear (belt ribs contact bottom of pulley grooves)	• Pulley(s) misaligned • Mismatch of belt and pulley groove widths • Abrasive environment • Rusted pulley(s) • Sharp or jagged pulley groove tips • Rubber deteriorated	• Align pulley(s) • Replace belt • Replace belt • Clean rust from pulley(s) • Replace pulley • Replace belt
Longitudinal belt cracking (cracks between two ribs)	• Belt has mistracked from pulley groove • Pulley groove tip has worn away rubber-to-tensile member	• Replace belt • Replace belt
Belt slips	• Belt slipping because of insufficient tension • Belt or pulley subjected to substance (belt dressing, oil, ethylene glycol) that has reduced friction • Driven component bearing failure • Belt glazed and hardened from heat and excessive slippage	• Adjust tension • Replace belt and clean pulleys • Replace faulty component bearing • Replace belt
"Groove jumping" (belt does not maintain correct position on pulley, or turns over and/or runs off pulleys)	• Insufficient belt tension • Pulley(s) not within design tolerance • Foreign object(s) in grooves	• Adjust belt tension • Replace pulley(s) • Remove foreign objects from grooves

Troubleshooting the Serpentine Drive Belt (cont.)

Problem	Cause	Solution
"Groove jumping" (belt does not maintain correct position on pulley, or turns over and/or runs off pulleys)	• Excessive belt speed • Pulley misalignment • Belt-to-pulley profile mismatched • Belt cordline is distorted	• Avoid excessive engine acceleration • Align pulley(s) • Install correct belt • Replace belt
Belt broken (Note: identify and correct problem before replacement belt is installed)	• Excessive tension • Tensile members damaged during belt installation • Belt turnover • Severe pulley misalignment • Bracket, pulley, or bearing failure	• Replace belt and adjust tension to specification • Replace belt • Replace belt • Align pulley(s) • Replace defective component and belt
Cord edge failure (tensile member exposed at edges of belt or separated from belt body)	• Excessive tension • Drive pulley misalignment • Belt contacting stationary object • Pulley irregularities • Improper pulley construction • Insufficient adhesion between tensile member and rubber matrix	• Adjust belt tension • Align pulley • Correct as necessary • Replace pulley • Replace pulley • Replace belt and adjust tension to specifications
Sporadic rib cracking (multiple cracks in belt ribs at random intervals)	• Ribbed pulley(s) diameter less than minimum specification • Backside bend flat pulley(s) diameter less than minimum • Excessive heat condition causing rubber to harden • Excessive belt thickness • Belt overcured • Excessive tension	• Replace pulley(s) • Replace pulley(s) • Correct heat condition as necessary • Replace belt • Replace belt • Adjust belt tension

GENERAL ENGINE SPECIFICATIONS

Years	Engine No. Cyl. Liters	Fuel System Type	SAE net Horsepower @ rpm	SAE net Torque ft. lbs. @ rpm	Bore × Stroke	Comp. Ratio	Oil Press. (psi.) @ 2000 rpm
1990	6-3.1L	TBI	120 @ 4200	175 @ 2200	3.50 × 3.40	8.5:1	15 @ 1100
1991	6-3.1L	TBI	120 @ 4200	175 @ 2200	3.50 × 3.40	8.5:1	15 @ 1100

TBI—Throttle Body Injection

VALVE SPECIFICATIONS

Years	Engine No. Cyl. Liters	Seat Angle (deg.)	Face Angle (deg.)	Spring Test Pressure (lbs. @ in.)	Spring Installed Height (in.)	Stem-to-Guide Clearance (in.) Intake	Stem-to-Guide Clearance (in.) Exhaust	Stem Diameter (in.) Intake	Stem Diameter (in.) Exhaust
1990	6-3.1L	46	45	191 @ 1.18	1.57	0.0010–0.0027	0.0010–0.0027	0.3410–0.3420	0.3410–0.3420
1991	6-3.1L	46	45	191 @ 1.18	1.57	0.0010–0.0027	0.0010–0.0027	0.3410–0.3420	0.3410–0.3420

CAMSHAFT SPECIFICATIONS
(All specifications in inches)

| Years | Engine No. Cyl. Liters | Journal Diameter | | | | | Bearing Clearance | Elevation | | End Play |
		1	2	3	4	5		Int.	Exh.	
1990	6-3.1L	1.867–1.881	1.867–1.881	1.867–1.881	1.867–1.881	—	0.0010–0.0040	0.230	0.261	—
1991	6-3.1L	1.867–1.881	1.867–1.881	1.867–1.881	1.867–1.881	—	0.0010–0.0040	0.230	0.261	—

CRANKSHAFT AND CONNECTING ROD SPECIFICATIONS
(All specifications in inches)

| Years | Engine No. Cyl. Liters | Crankshaft | | | | Connecting Rod | | |
		Main Bearing Journal Dia.	Main Bearing Oil Clearance	Shaft End Play	Thrust on No.	Journal Dia.	Oil Clearance	Side Clearance
1990	6-3.1L	2.6473–2.6483	0.0012–0.0027	0.0024–0.0083	3	1.9994–1.9983	0.0011–0.0032	0.0014–0.0267
1991	6-3.1L	2.6473–2.6483	0.0012–0.0027	0.0024–0.0083	3	1.9994–1.9983	0.0011–0.0032	0.0014–0.0267

PISTON AND RING SPECIFICATIONS
(All specifications in inches)

| Years | Engine No. Cyl. Liters | Ring Gap | | | Ring Side Clearance | | | Piston Clearance |
		#1 Compr.	#2 Compr.	Oil Control	#1 Compr.	#2 Compr.	Oil Control	
1990	6-3.1L	0.0010–0.020	0.020–0.028	0.010–0.030	0.002–0.0035	0.002–0.0035	0.008	0.0009–0.0022
1991	6-3.1L	0.0010–0.020	0.020–0.028	0.010–0.030	0.002–0.0035	0.002–0.0035	0.008	0.0009–0.0022

TORQUE SPECIFICATIONS
(All specifications in ft. lb.)

| Years | Engine No. Cyl. Liters | Cyl. Head | Conn. Rod | Main Bearing | Crankshaft Damper | Flywheel | Manifold | |
							Intake	Exhaust
1990	6-3.1L	①	39	72	75	31	②	24
1991	6-3.1L	①	39	72	75	31	②	24

① Tighten in 2 steps:
    1st step to 41 ft. lbs. in sequence
    2nd step an additional 90 degrees (1/4 turn)
② Tighten in 2 steps:
    1st step to 13 ft. lbs.
    2nd step to 19 ft. lbs.

Engine

REMOVAL AND INSTALLATION

1. Disconnect the negative battery cable.
2. Drain the cooling system. Disconnect the air flow tube from the air cleaner.
3. Disconnect the electrical connector from the ECM and push it through to the engine compartment. Disconnect the harness from the clips on the body and lay it across the engine.
4. Disconnect the engine harness at the bulkhead connector. Disconnect the throttle and TV cables.
5. Disconnect the fuel lines. Disconnect the transaxle shift linkage.
6. Disconnect the cooler lines at the radiator. Disconnect the radiator and heater hoses.
7. Remove the air conditioning compressor from the bracket and support it out of the way. Remove the upper engine support strut.
8. Raise and safely support the vehicle. Remove the front wheel and tire assemblies.
9. Remove the stabilizer bar. Disconnect the tie rod ends and the lower control arm ball joints.
10. Disconnect the halfhsafts and support them out of the way. Disconnect the steering shaft pinch bolt.
11. Remove the starter.
12. Disconnect the exhaust pipe at the manifold. Support the engine and sub-frame with a suitable jack.
13. Remove the sub-frame bolts and lower the engine/transaxle and subframe from the vehicle.

To install:

14. Raise the engine assembly into position and install the subframe bolts. Tighten to 35 ft. lbs.
15. Connect the exhaust pipe at the rear manifold. Install the starter.
16. Connect the steering shaft and install the pinch bolt. Connect the halfshafts to the transaxle.
17. Connect the lower control arm ball joints to the steering knuckles.
18. Install the stabilizer bar. Install the upper engine strut.
19. Install the wheel and tire assemblies. Lower the vehicle. Install the radiator and heater hoses.
20. Install the shift linkage. Connect the fuel lines and the throttle and TV cables.
21. Connect the harness to bulkhead connector. Connect the ECM harness to the ECM.
22. Connect the air cleaner hose and the radiator upper support.
23. Fill the cooling system. Install the air conditioning compressor.
24. Connect the negative battery cable.

Valve Cover

REMOVAL AND INSTALLATION

Left

1. Disconnect the negative battery cable.
2. Remove the air cleaner assembly.
3. Drain the cooling system.
4. Disconnect the engine harness at the EVRV and engine strut mount.
5. Disconnect the coolant tube hose at the water pump.
6. Remove the coolant tube bolt at the thermostat housing.
7. Remove the tube bracket nut and tube.
8. Remove the spark plug wire guide bracket.
9. Release the fuel system pressure and disconnect the fuel inlet and return lines at the TBI unit.
10. Disconnect the idle air control motor.

11. Disconnect the throttle position sensor.
12. Remove the PCV valve at the rocker cover.
13. Tap with a soft rubber mallet if necessary, and remove the rocker arm cover.

To install:

14. Clean the sealing surfaces on the cylinder head and rocker arm cover.
15. Properly seat a new gasket to the cover groove.
16. Apply RTV sealant in the notch. Install the rocker arm cover and tighten the retaining bolts to 89 inch lbs.
17. Install the PCV valve at the rocker arm cover.
18. Connect the throttle position sensor.
19. Connect the idle air control motor.
20. Connect the fuel inlet and return lines at the TBI unit.
21. Install the spark plug wire guide bracket.
22. Install the coolant tube bolt at the thermostat housing.
23. Connect the coolant tube hose at the water pump.
24. Connect the engine harness at the EVRV and engine strut mount.
25. Install the air cleaner assembly.
26. Fill the cooling system.
27. Connect the negative battery cable.

Right

1. Disconnect the negative battery cable.
2. Remove the air cleaner assembly.
3. Drain the cooling system.
4. Remove the throttle and T.V. bracket at the TBI unit.
5. Disconnect the necessary wires and vacuum hoses.
6. Remove the serpentine belt.
7. Remove the alternator and rear brace.
8. Disconnect the manifold coolant hose.
9. Tap with a soft rubber mallet if necessary, and remove the rocker arm cover.

To install:

10. Clean the sealing surfaces on the cylinder head and rocker arm cover.
11. Properly seat a new gasket to the cover groove.
12. Apply RTV sealant in the notch.
13. Install the rocker arm cover and tighten the retaining bolts to 89 inch lbs.

1. Oil indicator
2. Oil indicator tube
3. Bolt
4. Coolant tube assembly

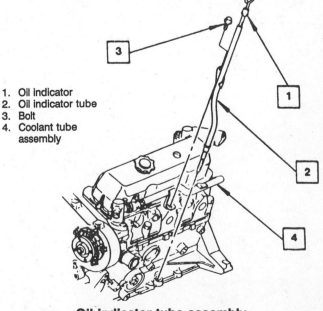

Oil indicator tube assembly

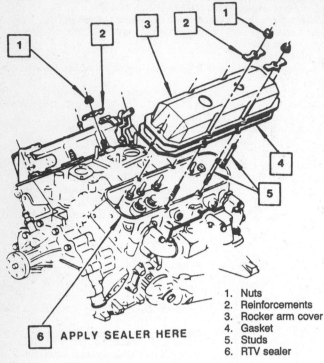

1. Nuts
2. Reinforcements
3. Rocker arm cover
4. Gasket
5. Studs
6. RTV sealer

APPLY SEALER HERE

Rocker arm cover installation

14. Install the rear alternator brace and alternator.
15. Install the serpentine belt.
16. Connect the wires and vacuum hoses.
17. Install the throttle and T.V. bracket at the TBI unit.
18. Install the air cleaner assembly.
19. Fill the cooling system.
20. Connect the negative battery cable.

Rocker Arm

REMOVAL AND INSTALLATION

1. Disconnect the negative battery cable.
2. Remove the rocker arm cover.
3. Remove the rocker arm retaining nut and remove the rocker arm. Keep them in order for reinstallation.
4. Remove the push rod guides and push rods, as necessary.
To install:
5. Install the push rod guides and push rods, as necessary.
6. Tnstall the rocker arms and adjust the valve lash.
7. Install the rocker cover and be sure to use new gaskets and RTV sealant.
8. Connect the negative battery cable.

VALVE LASH ADJUSTMENT

1. Remove the rocker covers.
2. With the No. 1 cylinder at **TDC** the following valves may be adjusted 1–½ turns past zero lash:
    a. Exhaust—1, 2, 3
    b. Intake—1, 5, 6

1. 4 bolts
2. Nut
3. Bolt
4. Bolt
5. Frame assembly
6. Wsaher
7. Nut

Engine mount and strut

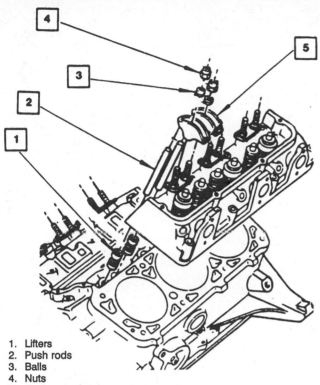

1. Lifters
2. Push rods
3. Balls
4. Nuts
5. Rocker arms

Exploded view of the valve mechanism

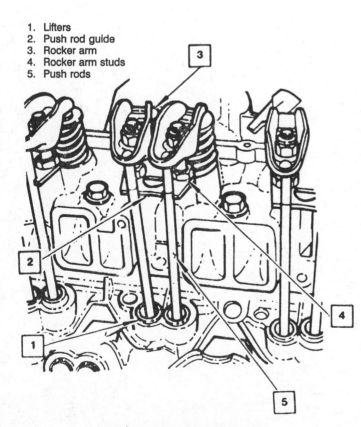

1. Lifters
2. Push rod guide
3. Rocker arm
4. Rocker arm studs
5. Push rods

Rocker ars and pushrods

3. Crank the engine 1 revolution to bring the No. 4 cylinder to **TDC** and adjust the following valves 1–½ turns past zero lash:
    a. Exhaust—4, 5, 6
    b. Intake—2, 3, 4
4. After all valves are adjusted, install the valve covers.

Thermostat

REMOVAL AND INSTALLATION

1. Disconnect the negative battery cable.
2. Drain the engine coolant.
3. Disconnect the upper radiator hose from the thermostat outlet.
4. Remove thew water outlet to thermostat housing attaching bolts and remove the outlet.
5. Remove the thermostat and gasket.
To install:
6. Clean the thermostat housing and water outlet mating surfaces.
7. Install the thermostat in the inlet manifold.
8. Position a new gasket and install the water outlet to the manifold.
9. Install the attaching bolts with sealer and torque the bolts to 18 ft. lbs. (25 Nm).
10. Refill the cooling system and connect the negative battery cable.

Intake Manifold

REMOVAL AND INSTALLATION

1. Disconnect the negative battery cable.
2. Drain the engine coolant.
3. Remove the rocker arm covers.
4. Remove the TBI unit from the manifold.
5. Remove the power steering pump and lay it aside.
6. Mark the position of the distributor cap and remove the distributor.
7. Remove the intake manifold retaining bolts and remove the intake manifold from the engine.

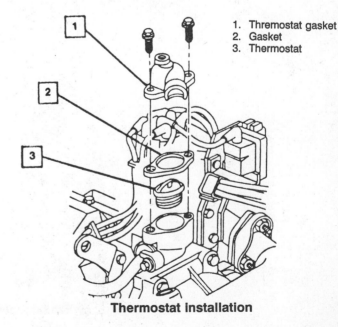

1. Thremostat gasket
2. Gasket
3. Thermostat

Thermostat installation

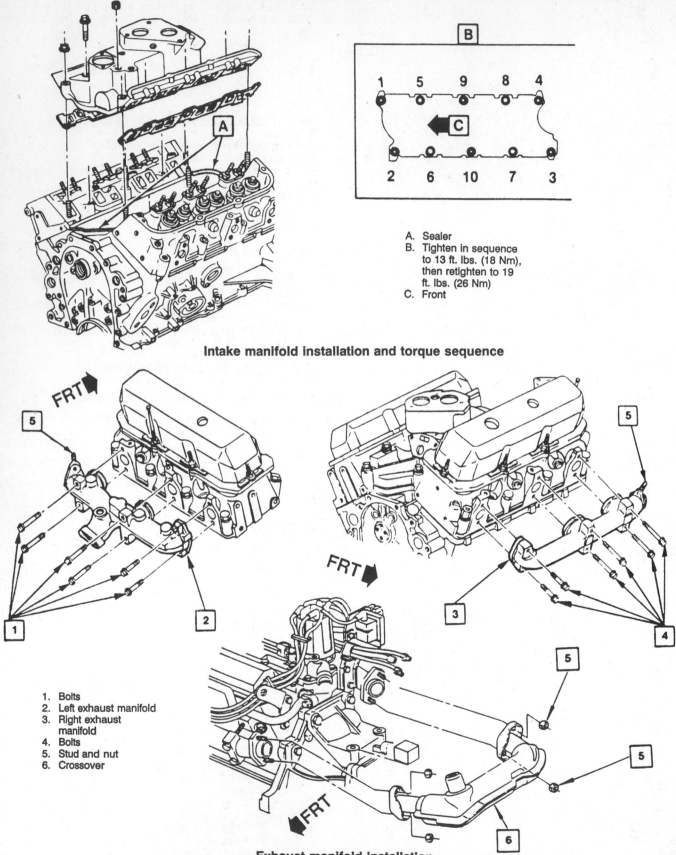

A. Sealer
B. Tighten in sequence
   to 13 ft. lbs. (18 Nm),
   then retighten to 19
   ft. lbs. (26 Nm)
C. Front

Intake manifold installation and torque sequence

1. Bolts
2. Left exhaust manifold
3. Right exhaust
   manifold
4. Bolts
5. Stud and nut
6. Crossover

Exhaust manifold installation

1. Bearing
2. Bearing
3. Bearing
4. Bearing
5. Piston
6. Bolt
7. Bolt
8. Plug
9. Rod
10. Bearing kit
11. Nut
12. Camshaft
13. Pin
14. Sprocket
15. Sensor
16. Nut
17. Cover
18. Plug
19. Plug
20. Pin
21. Sensor
22. Flywheel
23. Retainer
24. Bolt
25. Gasket
26. Adapter
27. Connector
28. Filter
29. Indicator
30. Tube
31. Pin
32. Seal
33. Crankshaft
34. Seal
35. Stud
36. Cord
37. Heater
38. Strap
39. Gasket
40. Pan
41. Shim
42. Motor
43. Stud
44. Bolt
45. Bolt
46. Stud
47. Bolt
48. Nut
49. Reinforcement
50. Cap
51. Gasket
52. Plug
53. Bolt
54. Pump
55. Shaft
56. Bolt
57. Bolt
58. Wsaher
59. Damper
60. Sprocket
61. Chain
62. Screw
63. Bolt
64. Pointer
65. Bolt
66. Seal
67. Key
68. Bolt
69. Bearing
70. Pulley
71. Pump
72. Gasket
73. Pulley

74. Bolt
75. Tensioner
76. Cover
78. Gasket

79. Damper
80. Bolt
81. Shield
82. Clip

83. Nut
84. Bolt
85. Clamp
86. Gasket

87. Adapter
88. Screw
89. Hose
90. Pipe

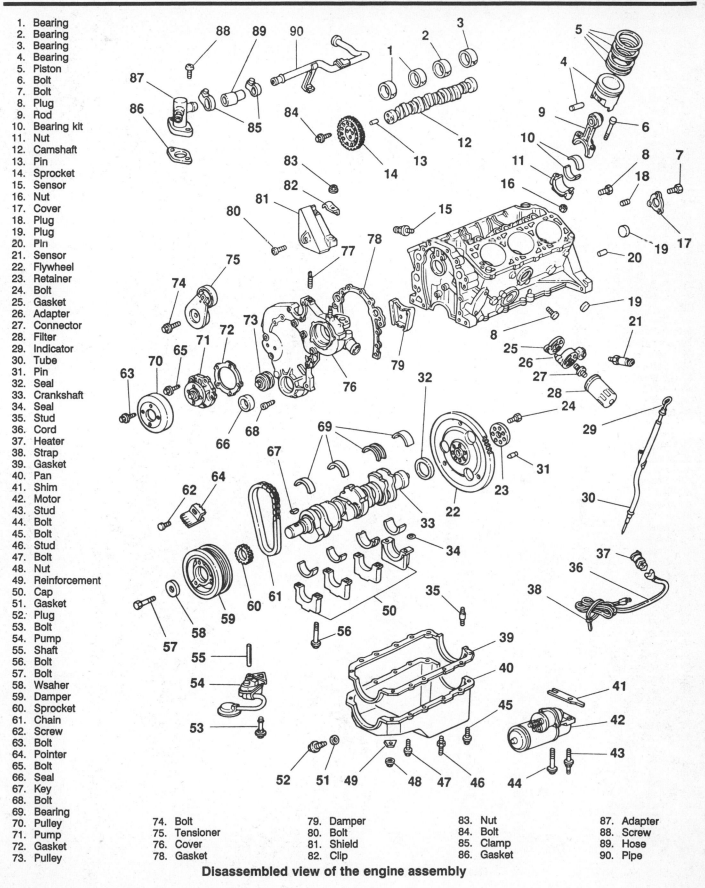

Disassembled view of the engine assembly

1. Distributor
2. Bolt
3. Hose
4. Valve
5. Grommet
6. Clamp
7. Cap
8. Clamp
9. Bolt
10. Outlet
11. Nut
12. Reinforcement
13. Thermostat
14. Stud
15. Bolt
16. Bolt
17. Cover
18. Gasket
19. Stud
20. Nut
21. Arm
22. Arm
23. Stud
24. Rod
25. Lifter
26. Key
27. Cap
28. Spring
29. Damper
30. Seal
31. Valve
32. Bracket
33. Valve
34. Coil
35. Bracket
36. Bolt
37. Bolt
38. Manifold
39. Harness
40. Bracket
41. Screw
42. Nut
43. Solenoid
44. Harness
45. Gasket
46. Gasket
47. Bracket
48. Stud
49. Bracket
50. Sensor
51. Head
52. Bolt
53. Gasket kit
54. Stud
55. Switch
56. Bolt
57. Bolt
58. Manifold
59. Gasket
60. Bolt
61. Bolt
62. Gasket
63. Sensor
64. Valve
65. Bolt
66. Plug
67. Pipe
68. Nipple
69. Throttle body injection
70. Switch
71. Bolt
72. Sensor
73. Pipe
74. Wire kit
75. Fitting
76. Pipe
77. Clip
78. Pipe

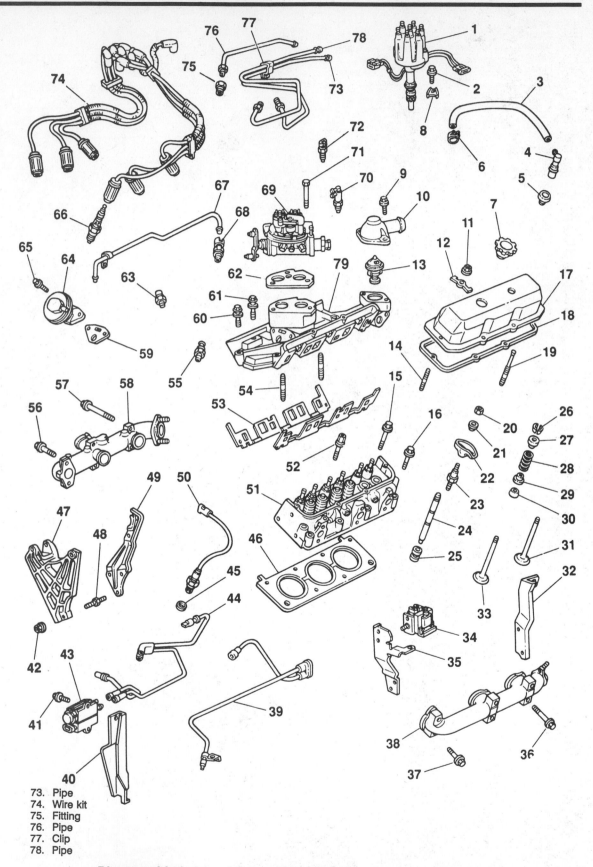

Disassembled view of the engine assembly

To install:

8. Clean the gasket material from the sealing surfaces.

9. Apply a $3/16$ in. bead of RTV sealer on each ridge and install a new intake manifold gasket.

10. Install the intake manifold and retaining bolts and torque in sequence to 13 ft. lbs. (18 Nm), then retighten in sequence to 19 ft. lbs. (26 Nm).

11. Install the rocker arm covers and the TBI unit.

12. Fill the cooling system and connect the negative battery cable.

Exhaust Manifold

REMOVAL AND INSTALLATION

Left

1. Disconnect the negative battery cable.

2. Remove the serpentine belt.

3. Remove the air conditioner compressor and lay to one side without disconnecting the refrigerant lines.

4. Remove the engine strut and engine strut bracket.

5. Disconnect the crossover pipe at the manifold.

6. Remove the exhaust manifold retaining bolts and remove the exhaust manifold.

To install:

7. Clean the mating surfaces, install the exhaust manifold and tighten the retaining bolts to 24 ft. lbs. (33 Nm).

8. Reconnect the crossover pipe.

9. Install the engine strut bracket and strut.

10. Install the air conditioning compressor.

11. Install the serpentine belt and connect the negative battery cable.

Right

1. Disconnect the negative battery cable.

2. Disconnect the oxygen sensor wire.

3. Disconnect the crossover pipe at the manifold.

4. Raise and support the vehicle safely.

5. Disconnect the exhaust pipe.

6. Safely support the frame at the rear center.

7. Remove the rear frame mount bolts and lower the frame 8–10 inches.

8. Remove the exhaust manifold retaining bolts and remove the exhaust manifold.

To install:

9. Clean the mating surfaces, install the exhaust manifold and tighten the retaining bolts to 24 ft. lbs. (33 Nm).

10. Raise the engine frame to the mounts and install the rear frame mount bolts. Tighten the nuts to 33 ft. lbs. (45 Nm).

11. Install the exhaust pipe and lower the vehicle.

12. Reconnect the crossover pipe.

13. Connect the oxygen sensor wire.

14. Connect the negative battery cable.

Air Conditioner Compressor

REMOVAL AND INSTALLATION

1. Disconnect the negative battery cable.

2. Discharge the air conditioning system as outlined in Section 1.

3. Disconnect the electrical connectors from the compressor.

4. Remove the serpentine belt from the compressor pulley by releasing the belt tension at the tensioner.

5. Remove the belt off of the compressor pulley.

6. Raise and support the vehicle safely.

7. Remove the front wheel for easier access to the compressor assembly.

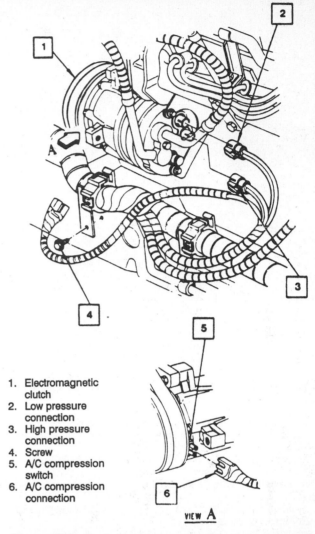

1. Electromagnetic clutch
2. Low pressure connection
3. High pressure connection
4. Screw
5. A/C compression switch
6. A/C compression connection

VIEW A

Air conditioner compressor electrical connections

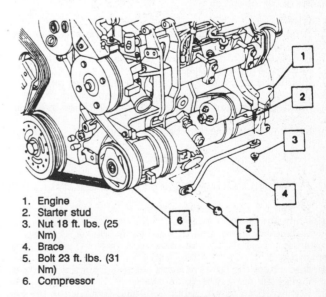

1. Engine
2. Starter stud
3. Nut 18 ft. lbs. (25 Nm)
4. Brace
5. Bolt 23 ft. lbs. (31 Nm)
6. Compressor

Air conditioner compressor brace

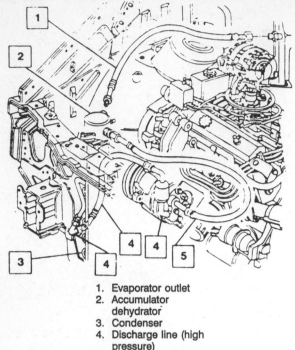

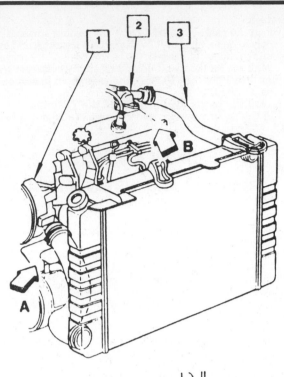

1. Evaporator outlet
2. Accumulator dehydrator
3. Condenser
4. Discharge line (high pressure)
5. Compressor suction line

Air conditioner compressor coupled hose assembly

8. Remove the right front wheel splash shield.
9. Remove the 2 bolts from the front engine bracket securing the front of the compressor.
10. Remove the 1 bolt from the rear engine bracket securing the rear of the compressor.
11. Remove the engine block stud nut securing the compressor brace.
12. Remove the 1 bolt attaching the brace to the compressor.
13. Remove the compressor.

NOTE: It may be necessary the rear mounting bracket and bolts for clearance.

To install:
14. Reposition the compressor and install the braces and retaining bolts and nuts.
15. Install the right front wheel splash shield and wheel.
16. Lower the vehicle safely.
17. Install the serpentine belt tot the compressor pulley.
18. Connect the electrical connectors to the compressor.
19. Charge the air conditioning system as outlined in Section 1.
20. Disconnect the negative battery cable.

Radiator

REMOVAL AND INSTALLATION

1. Disconnect the negative battery cable.
2. Drain the coolant from the radiator.
3. Disconnect the engine forward strut bracket at the radiator, loosen the bolt at the other end and swing the strut rearward.
4. Disconnect the forward lamp harness from the fan frame and unplug the fan connector.
5. Remove the fan attaching bolts and remove the fan and frame assembly.

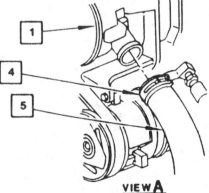

VIEW **A**

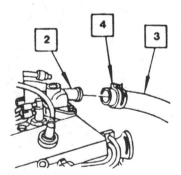

VIEW **B**

1. Water pump
2. Thermostat housing
3. Radiator inlet hose
4. Hose clamp
5. Radiator outlet hose

Coolant hose connections

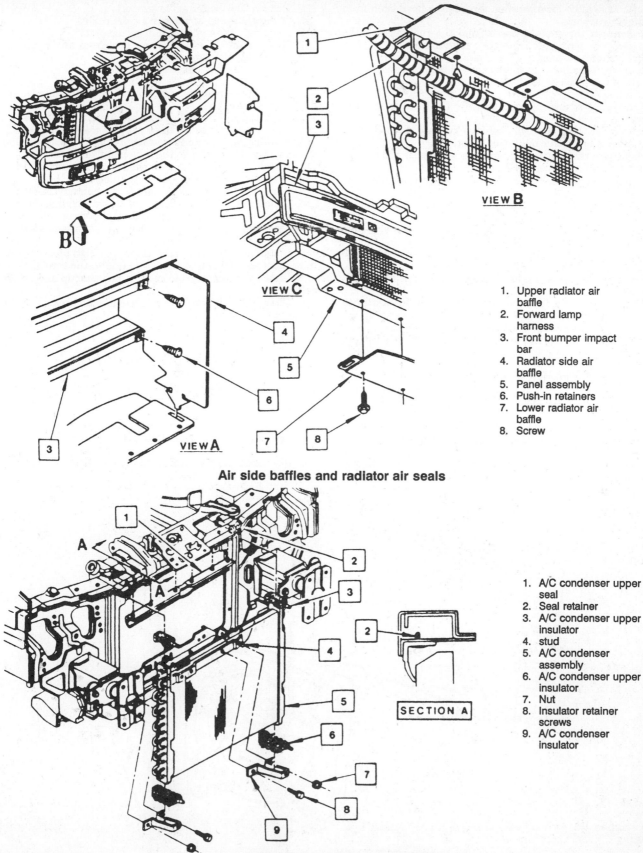

VIEW B

VIEW C

VIEW A

1. Upper radiator air baffle
2. Forward lamp harness
3. Front bumper impact bar
4. Radiator side air baffle
5. Panel assembly
6. Push-in retainers
7. Lower radiator air baffle
8. Screw

Air side baffles and radiator air seals

SECTION A

1. A/C condenser upper seal
2. Seal retainer
3. A/C condenser upper insulator
4. stud
5. A/C condenser assembly
6. A/C condenser upper insulator
7. Nut
8. Insulator retainer screws
9. A/C condenser insulator

Air conditioner condensor installation

6. Scribe the latch location then remove the hood latch from the radiator support.

7. Disconnect the coolant hoses from the radiator and the coolant recovery tank hose from the radiator neck.

8. Disconnect and plug the transaxle oil cooler lines.

9. Remove the radiator to support attaching bolts and clamps and remove the radiator from the vehicle.

To install:

10. If installing a new radiator, transfer the fittings from the old radiator.

11. Install the radiator to the vehicle, locating the bottom of the radiator in the lower mounting pads.

12. Install the radiator to support attaching bolts and clamps and torque to 88 inch lbs. (10 Nm).

13. Install the transaxle cooler lines and torque the nuts to 20 ft. lbs. (27 Nm).

14. Install the coolant hoses to the radiator and the coolant recovery hose to the radiator neck.

15. Install the hood latch to the radiator support and torque the bolts to 18 ft. lbs. (25 Nm).

16. Install the fan assembly and tighten the attaching bolts to 89 inch lbs. (10 Nm).

17. Connect the forward lamp harness to the fan frame and plug the fan connector.

18. Swing the engine forward strut and brace forward until the brace contacts the radiator support. Install the brace to the radiator support attaching bolts to 37 ft. lbs. (50 Nm).

19. Fill the cooling system and connect the negative battery cable.

Air Conditioner Condenser
REMOVAL AND INSTALLATION

1. Disconnect the negative battery cable.

2. Discharge the air conditioning system as noted in Section 1.

3. Disconnect the high pressure line to the condenser fitting and the liquid line at the condenser.

4. Remove the center grille support.

5. Remove the top and lower air deflector.

6. Disengage the upper and lower insulator.

7. Remove the upper condenser seal from the front engine compartment panel assembly.

8. Remove the condenser assembly.

To install:

9. Install the upper condenser seal to the engine compartment panel assembly.

10. Align the right and left seal retainers to the holes in the panel, then apply pressure to secure the seal to the panel.

11. Install the upper and lower insulators to the air conditioner condenser, making sure the tabs point forward.

12. Install the condenser with the insulators installed to the front engine compartment panel assembly.

13. Align the upper insulator tabs to the holes in the retainers.

14. Install the retainer to the lower tie bar aligning the retainer over the stud and engage the tab of the lower insulator.

15. Start the 2 inboard screws in the tie bar before installing the nuts, then install the nuts.

16. Install new O-rings and connect the high pressure line to the condenser fitting and the liquid line to the condenser.

17. Install the center grille support and the top and lower air deflectors.

18. Charge the air conditioner system and check for leaks as noted in Section 1.

Engine Cooling Fan
REMOVAL AND INSTALLATION

1. Disconnect the negative battery cable.

2. If necessary, disconnect the engine forward strut bracket at the radiator, loosen the bolt at the other end and swing the strut rearward.

3. Disconnect the forward lamp harness from the fan frame and unplug the fan connector.

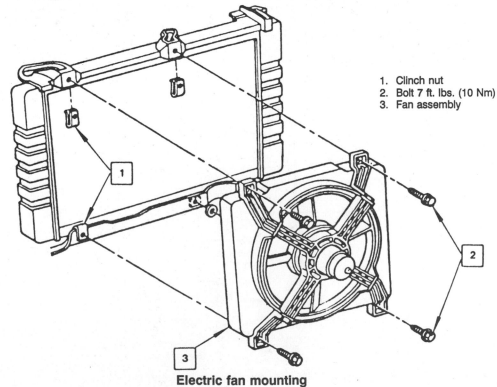

1. Clinch nut
2. Bolt 7 ft. lbs. (10 Nm)
3. Fan assembly

Electric fan mounting

4. Remove the fan attaching bolts and remove the fan and frame assembly.

5. Installation is the reverse of removal.

Water Pump

REMOVAL AND INSTALLATION

1. Disconnect the negative battery cable.
2. Drain the cooling system.
3. Disconnect the heater hose.
4. Remove the serpentine belt shield and using a ⅜ in. breaker bar, relieve the belt tension in the serpentine belt tensioner and remove the belt.
5. Remove the water pump pulley and remove the water pump.

To install:

6. Clean the water pump mating surfaces.
7. Install the water pump attaching bolts and torque the mounting bolts to 89 inch lbs.
8. Install the water pump pulley and attaching bolts.
9. Install the serpentine belt and shield.
10. Connect the heater hose and fill the cooling system.
11. Connect the negative battery cable.

Cylinder Head

REMOVAL AND INSTALLATION

Left

1. Disconnect the negative battery cable.
2. Drain the cooling system.
3. Remove the rocker arm covers.
4. Remove the intake manifold.
5. Disconnect the exhaust crossover pipe.
6. Remove the exhaust manifold.
7. Lower the vehicle and remove the oil level indicator tube bracket from the head.

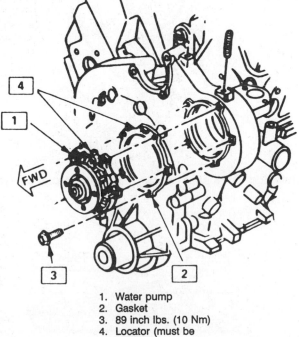

1. Water pump
2. Gasket
3. 89 inch lbs. (10 Nm)
4. Locator (must be vertical)

Water pump installation

HEAD TORQUE SEQUENCE

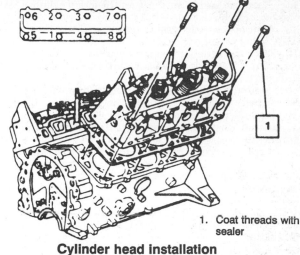

1. Coat threads with sealer

Cylinder head installation

8. Loosen the rocker arms enough to remove the pushrods.
9. Remove the cylinder head bolts and remove the cylinder head.

To install:

10. Clean the gasket surfaces on the head, cylinder block and intake manifold.
11. Position the new gasket over the dowel pins with THIS SIDE UP showing.
12. Place the cylinder head in position.
13. Coat the cylinder head bolt threads GM 1052080 sealer or equivalent, and install the bolts.
14. Tighten all the bolts in sequence to 41 ft. lbs. (55 Nm), then tighten all bolts in sequence an additional 90° (¼ turn).
15. Install the intake gasket.
16. Install the pushrods, making sure the lower ends are in the lifter seats.
17. Install the rocker arms and adjust the valve lash as follows:
   a. With the No. 1 cylinder at **TDC** the following valves may be adjusted 1–½ turns past zero lash:
   ● Exhaust – 1, 2, 3
   ● Intake – 1, 5, 6
   b. Crank the engine 1 revolution to bring the No. 4 cylinder to **TDC** and adjust the following valves 1–½ turns past zero lash:
   ● Exhaust – 4, 5, 6
   ● Intake – 2, 3, 4
18. After all valves are adjusted, install the intake manifold and valve covers.
19. Install the oil level indicator tube bracket to the head.
20. Install the exhaust manifold and connect the crossover pipe.
21. Fill the cooling system and connect the negative battery cable.

Right

1. Disconnect the negative battery cable.
2. Remove the air cleaner and intake hose.
3. Disconnect the exhaust crossover pipe.
4. Raise and support the vehicle safely and remove the exhaust manifold.
5. Lower the vehicle.
6. Remove the alternator assembly.
7. Remove the rocker arm covers and the intake manifold.
8. Loosen the rocker arms enough to remove the pushrods.
9. Remove the coil bracket.
10. Remove the cylinder head bolts and remove the cylinder head.

To install:

11. Clean the gasket surfaces on the head, cylinder block and intake manifold.

12. Position the new gasket over the dowel pins with THIS SIDE UP showing.

13. Place the cylinder head in position.

14. Coat the cylinder head bolt threads GM 1052080 sealer or equivalent, and install the bolts.

15. Tighten all the bolts in sequence to 41 ft. lbs. (55 Nm), then tighten all bolts in sequence an additional 90° (¼ turn).

16. Install the intake gasket.

17. Install the pushrods, making sure the lower ends are in the lifter seats.

18. Install the rocker arms and adjust the valve lash as follows:

    a. With the No. 1 cylinder at **TDC** the following valves may be adjusted 1–½ turns past zero lash:

- Exhaust–1, 2, 3
- Intake–1, 5, 6

    b. Crank the engine 1 revolution to bring the No. 4 cylinder to **TDC** and adjust the following valves 1–½ turns past zero lash:

- Exhaust–4, 5, 6
- Intake–2, 3, 4

19. After all valves are adjusted, install the intake manifold and valve covers.

20. Install the alternator assembly.

21. Raise and support the vehicle safely and install the exhaust manifold and connect the exhaust pipe.

22. Lower the vehicle and connect the crossover pipe.

23. Install the air cleaner and inlet pipe.

24. Install the coil bracket.

25. Connect the negative battery cable.

CLEANING AND INSPECTION

1. Refer to the Valves, Removal and Installation procedures in this section and remove the valve assemblies from the cylinder head.

2. Using a small wire power brush, clean the carbon from the combustion chambers and the valve ports.

3. Inspect the cylinder head for cracks in the exhaust ports, combustion chambers or external cracks to the water chamber.

4. Thoroughly clean the valve guides using a suitable wire bore brush.

NOTE: Excessive valve stem-to-bore clearance will cause excessive oil consumption and may cause valve breakage. Insufficient clearance will result in noisy and sticky functioning of the valve and disturb engine smoothness.

5. Measure the valve stem clearance as follows:

    a. Clamp a dial indicator on one side of the cylinder head rocker arm cover gasket rail.

    b. Locate the indicator so movement of the valve stem from side to side (crosswise to the head) will cause a direct move-

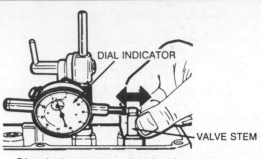

Check the stem-to-guide clearance

ment of the indicator stem. The indicator stem must contact the side of the valve stem just above the valve guide.

    c. Prop the valve head about ⅛ in. (2.0 mm) off the valve seat.

    d. Move the stem of the valve from side to side using light pressure to obtain a clearance reading. If the clearance exceeds specifications, it will be necessary to ream (for oversize valves) or knurl (raise the bore for original valves) the valve guides.

6. Inspect the rocker arm studs for wear or damage.

7. Install a dial micrometer into the valve guide and check the valve seat for concentricity.

RESURFACING

1. Using a straightedge, check the cylinder head for warpage.

2. If warpage exceeds 0.005 in. (127 mm), the cylinder head must be resurfaced. If more than 0.010 inch (0.25 mm) of metal must be removed from the head, it must be replaced. Resurfacing can be performed at most machine shops.

Checking valve seat concentricity with a dial gauge

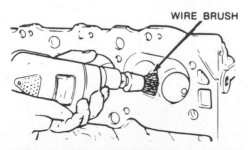

Remove the carbon from the cylinder head with a wire brush and electric drill

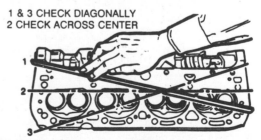

Check the cylinder head mating surface for warpage with a machinist's straightedge

NOTE: When resurfacing the cylinder head(s), the intake manifold mounting position is altered and must be corrected by machining a proportionate amount from the intake manifold flange.

Valves

REMOVAL AND INSTALLATION

Cylinder Head Removed

NOTE: The following procedures requires the use of a valve spring compressor tool J-5892–B or J-26513–A or their equivalent.

1. Refer to the Cylinder Head, Removal and Installation procedures in this section and remove the cylinder head.
2. Remove the rocker arm assemblies or the rocker arm nuts, the ball washers and the rocker arms, if not previously done.
3. Using a valve spring compressor tool, compress the valve springs and remove the stem keys. Release the compressor tool and the rotators or spring caps, the oil shedders, the springs and damper assemblies, then remove the oil seals and the valve spring shims.
4. Remove the valve from the cylinder head and place them in a rack in their proper sequence so they can be reassembled in their original positions. Discard any bent or damaged valves.
5. To install, use new oil seals and reverse the removal procedures. Refer to the Cylinder Head, Removal and Installation procedures in this section and adjust the valve lash.

1. Tool J–5892–B
2. Tool J–29833–B

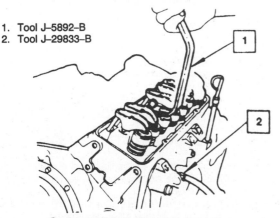

Compressing the valve spring

INSPECTION

Inspect the valve faces and seats (in the head) for pits, burned spots and other evidence of poor seating. If a valve face is in such bad shape that the head of the valve must be ground, in order to true up the face, discard the valve, because the sharp edge will run too hot. The correct angle for valve faces are 45°. We recommend the refacing be performed by a reputable machine shop.

Check the valve stem for scoring and burned spots. If not noticeably scored or damaged, clean the valve stem with solvent to remove all gum and varnish. Clean the valve guides using solvent and an expanding wire-type valve guide cleaner. If you have access to a dial indicator for measuring valve stem-to-guide clearance, mount it so the stem of the indicator is at 90° to the valve stem and as close to the valve guide as possible. Move the valve off its seat, then measure the valve guide-to-stem clearance by rocking the stem back and forth to actuate the dial indicator. Measure the valve stem diameter using a micrometer and compare to specifications to determine whether the stem or guide wear is responsible for the excess clearance. If a dial indi-

cator and micrometer are not available to you, take the cylinder head and valves to a reputable machine shop for inspection.

Some of the engines are equipped with valve rotators, which double as valve spring caps. In normal operation the rotators put a certain degree of wear on the tip of the valve stem; this wear appears as concentric rings on the stem tip. However, if the rotator is not working properly, the wear may appear as straight notches or X patterns across the valve stem tip. Whenever the valves are removed from the cylinder head, the tips should be inspected for improper pattern, which could indicate valve rotator problems. Valve stem tips will have to be ground flat if the rotator problems are severe.

REFACING

NOTE: All valve grinding operations should be performed by a qualified machine shop; only the valve lapping operation is recommended to be performed by the inexperienced mechanic.

Valve Lapping

When valve faces and seats have been refaced and/or recut, or if they are determined to be in good condition, the valves MUST BE lapped in to ensure efficient sealing when the valve closes against the seat.

1. Invert the cylinder head so the combustion chambers are facing upward.
2. Lightly lubricate the valve stems with clean engine oil and coat the valve seats with valve grinding compound. Install the valves in the cylinder head as numbered.
3. Attach the suction cup of a valve lapping tool to a valve head. You will probably have to moisten the cup to securely attach the tool to the valve.
4. Rotate the tool between the palms, changing position and lifting the tool often to prevent grooving. Lap the valve until a smooth polished seat is evident (you may have to add a bit more compound after some lapping is done).
5. Remove the valve and tool, then remove ALL traces of the grinding compound with a solvent-soaked rag or rinse the head with solvent.

NOTE: Valve lapping can also be done by fastening a suction cup to a piece of drill rod in a hand egg-beater type drill. Proceed as above, using the drill as a lapping tool. Due to the higher speeds involved when using the hand drill, care must be exercised to avoid grooving the seat. Lift the tool and change direction of rotation often.

Lapping the valves by hand

Valve Springs

REMOVAL AND INSTALLATION

If the cylinder head is removed from the engine, refer to the Valve, Removal and Installation procedures in this section and remove the valve spring.

NOTE: The following procedures requires the use of GM air adapter tool J–29833 or equivalent, and spring compressor tool J–5892–B or J–26513–A or their equivalents.

1. Refer to the Rocker Arm, Removal and Installation procedures in this section and remove the rocker arm nuts/bolts and the rocker arms.
2. Remove the spark plugs from the cylinders being worked on.
3. To remove the valve keepers, perform the following procedures:

a. Using the GM air adapter tool J–29833 or equivalent, install it into the spark plug hole.

b. Apply compressed air to the cylinder to hold the valves in place.

c. Install a rocker arm nut/bolt into the cylinder head.

d. Using the GM spring compressor tools J–5892–B or J–26513–A or their equivalents, compress the valve spring and remove the valve keepers.

e. Carefully release the spring pressure and remove the compressor tool.

4. Remove the valve cap, the shield and the spring.
5. Remove the O-ring seal and valve stem seal.
6. Inspect the valve spring, replace as necessary.
7. Lubricate the parts with engine oil, then install a new O-ring seal and valve stem seal onto each valve stem.
8. To complete the installation, adjust the valves and reverse the removal procedures. Start the engine, then check and/or adjust the timing.

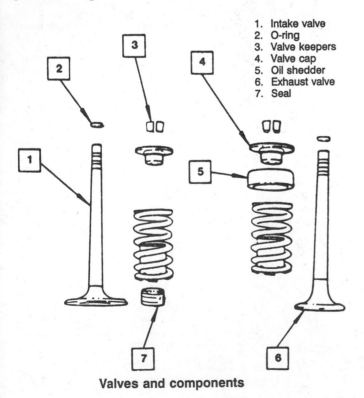

1. Intake valve
2. O-ring
3. Valve keepers
4. Valve cap
5. Oil shedder
6. Exhaust valve
7. Seal

Valves and components

INSPECTION

1. Position the valve spring on a flat, clean surface next to a square.
2. Measure the height of the spring and rotate it against the engine of the square to measure the distortion (out-of-roundness). If the spring height varies between the springs by more than $\frac{1}{16}$ in. (1.6mm) , replace the spring.
3. Using a valve spring tester, check the spring pressure at the installed and compressed height.

Valve Seats

REMOVAL AND INSTALLATION

The valve seats used on these engines are an integral part of the cylinder head and are not replaceable; they should be refaced, cleaned and lapped, ONLY. See the valve specifications chart for proper seat angle.

Valve Guides

REMOVAL AND INSTALLATION

These guides are not replaceable. The guides should be reamed to accommodate valves with oversized stems. Oversized stems are available in 0.089mm, 0.394mm and 0.775mm.

KNURLING

Valve guides which are not excessively worn or distorted may, in some cases, be knurled. knurling is a process in which metal is displaced and raised, thereby reducing clearance. Knurling also provides excellent oil control.

This procedure should only be performed by a qualified machine shop.

Valve Lifters

REMOVAL AND INSTALLATION

Valve lifters should be kept in order so they be reinstalled in their original position. Some engines will have both standard and oversize (O.S.) valve lifters.

Where O.S. lifters are used, the cylinder case will be marked with a dab of white paint **0.25mm O.S.** stamped on the lifter boss.

If a replacement is necessary, use lifters with a narrow flat ground along the lower ¾ of the lifter. These flats provide additional oil to the cam lobe and lifter surfaces.

1. Disconnect the negative battery cable.
2. Drain the cooling system.
3. Remove the rocker arm covers.
4. Remove the intake manifold.
5. Remove the rocker arm and pushrod and keep in a rack so they may be reinstalled in their original location.
6. Remove the valve lifter, and if to be reused, reinstalled in the original location.

To install:

7. Coat the bottom of the lifter with clean engine oil and install into position.
8. Install the pushrod and make sure it is seated in the lifter.
9. Coat the rocker arms and pivot balls with clean engine oil, place in their original position, install the nut and adjust the valve lash.
10. Install the intake manifold and valve covers.
11. Fill the cooling system and connect the negative battery cable.

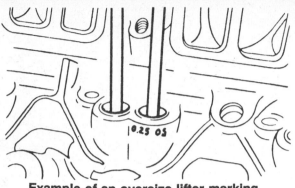

Example of an oversize lifter marking

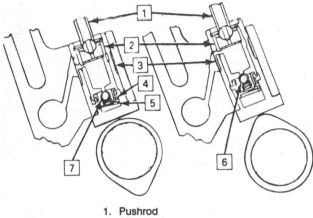

1. Pushrod
2. Plunger
3. Lifter body
4. Check ball spring
5. Plunger return spring
6. Check ball (closed)
7. Check ball (open)

Valve lifter operation

Oil Pan

REMOVAL AND INSTALLATION

1. Disconnect the negative battery cable. Remove the accessory drive belt.
2. Raise and safely support the vehicle.
3. Remove the crankshaft damper and pulley.
4. Drain the engine oil. Remove the flywheel shields.
5. Remove the starter. Support the engine from underneath with a suitable jack.
6. Remove the engine mounting bolts.
7. Raise the engine slightly.
8. Remove the oil pan bolts and the oil pan.

To install:

9. Clean the oil pan gasket mating surfaces, install a new oil pan gasket and install the oil pan. Tighten M8 oil pan bolts to 19 ft. lbs. (25 Nm) and the M6 oil pan bolts to 7 ft. lbs. (10 Nm).
10. Lower the engine and install the engine mounting bolts.
11. Install the starter and flywheel shields.
12. Install the crankshaft damper and pulley.
13. Lower the vehicle and install the accessory drive belt.
14. Refill the crankcase and connect the negative battery cable.

1. Frame assembly
2. Transaxle mounting bracket (point of support)
3. Oil pan
4. Transaxle fluid pan

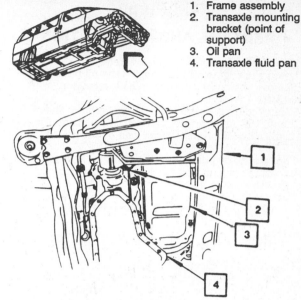

Support under the transxaxle mounting bracket

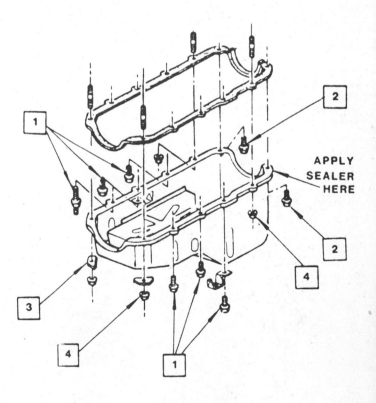

APPLY SEALER HERE

1. Bolts 100 inch lbs. (11 Nm)
2. Bolts 100 inch lbs. (11 Nm)
3. Reinforcements
4. Nuts 17 ft. lbs. (23 Nm)

Oil pan installation

Oil Pump

REMOVAL AND INSTALLATION

1. Raise and support the vehicle safely.
2. Drain the engine oil and remove the oil pan.
3. Remove the pump and drive shaft extension.

To install:

4. Clean the oil pan of oil and sludge, replace the oil filter.
5. Install the oil pump and drive shaft extension. Engage the drive shaft extension in the cover end of the distributor drive gear.
6. Tighten the oil pump mounting bolt to 30 ft. lbs. (40 Nm).
7. Install the oil pan and fill the crankcase with clean engine oil.

Timing Chain Front Cover

REMOVAL AND INSTALLATION

1. Disconnect the negative battery cable.
2. Drain the cooling system.
3. Remove the accessory drive belt and tensioner.
4. Remove the power steering pump.
5. Raise and safely support the vehicle. Remove the splash shield.
6. Drain the engine oil. Remove the crankshaft pulley and damper. Remove the starter and support it to the side.
7. Place a suitable jack under the engine-to-transaxle mount.
8. Remove the engine mount bolts and the engine mount. Raise the engine slightly.
9. Remove the lower front cover bolts and lower the oil pan. Remove the radiator hose at the water pump.
10. Remove the heater hose at the cooling system fill pipe. Remove the bypass and overflow hoses.
11. Remove the remaining front cover bolts and remove the front cover.

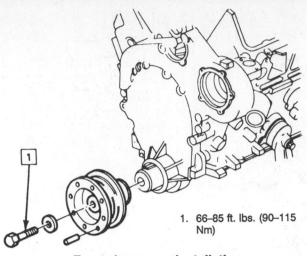

1. 66–85 ft. lbs. (90–115 Nm)

Front dampener installation

To install:

12. Clean all gasket mating surfaces. Install a new gasket in position on the engine block.
13. Apply sealer to the lower edges of the front cover. Install the front cover in position on the engine block. Tighten the upper bolts to 20 ft. lbs. (27 Nm).
14. Install the oil pan in position. Install the lower cover bolts and tighten to 28 ft. lbs. (38 Nm).
15. Install the engine mount to the engine and lower the engine into position.
16. Install the crankshaft damper and pulley. Install the flywheel cover and inner splash shield.
17. Install the starter. Connect the heater bypass hose an the slower radiator hose to the water pump. Lower the vehicle.

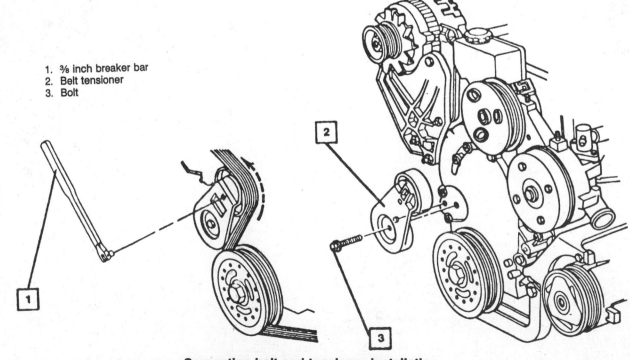

1. ⅜ inch breaker bar
2. Belt tensioner
3. Bolt

Serpentine belt and tensioner installation

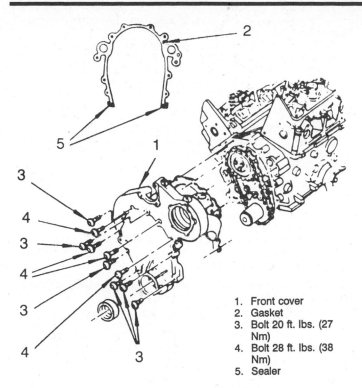

1. Front cover
2. Gasket
3. Bolt 20 ft. lbs. (27 Nm)
4. Bolt 28 ft. lbs. (38 Nm)
5. Sealer

Front cover installation

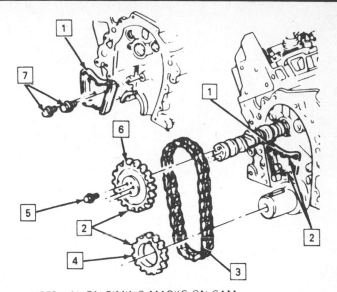

NOTE—ALIGN TIMING MARKS ON CAM & CRANK SPROCKETS USING ALIGNMENT MARKS ON DAMPER STAMPING OR CAST ALIGNMENT MARKS ON CYL & CASE

1. Damper
2. Alignment marks
3. Timing chain
4. Crankshaft sprocket
5. 21 ft. lbs. (28 Nm)
6. Camshaft sprocket

Timing chain and sprocket installation

18. Install the power steering pump bracket. Install the accessory drive belt and tensioner.
19. Refill the cooling system and the crankcase to the correct levels.
20. Connect the negative battery cable. Run the engine to normal operating temperature and check for leaks.

Front Cover Oil Seal

REPLACEMENT

The front cover seal can be replaced while the front cover is still on the vehicle. It is recommended by the manufacturer that the seal be replaced whenever the front cover is removed.
1. Disconnect the negative battery cable.
2. Remove the accessory drive belt.
3. Remove the crankshaft pulley and damper.
4. Using a suitable tool, pry the seal from the cover.
5. Lubricate the replacement seal with clean engine oil.
6. Using a suitable seal installer, position the seal on the crankshaft.
7. Install the crankshaft damper and pulley.
8. install the accessory drive belt.
9. Connect the negative battery cable.

Timing Chain and Sprockets

REMOVAL AND INSTALLATION

1. Disconnect the negative battery cable. Drain the coolant.
2. Remove the right front tire and wheel.
3. Remove the crankcase front cover assembly.
4. Crank the engine and align the timing marks on the cam and crank sprockets, using the alignment marks on the dampener stamping or the cast alignment marks on the cylinder and case.

5. Place the No. 1 piston at top dead center with the marks on the camshaft and crankshaft sprockets aligned.
6. Remove the bolts that hold the camshaft sprocket to the camshaft. This sprocket is a light press fit on the camshaft. If necessary, lightly tap the camshaft sprocket on the lower edge with a plastic mallet and remove the camshaft sprocket and chain.
7. Lock the crankshaft by freezing the flywheel with a prybar and remove the crankshaft sprocket, using a suitable gear puller.
To install:
8. Install the crankshaft sprocket using tool J 5590 or equivalent.
9. Install clean engine oil to the sprocket thrust surface.
10. Hold the sprocket with the chain hanging down and align the marks on the camshaft and crankshaft sprockets.
11. Align the dowel in the camshaft with the dowel hole in the camshaft sprocket.
12. Draw the camshaft sprocket onto the camshaft using the mounting bolts and torque to 18 ft. lbs. (24 Nm).
13. Lubricate the timing chain with clean engine oil.
14. Install the crankcase front cover.
15. Install the tire and wheel assembly.

Camshaft and Bearings

REMOVAL AND INSTALLATION

1. Disconnect the negative battery cable.
2. Drain the cooling system.
3. Remove the engine from the vehicle and support it in a suitable holding fixture.

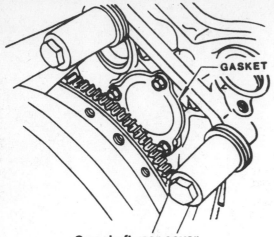

Camshaft rear cover

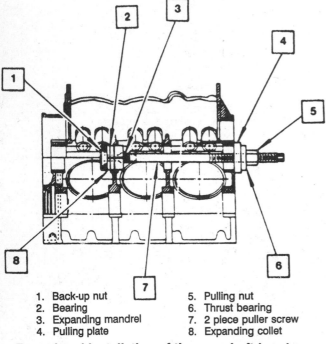

1. Back-up nut
2. Bearing
3. Expanding mandrel
4. Pulling plate
5. Pulling nut
6. Thrust bearing
7. 2 piece puller screw
8. Expanding collet

Reoval and installation of the camshaft bearings

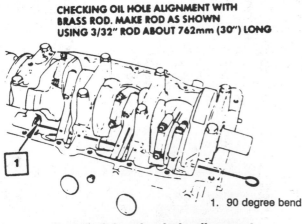

CHECKING OIL HOLE ALIGNMENT WITH BRASS ROD. MAKE ROD AS SHOWN USING 3/32" ROD ABOUT 762mm (30") LONG

1. 90 degree bend

Camshaft bearing hole alignment

4. Remove the intake manifold. Remove the valve cover and the valve train components.
5. Remove the front cover assembly.
6. Remove the timing chain and sprocket.
7. Remove the camshaft from the block by pulling it out. Use care not to damage the bearings.
8. If required, remove the camshaft bearings as follows:
   a. Using tool set J 33049 or equivalent, select the proper pilot, nut and thrust washer.
   b. Assemble the bearing puller, making sure that the puller engages a sufficient number of threads, and pull out the bearings.

To install:
9. Install the camshaft bearings as follows:
   a. Select the front, rear, and intermediate camshaft bearings.
   b. Select the proper pilot nut and thrust washer.
   c. Assemble the installing tool.
   d. Place the bearing onto the tool and index the oil hole(s) of the bearing with the oil passage(s) in the cylinder block. Pull the bearing into place.

WARNING: Correct alignment of the oil holes is critical for proper oil flow.

   e. With a piece of $^3/_{32}$ in. brass rod with a 90° bend at the end, probe the bearing oil holes and verify that they are properly aligned.
10. Lubricate the camshaft with Molykote or equivalent, before installation.
11. Install the camshaft into the cylinder block, use care not to damage the bearings.
12. Install the timing chain and sprocket. Make sure that the timing marks align correctly.
13. Install the front cover assembly.
14. Install the intake manifold assembly. Install the valve train components and the valve cover.
15. Install the engine into the vehicle.
16. Fill the cooling system to the correct level and connect the negative battery cable.

INSPECTION

Using solvent, degrease the camshaft and clean out all of the oil holes. Visually inspect the cam lobes and bearing journals for excessive wear. If a lobe is questionable, check all of the lobes as indicated. If a journal or lobe is worn, the camshaft must be reground or replaced.

NOTE: If a journal is worn, there is a good chance that the bushings are worn and need replacement.

If the lobes and journals appear intact, place the front and rear journals in V-blocks and rest a dial indicator on the center

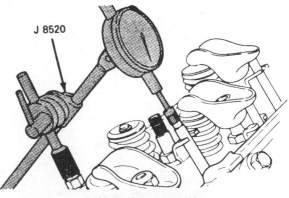

J 8520

Measuring cam lift

journal. Rotate the camshaft to check the straightness. If deviation exceeds 0.001 in. (0.0254mm), replace the camshaft.

Check the camshaft lobes with a micrometer, by measuring the lobes from the nose to the base and again at 90°. The lobe lift is determined by subtracting the second measurement from the first. If all of the exhaust and intake lobes are not identical, the camshaft must be reground or replace.

Pistons and Connecting Rods

REMOVAL AND INSTALLATION

1. Refer to the Engine, Removal and Installation procedures in this section and remove the engine from the vehicle.
2. Remove the intake manifold and the cylinder head(s).
3. Remove the oil pan and the oil pump assembly.
4. Stamp the cylinder number on the machined surfaces of the bolt bosses of the connecting rod and cap for identification when reinstalling. If the pistons are to be removed from the connecting rod, mark the cylinder number on the piston with a silver pencil or quick drying paint for proper cylinder identification and cap to rod location.

NOTE: **The cylinders are numbered 1–3–5 (left-to-right) on the rear side and 2–4–6 (left-to-right) on the front side, facing the vehicle.**

5. Examine the cylinder bore above the ring travel. If a ridge exists, remove it with a ridge reamer before attempting to remove the piston and rod assembly.
6. Remove the connecting rod bearing cap and bearing.
7. Install a ⅜ in. rubber guide hose over the rod bolt threads; this will prevent damage to the bearing journal and rod bolt threads.
8. Remove the rod and piston assembly through the top of the cylinder bore; remove the other rod and piston assemblies in the same manner.
9. Clean and inspect the engine block, the crankshaft, the pistons and the connecting rods.

CLEANING AND INSPECTION

Using a piston ring expanding tool, remove the piston rings from the pistons; any other method (screwdriver blades, pliers, etc.) usually results in the rings being bent, scratched or distorted and/or the piston itself being damaged.

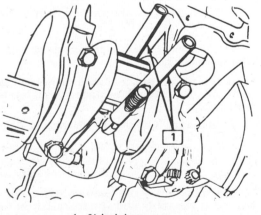

1. ⅜ inch hose as a guide

Install a ⅜ in. rubber guide hose over the rod bolt threads; this will prevent damage to the bearing journal and rod bolt threads

Pistons

Clean the varnish from the piston skirts and pins with a cleaning solvent. Do not wire brush any part of the piston. Clean the ring grooves with a groove cleaner and make sure the oil ring holes and slots are clean.

Inspect the piston for cracked ring lands, scuffed or damaged skirts, eroded areas at the top of the piston. Replace the pistons that are damaged or show signs of excessive wear.

Inspect the grooves for nicks of burrs that might cause the rings to hang up.

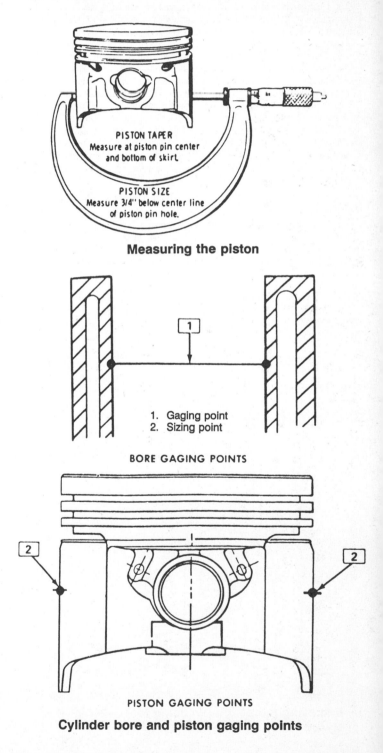

PISTON TAPER
Measure at piston pin center and bottom of skirt

PISTON SIZE
Measure 3/4" below center line of piston pin hole.

Measuring the piston

1. Gaging point
2. Sizing point

BORE GAGING POINTS

PISTON GAGING POINTS

Cylinder bore and piston gaging points

Measure the piston skirt, across the center line of the piston pin, and check the piston clearance.

Connecting Rods

Wash the connecting rods in cleaning solvent and dry with compressed air. Check for twisted or bent rods and inspect for nicks or cracks. Replace the connecting rods that are damaged.

Cylinder Bores

Using a telescoping gauge or an inside micrometer, measure the diameter of the cylinder bore, perpendicular (90°) to the piston pin, at 2½ in. (63.5mm) below the surface of the cylinder block. The difference between the 2 measurements is the piston clearance.

If the clearance is within specifications or slightly below, after the cylinders have been bored or honed, finish honing is all that is necessary, If the clearance is excessive, try to obtain a slightly larger piston to bring the clearance within specifications. If this is not possible obtain the first oversize piston and hone the cylinder or, if necessary, bore the cylinder to size. Generally, if the cylinder bore is tapered more than 0.005 in. (0.127mm) or is out-of-round more than 0.003 in. (0.0762mm), it is advisable to rebore for the smallest possible oversize piston and rings. After measuring, mark the pistons with a felt-tip pen for reference and for assembly.

NOTE: Boring of the cylinder block should be performed by a reputable machine shop with the proper equipment. In some cases, clean-up honing can be done with the cylinder block in the vehicle, but most excessive honing and all cylinder boring must be done with the block stripped and removed from the vehicle.

PISTON PIN REPLACEMENT

NOTE: The following procedure requires the use of J–24086–B or equivalent, piston pin remover/installer tool.

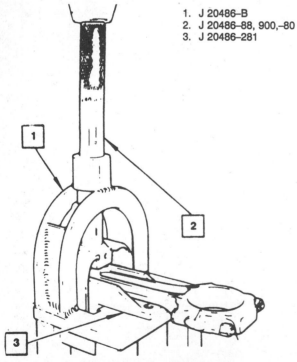

1. J 20486–B
2. J 20486–88, 900,–80
3. J 20486–281

Removing the piston pin using tool J–24086–B or equivalent

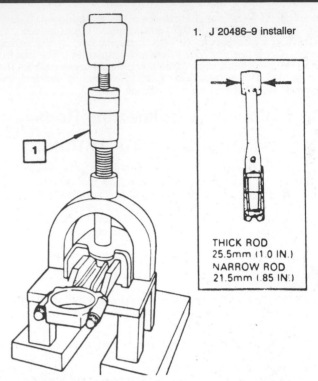

1. J 20486–9 installer

THICK ROD
25.5mm (1.0 IN.)
NARROW ROD
21.5mm (.85 IN.)

Installing the piston pin using tool J–24086–B or equivalent

Use care at all times when handling and servicing the connecting rods and pistons. To prevent possible damage to these units, do not clamp the rod or piston in a vise since they may become distorted. Do not allow the pistons to strike one another, against hard objects or bench surfaces, since distortion of the piston contour or nicks in the soft aluminum material may result.

1. Using an arbor press and the piston pin removal tool J–24086–B or equivalent, place the piston assembly in the tool and press the pin from the piston assembly.

NOTE: The piston and the piston pin are a matched set which are not serviced separately.

2. Using solvent, wash the varnish and oil from the parts, then inspect the parts for scuffing or wear.
3. Using a micrometer, measure the diameter of the piston pin. Using a inside micrometer or a dial bore gauge, measure the diameter of the piston bore.

NOTE: If the piston pin-to-piston clearance is in excess of 0.001 in. (0.0254mm), replace the piston and piston pin assembly.

4. Before installation, lubricate the piston pin and the piston bore with engine oil.
5. To install the piston pin into the piston assembly, use an arbor press, the assembly tool J–24086–B or equivalent, and press the piston pin into the piston/connecting rod assembly.

NOTE: When installing the piston pin into the piston/connecting rod assembly and the installation tool bottoms onto the support assembly, do not exceed 5000 lbs. of pressure for structural damage may occur to the tool.

6. After installing the piston pin, make sure that the piston has freedom of movement with the piston pin. The piston/connecting rod assembly is ready for installation into the engine block.

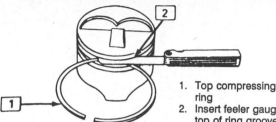

1. Top compressing ring
2. Insert feeler gauge at top of ring groove

Measuring piston ring side clearance

PISTON RING REPLACEMENT AND SIDE CLEARANCE MEASUREMENT

Check the pistons to see that the ring grooves and oil return holes have been properly cleaned. Slide a piston ring into its groove and check the side clearance with a feeler gauge. Make sure the feeler gauge is inserted between the ring and its lower land (lower edge of the groove), because any wear that occurs forms a step at the inner portion of the lower land. If the piston grooves have been worn to the extent that relatively high steps exist on the lower land, the piston should be replaced, because these will interfere with the operation of the new rings and ring clearances will be excessive. Piston rings are not furnished in oversize widths to compensate for ring groove wear.

Install the rings on the piston, bottom ring first, using a piston ring expander. There is a high risk of breaking or distorting the rings and/or scratching the piston, if the rings are installed by hand or other means.

Position the rings on the piston as illustrated; spacing of the various piston ring gaps is crucial to the proper oil retention and cylinder wear. When installing the new rings, refer to the installation diagram furnished with the new parts.

CHECKING RING END GAP

The piston ring end gap should be checked while the rings are removed from the pistons. Incorrect end gap indicates that the wrong size rings are being used; **ring breakage could result.**

1. Compress the new piston ring into a cylinder (one at a time).

2. Squirt some clean oil into the cylinder so the ring and the top 2 in. (51mm) of the cylinder wall are coated.

3. Using an inverted piston, push the ring approximately 1 in. (25.4mm) below the top of the cylinder.

4. Using a feeler gauge, measure the ring gap and compare it to the Ring Gap chart in this Section. Carefully remove the ring from the cylinder.

1. Feeler gauge
2. Piston ring
3. Ring positioned at bottom ring travel

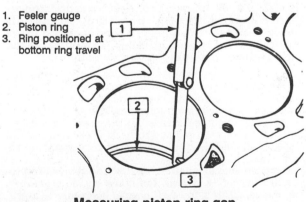

Measuring piston ring gap

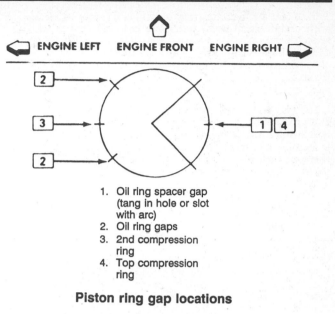

ENGINE LEFT   ENGINE FRONT   ENGINE RIGHT

1. Oil ring spacer gap (tang in hole or slot with arc)
2. Oil ring gaps
3. 2nd compression ring
4. Top compression ring

Piston ring gap locations

CONNECTING ROD BEARING REPLACEMENT

Replacement bearings are available in standard size and undersize (for reground crankshafts). Connecting rod-to-crankshaft bearing clearance is checked using Plastigage® at either the top or the bottom of each crank journal. The Plastigage® has a range of 0.001–0.003 in. (0.0254–0.0762mm).

1. Remove the rod cap with the bearing shell. Completely clean the bearing shell and the crank journal, blow any oil from the oil hole in the crankshaft; place the Plastigage® lengthwise along the bottom center of the lower bearing shell, then install the cap with the shell and torque the bolt or nuts to specification. Do not turn the crankshaft with the Plastigage® on the bearing.

2. Remove the bearing cap with the shell. The flattened Plastigage® will be found sticking to either the bearing shell or the crank journal. Do not remove it yet.

3. Use the scale printed on the Plastigage® envelope to measure the flattened material at its widest point. The number within the scale which most closely corresponds to the width of the Plastigage® indicates the bearing clearance in thousandths of an inch.

4. Check the specifications chart in this Section for the desired clearance. It is advisable to install a new bearing if the clearance exceeds 0.003 in. (0.0762mm); however, if the bearing is in good condition and is not being checked because of bearing noise, bearing replacement is not necessary.

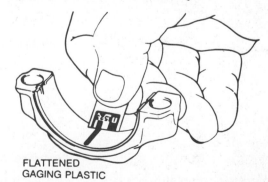

FLATTENED GAGING PLASTIC

Checking the bearing clearance with Plastigage®

5. If you are installing new bearings, try a standard size, then each undersize in order until one is found that is within the specified limits when checked for clearance with Plastigage®; each undersize shell has its size stamped on it.

6. When the proper size shell is found, clean off the Plastigage®, oil the bearing thoroughly, reinstall the cap with its shell and torque the rod bolt nuts to specifications.

NOTE: With the proper bearing selected and the nuts torqued, it should be possible to move the connecting rod back and forth freely on the crank journal as allowed by the specified connecting rod end clearance. If the rod cannot be moved, either the rod bearing is too far undersize or the rod is misaligned.

1. Piston
2. Arrow towards front of engine

J 8037

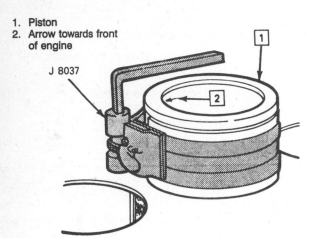

Piston and rod assembly

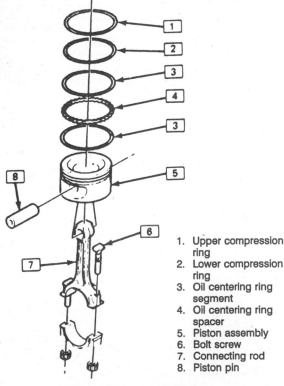

1. Upper compression ring
2. Lower compression ring
3. Oil centering ring segment
4. Oil centering ring spacer
5. Piston assembly
6. Bolt screw
7. Connecting rod
8. Piston pin

Piston ring compressor

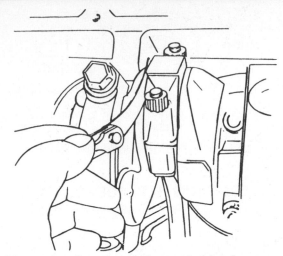

Measuring the connecting rod side clearance

INSTALLATION

NOTE: The following procedure requires the use of the ring compressor tool J-8037 or equivalent, and the ring installation tool.

Position the rings on the piston; **spacing of the various piston ring gaps is crucial to proper oil retention and even cylinder wear.** When installing new rings, refer to the installation diagram furnished with the new parts.

Install the connecting rod to the piston, making sure the piston installation notches and marks, if any, on the connecting rod are in proper relation to one another.

1. Make sure the connecting rod big-end bearings (including the end cap) are of the correct size and properly installed.

2. Fit rubber hoses over the connecting rod bolts to protect the crankshaft journals, as in the Piston Removal procedure. Lubricate the connecting rod bearings with clean engine oil.

3. Using the ring compressor tool J-8037 or equivalent, compress the rings around the piston head. Insert the piston assembly into the cylinder, so the notch (on top of the piston) faces the front of the engine.

4. Working under the engine, coat each crank journal with clean oil. Using a hammer handle, drive the connecting rod/piston assembly into the cylinder bore. Align the connecting rod (with bearing shell) onto the crankshaft journal.

5. Remove the rubber hoses from the studs. Install the bearing cap (with bearing shell) onto the connecting rod and the cap nuts. Torque the connecting rod cap nuts to 39 ft. lbs. (53 Nm)

NOTE: When more than one connecting rod/piston assembly are being installed, the connecting rod cap nuts should only be tightened enough to keep each rod in position until the all have been installed. This will ease the installation of the remaining piston assemblies.

6. Check the clearance between the sides of the connecting rods and the crankshaft using a feeler gauge. Spread the rods slightly with a small prybar to insert the feeler gauge. If the clearance is below the minimum tolerance, the rod may be machined to provide adequate clearance. If the clearance is excessive, substitute an unworn rod and recheck. If clearance is still outside specifications, the crankshaft must be welded and reground or replaced.

7. To complete the installation, reverse the removal procedures. Refill the cooling system. Refill the engine crankcase. Start the engine, allow it to reach normal operating temperatures and check for leaks.

Rear Main Seal

REMOVAL AND INSTALLATION

1. Remove the transaxle.
2. Remove the flywheel.
3. Insert a suitable prying tool through the dust lip and pry out the seal by moving the handle of the tool towards the end of the crankshaft, working around the entire circumference.

WARNING: Be careful not to nick or damage the outside diameter of the crankshaft with the pry tool.

To install:

4. Check for an O-ring in the rear main bearing cap.
5. Install a new seal, using tool J 34686 or equivalent, as follows:

   a. Apply a light coat of oil to the inside diameter of the new seal and install it over the mandrel. Slide the seal on the mandrel until the dust lip (back of the seal) bottoms squarely against the collar of the seal.

   b. Align the dowel pin of the tool with the dowel pin hole in the crankshaft and attach the tool to the crankshaft by hand or torque the attaching screw to 6 inch lbs.

   c. Turn the T handle of the tool so that the collar pushes the seal into the bore and turn the handle until the collar is tight against the case. This will insure that the seal is seated properly.

1. Alignment hole
2. Dust lip
3. Dowel pin
4. Collar
5. Mandrel
6. Ataching screws
7. Seals

Rear main seal installation

   d. Loosen the **T** handle of the tool until it comes to a stop. This will insure that the collar will be in the proper position for installing a new seal. Remove the attaching screws.
6. Check the seal and make sure it is seated squarely in the bore.
7. Install the flywheel and torque the retaining bolts to 52 ft. lbs. (71 Nm).
8. Install the transaxle.
9. Start the engine and check for leaks.

Flywheel

REMOVAL AND INSTALLATION

1. Remove the transaxle.
2. Use a suitable tool to prevent the crankshaft from rotating and remove the flywheel attaching bolts.
To install:
3. Apply thread lock compound to the flywheel retaining bolts, use a suitable tool to prevent the crankshaft from rotating and install the flywheel. Torque the bolts to 52 ft. lbs. (70 Nm).
4. Install the transaxle.

Crankshaft and Main Bearings

REMOVAL AND INSTALLATION

1. Refer to the Engine, Removal and Installation procedures in this section and remove the engine from the vehicle.

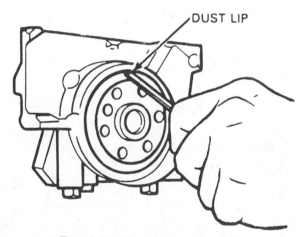

Removing the rear main seal

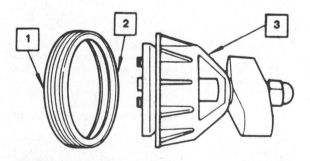

SPRING SIDE SEAL BORE
TO SEAL SURFACE TO BE
LUBRICATED WITH ENGINE
OIL BEFORE ASSEMBLY.

1. Spring side
2. Dust lip side
3. J–34686

Rear main seal installation tool

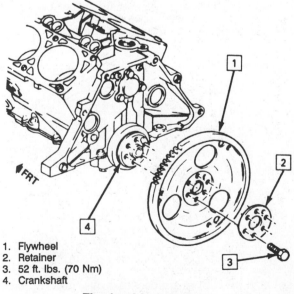

1. Flywheel
2. Retainer
3. 52 ft. lbs. (70 Nm)
4. Crankshaft

Flywheel installation

2. If equipped with a flywheel, remove it and mount the engine onto a workstand.

3. Disconnect the spark plug wires from the plugs, then remove the spark plugs.

4. Remove the drive belt pulley from the damper pulley/hub, the damper pulley/hub-to-crankshaft bolt, the damper pulley/hub from the crankshaft and the timing cover from the engine.

NOTE: After removing the damper pulley/hub from the crankshaft, be sure to remove the woodruff key from the crankshaft. When removing the damper pulley/hub from the crankshaft, the oil seal should be replaced.

5. Rotate the crankshaft, until the timing marks on the timing gears or sprockets align with each other, then remove the timing gear or sprocket from the crankshaft.

NOTE: After removing the timing gear or sprocket from the crankshaft, be sure to remove the woodruff key from the crankshaft.

6. Place a catch pan under the engine, remove the oil pan plug and drain the oil into the pan. Invert the engine and remove the oil pan from the engine.

7. Remove the oil pump.

8. Inspect the connecting rods and bearing caps for identification marks (numbers); if there are none, mark them for reassembly purposes.

9. Remove the connecting rod nuts and caps, then store them in the order of removal. Be sure to place short pieces of rubber hose on the connecting rod studs to prevent damaging the crankshaft bearing surfaces.

NOTE: When installing the rubber hoses onto the connecting rod studs, position the long tool so it may be used to push the connecting rod up into the bore.

10. Check the main bearing caps for identification marks, if not identified, mark them. Remove the main bearing caps and store them in order, for reassembly purposes; the caps must be reinstalled in their original position.

11. Remove the crankshaft, the main bearing inserts and the rear main oil seal, the rear main oil seal/retainer or the rear main oil shell sections.

NOTE: When removing the bearing shells, it is recommended to replace them with new ones.

12. Using solvent, clean all of the parts for inspection purposes. If necessary, replace any part that may be questionable.

13. To install, use new bearing shell inserts and check the bearing clearances using the Plastigage® method.

1. ⅜ inch guide hose

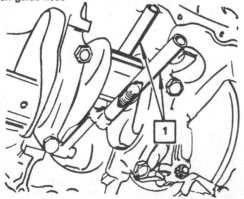

Install a ⅜ in. rubber guide hose over the rod bolt threads

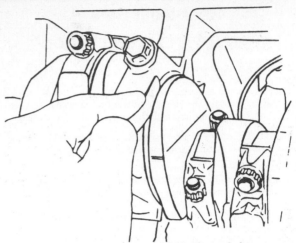

Measuring the crankshaft endplay

NOTE: If necessary, deliver the crankshaft to an automotive machine shop, have the crankshaft journals ground and new bearing shells matched.

14. Lubricate all of the parts and oil seals with clean engine oil.

15. Using a feeler gauge and a medium prybar, move the crankshaft forward-and-rearward, then the feeler gauge to check the crankshaft end play.

16. To complete the installation, use new gaskets (sealant if necessary) and reverse the removal procedures. Torque the main bearing cap-to-engine bolts to 72 ft. lbs. (98 Nm).Refill the cooling system (with the saved coolant) and the crankcase (with new oil). Start the engine, allow it to reach normal operating temperatures and check for leaks.

CLEANING AND INSPECTION

NOTE: The following procedure requires the use of a set of V-blocks, a dial indicator, an outside micrometer, an inside micrometer and Plastigage®.

1. Remove the bearing cap and wipe the oil from the crankshaft journal and outer/inner surfaces of the bearing shell.

2. To inspect the crankshaft bearing journals, perform the following procedures:

   a. Using a set of V-blocks and a dial indicator, inspect the main bearing journals for runout; if necessary, regrind the bearing journals.

   b. Using an outside micrometer, measure the main bearing journals for diameter and out-of-round conditions; if necessary, regrind the bearing journals.

   c. Install the main bearing caps and torque the nuts/bolts to specifications. Using an inside micrometer, inspect the main bearing journals in the engine block; if necessary, rebore the bearing seats in the engine block.

3. To inspect the main bearing surfaces, using the Plastigage® method, perform the following procedures:

   a. Using a piece of Plastigage® material, position it in the center of the main bearing surface(s).

   b. Install the main bearing cap(s) and torque the cap nuts/bolts to specifications.

NOTE: When the Plastigage® material is installed on the bearing surfaces, do not rotate the crankshaft.

   c. Remove the bearing caps and determine the bearing clearance by comparing the width of the flattened Plastigage® material at its widest point with the graduations on the gauging material conatainer.

NOTE: The number within the graduation on the envelope indicates the clearance in millimeters or thousandths of an inch. If the clearance is greater than allowed. Replace both bearing shells as a set. Recheck the clearance after replacing the shells. Refer to the Main Bearing Replacement in this section.

MAIN BEARING REPLACEMENT

Main bearing clearances must be corrected by the use of selective upper and lower shells. Under no circumstances should the use of shims behind the shells to compensate for wear be attempted. To install the main bearing shells, proceed as follows:

1. Refer to the Oil Pan, Removal and Installation procedures in this section and remove the oil pan.
2. Loosen all of the main bearing cap bolts.
3. Remove the bearing cap bolts, the caps and the lower bearing shell.
4. Insert a flattened cotter pin or a roll out pin in the oil passage hole in the crankshaft, then rotate the crankshaft in the direction opposite to the cranking rotation. The pin will contact the upper shell and roll it out.
5. The main bearing journals should be checked for roughness and wear. Slight roughness may be removed with a fine grit polishing cloth, saturated with engine oil. Burrs may be removed with a fine oil stone. If the journals are scored or ridged, the crankshaft must be replaced.

NOTE: The journals can be measured for out-of-round with the crankshaft installed by using a crankshaft caliper and inside micrometer or a main bearing micrometer. The upper bearing shell must be removed when measuring the crankshaft journals. Maximum out-of-round of the crankshaft journal must not exceed 0.0015 in. (0.038mm).

6. Clean the crankshaft journals and bearing caps thoroughly before installing the new main bearings.
7. Apply special lubricant, GM 1050169 or equivalent, to the thrust flanges of the bearing shells.
8. Place the new upper shell on the crankshaft journal with the locating tang in the correct position and rotate the shaft to turn it into place using a cotter pin or a roll out pin as during removal.
9. Place a new bearing shell in the bearing cap.
10. Lubricate the new bearings and the main bearing cap bolts with engine oil. Install the main bearing shells, the crankshaft and the main bearing caps. Using the Plastigage® method, check the bearing clearances. Using a feeler gauge, pry the crankshaft forward and rearward, then check for the crankshaft (thrust bearing) end play.

NOTE: In order to prevent the possibility of cylinder block and/or main bearing cap damage, the main bearing caps are to be tapped into their cylinder block cavity, using a brass or leather mallet before the bolts are installed. Do not use the bolts to pull the main bearing caps into their seats. Failure to observe this procedure may damage the cylinder block or bearing cap.

11. To complete the installation, use new oil seals, gaskets (sealant, if necessary) and reverse the removal procedures. Torque the main bearing cap-to-engine bolts to 72 ft. lbs. (98 Nm).

EXHAUST SYSTEM

Safety Precautions

For a number of reasons, exhaust system work can be the most dangerous type of work to perform on your car. Always observe the following precautions:
• Support the car extra securely. Not only will you often be working directly under it, but you'll frequently be using a lot of force, say, heavy hammer blows, to dislodge rusted parts. This can cause a car that's improperly supported to shift and possibly fall.
• Wear goggles. Exhaust system parts are always rusty. Metal chips can be dislodged, even when you're only turning rusted bolts. Attempting to pry pipes apart with a chisel makes the chips fly even more frequently.
• If you're using a cutting torch, keep it a great distance from either the fuel tank or lines. Stop what you're doing and feel the temperature of the fuel bearing pipes on the tank frequently. Even slight heat can expand and/or vaporize fuel, resulting in accumulated vapor, or even a liquid leak, near your torch.
• Watch where your hammer blows fall and make sure you hit squarely. You could easily tap a brake or fuel line when you hit an exhaust system part with a glancing blow. Inspect all lines and hoses in the area where you've been working.

———— CAUTION ————

Be very careful when working on or near the catalytic converter. External temperatures can reach 1,500°F (816°C) and more, causing severe burns. Removal or installation should be performed only on a cold exhaust system.

Special Tools

A number of special exhaust system tools can be purchased from local auto supply stores. A common one is a tail pipe expander, designed to enable you to join pipes of identical diameter.

It may also be quite helpful to use solvents designed to loosen rusted bolts or flanges. Soaking rusted parts the night before you do the job can speed the work of freeing rusted parts considerably. Remember that these solvents are often flammable. Apply only to parts after they are cool!

Front Exhaust Pipe

REMOVAL AND INSTALLATION

1. Raise and support the vehicle safely.
2. Support the catalytic converter and cut the front exhaust pipe at the converter, using a pipe cutter.
3. Unbolt the exhaust pipe at the exhaust manifold and remove the pipe.
4. Remove the intermediate hanger bolts.

To install:

5. File off the ridge on the cut end of the catalytic converter.
6. Install a repair sleeve over the replacement pipe and slide the pipe and sleeve over the converter opening.
7. Reconnect the exhaust system to the intermediate hanger.
8. Install the exhaust manifold seal, exhaust pipe springs and nuts. Torque the nuts to 18 ft. lbs. (25 Nm).
9. Install 2 new saddle/U-bolt clamps and torque to 26 ft. lbs. (35 Nm).

Catalytic Converter

REMOVAL AND INSTALLATION

1. Raise and support the vehicle safely.
2. Support the catalytic converter, cut the intermediate pipe and remove the converter.

To install:

3. Install repair sleeves over the pipe ends of the replacement catalytic converter.
4. Remove the ridges from the cut ends of the exhaust and intermediate pipes.
5. Install the replacement converter.
6. Install 2 new saddle/U-bolt clamps and torque to 26 ft. lbs. (35 Nm).

Muffler

REMOVAL AND INSTALLATION

1. Raise and support the vehicle safely.
2. Support the intermediate pipe and muffler.

3. Disconnect the tailpipe hanger and slide the muffler and tailpipe assembly off of the muffler hanger.

To install:

4. Trim the new muffler inlet pipe as required and install a repair sleeve.
5. Install the muffler assembly into the hangers and over the converter outlet pipe.
6. Install 2 new saddle/U-bolt clamps and torque to 26 ft. lbs. (35 Nm).

Tailpipe

REMOVAL AND INSTALLATION

1. Raise and support the vehicle safely.
2. Using a suitable pipe cutter, cut the tailpipe off and remove from the vehicle.

To install:

3. Cut the replacement tailpipe to the desired length.
4. Install a repair sleeve to the replacement tailpipe.
5. Fit the repair sleeve over the muffler and install the tailpipe.
6. Install 2 new saddle/U-bolt clamps and torque to 26 ft. lbs. (35 Nm).

Complete Exhaust

REMOVAL AND INSTALLATION

1. Raise and support the vehicle safely.
2. Support the exhaust system.
3. Unbolt the exhaust pipe from the exhaust manifold.
4. Remove all exhaust hanger bolts.
5. Remove the exhaust system from the vehicle.

To install:

6. Install the converter and exhaust pipe assembly with the repair sleeve attached.
7. Install the hanger bolts.
8. Install the muffler and tailpipe assembly.
9. Install the hanger bolts.
10. Install 2 new saddle/U-bolt clamps at the converter/intermediate pipe juncture and torque to 26 ft. lbs. (35 Nm).

1. Cutline
2. 2 in. sleeve
3. 2.5 in. sleeve
4. Muffler
5. Tailpipe
6. Intermediate pipe
7. Converter
8. Manifold pipe

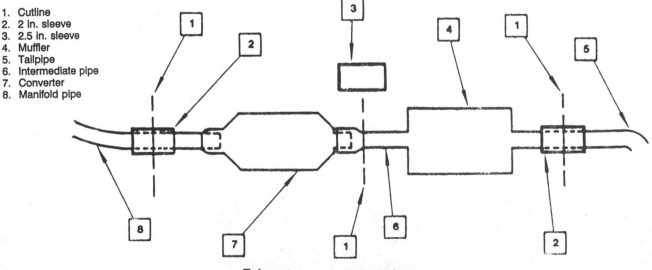

Exhaust system connections

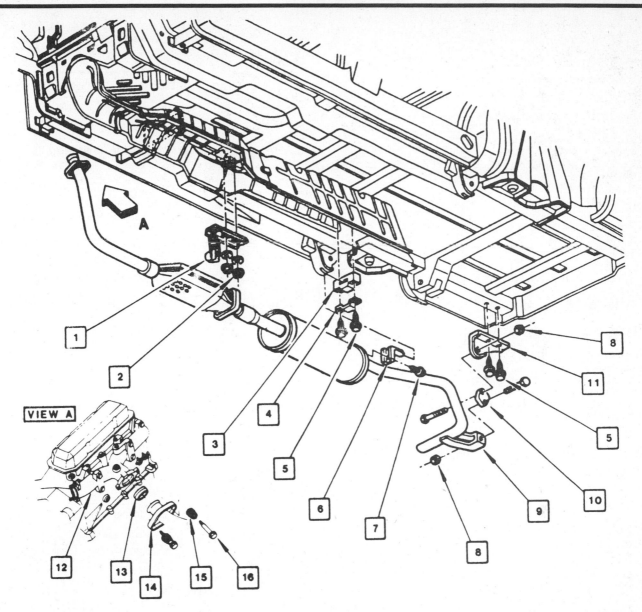

Exhaust system and hangers

1. Catalytic converter hanger assembly
2. Nut 14 ft. lbs. (20 Nm)
3. Insulator
4. Retainer
5. Screws 18 ft. lbs. (25 Nm)
6. Exhaust muffler hanger
7. Screw 7 ft. lbs. (10 Nm)
8. Nut
9. Tailpipe assembly
10. Insulator
11. Exhaust muffler hanger bracket asembly
12. Exhaust manifold
13. Exhaust manifold pipe seal assembly
14. Exhaust pipe assembly
15. Exhaust manifold pipe spring
16. Exhaust manifold pipe bolt 22 ft. lbs. (30 Nm)

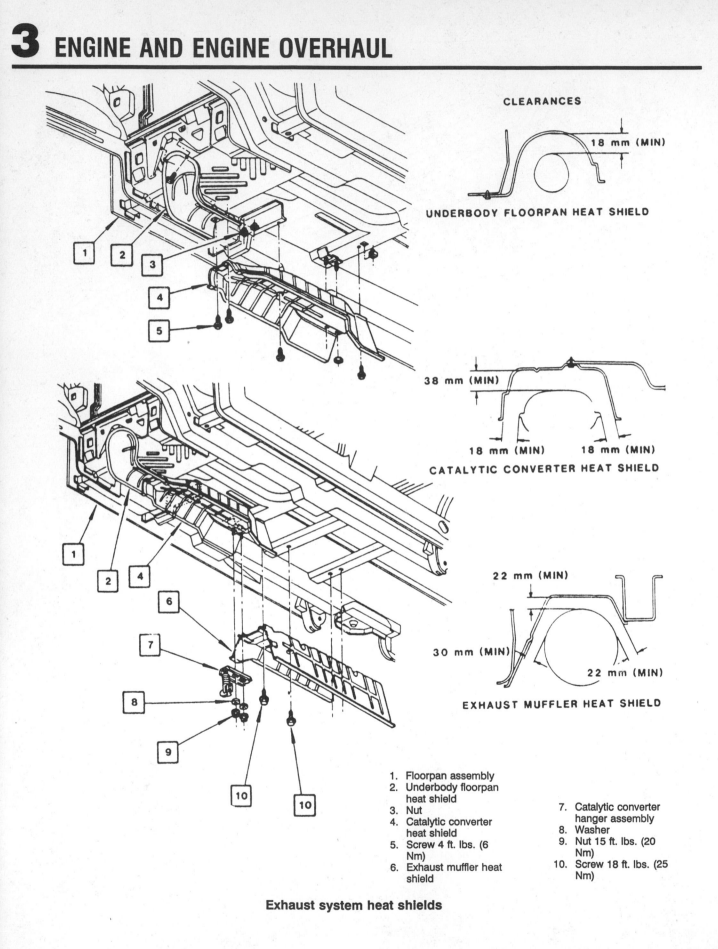

CLEARANCES

18 mm (MIN)

UNDERBODY FLOORPAN HEAT SHIELD

38 mm (MIN)

18 mm (MIN)   18 mm (MIN)

CATALYTIC CONVERTER HEAT SHIELD

22 mm (MIN)

30 mm (MIN)

22 mm (MIN)

EXHAUST MUFFLER HEAT SHIELD

1. Floorpan assembly
2. Underbody floorpan heat shield
3. Nut
4. Catalytic converter heat shield
5. Screw 4 ft. lbs. (6 Nm)
6. Exhaust muffler heat shield
7. Catalytic converter hanger assembly
8. Washer
9. Nut 15 ft. lbs. (20 Nm)
10. Screw 18 ft. lbs. (25 Nm)

Exhaust system heat shields

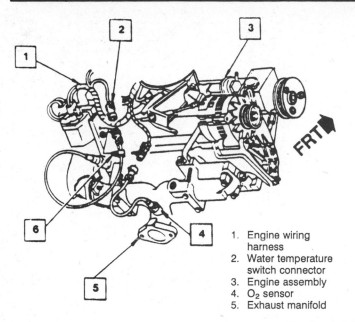

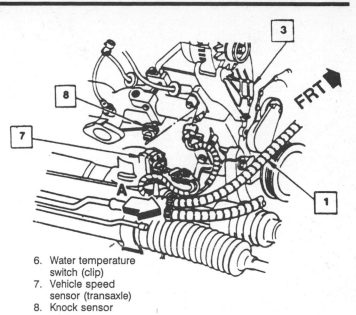

1. Engine wiring harness
2. Water temperature switch connector
3. Engine assembly
4. O$_2$ sensor
5. Exhaust manifold

6. Water temperature switch (clip)
7. Vehicle speed sensor (transaxle)
8. Knock sensor

Engine wiring—rear

1. Engine wiring harness leads
2. Transaxle assembly studs
3. Transaxle assembly
4. Engine wiring harness ground
5. Torque converter clutch
6. Transaxle assembly studs
7. Engine wiring harness

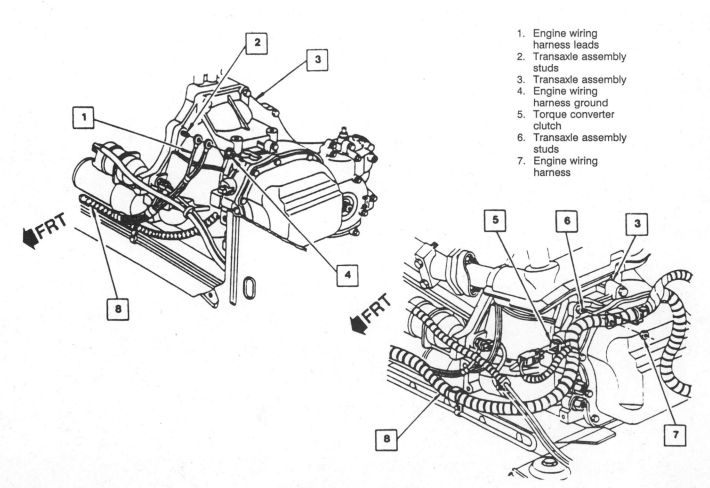

Engine wiring—left side

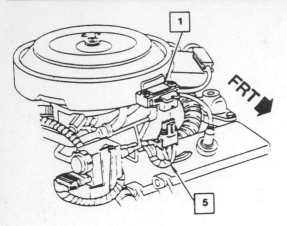

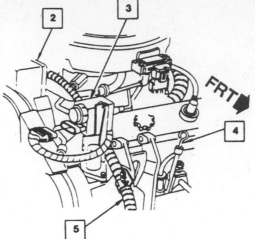

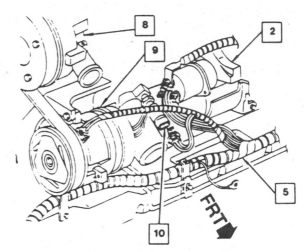

1. Manifold absolute pressure sensor
2. Engine assembly
3. Electronic vacuum regulator
4. Oil level indicator
5. Engine wiring harness
6. Throttle position control switch connector
7. Idle air control switch connector
8. Alternator
9. Air conditioner compressor
10. Oil pressure sensor connection

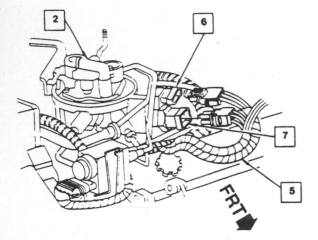

Engine wiring—front

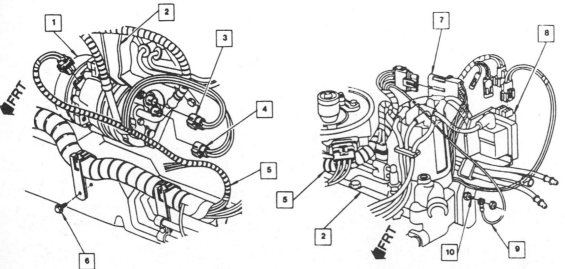

1. Air conditioner compressor
2. Engine assembly
3. Engine harness low pressure connection (BWN/GRN)
4. Engine harness high pressure connection (BWN/BLU)
5. Engine wiring harness
6. Screw
7. Engine assembly—distributor connection
8. Ignition coil
9. Engine wiring harness lead
10. Stud

Engine wiring—right side

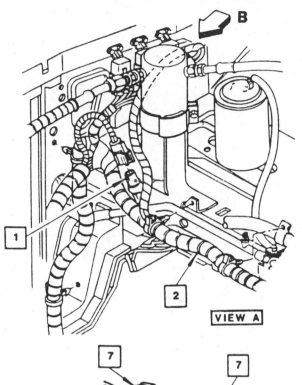

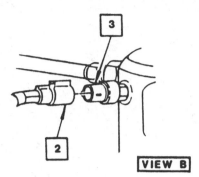

VIEW B

VIEW A

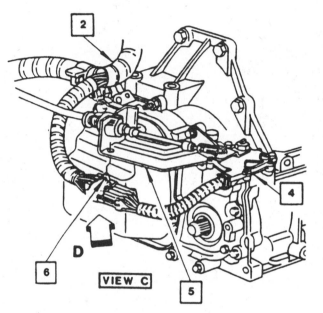

VIEW C

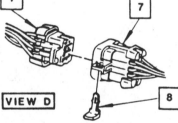

VIEW D

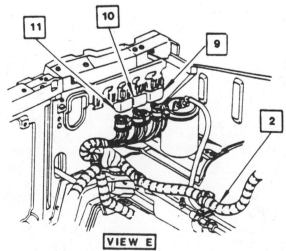

VIEW E

1. Refrigerent pressure and engine cooling fan switch
2. Engine wiring harness
3. Air conditioner pressure cycling switch
4. Automatic transaxle neutral start switch
5. Automatic transaxle range select lever cable to transaxle
6. Clip
7. Automatic transaxle neutral start switch connector
8. Connector retainer
9. Fuel pump relay
10. Engine cooling fan relay
11. Automatic transaxle neutral start switch connector

Engine wiring

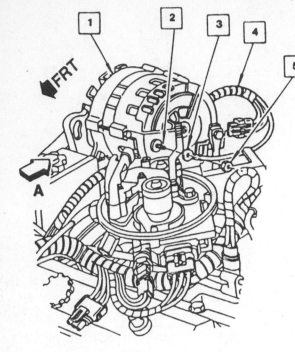

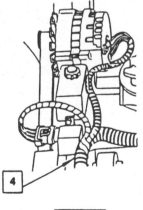

VIEW A

1. Alternator
2. Stud
3. Engine harness alternator lead
4. Engine wiring harness
5. Nut (38 inch lbs.)
6. Oil pressure sensor
7. Starter solenoid
8. Engine harness lead
9. Washer

Engine wiring—alternator and air conditioner compressor

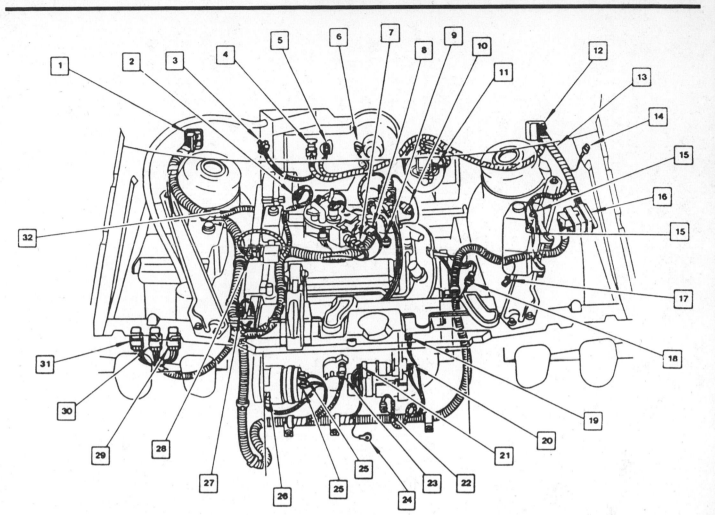

Engine harness wiring

1. Hard shell grommet
2. Alternator
3. Windshield wiper motor
4. High blower relay
5. Blower resistor assembly
6. Blower motor
7. Idle air control (IAC) sensor
8. Throttle position sensor
9. Engine temperature sensor
10. Distributor connector
11. Brake pressure switch
12. Hardshell grommet
13. Instrument panel wiring harness
14. Cruise control servo
15. Front and rear windshield wiper reservoir pumps
16. Instrument panel, engine and front lamp harness interconnect
17. Fuel pump prime connector
18. Transaxle selector switch (neutral start) connector
19. Transaxle Converter Clutch (TCC) switch
20. Engine wiring harness grounds
21. Starter solenoid
22. Engine cooling fan
23. Oil pressure sensor
24. Engine harness ground
25. Air conditioner compressor (hi and low pressure)
26. Air conditioner compressor clutch
27. Air conditioner schrader valve
28. Electronic vacuum regulator (EGR) valve
29. Air conditioner compressor control relay
30. Engine cooling fan relay
31. Fuel pump relay
32. Harness to electronic spark control (knock sensor), O_2 sensor, vehicle speed sensor, vehicle speed and water temperature switch

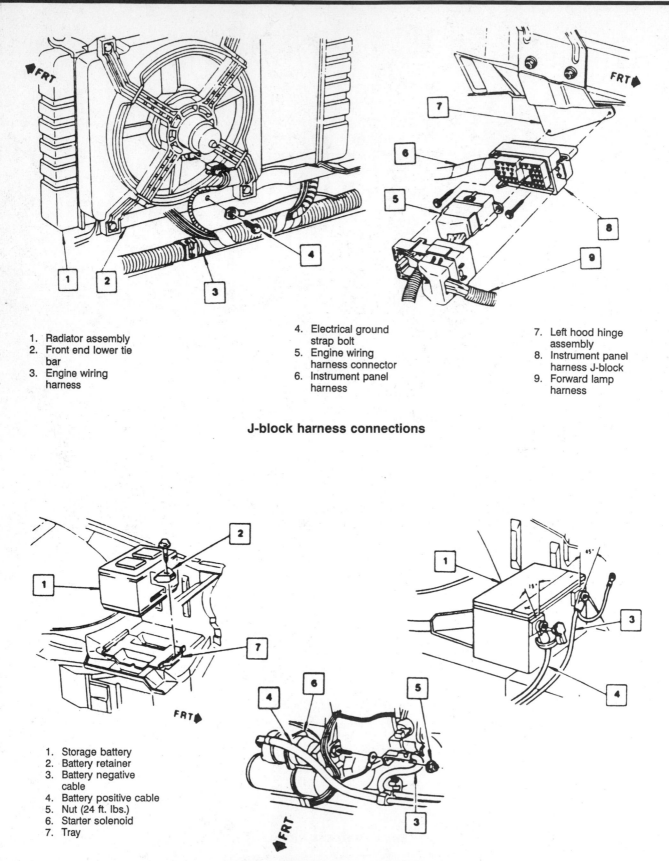

1. Radiator assembly
2. Front end lower tie bar
3. Engine wiring harness

4. Electrical ground strap bolt
5. Engine wiring harness connector
6. Instrument panel harness

7. Left hood hinge assembly
8. Instrument panel harness J-block
9. Forward lamp harness

J-block harness connections

1. Storage battery
2. Battery retainer
3. Battery negative cable
4. Battery positive cable
5. Nut (24 ft. lbs.)
6. Starter solenoid
7. Tray

Engine wiring—battery and starter

Emission Controls

4

QUICK REFERENCE INDEX

GENERAL INDEX

EMISSION CONTROLS

Positive Crankcase Ventilation (PCV)

OPERATION

The crankcase ventilation system (PCV) must be operating correctly to provide complete scavenging of the crankcase vapors. Fresh air is supplied to the crankcase from the air filter, mixed with the internal exhaust gases, passed through the PCV valve and into the intake manifold.

The PCV valve meters the flow at a rate depending upon the manifold vacuum. If the manifold vacuum is high, the PCV restricts the flow to the intake manifold. If abnormal, operating conditions occur, excessive amounts of internal exhaust gases back flow through the crankcase vent tube into the air filter to be burned by normal combustion.

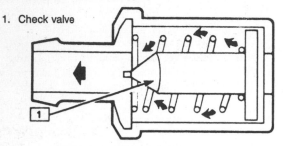

1. Check valve

Cross section of the PCV valve

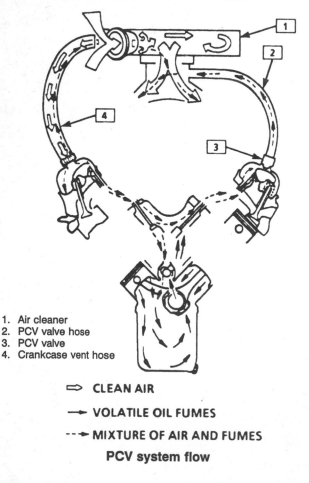

1. Air cleaner
2. PCV valve hose
3. PCV valve
4. Crankcase vent hose

⇨ CLEAN AIR

→ VOLATILE OIL FUMES

--→ MIXTURE OF AIR AND FUMES

PCV system flow

TESTING

If the engine is idling roughly, a quick check of the PCV valve can be made. While the engine is idling, pull the PCV valve from the valve cover, place your thumb over the end of the PCV valve and check for vacuum. If no vacuum exists, check for a plugged PCV valve, manifold port, hoses or deteriorated hoses. Turn the engine **OFF**, remove the PCV valve and shake it. Listen for the rattle of the check needle inside the valve. If it does not rattle, replace the valve.

The PCV system should be checked at every oil change and serviced every 30,000 miles.

NOTE: Never operate an engine without a PCV valve or a ventilation system, for it can become damaged.

REMOVAL AND INSTALLATION

1. Pull the PCV valve from the rocker arm cover grommet.
2. Remove the hose(s) from the PCV valve.
3. Shake the valve to make sure that it is not plugged.
4. To install, reverse the removal procedure.

Evaporative Emission Controls

OPERATION

The basic evaportative emission control system used on all vehicles is the charcoal canister storage method. This method transfers fuel vapor from the fuel tank to the activated carbon (charcoal) storage device (canister) to hold the vapors when the vehicle is not operating. When the engine is running, the fuel vapor is purged from the carbon element by the intake air flow and consumed in the normal combustion process.

Vapor Canister

Gasoline vapors from the fuel tank flow into the tube labeled tank. These vapors are absorbed into the carbon. The canister is purged progressively with throttle opening when the engine is running. Ambient air is allowed into the canister through the air tube in the top. The air mixes with the vapor and the mixture is drawn into the intake manifold.

Evaporative Emission System

This system has a thermostatic vacuum switch installed in the intake manifold coolant passage to sense engine coolant temperature. This switch has 2 ports and is located between the canister and the TBI unit. When the engine temperature is below 115°F (46°C), the switch is closed preventing purge of the canister. When the engine temperature is above 115°F (46°C), the switch is opens, allowing purge of the canister.

Tank Pressure Control Valve

The fuel tank pressure/vacuum relief is located inside the gas cap.

RESULTS OF INCORRECT OPERATION

1. Poor idling, stalling and poor drivability can be caused by the following:
   ● Damaged canister
   ● Hoses split, cracked and/or not connected to the proper tubes
2. Evidence of fuel loss or vapor odor can be caused by the following:
   ● Liquid fuel leaking from the fuel lines or TBI unit

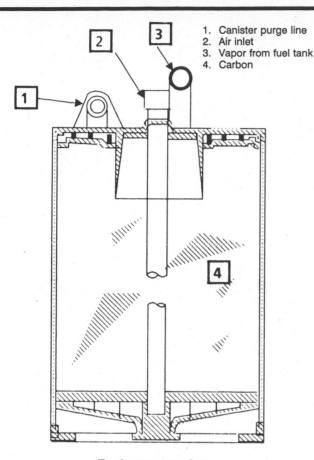

1. Canister purge line
2. Air inlet
3. Vapor from fuel tank
4. Carbon

Fuel vapor canister

- Cracked or damaged vapor canister
- Disconnected, misrouted, kinked, deteriorated or damaged vapor pipe or canister hoses
- Air cleaner or air cleaner gasket improperly seated

REMOVAL AND INSTALLATION

Vapor Canister

1. Tag and disconnect all hoses connected to the charcoal canister.
2. Loosen the retaining clamps and then lift out the canister.
3. Grasp the filter in the bottom of the canister with your fingers and pull it out. Replace it with a new one.
4. Install canister and tighten retaining clamps.
5. Install all hoses to canister.

NOTE: **Some models do not have replaceable filters.**

Exhaust Gas Recirculation System

OPERATION

The EGR system is used to lower NOx (oxides of nitrogen) emission levels caused by high combustion temperatures. It does this by decreasing combustion temperature.

The main element of the system is the EGR valve operated by vacuum, and mounted on the intake manifold.

The EGR valve feeds small amounts of exhaust gas back into the combustion chamber. The EGR valve is usually open under the following conditions:
1. Warm engine operation
2. Above idle speed
3. Throttle partly open
4. VSS signal greater than 2 mph (California)

The EGR valve should be closed at wide open throttle and idle.

EGR CONTROL

Electronic Vacuum Regulator Valve (EVRV)

To regulate EGR flow, an ECM controlled EVRV solenoid is used in the vacuum line. The ECM uses information from the following sensors to regulate the solenoid:
- Coolant Temperature Sensor (CTS)
- Throttle Position Sensor (TPS)
- Distributor (rpm signal)

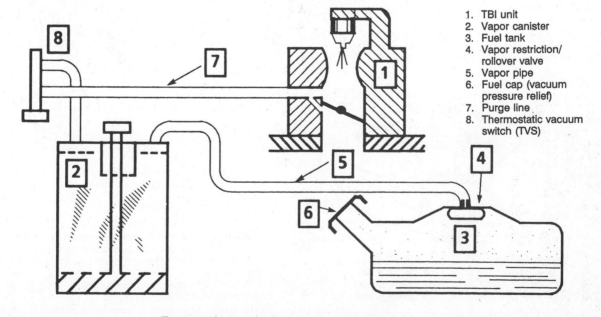

1. TBI unit
2. Vapor canister
3. Fuel tank
4. Vapor restriction/ rollover valve
5. Vapor pipe
6. Fuel cap (vacuum pressure relief)
7. Purge line
8. Thermostatic vacuum switch (TVS)

Evaporative emission control system

- MAP
- BARO

The EVRV regualtor uses "pulse width modulation". This means the ECM turns the solenoid ON and OFF many times a second and varies the amount of the ON time (pulse width) to vary the amount of EGR.

Port EGR Valve

This valve is controlled by a flexible diaphragm which is spring loaded to hold the valve closed. Vacuum applied to the top side of the diaphragm overcomes the spring pressure and opens the valve in the exhaust gas port. This allows exhaust gas to be pulled into the intake manifold and center the engine cylinders.

RESULTS OF INCORRECT OPERATION

1. Too much EGR flow (at idle, cruise, or cold operation) may result in any of the following conditions:
- Engine stops after cold start
- Engine stops at idle after deceleration
- Car surges during cruise
- Rough idle

2. Too little or no EGR flow allows combustion temperatures to get too high during acceleration and load conditions. This could cause the following:
- Spark knock (detonation)
- Engine overheating
- Emission test failure

REMOVAL AND INSTALLATION

EGR Valve

1. Disconnect the negative battery cable.
2. Remove the air cleaner assembly.
3. Disconnect the EGR vacuum hose at the valve.
4. Remove the EGR valve retaining bolts and remove the EGR valve from the manifold.

To install:

5. If reinstalling the old valve inspect the EGR valve passages for excessive build-up of deposits, and clean as necessary.

NOTE: Loose particles should be completely removed to prevent them from being ingested into the engine.

6. With a wire wheel buff the deposits from the mounting surfaces.

7. Install the EGR valve to the intake manifold using a new gasket and tighten the bolts to 18 ft. lbs. (25 Nm).

8. Install the vacuum hose to the valve.

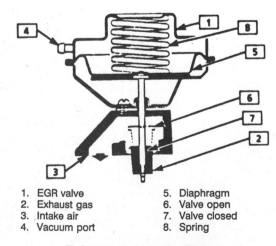

1. EGR valve
2. Exhaust gas
3. Intake air
4. Vacuum port
5. Diaphragm
6. Valve open
7. Valve closed
8. Spring

Exhaust gas recirculation

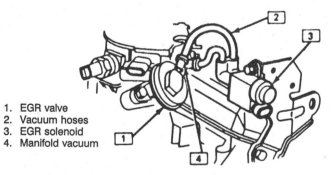

1. EGR valve
2. Gasket
3. 18 ft. lbs. (25 Nm)

FRT

EGR mounting

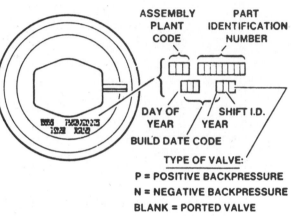

ASSEMBLY PLANT CODE

PART IDENTIFICATION NUMBER

DAY OF YEAR

SHIFT I.D.

YEAR

BUILD DATE CODE

TYPE OF VALVE:

P = POSITIVE BACKPRESSURE

N = NEGATIVE BACKPRESSURE

BLANK = PORTED VALVE

EGR valve identification

1. EGR valve
2. Vacuum hoses
3. EGR solenoid
4. Manifold vacuum

EGR and solenoid

9. Install the air cleaner assembly.
10. Connect the negative battery cable.

EGR Control Solenoid

1. Disconnect the negative battery cable.
2. Disconnect the electrical connector at the solenoid.
3. Disconnect the vacuum hoses at the solenoid.
4. Remove the retaining screw and regulator.

To install:

5. Install the solenoid and bracket and tighten the retaining screw to 35 inch lbs. (4 Nm).
6. Install the vacuum hoses and electrical connector.
7. Connect the negative battery cable.

Thermostaic Air Cleaner (THERMAC)

OPERATION

This system is designed to improve driveability and exhaust emissions when the engine is cold. Components added to the basic air cleaner assembly include a temperature sensor (connected to a manifold vacuum source), a vacuum diaphragm motor (connected to the temperature sensor) and an inlet damper door (installed in the air cleaner inlet snorkel). Additional components of the system include an exhaust manifold mounted heat stove and a hot air duct running from the heat source to the underside of the air cleaner snorkel.

When the engine is cold, the temperature sensor allows vacuum to pass through to the vacuum diaphragm motor. The vacuum acting on the vacuum motor causes the motor to close the damper door, which prohibits the introduction of cold, outside air to the air cleaner. The intake vacuum then pulls hot air, generated by the exhaust manifold, through the hot air duct and into the air cleaner. This heated air supply helps to more effectively vaporize the fuel mixture entering the engine. As the engine warms, the temperature sensor bleeds off vacuum to the vacuum motor, allowing the damper door to gradually open.

The usual problems with this system are leaking vacuum lines (which prevent proper operation of the sensor and/or motor); torn or rusted through hot air ducts and/or rusted through heat stoves (either condition will allow the introduction of too much cold air to the air cleaner). Visually check and replace these items as necessary. Should the system still fail to operate properly, disconnect the vacuum line from the vacuum motor and apply at least 7 in. Hg of vacuum directly to the motor from an outside vacuum source; the damper door should close. If the door does not close, either the vacuum motor is defective or the damper door and/or linkage is binding. If the door closes, but then gradually opens (with a steady vacuum source), the vacuum motor is defective.

RESULTS OF INCORRECT OPERATION

1. Hesitation during warm-up can be caused by the following:
- Heat stove tube disconnected
- Vacuum diaphragm motor inoperative (open to snorkel)
- No manifold vacuum
- Damper door does not move
- Missing air cleaner cover seal or loss cover
- Loose air cleaner
2. Lack of power, sluggish, spongy, or detonation on a hot engine can be caused by:
- Damper door does not open to the outside air
3. Temperature sensor doesn't bleed off vacuum

TESTING

Vacuum Motor

1. With the engine Off, disconnect the hose from the vacuum diaphragm motor.
2. Using a vacuum source, apply 7 in. Hg to the vacuum motor; the door should close and block off the outside air, completely.
3. Bend the vacuum hose (to trap the vacuum in the motor) and make sure that the door stays closed; if not, replace the vacuum motor.

NOTE: Before replacing the vacuum motor (if defective), be sure to check the motor linkage, for binding.

4. If the vacuum motor is OK and the problem still exists, check the temperature sensor.

Temperature Sensor

1. Remove the air cleaner cover and place a thermometer near the temperature sensor; the temperature MUST BE below 86°F (30°C). When the temperature is OK, replace the air cleaner.
2. Start the engine and allow it to idle. Watch the vacuum motor door, it should close immediately (if the engine is cool enough).
3. When the vacuum motor door starts to open, remove the air cleaner cover and read the thermometer, it should be about 131°F (55°C).
4. If the door does not respond correctly, replace the temperature sensor.

REMOVAL AND INSTALLATION

Vacuum Motor

1. Remove the air cleaner.
2. Disconnect the vacuum hose from the motor.
3. Using a $\frac{1}{16}$ in. (1.5mm) drill bit, drill out the spot welds, then enlarge as necessary to remove the retaining strap.
4. Remove the retaining strap.
5. Lift up the motor and cock it to one side to unhook the motor linkage at the control damper assembly.
6. Install the new vacuum motor as follows:
   a. Using a $\frac{7}{64}$ in. (2.8mm) drill bit, drill a hole in the snorkel tube at the center of the vacuum motor retaining strap.
   b. Insert the vacuum motor linkage into the control damper assembly.

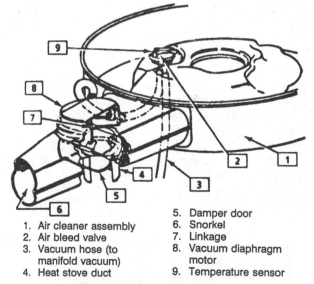

1. Air cleaner assembly
2. Air bleed valve
3. Vacuum hose (to manifold vacuum)
4. Heat stove duct
5. Damper door
6. Snorkel
7. Linkage
8. Vacuum diaphragm motor
9. Temperature sensor

THERMAC air cleaner

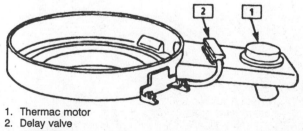

1. Thermac motor
2. Delay valve connector

THERMAC delay valve connection

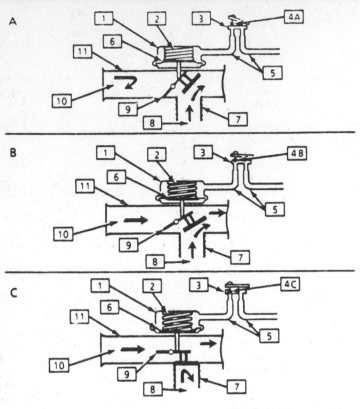

1. Vacuum diaphragm motor
2. Diaphragm spring
3. Temperature sensor
4A. Air bleed valve (closed)
4B. Air bleed valve (partially open)
4C. Air bleed valve (open)
5. Vacuum hoses
6. Diaphragm
7. Heat stove
8. Hot air (exhaust manifold)
9. Damper door
10. Outside inlet air
11. Snorkel
A. Hot air delivery mode
B. Regulating mode
C. Outside air delivery mode

THERMAC operation

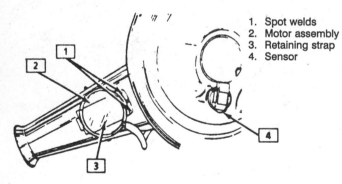

1. Spot welds
2. Motor assembly
3. Retaining strap
4. Sensor

Replacing the THERMAC vacuum motor

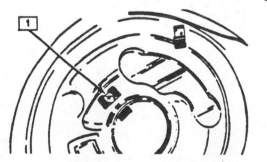

1. Sensor retaining clip

Replacing the THERMAC sensor

c. Use the motor retaining strap and a sheet metal screw to secure the retaining strap and motor to the snorkel tube.

NOTE: Make sure the screw does not interfere with the operation of the damper assembly; shorten the screw, if necessary.

Temperature Sensor

1. Remove the air cleaner.
2. Disconnect the hoses from the sensor.
3. Pry up the tabs on the sensor retaining clip and remove the clip and sensor from the air cleaner.
4. To install, reverse the removal procedures.

Oxygen Sensor

The exhaust Oxygen (O_2) sensor is mounted in the exhaust system where it can monitor the oxygen content of the exhaust gas stream.

For more information and testing of the Oxygen (O_2) sensor, please refer to the Electronic Engine Controls in this section.

WARNING: The Oxygen (O_2) sensor uses a permanently attached pigtail and connector. This pigtail should not be removed from the oxygen sensor. Damage or removal of the pigtail or connector could affect proper operation of the Oxygen (O_2) sensor.
The inline electrical connector and louvered and louvered end must be kept free of grease, dirt or other contaminants.

REMOVAL AND INSTALLATION

1. Disconnect the negative battery cable.

2. Remove the air cleaner assembly.
3. Disconnect the electrical connector.
4. Carefully back out the Oxygen (O₂) sensor.

WARNING: The Oxygen (O₂) sensor may be difficult to remove when the engine temperature is below 118°F (48°C). Excessive force may damage the threads in the exhaust manifold or exhaust pipe.

To install:

5. Coat the threads of the Oxygen (O₂) sensor with anti-sieze compound, if necessary.

NOTE: A special anti-sieze compound is used on the oxygen sensor threads. New or service sensors will already have the compound applied to the threads. If a sensor is removed from an engine, and, if for any reason it is to be reinstalled, the threads must have anti-seize compound applied before reinstallation.

6. Install the sensor and tighten to 30 ft. lbs. (41 Nm).
7. Install the electrical connector.
8. Install the air cleaner assembly.
9. Connect the negative battery cable.

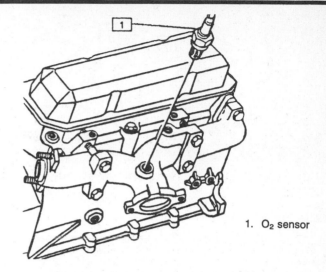

1. O₂ sensor

Oxygen (O₂) sensor installation

ELECTRONIC ENGINE CONTROLS

Electronic Control Module (ECM)

An Electronic Control Module (ECM) is designed to maintain exhaust emission levels at the federal standards while providing good driveability and fuel efficiency. The functions of the system are based on data gathered by the sensors and switches located throughout the vehicle. The ECM maintains control over fuel delivery, ignition, idle air flow, the fuel pump and other system components, while monitoring the system for faulty operation with its diagnostic capabilities. When it recognizes a problem it can alert the driver through the "Service Engine Soon" light, and store a code or codes to aid in making repairs. For service, the ECM has 2 parts: a controller (the ECM without the PROM) and a separate calibrator (PROM)

1. ECM
2. ECM harness connectors to the ECM
3. PROM access cover

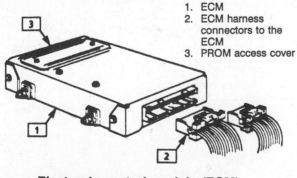

Electronic control module (ECM)

Programmable Read Only Memory (PROM)

NOTE: To prevent possibile Electrostatic Discharge damage to the PROM or ECM, do not touch the component leads, and do not remove the integrated circuit from the carrier.

To allow one model of ECM to be used foe many different vehicles, a device called a Calibrator or PROM, (Programmable Read Only Memory) is used. The PROM is located inside the ECM, and has information on the vehicle's weight, engine transmission, axle ratio, and several others. While one ECM part number can be used by many car lines, a PROM is very specific and must be used for the right car.

An ECM used for service (called a controller) comes without a PROM. The PROM from the old ECM must be carefully removed and installed in the new ECM. The ECM is located behind the right side sound insulator in the dash.

1. ECM
2. PROM (engine calibrator
3. PROM carrier
4. Calpak (as part of ECM)

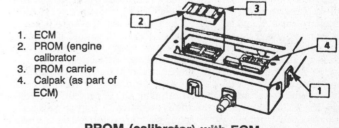

PROM (calibrator) with ECM

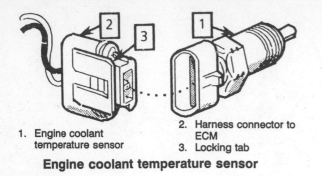

1. Engine coolant temperature sensor
2. Harness connector to ECM
3. Locking tab

Engine coolant temperature sensor

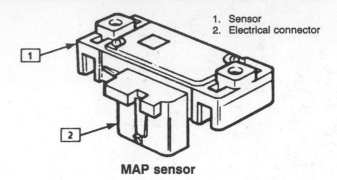

1. Sensor
2. Electrical connector

MAP sensor

ECM Function

The ECM supplies either 5 or 10 volts to power various sensors or switches. This is done through resistance in the ECM which are so high in value that a test light will not light when connected to the circuit. In some cases even an ordinary shop voltmeter will not give an accurate reading because its resistance is too low. therefore, a 10MΩ input impedance digital voltmeter is required to assure accurate voltage readings.

The ECM controls output circuits such as the injector, IAC cooling fan relay, etc. by controling the ground circuit through the transistors in the ECM.

Information Sensors

Engine Coolant Temperature Sensor

The coolant sensor is a thermister (a resistor) which changes value based on temperature) mounted in the engine coolant stream. Low coolant temperature produces a high resistance of $100,000\Omega$ at $-40°F$ ($-40°C$) while high temperature causes low resistance of 70Ω at $266°F$ ($130°$ C).

The ECM supplies a 5 volt signal to the coolant sensor thru a resistor in the ECM and measures the voltage. The voltage will be high when the engine is cold, and low when the engine is hot. By measuring the voltage, the ECM knows the engine coolant temperature. Engine coolant temperature affects most systems the ECM controls.

A failure in the coolant sensor circuit should set either a Code 14 or Code 15. Remember, these codes indicate a failure in the coolant temperature circuit, so proper use of the chart will lead to either repairing a wiring problem or replacing the sensor, to properly repair a problem.

MAP Sensor

The Manifold Absolute Pressure (MAP) Sensor measures the changes in the intake manifold pressure which result from engine load and speed changes, and converts this to a voltage output.

A closed throttle on engine coastdown would produce a relatively low MAP output, while a wide-open throttle would produce a high output. This high output is produced because the pressure inside the manifold is the same as outside the manifold, so you measure 100% of outside air pressure. Manifold Absolute Pressure (MAP) is the OPPOSITE of what you would measure on a vacuum gage. When manifold pressure is high, vacuum is low. The MAP sensor is also used to measure barometric pressure under certain conditions, which allows the ECM to automatically adjust for different altitudes.

The ECM sends a 5 volts reference signal to the MAP sensor. As the manifold pressure changes, the electrical resistance of the sensor also changes. By monitoring the sensor output voltage, the ECM knows the manifold pressure. A higher pressure, low vacuum (high voltage) requires more fuel, while a lower pressure, higher vacuum (low voltage) requires less fuel.

The ECM uses the MAP sensor to control fuel delivery and ignition timing.

A failure in the MAP sensor circuit should set a Code 33 or Code 34.

Oxygen (O_2) Sensor

The exhaust Oxygen (O_2) sensor is mounted in the exhaust system where it can monitor the oxygen content of the exhaust gas stream. The oxygen content in the exhaust reacts with the oxygen sensor to produce a voltage output. This voltage ranges from approximately 0.010 volt (high O_2 — lean mixture) to 0.9 volt (low O_2 — rich mixture).

By monitoring the voltage output of the O_2 sensor, the ECM will know what fuel mixture command to give to the injector (lean mixture — low voltage, rich command, rich mixture — high voltage, lean command). This voltage can be measured with a digital voltmeter having at least 10MΩ input impedance. Use of standard shop type voltmeters will result in very inaccurate readings.

An open O_2 sensor circuit, should set a Code 13. A shorted sensor circuit should set a Code 44. A high voltage in the circuit should set a Code 45. When any of these codes are set, the car will run in the "Open Loop" mode.

Throttle Position Sensor (TPS)

The Throttle Position Sensor (TPS) is connected to the throttle shaft on the TBI unit. It is a potentiometer with one end connected to 5 volts from the ECM and the other to ground. A third wire is connected to the ECM to measure the voltage from the TPS. As the throttle valve angle is changed (accelerator pedal moved), the output of the TPS also changes. At a closed throttle position, the output of the TPS is low (approximately 0.5 volt).

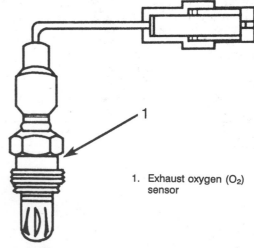

1. Exhaust oxygen (O_2) sensor

Exhaust oxygen (O_2) sensor

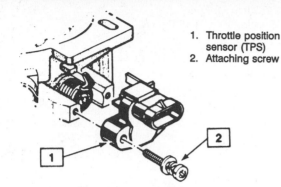

1. Throttle position sensor (TPS)
2. Attaching screw

Throttle position sensor (TPS)

As the throttle valve opens, the output increases so that, at wide-open throttle, the output voltage should be approximately 5 volts.

By monitoring the output voltage from the TPS, the ECM can determine fuel delivery based on throttle valve angle (driver demand). If the sensor CKT is open, the ECM will set a Trouble Code 22. If the circuit is shorted, the ECM will think the vehicle is at Wide Open Throttle (WOT), and a Trouble Code 21 will be set. A broken or loose TPS can cause intermittent bursts of fuel from the injector, and an unstable idel, because the ECM thinks the throttle is moving. Once a Trouble Code is set, the ECM will use an artificial value for TPS, and some vehicle performance will return.

On all engines, the TPS is not adjustable. The ECM uses the reading at idle for the zero reading, so no adjustment is necessary.

Knock Sensor

The knock sensor is mounted in the engine block. When abnormal engine vibrations (spark knock) are presnet, the sensor produces a voltage signal, which is sent to the ESC module.

Park/Neutral Switch

The Park/Neutral (P/N) switch indicates to the ECM when the transmission is in park or neutral. This information is used for the TCC, and the IAC valve operation.

NOTE: Vehicle should not be driven with Park/Neutral (P/N) switch disconnected as idle quality will be affected and a possible false Code 24 VSS.

Crank Signal

The ECM looks at the starter solenoid to tell when the engine is cranking. It uses this to tell when the car is in the Starting Mode.
If this signal is not available, the car may be hard to start in extremely cold weather.

A/C Request Signal

This signal tells the ECM that the A/C selector switch is turned "ON" and that the high side low pressure switch is closed. The ECM uses this to adjust the idle speed when the air conditioning is working.

Vehicle Speed Sensor (VSS)

The Vehicle Speed Sensor (VSS) sends a pulsing voltage signal the the ECM, which the ECM converts to miles per hour. This sensor mainly controls the operation the the TCC system.

Distributor Reference Signal

The distributor sends a signal to the ECM to tell it both engine rpm and crankshaft position.

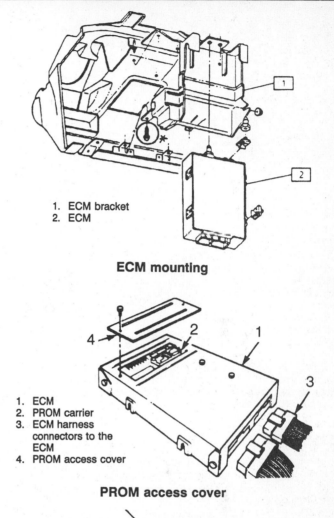

1. ECM bracket
2. ECM

ECM mounting

1. ECM
2. PROM carrier
3. ECM harness connectors to the ECM
4. PROM access cover

PROM access cover

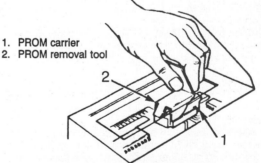

1. PROM carrier
2. PROM removal tool

The PROM is removed with a special removal tool

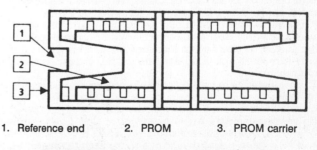

1. Reference end   2. PROM   3. PROM carrier

The PROM shown in the PROM carrier

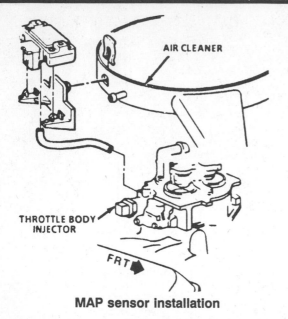

MAP sensor installation

DIAGNOSIS

Since the ECM can have a failure which may effect only one circuit, following the diagnostic procedures in this section can reliably tell when a failure has occurred in the ECM. Also, a Code 55 indicates a failure of the ECM.

If a diagnostic chart indicates that the ECM connections or ECM is the cause of a problem, and the ECM is replaced, but does not correct the problem, one of the following may be the reason:

• There is a problem with the ECM terminal connections — the diagnostic chart will say ECM connections or ECM. The terminals may have to be removed from the connector in order to check them properly.

• The ECM or PROM is not correct for the application — The incorrect ECM or PROM may cause a malfunction and may or may not set a code.

• The problem is intermittent — This means that the problem is not present at the time the system is being checked. In this case, make a careful physical inspection of all portions of the system involved.

• .Shorted solenoid, relay coil or harness — Solenoids and relays are turned "ON" and "OFF" by the ECM using internal electronic switches called "drivers." Each driver is part of a group of four called "Quad-Drivers."

• A shorted solenoid, relay coil or harness may cause an ECM to fail, and a replacement ECM to fail when it is installed. Use a short tester, J 34696, BT 8405, or equivalent, as a fast, accurate means of checking for a short circuit.

• The PROM may be faulty — Although the PROM rarely fails, it operates as part of the ECM. Therefore, it could be the cause of the problem. Substitute a known good PROM.

• The replacement ECM may be faulty — After the ECM is replaced, the system should be rechecked for proper operation. If the diagnostic chart again indicates the ECM is the problem, substitute a known good ECM. Although this is a rare condition, it could happen.

The components or circuits and the codes or charts, related to them are:

• Code 55 indicates a failure of the ECM.
• PROM — CHART 51.
• Coolant Temperature Sensor — CHARTS 14–15.
• MAP Sensor — CHART 33 or 34. To check the sensor with no code set, use CHART C–1D.

• TPS — CHARTS 21 or 22.
• P/N switch — CHART C–1A.
• Crank Signal — CHART C–1B
• O₂ Sensor — CHARTS 13, 44, 45.
• P/N Switch — CHART C–1A.
• A/C Request signal — If the A/C request signal is not reaching the ECM, it can cause rough idle, with A/C "ON." See "Rough Idle" in "Symptoms," section.
• VSS — CHART 24 and in TCC System.
• Distributor — CHART 42 and in EST system.
• Distributor — Chart and in the EST system.

ECM

A faulty ECM will be determined in the diagnostic charts, or by a Code 55.

PROM

An incorrect or faulty PROM, which is part of the ECM, may set a Code 51.

ECM Inputs

All of the sensors and input switches can be diagnosed by the use of a "Scan" tool. Following is a short description of how the sensors and switches can be diagnosed by the use of "Scan." The "Scan" can also be used to compare the values for a normal running engine with the engine you're diagnosing.

COOLANT TEMPERATURE SENSOR (CTS)

A "Scan" tool displays engine temperature in degrees centigrade and farenheit. After the engine is started, the temperature should rise steadily between 190–222°F (88–106°C), then stabilize when thermostat opens. A fault in the coolant sensor circuit should set a Code 14 or 15. The code charts also contain a chart to check for sensor resistance values relative to temperature.

MAP SENSOR

A "Scan" tool reads manifold pressure and will display volts and kPa of pressure.

Key "ON," engine stopped, (no vacuum), MAP will read high voltage or pressure, while at idle (high vacuum), MAP will read low voltage or pressure. Likewise, on acceleration, MAP will read high and on deceleration, will read low.

A failure in the MAP sensor, or circuit, should result in a Code 33 or 34.

OXYGEN (O₂) SENSOR

The "Scan" has several positions that will indicate the state of the exhaust gases, O₂ voltage, integrator, and block lear.

A problem in the O₂ sensor circuit should set a Code 13 (open circuit), Code 44 (lean O₂ indication), Code 45 (rich O₂ indication). Refer to applicable chart, if any of these codes were stored in memory

THROTTLE POSITION SENSOR (TPS)

A "Scan" tool displays throttle position in volts. The 3.1L should read under 1.25 volts, with throttle closed and ignition on, or at idle. Voltage should increase at a steady rate as throtttle is moved toward WOT.

The ECM has the ability to auto-zero the TPS voltage, if it is below about 1.25 volts. This means that any voltage less than 1.25 volts will be determined by the ECM to be 0% throttle. Some "Scan" tools have the ability to read the percentage of throttle angle and should read 0%, when the throttle is closed. A failure in the TPS, or circuit, should set a Code 21 or 22.

VEHICLE SPEED SENSOR (VSS)

A "Scan" tool reading should closely match with speedometer reading, with drive wheels turning. A failure in the VSS circuit should set a Code 24.

P/N SWITCH

A "Scan" tool should read "P-N-," when in park or neutral and "-R-DL," when in drive. This reading may vary with different makes of tools. Refer to CHART C-1A for P/N switch diagnosis.

A/C REQUEST SIGNAL

If the low pressure switch is closed and A/C is "ON," the A/C clutch should indicate "ON". See "ECM controlled Air conditioning".

Distributor Reference Signal

A "Scan" tool will read this signal and is displayed in rpm. See "Ignition System/(EST)".

KNOCK SIGNAL

A "Scan" tool will indicate when the ESC module signals the ECM that knock is present. See "Electronic Spark Control (ESC), System".

BASIC KNOWLEDGE AND TOOLS REQUIRED

To use this manual most effectively, a general understanding of basic electrical circuits and circuit testing tools is required. You should be familiar with wiring diagrams, the meaning of voltage, ohms, amps, the basic theories of electricity, and understand what happens in an open or shorted wire.

To perform system diagnosis, the use of a TECH 1 Diagnostic Computer or equivalent "Scan" tool is required. A tachometer, test light, ohmmeter, digital voltmeter with 10 megaohms impedance, vacuum gauge, and jumper wires are also required. Please become acquainted with the tools and their use before attempting to diagnose a vehicle.

DIAGNOSTIC INFORMATION

The diagnostic "tree" charts and functional checks in this manual are designed to locate a faulty circuit or component through logic based on the process of elimination.

Service Engine Soon Light

This light is on the instrument panel and has the following functions.
● It informs the driver that a problem has occurred and that the vehicle should be taken for service as soon as reasonably possible.
● It displays "Codes" stored by the ECM which help the technician diagnose system problems.
● It indicates "Open Loop" or "Closed Loop" operation.

As a bulb and system check, the light will come "ON" with the key "ON" and the engine not running. When the engine is started, the light will turn "OFF". If the light remains "ON", the self-diagnostic system has detected a problem. If the problem goes away, the light will go out in most cases after 10 seconds, but a Code will remain stored in the ECM.

When the light remains "ON" while the engine is running, or when a malfunction is suspected due to a driveability or emissions problem, a "Diagnostic Circuit Check" must be performed. These checks will expose malfunctions which may not be detected if other diagnostics are performed prematurely.

Intermittent "Service Engine Soon" Light

In the case of an "intermittent" problem, the **Service Engine Soon** light will light for 10 seconds and then will go out. However, the corresponding code will be stored in the memory of the ECM until the battery voltage to the ECM has been removed. When unexpected codes appear during the code reading

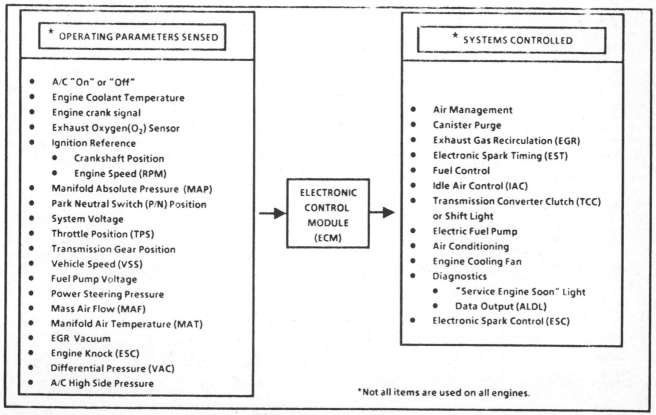

* OPERATING PARAMETERS SENSED	ELECTRONIC CONTROL MODULE (ECM)	* SYSTEMS CONTROLLED
● A/C "On" or "Off" ● Engine Coolant Temperature ● Engine crank signal ● Exhaust Oxygen(O_2) Sensor ● Ignition Reference 　● Crankshaft Position 　● Engine Speed (RPM) ● Manifold Absolute Pressure (MAP) ● Park Neutral Switch (P/N) Position ● System Voltage ● Throttle Position (TPS) ● Transmission Gear Position ● Vehicle Speed (VSS) ● Fuel Pump Voltage ● Power Steering Pressure ● Mass Air Flow (MAF) ● Manifold Air Temperature (MAT) ● EGR Vacuum ● Engine Knock (ESC) ● Differential Pressure (VAC) ● A/C High Side Pressure		● Air Management ● Canister Purge ● Exhaust Gas Recirculation (EGR) ● Electronic Spark Timing (EST) ● Fuel Control ● Idle Air Control (IAC) ● Transmission Converter Clutch (TCC) or Shift Light ● Electric Fuel Pump ● Air Conditioning ● Engine Cooling Fan ● Diagnostics 　● "Service Engine Soon" Light 　● Data Output (ALDL) ● Electronic Spark Control (ESC)

*Not all items are used on all engines.

ECM inputs and outputs

process, one can assume that these codes were set by an intermittent malfunction and could be helpful in diagnosing the system.

An intermittent code may or may not re-set. If it is an intermittent failure, a Diagnostic Code Chart is not used. A physical inspection of the applicable sub-system most often will resolve the problem. Most intermittent problems are caused by faulty electrical connections or wiring. Check all electrical connectors for damage or looseness

Reading Codes

The provision for communicating with the ECM is the Assembly Line Diagnostic Link (ALDL) connector. It is usually located under the instrument panel and is sometimes covered by a plastic cover labeled "DIAGNOSTIC CONNECTOR." It is used in the assembly plant to receive information in checking that the engine is operating properly before it leaves the plant. The code(s) stored in the ECM's memory can be read either through TECH 1 Diagnostic Computer, a hand-held diagnostic scanner plugged into the **ALDL** connector or by counting the number of flashes of the **Service Engine Soon** light when the diagnostic terminal of the **ALDL** connector is grounded. The **ALDL** connector terminal **B** (diagnostic terminal) is the second terminal from the right of the **ALDL** connector's top row. The terminal is most easily grounded by connecting it to terminal **A** (internal ECM ground), the terminal to the right of terminal **B** on top row of the **ALDL** connector.

Once terminals **A** and **B** have been connected, the ignition switch must be moved to the **ON** position, with the engine not running. At this point, the **Service Engine Soon** light should flash Code 12, 3 times consecutively. This would be the following flash sequence: "flash, pause, flash-flash, long pause, flash, pause, flash-flash, long pause, flash, pause, flash-flash." Code 12 indicates that the ECM's diagnostic system is operating. If Code 12 is not indicated, a problem is present within the diagnostic system itself, and should be addressed by consulting the appropriate diagnostic chart.

Following the output of Code 12, the **Service Engine Soon** light will indicate a diagnostic code 3 times if a code is present, or it will simply continue to output Code 12. If more than one diagnostic code has been stored in the ECM's memory, the codes will be output from the lowest to the highest, with each code being displayed 3 times.

Clearing Codes

To clear the codes from the memory of the ECM, either to determine if the malfunction will occur again or because repair has been completed, the ECM power feed must be disconnected for at least 30 seconds. Depending on how the vehicle is equipped, the ECM power feed can be disconnected at the positive battery terminal "pigtail," the inline fuseholder that originates at the positive connection at the battery, or the ECM fuse in the fuse block. (The nigative battery terminal may be discon-

nected, but other on-board memory data, such as preset radio tuning, will also be lost.)

WARNING: To prevent ECM damage, the key must be OFF when disconnecting or reconnecting ECM power.

When using a hand-held TECH 1 Diagnostic Computer, or "Scan" tool to read the codes, clearing the diagnostic codes is done in the same manner as in the above procedure.

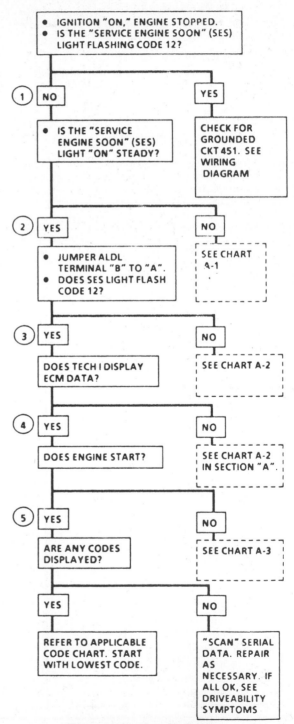

Diagnostic circuit check

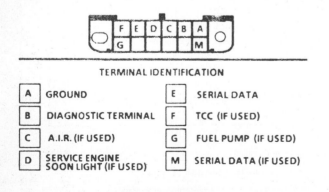

ALDL connector

Diagnostic Mode

When the Diagnostic terminal is grounded with the ignition ON and the engine not running, the system will enter what is called the Diagnostic Mode. In this mode the ECM will:

1. Display a Code 12 by flashing the **Service Engine Soon** light (indicating the system is operating correctly).

2. Display any stored codes by flashing the **Service Engine Soon** light. Each code will be flashed 3 times, then Code 12 will be flashed again.

3. Energize all ECM controlled relays and solenoids except fuel pump relay. This allows checking circuits which may be difficult to energize without driving the vehicle and being under particular operating conditions.

4. The IAC valve moves to its fully extended position on most models, blocking the idle air passage. This is useful in checking the minimum idle speed.

Field Service Mode

If the diagnostic terminal is grounded with the engine running, the system will enter the Field Service mode. In this mode, the **Service Engine Soon** light will indicate whether the system is in "Open Loop" or "Closed Loop."

In "Open Loop" the **Service Engine Soon** light flashes 2½ times per second.

In "Closed Loop," the light flashes once per second. Also, in "Closed Loop," the light will stay "OFF" most of the time if the system is running lean. It will stay "ON" most of the time if the system is running rich.

While the system is in Field Service Mode, new codes cannot be stored in the ECM and the "Closed Loop" timer is bypassed.

ECM Learing Ability

The ECM has a "learning" ability which allows it to make corrections for minor variations in the fuel system to improve driveability. If the battery is disconnected, to clear diagnostic codes or for other repair, the "learning" process resets and begins again. A change may be noted in the vehicle's performance. To "teach" the vehicle, ensure that the engine is at operating temperature. The vehicle should be driven at part throttle, with moderate acceleration and idle conditions until normal performance returns.

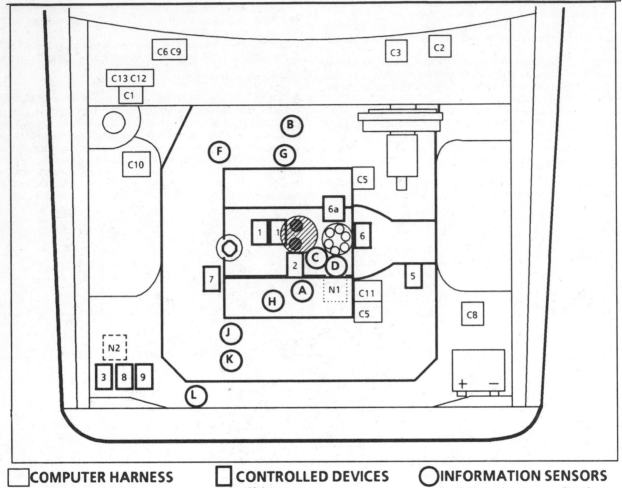

COMPUTER HARNESS

C1 Electronic Control Module
C2 ALDL diagnostic connector
C3 "SERVICE ENGINE SOON" light
C5 ECM harness grounds
C6 Fuse panel
C8 Fuel pump test connector
C9 Fuel pump fuse & ECM power
C10 Set timing connector
C11 Engine Grounds
C12 Electronic Spark Control Module
C13 Vehicle Speed Buffer

NOT ECM CONNECTED

N1 Crankcase vent valve (PCV)
N2 Fuel Vapor Canister

CONTROLLED DEVICES

1 Fuel injectors
2 Idle Air Control (IAC) motor
3 Fuel pump relay
5 Torque Converter Clutch (TCC) connector
6 EST distributor
6a Remote ignition coil
7 Electronic Vacuum Regulator Valve (EVRV) EGR
8 Cooling fan relay
9 A/C fan relay (if applicable)

INFORMATION SENSORS

A Manifold Absolute Pressure (MAP) (attached to air cleaner)
B Exhaust oxygen
C Throttle Position Sensor (TPS)
D Coolant temperature
F Vehicle Speed Sensor (VSS)
G Knock Sensor
H Oil Pressure Fuel Pump Switch
J A/C low pressure switch
K A/C high pressure switch
L Intermediate pressure A/C fan switch

Exhaust Gas Recirculation valve

Engine Component locations

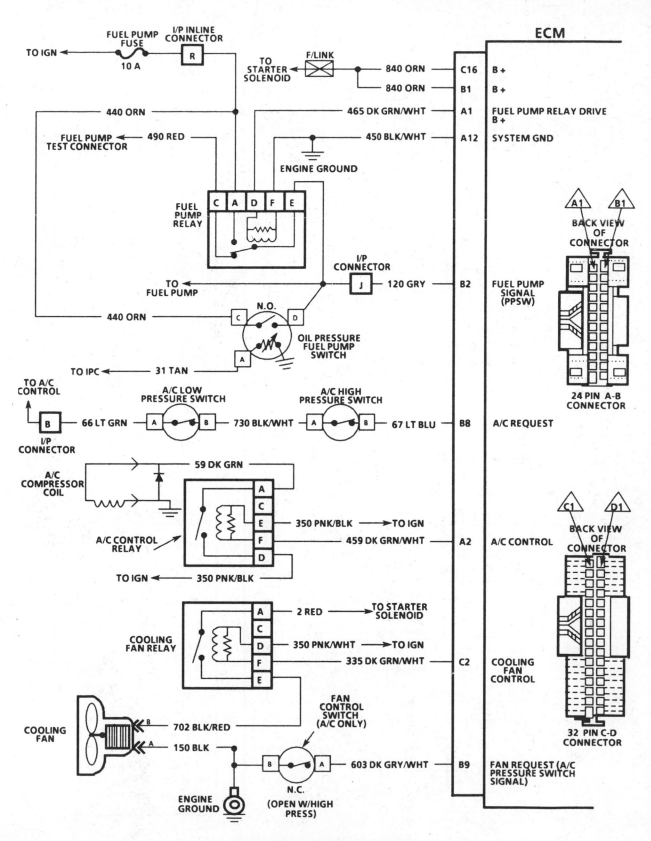

ECM wiring schematic (1 of 3)

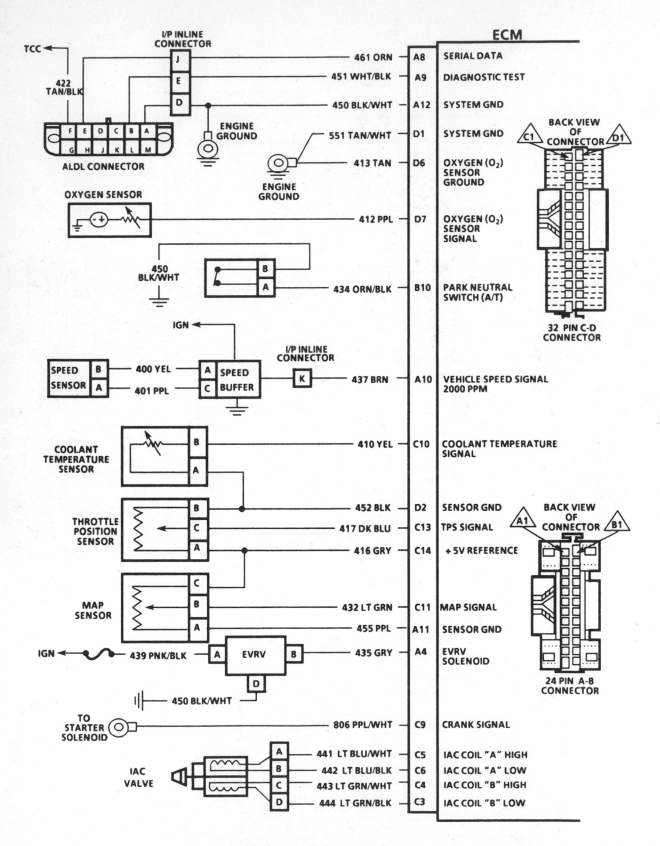

ECM wiring schematic (2 of 3)

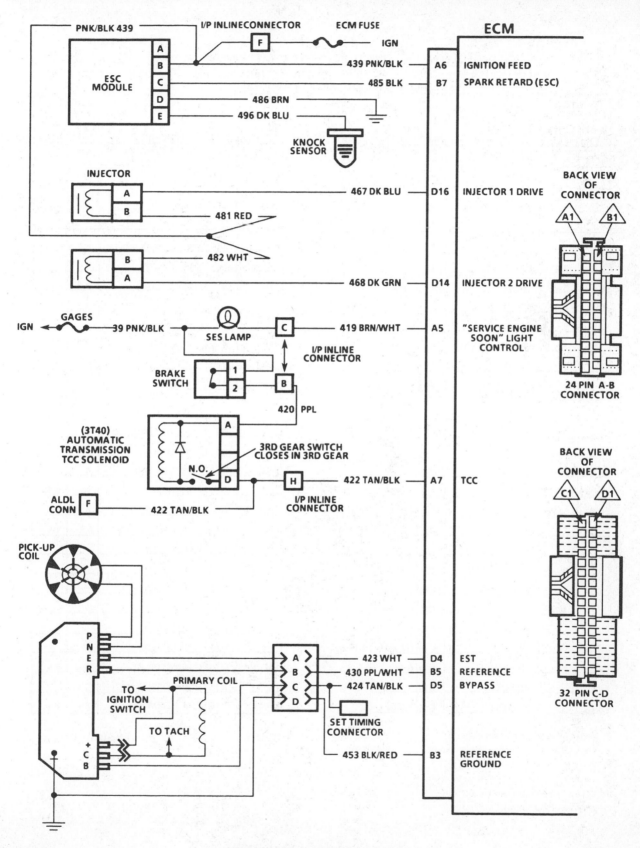

ECM wiring schematic (3 of 3)

THE FOLLOWING CONDITIONS MUST BE MET BEFORE TESTING:
- Engine at operating temperature • Engine idling in "Closed Loop" (for "Engine Run" column)
- "Test" terminal not grounded • ALDL tool not installed

VOLTAGE					
KEY "ON"	ENG. RUN	CIRCUIT	PIN	WIRE COLOR	
② 0	B+	FUEL PUMP RELAY DRIVE	A1	DK GRN/WHT	
... B+	B+	A/C CONTROL RELAY	A2	DK GRN/WHT	
		NOT USED	A3		
B+	B+	EVRV	A4	GRY	
0	B+	"SERVICE ENGINE SOON" CONTROL	A5	BRN/WHT	
B+	B+	IGN (ECM)	A6	PNK/BLK	
B+	B+	TCC SOLENOID	A7	TAN/BLK	
2-5	2-5	SERIAL DATA	A8	ORN	
5	5	DIAGNOSTIC TERMINAL	A9	WHT/BLK	
① 0 OR 12	0 OR 12	SPEED SENSOR SIGNAL	A10	BRN	
0	0	SENSOR GROUND	A11	PPL	
0	0	SYSTEM GROUND	A12	BLK/WHT	
0	0	PUSHER FAN CONTROL	C1	DK BLU WHT	
B+	B+	COOLING FAN RELAY	C2	DK GRN/WHT	
NOT USEABLE		IAC "B" LO	C3	LT GRN/BLK	
NOT USEABLE		IAC "B" HI	C4	LT GRN/WHT	
NOT USEABLE		IAC "A" HI	C5	LT BLU/WHT	
NOT USEABLE		IAC "A" LO	C6	LT BLU BLK	
		NOT USED	C7		
		NOT USED	C8		
⑦ 0	0	CRANK DISCRETE	C9	PPL/WHT	
⑤ 1.6	1.6	COOLANT TEMP. SIGNAL	C10	YEL	
③ 4.75	1.1	MAP SIGNAL	C11	LT GRN	
		NOT USED	C12		
.7	.7	TPS SIGNAL	C13	DK BLU	
5	5	TPS 5 VOLT REFERENCE	C14	GRY	
		NOT USED	C15		
B+	B+	BATTERY	C16	ORN	

A1   B1
BACK VIEW OF CONNECTOR
24 PIN A-B CONNECTOR

C1   D1
BACK VIEW OF CONNECTOR
32 PIN C-D CONNECTOR

			VOLTAGE		
WIRE COLOR	PIN	CIRCUIT	KEY "ON"	ENG. RUN	
ORN	B1	BATT 12 VOLTS	B+	B+	
GRY	B2	FUEL PUMP SIGNAL	0	B+	④
BLK/RED	B3	IGNITION GROUND	0	0	
	B4	NOT USED			
PPL/WHT	B5	DISTRIBUTOR REFERENCE HIGH	0	1.3	
	B6	NOT USED			
BLK	B7	ESC SIGNAL	9.2	9.3	
LT BLU	B8	A/C SIGNAL "OFF" / "ON"	0 / B+	0 / B+	
DK GRN/WHT	B9	INTER HD PRESS SW			
ORN/BLK	B10	PARK/NEUTRAL SW. SIGNAL (A/T)	0	0	⑥
	B11	NOT USED			
	B12	NOT USED			
TAN/WHT	D1	SYSTEM GROUND	0	0	
BLK	D2	SENSOR GROUND	0	0	
	D3	NOT USED			
WHT	D4	EST CONTROL	0	1.3	
TAN/BLK	D5	BYPASS	0	4.75	
TAN	D6	GROUND (O_2)	0	0	
PPL	D7	O_2 SENSOR SIGNAL	3.5	1.9	③
	D8	NOT USED			
	D9	NOT USED			
	D10	NOT USED			
	D11	NOT USED			
	D12	NOT USED			
	D13	NOT USED			
DK GRN	D14	INJECTOR #2	B+	B+	
	D15	NOT USED			
DK BLU	D16	INJECTOR #1	B+	B+	

① Varies from .60 to battery voltage, depending on position of drive wheels.
② 12 volts for first two seconds.
③ Varies.
④ 12 volts when fuel pump is running.
⑤ Varies with temperature.
⑥ Reads battery voltage in gear.
⑦ 12 volts, when engine is cranking.

ENGINE 3.1 L

ECM connector terminal end view

DIAGNOSTIC CIRCUIT CHECK

The Diagnostic Circuit Check is an organized approach to identifying a problem created by an electronic engine control system malfunction. It must be the starting point for any driveability complaint diagnosis, because it directs the service technician to the next logical step in diagnosing the complaint.

The "Scan Data" listed in the table may be used for comparison, after completing the diagnostic circuit check and finding the on-board diagnostics functioning properly and no trouble codes displayed. The "Typical Values" are an average of display values recorded from normally operating vehicles and are intended to represent what a normally functioning system would typically display.

A "SCAN" TOOL THAT DISPLAYS FAULTY DATA SHOULD NOT BE USED, AND THE PROBLEM SHOULD BE REPORTED TO THE MANUFACTURER. THE USE OF A FAULTY "SCAN" CAN RESULT IN MISDIAGNOSIS AND UNNECESSARY PARTS REPLACEMENT.

Only the parameters listed below are used in this manual for diagnosis. If a "Scan" tool reads other parameters, the values are not recommended by General Motors for use in diagnosis.

"SCAN" DATA

- RPM at a learned idle
- Closed Throttle
- Normal Operating Temperature
- Park or Neutral
- Closed Loop
- A/C OFF
- "Road Test" Mode on Tech I

"SCAN" Position	Units Displayed	Typical Data Value
Coolant Temp	C°/F°	88-106/190-222
Battery Voltage	volts	13.5 - 14.5
MAP	kPa, volts	30-45 / 1.04 - 1.83
Throttle Position	volts	.4 - 1.23
Oxygen (O_2) Sensor	mv	001 - 999 varies
Open/Closed Loop	open/closed	closed
Rich/Lean Flag	rich/lean	varies
O_2 Cross Counts	counts	greater than 1
Engine Speed	rpm	900 max. park or neutral / 650 ± 50 drive
Knock Signal	yes/no	no
Fuel Integrator	counts	varies
Block Learn	counts	110 - 138
Idle Air Control	counts	0-50 park or neutral / 5-15 drive
Park/Neutral	P-N / -R-DL	P-N
MPH KPH	mph/kph	0 / 0
Torque Converter Clutch	ON/OFF	OFF
A/C Clutch	ON/OFF	OFF

* Values are shown as typical scan values for vehicles operating under normal conditions. An "out of range" scan value indicates a suspected problem area and further diagnostics must be performed prior to replacing any parts.

DIAGNOSTIC CIRCUIT CHECK
3.1L (VIN D) "U" APV (TBI)

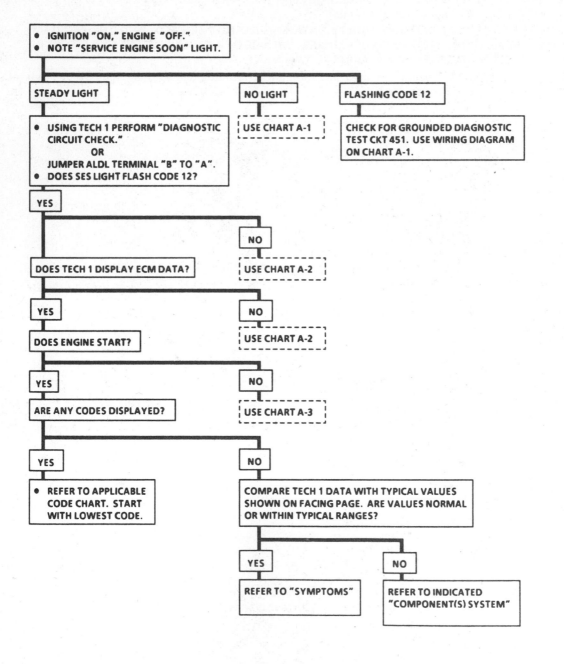

- IGNITION "ON," ENGINE "OFF."
- NOTE "SERVICE ENGINE SOON" LIGHT.

STEADY LIGHT

- USING TECH 1 PERFORM "DIAGNOSTIC CIRCUIT CHECK."
  OR
  JUMPER ALDL TERMINAL "B" TO "A".
- DOES SES LIGHT FLASH CODE 12?

NO LIGHT

USE CHART A-1

FLASHING CODE 12

CHECK FOR GROUNDED DIAGNOSTIC TEST CKT 451. USE WIRING DIAGRAM ON CHART A-1.

YES

NO

DOES TECH 1 DISPLAY ECM DATA?

USE CHART A-2

YES

NO

DOES ENGINE START?

USE CHART A-2

YES

NO

ARE ANY CODES DISPLAYED?

USE CHART A-3

YES

- REFER TO APPLICABLE CODE CHART. START WITH LOWEST CODE.

NO

COMPARE TECH 1 DATA WITH TYPICAL VALUES SHOWN ON FACING PAGE. ARE VALUES NORMAL OR WITHIN TYPICAL RANGES?

YES

REFER TO "SYMPTOMS"

NO

REFER TO INDICATED "COMPONENT(S) SYSTEM"

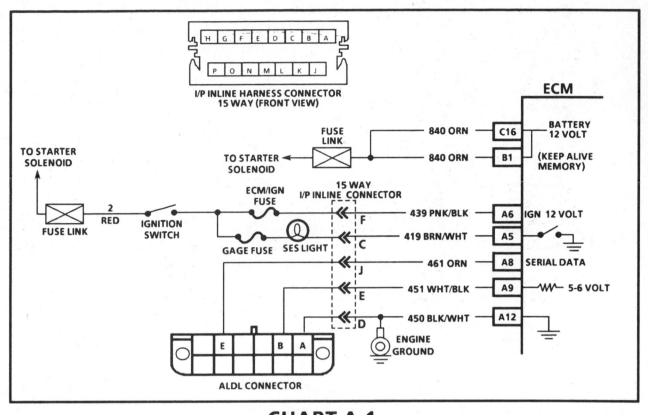

CHART A-1

NO "SERVICE ENGINE SOON" LIGHT
3.1L (VIN D) "U" APV (TBI)

Circuit Description:

There should always be a steady "Service Engine Soon" light, when the ignition is "ON" and engine stopped. Ignition voltage is supplied directly to the light bulb. The Electronic Control Module (ECM) will control the light and turn it "ON" by providing a ground path through CKT 419 to the ECM.

Test Description: Number(s) below refer to circled number(s) on the diagnostic chart..

1. Battery feed CKT 840 is protected by a fusible link and is connected to the starter solenoid.
2. Using a test light connected to 12 volts, probe each of the system ground circuits to be sure a good ground is present. See ECM terminal end view in front of this section for ECM pin locations of ground circuits.

Diagnostic Aids:

Engine runs OK, check:
- Faulty light bulb.
- CKT 419 open.
- Gage fuse blown. This will result in no oil, or generator lights, seat belt reminder, etc.
  Engine cranks, but will not run.
- Continuous battery - fuse or fusible link open.
- ECM ignition fuse open.
- Battery CKT 840 to ECM open.
- Ignition CKT 439 to ECM open.
- Poor connection to ECM.

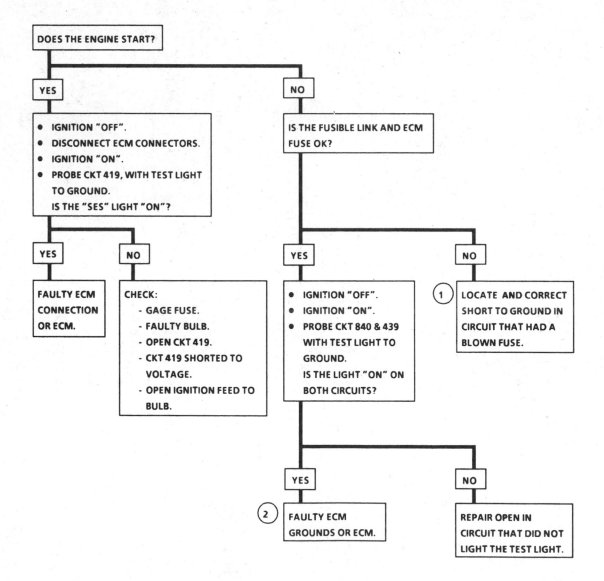

"NON-SCAN" DIAGNOSTICS

CHART A-1
NO "SERVICE ENGINE SOON" LIGHT
3.1L (VIN D) "U" APV (TBI)

DOES THE ENGINE START?

YES

- IGNITION "OFF".
- DISCONNECT ECM CONNECTORS.
- IGNITION "ON".
- PROBE CKT 419, WITH TEST LIGHT TO GROUND.
  IS THE "SES" LIGHT "ON"?

YES

FAULTY ECM CONNECTION OR ECM.

NO

CHECK:
- GAGE FUSE.
- FAULTY BULB.
- OPEN CKT 419.
- CKT 419 SHORTED TO VOLTAGE.
- OPEN IGNITION FEED TO BULB.

NO

IS THE FUSIBLE LINK AND ECM FUSE OK?

YES

- IGNITION "OFF".
- IGNITION "ON".
- PROBE CKT 840 & 439 WITH TEST LIGHT TO GROUND.
  IS THE LIGHT "ON" ON BOTH CIRCUITS?

NO

(1) LOCATE AND CORRECT SHORT TO GROUND IN CIRCUIT THAT HAD A BLOWN FUSE.

YES

(2) FAULTY ECM GROUNDS OR ECM.

NO

REPAIR OPEN IN CIRCUIT THAT DID NOT LIGHT THE TEST LIGHT.

CLEAR CODES AND CONFIRM "CLOSED LOOP" OPERATION AND NO "SERVICE ENGINE SOON" LIGHT.

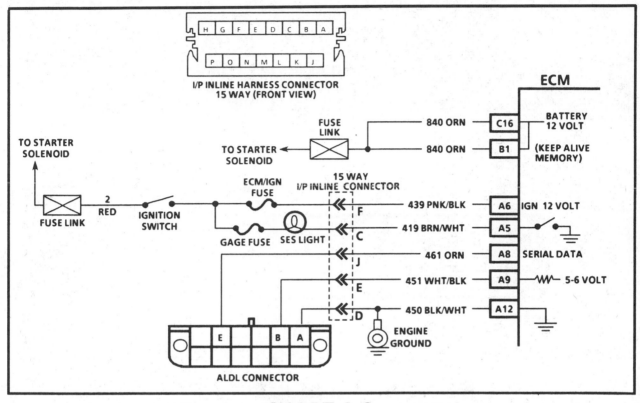

I/P INLINE HARNESS CONNECTOR
15 WAY (FRONT VIEW)

CHART A-2

NO ALDL DATA OR WON'T FLASH CODE 12
"SERVICE ENGINE SOON" LIGHT "ON" STEADY
3.1L (VIN D) "U" APV (TBI)

Circuit Description:

There should always be a steady "Service Engine Soon" light, when the ignition is "ON" and engine stopped. Ignition voltage is supplied directly to the light bulb. The Electronic Control Module (ECM) will turn the light "ON" by grounding CKT 419 at the ECM.

With the diagnostic terminal grounded, the light should flash a Code 12, followed by any trouble code(s) stored in memory.

A steady light suggests a short to ground in the light control CKT 419, or an open in diagnostic CKT 451.

Test Description: Number(s) below refer to circled number(s) on the diagnostic chart.

1. If there is a problem with the ECM that causes a "Scan" tool to not read Serial data, then the ECM should not flash a Code 12. If Code 12 does flash, be sure that the "Scan" tool is working properly on another vehicle. If the "Scan" is functioning properly and CKT 461 is OK, the MEM-CAL or ECM may be at fault for the NO ALDL symptom.

2. If the light goes "OFF," when the ECM connector is disconnected, then CKT 419 is not shorted to ground.

3. This step will check for an open diagnostic CKT 451.

4. At this point, the "Service Engine Soon" light wiring is OK. The problem is a faulty ECM or PROM. If Code 12 does not flash, the ECM should be replaced using the original PROM. Replace the PROM only after trying an ECM, as a defective PROM is an unlikely cause of the problem.

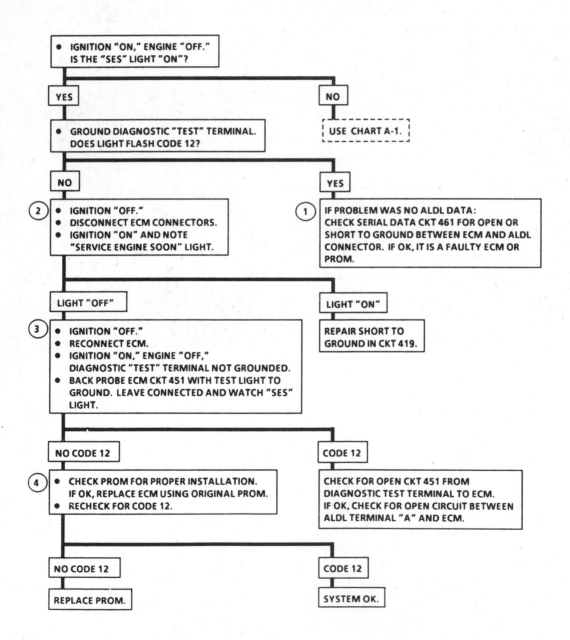

CHART A-2
NO ALDL DATA OR WON'T FLASH CODE 12
"SERVICE ENGINE SOON" LIGHT "ON" STEADY
3.1L (VIN D) "U" APV (TBI)

- IGNITION "ON," ENGINE "OFF." IS THE "SES" LIGHT "ON"?

YES

NO

- GROUND DIAGNOSTIC "TEST" TERMINAL. DOES LIGHT FLASH CODE 12?

USE CHART A-1.

NO

YES

2
- IGNITION "OFF."
- DISCONNECT ECM CONNECTORS.
- IGNITION "ON" AND NOTE "SERVICE ENGINE SOON" LIGHT.

1
IF PROBLEM WAS NO ALDL DATA: CHECK SERIAL DATA CKT 461 FOR OPEN OR SHORT TO GROUND BETWEEN ECM AND ALDL CONNECTOR. IF OK, IT IS A FAULTY ECM OR PROM.

LIGHT "OFF"

LIGHT "ON"

3
- IGNITION "OFF."
- RECONNECT ECM.
- IGNITION "ON," ENGINE "OFF," DIAGNOSTIC "TEST" TERMINAL NOT GROUNDED.
- BACK PROBE ECM CKT 451 WITH TEST LIGHT TO GROUND. LEAVE CONNECTED AND WATCH "SES" LIGHT.

REPAIR SHORT TO GROUND IN CKT 419.

NO CODE 12

CODE 12

4
- CHECK PROM FOR PROPER INSTALLATION. IF OK, REPLACE ECM USING ORIGINAL PROM.
- RECHECK FOR CODE 12.

CHECK FOR OPEN CKT 451 FROM DIAGNOSTIC TEST TERMINAL TO ECM. IF OK, CHECK FOR OPEN CIRCUIT BETWEEN ALDL TERMINAL "A" AND ECM.

NO CODE 12

CODE 12

REPLACE PROM.

SYSTEM OK.

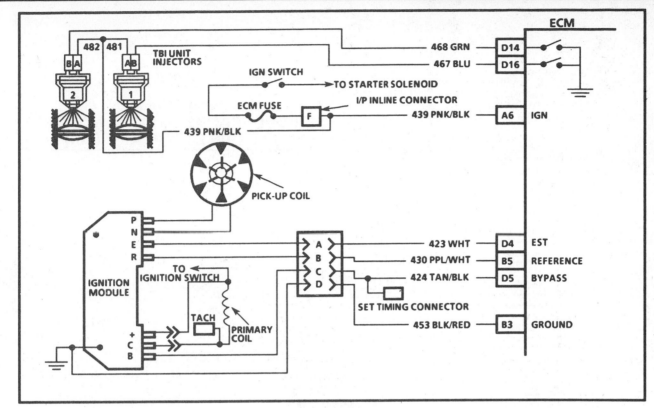

CHART A-3

(Page 1 of 2)
ENGINE CRANKS BUT WILL NOT RUN
3.1L (VIN D) "U" APV (TBI)

Circuit Description:

This chart assumes that battery condition and engine cranking speed are OK, and there is adequate fuel in the tank.

Test Description: Number(s) below refer to circled number(s) on the diagnostic chart.

1. A "Service Engine Soon" light "ON" is a basic test to determine if there is a 12 volts supply and ignition 12 volts to ECM. No ALDL may be due to an ECM problem and CHART A-2 will diagnose the ECM. If TPS is over 2.5 volts, the engine may be in the clear flood mode which will cause starting problems. The engine will not start without reference pulses and therefore, the "Scan" should read rpm (reference) during crank.

2. No spark may be caused by one of several components related to the ignition system. CHART C-4 will address all problems related to the causes of a no spark condition.

3. Fuel spray from the injector(s) indicates that fuel is available. However, the engine could be severely flooded due to too much fuel.

4. While cranking engine, there should be no fuel spray with injector disconnected. Replace an injector if it sprays fuel or drips like a leaking water faucet.

5. The fuel pressure will drop after the fuel pump stops running due to a controlled bleed in the fuel system. Use of the fuel pressure gage will determine if fuel system pressure is enough for engine to start and run.

6. No fuel spray from injector indicates a faulty fuel system or no ECM control of injector.

7. This test will determine if the ignition module is not generating the reference pulse, or if the wiring or ECM are at faulty by touching and removing a test light to 12 volts on CKT 430, a reference pulse should be generated. If injector test light blinks, the ECM and wiring are OK.

Diagnostic Aids:

- Water or foreign material can cause a no start during freezing weather.
- An EGR sticking open can cause a low air/fuel ratio during cranking.
- Fuel pressure: Low fuel pressure can result in a very lean air/fuel ratio. See CHART A-7.
- A grounded CKT 423 (EST) may cause a "No-Start" or a "Start then Stall" condition.

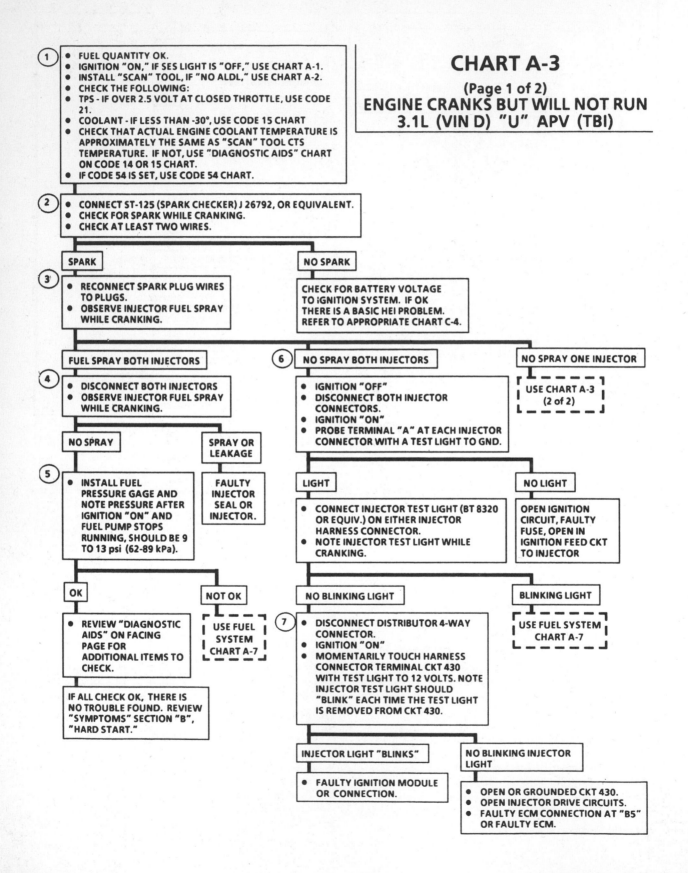

CHART A-3

(Page 1 of 2)
ENGINE CRANKS BUT WILL NOT RUN
3.1L (VIN D) "U" APV (TBI)

①
- FUEL QUANTITY OK.
- IGNITION "ON," IF SES LIGHT IS "OFF," USE CHART A-1.
- INSTALL "SCAN" TOOL, IF "NO ALDL," USE CHART A-2.
- CHECK THE FOLLOWING:
- TPS - IF OVER 2.5 VOLT AT CLOSED THROTTLE, USE CODE 21.
- COOLANT - IF LESS THAN -30°, USE CODE 15 CHART
- CHECK THAT ACTUAL ENGINE COOLANT TEMPERATURE IS APPROXIMATELY THE SAME AS "SCAN" TOOL CTS TEMPERATURE. IF NOT, USE "DIAGNOSTIC AIDS" CHART ON CODE 14 OR 15 CHART.
- IF CODE 54 IS SET, USE CODE 54 CHART.

②
- CONNECT ST-125 (SPARK CHECKER) J 26792, OR EQUIVALENT.
- CHECK FOR SPARK WHILE CRANKING.
- CHECK AT LEAST TWO WIRES.

SPARK

③
- RECONNECT SPARK PLUG WIRES TO PLUGS.
- OBSERVE INJECTOR FUEL SPRAY WHILE CRANKING.

NO SPARK

CHECK FOR BATTERY VOLTAGE TO IGNITION SYSTEM. IF OK THERE IS A BASIC HEI PROBLEM. REFER TO APPROPRIATE CHART C-4.

FUEL SPRAY BOTH INJECTORS

④
- DISCONNECT BOTH INJECTORS
- OBSERVE INJECTOR FUEL SPRAY WHILE CRANKING.

⑥ NO SPRAY BOTH INJECTORS

NO SPRAY ONE INJECTOR

USE CHART A-3 (2 of 2)

NO SPRAY

⑤
- INSTALL FUEL PRESSURE GAGE AND NOTE PRESSURE AFTER IGNITION "ON" AND FUEL PUMP STOPS RUNNING, SHOULD BE 9 TO 13 psi (62-89 kPa).

SPRAY OR LEAKAGE

FAULTY INJECTOR SEAL OR INJECTOR.

⑥
- IGNITION "OFF"
- DISCONNECT BOTH INJECTOR CONNECTORS.
- IGNITION "ON"
- PROBE TERMINAL "A" AT EACH INJECTOR CONNECTOR WITH A TEST LIGHT TO GND.

LIGHT

- CONNECT INJECTOR TEST LIGHT (BT 8320 OR EQUIV.) ON EITHER INJECTOR HARNESS CONNECTOR.
- NOTE INJECTOR TEST LIGHT WHILE CRANKING.

NO LIGHT

OPEN IGNITION CIRCUIT, FAULTY FUSE, OPEN IN IGNITION FEED CKT TO INJECTOR

OK

- REVIEW "DIAGNOSTIC AIDS" ON FACING PAGE FOR ADDITIONAL ITEMS TO CHECK.

IF ALL CHECK OK, THERE IS NO TROUBLE FOUND. REVIEW "SYMPTOMS" SECTION "B", "HARD START."

NOT OK

USE FUEL SYSTEM CHART A-7

NO BLINKING LIGHT

⑦
- DISCONNECT DISTRIBUTOR 4-WAY CONNECTOR.
- IGNITION "ON"
- MOMENTARILY TOUCH HARNESS CONNECTOR TERMINAL CKT 430 WITH TEST LIGHT TO 12 VOLTS. NOTE INJECTOR TEST LIGHT SHOULD "BLINK" EACH TIME THE TEST LIGHT IS REMOVED FROM CKT 430.

BLINKING LIGHT

USE FUEL SYSTEM CHART A-7

INJECTOR LIGHT "BLINKS"

- FAULTY IGNITION MODULE OR CONNECTION.

NO BLINKING INJECTOR LIGHT

- OPEN OR GROUNDED CKT 430.
- OPEN INJECTOR DRIVE CIRCUITS.
- FAULTY ECM CONNECTION AT "B5" OR FAULTY ECM.

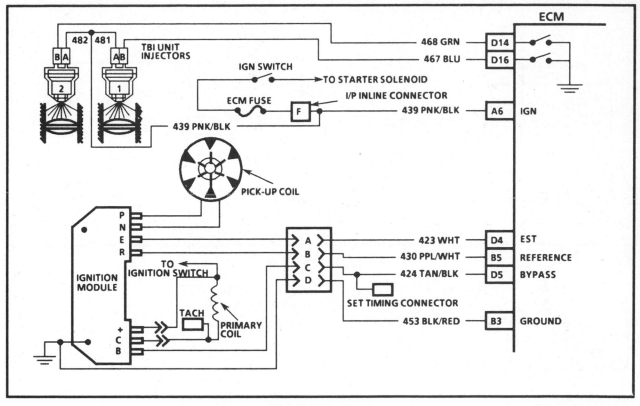

CHART A-3

(Page 2 of 2)
ENGINE CRANKS BUT WILL NOT RUN
3.1L (VIN D) "U" APV (TBI)

Circuit Description:
This chart assumes that battery condition and engine cranking speed are OK, and there is adequate fuel in the tank.

Test Description: Number(s) below refer to circled number(s) on the diagnostic chart.

1. No fuel spray from one injector indicates a faulty fuel injector or no ECM control of injector. If the test light "blinks" while cranking, then ECM control should be considered OK. Be sure test light makes good contact between connector terminals during test. The light may be a little dim when "blinking." This is due to current draw of the test light. How bright it "blinks" is not important.

2. CKT 481 and CKT 482 supply ignition voltage to the injectors. Probe each connector terminal with a test light to ground. There should be a light "ON" at one terminal. If the test light confirms ignition voltage at the connector, the ECM injector control CKT 467 or CKT 468 may be open. Reconnect the injector, and using a test light connected to ground, check for a light at the applicable ECM connector terminal ("D14" or "D16"). A light at this point indicates that the injector drive circuit involved is OK.

   If an ECM repeat failure has occurred, the injector is shorted. Replace the injector and ECM.

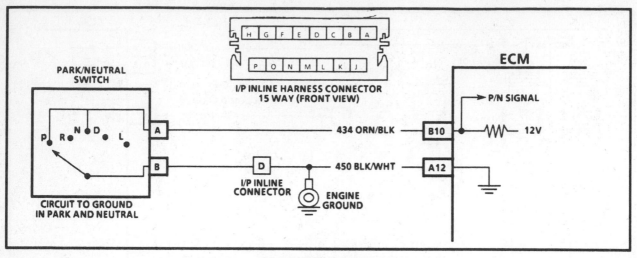

CHART C-1A
PARK/NEUTRAL (P/N) SWITCH DIAGNOSIS
(AUTO TRANSMISSION ONLY)
3.1L (VIN D) "U" APV (TBI)

Circuit Description:

The Park/Neutral (P/N) switch contacts are a part of the neutral start switch and are closed to ground in park or neutral, and open in drive ranges.

The ECM supplies ignition voltage through a current limiting resistor to CKT 434 and senses a closed switch, when the voltage on CKT 434 drops to less than one volt.

The ECM uses the P/N signal as one of the inputs to control:

> Idle Air Control (IAC).
> Vehicle Speed Sensor (VSS) Diagnostics.

Test Description: Number(s) below refer to circled number(s) on the diagnostic chart.

1. Checks for a closed switch to ground in park position. Different makes of "Scan" tools will read P/N differently. Refer to "Tool Operations" manual for type of display used.

2. Checks for an open switch in drive range.

3. Be sure "Scan" tool indicates drive, even while wiggling shifter to test for an intermittent or misadjusted switch in drive range.

CHART C-1A
PARK/NEUTRAL (P/N) SWITCH DIAGNOSIS
(AUTO TRANSMISSION ONLY)
3.1L (VIN D) "U" APV (TBI)

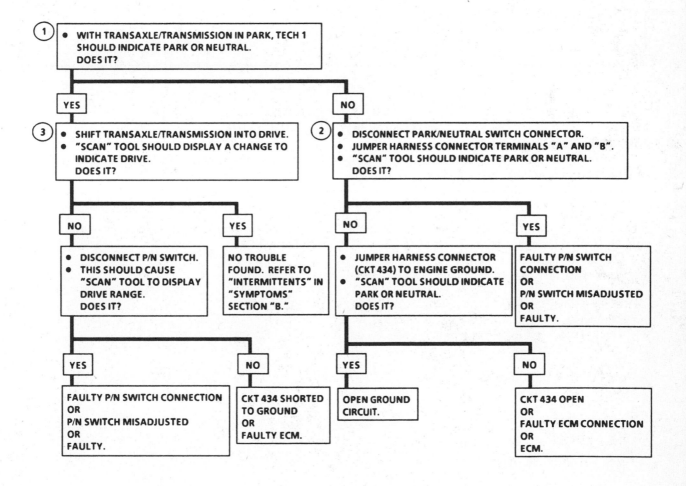

1 • WITH TRANSAXLE/TRANSMISSION IN PARK, TECH 1 SHOULD INDICATE PARK OR NEUTRAL. DOES IT?

YES | NO

3 • SHIFT TRANSAXLE/TRANSMISSION INTO DRIVE.
• "SCAN" TOOL SHOULD DISPLAY A CHANGE TO INDICATE DRIVE. DOES IT?

2 • DISCONNECT PARK/NEUTRAL SWITCH CONNECTOR.
• JUMPER HARNESS CONNECTOR TERMINALS "A" AND "B".
• "SCAN" TOOL SHOULD INDICATE PARK OR NEUTRAL. DOES IT?

NO | YES | NO | YES

• DISCONNECT P/N SWITCH.
• THIS SHOULD CAUSE "SCAN" TOOL TO DISPLAY DRIVE RANGE. DOES IT?

NO TROUBLE FOUND. REFER TO "INTERMITTENTS" IN "SYMPTOMS" SECTION "B."

• JUMPER HARNESS CONNECTOR (CKT 434) TO ENGINE GROUND.
• "SCAN" TOOL SHOULD INDICATE PARK OR NEUTRAL. DOES IT?

FAULTY P/N SWITCH CONNECTION OR P/N SWITCH MISADJUSTED OR FAULTY.

YES | NO | YES | NO

FAULTY P/N SWITCH CONNECTION OR P/N SWITCH MISADJUSTED OR FAULTY.

CKT 434 SHORTED TO GROUND OR FAULTY ECM.

OPEN GROUND CIRCUIT.

CKT 434 OPEN OR FAULTY ECM CONNECTION OR ECM.

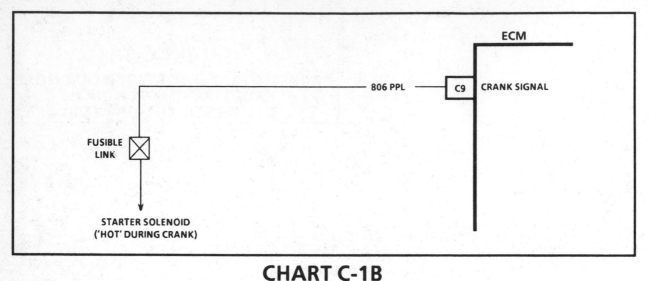

CHART C-1B
CRANK SIGNAL
3.1L (VIN D) "U" APV (TBI)

Circuit Description:

Crank signal is a 12 volt signal to the ECM during cranking to allow enrichment and cancel diagnostics until engine is running and 12 volts is no longer on the circuit.

Test Description: Number(s) below refer to circled number(s) on the diagnostic chart.

1. Checks for normal (cranking) voltage to terminal "C9" of ECM. Test light should be "ON" during cranking.

2. Checks to determine if source of blown fuse was a faulty ECM.

CHART C-1B
CRANK SIGNAL
3.1L (VIN D) "U" APV (TBI)

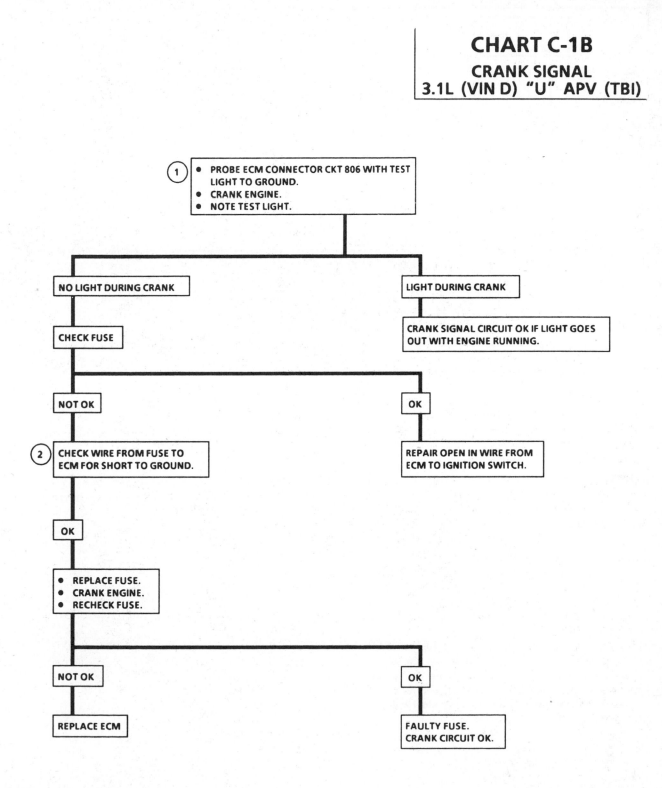

1
- PROBE ECM CONNECTOR CKT 806 WITH TEST LIGHT TO GROUND.
- CRANK ENGINE.
- NOTE TEST LIGHT.

NO LIGHT DURING CRANK

LIGHT DURING CRANK

CHECK FUSE

CRANK SIGNAL CIRCUIT OK IF LIGHT GOES OUT WITH ENGINE RUNNING.

NOT OK

OK

2 CHECK WIRE FROM FUSE TO ECM FOR SHORT TO GROUND.

REPAIR OPEN IN WIRE FROM ECM TO IGNITION SWITCH.

OK

- REPLACE FUSE.
- CRANK ENGINE.
- RECHECK FUSE.

NOT OK

OK

REPLACE ECM

FAULTY FUSE. CRANK CIRCUIT OK.

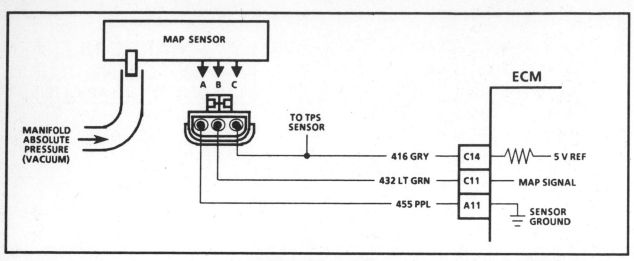

CHART C-1D

MANIFOLD ABSOLUTE PRESSURE (MAP) VOLTAGE OUTPUT CHECK
3.1L (VIN D) "U" APV (TBI)

Circuit Description:

The Manifold Absolute Pressure (MAP) sensor measures the changes in the intake manifold pressure which result from engine load (intake manifold vacuum) and rpm changes; and converts these into a voltage output. The ECM sends a 5 volt reference voltage to the MAP sensor. As the manifold pressure changed, the output voltage of the sensor also changes. By monitoring the sensor output voltage, the ECM knows the manifold pressure. A lower pressure (low voltage) output voltage will be about 1 - 2 volts at idle. While higher pressure (high voltage) output voltage will be about 4 - 4.8 at Wide Open Throttle (WOT). The MAP sensor is also used, under certain conditions, to measure barometric pressure, allowing the ECM to make adjustments for different altitudes. The ECM uses the MAP sensor to control fuel delivery and ignition timing.

Test Description: Number(s) below refer to circled number(s) on the diagnostic chart.

⚠ Important

● Be sure to use the same Diagnostic Test Equipment for all measurements.

1. When comparing "Scan" readings to a known good vehicle, it is important to compare vehicles that use a MAP sensor having the same color insert or having the same "Hot Stamped" number. See figures on facing page.

2. Applying 34 kPa (10" Hg) vacuum to the MAP sensor should cause the voltage to be 1.5 to 2.1 volts less than the voltage at Step 1. Upon applying vacuum to the sensor, the change in voltage should be instantaneous. A slow voltage change indicates a faulty sensor.

3. Check vacuum hose to sensor for leaking or restriction. Be sure that no other vacuum devices are connected to the MAP hose.

NOTE: Make sure electrical connector remains securely fastened.

4. Disconnect sensor from bracket and twist sensor by hand (only) to check for intermittent connection. Output changes greater than .10 volt indicate a bad sensor.

CHART C-1D
MANIFOLD ABSOLUTE PRESSURE (MAP) VOLTAGE OUTPUT CHECK
3.1L (VIN D) "U" APV (TBI)

NOTE: THIS CHART ONLY APPLIES TO MAP SENSORS HAVING GREEN OR BLACK COLOR KEY INSERT (SEE BELOW).

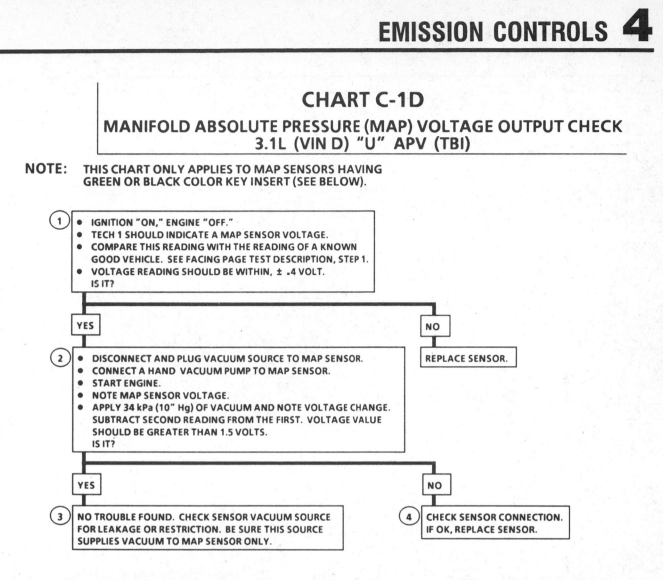

1
- IGNITION "ON," ENGINE "OFF."
- TECH 1 SHOULD INDICATE A MAP SENSOR VOLTAGE.
- COMPARE THIS READING WITH THE READING OF A KNOWN GOOD VEHICLE. SEE FACING PAGE TEST DESCRIPTION, STEP 1.
- VOLTAGE READING SHOULD BE WITHIN, ± .4 VOLT. IS IT?

YES   **NO**

NO → REPLACE SENSOR.

2
- DISCONNECT AND PLUG VACUUM SOURCE TO MAP SENSOR.
- CONNECT A HAND VACUUM PUMP TO MAP SENSOR.
- START ENGINE.
- NOTE MAP SENSOR VOLTAGE.
- APPLY 34 kPa (10" Hg) OF VACUUM AND NOTE VOLTAGE CHANGE. SUBTRACT SECOND READING FROM THE FIRST. VOLTAGE VALUE SHOULD BE GREATER THAN 1.5 VOLTS. IS IT?

YES   **NO**

3 NO TROUBLE FOUND. CHECK SENSOR VACUUM SOURCE FOR LEAKAGE OR RESTRICTION. BE SURE THIS SOURCE SUPPLIES VACUUM TO MAP SENSOR ONLY.

4 CHECK SENSOR CONNECTION. IF OK, REPLACE SENSOR.

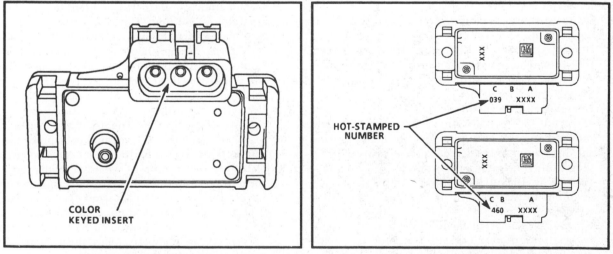

COLOR KEYED INSERT

HOT-STAMPED NUMBER

C B A
039 XXXX

C B A
460 XXXX

Figure 1 - Color Key Insert

Figure 2 - Hot-Stamped Number

"AFTER REPAIRS," CONFIRM "CLOSED LOOP" OPERATION AND NO "SERVICE ENGINE SOON" LIGHT.

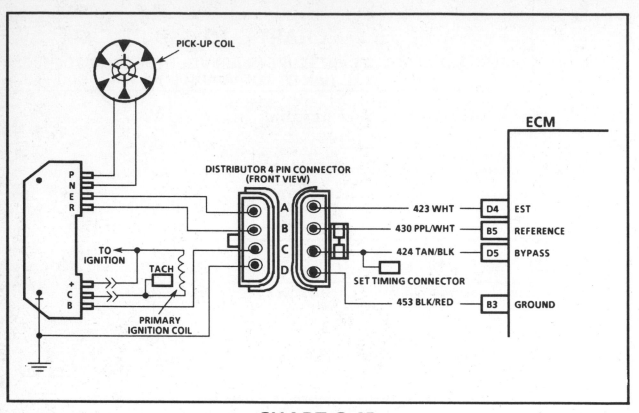

CHART C-4B

IGNITION SYSTEM CHECK
(REMOTE COIL/SEALED MODULE CONNECTOR DISTRIBUTOR)
3.1L (VIN D) "U" APV (TBI)

Test Description: Number(s) below refer to circled number(s) on the diagnostic chart.

1. Two wires are checked, to ensure that an open is not present in a spark plug wire.

1A. If spark occurs with EST connector disconnected, pick-up coil output is too low for EST operation.

2. A spark indicates the problem must be the distributor cap or rotor.

3. Normally, there should be battery voltage at the "C" and "+" terminals. Low voltage would indicate an open or a high resistance circuit from the distributor to the coil or ignition switch. If "C" terminal voltage was low, but "+" terminal voltage is 10 volts or more, circuit from "C" terminal to ignition coil or ignition coil primary winding is open.

4. Checks for a shorted module or grounded circuit from the ignition coil to the module. The distributor module should be turned "OFF," so normal voltage should be about 12 volts.
If the module is turned "ON," the voltage would be low, but above 1 volt. This could cause the ignition coil to fail from excessive heat.
With an open ignition coil primary winding, a

small amount of voltage will leak through the module from the "Batt" to the "tach" terminal.

5. Applying a voltage (1.5 to 8 volts) to module terminal "P" should turn the module "ON" and the tach. term. voltage should drop to about 7-9 volts. This test will determine whether the module or coil is faulty or if the pick-up coil is not generating the proper signal to turn the module "ON." This test can be performed by using a DC battery with a rating of 1.5 to 8 volts. The use of the test light is mainly to allow the "P" terminal to be probed more easily. Some digital multi-meters can also be used to trigger the module by selecting ohms, usually the diode position. In this position the meter may have a voltage across it's terminals which can be used to trigger the module. The voltage in the ohm's position can be checked by using a second meter or by checking the manufacturer's specification of the tool being used.

6. This should turn "OFF" the module and cause a spark. If no spark occurs, the fault is most likely in the ignition coil because most module problems would have been found before this point in theprocedure. A module tester could determine which is at fault.

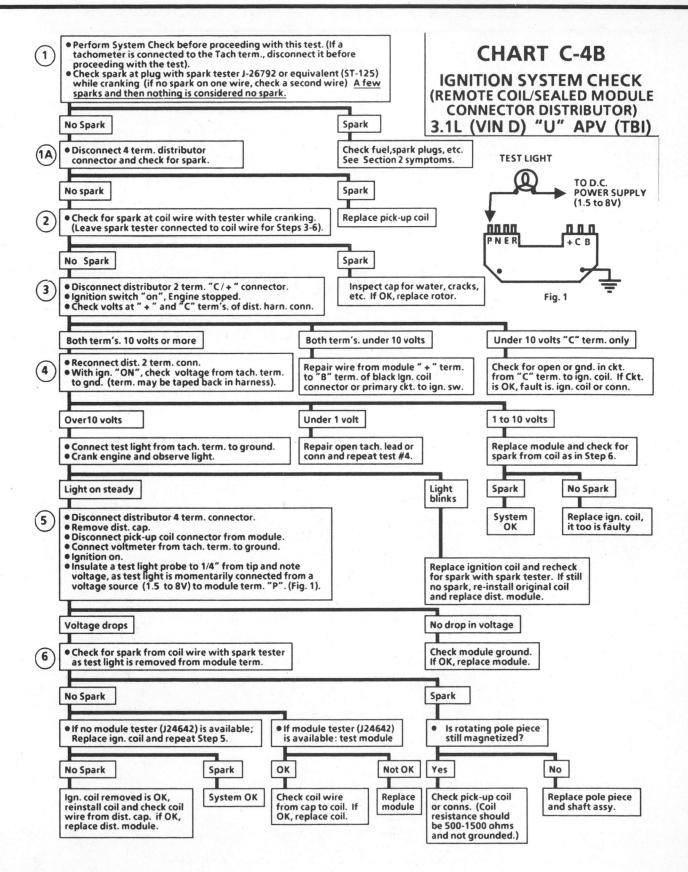

CHART C-4B

IGNITION SYSTEM CHECK
(REMOTE COIL/SEALED MODULE
CONNECTOR DISTRIBUTOR)
3.1L (VIN D) "U" APV (TBI)

(1)
- Perform System Check before proceeding with this test. (If a tachometer is connected to the Tach term., disconnect it before proceeding with the test).
- Check spark at plug with spark tester J-26792 or equivalent (ST-125) while cranking (if no spark on one wire, check a second wire) A few sparks and then nothing is considered no spark.

| No Spark | | Spark |

(1A)
- Disconnect 4 term. distributor connector and check for spark.

Check fuel, spark plugs, etc. See Section 2 symptoms.

TEST LIGHT

TO D.C. POWER SUPPLY (1.5 to 8V)

P N E R   + C B

Fig. 1

| No spark | | Spark |

(2)
- Check for spark at coil wire with tester while cranking. (Leave spark tester connected to coil wire for Steps 3-6).

Replace pick-up coil

| No Spark | | Spark |

(3)
- Disconnect distributor 2 term. "C / + " connector.
- Ignition switch "on", Engine stopped.
- Check volts at " + " and "C" term's. of dist. harn. conn.

Inspect cap for water, cracks, etc. If OK, replace rotor.

| Both term's. 10 volts or more | Both term's. under 10 volts | Under 10 volts "C" term. only |

(4)
- Reconnect dist. 2 term. conn.
- With ign. "ON", check voltage from tach. term. to gnd. (term. may be taped back in harness).

Repair wire from module " + " term. to "B" term. of black Ign. coil connector or primary ckt. to ign. sw.

Check for open or gnd. in ckt. from "C" term. to ign. coil. If Ckt. is OK, fault is. ign. coil or conn.

| Over 10 volts | Under 1 volt | 1 to 10 volts |

- Connect test light from tach. term. to ground.
- Crank engine and observe light.

Repair open tach. lead or conn and repeat test #4.

Replace module and check for spark from coil as in Step 6.

| Light on steady | | Light blinks | | Spark | No Spark |

(5)
- Disconnect distributor 4 term. connector.
- Remove dist. cap.
- Disconnect pick-up coil connector from module.
- Connect voltmeter from tach. term. to ground.
- Ignition on.
- Insulate a test light probe to 1/4" from tip and note voltage, as test light is momentarily connected from a voltage source (1.5 to 8V) to module term. "P". (Fig. 1).

System OK

Replace ign. coil, it too is faulty

Replace ignition coil and recheck for spark with spark tester. If still no spark, re-install original coil and replace dist. module.

| Voltage drops | | No drop in voltage |

(6)
- Check for spark from coil wire with spark tester as test light is removed from module term.

Check module ground. If OK, replace module.

| No Spark | | Spark |

- If no module tester (J24642) is available; Replace ign. coil and repeat Step 5.

- If module tester (J24642) is available: test module

- Is rotating pole piece still magnetized?

| No Spark | Spark | OK | Not OK | Yes | No |

Ign. coil removed is OK, reinstall coil and check coil wire from dist. cap. if OK, replace dist. module.

System OK

Check coil wire from cap to coil. If OK, replace coil.

Replace module

Check pick-up coil or conns. (Coil resistance should be 500-1500 ohms and not grounded.)

Replace pole piece and shaft assy.

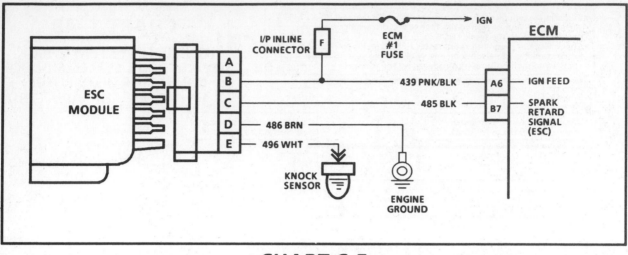

CHART C-5

ELECTRONIC SPARK CONTROL (ESC) SYSTEM CHECK
(ENGINE KNOCK, POOR PERFORMANCE, OR POOR ECONOMY)
3.1L (VIN D) "U" APV (TBI)

Circuit Description:

Electronic Spark Control (ESC) is accomplished with a module that sends a voltage signal to the ECM. As the knock sensor detects engine knock, the voltage from the ESC module to the ECM is reduced and this signals the ECM to retard timing, if engine rpm is over about 1500 or vehicle speed is greater than 10 mph.

Test Description: Number(s) below refer to circled number(s) on the diagnostic chart.

1. If a Code 43 is not set, but a knock signal is indicated while running above 1500 rpm, listen for an internal engine noise. Under a no load condition, there should not be any detonation, and if knock is indicated, an internal engine problem may exist.

2. Usually a knock signal can be generated by tapping on the right exhaust manifold. This test can also be performed at idle. Test number 1 was run above 1500 rpm, to determine if a constant knock signal was present, which would affect engine performance.

3. This tests whether the knock signal is due to the sensor, a basic engine problem, or the ESC module.

4. If the module ground circuit is faulty, the ESC module will not function correctly. The test light should light indicating the ground circuit is OK.

5. Contacting CKT 496, with a test light to 12 volts, should generate a knock signal to determine whether the knock sensor is faulty, or the ESC module can't recognize a knock signal.

CHART C-5

ELECTRONIC SPARK CONTROL (ESC) SYSTEM CHECK
(ENGINE KNOCK, POOR PERFORMANCE, OR POOR ECONOMY)
3.1L (VIN D) "U" APV (TBI)

THIS CHART SHOULD BE USED AFTER ALL OTHER CAUSES OF SPARK KNOCK HAVE BEEN CHECKED. I.E., TIMING, EGR, ENGINE TEMPERATURE OR EXCESSIVE ENGINE NOISE, ETC. IF CODE 43 IS SET, USE THAT CHART FIRST.

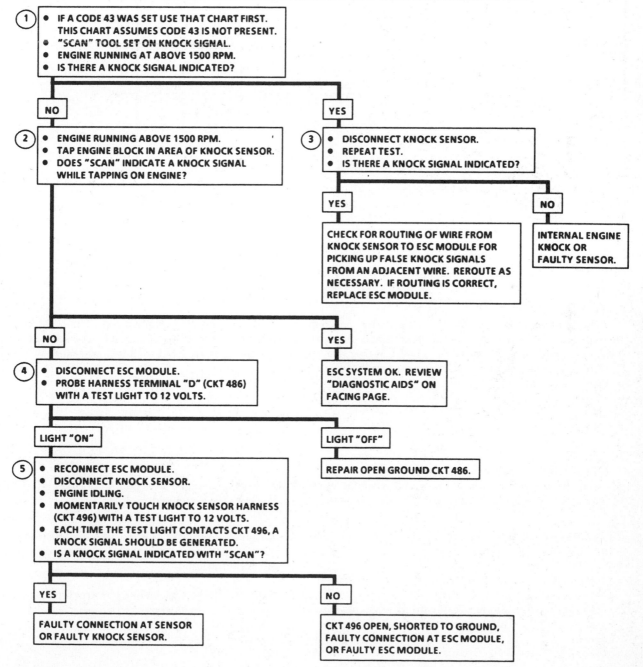

1
- IF A CODE 43 WAS SET USE THAT CHART FIRST. THIS CHART ASSUMES CODE 43 IS NOT PRESENT.
- "SCAN" TOOL SET ON KNOCK SIGNAL.
- ENGINE RUNNING AT ABOVE 1500 RPM.
- IS THERE A KNOCK SIGNAL INDICATED?

NO

2
- ENGINE RUNNING ABOVE 1500 RPM.
- TAP ENGINE BLOCK IN AREA OF KNOCK SENSOR.
- DOES "SCAN" INDICATE A KNOCK SIGNAL WHILE TAPPING ON ENGINE?

YES

3
- DISCONNECT KNOCK SENSOR.
- REPEAT TEST.
- IS THERE A KNOCK SIGNAL INDICATED?

YES

CHECK FOR ROUTING OF WIRE FROM KNOCK SENSOR TO ESC MODULE FOR PICKING UP FALSE KNOCK SIGNALS FROM AN ADJACENT WIRE. REROUTE AS NECESSARY. IF ROUTING IS CORRECT, REPLACE ESC MODULE.

NO

INTERNAL ENGINE KNOCK OR FAULTY SENSOR.

NO

4
- DISCONNECT ESC MODULE.
- PROBE HARNESS TERMINAL "D" (CKT 486) WITH A TEST LIGHT TO 12 VOLTS.

YES

ESC SYSTEM OK. REVIEW "DIAGNOSTIC AIDS" ON FACING PAGE.

LIGHT "ON"

5
- RECONNECT ESC MODULE.
- DISCONNECT KNOCK SENSOR.
- ENGINE IDLING.
- MOMENTARILY TOUCH KNOCK SENSOR HARNESS (CKT 496) WITH A TEST LIGHT TO 12 VOLTS.
- EACH TIME THE TEST LIGHT CONTACTS CKT 496, A KNOCK SIGNAL SHOULD BE GENERATED.
- IS A KNOCK SIGNAL INDICATED WITH "SCAN"?

LIGHT "OFF"

REPAIR OPEN GROUND CKT 486.

YES

FAULTY CONNECTION AT SENSOR OR FAULTY KNOCK SENSOR.

NO

CKT 496 OPEN, SHORTED TO GROUND, FAULTY CONNECTION AT ESC MODULE, OR FAULTY ESC MODULE.

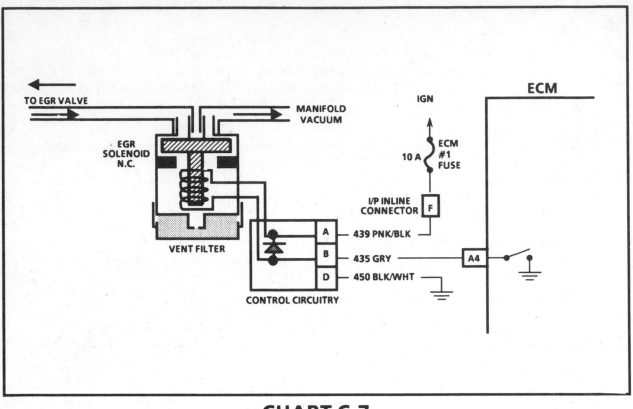

CHART C-7
EGR SYSTEM CHECK
3.1L (VIN D) "U" APV (TBI)

Circuit Description:

The EGR valve is controlled by a normally open regulator with a normally open air bleed. The ECM signals the regulator to control the amount of air bleed. As more air is allowed to bleed, less vacuum can be applied to the EGR valve, resulting in less EGR. The ECM diagnoses the system using an internal EGR test procedure.

The ECM control, of the EGR, is based on the following inputs:

- Engine coolant temperature.
- TPS - "OFF" idle.
- MAP.
- BARO.
- TCC.
- Engine rpm.

If Code 24 is stored, use that chart first.

Code 32 will detect a faulty solenoid, vacuum supply, EGR valve or plugged passage. This chart checks for plugged EGR passages, a sticking EGR valve, or a stuck open or inoperative solenoid.

Test Description: Number(s) below refer to circled number(s) on the diagnostic chart.

1. With the ignition "ON," engine stopped, the solenoid should not be energized and vacuum should not pass to the EGR valve.
2. Grounding the diagnostic terminal will energize the solenoid and allow vacuum to pass to valve.

3. Checks for plugged EGR passages. If passages are plugged, the engine may have severe detonation on acceleration.

NOTE: Vehicle speed must be greater than 2 mph for California vehicles.

CHART C-7
EGR SYSTEM CHECK
3.1L (VIN D) "U" APV (TBI)

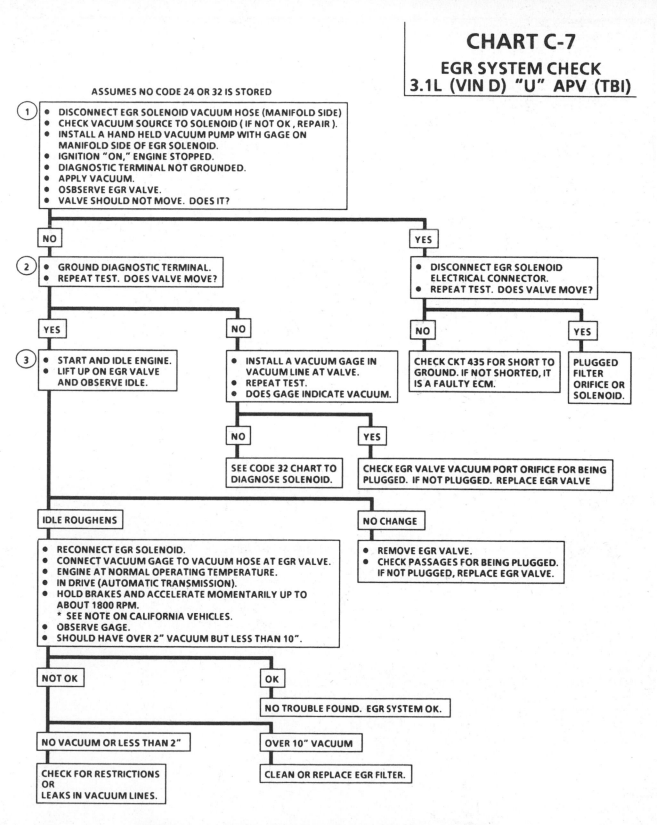

ASSUMES NO CODE 24 OR 32 IS STORED

1
- DISCONNECT EGR SOLENOID VACUUM HOSE (MANIFOLD SIDE)
- CHECK VACUUM SOURCE TO SOLENOID (IF NOT OK , REPAIR).
- INSTALL A HAND HELD VACUUM PUMP WITH GAGE ON MANIFOLD SIDE OF EGR SOLENOID.
- IGNITION "ON," ENGINE STOPPED.
- DIAGNOSTIC TERMINAL NOT GROUNDED.
- APPLY VACUUM.
- OSBSERVE EGR VALVE.
- VALVE SHOULD NOT MOVE. DOES IT?

NO

YES

2
- GROUND DIAGNOSTIC TERMINAL.
- REPEAT TEST. DOES VALVE MOVE?

- DISCONNECT EGR SOLENOID ELECTRICAL CONNECTOR.
- REPEAT TEST. DOES VALVE MOVE?

YES **NO** **NO** **YES**

3
- START AND IDLE ENGINE.
- LIFT UP ON EGR VALVE AND OBSERVE IDLE.

- INSTALL A VACUUM GAGE IN VACUUM LINE AT VALVE.
- REPEAT TEST.
- DOES GAGE INDICATE VACUUM.

CHECK CKT 435 FOR SHORT TO GROUND. IF NOT SHORTED, IT IS A FAULTY ECM.

PLUGGED FILTER ORIFICE OR SOLENOID.

NO **YES**

SEE CODE 32 CHART TO DIAGNOSE SOLENOID.

CHECK EGR VALVE VACUUM PORT ORIFICE FOR BEING PLUGGED. IF NOT PLUGGED. REPLACE EGR VALVE

IDLE ROUGHENS

NO CHANGE

- RECONNECT EGR SOLENOID.
- CONNECT VACUUM GAGE TO VACUUM HOSE AT EGR VALVE.
- ENGINE AT NORMAL OPERATING TEMPERATURE.
- IN DRIVE (AUTOMATIC TRANSMISSION).
- HOLD BRAKES AND ACCELERATE MOMENTARILY UP TO ABOUT 1800 RPM.
  * SEE NOTE ON CALIFORNIA VEHICLES.
- OBSERVE GAGE.
- SHOULD HAVE OVER 2" VACUUM BUT LESS THAN 10".

- REMOVE EGR VALVE.
- CHECK PASSAGES FOR BEING PLUGGED. IF NOT PLUGGED, REPLACE EGR VALVE.

NOT OK

OK

NO TROUBLE FOUND. EGR SYSTEM OK.

NO VACUUM OR LESS THAN 2"

OVER 10" VACUUM

CHECK FOR RESTRICTIONS OR LEAKS IN VACUUM LINES.

CLEAN OR REPLACE EGR FILTER.

CONFIRM "CLOSED LOOP" OPERATION AND NO "SERVICE ENGINE SOON" LIGHT.

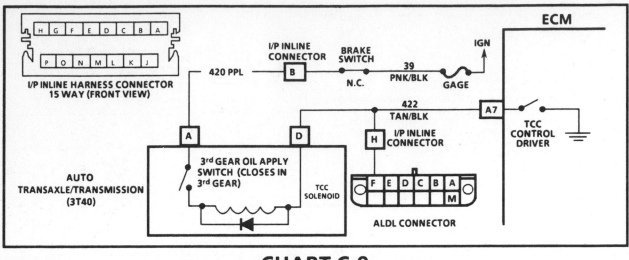

CHART C-8

TORQUE CONVERTER CLUTCH (TCC) - 3T40
(ELECTRICAL DIAGNOSIS)
3.1L (VIN D) "U" APV (TBI)

Circuit Description:

The purpose of the Torque Converter Clutch (TCC) feature is to eliminate the power loss of the torque converter stage when the vehicle is in a cruise condition. This allows for the convenience of the automatic transaxle and the fuel economy of a manual transaxle. The TCC can remain engaged as low as 23 mph.

Fused battery ignition is supplied to the TCC solenoid through the brake switch, and the third gear apply switch. The ECM will engage TCC by grounding CKT 422 to energize the solenoid.

TCC will engage when

● Engine warmed up.
● Vehicle speed above a calibrated value (about 32 mph 51 km/h).
● Throttle Position Sensor (TPS) output not changing, indicating a steady road speed.
● Third gear switch closed.
● Brake switch closed.

Test Description: Number(s) below refer to circled number(s) on the diagnostic chart.

1. Light "OFF" confirms the third gear apply switch is open.
2. At 25 mph the transaxle/transmission third gear apply switch should close. Test light will come "ON" and confirm battery supply and closed brake switch.
3. Grounding the diagnostic terminal with ignition "ON," engine "OFF," should energize the TCC solenoid by grounding CKT 422. This test checks the ability of the ECM to supply a ground to the TCC solenoid. The test light connected from 12 volts to ALDL terminal "F" will turn "ON," as CKT 422 is grounded.

Diagnostic Aids:

A "Scan" tool only indicates when the ECM has turned "ON" the TCC driver, and this does not confirm that the TCC has engaged. To determine if TCC is functioning properly, engine rpm should decrease when the "Scan" tool indicates the TCC driver has turned "ON."

CHART C-8A
TORQUE CONVERTER CLUTCH (TCC) - 3T40 (ELECTRICAL DIAGNOSIS) 3.1L (VIN D) "U" APV (TBI)

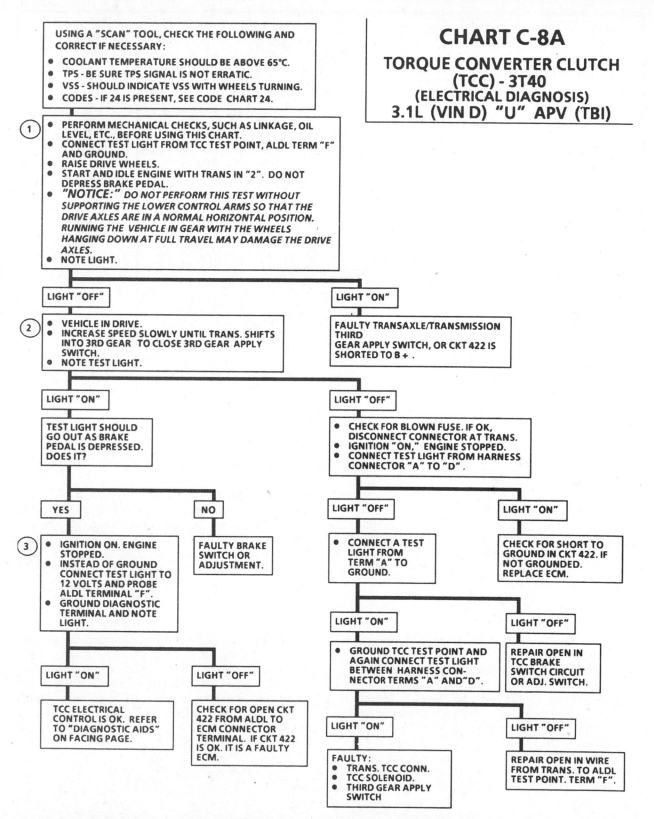

USING A "SCAN" TOOL, CHECK THE FOLLOWING AND CORRECT IF NECESSARY:
- COOLANT TEMPERATURE SHOULD BE ABOVE 65°C.
- TPS - BE SURE TPS SIGNAL IS NOT ERRATIC.
- VSS - SHOULD INDICATE VSS WITH WHEELS TURNING.
- CODES - IF 24 IS PRESENT, SEE CODE CHART 24.

1
- PERFORM MECHANICAL CHECKS, SUCH AS LINKAGE, OIL LEVEL, ETC., BEFORE USING THIS CHART.
- CONNECT TEST LIGHT FROM TCC TEST POINT, ALDL TERM "F" AND GROUND.
- RAISE DRIVE WHEELS.
- START AND IDLE ENGINE WITH TRANS IN "2". DO NOT DEPRESS BRAKE PEDAL.
- *"NOTICE:" DO NOT PERFORM THIS TEST WITHOUT SUPPORTING THE LOWER CONTROL ARMS SO THAT THE DRIVE AXLES ARE IN A NORMAL HORIZONTAL POSITION. RUNNING THE VEHICLE IN GEAR WITH THE WHEELS HANGING DOWN AT FULL TRAVEL MAY DAMAGE THE DRIVE AXLES.*
- NOTE LIGHT.

LIGHT "OFF"

LIGHT "ON"

FAULTY TRANSAXLE/TRANSMISSION THIRD GEAR APPLY SWITCH, OR CKT 422 IS SHORTED TO B + .

2
- VEHICLE IN DRIVE.
- INCREASE SPEED SLOWLY UNTIL TRANS. SHIFTS INTO 3RD GEAR TO CLOSE 3RD GEAR APPLY SWITCH.
- NOTE TEST LIGHT.

LIGHT "ON"

LIGHT "OFF"

TEST LIGHT SHOULD GO OUT AS BRAKE PEDAL IS DEPRESSED. DOES IT?

- CHECK FOR BLOWN FUSE. IF OK, DISCONNECT CONNECTOR AT TRANS.
- IGNITION "ON," ENGINE STOPPED.
- CONNECT TEST LIGHT FROM HARNESS CONNECTOR "A" TO "D" .

YES

NO

FAULTY BRAKE SWITCH OR ADJUSTMENT.

LIGHT "OFF"

LIGHT "ON"

3
- IGNITION ON. ENGINE STOPPED.
- INSTEAD OF GROUND CONNECT TEST LIGHT TO 12 VOLTS AND PROBE ALDL TERMINAL "F".
- GROUND DIAGNOSTIC TERMINAL AND NOTE LIGHT.

- CONNECT A TEST LIGHT FROM TERM "A" TO GROUND.

CHECK FOR SHORT TO GROUND IN CKT 422. IF NOT GROUNDED. REPLACE ECM.

LIGHT "ON"

LIGHT "OFF"

TCC ELECTRICAL CONTROL IS OK. REFER TO "DIAGNOSTIC AIDS" ON FACING PAGE.

CHECK FOR OPEN CKT 422 FROM ALDL TO ECM CONNECTOR TERMINAL. IF CKT 422 IS OK. IT IS A FAULTY ECM.

LIGHT "ON"

LIGHT "OFF"

- GROUND TCC TEST POINT AND AGAIN CONNECT TEST LIGHT BETWEEN HARNESS CONNECTOR TERMS "A" AND"D".

REPAIR OPEN IN TCC BRAKE SWITCH CIRCUIT OR ADJ. SWITCH.

LIGHT "ON"

LIGHT "OFF"

FAULTY:
- TRANS. TCC CONN.
- TCC SOLENOID.
- THIRD GEAR APPLY SWITCH

REPAIR OPEN IN WIRE FROM TRANS. TO ALDL TEST POINT. TERM "F".

CLEAR CODES AND CONFIRM "CLOSED LOOP" OPERATION AND NO "SERVICE ENGINE SOON" LIGHT.

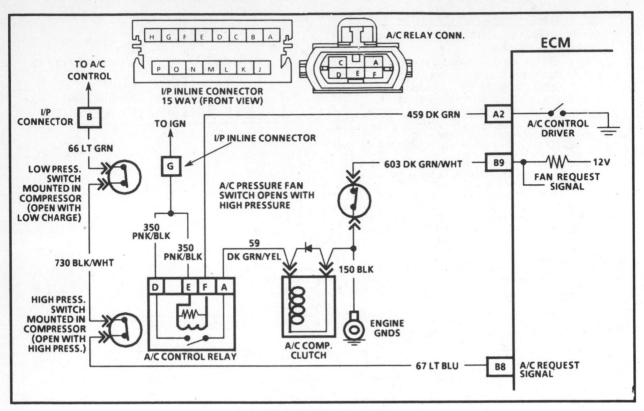

CHART C-10

A/C CLUTCH CONTROL CIRCUIT DIAGNOSIS
3.1L (VIN D) "U" APV (TBI)

Circuit Description:

The A/C clutch control relay is ECM controlled to delay A/C clutch engagement about 8 seconds after A/C is turned "ON." This allows the IAC to adjust engine rpm, before the A/C clutch engages. The ECM, also, causes the relay to disengage the A/C clutch during Wide Open Throttle (WOT), or if engine is overheating. The A/C clutch control relay is energized, when the ECM provides a ground path for CKT 459. The low pressure switch will open if A/C pressure is less than 40 psi (276 kPa). The high pressure switch will open, if A/C pressure exceeds about 440 psi (3034 kPa). The A/C pressure fan switch opens to turn the fan "ON," when A/C pressure exceeds about 200 psi (1380 kPa).

Test Description: Number(s) below refer to circled number(s) on the diagnostic chart.

1. The ECM will only energize the A/C relay, when the engine is running. This test will determine if the relay or CKT 459 is faulty.
2. In order for the clutch to properly be engaged, the low pressure switch must be closed to provide 12 volts to the relay, and the high pressure switch must be closed, so the A/C request (12 volts) will be present at the ECM.
3. Determines if the signal is reaching the ECM on CKT 67 from the A/C control panel. Signal should only be present when the A/C mode or defrost mode has been selected.
4. With the engine idling and A/C "ON," the ECM should be grounding CKT 459, which should cause the test light to be "ON."

Diagnostic Aids:

If complaint was insufficient cooling, the problem may be caused by a inoperative cooling fan, or A/C pressure fan switch. The engine cooling fan should turn "ON," when A/C pressure exceeds a value to open the switch, which causes the ECM to energize the cooling fan relay. See CHART C-12, for cooling fan diagnosis. If fan operates correctly, see HEATING AND AIR CONDITIONING

CHART C-10
A/C CLUTCH CONTROL CIRCUIT DIAGNOSIS
3.1L (VIN D) "U" APV (TBI)

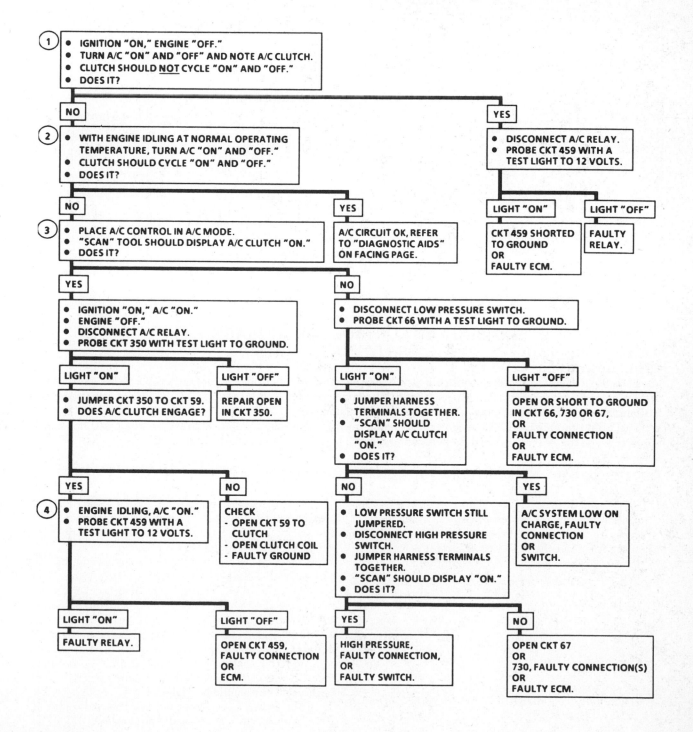

1
- IGNITION "ON," ENGINE "OFF."
- TURN A/C "ON" AND "OFF" AND NOTE A/C CLUTCH.
- CLUTCH SHOULD <u>NOT</u> CYCLE "ON" AND "OFF."
- DOES IT?

NO

YES

- DISCONNECT A/C RELAY.
- PROBE CKT 459 WITH A TEST LIGHT TO 12 VOLTS.

2
- WITH ENGINE IDLING AT NORMAL OPERATING TEMPERATURE, TURN A/C "ON" AND "OFF."
- CLUTCH SHOULD CYCLE "ON" AND "OFF."
- DOES IT?

LIGHT "ON"

CKT 459 SHORTED TO GROUND
OR
FAULTY ECM.

LIGHT "OFF"

FAULTY RELAY.

NO

YES

A/C CIRCUIT OK, REFER TO "DIAGNOSTIC AIDS" ON FACING PAGE.

3
- PLACE A/C CONTROL IN A/C MODE.
- "SCAN" TOOL SHOULD DISPLAY A/C CLUTCH "ON."
- DOES IT?

YES

NO

- IGNITION "ON," A/C "ON."
- ENGINE "OFF."
- DISCONNECT A/C RELAY.
- PROBE CKT 350 WITH TEST LIGHT TO GROUND.

- DISCONNECT LOW PRESSURE SWITCH.
- PROBE CKT 66 WITH A TEST LIGHT TO GROUND.

LIGHT "ON"

- JUMPER CKT 350 TO CKT 59.
- DOES A/C CLUTCH ENGAGE?

LIGHT "OFF"

REPAIR OPEN IN CKT 350.

LIGHT "ON"

- JUMPER HARNESS TERMINALS TOGETHER.
- "SCAN" SHOULD DISPLAY A/C CLUTCH "ON."
- DOES IT?

LIGHT "OFF"

OPEN OR SHORT TO GROUND IN CKT 66, 730 OR 67,
OR
FAULTY CONNECTION
OR
FAULTY ECM.

YES

4
- ENGINE IDLING, A/C "ON."
- PROBE CKT 459 WITH A TEST LIGHT TO 12 VOLTS.

NO

CHECK
- OPEN CKT 59 TO CLUTCH
- OPEN CLUTCH COIL
- FAULTY GROUND

NO

- LOW PRESSURE SWITCH STILL JUMPERED.
- DISCONNECT HIGH PRESSURE SWITCH.
- JUMPER HARNESS TERMINALS TOGETHER.
- "SCAN" SHOULD DISPLAY "ON."
- DOES IT?

YES

A/C SYSTEM LOW ON CHARGE, FAULTY CONNECTION
OR
SWITCH.

LIGHT "ON"

FAULTY RELAY.

LIGHT "OFF"

OPEN CKT 459, FAULTY CONNECTION
OR
ECM.

YES

HIGH PRESSURE, FAULTY CONNECTION,
OR
FAULTY SWITCH.

NO

OPEN CKT 67
OR
730, FAULTY CONNECTION(S)
OR
FAULTY ECM.

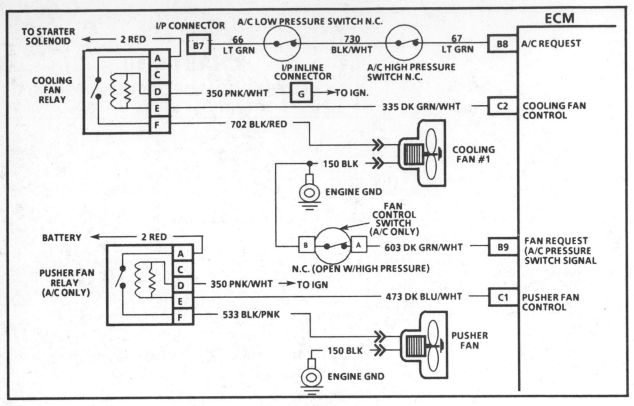

CHART C-12

(Page 1 of 2)
COOLANT FAN CONTROL CIRCUIT DIAGNOSIS
3.1L (VIN D) "U" APV (TBI)

Circuit Description:

The electric cooling fan is controlled by the ECM, based on inputs from the coolant temperature sensor, the A/C fan control switch, and vehicle speed. The ECM controls the fan by grounding CKT 335, which energizes the fan control relay. Battery voltage is then supplied to the fan motor.

The ECM grounds CKT 335, when coolant temperature is over about 106°C (223°F), or when A/C has been requested, and the fan control switch opens with high A/C pressure, about 200 psi (1380 kPa).

Test Description: Number(s) below refer to circled number(s) on the diagnostic chart.

1. With the diagnostic terminal grounded, the cooling fan control driver will close, which should energize the fan control relay.
2. If the A/C fan control switch or circuit is open, the fan would run whenever A/C is requested.
3. With A/C clutch engaged, the A/C fan control switch should open, when A/C high pressure exceeds about 1380 kPa (200 psi). This signal should cause the ECM to energize the fan control relay.

Diagnostic Aids:

If the owner complained of an overheating problem, it must be determined if the complaint was due to an actual boil over, or the hot light, or temperature gage indicated over heating.

If the gage, or light, indicates overheating, but no boil over is detected, the gage circuit should be checked. The gage accuracy can also be checked by comparing the coolant sensor reading using a "Scan" tool and comparing its reading with the gage reading.

If the engine is actually overheating, and the gage indicates overheating, but the cooling fan is not coming "ON," and the "Scan" indicates normal readings, the coolant sensor has probably shifted out of calibration and should be replaced.

If the engine is overheating, and the cooling fan is "ON," the cooling system should be checked.

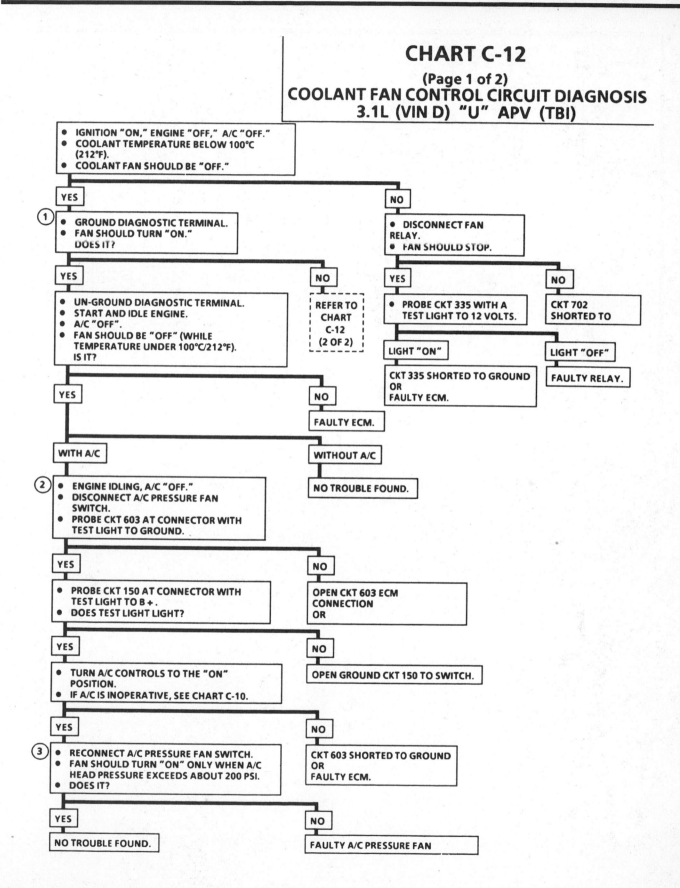

CHART C-12
(Page 1 of 2)
COOLANT FAN CONTROL CIRCUIT DIAGNOSIS
3.1L (VIN D) "U" APV (TBI)

- IGNITION "ON," ENGINE "OFF," A/C "OFF."
- COOLANT TEMPERATURE BELOW 100°C (212°F).
- COOLANT FAN SHOULD BE "OFF."

YES

①
- GROUND DIAGNOSTIC TERMINAL.
- FAN SHOULD TURN "ON." DOES IT?

YES
- UN-GROUND DIAGNOSTIC TERMINAL.
- START AND IDLE ENGINE.
- A/C "OFF".
- FAN SHOULD BE "OFF" (WHILE TEMPERATURE UNDER 100°C/212°F). IS IT?

YES

WITH A/C

②
- ENGINE IDLING, A/C "OFF."
- DISCONNECT A/C PRESSURE FAN SWITCH.
- PROBE CKT 603 AT CONNECTOR WITH TEST LIGHT TO GROUND.

YES
- PROBE CKT 150 AT CONNECTOR WITH TEST LIGHT TO B +.
- DOES TEST LIGHT LIGHT?

YES
- TURN A/C CONTROLS TO THE "ON" POSITION.
- IF A/C IS INOPERATIVE, SEE CHART C-10.

YES

③
- RECONNECT A/C PRESSURE FAN SWITCH.
- FAN SHOULD TURN "ON" ONLY WHEN A/C HEAD PRESSURE EXCEEDS ABOUT 200 PSI.
- DOES IT?

YES

NO TROUBLE FOUND.

NO (from branch under ① GROUND DIAGNOSTIC)
REFER TO CHART C-12 (2 OF 2)

NO (under UN-GROUND)
FAULTY ECM.

WITHOUT A/C
NO TROUBLE FOUND.

NO (under ②)
OPEN CKT 603 ECM CONNECTION OR

NO
OPEN GROUND CKT 150 TO SWITCH.

NO
CKT 603 SHORTED TO GROUND OR FAULTY ECM.

NO
FAULTY A/C PRESSURE FAN

NO (top right)
- DISCONNECT FAN RELAY.
- FAN SHOULD STOP.

YES
- PROBE CKT 335 WITH A TEST LIGHT TO 12 VOLTS.

LIGHT "ON"
CKT 335 SHORTED TO GROUND OR FAULTY ECM.

NO
CKT 702 SHORTED TO

LIGHT "OFF"
FAULTY RELAY.

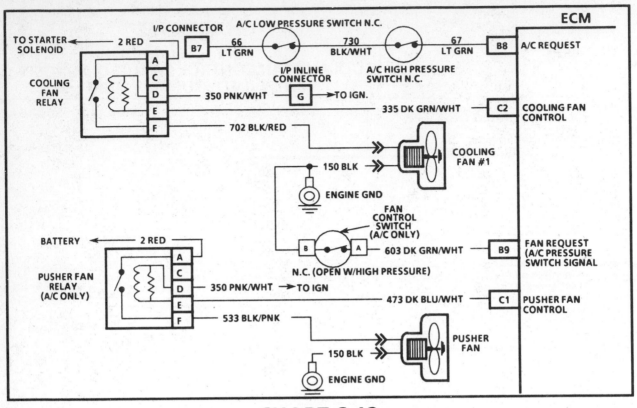

CHART C-12

(Page 2 of 2)
COOLANT FAN CONTROL CIRCUIT DIAGNOSIS
3.1L (VIN D) "U" APV (TBI)

Test Description: Number(s) below refer to circled number(s) on the diagnostic chart.

1. 12 volts should be available to both terminals "A" & "D", when the ignition is "ON."
2. This test checks the ability of the ECM to ground CKT 335. The "Service Engine Soon" light should also be flashing at this point. If it isn't flashing, see CHART A-2.

3. If the fan does not turn "ON" at this point, CKT 702 or CKT 150 is open, or the cooling fan motor is faulty.

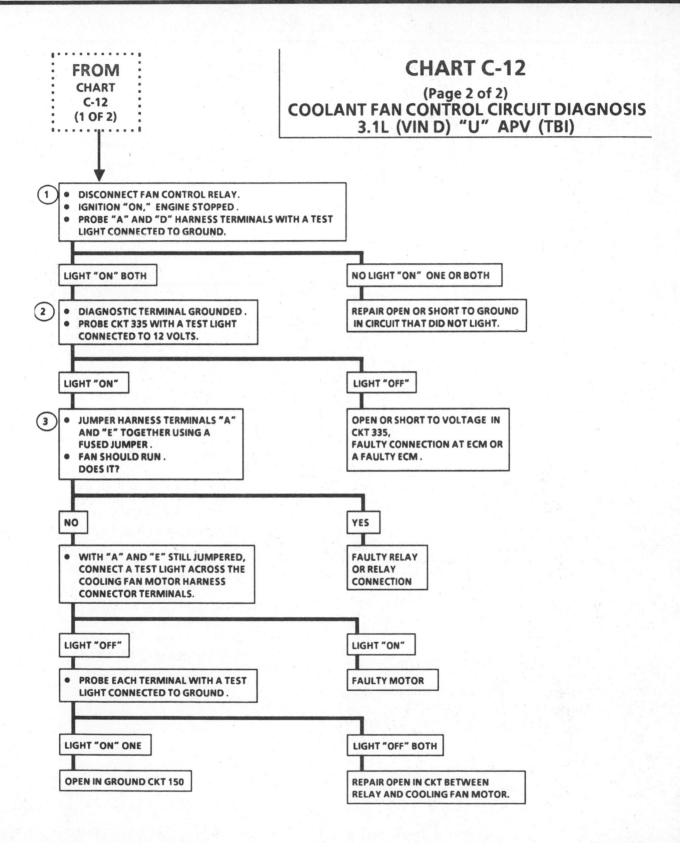

FROM
CHART
C-12
(1 OF 2)

CHART C-12
(Page 2 of 2)
COOLANT FAN CONTROL CIRCUIT DIAGNOSIS
3.1L (VIN D) "U" APV (TBI)

1
- DISCONNECT FAN CONTROL RELAY.
- IGNITION "ON," ENGINE STOPPED.
- PROBE "A" AND "D" HARNESS TERMINALS WITH A TEST LIGHT CONNECTED TO GROUND.

LIGHT "ON" BOTH

NO LIGHT "ON" ONE OR BOTH

2
- DIAGNOSTIC TERMINAL GROUNDED.
- PROBE CKT 335 WITH A TEST LIGHT CONNECTED TO 12 VOLTS.

REPAIR OPEN OR SHORT TO GROUND IN CIRCUIT THAT DID NOT LIGHT.

LIGHT "ON"

LIGHT "OFF"

3
- JUMPER HARNESS TERMINALS "A" AND "E" TOGETHER USING A FUSED JUMPER.
- FAN SHOULD RUN. DOES IT?

OPEN OR SHORT TO VOLTAGE IN CKT 335,
FAULTY CONNECTION AT ECM OR A FAULTY ECM.

NO

YES

- WITH "A" AND "E" STILL JUMPERED, CONNECT A TEST LIGHT ACROSS THE COOLING FAN MOTOR HARNESS CONNECTOR TERMINALS.

FAULTY RELAY OR RELAY CONNECTION

LIGHT "OFF"

LIGHT "ON"

- PROBE EACH TERMINAL WITH A TEST LIGHT CONNECTED TO GROUND.

FAULTY MOTOR

LIGHT "ON" ONE

LIGHT "OFF" BOTH

OPEN IN GROUND CKT 150

REPAIR OPEN IN CKT BETWEEN RELAY AND COOLING FAN MOTOR.

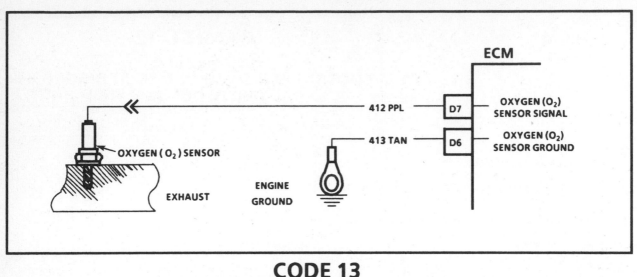

CODE 13
OXYGEN (O₂) SENSOR CIRCUIT
(OPEN CIRCUIT)
3.1L (VIN D) "U" APV (TBI)

Circuit Description:

The ECM supplies a voltage of about .45 volt between terminals "D7" and "D6". (If measured with a 10 megohm digital voltmeter, this may read as low as .32 volt.) The Oxygen (O₂) sensor varies the voltage within a range of about 1 volt if the exhaust is rich, down through about .01 volt if exhaust is lean.

The sensor is like an open circuit and produces no voltage when it is below 315°C (600°F). An open sensor circuit or cold sensor causes "Open Loop" operation.

Test Description: Number(s) below refer to circled number(s) on the diagnostic chart.
1. Code 13 will set:
   - No Code 21 or Code 22.
   - Coolant temperature above 70°C (158°F).
   - At least 2 minutes engine time after start.
   - Oxygen (O₂) signal voltage steady between .35 and .55 volt.
   - Throttle position sensor signal above 5% (about .3 volt above closed throttle voltage).
   - All conditions must be met for about 60 seconds.
     If the conditions for a Code 13 exist, the system will not go "Closed Loop."
2. This will determine if the sensor is at fault or the wiring or ECM is the cause of the Code 13.

3. In doing this test, use only a high impedance digital volt ohmmeter. This test checks the continuity of CKT 412 and CKT 413. If CKT 413 is open, the ECM voltage on CKT 412 will be over .6 volt (600 mV).

Diagnostic Aids:

Normal "Scan" voltage varies between 100 mV to 999 mV (.1 and 1.0 volt), while in "Closed Loop." Code 13 sets in one minute, if voltage remains between .35 and .55 volt, but the system will go "Open Loop" in about 15 seconds.

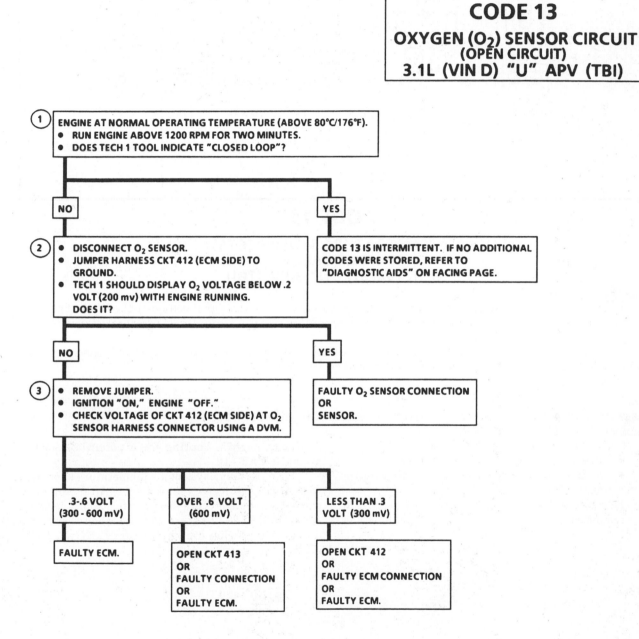

CODE 13
OXYGEN (O$_2$) SENSOR CIRCUIT
(OPEN CIRCUIT)
3.1L (VIN D) "U" APV (TBI)

1 ENGINE AT NORMAL OPERATING TEMPERATURE (ABOVE 80°C/176°F).
- RUN ENGINE ABOVE 1200 RPM FOR TWO MINUTES.
- DOES TECH 1 TOOL INDICATE "CLOSED LOOP"?

NO

YES

2
- DISCONNECT O$_2$ SENSOR.
- JUMPER HARNESS CKT 412 (ECM SIDE) TO GROUND.
- TECH 1 SHOULD DISPLAY O$_2$ VOLTAGE BELOW .2 VOLT (200 mv) WITH ENGINE RUNNING. DOES IT?

CODE 13 IS INTERMITTENT. IF NO ADDITIONAL CODES WERE STORED, REFER TO "DIAGNOSTIC AIDS" ON FACING PAGE.

NO

YES

3
- REMOVE JUMPER.
- IGNITION "ON," ENGINE "OFF."
- CHECK VOLTAGE OF CKT 412 (ECM SIDE) AT O$_2$ SENSOR HARNESS CONNECTOR USING A DVM.

FAULTY O$_2$ SENSOR CONNECTION
OR
SENSOR.

.3-.6 VOLT (300 - 600 mV)

OVER .6 VOLT (600 mV)

LESS THAN .3 VOLT (300 mV)

FAULTY ECM.

OPEN CKT 413
OR
FAULTY CONNECTION
OR
FAULTY ECM.

OPEN CKT 412
OR
FAULTY ECM CONNECTION
OR
FAULTY ECM.

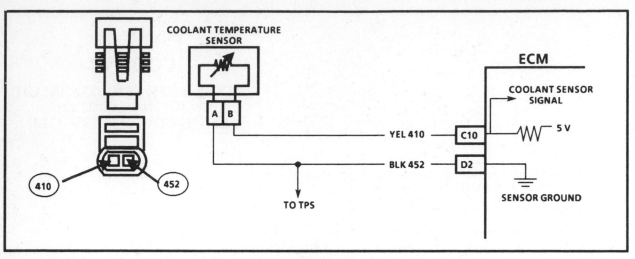

CODE 14

COOLANT TEMPERATURE SENSOR (CTS) CIRCUIT
(HIGH TEMPERATURE INDICATED)
3.1L (VIN D) "U" APV (TBI)

Circuit Description:

The Coolant Temperature Sensor (CTS) uses a thermistor to control the signal voltage to the ECM. The ECM applies a voltage on CKT 410 to the sensor. When the engine is cold the sensor (thermistor) resistance is high, therefore the ECM will see high signal voltage.

As the engine warms, the sensor resistance becomes less, and the voltage drops. At normal engine operating temperature 88 to 106°C (190 to 222°F) the voltage will measure about .5 to 1.1 volts.

Test Description: Number(s) below refer to circled number(s) on the diagnostic chart.

1. Code 14 will set if:
   - Engine running longer than 6 seconds.
   - Signal voltage indicates a coolant temperature above 135°C (275°F).
2. This test will determine if CKT 410 is shorted to ground which will cause the conditions for Code 14.

Diagnostic Aids:

Check harness routing for a potential short to ground in CKT 410.

"Scan" tool displays engine temperature in degrees centigrade and degrees fahrenheit. After engine is started, the temperature should rise steadily between 88-106°C (190-222°F) then stabilize when thermostat opens. The cooling fan should turn "ON" at 106°C (222°).

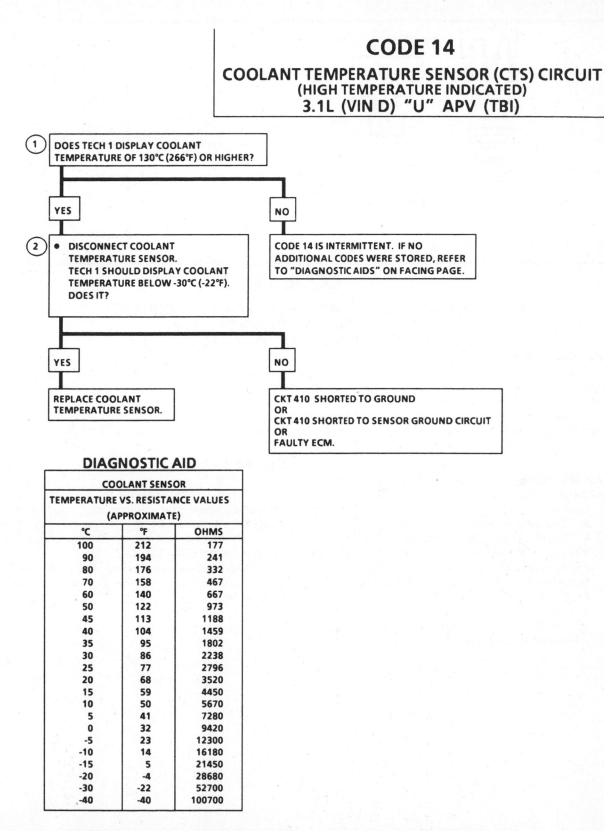

CODE 14
COOLANT TEMPERATURE SENSOR (CTS) CIRCUIT
(HIGH TEMPERATURE INDICATED)
3.1L (VIN D) "U" APV (TBI)

① DOES TECH 1 DISPLAY COOLANT TEMPERATURE OF 130°C (266°F) OR HIGHER?

YES

NO

② • DISCONNECT COOLANT TEMPERATURE SENSOR. TECH 1 SHOULD DISPLAY COOLANT TEMPERATURE BELOW -30°C (-22°F). DOES IT?

CODE 14 IS INTERMITTENT. IF NO ADDITIONAL CODES WERE STORED, REFER TO "DIAGNOSTIC AIDS" ON FACING PAGE.

YES

NO

REPLACE COOLANT TEMPERATURE SENSOR.

CKT 410 SHORTED TO GROUND
OR
CKT 410 SHORTED TO SENSOR GROUND CIRCUIT
OR
FAULTY ECM.

DIAGNOSTIC AID

COOLANT SENSOR		
TEMPERATURE VS. RESISTANCE VALUES		
(APPROXIMATE)		
°C	°F	OHMS
100	212	177
90	194	241
80	176	332
70	158	467
60	140	667
50	122	973
45	113	1188
40	104	1459
35	95	1802
30	86	2238
25	77	2796
20	68	3520
15	59	4450
10	50	5670
5	41	7280
0	32	9420
-5	23	12300
-10	14	16180
-15	5	21450
-20	-4	28680
-30	-22	52700
-40	-40	100700

"AFTER REPAIRS," REFER TO CODE CRITERIA ON FACING PAGE AND CONFIRM CODE DOES NOT RESET.

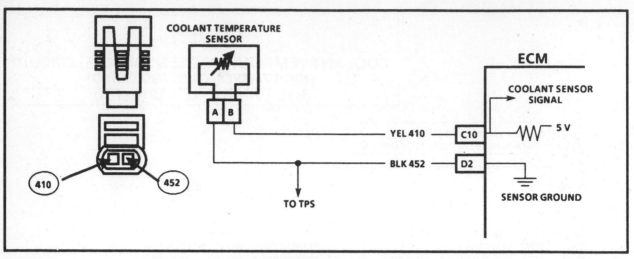

CODE 15
COOLANT TEMPERATURE SENSOR (CTS) CIRCUIT
(LOW TEMPERATURE INDICATED)
3.1L (VIN D) "U" APV (TBI)

Circuit Description:

The Coolant Temperature Sensor (CTS) uses a thermistor to control the signal voltage to the ECM. The ECM applies a voltage on CKT 410 to the sensor. When the engine is cold the sensor (thermistor) resistance is high, therefore the ECM will see high signal voltage.

As the engine warms, the sensor resistance becomes less, and the voltage drops. At normal engine operating temperature 88 to 106°C (190 to 222°F) the voltage will measure about .5 to 1.1 volts at the ECM.

Test Description: Number(s) below refer to circled number(s) on the diagnostic chart.
1. Code 15 will set if:
   - Engine running longer than 30 seconds.
   - Coolant temperature less than -33°C (-27°F).
2. This test simulates a Code 14. If the ECM recognizes the low signal voltage, (high temperature) and "Scan" reads 130°C or above, the ECM and wiring are OK.
3. This test will determine if CKT 410 is open. There should be 5 volts present at sensor connector if measured with a DVM.

Diagnostic Aids:

A "Scan" tool reads engine temperature in degrees centigrade and degrees fahrenheit. After engine is started the temperature should rise steadily between 88°C (106°F) then stabilize when thermostat opens. The fan will turn "ON" at 106°C (222°F).

If Code 21 is also set, check CKT 452 for faulty wiring or connections. Check terminals at sensor for good contact.

CODE 15
COOLANT TEMPERATURE SENSOR (CTS) CIRCUIT
(LOW TEMPERATURE INDICATED)
3.1L (VIN D) "U" APV (TBI)

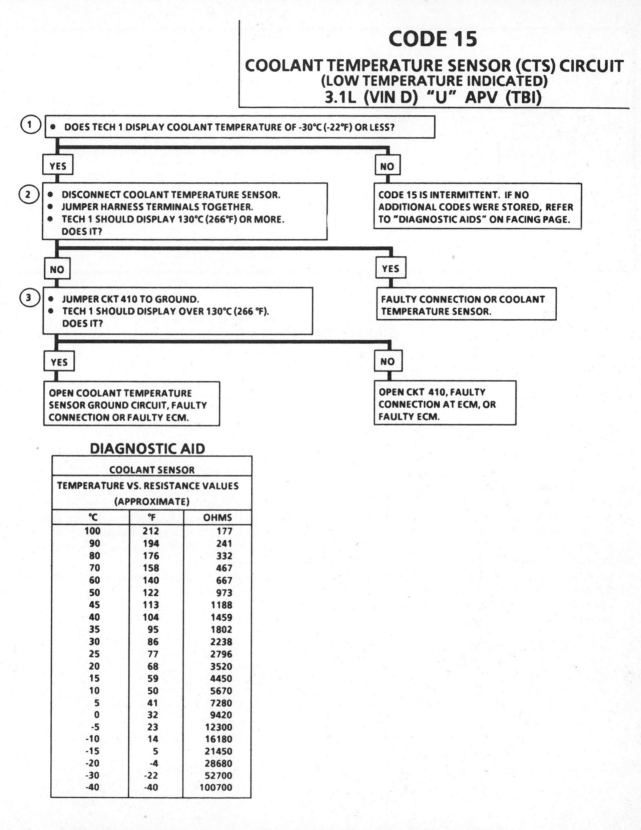

(1)
- DOES TECH 1 DISPLAY COOLANT TEMPERATURE OF -30°C (-22°F) OR LESS?

YES

(2)
- DISCONNECT COOLANT TEMPERATURE SENSOR.
- JUMPER HARNESS TERMINALS TOGETHER.
- TECH 1 SHOULD DISPLAY 130°C (266°F) OR MORE. DOES IT?

NO

NO

CODE 15 IS INTERMITTENT. IF NO ADDITIONAL CODES WERE STORED, REFER TO "DIAGNOSTIC AIDS" ON FACING PAGE.

YES

(3)
- JUMPER CKT 410 TO GROUND.
- TECH 1 SHOULD DISPLAY OVER 130°C (266 °F). DOES IT?

FAULTY CONNECTION OR COOLANT TEMPERATURE SENSOR.

YES

NO

OPEN COOLANT TEMPERATURE SENSOR GROUND CIRCUIT, FAULTY CONNECTION OR FAULTY ECM.

OPEN CKT 410, FAULTY CONNECTION AT ECM, OR FAULTY ECM.

DIAGNOSTIC AID

COOLANT SENSOR		
TEMPERATURE VS. RESISTANCE VALUES (APPROXIMATE)		
°C	°F	OHMS
100	212	177
90	194	241
80	176	332
70	158	467
60	140	667
50	122	973
45	113	1188
40	104	1459
35	95	1802
30	86	2238
25	77	2796
20	68	3520
15	59	4450
10	50	5670
5	41	7280
0	32	9420
-5	23	12300
-10	14	16180
-15	5	21450
-20	-4	28680
-30	-22	52700
-40	-40	100700

"AFTER REPAIRS," REFER TO CODE CRITERIA ON FACING PAGE AND CONFIRM CODE DOES NOT RESET.

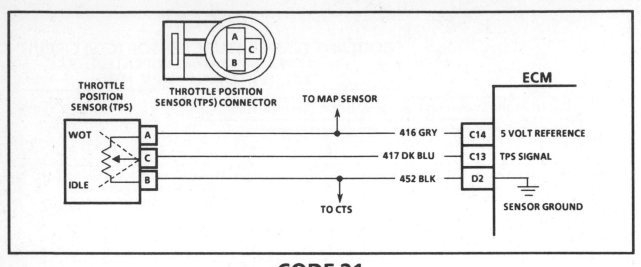

CODE 21
THROTTLE POSITION SENSOR (TPS) CIRCUIT
(SIGNAL VOLTAGE HIGH)
3.1L (VIN D) "U" APV (TBI)

Circuit Description:

The Throttle Position Sensor (TPS) provides a voltage signal that changes relative to the throttle blade. Signal voltage will vary from about .5 at idle to about 4.5 volts at Wide Open Throttle (WOT).

The TPS signal is one of the most important inputs used by the ECM for fuel control and for most of the ECM control outputs.

Test Description: Number(s) below refer to circled number(s) on the diagnostic chart.

1. Code 21 will set if:
   - TPS signal voltage is greater than 3.1 volts.
   - All conditions met for 2 seconds.
   - MAP less than 52 kPa.
2. With the TPS sensor disconnected, the TPS voltage should go low if the ECM and wiring are OK.
3. Probing CKT 452 with a test light to 12 volts checks the sensor ground circuit. A faulty sensor ground will cause a Code 21.

Diagnostic Aids:

A "Scan" tool reads throttle position in volts. Should read less than 1.25 volts with throttle closed and ignition "ON" or at idle. Voltage should increase at a steady rate as throttle is moved toward Wide Open Throttle (WOT).

An open in CKT 452 will result in a Code 21.

CODE 21
THROTTLE POSITION SENSOR (TPS) CIRCUIT
(SIGNAL VOLTAGE HIGH)
3.1L (VIN D) "U" APV (TBI)

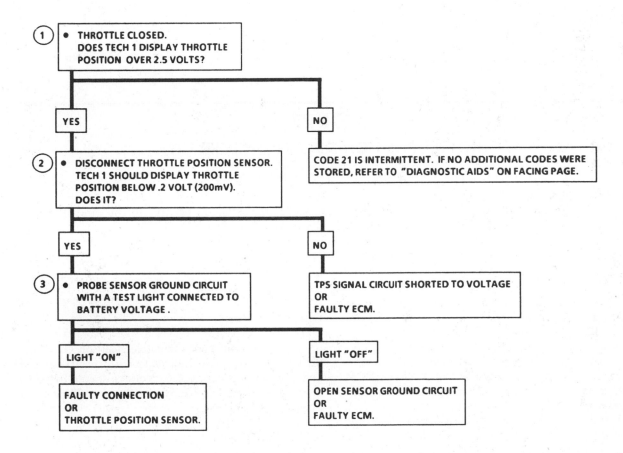

1. • THROTTLE CLOSED.
     DOES TECH 1 DISPLAY THROTTLE POSITION OVER 2.5 VOLTS?

YES

NO

2. • DISCONNECT THROTTLE POSITION SENSOR.
     TECH 1 SHOULD DISPLAY THROTTLE POSITION BELOW .2 VOLT (200mV).
     DOES IT?

CODE 21 IS INTERMITTENT. IF NO ADDITIONAL CODES WERE STORED, REFER TO "DIAGNOSTIC AIDS" ON FACING PAGE.

YES

NO

3. • PROBE SENSOR GROUND CIRCUIT WITH A TEST LIGHT CONNECTED TO BATTERY VOLTAGE .

TPS SIGNAL CIRCUIT SHORTED TO VOLTAGE
OR
FAULTY ECM.

LIGHT "ON"

LIGHT "OFF"

FAULTY CONNECTION
OR
THROTTLE POSITION SENSOR.

OPEN SENSOR GROUND CIRCUIT
OR
FAULTY ECM.

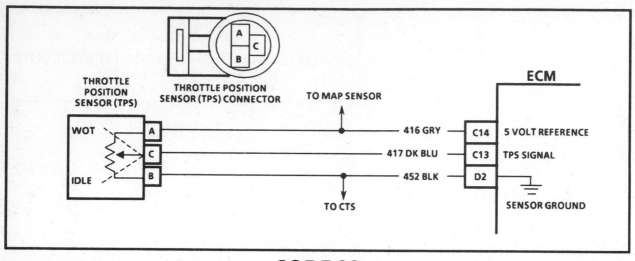

CODE 22
THROTTLE POSITION SENSOR (TPS) CIRCUIT
(SIGNAL VOLTAGE LOW)
3.1L (VIN D) "U" APV (TBI)

Circuit Description:

The Throttle Position Sensor (TPS) provides a voltage signal that changes relative to the throttle blade. Signal voltage will vary from about .5 at idle to about 4.5 volts at Wide Open Throttle (WOT).

The TPS signal is one of the most important inputs used by the ECM for fuel control and for most of the ECM control outputs.

Test Description: Number(s) below refer to circled number(s) on the diagnostic chart.

1. Code 22 will set if:
   - Engine is running.
   - TPS signal voltage is less than about .2 volt.
2. Simulates Code 21: (high voltage) If the ECM recognizes the high signal voltage then the ECM and wiring are OK.
3. TPS check. The TPS has an "Auto Zeroing" feature. This means that the ECM has the ability to auto-zero the TPS voltage, if it is below about 1.25 volts at idle. The ECM will use this value to be 0% throttle. The TPS is not adjustable. If the TPS voltage is out of the "Auto Zeroing Range," check for binding or sticking cruise control or throttle cables. If OK, replace the TPS.
4. This simulates a high signal voltage to check for an open CKT 417.

Diagnostic Aids:

A "Scan" tool reads throttle position in volts. Should read less than 1.25 volts with throttle closed and ignition "ON" or at idle. Voltage should increase at a steady rate as throttle is moved toward Wide Open Throttle (WOT).

An open or short to ground in CKT 416 or CKT 417 will result in a Code 22.

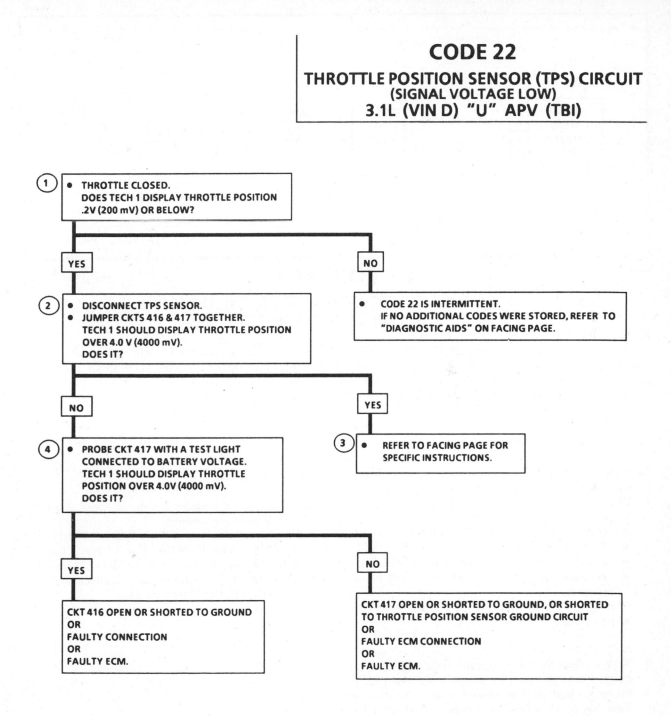

CODE 22
THROTTLE POSITION SENSOR (TPS) CIRCUIT
(SIGNAL VOLTAGE LOW)
3.1L (VIN D) "U" APV (TBI)

1
- THROTTLE CLOSED.
  DOES TECH 1 DISPLAY THROTTLE POSITION
  .2V (200 mV) OR BELOW?

YES

NO

2
- DISCONNECT TPS SENSOR.
- JUMPER CKTS 416 & 417 TOGETHER.
  TECH 1 SHOULD DISPLAY THROTTLE POSITION
  OVER 4.0 V (4000 mV).
  DOES IT?

- CODE 22 IS INTERMITTENT.
  IF NO ADDITIONAL CODES WERE STORED, REFER TO
  "DIAGNOSTIC AIDS" ON FACING PAGE.

NO

YES

4
- PROBE CKT 417 WITH A TEST LIGHT
  CONNECTED TO BATTERY VOLTAGE.
  TECH 1 SHOULD DISPLAY THROTTLE
  POSITION OVER 4.0V (4000 mV).
  DOES IT?

3
- REFER TO FACING PAGE FOR
  SPECIFIC INSTRUCTIONS.

YES

NO

CKT 416 OPEN OR SHORTED TO GROUND
OR
FAULTY CONNECTION
OR
FAULTY ECM.

CKT 417 OPEN OR SHORTED TO GROUND, OR SHORTED
TO THROTTLE POSITION SENSOR GROUND CIRCUIT
OR
FAULTY ECM CONNECTION
OR
FAULTY ECM.

"AFTER REPAIRS," REFER TO CODE CRITIERIA ON FACING PAGE AND CONFIRM CODE DOES NOT RESET.

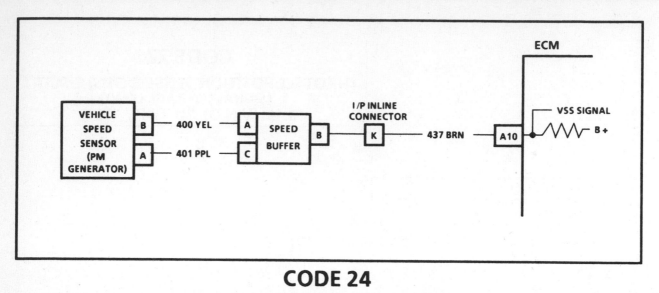

CODE 24
VEHICLE SPEED SENSOR (VSS) CIRCUIT
3.1L (VIN D) "U" APV (TBI)

Circuit Description:

The ECM applies and monitors 12 volts on CKT 437. CKT 437 connects to the vehicle speed buffer which alternately grounds CKT 437 when drive wheels are turning. This pulsing action takes place about 2000 times per mile and the ECM will calculate vehicle speed based on the time between "pulses."

"Scan" reading should closely match with speedometer reading with drive wheels turning.

Test Description: Number(s) below refer to circled number(s) on the diagnostic chart.

1. Code 24 will set if vehicle speed is less than 2 mph when:
   - Engine speed is greater than 1400 rpm.
   - TPS is greater than 5%.
   - Load condition is less than 25 kPa of vacuum.
   - All conditions met and accumulated for 30 seconds.

   Disregard Code 24 that sets when drive wheels are not turning.

2. 8-12 volts, at the I/P connector, indicates CKT 437 is open between the I/P connector and the VSS, or there is a faulty vehicle speed sensor. A voltage of less than 1 volt, at the I/P connector, indicates that CKT 437 wire is shorted to ground. If, after disconnecting CKT 437 at the vehicle speed buffer, the voltage reads above 10 volts, the vehicle speed buffer is faulty. If voltage remains less than 8 volts, then CKT 437 wire is grounded. If 437 is not grounded, there is a faulty connection at the ECM, or a faulty ECM.

Diagnostic Aids:

"Scan" should indicate a vehicle speed whenever the drive wheels are turning.

A faulty or misadjusted Park/Neutral (P/N) switch can result in a false Code 24. Use a "Scan" tool and check for proper signal while in drive. Refer to CHART C-1A for P/N switch diagnosis check.

If all OK, refer to "Intermittents"

CODE 24
VEHICLE SPEED SENSOR (VSS) CIRCUIT
3.1L (VIN D) "U" APV (TBI)

DISREGARD CODE 24 IF SET WHILE DRIVE WHEELS ARE NOT TURNING.

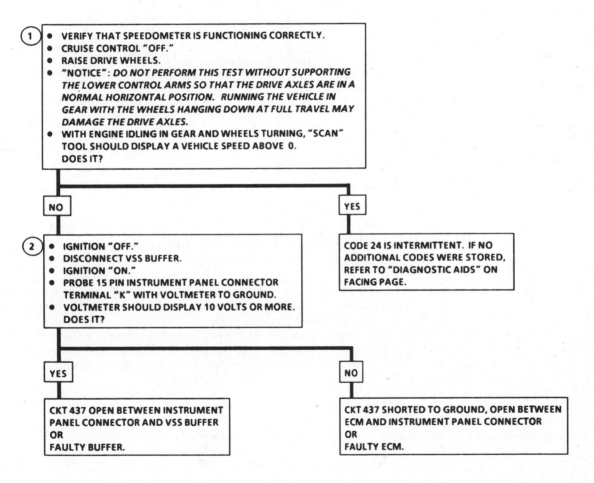

1
- VERIFY THAT SPEEDOMETER IS FUNCTIONING CORRECTLY.
- CRUISE CONTROL "OFF."
- RAISE DRIVE WHEELS.
- "NOTICE": *DO NOT PERFORM THIS TEST WITHOUT SUPPORTING THE LOWER CONTROL ARMS SO THAT THE DRIVE AXLES ARE IN A NORMAL HORIZONTAL POSITION. RUNNING THE VEHICLE IN GEAR WITH THE WHEELS HANGING DOWN AT FULL TRAVEL MAY DAMAGE THE DRIVE AXLES.*
- WITH ENGINE IDLING IN GEAR AND WHEELS TURNING, "SCAN" TOOL SHOULD DISPLAY A VEHICLE SPEED ABOVE 0. DOES IT?

NO

YES

2
- IGNITION "OFF."
- DISCONNECT VSS BUFFER.
- IGNITION "ON."
- PROBE 15 PIN INSTRUMENT PANEL CONNECTOR TERMINAL "K" WITH VOLTMETER TO GROUND.
- VOLTMETER SHOULD DISPLAY 10 VOLTS OR MORE. DOES IT?

CODE 24 IS INTERMITTENT. IF NO ADDITIONAL CODES WERE STORED, REFER TO "DIAGNOSTIC AIDS" ON FACING PAGE.

YES

NO

CKT 437 OPEN BETWEEN INSTRUMENT PANEL CONNECTOR AND VSS BUFFER
OR
FAULTY BUFFER.

CKT 437 SHORTED TO GROUND, OPEN BETWEEN ECM AND INSTRUMENT PANEL CONNECTOR
OR
FAULTY ECM.

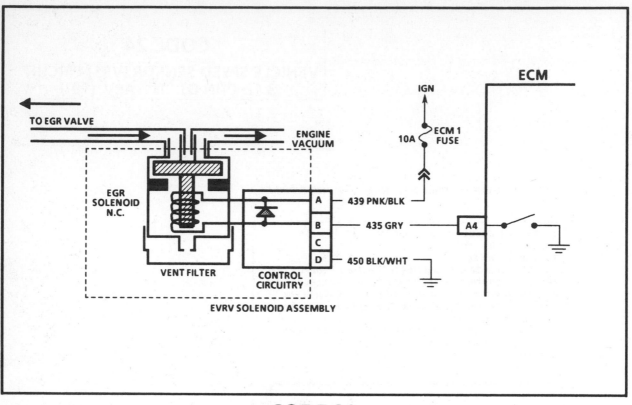

CODE 32

EXHAUST GAS RECIRCULATION (EGR) CIRCUIT
3.1L (VIN D) "U" APV (TBI)

Circuit Description:

The ECM operates a regulator to control the Exhaust Gas Recirculation (EGR) valve. This regulator normally allows for only a small amount of vacuum to pass. By providing a ground path, the ECM energizes the regulator which then allows enough vacuum to pass to open the EGR valve.

The ECM monitors EGR effectiveness by de-energizing the EGR control regulator thereby reducing vacuum to the EGR valve diaphragm. With the EGR valve closed, fuel integrator counts will be greater than they were during normal EGR operation. If the change is not within the calibrated window, a Code 32 will be set.

The ECM will check EGR operation when:
- Vehicle speed is above 80 km/h (50 mph).
- Engine vacuum is between 12.5 and 55 kPa (1.8 and 7.4 psi).
- Throttle position between 5 and 30%.
- All conditions met twice for 60 seconds.

Test Description: Number(s) below refer to circled number(s) on the diagnostic chart.

1. With the ignition "ON," engine stopped, the regulator should not be energized and minimum vacuum should pass to the EGR valve. Grounding the diagnostic terminal will energize the regulator and allow vacuum to pass to valve.

2. Checks for plugged EGR passages. If passages are plugged, the engine may have severe detonation on acceleration.

NOTE: Vehicle speed must be greater than 2 mph for California vehicles.

CODE 32
EXHAUST GAS RECIRCULATION (EGR) CIRCUIT
3.1L (VIN D) "U" APV (TBI)

IF ANY OTHER CODES ARE STORED, DIAGNOSE THEM FIRST.

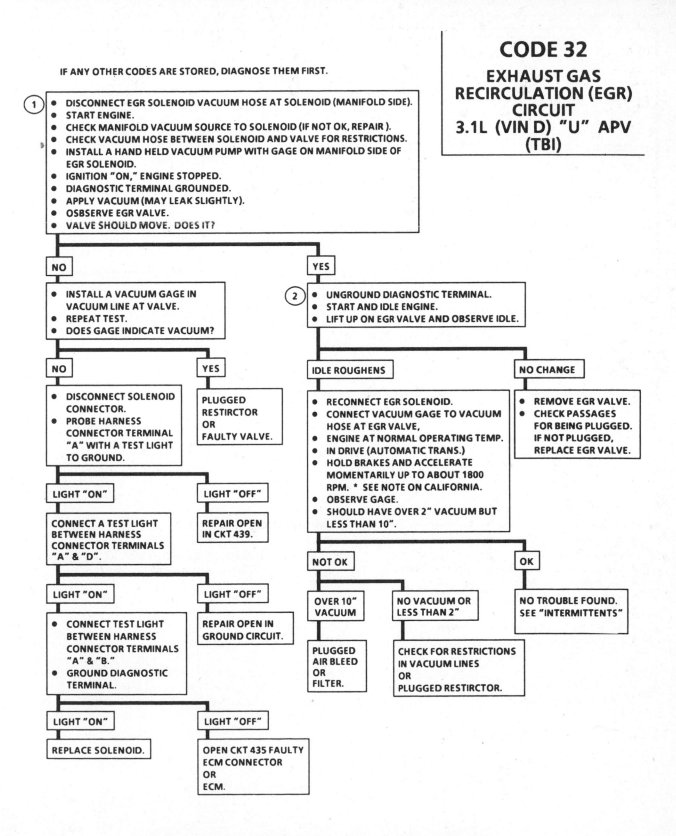

1
- DISCONNECT EGR SOLENOID VACUUM HOSE AT SOLENOID (MANIFOLD SIDE).
- START ENGINE.
- CHECK MANIFOLD VACUUM SOURCE TO SOLENOID (IF NOT OK, REPAIR).
- CHECK VACUUM HOSE BETWEEN SOLENOID AND VALVE FOR RESTRICTIONS.
- INSTALL A HAND HELD VACUUM PUMP WITH GAGE ON MANIFOLD SIDE OF EGR SOLENOID.
- IGNITION "ON," ENGINE STOPPED.
- DIAGNOSTIC TERMINAL GROUNDED.
- APPLY VACUUM (MAY LEAK SLIGHTLY).
- OSBSERVE EGR VALVE.
- VALVE SHOULD MOVE. DOES IT?

NO

- INSTALL A VACUUM GAGE IN VACUUM LINE AT VALVE.
- REPEAT TEST.
- DOES GAGE INDICATE VACUUM?

YES

2
- UNGROUND DIAGNOSTIC TERMINAL.
- START AND IDLE ENGINE.
- LIFT UP ON EGR VALVE AND OBSERVE IDLE.

NO
- DISCONNECT SOLENOID CONNECTOR.
- PROBE HARNESS CONNECTOR TERMINAL "A" WITH A TEST LIGHT TO GROUND.

YES
PLUGGED RESTIRCTOR OR FAULTY VALVE.

IDLE ROUGHENS
- RECONNECT EGR SOLENOID.
- CONNECT VACUUM GAGE TO VACUUM HOSE AT EGR VALVE,
- ENGINE AT NORMAL OPERATING TEMP.
- IN DRIVE (AUTOMATIC TRANS.)
- HOLD BRAKES AND ACCELERATE MOMENTARILY UP TO ABOUT 1800 RPM. * SEE NOTE ON CALIFORNIA.
- OBSERVE GAGE.
- SHOULD HAVE OVER 2" VACUUM BUT LESS THAN 10".

NO CHANGE
- REMOVE EGR VALVE.
- CHECK PASSAGES FOR BEING PLUGGED. IF NOT PLUGGED, REPLACE EGR VALVE.

LIGHT "ON"

CONNECT A TEST LIGHT BETWEEN HARNESS CONNECTOR TERMINALS "A" & "D".

LIGHT "OFF"

REPAIR OPEN IN CKT 439.

NOT OK

OK

LIGHT "ON"
- CONNECT TEST LIGHT BETWEEN HARNESS CONNECTOR TERMINALS "A" & "B."
- GROUND DIAGNOSTIC TERMINAL.

LIGHT "OFF"
REPAIR OPEN IN GROUND CIRCUIT.

OVER 10" VACUUM

NO VACUUM OR LESS THAN 2"

NO TROUBLE FOUND. SEE "INTERMITTENTS"

PLUGGED AIR BLEED OR FILTER.

CHECK FOR RESTRICTIONS IN VACUUM LINES OR PLUGGED RESTIRCTOR.

LIGHT "ON"
REPLACE SOLENOID.

LIGHT "OFF"
OPEN CKT 435 FAULTY ECM CONNECTOR OR ECM.

CONFIRM "CLOSED LOOP" OPERATION AND NO "SERVICE ENGINE SOON" LIGHT.

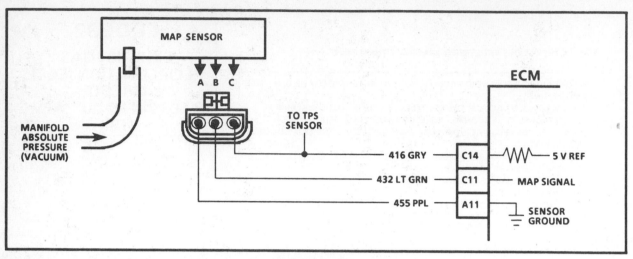

CODE 33

MANIFOLD ABSOLUTE PRESSURE (MAP) SENSOR CIRCUIT
(SIGNAL VOLTAGE HIGH - LOW VACUUM)
3.1L (VIN D) "U" APV (TBI)

Circuit Description:

The Manifold Absolute Pressure (MAP) sensor responds to changes in manifold pressure (vacuum). The ECM receives this information as a signal voltage that will vary from about 1-1.5 volts at idle to 4-4.5 volts at Wide Open Throttle (WOT). Signals will vary depending on altitude.

A "Scan" displays manifold pressure in volts. Low pressure (high vacuum) reads a low voltage while a high pressure (low vacuum) reads a high voltage.

If the MAP sensor fails the ECM will substitute a fixed MAP value and use the Throttle Position Sensor (TPS) to control fuel delivery.

Test Description: Number(s) below refer to circled number(s) on the diagnostic chart.

1. Code 33 will set when:
   - Signal is too high (kPa greater than 80 kPa).
   - TPS less than 4%.
   - Engine is running.
   - No Code 21 or Code 22.
   - Vehicle speed is less than 2 mph.
   - All conditions met for more than 5 seconds.
   Engine misfire or a low unstable idle may set Code 33.
2. If the ECM recognizes the low MAP signal, the ECM and wiring are OK.

Diagnostic Aids:

If idle is rough or unstable refer to "Symptoms," Section "6E2-B" for items which can cause an unstable idle.

An open in CKT 455 or the connection will result in a Code 33.

With the ignition "ON," and the engine stopped, the manifold pressure is equal to atmospheric pressure and the signal voltage will be high. This information is used by the ECM as an indication of vehicle altitude and is referred to as BARO. Comparison of this BARO reading with a known good vehicle with the same sensor is a good way to check accuracy of a "suspect" sensor. Reading should be the same ± .4 volt.

Refer to "Intermittents"

CODE 33
MANIFOLD ABSOLUTE PRESSURE (MAP) SENSOR CIRCUIT
(SIGNAL VOLTAGE HIGH - LOW VACUUM)
3.1L (VIN D) "U" APV (TBI)

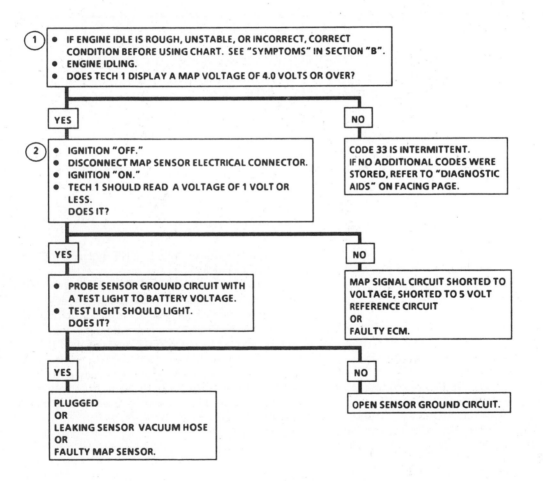

1
- IF ENGINE IDLE IS ROUGH, UNSTABLE, OR INCORRECT, CORRECT CONDITION BEFORE USING CHART. SEE "SYMPTOMS" IN SECTION "B".
- ENGINE IDLING.
- DOES TECH 1 DISPLAY A MAP VOLTAGE OF 4.0 VOLTS OR OVER?

YES

NO

2
- IGNITION "OFF."
- DISCONNECT MAP SENSOR ELECTRICAL CONNECTOR.
- IGNITION "ON."
- TECH 1 SHOULD READ A VOLTAGE OF 1 VOLT OR LESS.
  DOES IT?

CODE 33 IS INTERMITTENT.
IF NO ADDITIONAL CODES WERE STORED, REFER TO "DIAGNOSTIC AIDS" ON FACING PAGE.

YES

NO

- PROBE SENSOR GROUND CIRCUIT WITH A TEST LIGHT TO BATTERY VOLTAGE.
- TEST LIGHT SHOULD LIGHT.
  DOES IT?

MAP SIGNAL CIRCUIT SHORTED TO VOLTAGE, SHORTED TO 5 VOLT REFERENCE CIRCUIT
OR
FAULTY ECM.

YES

NO

PLUGGED
OR
LEAKING SENSOR VACUUM HOSE
OR
FAULTY MAP SENSOR.

OPEN SENSOR GROUND CIRCUIT.

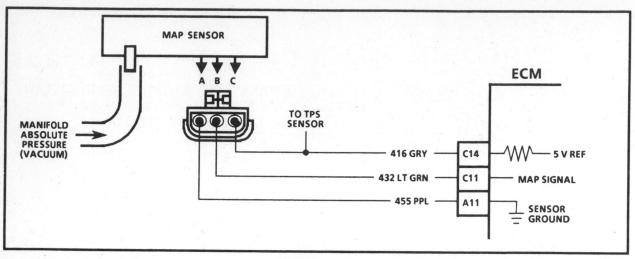

CODE 34

MANIFOLD ABSOLUTE PRESSURE (MAP) SENSOR CIRCUIT
(SIGNAL VOLTAGE LOW - HIGH VACUUM)
3.1L (VIN D) "U" APV (TBI)

Circuit Description:

The Manifold Absolute Pressure (MAP) sensor responds to changes in manifold pressure (vacuum). The ECM receives this information as a signal voltage that will vary from about 1-1.5 volts at idle to 4-4.5 volts at Wide Open Throttle (WOT). Signals will vary depending on altitude.

If the MAP sensor fails the ECM will substitute a fixed MAP value and use the Throttle Position Sensor (TPS) to control fuel delivery.

Test Description: Number(s) below refer to circled number(s) on the diagnostic chart.

1. Code 34 will set when:
   - No Code 21.
   - Engine speed less than 1200 rpm.
   - Signal is too low (kPa less than 14).
     OR
   - No Code 21.
   - Engine speed greater than 1200 rpm.
   - MAP sensor reading is less than 14 kPa.
   - TPS is greater than 15%.
2. If the ECM recognizes the high MAP signal, the ECM and wiring are OK.
3. The "Scan" tool may not display 12 volts. The important thing is that the ECM recognizes the voltage as more than 4 volts, indicating that the ECM and CKT 432 are OK.

Diagnostic Aids:

An intermittent open in CKT 432 or CKT 416 will result in a Code 34.

With the ignition "ON," and the engine stopped, the manifold pressure is equal to atmospheric pressure and the signal voltage will be high. This information is used by the ECM as an indication of vehicle altitude and is referred to as BARO. Comparison of this BARO reading with a known good vehicle with the same sensor is a good way to check accuracy of a "suspect" sensor. Reading should be the same ± .4 volt.

Also CHART C-1D can be used to test the MAP sensor.

CODE 34
MANIFOLD ABSOLUTE PRESSURE (MAP) SENSOR CIRCUIT
(SIGNAL VOLTAGE LOW - HIGH VACUUM)
3.1L (VIN D) "U" APV (TBI)

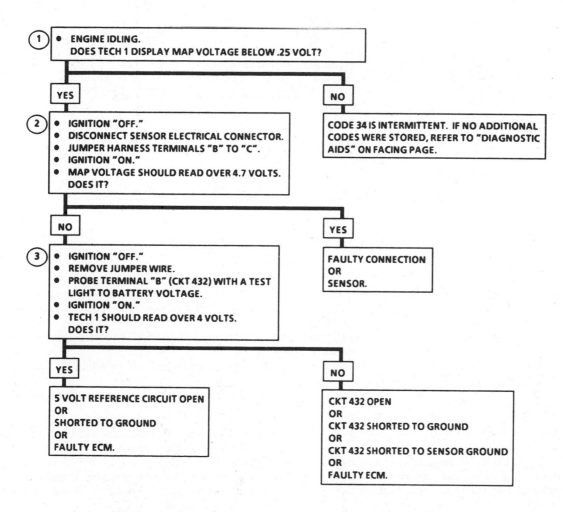

1
- ENGINE IDLING.
  DOES TECH 1 DISPLAY MAP VOLTAGE BELOW .25 VOLT?

YES   **NO**

2
- IGNITION "OFF."
- DISCONNECT SENSOR ELECTRICAL CONNECTOR.
- JUMPER HARNESS TERMINALS "B" TO "C".
- IGNITION "ON."
- MAP VOLTAGE SHOULD READ OVER 4.7 VOLTS. DOES IT?

CODE 34 IS INTERMITTENT. IF NO ADDITIONAL CODES WERE STORED, REFER TO "DIAGNOSTIC AIDS" ON FACING PAGE.

NO   **YES**

3
- IGNITION "OFF."
- REMOVE JUMPER WIRE.
- PROBE TERMINAL "B" (CKT 432) WITH A TEST LIGHT TO BATTERY VOLTAGE.
- IGNITION "ON."
- TECH 1 SHOULD READ OVER 4 VOLTS. DOES IT?

FAULTY CONNECTION
OR
SENSOR.

YES   **NO**

5 VOLT REFERENCE CIRCUIT OPEN
OR
SHORTED TO GROUND
OR
FAULTY ECM.

CKT 432 OPEN
OR
CKT 432 SHORTED TO GROUND
OR
CKT 432 SHORTED TO SENSOR GROUND
OR
FAULTY ECM.

"AFTER REPAIRS," REFER TO CODE CRITERIA ON FACING PAGE AND CONFIRM CODE DOES NOT RESET.

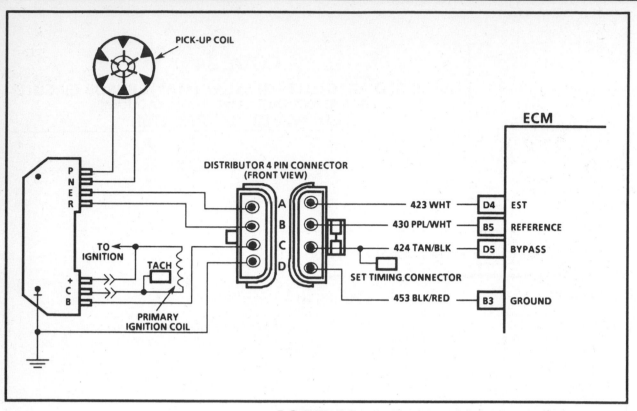

CODE 42
ELECTRONIC SPARK TIMING (EST) CIRCUIT
3.1L (VIN D) "U" APV (TBI)

Circuit Description:

When the system is running on the ignition module, that is, no voltage on the bypass line, the ignition module grounds the EST signal. The ECM expects to see no voltage on the EST line during this condition. If it sees a voltage, it sets Code 42 and will not go into the EST mode.

When the rpm for EST is reached (about 500 rpm), and bypass voltage applied, the EST should no longer be grounded in the ignition module so the EST voltage should be varying.

If the bypass line is open or grounded (as when timing is set), the ignition module will not switch to EST mode so the EST voltage will be low and Code 42 will be set.

If the EST line is grounded, the ignition module will switch to EST, but because the line is grounded, there will be no EST signal. A Code 42 will be set.

Test Description: Number(s) below refer to circled number(s) on the diagnostic chart.

1. Code 42 means the ECM has seen an open or short to ground in the EST or bypass circuits. This test confirms Code 42 and that the fault causing the code is present.
2. Checks for a normal EST ground path through the ignition module. An EST CKT 423 shorted to ground will also read less than 500 ohms; however, this will be checked later.
3. As the test light voltage touches CKT 424, the module should switch causing the ohmmeter to "overrange" if the meter is in the 1000-2000 ohms position. Selecting the 10-20,000 ohms position will indicate above 5000 ohms. The important thing is that the module "switched."

4. The module did not switch and this step checks for:
   - EST CKT 423 shorted to ground.
   - Bypass CKT 424 open.
   - Faulty ignition module connection or module.
5. Confirms that Code 42 is a faulty ECM and not an intermittent in CKT 423 or CKT 424.

Diagnostic Aids:

If a Code 42 was stored and the customer complains of a "Hard Start," the problem is most likely a grounded EST line (CKT 423).

A PROM not fully seated in the ECM can result in a Code 42. A Code 42 will set if base timing was checked or set by grounding the set timing connector.

Refer to "Intermittents"

CODE 42
ELECTRONIC SPARK TIMING (EST) CIRCUIT
3.1L (VIN D) "U" APV (TBI)

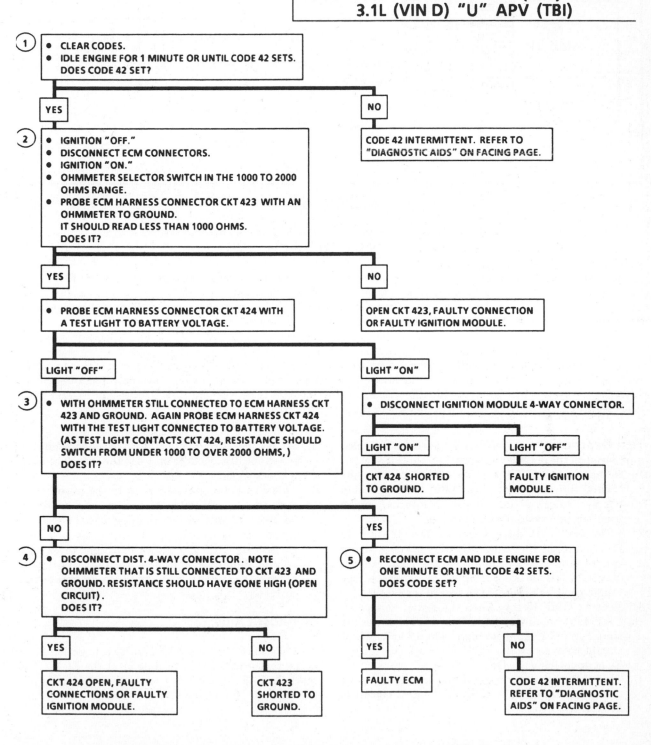

1
- CLEAR CODES.
- IDLE ENGINE FOR 1 MINUTE OR UNTIL CODE 42 SETS. DOES CODE 42 SET?

YES

2
- IGNITION "OFF."
- DISCONNECT ECM CONNECTORS.
- IGNITION "ON."
- OHMMETER SELECTOR SWITCH IN THE 1000 TO 2000 OHMS RANGE.
- PROBE ECM HARNESS CONNECTOR CKT 423 WITH AN OHMMETER TO GROUND. IT SHOULD READ LESS THAN 1000 OHMS. DOES IT?

NO

CODE 42 INTERMITTENT. REFER TO "DIAGNOSTIC AIDS" ON FACING PAGE.

YES

- PROBE ECM HARNESS CONNECTOR CKT 424 WITH A TEST LIGHT TO BATTERY VOLTAGE.

NO

OPEN CKT 423, FAULTY CONNECTION OR FAULTY IGNITION MODULE.

LIGHT "OFF"

3
- WITH OHMMETER STILL CONNECTED TO ECM HARNESS CKT 423 AND GROUND. AGAIN PROBE ECM HARNESS CKT 424 WITH THE TEST LIGHT CONNECTED TO BATTERY VOLTAGE. (AS TEST LIGHT CONTACTS CKT 424, RESISTANCE SHOULD SWITCH FROM UNDER 1000 TO OVER 2000 OHMS.) DOES IT?

LIGHT "ON"

- DISCONNECT IGNITION MODULE 4-WAY CONNECTOR.

LIGHT "ON"

CKT 424 SHORTED TO GROUND.

LIGHT "OFF"

FAULTY IGNITION MODULE.

NO

4
- DISCONNECT DIST. 4-WAY CONNECTOR. NOTE OHMMETER THAT IS STILL CONNECTED TO CKT 423 AND GROUND. RESISTANCE SHOULD HAVE GONE HIGH (OPEN CIRCUIT). DOES IT?

YES

5
- RECONNECT ECM AND IDLE ENGINE FOR ONE MINUTE OR UNTIL CODE 42 SETS. DOES CODE SET?

YES

CKT 424 OPEN, FAULTY CONNECTIONS OR FAULTY IGNITION MODULE.

NO

CKT 423 SHORTED TO GROUND.

YES

FAULTY ECM

NO

CODE 42 INTERMITTENT. REFER TO "DIAGNOSTIC AIDS" ON FACING PAGE.

CLEAR CODES AND CONFIRM "CLOSED LOOP" OPERATION AND NO "SERVICE ENGINE SOON" LIGHT.

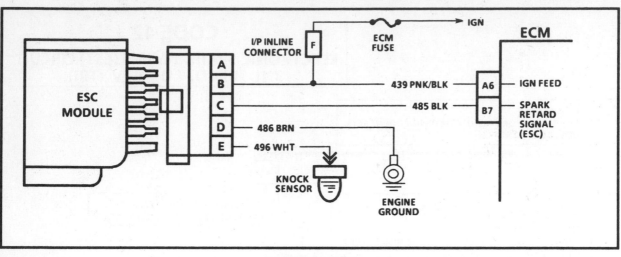

CODE 43
ELECTRONIC SPARK CONTROL (ESC) CIRCUIT
3.1L (VIN D) "U" APV (TBI)

Circuit Description:

Electronic Spark Control (ESC) is accomplished with a module that sends a voltage signal to the ECM. As the knock sensor detects engine knock, the voltage from the ESC module to the ECM drops, and this signals the ECM to retard timing. The ECM will retard the timing when knock is detected if: coolant temperature is above 35°C, rpm is at least 1500 or vehicle speed is greater than 10 mph, and battery voltage is at least 9 volts.

Code 43 means the ECM has seen low voltage at CKT 485 terminal "B7" for longer than 5 seconds with the engine running or the system has failed the functional check.

This system performs a functional check once per start up to check the ESC system. To perform this test, the ECM will advance the spark up to 20° if no knock has been detected. If no knock has been detected after 20° of advance, the system has failed the functional check. When coolant is between 90°-115°C (194°-239°F), and high load conditions are met, the ECM will then check the signal at "B7".

Test Description: Number(s) below refer to circled number(s) on the diagnostic chart.

1. If the conditions for a Code 43 are present the "Scan" will always display "YES." There should not be a knock at idle unless an internal engine problem, or a system problem exists.
2. This test will determine if the system is functioning at this time. Usually a knock signal can be generated by tapping on the right exhaust manifold. If no knock signal is generated try tapping on block close to the area of the sensor.
3. Because Code 43 sets when the signal voltage on CKT 485 remains low this test should cause the signal on CKT 485 to go high. The 12 volts signal should be seen by the ECM as "no knock" if the ECM and wiring are OK.
4. This test will determine if the knock signal is being detected on CKT 496 or if the ESC module is at fault.

5. If CKT 496 is routed to close to secondary ignition wires the ESC module may see the interference as a knock signal.
6. This checks the ground circuit to the module. An open ground will cause the voltage on CKT 485 to be about 12 volts which would cause the Code 43 functional test to fail.
7. Contacting CKT 496 with a test light to 12 volts should generate a knock signal. This will determine if the ESC module is operating correctly.

Diagnostic Aids:

Code 43 can be caused by a faulty connection at the knock sensor at the ESC module or at the ECM. Also check CKT 485 for possible open or short to ground.

Refer to "Intermittents"

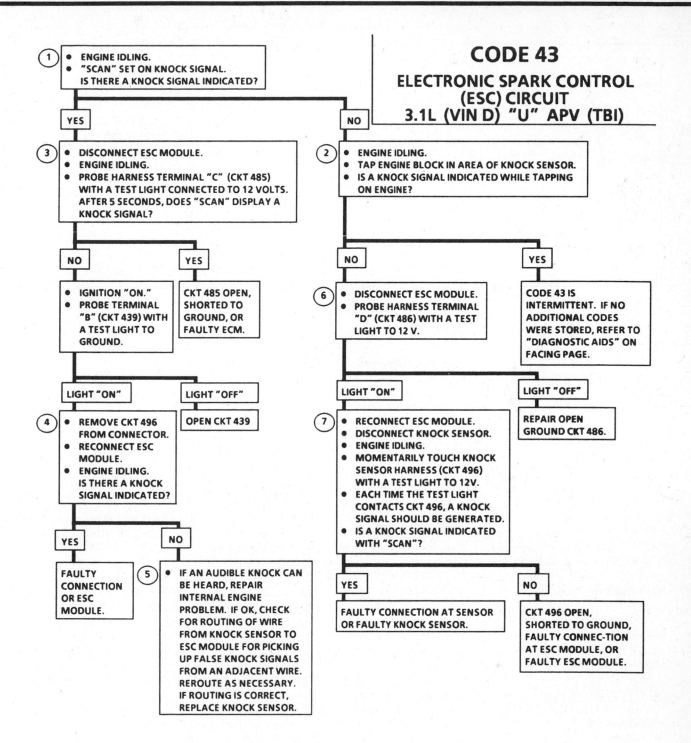

CODE 43
ELECTRONIC SPARK CONTROL (ESC) CIRCUIT
3.1L (VIN D) "U" APV (TBI)

1
- ENGINE IDLING.
- "SCAN" SET ON KNOCK SIGNAL. IS THERE A KNOCK SIGNAL INDICATED?

YES | **NO**

3
- DISCONNECT ESC MODULE.
- ENGINE IDLING.
- PROBE HARNESS TERMINAL "C" (CKT 485) WITH A TEST LIGHT CONNECTED TO 12 VOLTS. AFTER 5 SECONDS, DOES "SCAN" DISPLAY A KNOCK SIGNAL?

2
- ENGINE IDLING.
- TAP ENGINE BLOCK IN AREA OF KNOCK SENSOR.
- IS A KNOCK SIGNAL INDICATED WHILE TAPPING ON ENGINE?

NO | **YES**

- IGNITION "ON."
- PROBE TERMINAL "B" (CKT 439) WITH A TEST LIGHT TO GROUND.

CKT 485 OPEN, SHORTED TO GROUND, OR FAULTY ECM.

6
- DISCONNECT ESC MODULE.
- PROBE HARNESS TERMINAL "D" (CKT 486) WITH A TEST LIGHT TO 12 V.

CODE 43 IS INTERMITTENT. IF NO ADDITIONAL CODES WERE STORED, REFER TO "DIAGNOSTIC AIDS" ON FACING PAGE.

LIGHT "ON" | **LIGHT "OFF"**

4
- REMOVE CKT 496 FROM CONNECTOR.
- RECONNECT ESC MODULE.
- ENGINE IDLING. IS THERE A KNOCK SIGNAL INDICATED?

OPEN CKT 439

LIGHT "ON" | **LIGHT "OFF"**

7
- RECONNECT ESC MODULE.
- DISCONNECT KNOCK SENSOR.
- ENGINE IDLING.
- MOMENTARILY TOUCH KNOCK SENSOR HARNESS (CKT 496) WITH A TEST LIGHT TO 12V.
- EACH TIME THE TEST LIGHT CONTACTS CKT 496, A KNOCK SIGNAL SHOULD BE GENERATED.
- IS A KNOCK SIGNAL INDICATED WITH "SCAN"?

REPAIR OPEN GROUND CKT 486.

YES | **NO**

FAULTY CONNECTION OR ESC MODULE.

5
- IF AN AUDIBLE KNOCK CAN BE HEARD, REPAIR INTERNAL ENGINE PROBLEM. IF OK, CHECK FOR ROUTING OF WIRE FROM KNOCK SENSOR TO ESC MODULE FOR PICKING UP FALSE KNOCK SIGNALS FROM AN ADJACENT WIRE. REROUTE AS NECESSARY. IF ROUTING IS CORRECT, REPLACE KNOCK SENSOR.

YES | **NO**

FAULTY CONNECTION AT SENSOR OR FAULTY KNOCK SENSOR.

CKT 496 OPEN, SHORTED TO GROUND, FAULTY CONNEC-TION AT ESC MODULE, OR FAULTY ESC MODULE.

"AFTER REPAIRS," CONFIRM "CLOSED LOOP" OPERATION AND NO "SERVICE ENGINE SOON" LIGHT.

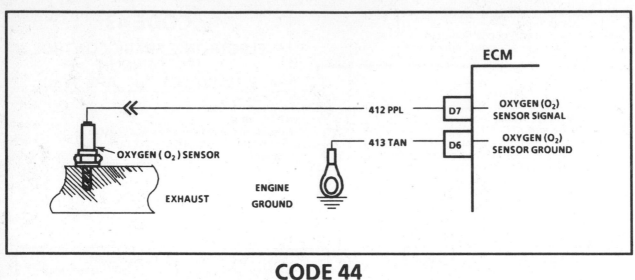

CODE 44

OXYGEN (O₂) SENSOR CIRCUIT
(LEAN EXHAUST INDICATED)
3.1L (VIN D) "U" APV (TBI)

Circuit Description:

The ECM supplies a voltage of about .45 volt between terminals "D6" and "D7". (If measured with a 10 megohm digital voltmeter, this may read as low as .32 volt.) The Oxygen (O₂) sensor varies the voltage within a range of about 1 volt if the exhaust is rich, down through about .01 volt if exhaust is lean.

The sensor is like an open circuit and produces no voltage when it is below about 315°C (600°F). An open sensor circuit or cold sensor causes "Open Loop" operation.

Test Description: Number(s) below refer to circled number(s) on the diagnostic chart.

1. Code 44 is set when:
   - Oxygen (O₂) sensor signal voltage is less than .150 volt for 3 minutes.
   - System is operating in "Closed Loop."

Diagnostic Aids:

Using the "Scan," observe the block learn values at different rpm and air flow conditions to determine when the Code 44 may have been set. If the conditions for Code 44 exist, the block learn values will be around 172.

- OXYGEN (O₂) Sensor Wire. Sensor pigtail may be mispositioned and contacting the exhaust manifold.
- Check for intermittent ground in wire between connector and sensor.

- MAP Sensor A (MAP) sensor output that causes the ECM to sense a higher than normal vacuum will cause the system to go lean. Disconnect the MAP sensor and if the lean condition is gone, replace the sensor.
- Lean Injector(s).
- Fuel Contamination. Water, even in small amounts, near the in-tank fuel pump inlet can be delivered to the injectors. The water causes a lean exhaust and can set a Code 44.
- Fuel Pressure. System will be lean if pressure is too low. It may be necessary to monitor fuel pressure while driving the car at various road speeds and/or loads to confirm. See "Fuel System Diagnosis" CHART A-7.
- Exhaust Leaks. If there is an exhaust leak, the engine can pull outside air into the exhaust and past the sensor. Vacuum or crankcase leaks can cause a lean condition.
- If the above are OK, it is a faulty Oxygen (O₂) sensor.

CODE 44

OXYGEN SENSOR CIRCUIT
(LEAN EXHAUST INDICATED)
3.1L (VIN D) "U" APV (TBI)

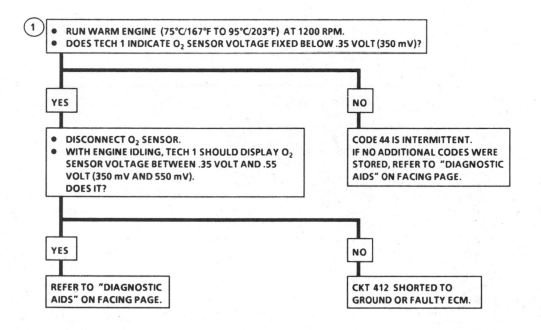

1
- RUN WARM ENGINE (75°C/167°F TO 95°C/203°F) AT 1200 RPM.
- DOES TECH 1 INDICATE O_2 SENSOR VOLTAGE FIXED BELOW .35 VOLT (350 mV)?

YES

- DISCONNECT O_2 SENSOR.
- WITH ENGINE IDLING, TECH 1 SHOULD DISPLAY O_2 SENSOR VOLTAGE BETWEEN .35 VOLT AND .55 VOLT (350 mV AND 550 mV). DOES IT?

NO

CODE 44 IS INTERMITTENT. IF NO ADDITIONAL CODES WERE STORED, REFER TO "DIAGNOSTIC AIDS" ON FACING PAGE.

YES

REFER TO "DIAGNOSTIC AIDS" ON FACING PAGE.

NO

CKT 412 SHORTED TO GROUND OR FAULTY ECM.

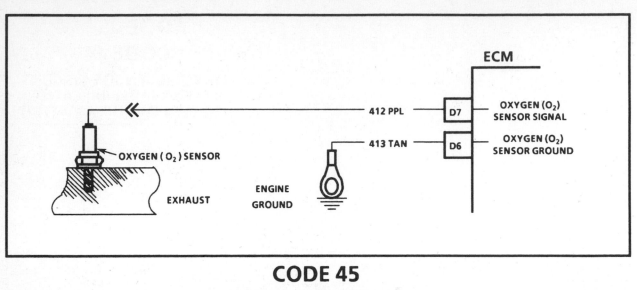

CODE 45
OXYGEN (O₂) SENSOR CIRCUIT
(RICH EXHAUST INDICATED)
3.1L (VIN D) "U" APV (TBI)

Circuit Description:

The ECM supplies a voltage of about .45 volt between terminals "D6" and "D7". (If measured with a 10 megohm digital voltmeter, this may read as low as .32 volt.) The Oxygen (O_2) sensor varies the voltage within a range of about 1 volt if the exhaust is rich, down through about .01 volt if exhaust is lean.

The sensor is like an open circuit and produces no voltage when it is below about 315°C (600°F). An open sensor circuit or cold sensor causes "Open Loop" operation.

Test Description: Number(s) below refer to circled number(s) on the diagnostic chart.
1. Code 45 is set when:
   - Oxygen (O_2) sensor signal voltage greater than .700 volt for 50 seconds.
   - Throttle position is between 0% and 99.6%.
   - System is operating in "Closed Loop."

Diagnostic Aids:

Using the "Scan," observe the block learn values at different rpm conditions to determine when the Code 45 may have been set. If the conditions for Code 45 exist, the block learn values will be around 90.
- Fuel Pressure. System will go rich if pressure is too high. The ECM can compensate for some increase. However, if it gets too high, a Code 45 may be set. See "Fuel System Diagnosis" CHART A-7.
- Leaking injector. See CHART A-7.
- Check for fuel contaminated oil.

- HEI Shielding. An open ground CKT 453 (ignition system reference low) may result in EMI, or induced electrical "noise." The ECM looks at this "noise" as reference pulses. The additional pulses result in a higher than actual engine speed signal. The ECM then delivers too much fuel, causing system to go rich. Engine tachometer will also show higher than actual engine speed, which can help in diagnosing this problem.
- Canister purge. Check for fuel saturation. If full of fuel, check canister control and hoses. See EVAPORATIVE EMISSION CONTROL SYSTEM (EECS)
- MAP sensor. An output that causes the ECM to sense a lower than normal vacuum can cause the system to go rich. Disconnecting the MAP sensor will allow the ECM to set a fixed value for the sensor. Substitute a different MAP sensor if the the rich condition is gone while the sensor is disconnected.
- TPS. An intermittent TPS output will cause the system to go rich, due to a false indication of the engine accelerating.

CODE 45

OXYGEN (O_2) SENSOR CIRCUIT
(RICH EXHAUST INDICATED)
3.1L (VIN D) "U" APV (TBI)

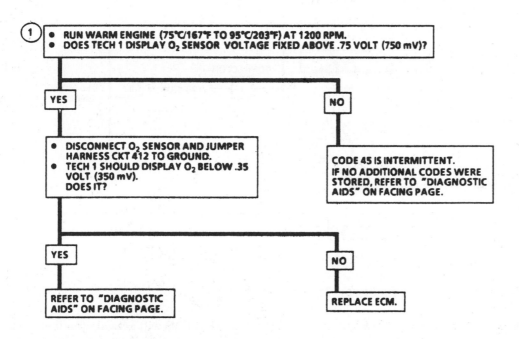

1
- RUN WARM ENGINE (75°C/167°F TO 95°C/203°F) AT 1200 RPM.
- DOES TECH 1 DISPLAY O_2 SENSOR VOLTAGE FIXED ABOVE .75 VOLT (750 mV)?

YES

- DISCONNECT O_2 SENSOR AND JUMPER HARNESS CKT 412 TO GROUND.
- TECH 1 SHOULD DISPLAY O_2 BELOW .35 VOLT (350 mV). DOES IT?

NO

CODE 45 IS INTERMITTENT.
IF NO ADDITIONAL CODES WERE STORED, REFER TO "DIAGNOSTIC AIDS" ON FACING PAGE.

YES

REFER TO "DIAGNOSTIC AIDS" ON FACING PAGE.

NO

REPLACE ECM.

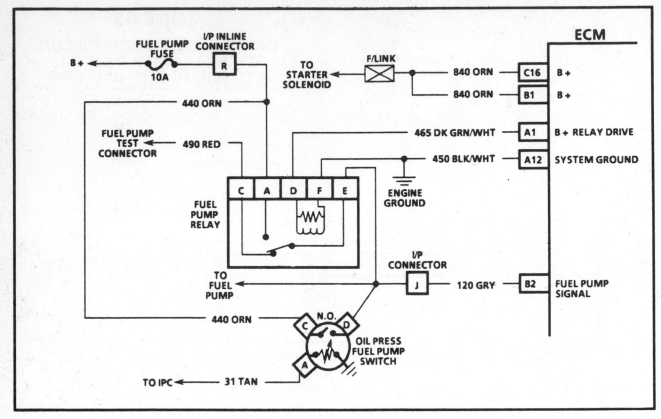

CODE 54

FUEL PUMP CIRCUIT
(LOW VOLTAGE)
3.1L (VIN D) "U" APV (TBI)

Circuit Description:

When the ignition switch is turned "ON," the Electronic Control Module (ECM) will activate the fuel pump relay and run the in-tank fuel pump. The fuel pump will operate as long as the engine is cranking or running, and the ECM is receiving ignition reference pulses.

If there are no reference pulses, the ECM will shut "OFF" the fuel pump within 2 seconds after key "ON."

Should the fuel pump relay, or the 12 volt relay drive from the ECM fail, the fuel pump will be run through an oil pressure switch back-up circuit.

Diagnostic Aids:

An inoperative fuel pump relay can result in long cranking times, particularly if the engine is cold or engine oil pressure is low. The extended crank period is caused by the time necessary for oil pressure to build enough to close the oil pressure switch and turn "ON" the fuel pump.

CODE 54
FUEL PUMP CIRCUIT
(LOW VOLTAGE)
3.1L (VIN D) "U" APV (TBI)

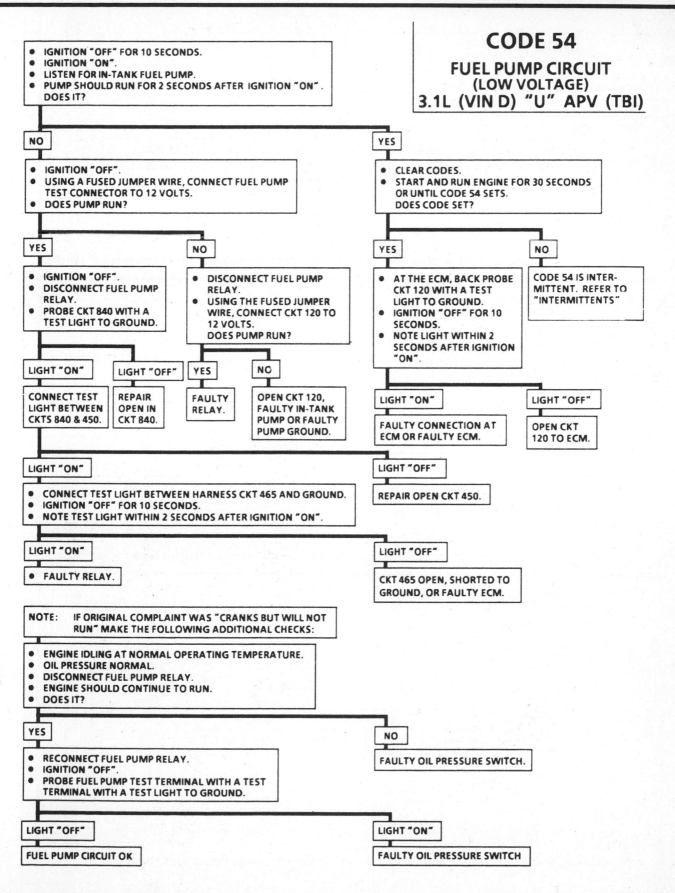

- IGNITION "OFF" FOR 10 SECONDS.
- IGNITION "ON".
- LISTEN FOR IN-TANK FUEL PUMP.
- PUMP SHOULD RUN FOR 2 SECONDS AFTER IGNITION "ON".
  DOES IT?

NO

- IGNITION "OFF".
- USING A FUSED JUMPER WIRE, CONNECT FUEL PUMP TEST CONNECTOR TO 12 VOLTS.
- DOES PUMP RUN?

YES

- IGNITION "OFF".
- DISCONNECT FUEL PUMP RELAY.
- PROBE CKT 840 WITH A TEST LIGHT TO GROUND.

NO

- DISCONNECT FUEL PUMP RELAY.
- USING THE FUSED JUMPER WIRE, CONNECT CKT 120 TO 12 VOLTS.
  DOES PUMP RUN?

LIGHT "ON"

CONNECT TEST LIGHT BETWEEN CKTS 840 & 450.

LIGHT "OFF"

REPAIR OPEN IN CKT 840.

YES

FAULTY RELAY.

NO

OPEN CKT 120, FAULTY IN-TANK PUMP OR FAULTY PUMP GROUND.

LIGHT "ON"

- CONNECT TEST LIGHT BETWEEN HARNESS CKT 465 AND GROUND.
- IGNITION "OFF" FOR 10 SECONDS.
- NOTE TEST LIGHT WITHIN 2 SECONDS AFTER IGNITION "ON".

LIGHT "ON"

- FAULTY RELAY.

NOTE: IF ORIGINAL COMPLAINT WAS "CRANKS BUT WILL NOT RUN" MAKE THE FOLLOWING ADDITIONAL CHECKS:

- ENGINE IDLING AT NORMAL OPERATING TEMPERATURE.
- OIL PRESSURE NORMAL.
- DISCONNECT FUEL PUMP RELAY.
- ENGINE SHOULD CONTINUE TO RUN.
- DOES IT?

YES

- RECONNECT FUEL PUMP RELAY.
- IGNITION "OFF".
- PROBE FUEL PUMP TEST TERMINAL WITH A TEST TERMINAL WITH A TEST LIGHT TO GROUND.

NO

FAULTY OIL PRESSURE SWITCH.

LIGHT "OFF"

FUEL PUMP CIRCUIT OK

LIGHT "ON"

FAULTY OIL PRESSURE SWITCH

YES

- CLEAR CODES.
- START AND RUN ENGINE FOR 30 SECONDS OR UNTIL CODE 54 SETS.
  DOES CODE SET?

YES

- AT THE ECM, BACK PROBE CKT 120 WITH A TEST LIGHT TO GROUND.
- IGNITION "OFF" FOR 10 SECONDS.
- NOTE LIGHT WITHIN 2 SECONDS AFTER IGNITION "ON".

NO

CODE 54 IS INTERMITTENT. REFER TO "INTERMITTENTS"

LIGHT "ON"

FAULTY CONNECTION AT ECM OR FAULTY ECM.

LIGHT "OFF"

OPEN CKT 120 TO ECM.

LIGHT "OFF"

REPAIR OPEN CKT 450.

LIGHT "OFF"

CKT 465 OPEN, SHORTED TO GROUND, OR FAULTY ECM.

CODE 51

PROM ERROR
(FAULTY OR INCORRECT PROM)
3.1L (VIN D) "U" APV (TBI)

CHECK THAT ALL PINS ARE FULLY INSERTED IN THE SOCKET. IF OK, REPLACE PROM, CLEAR MEMORY AND RECHECK. IF CODE 51 REAPPEARS, REPLACE ECM.

CLEAR ALL CODES AND CONFIRM "CLOSED LOOP" OPERATION AND NO "SERVICE ENGINE SOON" LIGHT

CODE 52

CAL-PAK ERROR
(FAULTY OR INCORRECT CAL-PAK)
3.1L (VIN D) "U" APV (TBI)

REPLACE ELECTRONIC CONTROL MODULE (ECM).

CLEAR ALL CODES AND CONFIRM "CLOSED LOOP" OPERATION AND NO "SERVICE ENGINE SOON" LIGHT

CODE 55

ECM ERROR
3.1L (VIN D) "U" APV (TBI)

REPLACE ELECTRONIC CONTROL MODULE (ECM).

CLEAR ALL CODES AND CONFIRM "CLOSED LOOP" OPERATION AND NO "SERVICE ENGINE SOON" LIGHT

VACUUM DIAGRAMS

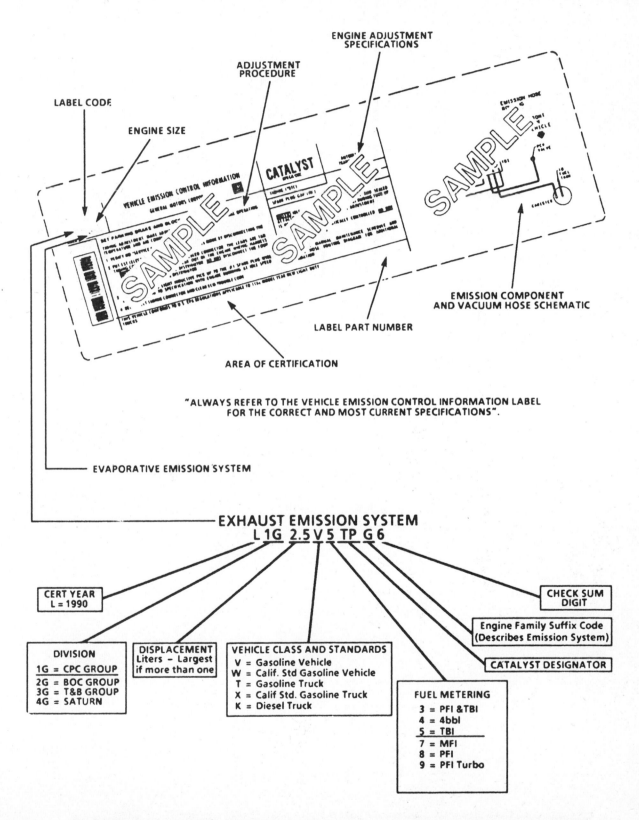

"ALWAYS REFER TO THE VEHICLE EMISSION CONTROL INFORMATION LABEL
FOR THE CORRECT AND MOST CURRENT SPECIFICATIONS".

An example of a Vehicle Emission Control Label, located in the engine compartment

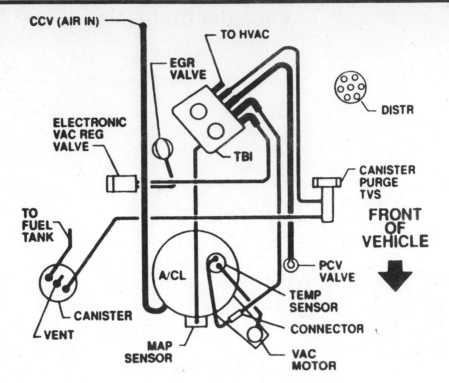

Emission hose routing. Use the emission hose routing illustrated on the Vehicle Emission Control Label, located in the engine compartment, if it differs from the above.

Fuel System

5

FUEL INJECTION SYSTEM

Electric Fuel Pump

The electric fuel pump is attached to the fuel meter assembly, located in the fuel tank.

REMOVAL AND INSTALLATION

NOTE: The following procedure requires the use of the GM Fuel Gauge Sending Unit Spanner Wrench No. J–35731 or equivalent.

—————————— CAUTION ——————————

Before removing any component of the fuel system, be sure to reduce the fuel pressure in the system. The pressure regulator contains an orifice in the fuel system; when the engine is turned Off, the pressure in the system will bleed down within a few minutes.

1. If the fuel system has been in use, turn the ignition switch Off and allow the system time to reduce the fuel pressure.
2. Disconnect the negative battery terminal from the battery.

NOTE: Be sure to keep a Class B (dry chemical) fire extinguisher nearby.

—————————— CAUTION ——————————

Due to the possibility of fire or explosion, never drain or store gasoline in an open container.

3. Remove the fuel tank as outlined in this section.

N0TE: If the nylon fuel feed or return lines becomes kinked, and cannot be straightened, they must be replaced. Do not attempt to repair sections of the nylon fuel lines.

4. Disconnect the fuel feed and return line quick-connect fittings at the fuel level meter as follows:
   a. Grasp both ends of one fuel line fitting connection and twist the quick connect fitting ¼ turn in each direction to loosen any dirt within the fitting. Repeat for the other fuel line fitting.
   b. Squeeze the plastic tabs of the male end connector and pull the connection apart. Repeat for the return line fitting.
5. Disconnect the fuel level meter electrical connector.
6. Using tool No. J–35731 or equivalent, remove the cam locking ring (fuel sending unit) counterclockwise, then lift the sending unit and O-ring from the fuel tank. Discard the O-ring.
7. Remove the fuel pump from the fuel sending unit, by performing the following procedures:
   a. Support the pump with one hand and grasp the filter with the other hand, rotate the filter in one direction and pull off of the pump.
   b. Remove the deflector and discard the filter.
8. Disconnect the fuel pump electrical connector.
9. Loosen the 2 connecting clamps.
10. Place the fuel level meter upside down on a bench.
11. Pull the pump downward to remove from the mounting bracket, then tilt the pump outward and remove from the connecting hose.
12. Remove and discard the connecting hose and clamps.

WARNING: Do not run the pump unless sumerged in fuel.

To install:
13. Assemble the rubber bumper on the fuel pump.
14. Install the new connecting hose and clamps on the fuel feed tube, but do not tighten the clamps at this time.
15. Position the fuel level meter assembly upside down and install th fuel pump between the connecting hose and mounting bracket.
16. Install the center connecting hose between the fuel pump and the fuel feed tube. Tighten the clamps so that 5–8 teeth are engaged.
17. Install the fuel pump electrical connector.
18. Support the pump with one hand and position the deflector on the fuel pump.
19. Install a NEW pump filter in the same direction as noted during disassembly. Push on the outer edge of the ferrule until it is fully seated.
20. Install a new O-ring and install the fuel meter assembly.
21. Using tool No. J–35731 or equivalent, install the cam locking ring (fuel meter assembly) clockwise.
22. Apply a few drops of engine oil to both the male tube ends of the fuel level meter and push the connectors together to cause the retaining tabs to snap into place.
23. Once installed pull on both ends of each connection to make sure they are secure.
24. Install the fuel tank vapor line and clamp.
25. Install the fuel level meter electrical connector on the fuel tank routing clamps.
26. Install the fuel tank as outlined in this section.
27. Add fuel then install the fuel filler cap.
28. Connect the negative battery cable.

TESTING

For testing of the fuel pump, refer to the Fuel System Diagnosis Charts at the end of this section

Fuel Pump Relay

The fuel pump relay is mounted on the right-side of the engine compartment behind the headlamp. Check for loose electrical connections; no other service is possible, except replacement. For diagnosis of the fuel pump relay circuit, please refer to the Code 54 Diagnosis chart in this section and also in Section 4.

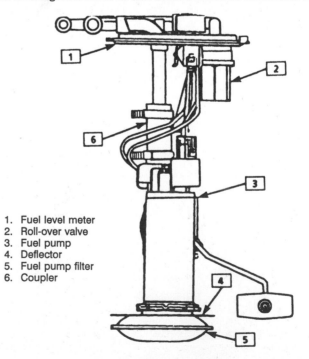

1. Fuel level meter
2. Roll-over valve
3. Fuel pump
4. Deflector
5. Fuel pump filter
6. Coupler

Fuel level meter assembly

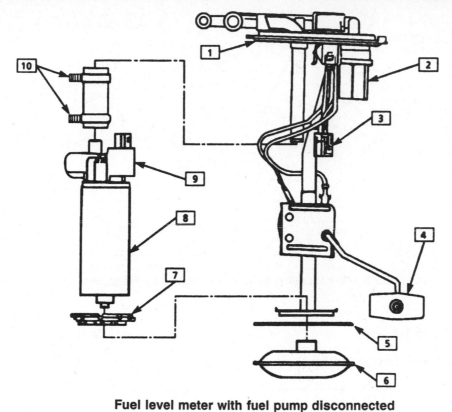

1. Fuel level meter
2. Roll-over valve
3. Fuel pump electrical connector
4. Float
5. Deflector
6. Fuel pump filter
7. Rubber bumper
8. Fuel pump
9. Coupler
10. Clamps

Fuel level meter with fuel pump disconnected

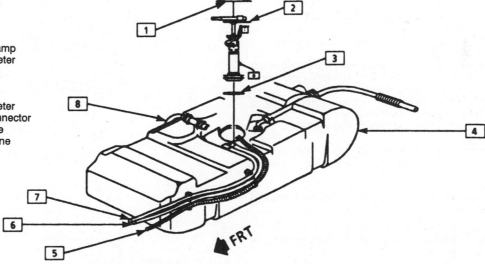

1. Retaining clamp
2. Fuel level meter assembly
3. O-ring
4. Fuel tank
5. Fuel level meter electrical connector
6. Fuel feed line
7. Fuel return line

Fuel level meter with fuel pump removal

REMOVAL AND INSTALLATION

1. Disconnect the negative battery terminal from the battery.
2. Disconnect the relay/electrical connector assembly from the bracket.
3. Pull the fuel pump relay from the electrical connector.

FUEL PRESSURE RELIEF

Allow the engine to set for 5–10 minutes; this will allow the orifice (in the fuel system) to bleed off the pressure. Remove the fuel tank cap.

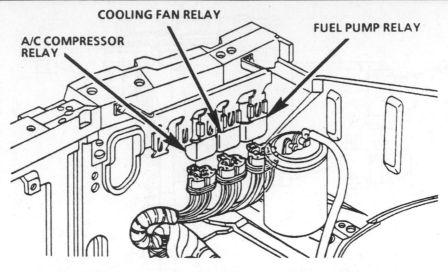

Fuel pump relay location behind the right side headlamp

COOLING FAN RELAY

A/C COMPRESSOR RELAY

FUEL PUMP RELAY

Throttle Body Unit

REMOVAL AND INSTALLATION

—— CAUTION ——

Before removing any component of the fuel system (TBI models), be sure to reduce the fuel pressure in the system. The pressure regulator (TBI models) contains an orifice in the fuel system; when the engine is turned Off, the pressure in the system will bleed down within a few minutes.

1. Refer to the Fuel Pressure Relief procedures in this section and reduce the pressure in the fuel system.
2. Disconnect the negative battery cable.
3. Remove the air cleaner.
4. Disconnect the electrical connectors from the idle air control valve, the throttle position sensor and the fuel injectors.
5. Disconnect the injector wiring harness.
6. Disconnect the throttle cable, the cruise control cable, if equipped, and the transmission control cable.
7. Label and disconnect the vacuum hoses and PCV hose from the throttle body.
8. Place a rag (to catch the excess fuel) under the fuel line-to-throttle body connection, then disconnect the fuel line from the throttle body.

NOTE: Use a back-up wrench on the TBI fuel nuts to prevent them from turning.

9. Remove the fuel line O-rings and discard.
10. Remove the TBI attaching bolts and nuts and remove the TBI unit. Discard the gasket.

To install:

11. Place a cloth in the intake manifold to prevent dirt from entering the engine.
12. Using a putty knife (if necessary), clean the gasket mounting surfaces.
13. Use a new gasket. Install the gasket, throttle body and mounting bolts. Torque the throttle body-to-intake manifold nuts/bolts to 18 ft. lbs. (25 Nm).
14. Use new O-rings and connect the fuel lines to the throttle body. Use a back-up wrench and tighten the nuts to 20 ft. lbs. (27 Nm).
15. Connect the vacuum hoses to the throttle body.
16. Install the cable support bracket and tighten the screws to 88 inch lbs.

1. Bolt
2. TBI unit
3. Gasket (installed with stripe facing up)
4. Engine intake manifold

TBI unit installation

TPS SIDE

THROTTLE LEVER OR CAM SIDE

ASSEMBLY PART NUMBER

DAY OF YEAR

LAST DIGIT OF YEAR

PLANT CODE

Fuel injector part number location

17. Install the throttle cable, transmission control cable and cruise control cable, if equipped.

18. Connect the electrical connectors to the idle air control valve, the throttle position sensor and the fuel injectors. Make sure all the connectors are fully seated and latched.

19. Connect the negative battery cable.

20. Turn the ignition switch to the **ON** position for 2 seconds then turn to the **OFF** position for 10 seconds. Again turn the switch to the **ON** position and check for leaks. With the engine **OFF**, depress the accelerator pedal to the floor and release it, to see if the pedal returns freely.

21. Install the air cleaner assembly.

22. Reset the IAC valve pintle position as follows:
    a. Depress the accelerator pedal slightly.
    b. Start and run the engine for 3 seconds.
    c. Turn the ignition **OFF** for 10 seconds.
    d. Restart the engine and check for proper idle operation.

INJECTOR REPLACEMENT

CAUTION

When removing the injector(s), be careful not to damage the electrical connector pins (on top of the injector), the injector fuel filter and the nozzle. The fuel injector is serviced as a complete assembly ONLY, it is an electrical component and should not be immersed in any kind of cleaner.

1. Remove the air cleaner. Disconnect the negative battery terminal from the battery.

2. Refer to the Fuel Pressure Relief procedures in this section and relieve the fuel pressure.

3. At the injector connector, squeeze the two tabs together and pull it straight up.

4. Remove the fuel meter cover and leave the cover gasket in place.

5. Using a small pry bar and carefully lift the injector until it is free from the fuel meter body.

6. Remove the lower small O-ring from the nozzle end of the injector and discard.

7. Discard the fuel meter cover gasket.

8. Remove the upper, large O-ring from the top of the injector cavity and discard.

To install:

9. Lubricate the new upper (large) O-ring with clean engine oil, and install in the counterbore of the fuel meter body. Make sure it is seated properly.

CAUTION

When installing an injector, install the upper O-ring before the injector to ensure proper seating of the O-ring. Reversing these steps could result in a fuel leak and possible fire.

10. Lubricate the new lower (small) O-ring with clean engine oil, and install on the nozzle end of the injector. Push the O-ring on far enough to contact the filter.

11. Install the fuel injector as follows:
    a. Align the raised lug on the injector base with the notch on the fuel meter body cavity.
    b. Push down on the injector until it is fully seated in the fuel meter body.

NOTE: The electrical terminals of the injector should be parallel with the throttle shaft.

12. Install a new pressure regulator dust seal, fuel meter outlet gasket and cover gasket.

13. Install the fuel meter cover assembly.

14. Apply Loctite®262 or equivalent to the screw threads, then install the fuel meter cover attaching screws. Tighten the screws to 27 inch lbs.

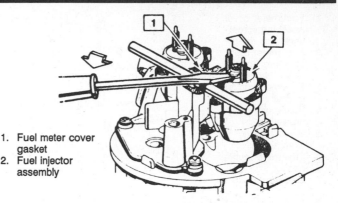

1. Fuel meter cover gasket
2. Fuel injector assembly

Removing the fuel injector

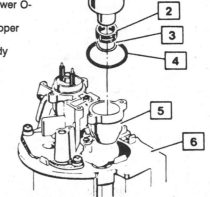

1. Fuel injector assembly
2. Fuel injector inlet filter
3. Fuel injector lower O-ring
4. Fuel injector upper O-ring
5. Fuel meter body assembly
6. Throttle body assembly

Fuel injector and O-rings

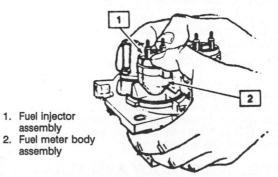

1. Fuel injector assembly
2. Fuel meter body assembly

Installing the fuel injector

15. Install the electrical connectors to the injectors.

16. Connect the negative battery cable.

FUEL METER COVER REPLACEMENT

NOTE: The fuel meter cover and pressure regulator are serviced as a complete assembly only.

1. Fuel meter cover attaching screw assembly (long)
2. Fuel meter cover attaching screw assembly (short)
3. Fuel meter cover gasket
4. Fuel meter body assembly
5. Throttle body assembly
6. Fuel meter outlet gasket
7. Pressure regulator seal
8. Fuel meter cover assembly

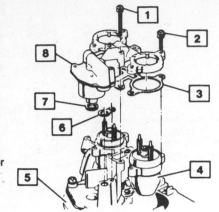

Fuel meter cover assembly

1. Fuel meter body assembly
2. Gasket
3. Fuel outlet nut gasket
4. Fuel outlet nut
5. Fuel return line O-ring
6. Fuel inlet line O-ring
7. Fuel inlet nut
8. Fuel inlet nut gasket
9. Throttle body assembly
10. Attaching screw

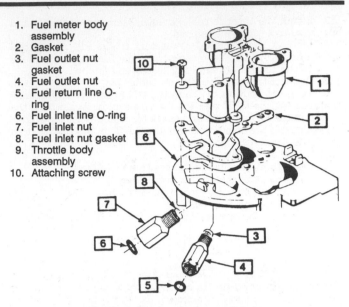

Fuel meter body assembly

─────── CAUTION ───────

Do not remove the screws securing the pressure regulator to the fuel meter cover. The regulator includes a spring, which if released, could cause personal injury. Disassembly might also result in a fuel leak between the diaphragm and the regulator container.

1. Disconnect the negative battery cable.
2. Release the fuel system pressure.
3. Remove the air cleaner assembly.
4. Disconnect the electrical connectors at the injectors by squeezing the 2 tabs together and pulling it straight up.
5. Remove the fuel meter cover attaching screws and remove the fuel meter cover.

NOTE: When removing the fuel meter cover screws, note the location of the 2 short screws.

To install:
6. Clean the gasket sealing surfaces and install a new pressure regulator dust seal, fuel meter outlet passage gasket and cover gasket.

WARNING: Do not immerse the fuel meter cover (with pressure regulator) in cleaner, as damage to the pressure regulator diaphragm could occur.

7. Install the fuel meter cover. Apply Loctite 262 or equivalent to the screw threads and install and torque the screws to 27 inch lbs. (3.0 Nm).

NOTE: Install the short screws next to the injectors.

8. Reconnect the injector electrical connectors.
9. Connect the negative battery cable.
10. Turn the ignition switch to the **ON** position for 2 seconds then turn to the **OFF** position for 10 seconds. Again turn the switch to the **ON** position and check for leaks.
11. Install the air cleaner assembly.

FUEL METER BODY ASSEMBLY

1. Remove the air cleaner. Disconnect the negative battery terminal from the battery.
2. Refer to the Fuel Pressure Relief procedures in this section and relieve the fuel pressure.
3. At the injector connector, squeeze the two tabs together and pull it straight up.
4. Remove the fuel meter cover and fuel injectors.
5. Disconnect the fuel feed and return lines.
6. Remove the fuel line O-rings and discard.
7. Remove the fuel inlet and outlet nuts and gaskets from the fuel meter body assembly.

NOTE: Remember the locations of the nuts, for proper reassembly later. The inlet nut has a larger passage than the outlet nut.

8. Remove the fuel meter body to throttle body attaching screws.
9. Remove the fuel meter body and gasket from the throttle body.
To install:
10. Properly position a new fuel meter body gasket to the throttle body.
11. Place the fuel meter body on the throttle body.
12. If there is no thread locking compound on the retaining screws, apply Loctite 262 or equivalent, to the threads, then install the screws and tighten to 35 inch lbs. (4.0 Nm).
13. Install the fuel inlet and outlet nuts with new gaskets. Tighten the inlet nut to 30 ft. lbs.(40 Nm) and the outlet nut to 21 ft. lbs. (29 Nm).
14. Install new O-rings on the fuel feed and return lines and connect the lines. Tighten the line nuts to 20 ft. lbs. (27 Nm).

WARNING: Use a back-up wrench on the TBI fuel nuts to keep them from turning.

15. Install the fuel injectors and the fuel meter cover.
16. Install the electrical connectors to the injectors.
17. Connect the negative battery cable.
18. Turn the ignition switch to the **ON** position for 2 seconds then turn to the **OFF** position for 10 seconds. Again turn the switch to the **ON** position and check for leaks.
19. Install the air cleaner assembly.

IDLE AIR CONTROL (IAC) VALVE REPLACEMENT

1. Disconnect the negative battery terminal from the battery.
2. Remove the air cleaner assembly.
3. Disconnect the electrical connector from the idle air control valve.
4. Remove the idle air control valve assembly.

NOTE: If the IAC valve has been in service, do not push or pull on the IAC valve pintle. The force required to move the pintle may damage the threads on the worm drive.

To install:

NOTE: If installing a new IAC valve, be sure to replace with an identical part. The IAC pintle shape and diameter are designed for a specific application.

5. If installing a new IAC valve, the distance between the tip of the IAC valve pintle and the mounting surface should be 28 mm. If greater than 28 mm, use finger pressure to slowly retract the pintle. This force will not cause damage to the valve.
6. Install the IAC valve and gasket.
7. Using a socket or box wrench on the valve hex, tighten the valve to 13 ft. lbs. (18 Nm).
8. Connect the IAC valve electrical connector.
9. Install the air cleaner assembly.

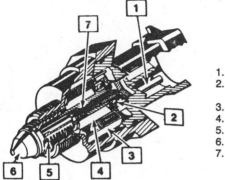

1. Terminal pins
2. Ball bearing assembly
3. Stator assembly
4. Rotor assembly
5. Spring
6. Pintle
7. Lead screw

Cross section of the Idle Air Control (IAC) valve

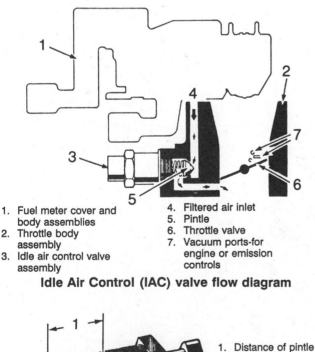

1. Fuel meter cover and body assemblies
2. Throttle body assembly
3. Idle air control valve assembly
4. Filtered air inlet
5. Pintle
6. Throttle valve
7. Vacuum ports-for engine or emission controls

Idle Air Control (IAC) valve flow diagram

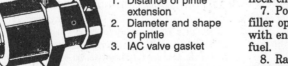

1. Distance of pintle extension
2. Diameter and shape of pintle
3. IAC valve gasket

Idle Air Control (IAC) valve pintle extension

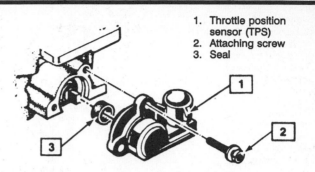

1. Throttle position sensor (TPS)
2. Attaching screw
3. Seal

Throttle position sensor installation

10. Reset the IAC valve pintle position as follows:
    a. Depress the accelerator pedal slightly.
    b. Start and run the engine for 5 seconds.
    c. Turn the ignition **OFF** for 10 seconds.
    d. Restart the engine and check for proper idle operation.
11. The vehicle may have to driven a few miles before the IAC valve will return to normal.

THROTTLE POSITION SENSOR (TPS) REPLACEMENT

1. Disconnect the negative (−) battery cable.2. Remove the air cleaner assembly.
3. Disconnect the electrical connector from the throttle position sensor (TPS).
4. Remove the throttle position sensor mounting screws and remove the throttle position sensor and seal.
To install:
5. Install the throttle position sensor and seal. Line up the TPS lever with the TPS drive lever on the throttle body.
6. Coat the retaining screws with Loctite® (thread locking compound) No. 262. Install the mounting screws and torque to 18 inch lbs. (2.0 Nm).
7. Connect the electrical connector to the throttle position sensor.
8. Connect the negative (−) battery cable and install the air cleaner.
9. Start the engine and check for proper operation.

Fuel Tank

REMOVAL AND INSTALLATION

1. Disconnect the negative battery cable.
2. Relieve the fuel system pressure.
3. Block the front wheels and raise and support the rear of the vehicle safely. The rear bumper should be at least 28 in. (711mm) above the ground.
4. Loosen the fuel filler neck connecting tube clamp at the tank.
5. Wrap a shop towel around the fuel filter neck connecting tube and slowly remove the fuel filler neck connecting tube from the fuel tank.
6. Using a 18 in. (457mm) socket extension, push the filler neck check-ball into the tank.
7. Position a siphon hose into the fuel tank through the fuel filler opening. Place the other end into a approved container with enough capacity to hold the fuel in the tank. Siphon the fuel.
8. Raise the vehicle to gain access to the fuel tank. Make sure the vehicle is safely supported.
9. Disconnect the tail pipe hanger attaching bolt.
10. Remove the muffler hanger attaching bolts and remove the muffler hanger.

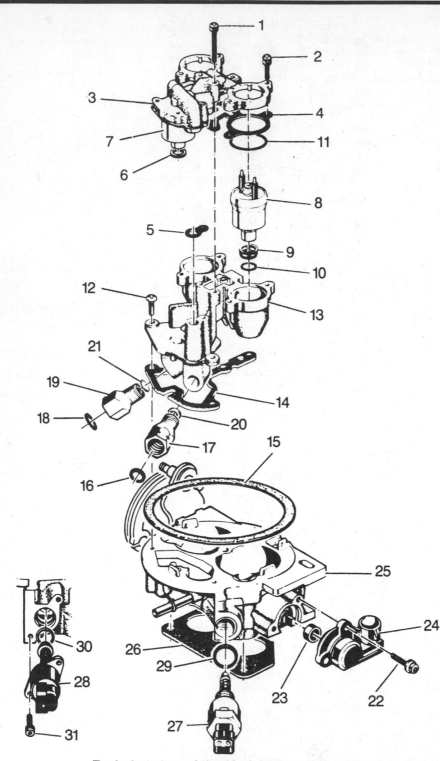

1. Fuel meter screw
2. Fuel meter cover attaching screw (short)
3. Fuel meter cover assembly
4. Fuel meter cover gasket
5. Fuel meter outlet gasket
6. Pressure regulator seal
7. Pressure regulator
8. Fuel injector assembly
9. Fuel injector inlet filter
10. Fuel injector lower O-ring
11. Fuel injector upper O-ring
12. Fuel meter body screw
13. Fuel meter body assembly
14. Gasket
15. Air cleaner gasket
16. Fuel return line O-ring
17. Fuel outlet nut
18. Fuel inlet line O-ring
19. Fuel inlet nut
20. Fuel outlet nut gasket
21. Fuel outlet nut gasket
22. TPS attaching screw
23. TPS seal
24. TPS sensor
25. Throttle body assembly
26. Flange gasket
27. Idle air control valve (thread mounted)
28. Idle air control valve (flange mounted)
29. Idle air control valve gasket
30. Idle air control valve O-ring
31. Idle air control valve attaching screw

Exploded view of the Model 220 throttle body injection unit assembly

11. Loosen the converter hanger attaching nuts.

12. Remove the 2 heat shield attaching screws and note the position for reassembly.

13. Support the exhaust and move the heat shield to gain the access to the right side of the fuel tank retaining strap attaching bolts.

14. Remove the in-line fuel filter body clips.

NOTE: If the nylon fuel feed or return lines becomes kinked, and cannot be straightened, they must be replaced. Do not attempt to repair sections of the nylon fuel lines.

15. Disconnect the quick-connect fitting at the inlet side of the in-line fuel filter, and return line fitting near the in-line fuel filter as follows:

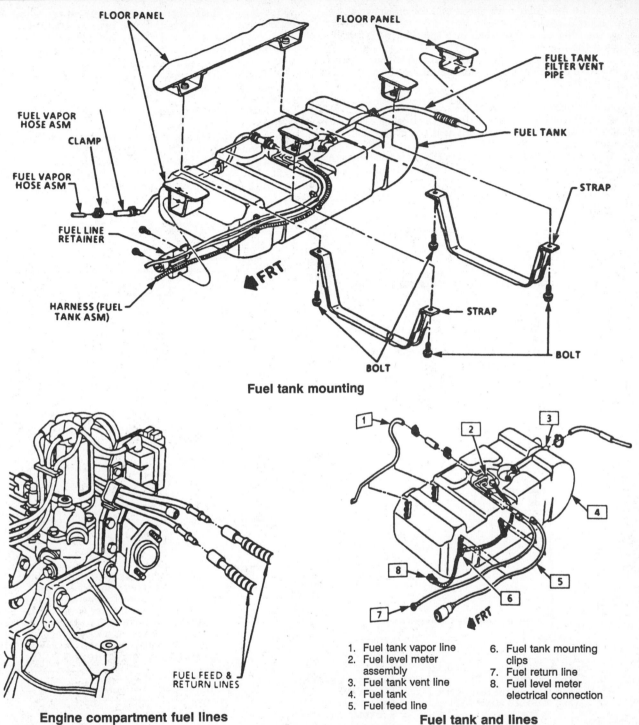

Fuel tank mounting

Engine compartment fuel lines

1. Fuel tank vapor line
2. Fuel level meter assembly
3. Fuel tank vent line
4. Fuel tank
5. Fuel feed line
6. Fuel tank mounting clips
7. Fuel return line
8. Fuel level meter electrical connection

Fuel tank and lines

a. Grasp both ends of one fuel line fitting connection and twist the quick connect fitting ¼ turn in each direction to loosen any dirt within the fitting. Repeat for the other fuel line fitting.

b. Squeeze the plastic tabs of the male end connector and pull the connection apart. Repeat for the return line fitting.

16. Disconnect the fuel level meter electrical connector.
17. Disconnect the vapor hose at the fuel tank.
18. Disconnect the vent hose at the fuel tank.
19. With the aid of an assistant, support the fuel tank and re-move the left and right tank retaining strap attaching bolts and remove the tank.

20. As necessary, remove the fuel meter assembly (which includes the fuel pump), as outlined under Electric Fuel Pump removal, in this section.
21. Remove the filler neck check-ball.

To install:
22. If the fuel tank is replaced, transfer the fuel feed and re-turn lines from the mounting clips, the vapor hose from the mounting clips and the vent hose from the vent hose fitting.

23. Check the fuel filler neck check-ball for cracks and holes and replace as necessary.

24. Pop the filler neck check-ball into the filler neck tube.

25. Install the fuel level meter.

26. With the aid of an assistant, position and support the fuel tank and install the left and right tank retaining strap attaching bolts and tighten to 18 ft. lbs.

27. Connect the vent and vapor hoses.

28. Connect the fuel meter level electrical connector.

29. Connect the quick-connect fitting at the inlet side of the in-line fuel filter, and return line fitting near the in-line fuel filter as follows:

a. Apply a few drops of engine oil to the male tube ends and push the connectors together to cause the retaining tabs to snap into place.

b. Once installed pull on both ends of each connection to make sure they are secure.

30. Position the fuel level meter electrical connector and fuel return line under the in-line fuel filter bracket.

31. Install the in-line fuel filter and new body clips.

32. Reposition the heat shield as noted during removal and tighten the retaining screws to 18 ft. lbs.

33. Tighten the converter hanger attaching bolts to 20 ft. lbs.

34. Install the muffler hanger and attching bolts and tighten to 18 ft. lbs.

35. Install the tailpipe hanger attaching bolt and tighten to 20 ft. lbs.

36. Lower the vehicle, add fuel and install the fuel filler cap.

37. Connect the negative battery cable.

38. Turn the ignition switch to the **ON** position for 2 seconds then turn to the **OFF** position for 5 seconds. Again turn the switch to the **ON** position and check for leaks.

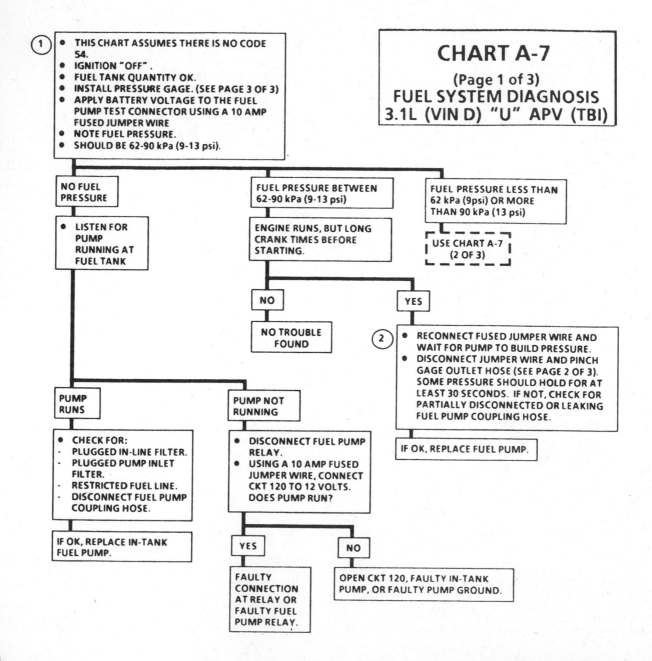

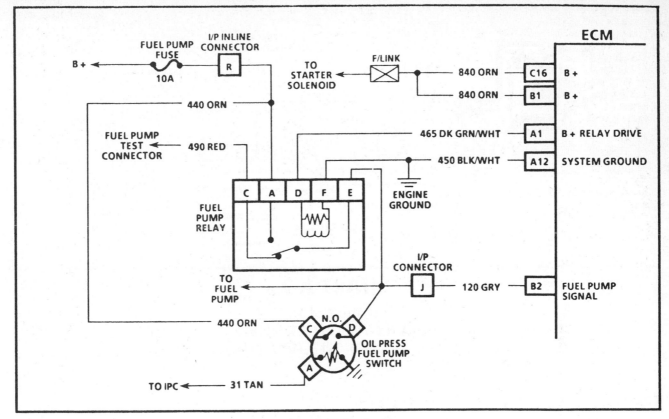

CHART A-7

(Page 1 of 3)
FUEL SYSTEM DIAGNOSIS
3.1L (VIN D) "U" APV (TBI)

Circuit Description:

When the ignition switch is turned "ON," the Electronic Control Module (ECM) will turn "ON" the in-tank fuel pump. It will remain "ON" as long as the engine is cranking or running, and the ECM is receiving ignition reference pulses.

If there are no reference pulses, the ECM will shut "OFF" the fuel pump within 2 seconds after key "ON."

The pump will deliver fuel to the TBI unit where the system pressure is controlled to 62 to 90 kPa (9 to 13 psi). Excess fuel is then returned to the fuel tank.

The fuel pump test terminal is located in the left side of the engine compartment. When the engine is stopped, the pump can be turned "ON" by applying battery voltage to the test terminal.

Test Description: Number(s) below refer to circled number(s) on the diagnostic chart.

1. Fuel pressure should be noted while fuel pump is running. Fuel pressure will drop immediately after fuel pump stops running due to a controlled bleed in the fuel system.

2. Restricting the fuel supply line between the gage and TBI unit and turning the pump "ON" will determine if the fuel pump can supply enough fuel pressure at the injector to operate properly, above 62 kPa (9 psi).

Diagnostic Aids:

Improper fuel system pressure can result in one of the following symptoms:

- Cranks, but won't run.
- Code 44.
- Code 45.
- Cuts out, may feel like ignition problem.
- Poor fuel economy, loss of power.
- Hesitation.

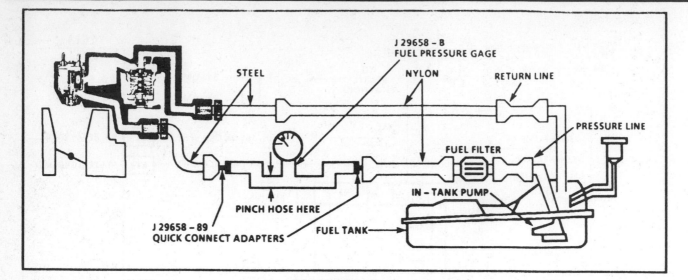

CHART A-7

(Page 2 of 3)
FUEL SYSTEM DIAGNOSIS
3.1L (VIN D) "U" APV (TBI)

Test Description: Number(s) below refer to circled number(s) on the diagnostic chart.

1. Pressure less than 62 kPa (9 psi) falls into two areas:
   - Regulated less pressure under 62 kPa (9 psi). Amount of fuel to injectors OK but, pressure is too low. System will be lean and may set Code 44. Also, hard starting cold and poor overall performance.
   - Restricted flow causing pressure drop. Normally, a vehicle with a fuel pressure of less than 62 kPa (9 psi) at idle will not be driveable. However, if the pressure drop occurs only while driving, the engine will normally surge then stop as pressure begins to drop rapidly.

2. Turning the fuel pump "ON" and restricting fuel flow at the fuel pressure gage (as shown) will determine if the fuel pump can supply enough fuel pressure to the injector to operate properly, above 62 kPa (9 psi).

3. This test determines if the high fuel pressure is due to a restricted fuel return line or a throttle body pressure regulator problem. Apply battery voltage to the fuel pump "test" connector only long enough to get an accurate fuel pressure reading.

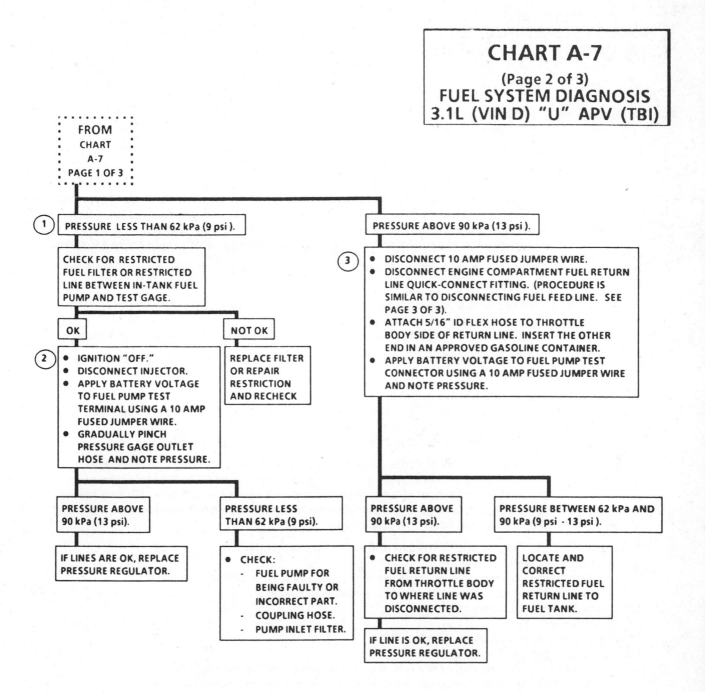

CHART A-7
(Page 2 of 3)
FUEL SYSTEM DIAGNOSIS
3.1L (VIN D) "U" APV (TBI)

FROM
CHART
A-7
PAGE 1 OF 3

① PRESSURE LESS THAN 62 kPa (9 psi).

CHECK FOR RESTRICTED
FUEL FILTER OR RESTRICTED
LINE BETWEEN IN-TANK FUEL
PUMP AND TEST GAGE.

OK

NOT OK

② • IGNITION "OFF."
• DISCONNECT INJECTOR.
• APPLY BATTERY VOLTAGE
  TO FUEL PUMP TEST
  TERMINAL USING A 10 AMP
  FUSED JUMPER WIRE.
• GRADUALLY PINCH
  PRESSURE GAGE OUTLET
  HOSE AND NOTE PRESSURE.

REPLACE FILTER
OR REPAIR
RESTRICTION
AND RECHECK

PRESSURE ABOVE
90 kPa (13 psi).

IF LINES ARE OK, REPLACE
PRESSURE REGULATOR.

PRESSURE LESS
THAN 62 kPa (9 psi).

• CHECK:
  - FUEL PUMP FOR
    BEING FAULTY OR
    INCORRECT PART.
  - COUPLING HOSE.
  - PUMP INLET FILTER.

PRESSURE ABOVE 90 kPa (13 psi).

③ • DISCONNECT 10 AMP FUSED JUMPER WIRE.
• DISCONNECT ENGINE COMPARTMENT FUEL RETURN
  LINE QUICK-CONNECT FITTING. (PROCEDURE IS
  SIMILAR TO DISCONNECTING FUEL FEED LINE. SEE
  PAGE 3 OF 3).
• ATTACH 5/16" ID FLEX HOSE TO THROTTLE
  BODY SIDE OF RETURN LINE. INSERT THE OTHER
  END IN AN APPROVED GASOLINE CONTAINER.
• APPLY BATTERY VOLTAGE TO FUEL PUMP TEST
  CONNECTOR USING A 10 AMP FUSED JUMPER WIRE
  AND NOTE PRESSURE.

PRESSURE ABOVE
90 kPa (13 psi).

PRESSURE BETWEEN 62 kPa AND
90 kPa (9 psi - 13 psi).

• CHECK FOR RESTRICTED
  FUEL RETURN LINE
  FROM THROTTLE BODY
  TO WHERE LINE WAS
  DISCONNECTED.

LOCATE AND
CORRECT
RESTRICTED FUEL
RETURN LINE TO
FUEL TANK.

IF LINE IS OK, REPLACE
PRESSURE REGULATOR.

CHART A-7
(Page 3 of 3)
FUEL SYSTEM DIAGNOSIS
3.1L (VIN D) "U" APV (TBI)

FUEL PRESSURE CHECK

Tools Required: J 29658-B - Fuel Pressure Gage
J 29658-89 - Fuel Pressure Quick Connect Adapters
. J 37088 - Fuel Line Quick-Connect Separators

CAUTION: To Reduce the Risk of Fire and Personal Injury:
- It is necessary to relieve fuel system pressure before connecting a fuel pressure gage.
- A small amount of fuel may be released when disconnecting the fuel lines. Cover fuel line fittings with a shop towel before disconnecting, to catch any fuel that may leak out. Place towel in approved container when disconnect is completed.
- Do not pinch or restrict nylon fuel lines to avoid severing, which could cause a fuel leak.

NOTICE: • If nylon fuel lines become kinked, and cannot be straightened, they must be replaced.

1. Disconnect negative battery terminal.
2. Loosen fuel filler cap to relieve fuel tank pressure. (Do not tighten at this time.)
3. Locate engine compartment fuel feed quick-connect fitting.
4. Grasp both ends of fitting, twist female end ¼ turn in each direction to loosen any dirt in fitting.

CAUTION: Safety glasses must be worn when using compressed air, as flying dirt particles may cause eye injury.

5. Using compressed air, blow dirt out of quick-connect fitting.
6. Choose correct tool from separator tool set J 37088 for size of fitting. Insert tool into female end of connector, then push inward to release male connector.
7. Connect gage quick-connect adapters J 29658-89 to fuel pressure gage J 29658-B.

CAUTION: To Reduce the Risk of Fire and Personal Injury: Before connecting fuel line quick-connect fittings, always apply a few drops of clean engine oil to the male tube ends. This will ensure proper reconnection and prevent a possible fuel leak. (During normal operation, the O-rings located inside the female connector will swell and may prevent proper reconnection if not lubricated.)

8. Lubricate the male tube end of the fuel line and the gage adapter with engine oil.
9. Connect fuel pressure gage.
   - Push connectors together to cause the retaining tabs/fingers to snap into place.
   - Once installed, pull on both ends of each connection to make sure it is secure.
10. Connect negative battery terminal.
11. Check fuel pressure.
12. Disconnect negative battery terminal.
13. Disconnect fuel pressure gage.
14. Lubricate the male tube end of the fuel line, and reconnect quick-connect fitting.
    - Push connector together to cause the retaining tabs/fingers to snap into place.
    - Once installed, pull on both ends of connection to make sure it is secure.
15. Tighten fuel filler cap.
16. Connect negative battery terminal.
17. Cycle ignition "ON" and "OFF" twice, waiting ten seconds between cycles, then check for fuel leaks.

"AFTER REPAIRS," CONFIRM "CLOSED LOOP" OPERATION AND NO "SERVICE ENGINE SOON" LIGHT.

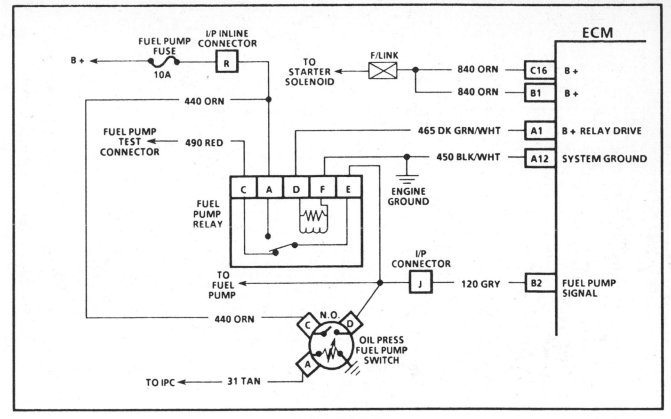

CODE 54

FUEL PUMP CIRCUIT
(LOW VOLTAGE)
3.1L (VIN D) "U" APV (TBI)

Circuit Description:

When the ignition switch is turned "ON," the Electronic Control Module (ECM) will activate the fuel pump relay and run the in-tank fuel pump. The fuel pump will operate as long as the engine is cranking or running, and the ECM is receiving ignition reference pulses.

If there are no reference pulses, the ECM will shut "OFF" the fuel pump within 2 seconds after key "ON."

Should the fuel pump relay, or the 12 volt relay drive from the ECM fail, the fuel pump will be run through an oil pressure switch back-up circuit.

Diagnostic Aids:

An inoperative fuel pump relay can result in long cranking times, particularly if the engine is cold or engine oil pressure is low. The extended crank period is caused by the time necessary for oil pressure to build enough to close the oil pressure switch and turn "ON" the fuel pump.

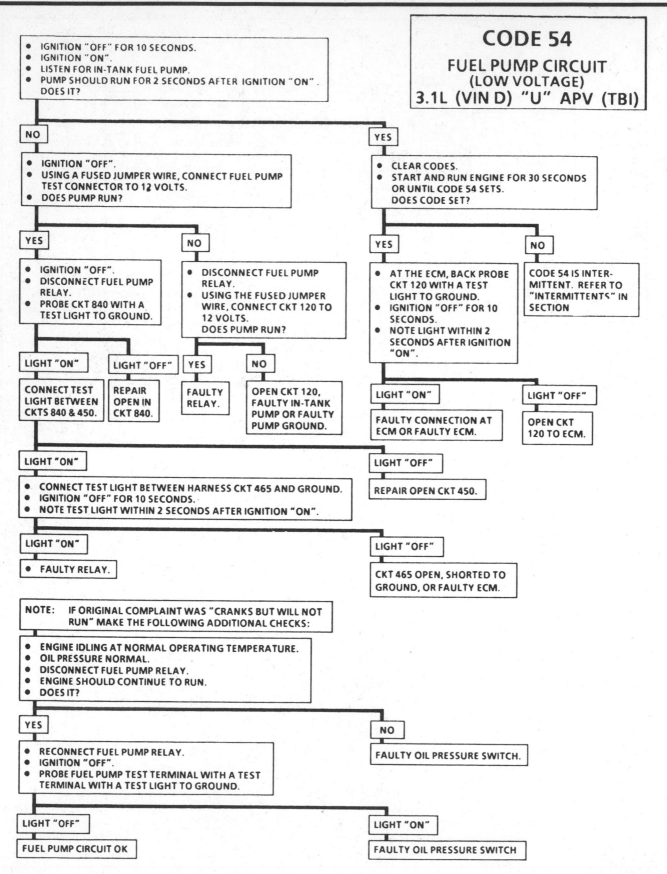

CODE 54
FUEL PUMP CIRCUIT
(LOW VOLTAGE)
3.1L (VIN D) "U" APV (TBI)

- IGNITION "OFF" FOR 10 SECONDS.
- IGNITION "ON".
- LISTEN FOR IN-TANK FUEL PUMP.
- PUMP SHOULD RUN FOR 2 SECONDS AFTER IGNITION "ON".
  DOES IT?

NO

- IGNITION "OFF".
- USING A FUSED JUMPER WIRE, CONNECT FUEL PUMP TEST CONNECTOR TO 12 VOLTS.
- DOES PUMP RUN?

YES

- IGNITION "OFF".
- DISCONNECT FUEL PUMP RELAY.
- PROBE CKT 840 WITH A TEST LIGHT TO GROUND.

NO

- DISCONNECT FUEL PUMP RELAY.
- USING THE FUSED JUMPER WIRE, CONNECT CKT 120 TO 12 VOLTS.
  DOES PUMP RUN?

LIGHT "ON"

CONNECT TEST LIGHT BETWEEN CKTS 840 & 450.

LIGHT "OFF"

REPAIR OPEN IN CKT 840.

YES

FAULTY RELAY.

NO

OPEN CKT 120, FAULTY IN-TANK PUMP OR FAULTY PUMP GROUND.

LIGHT "ON"

- CONNECT TEST LIGHT BETWEEN HARNESS CKT 465 AND GROUND.
- IGNITION "OFF" FOR 10 SECONDS.
- NOTE TEST LIGHT WITHIN 2 SECONDS AFTER IGNITION "ON".

LIGHT "ON"

- FAULTY RELAY.

NOTE: IF ORIGINAL COMPLAINT WAS "CRANKS BUT WILL NOT RUN" MAKE THE FOLLOWING ADDITIONAL CHECKS:

- ENGINE IDLING AT NORMAL OPERATING TEMPERATURE.
- OIL PRESSURE NORMAL.
- DISCONNECT FUEL PUMP RELAY.
- ENGINE SHOULD CONTINUE TO RUN.
- DOES IT?

YES

- RECONNECT FUEL PUMP RELAY.
- IGNITION "OFF".
- PROBE FUEL PUMP TEST TERMINAL WITH A TEST TERMINAL WITH A TEST LIGHT TO GROUND.

LIGHT "OFF"

FUEL PUMP CIRCUIT OK

NO

FAULTY OIL PRESSURE SWITCH.

LIGHT "ON"

FAULTY OIL PRESSURE SWITCH

YES

- CLEAR CODES.
- START AND RUN ENGINE FOR 30 SECONDS OR UNTIL CODE 54 SETS.
  DOES CODE SET?

YES

- AT THE ECM, BACK PROBE CKT 120 WITH A TEST LIGHT TO GROUND.
- IGNITION "OFF" FOR 10 SECONDS.
- NOTE LIGHT WITHIN 2 SECONDS AFTER IGNITION "ON".

NO

CODE 54 IS INTERMITTENT. REFER TO "INTERMITTENTS" IN SECTION

LIGHT "ON"

FAULTY CONNECTION AT ECM OR FAULTY ECM.

LIGHT "OFF"

OPEN CKT 120 TO ECM.

LIGHT "OFF"

REPAIR OPEN CKT 450.

LIGHT "OFF"

CKT 465 OPEN, SHORTED TO GROUND, OR FAULTY ECM.

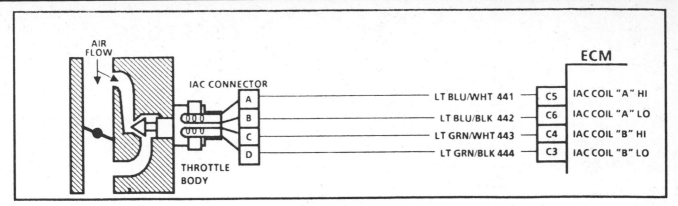

CHART C-2C
IDLE AIR CONTROL (IAC) VALVE CHECK
3.1L (VIN D) "U" APV (TBI)

Circuit Description:

The ECM controls engine idle speed with the IAC valve. To increase idle speed, the ECM retracts the IAC valve pintle away from its seat, allowing more air to pass by the throttle bore. To decrease idle speed, it extends the IAC valve pintle towards its seat, reducing bypass air flow. A "Scan" tool will read the ECM commands to the IAC valve in counts. Higher the counts, indicate more air bypass (higher idle). The lower the counts indicate less air is allowed to bypass (lower idle).

Test Description: Number(s) below refer to circled number(s) on the diagnostic chart.

1. The IAC tester is used to extend and retract the IAC valve. Valve movement is verified by an engine speed change. If no change in engine speed occurs, the valve can be retested when removed from the throttle body.

2. This step checks the quality of the IAC movement in Step 1. Between 700 rpm and about 1500 rpm, the engine speed should change smoothly with each flash of the tester light in both extend and retract. If the IAC valve is retracted beyond the control range (about 1500 rpm), it may take many flashes in the extend position before engine speed will begin to drop. This is normal on certain engines, fully extending IAC may cause engine stall. This may be normal.

3. Steps 1 and 2 verified proper IAC valve operation while this step checks the IAC circuits. Each lamp on the mode light should flash red and green while the IAC valve is cycled. While the sequence of color is not important if either light is "OFF" or does not flash red and green, check the circuits for faults, beginning with poor terminal contacts.

Diagnostic Aids:

A slow, unstable, or fast idle may be caused by a non-IAC system problem that cannot be overcome by the IAC valve. Out of control range IAC "Scan" tool counts will be above 60 if idle is too low, and "0" counts, if idle is too high. The following checks should be made to repair a non-IAC system problem:

- Vacuum Leak (High Idle) - If idle is too high, stop the engine. Fully extend (low) IAC with tester. Start engine. If idle speed is above 800 rpm, locate and correct vacuum leak including PCV system. Also check for binding of throttle blade or linkage.
- System too lean (High Air/Fuel Ratio) - The idle speed may be too high or too low. Engine speed may vary up and down and disconnecting IAC valve does not help. Code 44 may set.
  "Scan" O_2 voltage will be less than 300 mV (.3 volt). Check for low regulated fuel pressure, water in fuel, or restricted injector.
- System too rich (Low Air/Fuel Ratio) - The idle speed will be too low. "Scan" tool IAC counts will usually be above 80. System is obviously rich and may exhibit black smoke in exhaust.
  "Scan" tool O_2 voltage will be fixed above 800 mV (.8 volt).
  Check for high fuel pressure, leaking or sticking injector. Silicone contaminated O_2 sensors "Scan" voltage will be slow to respond.
- Throttle Body - Remove IAC valve and inspect bore for foreign material.
- IAC Valve Electrical Connections - IAC valve connections should be carefully checked for proper contact.
- PCV Valve - An incorrect or faulty PCV valve may result in an incorrect idle speed.
- Refer to "Rough, Unstable, Incorrect Idle or Stalling" in "Symptoms" Section "6E2-B".
- If intermittent poor driveability or idle symptoms are resolved by disconnecting the IAC, carefully re-check connections, valve terminal resistance or replace IAC.

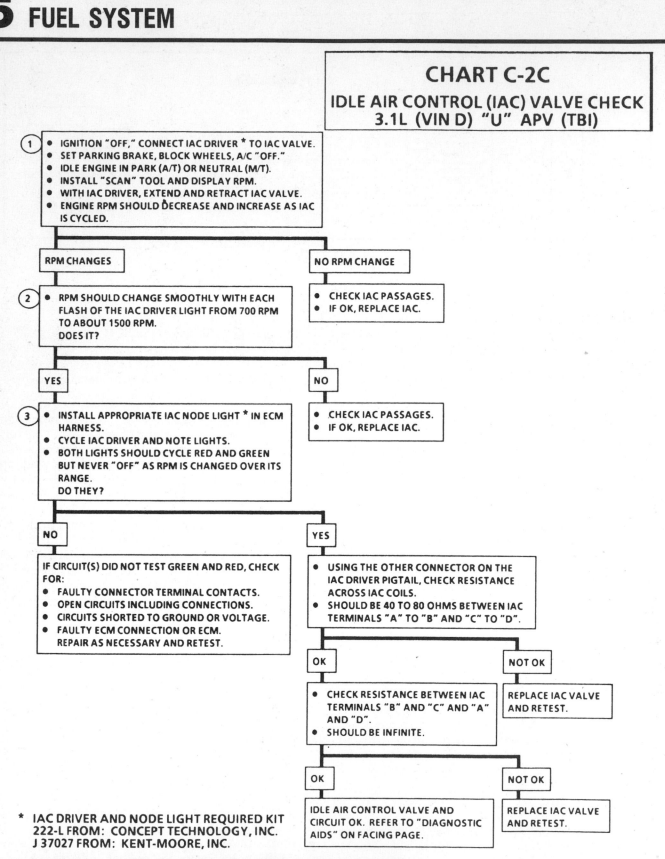

CHART C-2C
IDLE AIR CONTROL (IAC) VALVE CHECK
3.1L (VIN D) "U" APV (TBI)

1
- IGNITION "OFF," CONNECT IAC DRIVER * TO IAC VALVE.
- SET PARKING BRAKE, BLOCK WHEELS, A/C "OFF."
- IDLE ENGINE IN PARK (A/T) OR NEUTRAL (M/T).
- INSTALL "SCAN" TOOL AND DISPLAY RPM.
- WITH IAC DRIVER, EXTEND AND RETRACT IAC VALVE.
- ENGINE RPM SHOULD DECREASE AND INCREASE AS IAC IS CYCLED.

RPM CHANGES

NO RPM CHANGE

2
- RPM SHOULD CHANGE SMOOTHLY WITH EACH FLASH OF THE IAC DRIVER LIGHT FROM 700 RPM TO ABOUT 1500 RPM. DOES IT?

- CHECK IAC PASSAGES.
- IF OK, REPLACE IAC.

YES

NO

3
- INSTALL APPROPRIATE IAC NODE LIGHT * IN ECM HARNESS.
- CYCLE IAC DRIVER AND NOTE LIGHTS.
- BOTH LIGHTS SHOULD CYCLE RED AND GREEN BUT NEVER "OFF" AS RPM IS CHANGED OVER ITS RANGE. DO THEY?

- CHECK IAC PASSAGES.
- IF OK, REPLACE IAC.

NO

YES

IF CIRCUIT(S) DID NOT TEST GREEN AND RED, CHECK FOR:
- FAULTY CONNECTOR TERMINAL CONTACTS.
- OPEN CIRCUITS INCLUDING CONNECTIONS.
- CIRCUITS SHORTED TO GROUND OR VOLTAGE.
- FAULTY ECM CONNECTION OR ECM. REPAIR AS NECESSARY AND RETEST.

- USING THE OTHER CONNECTOR ON THE IAC DRIVER PIGTAIL, CHECK RESISTANCE ACROSS IAC COILS.
- SHOULD BE 40 TO 80 OHMS BETWEEN IAC TERMINALS "A" TO "B" AND "C" TO "D".

OK

NOT OK

- CHECK RESISTANCE BETWEEN IAC TERMINALS "B" AND "C" AND "A" AND "D".
- SHOULD BE INFINITE.

REPLACE IAC VALVE AND RETEST.

OK

NOT OK

IDLE AIR CONTROL VALVE AND CIRCUIT OK. REFER TO "DIAGNOSTIC AIDS" ON FACING PAGE.

REPLACE IAC VALVE AND RETEST.

* IAC DRIVER AND NODE LIGHT REQUIRED KIT 222-L FROM: CONCEPT TECHNOLOGY, INC. J 37027 FROM: KENT-MOORE, INC.

CLEAR CODES, CONFIRM "CLOSED LOOP" OPERATION, NO "SERVICE ENGINE SOON" LIGHT, PERFORM IAC RESET PROCEDURE PER APPLICABLE SERVICE MANUAL AND VERIFY CONTROLLED IDLE SPEED IS CORRECT.

6 Chassis Electrical

UNDERSTANDING BASIC ELECTRICITY

At the rate which both import and domestic manufacturers are incorporating electronic control systems into their production lines, it won't be long before every new vehicle is equipped with one or more on-board computer. These electronic components (with no moving parts) should theoretically last the life of the vehicle, provided nothing external happens to damage the circuits or memory chips.

While it is true that electronic components should never wear out, in the real world malfunctions do occur. It is also true that any computer-based system is extremely sensitive to electrical voltages and cannot tolerate careless or haphazard testing or service procedures. An inexperienced individual can literally do major damage looking for a minor problem by using the wrong kind of test equipment or connecting test leads or connectors with the ignition switch ON. When selecting test equipment, make sure the manufacturers instructions state that the tester is compatible with whatever type of electronic control system is being serviced. Read all instructions carefully and double check all test points before installing probes or making any test connections.

The following section outlines basic diagnosis techniques for dealing with computerized automotive control systems. Along with a general explanation of the various types of test equipment available to aid in servicing modern electronic automotive systems, basic repair techniques for wiring harnesses and connectors is given. Read the basic information before attempting any repairs or testing on any computerized system, to provide the background of information necessary to avoid the most common and obvious mistakes that can cost both time and money. Although the replacement and testing procedures are simple in themselves, the systems are not, and unless one has a thorough understanding of all components and their function within a particular computerized control system, the logical test sequence these systems demand cannot be followed. Minor malfunctions can make a big difference, so it is important to know how each component affects the operation of the overall electronic system to find the ultimate cause of a problem without replacing good components unnecessarily. It is not enough to use the correct test equipment; the test equipment must be used correctly.

Safety Precautions

——————— CAUTION ———————

Whenever working on or around any computer based microprocessor control system, always observe these general precautions to prevent the possibility of personal injury or damage to electronic components.

• Never install or remove battery cables with the key ON or the engine running. Jumper cables should be connected with the key OFF to avoid power surges that can damage electronic control units. Engines equipped with computer controlled systems should avoid both giving and getting jump starts due to the possibility of serious damage to components from arcing in the engine compartment when connections are made with the ignition ON.

• Always remove the battery cables before charging the battery. Never use a high output charger on an installed battery or attempt to use any type of "hot shot" (24 volt) starting aid.

• Exercise care when inserting test probes into connectors to insure good connections without damaging the connector or spreading the pins. Always probe connectors from the rear (wire) side, NOT the pin side, to avoid accidental shorting of terminals during test procedures.

• Never remove or attach wiring harness connectors with the ignition switch ON, especially to an electronic control unit.

• Do not drop any components during service procedures and never apply 12 volts directly to any component (like a solenoid or relay) unless instructed specifically to do so. Some component electrical windings are designed to safely handle only 4 or 5 volts and can be destroyed in seconds if 12 volts are applied directly to the connector.

• Remove the electronic control unit if the vehicle is to be placed in an environment where temperatures exceed approximately 176°F (80°C), such as a paint spray booth or when arc or gas welding near the control unit location in the car.

ORGANIZED TROUBLESHOOTING

When diagnosing a specific problem, organized troubleshooting is a must. The complexity of a modern automobile demands that you approach any problem in a logical, organized manner. There are certain troubleshooting techniques that are standard:

1. Establish when the problem occurs. Does the problem appear only under certain conditions? Were there any noises, odors, or other unusual symptoms?

2. Isolate the problem area. To do this, make some simple tests and observations; then eliminate the systems that are working properly. Check for obvious problems such as broken wires, dirty connections or split or disconnected vacuum hoses. Always check the obvious before assuming something complicated is the cause.

3. Test for problems systematically to determine the cause once the problem area is isolated. Are all the components functioning properly? Is there power going to electrical switches and motors? Is there vacuum at vacuum switches and/or actuators? Is there a mechanical problem such as bent linkage or loose mounting screws? Doing careful, systematic checks will often turn up most causes on the first inspection without wasting time checking components that have little or no relationship to the problem.

4. Test all repairs after the work is done to make sure that the problem is fixed. Some causes can be traced to more than one component, so a careful verification of repair work is important to pick up additional malfunctions that may cause a problem to reappear or a different problem to arise. A blown fuse, for example, is a simple problem that may require more than another fuse to repair. If you don't look for a problem that caused a fuse to blow, for example, a shorted wire may go undetected.

Experience has shown that most problems tend to be the result of a fairly simple and obvious cause, such as loose or corroded connectors or air leaks in the intake system; making careful inspection of components during testing essential to quick and accurate troubleshooting. Special, hand held computerized testers designed specifically for diagnosing the Computer Command Control system are available from a variety of aftermarket sources, as well as from the vehicle manufacturer, but care should be taken that any test equipment being used is designed to diagnose that particular computer controlled system accurately without damaging the control module (ECM) or components being tested.

NOTE: Pinpointing the exact cause of trouble in an electrical system can sometimes only be accomplished by the use of special test equipment. The following describes commonly used test equipment and explains how to put it to best use in diagnosis. In addition to the information covered below, the manufacturer's instructions booklet provided with the tester should be read and clearly understood before attempting any test procedures.

TEST EQUIPMENT

Jumper Wires

Jumper wires are simple, yet extremely valuable, pieces of

test equipment. Jumper wires are merely wires that are used to bypass sections of a circuit. The simplest type of jumper wire is merely a length of multistrand wire with an alligator clip at each end. Jumper wires are usually fabricated from lengths of standard automotive wire and whatever type of connector (alligator clip, spade connector or pin connector) that is required for the particular vehicle being tested. The well equipped tool box will have several different styles of jumper wires in several different lengths. Some jumper wires are made with three or more terminals coming from a common splice for special purpose testing. In cramped, hard-to-reach areas it is advisable to have insulated boots over the jumper wire terminals in order to prevent accidental grounding, sparks, and possible fire, especially when testing fuel system components.

Jumper wires are used primarily to locate open electrical circuits, on either the ground (−) side of the circuit or on the hot (+) side. If an electrical component fails to operate, connect the jumper wire between the component and a good ground. If the component operates only with the jumper installed, the ground circuit is open. If the ground circuit is good, but the component does not operate, the circuit between the power feed and component is open. You can sometimes connect the jumper wire directly from the battery to the hot terminal of the component, but first make sure the component uses 12 volts in operation. Some electrical components, such as fuel injectors, are designed to operate on about 4 volts and running 12 volts directly to the injector terminals can burn out the wiring. By inserting an inline fuseholder between a set of test leads, a fused jumper wire can be used for bypassing open circuits. Use a 5 amp fuse to provide protection against voltage spikes. When in doubt, use a voltmeter to check the voltage input to the component and measure how much voltage is being applied normally. By moving the jumper wire successively back from the lamp toward the power source, you can isolate the area of the circuit where the open is located. When the component stops functioning, or the power is cut off, the open is in the segment of wire between the jumper and the point previously tested.

CAUTION

Never use jumpers made from wire that is of lighter gauge than used in the circuit under test. If the jumper wire is of too small gauge, it may overheat and possibly melt. Never use jumpers to bypass high resistance loads (such as motors) in a circuit. Bypassing resistances, in effect, creates a short circuit which may, in turn, cause damage and fire. Never use a jumper for anything other than temporary bypassing of components in a circuit.

12 Volt Test Light

The 12 volt test light is used to check circuits and components while electrical current is flowing through them. It is used for voltage and ground tests. Twelve volt test lights come in different styles but all have three main parts; a ground clip, a probe, and a light. The most commonly used 12 volt test lights have pick-type probes. To use a 12 volt test light, connect the ground clip to a good ground and probe wherever necessary with the pick. The pick should be sharp so that it can penetrate wire insulation to make contact with the wire, without making a large hole in the insulation. The wrap-around light is handy in hard to reach areas or where it is difficult to support a wire to push a probe pick into it. To use the wrap around light, hook the wire to probed with the hook and pull the trigger. A small pick will be forced through the wire insulation into the wire core.

CAUTION

Do not use a test light to probe electronic ignition spark plug or coil wires. Never use a pick-type test light to probe wiring on computer controlled systems unless specifically instructed to do so. Any wire insulation that is pierced by the test light probe should be taped and sealed with silicone after testing.

Like the jumper wire, the 12 volt test light is used to isolate opens in circuits. But, whereas the jumper wire is used to bypass the open to operate the load, the 12 volt test light is used to locate the presence of voltage in a circuit. If the test light glows, you know that there is power up to that point; if the 12 volt test light does not glow when its probe is inserted into the wire or connector, you know that there is an open circuit (no power). Move the test light in successive steps back toward the power source until the light in the handle does glow. When it does glow, the open is between the probe and point previously probed.

NOTE: The test light does not detect that 12 volts (or any particular amount of voltage) is present; it only detects that some voltage is present. It is advisable before using the test light to touch its terminals across the battery posts to make sure the light is operating properly.

Self-Powered Test Light

The self-powered test light usually contains a 1.5 volt penlight battery. One type of self-powered test light is similar in design to the 12 volt test light. This type has both the battery and the light in the handle and pick-type probe tip. The second type has the light toward the open tip, so that the light illuminates the contact point. The self-powered test light is dual purpose piece of test equipment. It can be used to test for either open or short circuits when power is isolated from the circuit (continuity test). A powered test light should not be used on any computer controlled system or component unless specifically instructed to do so. Many engine sensors can be destroyed by even this small amount of voltage applied directly to the terminals.

Open Circuit Testing

To use the self-powered test light to check for open circuits, first isolate the circuit from the vehicle's 12 volt power source by disconnecting the battery or wiring harness connector. Connect the test light ground clip to a good ground and probe sections of the circuit sequentially with the test light. (start from either end of the circuit). If the light is out, the open is between the probe and the circuit ground. If the light is on, the open is between the probe and end of the circuit toward the power source.

Short Circuit Testing

By isolating the circuit both from power and from ground, and using a self-powered test light, you can check for shorts to ground in the circuit. Isolate the circuit from power and ground. Connect the test light ground clip to a good ground and probe any easy-to-reach test point in the circuit. If the light comes on, there is a short somewhere in the circuit. To isolate the short, probe a test point at either end of the isolated circuit (the light should be on). Leave the test light probe connected and open connectors, switches, remove parts, etc., sequentially, until the light goes out. When the light goes out, the short is between the last circuit component opened and the previous circuit opened.

NOTE: The 1.5 volt battery in the test light does not provide much current. A weak battery may not provide enough power to illuminate the test light even when a complete circuit is made (especially if there are high resistances in the circuit). Always make sure that the test battery is strong. To check the battery, briefly touch the ground clip to the probe; if the light glows brightly the battery is strong enough for testing. Never use a self-powered test light to perform checks for opens or shorts when power is applied to the electrical system under test. The 12 volt vehicle power will quickly burn out the 1.5 volt light bulb in the test light.

Voltmeter

A voltmeter is used to measure voltage at any point in a circuit, or to measure the voltage drop across any part of a circuit. It can also be used to check continuity in a wire or circuit by indicating current flow from one end to the other. Voltmeters usually have various scales on the meter dial and a selector switch to allow the selection of different voltages. The voltmeter has a positive and a negative lead. To avoid damage to the meter, always connect the negative lead to the negative (−) side of circuit (to ground or nearest the ground side of the circuit) and connect the positive lead to the positive (+) side of the circuit (to the power source or the nearest power source). Note that the negative voltmeter lead will always be black and that the positive voltmeter will always be some color other than black (usually red). Depending on how the voltmeter is connected into the circuit, it has several uses.

A voltmeter can be connected either in parallel or in series with a circuit and it has a very high resistance to current flow. When connected in parallel, only a small amount of current will flow through the voltmeter current path; the rest will flow through the normal circuit current path and the circuit will work normally. When the voltmeter is connected in series with a circuit, only a small amount of current can flow through the circuit. The circuit will not work properly, but the voltmeter reading will show if the circuit is complete or not.

Available Voltage Measurement

Set the voltmeter selector switch to the 20V position and connect the meter negative lead to the negative post of the battery. Connect the positive meter lead to the positive post of the battery and turn the ignition switch ON to provide a load. Read the voltage on the meter or digital display. A well charged battery should register over 12 volts. If the meter reads below 11.5 volts, the battery power may be insufficient to operate the electrical system properly. This test determines voltage available from the battery and should be the first step in any electrical trouble diagnosis procedure. Many electrical problems, especially on computer controlled systems, can be caused by a low state of charge in the battery. Excessive corrosion at the battery cable terminals can cause a poor contact that will prevent proper charging and full battery current flow.

Normal battery voltage is 12 volts when fully charged. When the battery is supplying current to one or more circuits it is said to be "under load". When everything is off the electrical system is under a "no-load" condition. A fully charged battery may show about 12.5 volts at no load; will drop to 12 volts under medium load; and will drop even lower under heavy load. If the battery is partially discharged the voltage decrease under heavy load may be excessive, even though the battery shows 12 volts or more at no load. When allowed to discharge further, the battery's available voltage under load will decrease more severely. For this reason, it is important that the battery be fully charged during all testing procedures to avoid errors in diagnosis and incorrect test results.

Voltage Drop

When current flows through a resistance, the voltage beyond the resistance is reduced (the larger the current, the greater the reduction in voltage). When no current is flowing, there is no voltage drop because there is no current flow. All points in the circuit which are connected to the power source are at the same voltage as the power source. The total voltage drop always equals the total source voltage. In a long circuit with many connectors, a series of small, unwanted voltage drops due to corrosion at the connectors can add up to a total loss of voltage which impairs the operation of the normal loads in the circuit.

INDIRECT COMPUTATION OF VOLTAGE DROPS

1. Set the voltmeter selector switch to the 20 volt position.
2. Connect the meter negative lead to a good ground.

3. Probe all resistances in the circuit with the positive meter lead.
4. Operate the circuit in all modes and observe the voltage readings.

DIRECT MEASUREMENT OF VOLTAGE DROPS

1. Set the voltmeter switch to the 20 volt position.
2. Connect the voltmeter negative lead to the ground side of the resistance load to be measured.
3. Connect the positive lead to the positive side of the resistance or load to be measured.
4. Read the voltage drop directly on the 20 volt scale.

Too high a voltage indicates too high a resistance. If, for example, a blower motor runs too slowly, you can determine if there is too high a resistance in the resistor pack. By taking voltage drop readings in all parts of the circuit, you can isolate the problem. Too low a voltage drop indicates too low a resistance. If, for example, a blower motor runs too fast in the MED and/or LOW position, the problem can be isolated in the resistor pack by taking voltage drop readings in all parts of the circuit to locate a possibly shorted resistor. The maximum allowable voltage drop under load is critical, especially if there is more than one high resistance problem in a circuit because all voltage drops are cumulative. A small drop is normal due to the resistance of the conductors.

HIGH RESISTANCE TESTING

1. Set the voltmeter selector switch to the 4 volt position.
2. Connect the voltmeter positive lead to the positive post of the battery.
3. Turn on the headlights and heater blower to provide a load.
4. Probe various points in the circuit with the negative voltmeter lead.
5. Read the voltage drop on the 4 volt scale. Some average maximum allowable voltage drops are:

FUSE PANEL — 7 volts
IGNITION SWITCH — 5 volts
HEADLIGHT SWITCH — 7 volts
IGNITION COIL (+) — 5 volts
ANY OTHER LOAD — 1.3 volts

NOTE: Voltage drops are all measured while a load is operating; without current flow, there will be no voltage drop.

Ohmmeter

The ohmmeter is designed to read resistance (ohms) in a circuit or component. Although there are several different styles of ohmmeters, all will usually have a selector switch which permits the measurement of different ranges of resistance (usually the selector switch allows the multiplication of the meter reading by 10, 100, 1,000, and 10,000). A calibration knob allows the meter to be set at zero for accurate measurement. Since all ohmmeters are powered by an internal battery (usually 9 volts), the ohmmeter can be used as a self-powered test light. When the ohmmeter is connected, current from the ohmmeter flows through the circuit or component being tested. Since the ohmmeter's internal resistance and voltage are known values, the amount of current flow through the meter depends on the resistance of the circuit or component being tested.

The ohmmeter can be used to perform continuity test for opens or shorts (either by observation of the meter needle or as a self-powered test light), and to read actual resistance in a circuit. It should be noted that the ohmmeter is used to check the resistance of a component or wire while there is no voltage applied to the circuit. Current flow from an outside voltage source (such as the vehicle battery) can damage the ohmmeter, so the circuit or component should be isolated from the vehicle electrical system before any testing is done. Since the ohmmeter uses its own voltage source, either lead can be connected to any test point.

NOTE: **When checking diodes or other solid state components, the ohmmeter leads can only be connected one way in order to measure current flow in a single direction. Make sure the positive (+) and negative (−) terminal connections are as described in the test procedures to verify the one-way diode operation.**

In using the meter for making continuity checks, do not be concerned with the actual resistance readings. Zero resistance, or any resistance readings, indicate continuity in the circuit. Infinite resistance indicates an open in the circuit. A high resistance reading where there should be none indicates a problem in the circuit. Checks for short circuits are made in the same manner as checks for open circuits except that the circuit must be isolated from both power and normal ground. Infinite resistance indicates no continuity to ground, while zero resistance indicates a dead short to ground.

RESISTANCE MEASUREMENT

The batteries in an ohmmeter will weaken with age and temperature, so the ohmmeter must be calibrated or "zeroed" before taking measurements. To zero the meter, place the selector switch in its lowest range and touch the two ohmmeter leads together. Turn the calibration knob until the meter needle is exactly on zero.

NOTE: **All analog (needle) type ohmmeters must be zeroed before use, but some digital ohmmeter models are automatically calibrated when the switch is turned on. Self-calibrating digital ohmmeters do not have an adjusting knob, but its a good idea to check for a zero readout before use by touching the leads together. All computer controlled systems require the use of a digital ohmmeter with at least 10 megohms impedance for testing. Before any test procedures are attempted, make sure the ohmmeter used is compatible with the electrical system or damage to the on-board computer could result.**

To measure resistance, first isolate the circuit from the vehicle power source by disconnecting the battery cables or the harness connector. Make sure the key is OFF when disconnecting any components or the battery. Where necessary, also isolate at least one side of the circuit to be checked to avoid reading parallel resistances. Parallel circuit resistances will always give a lower reading than the actual resistance of either of the branches. When measuring the resistance of parallel circuits, the total resistance will always be lower than the smallest resistance in the circuit. Connect the meter leads to both sides of the circuit (wire or component) and read the actual measured ohms on the meter scale. Make sure the selector switch is set to the proper ohm scale for the circuit being tested to avoid misreading the ohmmeter test value.

WARNING: **Never use an ohmmeter with power applied to the circuit. Like the self-powered test light, the ohmmeter is designed to operate on its own power supply. The normal 12 volt automotive electrical system current could damage the meter!**

Ammeters

An ammeter measures the amount of current flowing through a circuit in units called amperes or amps. Amperes are units of electron flow which indicate how fast the electrons are flowing through the circuit. Since Ohms Law dictates that current flow in a circuit is equal to the circuit voltage divided by the total circuit resistance, increasing voltage also increases the current level (amps). Likewise, any decrease in resistance will increase the amount of amps in a circuit. At normal operating voltage, most circuits have a characteristic amount of amperes, called "current draw" which can be measured using an ammeter. By referring to a specified current draw rating, measuring

the amperes, and comparing the two values, one can determine what is happening within the circuit to aid in diagnosis. An open circuit, for example, will not allow any current to flow so the ammeter reading will be zero. More current flows through a heavily loaded circuit or when the charging system is operating.

An ammeter is always connected in series with the circuit being tested. All of the current that normally flows through the circuit must also flow through the ammeter; if there is any other path for the current to follow, the ammeter reading will not be accurate. The ammeter itself has very little resistance to current flow and therefore will not affect the circuit, but it will measure current draw only when the circuit is closed and electricity is flowing. Excessive current draw can blow fuses and drain the battery, while a reduced current draw can cause motors to run slowly, lights to dim and other components to not operate properly. The ammeter can help diagnose these conditions by locating the cause of the high or low reading.

Multimeters

Different combinations of test meters can be built into a single unit designed for specific tests. Some of the more common combination test devices are known as Volt/Amp testers, Tach/Dwell meters, or Digital Multimeters. The Volt/Amp tester is used for charging system, starting system or battery tests and consists of a voltmeter, an ammeter and a variable resistance carbon pile. The voltmeter will usually have at least two ranges for use with 6, 12 and 24 volt systems. The ammeter also has more than one range for testing various levels of battery loads and starter current draw and the carbon pile can be adjusted to offer different amounts of resistance. The Volt/Amp tester has heavy leads to carry large amounts of current and many later models have an inductive ammeter pickup that clamps around the wire to simplify test connections. On some models, the ammeter also has a zero-center scale to allow testing of charging and starting systems without switching leads or polarity. A digital multimeter is a voltmeter, ammeter and ohmmeter combined in an instrument which gives a digital readout. These are often used when testing solid state circuits because of their high input impedance (usually 10 megohms or more).

The tach/dwell meter combines a tachometer and a dwell (cam angle) meter and is a specialized kind of voltmeter. The tachometer scale is marked to show engine speed in rpm and the dwell scale is marked to show degrees of distributor shaft rotation. In most electronic ignition systems, dwell is determined by the control unit, but the dwell meter can also be used to check the duty cycle (operation) of some electronic engine control systems. Some tach/dwell meters are powered by an internal battery, while others take their power from the car battery in use. The battery powered testers usually require calibration much like an ohmmeter before testing.

Special Test Equipment

A variety of diagnostic tools are available to help troubleshoot and repair computerized engine control systems. The most sophisticated of these devices are the console type engine analyzers that usually occupy a garage service bay, but there are several types of aftermarket electronic testers available that will allow quick circuit tests of the engine control system by plugging directly into a special connector located in the engine compartment or under the dashboard. Several tool and equipment manufacturers offer simple, hand held testers that measure various circuit voltage levels on command to check all system components for proper operation. Although these testers usually cost about $300–500, consider that the average computer control module (or ECM) can cost just as much and the money saved by not replacing perfectly good sensors or components in an attempt to correct a problem could justify the purchase price of a special diagnostic tester the first time it's used.

These computerized testers can allow quick and easy test measurements while the engine is operating or while the car is being driven. In addition, the on-board computer memory can be read to access any stored trouble codes; in effect allowing the computer to tell you where it hurts and aid trouble diagnosis by pinpointing exactly which circuit or component is malfunctioning. In the same manner, repairs can be tested to make sure the problem has been corrected. The biggest advantage these special testers have is their relatively easy hookups that minimize or eliminate the chances of making the wrong connections and getting false voltage readings or damaging the computer accidentally.

NOTE: It should be remembered that these testers check voltage levels in circuits; they don't detect mechanical problems or failed components if the circuit voltage falls within the preprogrammed limits stored in the tester PROM unit. Also, most of the hand held testes are designed to work only on one or two systems made by a specific manufacturer.

A variety of aftermarket testers are available to help diagnose different computerized control systems. Owatonna Tool Company (OTC), for example, markets a device called the OTC Monitor which plugs directly into the assembly line diagnostic link (ALDL). The OTC tester makes diagnosis a simple matter of pressing the correct buttons and, by changing the internal PROM or inserting a different diagnosis cartridge, it will work on any model from full size to subcompact, over a wide range of years. An adapter is supplied with the tester to allow connection to all types of ALDL links, regardless of the number of pin terminals used. By inserting an updated PROM into the OTC tester, it can be easily updated to diagnose any new modifications of computerized control systems.

Wiring Harnesses

The average automobile contains about ½ mile of wiring, with hundreds of individual connections. To protect the many wires from damage and to keep them from becoming a confusing tangle, they are organized into bundles, enclosed in plastic or taped together and called wire harnesses. Different wiring harnesses serve different parts of the vehicle. Individual wires are color coded to help trace them through a harness where sections are hidden from view.

A loose or corroded connection or a replacement wire that is too small for the circuit will add extra resistance and an additional voltage drop to the circuit. A ten percent voltage drop can result in slow or erratic motor operation, for example, even though the circuit is complete. Automotive wiring or circuit conductors can be in any one of three forms:
1. Single strand wire
2. Multistrand wire
3. Printed circuitry

Single strand wire has a solid metal core and is usually used inside such components as alternators, motors, relays and other devices. Multistrand wire has a core made of many small strands of wire twisted together into a single conductor. Most of the wiring in an automotive electrical system is made up of multistrand wire, either as a single conductor or grouped together in a harness. All wiring is color coded on the insulator, either as a solid color or as a colored wire with an identification stripe. A printed circuit is a thin film of copper or other conductor that is printed on an insulator backing. Occasionally, a printed circuit is sandwiched between two sheets of plastic for more protection and flexibility. A complete printed circuit, consisting of conductors, insulating material and connectors for lamps or other components is called a printed circuit board. Printed circuitry is used in place of individual wires or harnesses in places where space is limited, such as behind instrument panels.

Wire Gauge

Since computer controlled automotive electrical systems are

very sensitive to changes in resistance, the selection of properly sized wires is critical when systems are repaired. The wire gauge number is an expression of the cross section area of the conductor. The most common system for expressing wire size is the American Wire Gauge (AWG) system.

Wire cross section area is measured in circular mils. A mil is $\frac{1}{1000}$ in. (0.001 in.); a circular mil is the area of a circle one mil in diameter. For example, a conductor ¼ in. in diameter is 0.250 in. or 250 mils. The circular mil cross section area of the wire is 250 squared (250^2) or 62,500 circular mils. Imported car models usually use metric wire gauge designations, which is simply the cross section area of the conductor in square millimeters (mm^2).

Gauge numbers are assigned to conductors of various cross section areas. As gauge number increases, area decreases and the conductor becomes smaller. A 5 gauge conductor is smaller than a 1 gauge conductor and a 10 gauge is smaller than a 5 gauge. As the cross section area of a conductor decreases, resistance increases and so does the gauge number. A conductor with a higher gauge number will carry less current than a conductor with a lower gauge number.

NOTE: Gauge wire size refers to the size of the conductor, not the size of the complete wire. It is possible to have two wires of the same gauge with different diameters because one may have thicker insulation than the other.

12 volt automotive electrical systems generally use 10, 12, 14, 16 and 18 gauge wire. Main power distribution circuits and larger accessories usually use 10 and 12 gauge wire. Battery cables are usually 4 or 6 gauge, although 1 and 2 gauge wires are occasionally used. Wire length must also be considered when making repairs to a circuit. As conductor length increases, so does resistance. An 18 gauge wire, for example, can carry a 10 amp load for 10 feet without excessive voltage drop; however if a 15 foot wire is required for the same 10 amp load, it must be a 16 gauge wire.

An electrical schematic shows the electrical current paths when a circuit is operating properly. It is essential to understand how a circuit works before trying to figure out why it does not. Schematics break the entire electrical system down into individual circuits and show only one particular circuit. In a schematic, no attempt is made to represent wiring and components as they physically appear on the vehicle; switches and other components are shown as simply as possible. Face views of harness connectors show the cavity or terminal locations in all multi-pin connectors to help locate test points.

If you need to backprobe a connector while it is on the component, the order of the terminals must be mentally reversed. The wire color code can help in this situation, as well as a keyway, lock tab or other reference mark.

NOTE: Some wiring diagrams are included in this book. As trucks have become more complex and available with longer option lists, wiring diagrams have grown in size and complexity. It has become almost impossible to provide a readable reproduction of a wiring diagram in a book this size.

WIRING REPAIR

Soldering is a quick, efficient method of joining metals permanently. Everyone who has the occasion to make wiring repairs should know how to solder. Electrical connections that are soldered are far less likely to come apart and will conduct electricity much better than connections that are only "pig-tailed" together. The most popular (and preferred) method of soldering is with an electrical soldering gun. Soldering irons are available in many sizes and wattage ratings. Irons with higher wattage ratings deliver higher temperatures and recover lost heat faster. A small soldering iron rated for no more than 50 watts is recommended, especially on electrical systems where excess heat can damage the components being soldered.

There are three ingredients necessary for successful soldering; proper flux, good solder and sufficient heat. A soldering flux is necessary to clean the metal of tarnish, prepare it for soldering and to enable the solder to spread into tiny crevices. When soldering, always use a resin flux or resin core solder which is non-corrosive and will not attract moisture once the job is finished. Other types of flux (acid core) will leave a residue that will attract moisture and cause the wires to corrode. Tin is a unique metal with a low melting point. In a molten state, it dissolves and alloys easily with many metals. Solder is made by mixing tin with lead. The most common proportions are 40/60, 50/50 and 60/40, with the percentage of tin listed first. Low priced solders usually contain less tin, making them very difficult for a beginner to use because more heat is required to melt the solder. A common solder is 40/60 which is well suited for all-around general use, but 60/40 melts easier, has more tin for a better joint and is preferred for electrical work.

Soldering Techniques

Successful soldering requires that the metals to be joined be heated to a temperature that will melt the solder—usually 360–460°F (182–238°C). Contrary to popular belief, the purpose of the soldering iron is not to melt the solder itself, but to heat the parts being soldered to a temperature high enough to melt the solder when it is touched to the work. Melting flux-cored solder on the soldering iron will usually destroy the effectiveness of the flux.

NOTE: Soldering tips are made of copper for good heat conductivity, but must be "tinned" regularly for quick transference of heat to the project and to prevent the solder from sticking to the iron. To "tin" the iron, simply heat it and touch the flux-cored solder to the tip; the solder will flow over the hot tip. Wipe the excess off with a clean rag, but be careful as the iron will be hot.

After some use, the tip may become pitted. If so, simply dress the tip smooth with a smooth file and "tin" the tip again. An old saying holds that "metals well cleaned are half soldered." Flux-cored solder will remove oxides but rust, bits of insulation and oil or grease must be removed with a wire brush or emery cloth. For maximum strength in soldered parts, the joint must start off clean and tight. Weak joints will result in gaps too wide for the solder to bridge.

If a separate soldering flux is used, it should be brushed or swabbed on only those areas that are to be soldered. Most solders contain a core of flux and separate fluxing is unnecessary. Hold the work to be soldered firmly. It is best to solder on a wooden board, because a metal vise will only rob the piece to be soldered of heat and make it difficult to melt the solder. Hold the soldering tip with the broadest face against the work to be soldered. Apply solder under the tip close to the work, using enough solder to give a heavy film between the iron and the piece being soldered, while moving slowly and making sure the solder melts properly. Keep the work level or the solder will run to the lowest part and favor the thicker parts, because these require more heat to melt the solder. If the soldering tip overheats (the solder coating on the face of the tip burns up), it should be retinned. Once the soldering is completed, let the soldered joint stand until cool. Tape and seal all soldered wire splices after the repair has cooled.

Wire Harness and Connectors

The on-board computer (ECM) wire harness electrically connects the control unit to the various solenoids, switches and sensors used by the control system. Most connectors in the engine compartment or otherwise exposed to the elements are protected against moisture and dirt which could create oxidation and deposits on the terminals. This protection is important because of the very low voltage and current levels used by the computer and sensors. All connectors have a lock which secures the male and female terminals together, with a secondary lock holding the seal and terminal into the connector. Both terminal locks must be released when disconnecting ECM connectors.

These special connectors are weather-proof and all repairs require the use of a special terminal and the tool required to service it. This tool is used to remove the pin and sleeve terminals. If removal is attempted with an ordinary pick, there is a good chance that the terminal will be bent or deformed. Unlike standard blade type terminals, these terminals cannot be straightened once they are bent. Make certain that the connectors are properly seated and all of the sealing rings in place when connecting leads. On some models, a hinge-type flap provides a backup or secondary locking feature for the terminals. Most secondary locks are used to improve the connector reliability by retaining the terminals if the small terminal lock tangs are not positioned properly.

Molded-on connectors require complete replacement of the connection. This means splicing a new connector assembly into the harness. All splices in on-board computer systems should be soldered to insure proper contact. Use care when probing the connections or replacing terminals in them as it is possible to short between opposite terminals. If this happens to the wrong terminal pair, it is possible to damage certain components. Always use jumper wires between connectors for circuit checking and never probe through weatherproof seals.

Open circuits are often difficult to locate by sight because corrosion or terminal misalignment are hidden by the connectors. Merely wiggling a connector on a sensor or in the wiring harness may correct the open circuit condition. This should always be considered when an open circuit or a failed sensor is indicated. Intermittent problems may also be caused by oxidized or loose connections. When using a circuit tester for diagnosis, always probe connections from the wire side. Be careful not to damage sealed connectors with test probes.

All wiring harnesses should be replaced with identical parts, using the same gauge wire and connectors. When signal wires are spliced into a harness, use wire with high temperature insulation only. With the low voltage and current levels found in the system, it is important that the best possible connection at all wire splices be made by soldering the splices together. It is seldom necessary to replace a complete harness. If replacement is necessary, pay close attention to insure proper harness routing. Secure the harness with suitable plastic wire clamps to prevent vibrations from causing the harness to wear in spots or contact any hot components.

NOTE: Weatherproof connectors cannot be replaced with standard connectors. Instructions are provided with replacement connector and terminal packages. Some wire harnesses have mounting indicators (usually pieces of colored tape) to mark where the harness is to be secured.

In making wiring repairs, it's important that you always replace damaged wires with wires that are the same gauge as the wire being replaced. The heavier the wire, the smaller the gauge number. Wires are color-coded to aid in identification and whenever possible the same color coded wire should be used for replacement. A wire stripping and crimping tool is necessary to install solderless terminal connectors. Test all crimps by pulling on the wires; it should not be possible to pull the wires out of a good crimp.

Wires which are open, exposed or otherwise damaged are repaired by simple splicing. Where possible, if the wiring harness is accessible and the damaged place in the wire can be located, it is best to open the harness and check for all possible damage. In an inaccessible harness, the wire must be bypassed with a new insert, usually taped to the outside of the old harness.

When replacing fusible links, be sure to use fusible link wire, NOT ordinary automotive wire. Make sure the fusible segment is of the same gauge and construction as the one being replaced and double the stripped end when crimping the terminal connector for a good contact. The melted (open) fusible link segment of the wiring harness should be cut off as close to the harness as possible, then a new segment spliced in as described. In the case of a damaged fusible link that feeds two harness wires, the harness connections should be replaced with two fusible link wires so that each circuit will have its own separate protection.

NOTE: Most of the problems caused in the wiring harness are due to bad ground connections. Always check all vehicle ground connections for corrosion or looseness before performing any power feed checks to eliminate the chance of a bad ground affecting the circuit.

Repairing Hard Shell Connectors

Unlike molded connectors, the terminal contacts in hard shell connectors can be replaced. Weatherproof hard-shell connectors with the leads molded into the shell have non-replaceable terminal ends. Replacement usually involves the use of a special terminal removal tool that depress the locking tangs (barbs) on the connector terminal and allow the connector to be removed from the rear of the shell. The connector shell should be replaced if it shows any evidence of burning, melting, cracks, or breaks. Replace individual terminals that are burnt, corroded, distorted or loose.

NOTE: The insulation crimp must be tight to prevent the insulation from sliding back on the wire when the wire is pulled. The insulation must be visibly compressed under the crimp tabs, and the ends of the crimp should be turned in for a firm grip on the insulation.

The wire crimp must be made with all wire strands inside the crimp. The terminal must be fully compressed on the wire strands with the ends of the crimp tabs turned in to make a firm grip on the wire. Check all connections with an ohmmeter to insure a good contact. There should be no measurable resistance between the wire and the terminal when connected.

Mechanical Test Equipment

Vacuum Gauge

Most gauges are graduated in inches of mercury (in.Hg), although a device called a manometer reads vacuum in inches of water (in. H_2O). The normal vacuum reading usually varies between 18 and 22 in.Hg at sea level. To test engine vacuum, the vacuum gauge must be connected to a source of manifold vacuum. Many engines have a plug in the intake manifold which can be removed and replaced with an adapter fitting. Connect the vacuum gauge to the fitting with a suitable rubber hose or, if no manifold plug is available, connect the vacuum gauge to any device using manifold vacuum, such as EGR valves, etc. The vacuum gauge can be used to determine if enough vacuum is reaching a component to allow its actuation.

Hand Vacuum Pump

Small, hand-held vacuum pumps come in a variety of designs. Most have a built-in vacuum gauge and allow the component to be tested without removing it from the vehicle. Operate the pump lever or plunger to apply the correct amount of vacuum required for the test specified in the diagnosis routines. The level of vacuum in inches of Mercury (in.Hg) is indicated on the pump gauge. For some testing, an additional vacuum gauge may be necessary.

Intake manifold vacuum is used to operate various systems and devices on late model vehicles. To correctly diagnose and solve problems in vacuum control systems, a vacuum source is necessary for testing. In some cases, vacuum can be taken from the intake manifold when the engine is running, but vacuum is normally provided by a hand vacuum pump. These hand vacuum pumps have a built-in vacuum gauge that allow testing while the device is still attached to the component. For some tests, an additional vacuum gauge may be necessary.

HEATING AND AIR CONDITIONING

Front Blower Motor

REMOVAL AND INSTALLATION

1. Disconnect the negative battery cable.
2. Remove the engine air cleaner.
3. Disconnect the left windshield wiper transmission arm linkage.
4. Disconnect the blower motor electrical harness.
5. Remove the blower motor retaining screws and remove the blower motor assembly.
6. Installation is the reverse of removal.

Rear Auxiliary Blower Motor

REMOVAL AND INSTALLATION

1. Disconnect the negative battery cable.
2. Remove the left front quarter trim panel.
3. Remove the motor housing to case screws.
4. Remove the motor housing assembly.
5. Remove the fan retaining nut and remove the fan from the motor.
6. Installation is the reverse of removal.

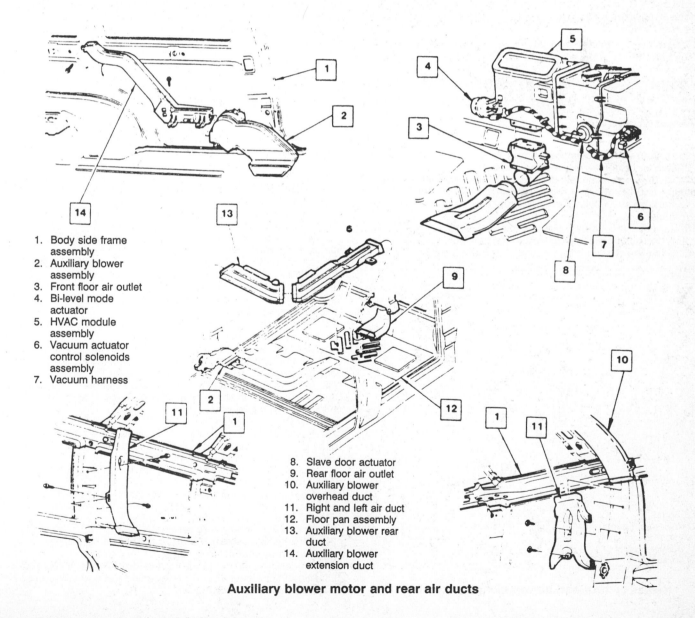

1. Relay assembly
2. A/C heater module
3. Resistor assembly
4. Blower motor

Front blower motor, resistor and relay installation

Heater Core

REMOVAL AND INSTALLATION

1. Disconnect the negative battery cable.
2. Drain the cooling system.

───────── **CAUTION** ─────────

When draining the coolant, keep in mind that cats and dogs are attracted by the ethylene glycol antifreeze, and are quite likely to drink any that is left in an uncovered container or in puddles on the ground. This will prove fatal in sufficient quantity. Always drain the coolant into a sealable container. Coolant should be reused unless it is contaminated or several years old.

3. Disconnect the heater hoses.
4. Remove the right side sound insulator from under the instrument panel.
5. Remove the glove box.
6. Disconnect the vacuum hoses and wiring from in front of the heater core cover.

1. Body side frame assembly
2. Auxiliary blower assembly
3. Front floor air outlet
4. Bi-level mode actuator
5. HVAC module assembly
6. Vacuum actuator control solenoids assembly
7. Vacuum harness
8. Slave door actuator
9. Rear floor air outlet
10. Auxiliary blower overhead duct
11. Right and left air duct
12. Floor pan assembly
13. Auxiliary blower rear duct
14. Auxiliary blower extension duct

Auxiliary blower motor and rear air ducts

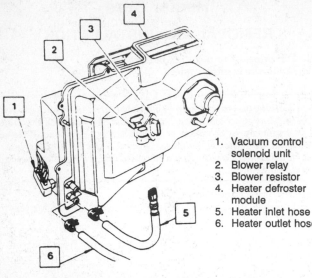

1. Vacuum control solenoid unit
2. Blower relay
3. Blower resistor
4. Heater defroster module
5. Heater inlet hose
6. Heater outlet hose

Heater hose connections at the module.

7. Remove the heater core cover and remove the heater core.
8. Installation is the reverse of the removal procedure.

Heater Control and Blower Switch Assembly

REMOVAL AND INSTALLATION

1. Disconnect the negative battery cable.
2. Remove the steering column lower trim cover.
3. Remove the glove box door by holding at the bottom while opening and lifting up and pulling from the door stops.
4. Remove the 4 trim plate retaining screws and remove the trim plate.
5. Loosen the 2 screws retaining the heater-HVAC control assembly to the left side of the accessory mounting bracket.
6. Slide the control assembly out from the bracket

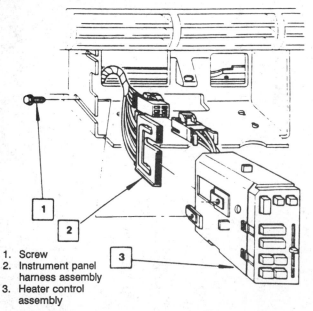

1. Screw
2. Instrument panel harness assembly
3. Heater control assembly

Heater control and blower switch assembly

7. Disconnect the 2 instrument panel electrical harness connectors attached to the rear side of the control assembly.
8. Remove the heater control assembly.

To install:

9. Connect the 2 instrument panel electrical harness connectors attached to the rear side of the control assembly.
10. Slide the control assembly into the accessory housing bracket and secure with the retaining screws.
11. Install the trim plate and 4 retaining screws.
12. Install the glove box door and steering column trim cover.
13. Connect the negative battery cable.

Evaporator Core

REMOVAL AND INSTALLATION

1. Disconnect the negative battery cable.
2. Drain the cooling system.

─────────── CAUTION ───────────

When draining the coolant, keep in mind that cats and dogs are attracted by the ethylene glycol antifreeze, and are quite likely to drink any that is left in an uncovered container or in puddles on the ground. This will prove fatal in sufficient quantity. Always drain the coolant into a sealable container. Coolant should be reused unless it is contaminated or several years old.

3. Disconnect the heater core inlet and outlet hoses.
4. Blow air through the heater core nipples to remove the coolant from the heater core.
5. Discharge the air conditioning system as outlined in Section 1.
6. Disconnect the inlet and outlet pipes at the evaporator.
7. Remove the left side instrument panel sound insulator panel as follows:
   a. Remove the nut from the retainer/stud on the lower trim pad.
   b. Remove the screw fastening the right side panel to the trim pad.
   c. Remove the bolt and nut fastening panel to the trim pad.
   d. Remove the left side sound insulator
8. Remove the 2 screws attaching the vacuum electric solenoid to the heater core cover.
9. Disconnect the electrical harness connector to the solenoid.
10. Remove the 6 screws attaching the heater core cover to the air conditioning module assembly.
11. Remove the heater core assembly.
12. Remove the upper instrument panel trim pad assembly as outlined later in this section.
13. Disconnect the temperature motor harness connector.
14. Remove the 4 screws attaching the temperature door/slave door housing.
15. Remove the 4 bolts from the engine compartment side of the cowl that attach the evaportor core to the evaporator cover and remove the evaporator.

To install:

16. Reposition the evaporator and install the 4 retaining bolts to the engine compartment side of the cowl that attach the evaporator core to the evaporator cover.
17. Install the 4 screws attaching the temperature door/slave door housing.
18. Connect the temperature motor harness connector.
19. Install the upper instrument panel trim pad assembly as outlined later in this section.
20. Install the heater core assembly.
21. Install the 6 screws attaching the heater core cover to the air conditioning module assembly
22. Connect the electrical harness connector to the solenoid.
23. Install the upper instrument panel trim pad assembly as outlined later in this section.

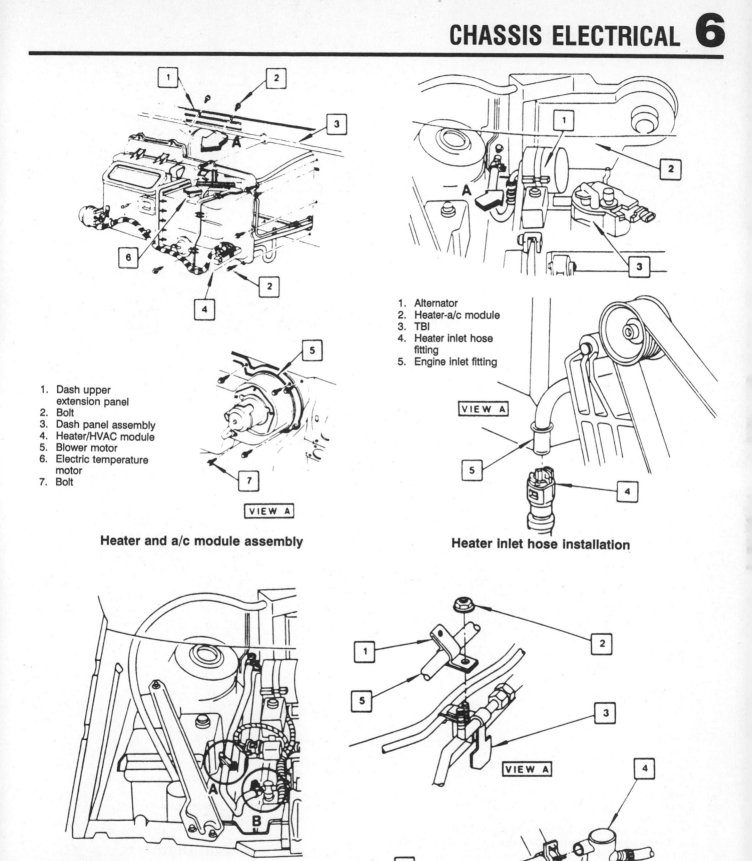

1. Dash upper
   extension panel
2. Bolt
3. Dash panel assembly
4. Heater/HVAC module
5. Blower motor
6. Electric temperature
   motor
7. Bolt

VIEW A

Heater and a/c module assembly

1. Alternator
2. Heater-a/c module
3. TBI
4. Heater inlet hose
   fitting
5. Engine inlet fitting

VIEW A

Heater inlet hose installation

1. Clip
2. Nut
3. Left upper side rail
4. Water pump
5. Heater outlet hose

VIEW A

VIEW B

Heater outlet hose installation

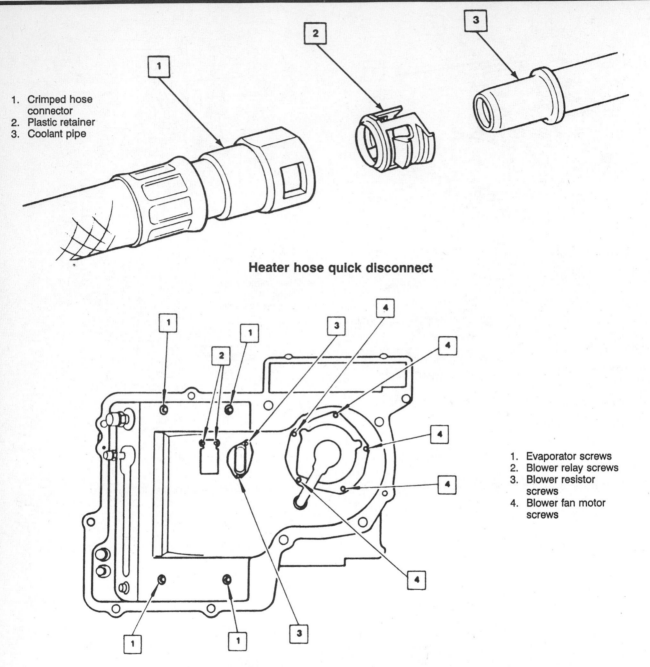

1. Crimped hose connector
2. Plastic retainer
3. Coolant pipe

Heater hose quick disconnect

1. Evaporator screws
2. Blower relay screws
3. Blower resistor screws
4. Blower fan motor screws

HVAC module assembly mounting screws

24. Install the heater core assembly.
25. Install the 6 screws attaching the heater core cover to the air conditioning module assembly
26. Connect the electrical harness connector to the solenoid.
27. Install the 2 screws attaching the vacuum electric solenoid to the heater core cover.
28. Install the left side instrument panel sound insulator panel.
29. Connect the inlet and outlet pipes at the evaporator.
30. Charge the air conditioning system as outlined in Section 1.
31. Connect the heater core inlet and outlet hoses.

32. Fill the cooling system.
33. Connect the negative battery cable.

Accumulator

REMOVAL AND INSTALLATION

NOTE: The accumulator should not be replaced un-

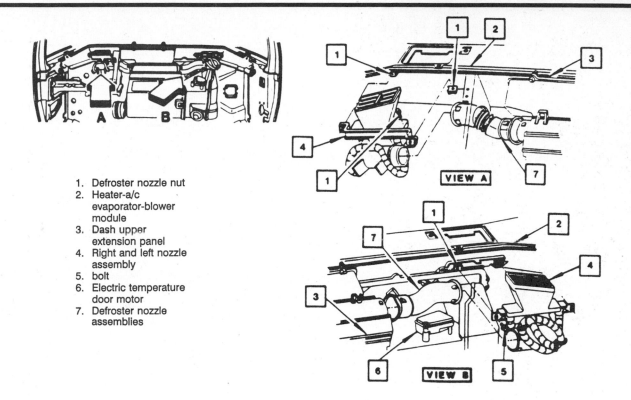

1. Defroster nozzle nut
2. Heater-a/c evaporator-blower module
3. Dash upper extension panel
4. Right and left nozzle assembly
5. bolt
6. Electric temperature door motor
7. Defroster nozzle assemblies

Temperature door motor, defroster nozzles and ducts

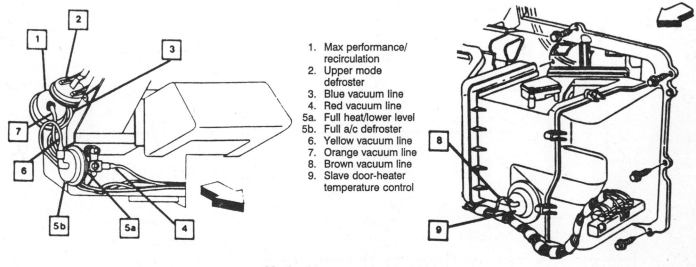

1. Max performance/recirculation
2. Upper mode defroster
3. Blue vacuum line
4. Red vacuum line
5a. Full heat/lower level
5b. Full a/c defroster
6. Yellow vacuum line
7. Orange vacuum line
8. Brown vacuum line
9. Slave door-heater temperature control

Mode door vacuum actuators

less the outer shell is perforated or the system is opened to air for an extended period of time.

1. Disconnect the negative battery cable.
2. Discharge and evacuate the air conditioning system.
3. Disconnect the low pressure return lines at both the inlet and outlet accumulator connections.
4. Loosen the lower bracket bolt and spread the bracket.
5. Rotate the accumulator to loosen and remove.

To install:

6. Position the accumulator into the bracket and tighten the clamp bolt.
7. Install new O-rings in the fittings and connect the low pressure lines at the inlet and outlet connections on the accumulator.
8. Connect the negative battery cable.
9. Charge and leak test the air conditioning system as outlined in Section 1.

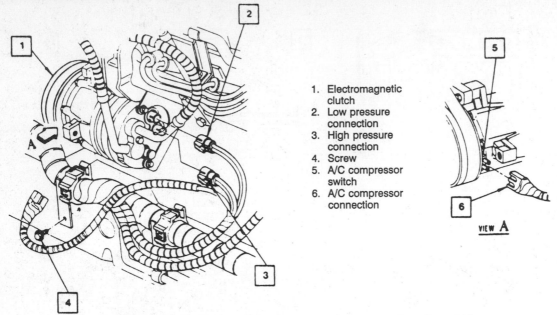

1. Electromagnetic clutch
2. Low pressure connection
3. High pressure connection
4. Screw
5. A/C compressor switch
6. A/C compressor connection

VIEW A

High-low pressure compressor compressor cut-off switches

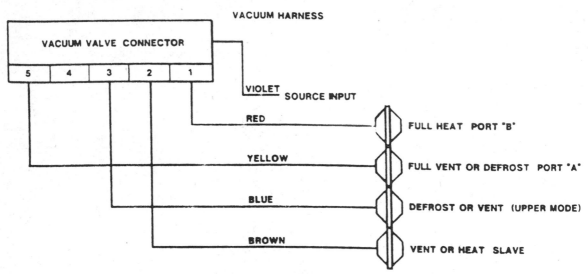

VACUUM HARNESS

VACUUM VALVE CONNECTOR

| 5 | 4 | 3 | 2 | 1 |

VIOLET SOURCE INPUT

RED — FULL HEAT PORT "B"

YELLOW — FULL VENT OR DEFROST PORT "A"

BLUE — DEFROST OR VENT (UPPER MODE)

BROWN — VENT OR HEAT SLAVE

VACUUM VALVE LOGIC - MODE LEVER POSITIONS

PORT	OFF	MAX A/C	NORM A/C	BI LEVEL	VENT	HEATER	DEFROST	DEFOG
LOWER MODE HEATER	VENT	VENT	VENT	VENT	VENT	VAC	VENT	VENT
SLAVE DOOR	VENT	VAC	VAC	VAC	VAC	VENT	VENT	VENT
UPPER MODE DEFROST A/C	VENT	VAC	VAC	VAC	VAC	VENT	VENT	VENT
LOWER MODE A/C DEFROST	VENT	VAC	VAC	VENT	VAC	VENT	VAC	VENT

Heater and a/c control vacuum logic

| STEP | CONTROL SETTINGS | | | | | | SYSTEM RESPONSE | | | | |
	MODE BUTTON	LITE ON	TEMP SETT	BLOWER FAN SW FRT	BLOWER FAN SW RR	BLOWER SPEED	RR OPT AUX. DUCT	HEATER OUTLETS	A C I P OUTLETS	DEF OUTLETS	SIDE WDO DEF
1	OFF	YES	FULL HOT	HI	OFF	OFF	NO AIR FLOW	NO AIR FLOW	NO AIR FLOW	NO AIR FLOW	NO AIR FLOW
2	DEFR.	YES	FULL HOT	HI	OFF	HI	NO AIR FLOW	AIR FLOW	NO AIR FLOW	HOT AIR FLOW	SOME HOT AIR FLOW
3	MIX	YES	FULL HOT	HI	OFF	HI	SOME AIR FLOW	HOT AIR FLOW	NO AIR FLOW	HOT AIR FLOW	SOME HOT AIR FLOW
4	HEATER	YES	FULL HOT	HI	OFF	HI	AIR FLOW	HOT AIR FLOW	NO AIR FLOW	SOME AIR FLOW	SOME HOT AIR FLOW
5	BI-LEVEL	YES	FULL COLD	HI	OFF	HI	SOME AIR FLOW	AIR FLOW	COOL AIR FLOW	SOME AIR FLOW	SOME AIR FLOW
6	VENT	YES	FULL HOT	HI	OFF	HI	SOME AIR FLOW	NO AIR FLOW	HOT AIR FLOW	NO AIR FLOW	SOME AIR FLOW
7	VENT	YES	FULL COLD	HI	OFF	HI	SOME AIR FLOW	NO AIR FLOW	COOL AIR FLOW	NO AIR FLOW	SOME AIR FLOW
8	VENT	YES	FULL COLD	LOW	OFF	LOW	SOME AIR FLOW	NO AIR FLOW	COOL AIR FLOW	NO AIR FLOW	SOME AIR FLOW
9	HEATER	YES	FULL HOT	LOW	HI	LOW HI	HOT AIR FLOW	SOME HOT AIR FLOW	NO AIR FLOW	SOME AIR FLOW	SOME AIR FLOW

- TEMPERATURE DOOR ACTUATOR MOTOR SHOULD BE HEARD DURING TEMPERATURE SETTING CHANGES. AND NOTICEABLE BLOWER SPEED INCREASE MUST OCCUR FROM LOW TO MID. TO MID₂ AND HIGH

- CHECK TEMPERATURE LEVER FOR EFFORT AND TRAVEL (COLD TO HOT). (TEMPERATURE CHANGE SHOULD OCCUR).

- CHECK FOR AIR FLOW AS DEFINED IN SYSTEM RESPONSE

- ALL I.P. OUTLETS MUST BE CHECKED FOR: 1) BARREL ROTATION. 2) VANE OPERATION. 3) BARREL AND VANES MUST HOLD PRESENT POSITION IN HI BLOWER OPERATION.

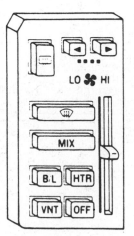

Heater functional test chart

CHECK ALL ELECTRICAL CONNECTIONS AND GROUNDS FOR PROPER
CONNECTION. REFER TO SECTION 8A.

SIT IN THE VEHICLE WITH THE DOORS AND WINDOWS CLOSED. WITH THE IGNITION ON
AND THE ENGINE OFF, START WITH THE BLOWER ON HIGH, IN VENT MODE AND THE
TEMPERATURE LEVER ON FULL COLD. CYCLE THROUGH BLOWER SPEEDS, MODES AND
TEMPERATURE VALVE POSITIONS TO FIND WHERE THE NOISE OCCURS AND WHERE THE
NOISE DOES NOT OCCUR. TRY TO DEFINE THE TYPE OF NOISE: AIR RUSH, WHINE,
TICK/CLICK, SQUEAL/SCREECH, FLUTTER, RUMBLE OR SCRAPING NOISE. CHART
BELOW SHOULD BE COMPLETELY FILLED IN AT COMPLETION.

A CONSTANT AIR RUSH NOISE IS TYPICAL OF ALL SYSTEMS ON HIGH BLOWER. SOME
SYSTEMS AND MODES (USUALLY DEFROSTER) MAY BE WORSE THAN OTHERS. CHECK
ANOTHER VEHICLE IF POSSIBLE (SAME MODEL) TO DETERMINE IF THE NOISE IS
TYPICAL OF THE SYSTEM AS DESIGNED.

INDICATE THE TYPE OF NOISE AND WHERE IT OCCURS:

	VENT		HEATER		DEFROST	
	FULL COLD	FULL HOT	FULL COLD	FULL HOT	FULL COLD	FULL HOT
LOW BLOWER						
M2						
M3						
HIGH BLOWER						

A — WHINE, B — CLICK/TICK, C — SQUEAL/SCREECH, D — FLUTTER, E — RUMBLE,
F — SCRAPING, G — AIR RUSH, H — OTHER, DESCRIBE _____

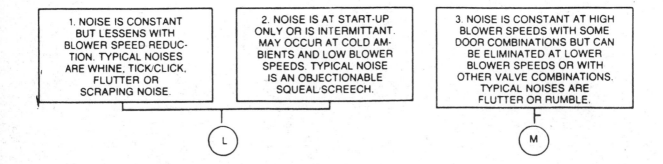

1. NOISE IS CONSTANT BUT LESSENS WITH BLOWER SPEED REDUCTION. TYPICAL NOISES ARE WHINE, TICK/CLICK, FLUTTER OR SCRAPING NOISE.

2. NOISE IS AT START-UP ONLY OR IS INTERMITTANT. MAY OCCUR AT COLD AMBIENTS AND LOW BLOWER SPEEDS. TYPICAL NOISE IS AN OBJECTIONABLE SQUEAL/SCREECH.

3. NOISE IS CONSTANT AT HIGH BLOWER SPEEDS WITH SOME DOOR COMBINATIONS BUT CAN BE ELIMINATED AT LOWER BLOWER SPEEDS OR WITH OTHER VALVE COMBINATIONS. TYPICAL NOISES ARE FLUTTER OR RUMBLE.

L   M

Blower noise diagnosis

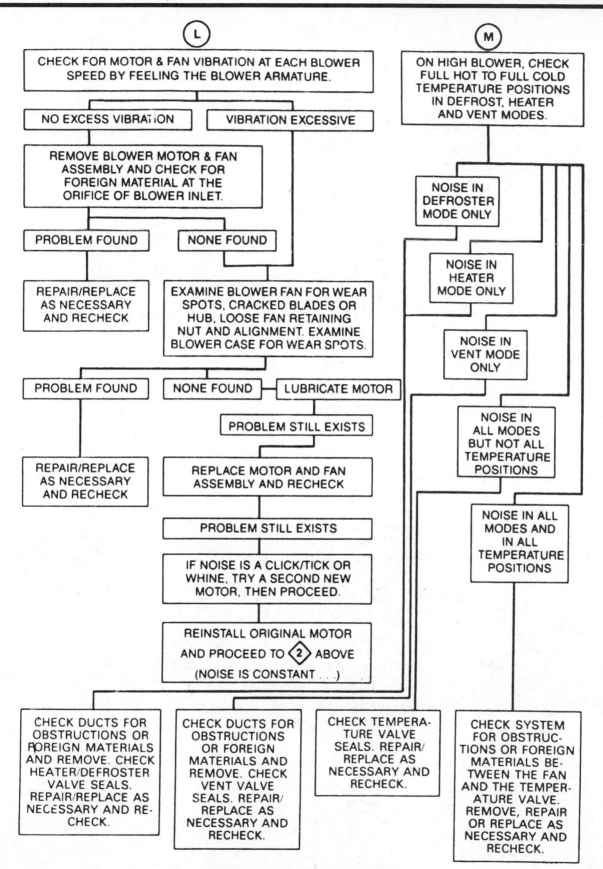

Blower noise diagnosis (cont.)

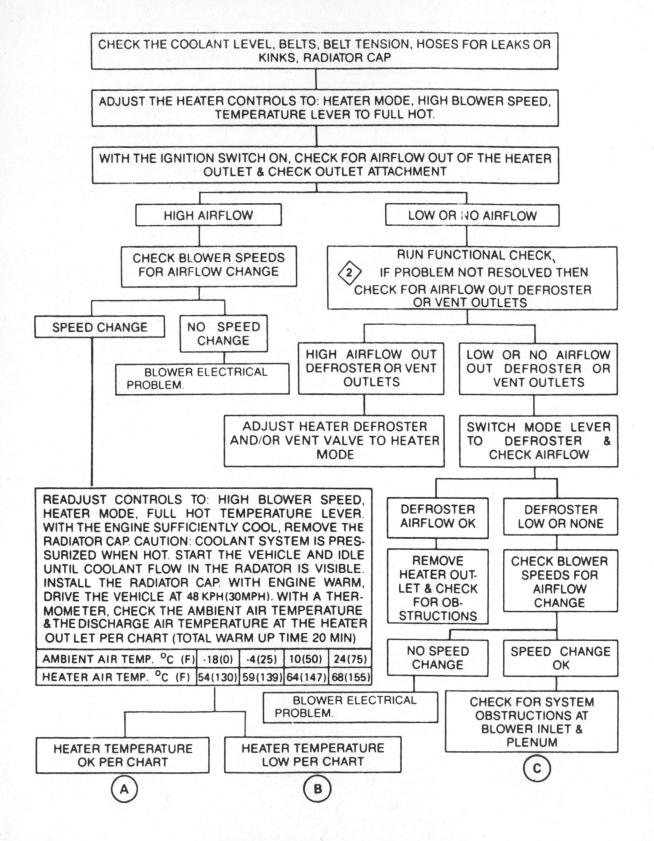

Insufficient heating and defrosting diagnosis

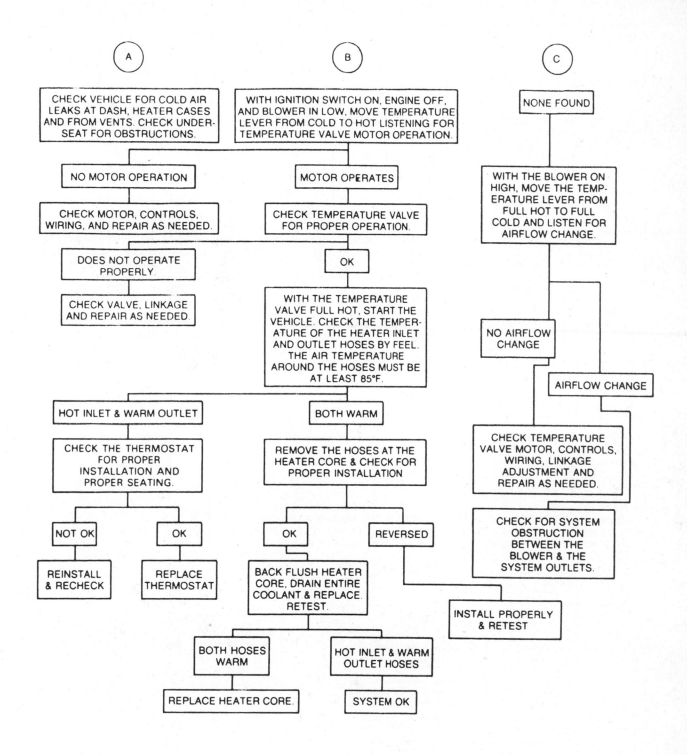

Insufficient heating and defrosting diagnosis (cont.)

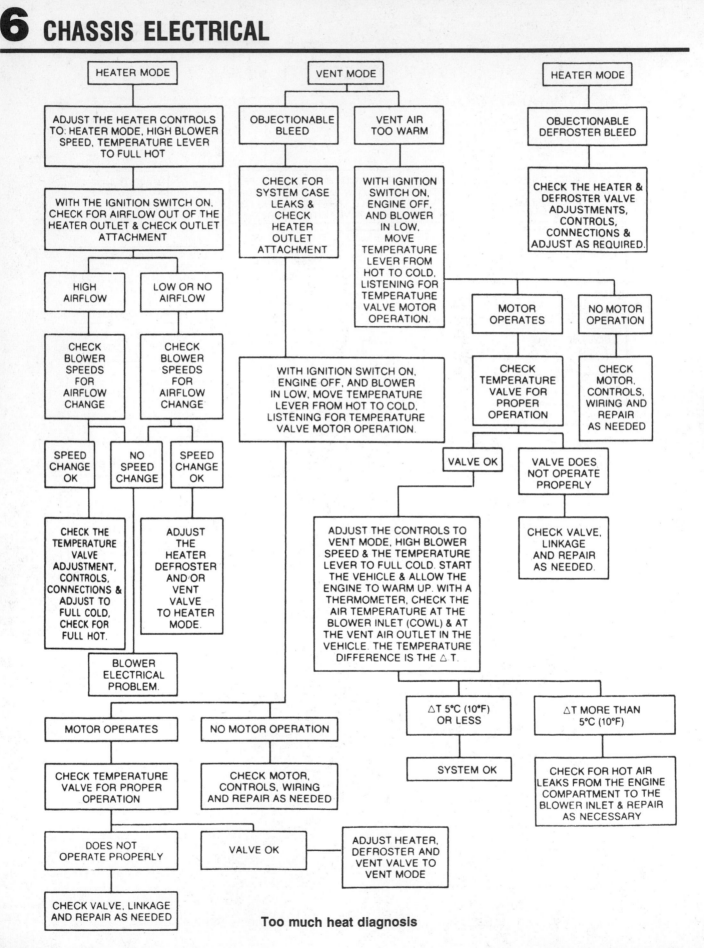

Too much heat diagnosis

RADIO AND CASSETTE PLAYER

REMOVAL AND INSTALLATION

1. Disconnect the negative battery cable.
2. Remove the steering column opening filler panel.
3. Remove the right side sound insulator panel.
4. Remove the accessory trim panel.
5. Loosen the 2 nuts at the bottom of the radio.
6. Remove the 2 screws attaching the radio bracket to the instrument panel lower trim pad assembly.
7. Slide the radio assembly out from the accessory housing.
8. Disconnect the antenna lead-in cable from the radio.
9. Disconnect the instrument panel electrical harness connectors from the radio and remove the radio assembly.

To install:

10. Connect the instrument panel electrical harness connectors and the antenna lead-in cable to the radio.
11. Slide the radio assembly into the accessory housing.
12. Install the 2 screws attaching the radio bracket to the instrument panel lower trim pad assembly.
13. Tighten the 2 nuts at the bottom of the radio.
14. Install the accessory trim panel.
15. Install the right side sound insulator panel.

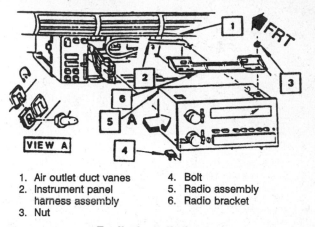

1. Air outlet duct vanes
2. Instrument panel harness assembly
3. Nut
4. Bolt
5. Radio assembly
6. Radio bracket

Radio installation

16. Install the steering column opening filler panel.
17. Connect the negative battery cable.

WINDSHIELD WIPERS

Wiper Blade

REMOVAL AND INSTALLATION

Front

1. Place the wiper arm at the outer wipe position.
2. Lift the blade retainer spring tab.
3. Remove the blade assembly from the arm.

To install:

4. Snap the blade assembly onto the pivot pin.
5. Park the blade and arm assembly.

Rear

1. Insert a suitable tool into the blade retainer slot over the spring.
2. Pivot the tool so that the tip of the tool presses downward on the retainer spring, releasing the pin off the wiper arm.

To install:

3. Install the wiper blade assembly by pressing the pin of of the wiper arm into the blade retainer until the pin is engaged.

Wiper Arm

REMOVAL AND INSTALLATION

Front

NOTE: This procedure requires the use of a wiper arm puller tool No. J-22888D or equivalent and a pin or pop rivet.

1. Disconnect the washer hoses.
2. Remove the nut cover from each wiper arm nut by twisting with a 17mm socket until the cover cracks (breaks). Discard the nut cover(s).

NOTE: Do not use a screwdriver to pry off the nut cover(s).

3. Remove the nut from the wiper arm.
4. Lift the wiper arm and insert a suitable pin or pop rivet completely through the 2 holes located next to the pivot of the arm. Use tool No. J-22888D or equivalent with 35 legs and 90 tip to remove the arm from the drive shaft.

To install:

5. Run and park the wiper motor.
6. Install the wiper arm on the drive shaft.
7. Install the nut on the drive shaft finger tight, then remove the pin, that was inserted near the pivot arm.

NOTE: It may be necessary to allow for some movement of the arm when the nut is being tightened. If the arm moves away from the desired alignment mark, loosen the nut and reposition the arm by moving the blade tip. Retighten the tip.

8. If installing the driver's side wiper arm and blade, measure from the tip of blade to the bottom edge of the glass. This must be approximately 147mm (5.8 in.).

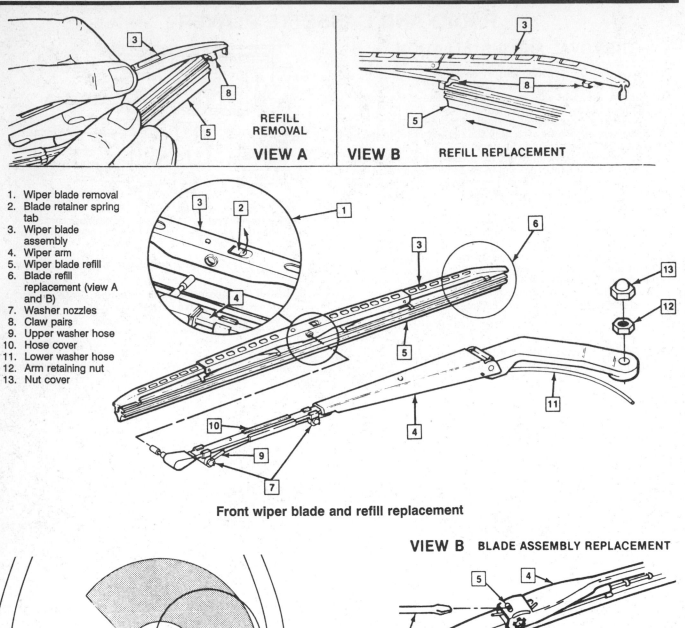

REFILL REMOVAL

VIEW A

VIEW B REFILL REPLACEMENT

1. Wiper blade removal
2. Blade retainer spring tab
3. Wiper blade assembly
4. Wiper arm
5. Wiper blade refill
6. Blade refill replacement (view A and B)
7. Washer nozzles
8. Claw pairs
9. Upper washer hose
10. Hose cover
11. Lower washer hose
12. Arm retaining nut
13. Nut cover

Front wiper blade and refill replacement

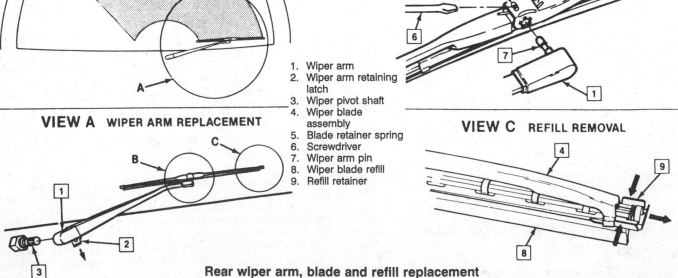

VIEW B BLADE ASSEMBLY REPLACEMENT

VIEW A WIPER ARM REPLACEMENT

1. Wiper arm
2. Wiper arm retaining latch
3. Wiper pivot shaft
4. Wiper blade assembly
5. Blade retainer spring
6. Screwdriver
7. Wiper arm pin
8. Wiper blade refill
9. Refill retainer

VIEW C REFILL REMOVAL

Rear wiper arm, blade and refill replacement

1. Pin or pop rivet
2. Tool J–22888D
3. 35 legs
4. 90 tip

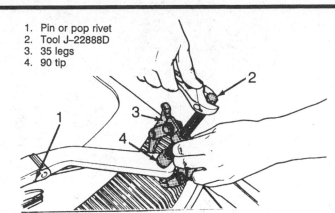

Wiper arm removal

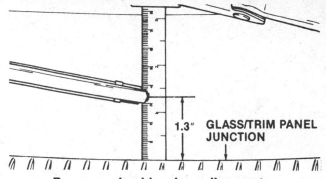

1.3″ **GLASS/TRIM PANEL JUNCTION**

Passenger's side wiper alignment

9. If installing the passenger's side wiper arm and blade, measure from the tip of blade to the bottom edge of the glass. This must be approximately 33mm (1.3 in.).
10. Tighten the wiper arm nut to 29.5 ft. lbs. (40 Nm).
11. Install a new nut cover and connect the washer hose.

Rear

1. Lift the wiper arm from the window and pull the retaining latch.
2. Remove the wiper arm from the pivot shaft.
To install:
3. Run the wiper motor to the park position.
4. Install the head of the wiper arm on the serrated wiper pivot shaft in position where the wiper blade will rest in the proper parked position.
5. Lift the arm extension and push in the retaining latch when the head is fully seated on the pivot shaft.

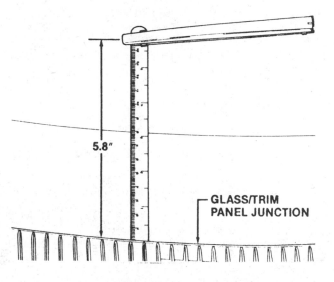

5.8″

GLASS/TRIM PANEL JUNCTION

Driver'side wiper alignment

Wiper Motor
REMOVAL AND INSTALLATION

Front
1990

1. Remove the wiper module assembly as outlined in this section.

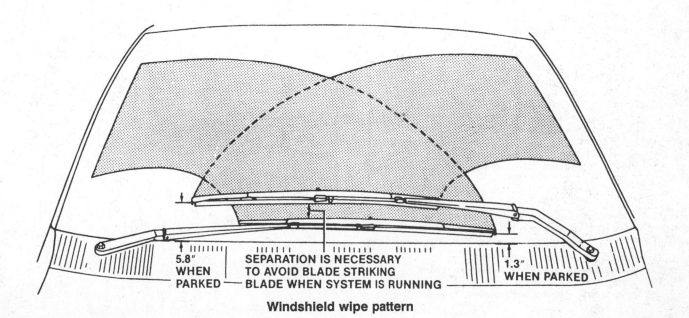

5.8″ WHEN PARKED — SEPARATION IS NECESSARY TO AVOID BLADE STRIKING BLADE WHEN SYSTEM IS RUNNING — 1.3″ WHEN PARKED

Windshield wipe pattern

1. 8 mm socket

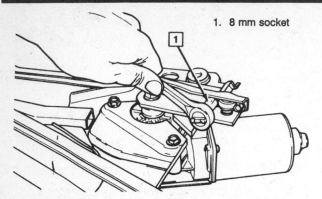

Loosening the socket screw and lockwasher assemblies on the front wiper motor

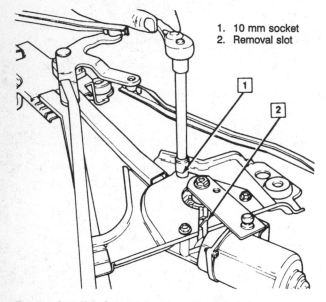

1. 10 mm socket
2. Removal slot

Removing the front wiper motor retaining screws

2. Using a 8mm socket, loosen the 2 crank arm socket screw and lockwashers until the socket releases from the crank arm ball.

3. Run the wipers to the park position.

4. Remove the 3 wiper motor retaining screws and remove the wiper motor from the frame.

To install:

5. Make sure the wiper motor is in the park position.

6. Position the wiper motor to the frame and install the 3 wiper motor retaining screws.

7. Using a 8mm socket, tighten the 2 crank arm socket screw and lockwashers.

8. Install the wiper module assembly as outlined in this section.

1991

NOTE: Because of a new wiper motor bracket design, the wiper motor can be removed from the vehicle without removing the complete wiper module.

1. Disconnect the negative battery cable.

2. Disconnect the harness from the wiper motor.

3. Using a 8mm socket, loosen the 2 crank arm socket screw and lockwashers until the socket releases from the crank arm ball.

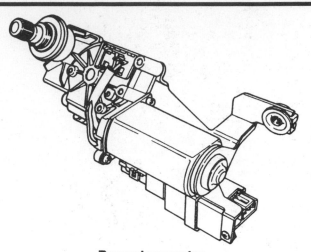

Rear wiper motor

NOTE: Do not remove the crank arm from the motor.

4. Using a 10mm socket, remove the 3 motor retaining screws.

5. Slide the motor out of the slot in the bracket.

To install:

6. Make sure the wipers are in the park position.

7. Slide the motor into the slot in the bracket.

8. Using a 10mm socket, install the 3 motor retaining screws and tighten to 49–80 inch lbs. (5.5–9.0 Nm).

9. Using a 8mm socket, tighten the 2 crank arm socket screw and lockwashers.

10. Connect the harness to the wiper motor.

11. Connect the negative battery cable.

Rear

1. Disconnect the negative battery cable.

2. Remove the tailgate inner trim finish panel as outlined in Section 10.

3. Disconnect the wiring harness from the motor.

4. Remove the 2 motor retaining screws from the grommets and the retaining nut at the pivot and spacer on the tailgate.

5. Remove the motor from the vehicle.

6. Installation is the reverse of removal.

Wiper Module Assembly

REMOVAL AND INSTALLATION

1. Run the wipers to the park position.

2. Disconnect the negative battery cable.

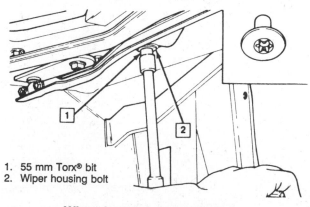

1. 55 mm Torx® bit
2. Wiper housing bolt

Wiper housing bolt removal

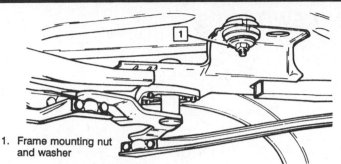

1. Frame mounting nut
   and washer

Removing the 3 module frame mounting nut and washer assemblies.

Wiper module removal

3. Remove the wiper arms as outlined in this section.
4. Remove the air cleaner assembly.
5. Disconnect the harness from the wiper motor.
6. Using a 55mm Torx® bit, remove the wiper housing bolt.
7. Using a 10mm socket, remove the 3 frame mounting nut and washer assemblies and remove the module from the vehicle.

To install:

7. Reposition the module, install the 3 frame mounting nut and washer assemblies. Install the center nut and washer first, then install the 2 outer nut and washer assemblies, followed by the wiper housing bolt. Tighten all to 71–89 inch lbs. (8–10 Nm).
8. Connect the harness from the wiper motor.
9. Install the air cleaner assembly.
10. Connect the negative battery cable.

Wiper Linkage

REMOVAL AND INSTALLATION

1. Remove the wiper module as outlined in this section.
2. Using a 8mm socket, loosen the 6 socket screw and lock-washers assemblies until each of the 3 sockets releases from the respective ball.
3. Using a 10mm socket, remove the 3 bell housing scerws.
4. Installation is the reverse of removal. Tighten the 6 screw and lockwasher assemblies to 49–80 inch lbs. (5.5–9.0 Nm).

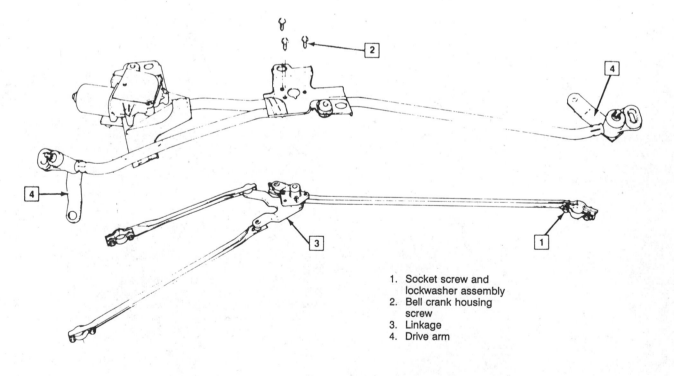

1. Socket screw and
   lockwasher assembly
2. Bell crank housing
   screw
3. Linkage
4. Drive arm

Exploded view of the wiper linkage

INSTRUMENTS AND SWITCHES

Instrument Cluster

REMOVAL AND INSTALLATION

1. Disconnect the negative battery cable.
2. Open the glove box door to access the 2 screws securing the lower instrument panel trim pad assembly to the instrument panel pad assembly.
3. Remove the 2 screws securing the instrument cluster trim panel to the instrument panel pad.
4. Remove the screw retaining the headlamp switch pod to the cluster trim panel and remove the headlamp switch pod. Disconnect the wiring harness to the pod.
5. Remove the screw retaining the windshield wiper switch pod to the cluster trim panel and remove the wiper switch pod. Disconnect the wiring harness to the pod.
6. Remove the 2 screws behind each switch pod securing the cluster trim panel to the left and right instrument cluster mounting brackets.
7. Remove the steering column opening filler.
8. Disconnect the **PNDRL** cable clip.
9. Disconnect the instrument panel harness connector to the instrument cluster.
10. Remove the 2 screws on each side from the left and right cluster retainer brackets and remove the instruments cluster.

To install:

11. Reposition the instrument cluster and install the 2 screws on each side to the left and right cluster retainer brackets.
12. Connect the instrument panel harness connector to the instrument cluster.
13. Connect the **PNDRL** cable clip.
14. Install the steering column opening filler.
15. Install the 2 screws behind each switch pod securing the cluster trim panel to the left and right instrument cluster mounting brackets.
16. Install the screw retaining the windshield wiper switch pod to the cluster trim panel and connect the wiring harness to the pod.
17. Install the 2 screws securing the instrument cluster trim panel to the instrument panel pad.
18. Open the glove box door and install the 2 screws securing the lower instrument panel trim pad assembly to the instrument panel pad assembly.
19. Connect the negative battery cable.

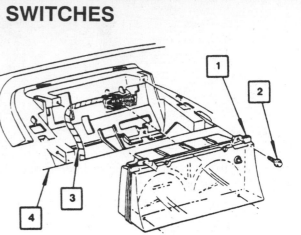

1. Instrument cluster
2. Screw
3. Instrument panel harness assembly
4. Instrument panel lower trim pad assembly

Instrument cluster

Windshield Wiper Switch

REMOVAL AND INSTALLATION

Lumina APV

1. Disconnect the negative battery cable.
2. Remove the wiring protector cover underneath the column.
3. Disconnect the multi-function switch.
4. Disconnect the cruise control wire.
5. Remove the switch.
6. Installation is the reverse of removal. Feed the cruise control wire into the column using piano wire or something similar.

Trans Sport and Silhouette

1. Disconnect the negative battery cable.
2. Grip the pod and carefully pull the wiper switch out to release the 2 spring retaining clips.
3. Disconnect the electrical connector and remove the switch.
4. Installation is the reverse of removal.

Rear Window Wiper Switch

REMOVAL AND INSTALLATION

1. Disconnect the negative battery cable.
2. Grip the pod and carefully pull the wiper switch out to release the 2 spring retaining clips.
3. Disconnect the electrical connector and remove the switch.
4. Installation is the reverse of removal.

Headlight Switch

REMOVAL AND INSTALLATION

1. Disconnect the negative battery cable.
2. Remove the left retaining screw under the trim pad.
3. Disconnect the electrical connector and remove the switch pod.
4. Installation is the reverse of removal.

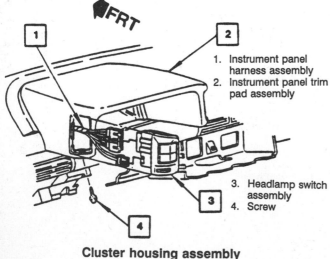

1. Instrument panel harness assembly
2. Instrument panel trim pad assembly
3. Headlamp switch assembly
4. Screw

Cluster housing assembly

1. Instrument panel harness assembly
2. Instrument panel trim pad assembly

3. Headlamp switch assembly
4. Screw

Headlight switch installation

Instrument Panel Assembly

REMOVAL AND INSTALLATION

Upper Trim Panel

The upper trim panel, sometimes referred to as the plenum (closeout) panel, is attached to the instrument panel lower trim pad by 5 bolts. Two bolts are accessed by removing the plastic defroster vent grilles. The remaining 3 bolts secure the trim panel to the dash upper extension and cowl panels.

1. Remove the 2 plastic defroster vent grilles.
2. Remove the 5 panel retaining screws.
3. Lift up on the rear of the trim panel and pull rearward to release the front of the panel.
4. Remove the upper trim panel assembly.

To install:

5. Reposition the upper trim panel and align the holes in the panel with the holes in the extension and cowl panels.
6. Install the 5 retaining screws.

Dash Panel Upper Insulator

1. Remove the push-on insulator retainers.
2. Remove the dash panel upper insulator.

To install:

3. Align the holes in the insulator with the studs on the underside of the dash upper extension panel.
4. Push the retainers on the studs to secure the insulator in place.

Instrument Panel Pad Assembly

1. Remove the 6 screws retaining the instrument panel trim pad to the instrument panel lower trim pad. Two screws are hidden under the adjacent side window deflector grilles.
2. Disconnect the daytime running lights sensor attached to the pad under the front left side speaker grille. Canadian option only).
3. Lift the instrument panel trim pad up and pull the pad rearward to disengage the pad from the 4 slots in the instrument panel lower trim pad.
4. Remove the instrument panel trim pad assembly.

To install:

5. Reposition the trim pad in the 4 slots in the lower trim pad.
6. Connect the daytime running lights sensor attached to the pad under the front left side speaker grille, if so equipped.
7. Install the 6 screws retaining the instrument panel trim pad to the instrument panel lower trim pad.

Lower Trim Pad Assembly

The lower trim pad bears the load of the entire instrument panel assembly. It is supported by the steering column support, a center support bracket, a lower brace, and 2 outer support brackets attached to the left and right body side hinge (A) pillars.

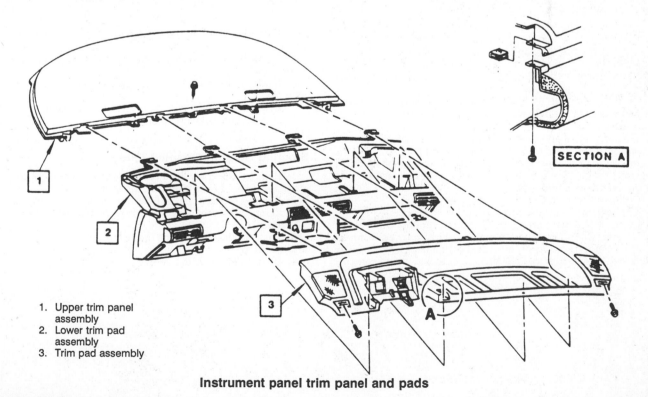

1. Upper trim panel assembly
2. Lower trim pad assembly
3. Trim pad assembly

SECTION A

Instrument panel trim panel and pads

To remove and replace the lower trim pad assembly, several of the instrument panel and engine electrical harness(es) connections must be disconnected.

1. Disconnect the negative battery cable.
2. Remove the front passenger seat for easier access to the lower trim pad.
3. Remove the instrument panel cluster housing.
4. Remove the upper instrument panel trim panel assembly.
5. Remove the right and left sound insulator panels.
6. Remove the steering column opening filler panel.
7. Remove the upper instrument panel trim pad assembly.
8. Disconnect the brake cable from the release handle.
9. Remove the brake release handle.
10. Disconnect the hood latch cable to hood release handle.
11. Remove the hood release handle.
12. Remove the left and right side lower A-pillar kick panels.
13. Disconnect the instrument panel electrical harness from the crosscar harness J-block connectors.
14. Disconnect the instrument panel electrical harness from the body harness J-block connectors.
15. Lower the steering column to rest on the driver's seat to allow clearance when removing and replacing the instrument panel lower pad assembly.
16. Disconnect the instrument panel electrical harness from the engine harness J-block connectors, near left side shock tower in the engine compartment.
17. Disconnect the instrument panel electrical connectors from the DLR resistor relay, both windshield wiper solvent pumps, brake (low hydraulic fluid) warning, blower motor, resistor block, high blower fan relay and windshield wiper motor.
18. Disconnect the instrument panel ground (lugs) connections to the vehicle space frame (behind the driver's side lower A-pillar kick panel).
19. Disconnect the instrument panel electrical harness connections to the steering column electrical components, such as the hazard switch, ignition switch, turn signals and cruise control.

WARNING: Provide temporary support for the instrument panel lower trim panel assembly while the load bearing support braces are disconnected.

20. Disconnect the instrument panel center support bracket.
21. Disconnect the instrument panel lower support.
22. Disconnect the instrument panel lower brace.
23. Push the engine compartment side of the instrument panel electrical harness through the left side bulkhead grommet access hole into the passenger compartment.
24. With the aid of an assistant lift the instrument panel lower trim pad from the vehicle and place in a clean area.

To install:
25. With the aid of an assistant lift the instrument panel lower trim pad into the vehicle and temporarily support it.
26. Push the passenger side of the instrument panel electrical harness through the left side bulkhead grommet access hole into the engine compartment.
27. Connect the instrument panel lower brace.
28. Connect the instrument panel lower support.
29. Connect the instrument panel center support bracket.
30. Connect the instrument panel electrical harness connections to the steering column electrical components, such as the hazard switch, ignition switch, turn signals and cruise control.

31. Connect the instrument panel ground (lugs) connections to the vehicle space frame (behind the driver's side lower A-pillar kick panel).
32. Connect the instrument panel electrical connectors to the DLR resistor relay, both windshield wiper solvent pumps, brake (low hydraulic fluid) warning, blower motor, resistor block, high blower fan relay and windshield wiper motor.
33. Connect the instrument panel electrical harness to the engine harness J-block connectors, near left side shock tower in the engine compartment.
34. Reinstall the steering column back into position.
35. Connect the instrument panel electrical harness to the body harness J-block connectors.
36. Connect the instrument panel electrical harness from the crosscar harness J-block connectors.
37. Install the left and right side lower A-pillar kick panels.
38. Install the hood release handle.
39. Connect the hood latch cable to hood release handle.
40. Install the brake release handle.
41. Connect the brake cable to the release handle.
42. Install the upper instrument panel trim pad assembly.
43. Install the steering column opening filler panel.
44. Install the right and left sound insulator panels.
45. Install the instrument panel cluster housing.
46. Install the front passenger seat.
48. Connect the negative battery cable.

Sound Insulator Panels

LEFT

1. Remove the nut from the retainer/stud on the lower trim pad.
2. Remove the screw retaining the right side panel to the trim pad.
3. Remove the bolt and nut fastening the panel to the trim pad.
4. Remove the nut from the panel tab.
5. Remove the left side sound insulator panel.
6. Installation is the reverse of removal.

RIGHT

1. Remove the screw fastening the left and right insulator panel.
2. Remove the screw retaining the insulator panel to the lower trim pad.
3. Remove the nuts from the retainers/studs on the lower trim pad.
4. Remove the right side sound insulator panel.
5. Installation is the reverse of removal.

Steering Column Opening Filler

1. Remove the 3 screws attaching the filler panel to the instrument panel lower trim pad assembly.
2. Remove the filler panel from the slots in the lower trim pad by pulling to the rear and downward to release the clips.
To install:
3. Position the filler to the lower trim pad, inserting the clips into the slots.
4. Install the retaining screws.

1. Plenum panel
   assembly
2. Screw
3. Instrument panel
   lower trim pad
   assembly
4. Instrument panel
   lower support
5. Screw
6. Body wiring harness
7. Instrument panel
   lower brace
8. Nut
9. Screw
10. Steering column
    lower support

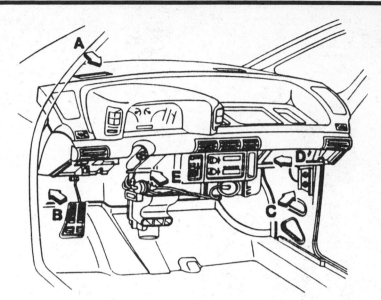

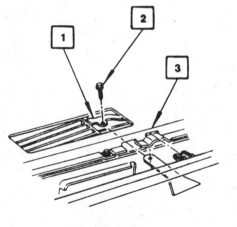

VIEW A

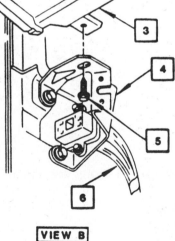

VIEW B

VIEW C

VIEW E

VIEW D

Lower trim pad load supports

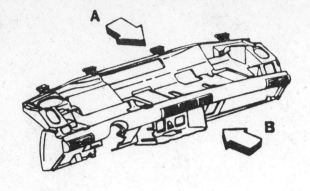

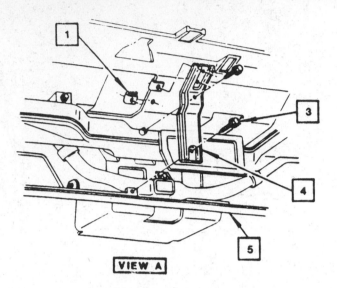

VIEW A

1. J-nut
2. Dash upper extension panel
3. Screw
4. Instrument panel center support bracket
5. Instrument panel lower trim pad
6. HVAC module assembly
7. Instrument panel lower brace
8. Temperature valve electric motor

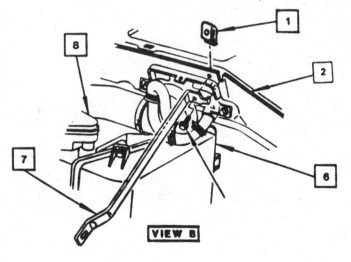

VIEW B

Instrument panel center support and lower braces

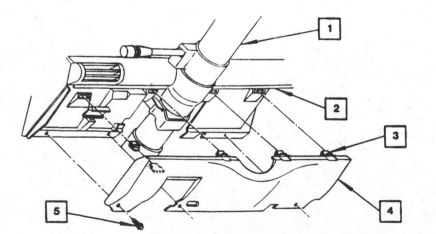

1. Steering column
2. Instrument panel lower trim pad assembly
3. Retaining clips
4. Steering column opening filler assembly
5. Bolt

Steering column opening filler

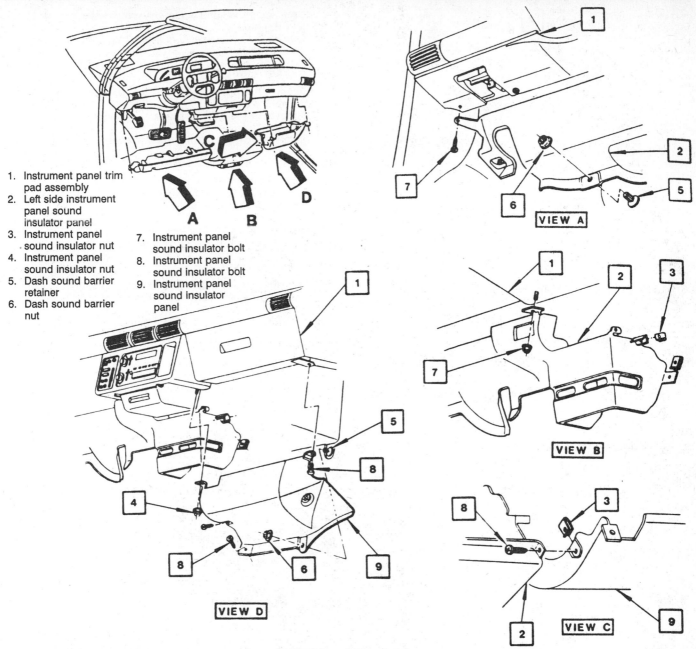

1. Instrument panel trim pad assembly
2. Left side instrument panel sound insulator panel
3. Instrument panel sound insulator nut
4. Instrument panel sound insulator nut
5. Dash sound barrier retainer
6. Dash sound barrier nut

7. Instrument panel sound insulator bolt
8. Instrument panel sound insulator bolt
9. Instrument panel sound insulator panel

Sound insulator panels

LIGHTING

Headlight Assembly or Bulb

REMOVAL AND INSTALLATION

1. Open the hood.

2. Disconnect the negative battery cable.
3. Use a pair of pliers and pull out the 2 retainers at the top of the assembly.
4. Remove the 1 bolt at the bottom rear of the assembly.
5. Pull the assembly forward and disconnect the electrical connectors.

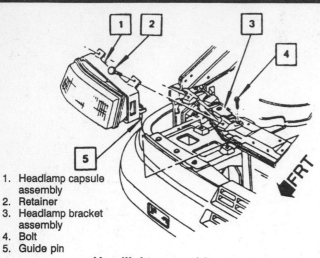

1. Headlamp capsule assembly
2. Retainer
3. Headlamp bracket assembly
4. Bolt
5. Guide pin

Headlight assembly

6. Remove the bulb(s) from the assembly, if replacing.

To install:

7. Install the bulb(s) to the assembly, if replacing.
8. Connect the electrical connectors.
9. Install the 1 bolt at the bottom rear of the assembly.
10. Install the 2 retainers by pushing in place.
11. Connect the negative battery cable and close the hood.

Signal and Marker Lights

REMOVAL AND INSTALLATION

Front Parking or Turn Signal Light

1. Reach under the vehicle and disconnect socket from the light assembly.
2. Remove the bulb from the socket, if replacing.

3. If replacing the lamp assembly, remove the 1 screw at the bottom of the bumper.
4. Remove the lamp assembly by pulling from the rear.
5. Installation is the reverse of removal.

Side Marker Lights

1. Remove the thumb screw and pull the lamp assembly out from the vehicle.
2. Remove the socket from the lamp assembly and replace the bulb as necessary.
3. Install the lamp assembly in the reverse of removal.

Rear Taillight, Stop and Turn Signal Lights

1. Support the liftgate.
2. Remove the 2 screws holding the rear tailamp housing assembly and pull the assembly out.
3. Remove the socket from the lamp assembly and replace the bulb as necessary.
4. Installation is the reverse of removal.

License Plate Light

1. Remove the 2 Torx® screws and remove the light assembly.
2. Remove the socket from the lamp assembly and replace the bulb as necessary.
3. Installation is the reverse of removal.

Dome and Reading Lights

1. Remove the lens by pulling down.
2. Remove the bulb(s) as necessary.
3. If removing the light assembly, disconnect the 2 push clips with a pair of pliers.
4. Pull the assembly down and and disconnect the electrical connector.
5. Installation is the reverse of removal. Replace with new clips, if necessary.

Door Courtesy Light

1. Remove the stepwell lamp assembly from the opening in

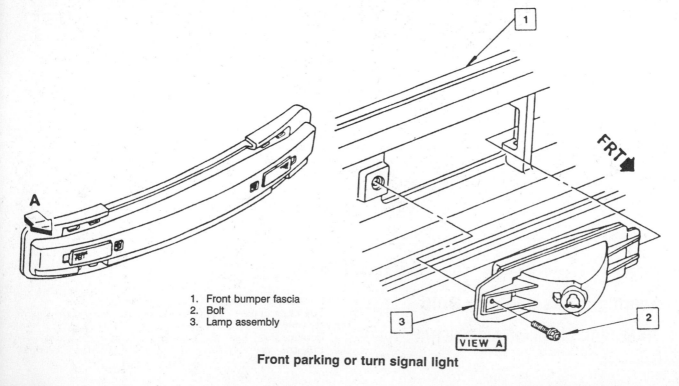

1. Front bumper fascia
2. Bolt
3. Lamp assembly

Front parking or turn signal light

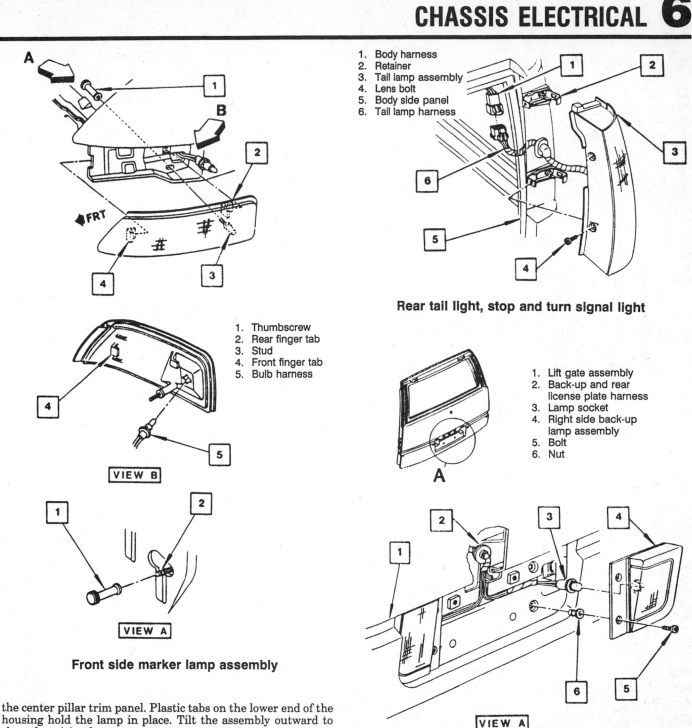

1. Body harness
2. Retainer
3. Tail lamp assembly
4. Lens bolt
5. Body side panel
6. Tail lamp harness

Rear tail light, stop and turn signal light

1. Thumbscrew
2. Rear finger tab
3. Stud
4. Front finger tab
5. Bulb harness

VIEW B

VIEW A

Front side marker lamp assembly

1. Lift gate assembly
2. Back-up and rear license plate harness
3. Lamp socket
4. Right side back-up lamp assembly
5. Bolt
6. Nut

A

VIEW A

License plate and back-up lights

the center pillar trim panel. Plastic tabs on the lower end of the housing hold the lamp in place. Tilt the assembly outward to clear the wiring harness connector.

2. Disconnect the wiring harness connector.

3. Remove the lamp assembly and replace the bulb as necessary.

4. Installation is the reverse of removal.

Instrument Panel Courtesy Lights

LEFT SIDE

NOTE: The housing for the left courtesy light is part of the left sound insulator.

1. Remove the screws holding the left sound insulator.

2. Remove the sound insulator and remove the bulb from the socket.

3. Installation is the reverse of removal.

RIGHT SIDE

1. Remove the screws holding the left sound insulator and remove the left sound insulator.

2. Remove the screws holding the right sound insulator and remove the right sound insulator.

3. Remove the socket from the assembly.

4. Remove the bulb from the socket, if replacing.

5. Remove the light retaining screw and remove the light assembly.

6. Installation is the reverse of removal.

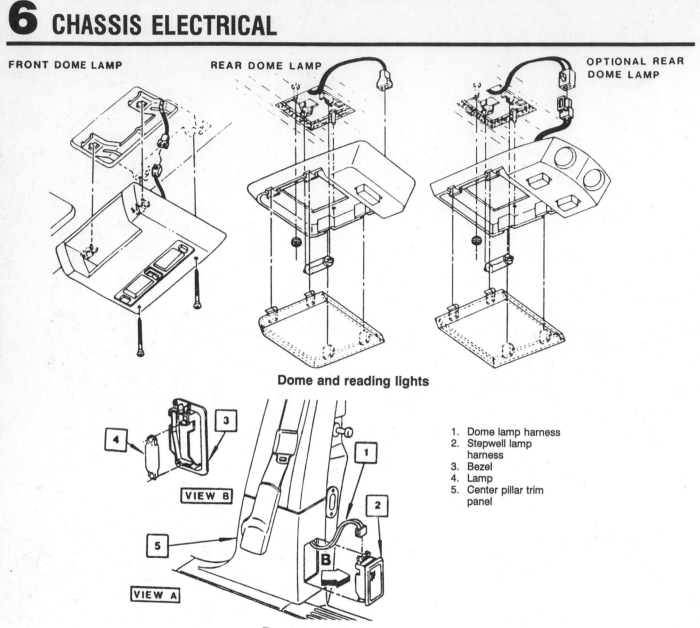

FRONT DOME LAMP

REAR DOME LAMP

OPTIONAL REAR DOME LAMP

Dome and reading lights

1. Dome lamp harness
2. Stepwell lamp harness
3. Bezel
4. Lamp
5. Center pillar trim panel

VIEW B

VIEW A

Door stepwell courtesy lamp

LOCATION	BULB NUMBER
Exterior	
Headlight, Outer, (Halogen)	9006•
Headlight, Inner, (Halogen)	9005•
Front Park and Turn Signal	2358NA
Front Sidemarker	9438068
Rear Stop and Turn Signal	2057
Rear Taillight	194
License Plate	194
Backup	3057
Underhood	561
Interior	
Front Ashtray	194
Rear Cigarette Lighter/Ashtray	194
Front Courtesy	194

Side Door Stepwell	561
Glove Box	194
Front and Rear Dome	561
Front Reading	562
Rear Reading	906
Instruments and Controls	
Illumination	161
Oil and Volts gage	37
Warning Indicators	74/161
Heater and A/C Control	Not Serviceable
Radio	Not Serviceable
Light Switch and Wiper controls	TSS7008A-9753/ BQ245-36206A

•Bulb and socket are serviced as an assembly.

Light bulb identification

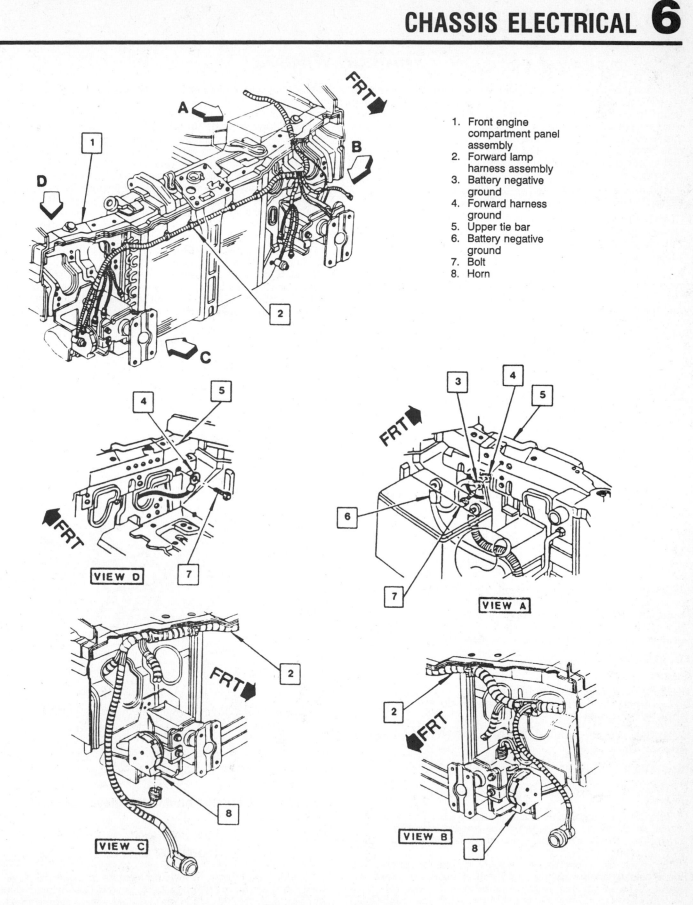

1. Front engine compartment panel assembly
2. Forward lamp harness assembly
3. Battery negative ground
4. Forward harness ground
5. Upper tie bar
6. Battery negative ground
7. Bolt
8. Horn

VIEW D

VIEW A

VIEW C

VIEW B

Forward lamp harness

TRAILER WIRING

Wiring the van for towing is fairly easy. There are a number of good wiring kits available and these should be used, rather than trying to design your own. All trailers will need brake lights and turn signals as well as tail lights and side marker lights. Most states require extra marker lights for overly wide trailers. Also, most states have recently required back-up lights for trailers, and most trailer manufacturers have been building trailers with back-up lights for several years.

Additionally, some Class I, most Class II and just about all Class III trailers will have electric brakes.

Add to this number an accessories wire, to operate trailer internal equipment or to charge the trailer's battery, and you can have as many as seven wires in the harness.

Determine the equipment on your trailer and buy the wiring kit necessary. The kit will contain all the wires needed, plus a plug adapter set which included the female plug, mounted on the bumper or hitch, and the male plug, wired into, or plugged into the trailer harness.

When installing the kit, follow the manufacturer's instruc-tions. The color coding of the wires is standard throughout the industry.

One point to note: some domestic vehicles, and most imported vehicles, have separate turn signals. On most domestic vehicles, the brake lights and rear turn signals operate with the same bulb. For those vehicles with separate turn signals, you can pur-chase an isolation unit so that the brake lights won't blink whenever the turn signals are operated, or, you can go to your local electronics supply house and buy four diodes to wire in se-ries with the brake and turn signal bulbs. Diodes will isolate the brake and turn signals. The choice is yours. The isolation units are simple and quick to install, but far more expensive than the diodes. The diodes, however, require more work to install prop-erly, since they require the cutting of each bulb's wire and sol-dering in place of the diode.

One, final point, the best kits are those with a spring loaded cover on the vehicle mounted socket. This cover prevent dirt and moisture from corroding the terminals. Never let the vehi-cle socket hang loosely; always mount it securely to the bumper or hitch.

CIRCUIT PROTECTION

Fuses

REPLACEMENT

The fuses are of the miniaturized (compact) size and are locat-ed on a fuse block, they provide increased circuit protection and reliability. Access to the fuse block is gained through the glove box opening. Each fuse receptacle is marked as to the circuit it protects and the correct amperage of the fuse.

REPLACEMENT

1. Pull the fuse from the fuse block.
2. Inspect the fuse element (through the clear plastic body) to the blade terminal for defects.

NOTE: When replacing the fuse, DO NOT use one of a higher amperage.

3. To install, reverse the removal procedures.

Convenience Center

The Convenience Center is a mounted to a bracket behind the glove compartment. It contains the hazard warning flasher, horn relay, circuit breakers, chime module and air conditioner low fan relay.

To reach the convenience center components, remove the glove compartment and the right sound insulator panel. Re-move the hazard flasher, horn relay and circuit breakers by pull-ing the unit straight out. On the chime module, release the lock-ing tab first.

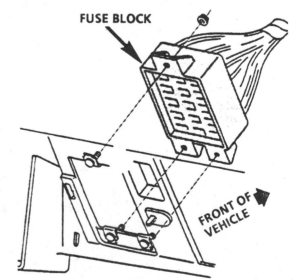

Fuse box is located behind the glove compartment door

Fusible Links

In addition to fuses, the wiring harness incorporates fusible links (in the battery feed circuits) to protect the wiring. Fusible links are 4 in. (102mm) sections of copper wire, 4 gauges smaller than the circuit(s) they are protecting, designed to melt under

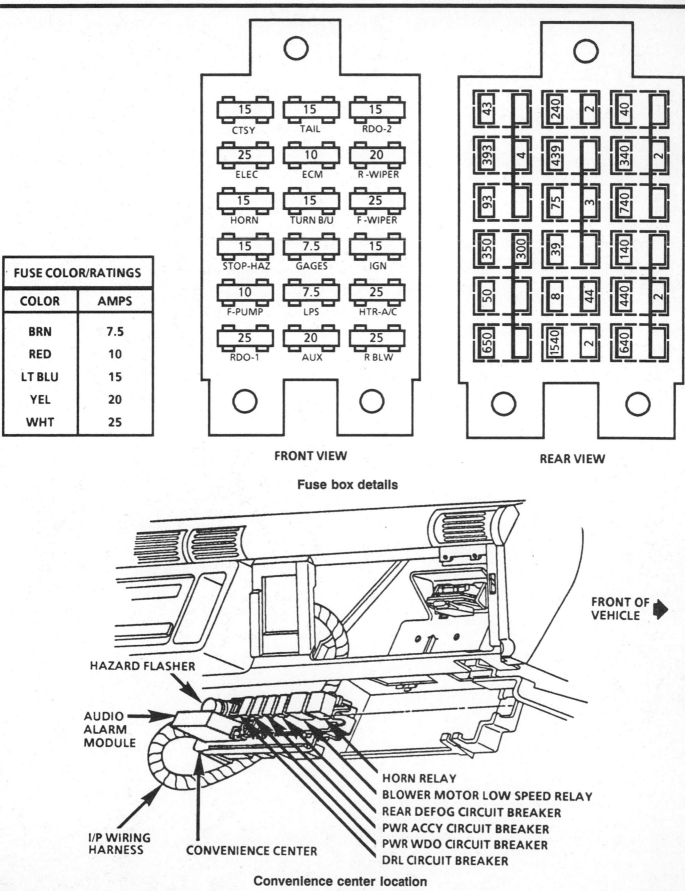

FUSE COLOR/RATINGS	
COLOR	AMPS
BRN	7.5
RED	10
LT BLU	15
YEL	20
WHT	25

FRONT VIEW

REAR VIEW

Fuse box details

HAZARD FLASHER

AUDIO
ALARM
MODULE

I/P WIRING
HARNESS

CONVENIENCE CENTER

FRONT OF
VEHICLE

HORN RELAY
BLOWER MOTOR LOW SPEED RELAY
REAR DEFOG CIRCUIT BREAKER
PWR ACCY CIRCUIT BREAKER
PWR WDO CIRCUIT BREAKER
DRL CIRCUIT BREAKER

Convenience center location

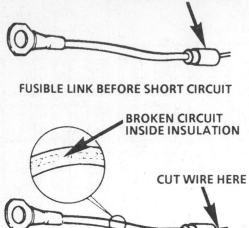

CONNECTOR COVERING

FUSIBLE LINK BEFORE SHORT CIRCUIT

BROKEN CIRCUIT INSIDE INSULATION

CUT WIRE HERE

FUSIBLE LINK AFTER SHORT CIRCUIT

Good and damaged fusible links

electrical overload. There are four different gauge sizes used. The fusible links are color coded so that they may be installed in their original positions.

REPLACEMENT

• Fusible link B — Rust colored, charging and starting circuit, connected to the starter solenoid.
• Fusible link C — Rust colored, TBI circuit, located at junction block, in the engine compartment, on the left side wheelhouse opening.
• Fusible link H — Rust colored, charging and starting circuit, connected to the starter solenoid.
• Fusible link J — RUST colored, coolant fan circuit, connected to the starter solenoid.
• Fusible link Y — Rust colored, headlight circuit, located at junction block, in the engine compartment, on the left side wheelhouse opening.
• Fusible link X — Rust colored, heater circuit, located at junction block, in the engine compartment, on the left side wheelhouse opening.
• Fusible link X — Rust colored, TBI circuit, located at junction block, in the engine compartment, on the left side wheelhouse opening.

• Fusible link X — Rust colored, charging and starting circuit, located at junction block, in the engine compartment, on the left side wheelhouse opening.
1. Disconnect the negative battery terminal from the battery.
2. Locate the cause of the problem and repair before replacing the link.
3. Locate the burned out link.
4. Strip away the melted insulation and cut the burned link ends from the wire.
5. Strip the wire back ½ in. (13mm) to allow soldering of the new link.
6. Using a new fusible link 4 gauges smaller than the protected circuit and approximately 10 in. (254mm) long, solder it into the circuit.

NOTE: Whenever splicing a new wire, always bond the splice with rosin core solder, then cover with electrical tape. Using acid core solder may cause corrosion.

7. Tape and seal all splices with silicone to weatherproof repairs.
8. After taping the wire, tape the electrical harness leaving an exposed 5 in. (127mm) loop of wire.
9. Reconnect the battery.

Circuit Breakers

A circuit breaker is an electrical switch which breaks the circuit in case of an overload. The rear defogger, power accessories, power windows and Daytime Running Light (DRL) circuit breakers are located in the convenience center (see above). The circuit breaker will remain open until the short or overload condition in the circuit is corrected.

RESETTING

Locate the circuit breaker in the convenience center, then push the circuit breaker in until it locks. If the circuit breaker kicks itself Off again, locate and correct the problem in the electrical circuit.

Flashers

The turn signal flasher is mounted under the instrument panel above the parking brake.
The hazard flasher is mounted in the convenience center. The convenience center is located behind the glove compartment (See above).

Troubleshooting Basic Turn Signal and Flasher Problems

Most problems in the turn signals or flasher system can be reduced to defective flashers or bulbs, which are easily replaced. Occasionally, problems in the turn signals are traced to the switch in the steering column, which will require professional service.

F = Front   R = Rear   ● = Lights off   o = Lights on

Problem		Solution
Turn signals light, but do not flash		· Replace the flasher
No turn signals light on either side		· Check the fuse. Replace if defective. · Check the flasher by substitution · Check for open circuit, short circuit or poor ground
Both turn signals on one side don't work		· Check for bad bulbs · Check for bad ground in both housings
One turn signal light on one side doesn't work		· Check and/or replace bulb · Check for corrosion in socket. Clean contacts. · Check for poor ground at socket
Turn signal flashes too fast or too slow		· Check any bulb on the side flashing too fast. A heavy-duty bulb is probably installed in place of a regular bulb. · Check the bulb flashing too slow. A standard bulb was probably installed in place of a heavy-duty bulb. · Check for loose connections or corrosion at the bulb socket
Indicator lights don't work in either direction		· Check if the turn signals are working · Check the dash indicator lights · Check the flasher by substitution

Troubleshooting Basic Turn Signal and Flasher Problems

Most problems in the turn signals or flasher system can be reduced to defective flashers or bulbs, which are easily replaced. Occasionally, problems in the turn signals are traced to the switch in the steering column, which will require professional service.

F = Front   R = Rear   • = Lights off   o = Lights on

Problem		Solution
One indicator light doesn't light		• On systems with 1 dash indicator: See if the lights work on the same side. Often the filaments have been reversed in systems combining stoplights with taillights and turn signals. Check the flasher by substitution • On systems with 2 indicators: Check the bulbs on the same side Check the indicator light bulb Check the flasher by substitution

Troubleshooting Basic Lighting Problems

Problem	Cause	Solution
Lights		
One or more lights don't work, but others do	• Defective bulb(s) • Blown fuse(s) • Dirty fuse clips or light sockets • Poor ground circuit	• Replace bulb(s) • Replace fuse(s) • Clean connections • Run ground wire from light socket housing to car frame
Lights burn out quickly	• Incorrect voltage regulator setting or defective regulator • Poor battery/alternator connections	• Replace voltage regulator • Check battery/alternator connections
Lights go dim	• Low/discharged battery • Alternator not charging • Corroded sockets or connections • Low voltage output	• Check battery • Check drive belt tension; repair or replace alternator • Clean bulb and socket contacts and connections • Replace voltage regulator
Lights flicker	• Loose connection • Poor ground • Circuit breaker operating (short circuit)	• Tighten all connections • Run ground wire from light housing to car frame • Check connections and look for bare wires
Lights "flare"—Some flare is normal on acceleration—if excessive, see "Lights Burn Out Quickly"	• High voltage setting	• Replace voltage regulator

Troubleshooting Basic Lighting Problems

Problem	Cause	Solution
Lights glare—approaching drivers are blinded	• Lights adjusted too high • Rear springs or shocks sagging • Rear tires soft	• Have headlights aimed • Check rear springs/shocks • Check/correct rear tire pressure

Turn Signals

Problem	Cause	Solution
Turn signals don't work in either direction	• Blown fuse • Defective flasher • Loose connection	• Replace fuse • Replace flasher • Check/tighten all connections
Right (or left) turn signal only won't work	• Bulb burned out • Right (or left) indicator bulb burned out • Short circuit	• Replace bulb • Check/replace indicator bulb • Check/repair wiring
Flasher rate too slow or too fast	• Incorrect wattage bulb • Incorrect flasher	• Flasher bulb • Replace flasher (use a variable load flasher if you pull a trailer)
Indicator lights do not flash (burn steadily)	• Burned out bulb • Defective flasher	• Replace bulb • Replace flasher
Indicator lights do not light at all	• Burned out indicator bulb • Defective flasher	• Replace indicator bulb • Replace flasher

Troubleshooting Basic Dash Gauge Problems

Problem	Cause	Solution
Coolant Temperature Gauge		
Gauge reads erratically or not at all	• Loose or dirty connections • Defective sending unit • Defective gauge	• Clean/tighten connections • Bi-metal gauge: remove the wire from the sending unit. Ground the wire for an instant. If the gauge registers, replace the sending unit. • Magnetic gauge: disconnect the wire at the sending unit. With ignition ON gauge should register COLD. Ground the wire; gauge should register HOT.

Ammeter Gauge—Turn Headlights ON (do not start engine). Note reaction

Problem	Cause	Solution
Ammeter shows charge Ammeter shows discharge Ammeter does not move	• Connections reversed on gauge • Ammeter is OK • Loose connections or faulty wiring • Defective gauge	• Reinstall connections • Nothing • Check/correct wiring • Replace gauge

Troubleshooting Basic Dash Gauge Problems

Problem	Cause	Solution
Oil Pressure Gauge		
Gauge does not register or is inaccurate	• On mechanical gauge, Bourdon tube may be bent or kinked	• Check tube for kinks or bends preventing oil from reaching the gauge
	• Low oil pressure	• Remove sending unit. Idle the engine briefly. If no oil flows from sending unit hole, problem is in engine.
	• Defective gauge	• Remove the wire from the sending unit and ground it for an instant with the ignition ON. A good gauge will go to the top of the scale.
	• Defective wiring	• Check the wiring to the gauge. If it's OK and the gauge doesn't register when grounded, replace the gauge.
	• Defective sending unit	• If the wiring is OK and the gauge functions when grounded, replace the sending unit
All Gauges		
All gauges do not operate	• Blown fuse	• Replace fuse
	• Defective instrument regulator	• Replace instrument voltage regulator
All gauges read low or erratically	• Defective or dirty instrument voltage regulator	• Clean contacts or replace
All gauges pegged	• Loss of ground between instrument voltage regulator and car	• Check ground
	• Defective instrument regulator	• Replace regulator
Warning Lights		
Light(s) do not come on when ignition is ON, but engine is not started	• Defective bulb	• Replace bulb
	• Defective wire	• Check wire from light to sending unit
	• Defective sending unit	• Disconnect the wire from the sending unit and ground it. Replace the sending unit if the light comes on with the ignition ON.
Light comes on with engine running	• Problem in individual system	• Check system
	• Defective sending unit	• Check sending unit (see above)

Troubleshooting Basic Windshield Wiper Problems

Problem	Cause	Solution
Electric Wipers		
Wipers do not operate— Wiper motor heats up or hums	• Internal motor defect • Bent or damaged linkage • Arms improperly installed on linking pivots	• Replace motor • Repair or replace linkage • Position linkage in park and reinstall wiper arms
Electric Wipers		
Wipers do not operate— No current to motor	• Fuse or circuit breaker blown • Loose, open or broken wiring • Defective switch • Defective or corroded terminals • No ground circuit for motor or switch	• Replace fuse or circuit breaker • Repair wiring and connections • Replace switch • Replace or clean terminals • Repair ground circuits
Wipers do not operate— Motor runs	• Linkage disconnected or broken	• Connect wiper linkage or replace broken linkage
Vacuum Wipers		
Wipers do not operate	• Control switch or cable inoperative • Loss of engine vacuum to wiper motor (broken hoses, low engine vacuum, defective vacuum/fuel pump) • Linkage broken or disconnected • Defective wiper motor	• Repair or replace switch or cable • Check vacuum lines, engine vacuum and fuel pump • Repair linkage • Replace wiper motor
Wipers stop on engine acceleration	• Leaking vacuum hoses • Dry windshield • Oversize wiper blades • Defective vacuum/fuel pump	• Repair or replace hoses • Wet windshield with washers • Replace with proper size wiper blades • Replace pump

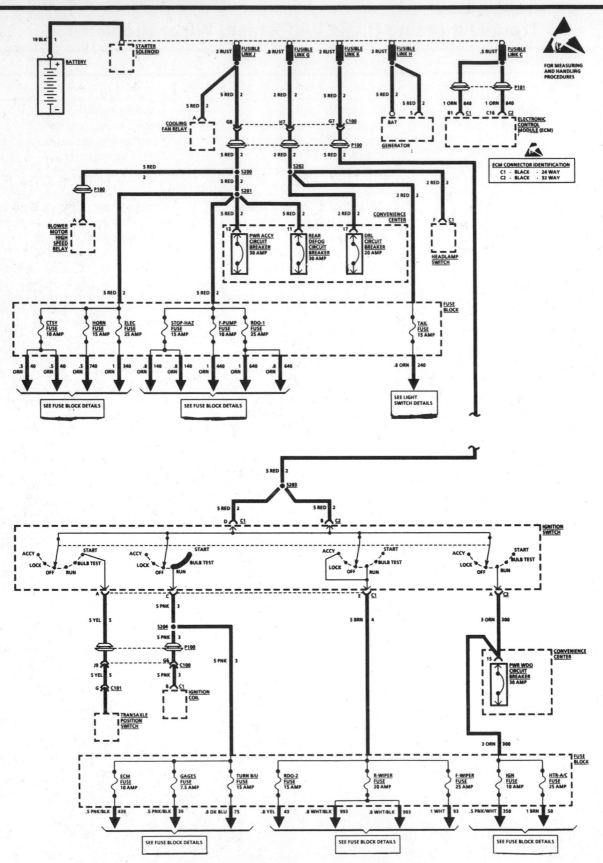

Power distribution — 1990 Lumina APV

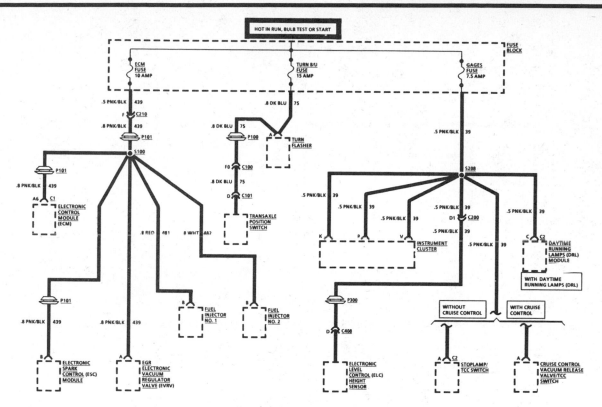

Fuse block details (ECM fuse, turn/back-up fuse and gauges fuse) — 1990 Lumina APV

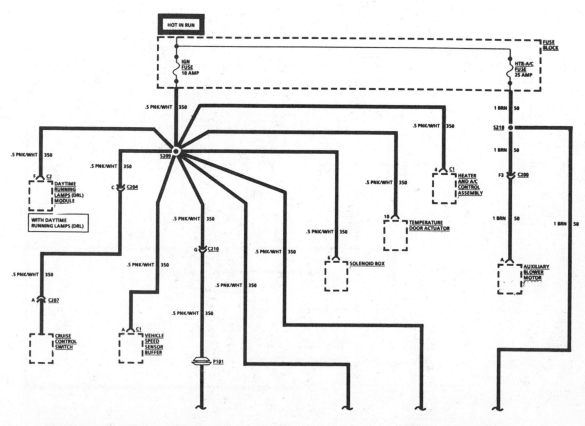

Fuse block details (Ignition fuse and heater/a/c fuse) — 1990 Lumina APV

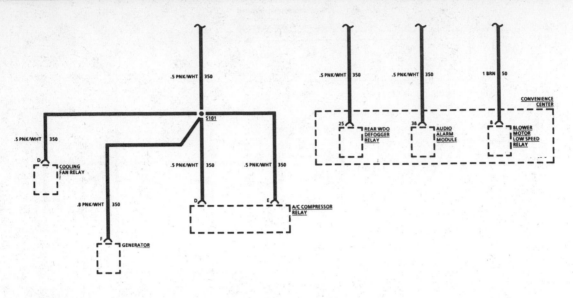

Fuse block details (Ignition fuse and heater/a/c fuse) (cont.) — 1990 Lumina APV

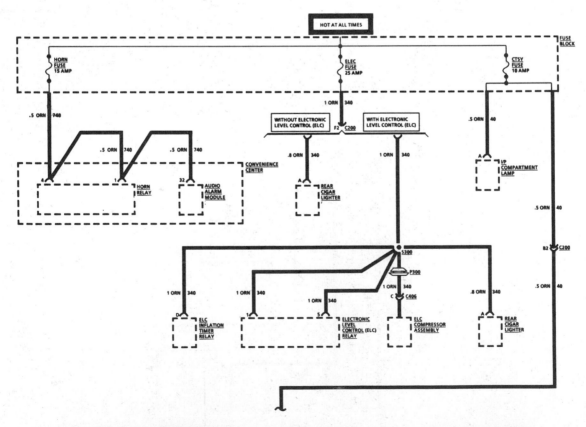

Fuse block details (horn fuse, elec fuse and ctsy fuse) — 1990 Lumina APV

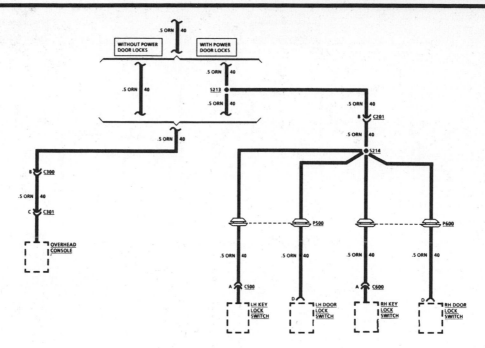

Fuse block details (horn fuse, elec fuse and ctsy fuse) (cont.) — 1990 Lumina APV

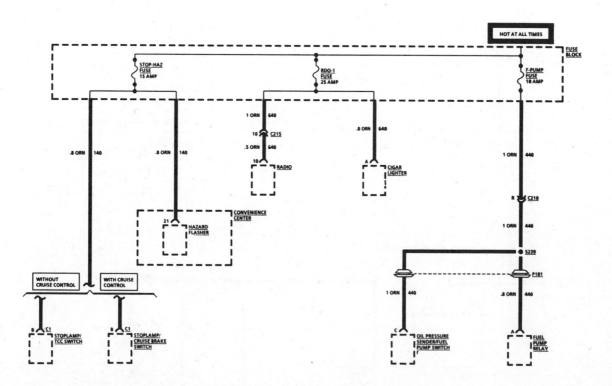

Fuse block details (stop-haz fuse, rdo-1 fuse and f- pump fuse) — 1990 Lumina APV

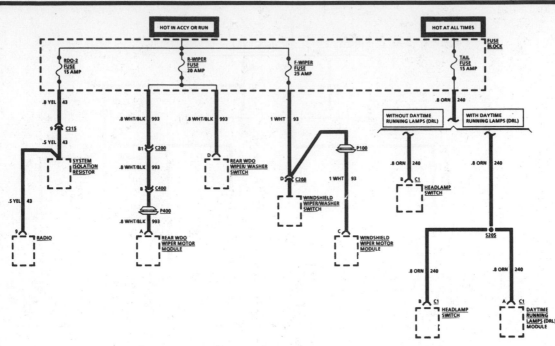

Fuse block details (rdo-2 fuse, r-wiper fuse, f-wiper fuse and tail fuse) — 1990 Lumina APV

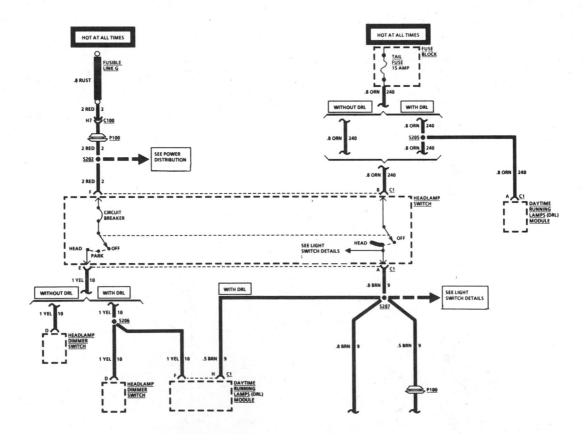

Light switch details — 1990 Lumina APV

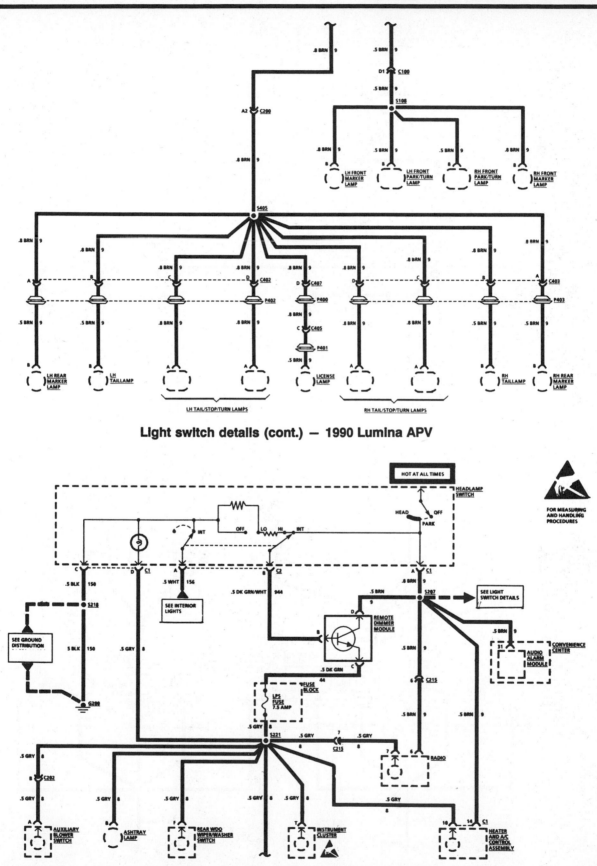

Light switch details (cont.) — 1990 Lumina APV

Light switch details (cont.) — 1990 Lumina APV

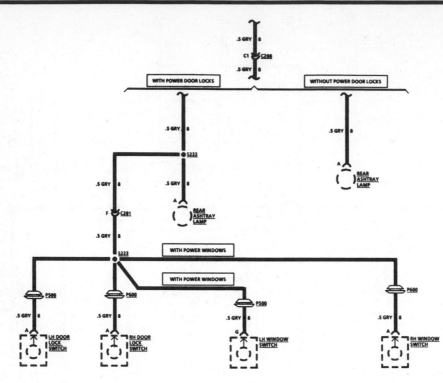

Light switch details (cont.) — 1990 Lumina APV

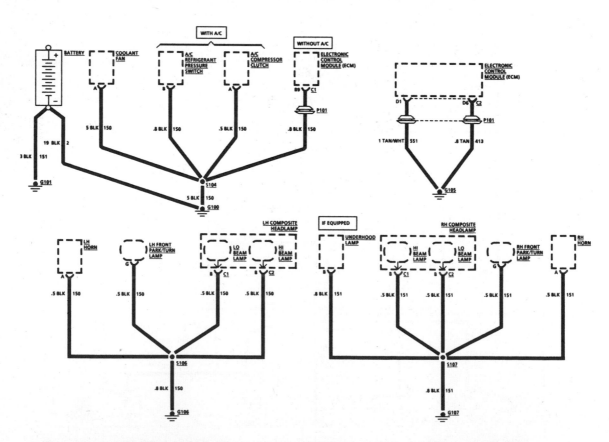

Ground distribution: (G100, G101, G105, G106 and G107) — 1990 Lumina APV

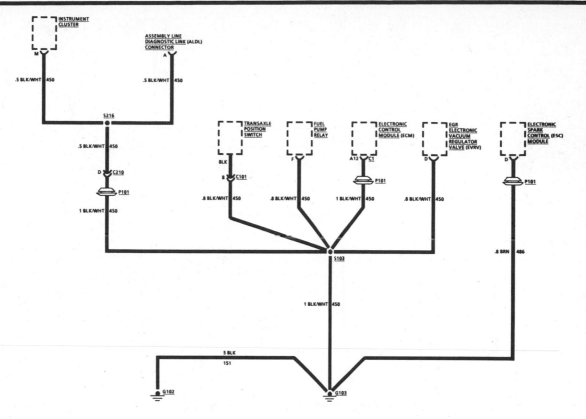

Ground distribution: (G102 and G103) — 1990 Lumina APV

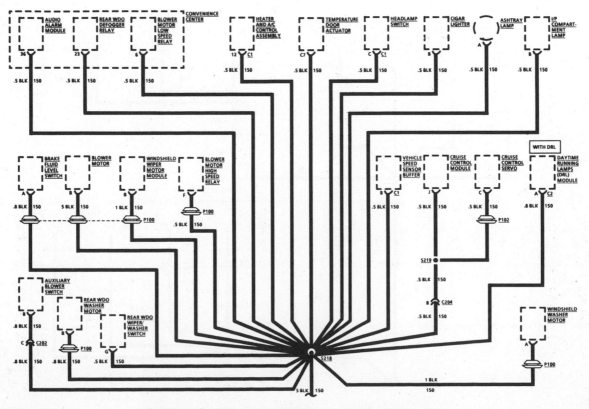

Ground distribution: (G200) — 1990 Lumina APV

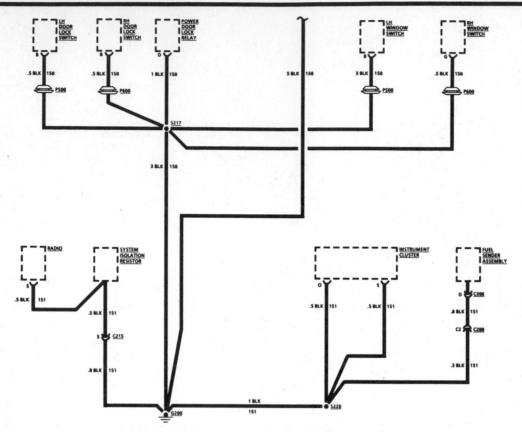

Ground distribution: (G200) (cont.) — 1990 Lumina APV

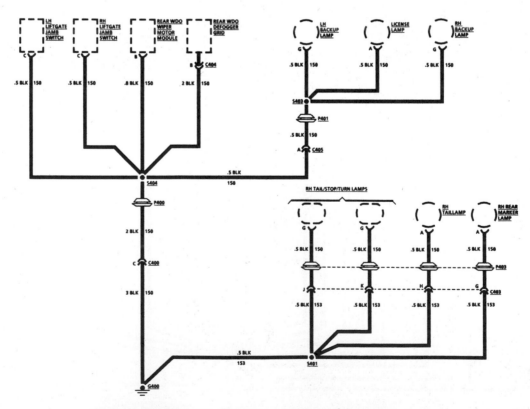

Ground distribution: (G400) — 1990 Lumina APV

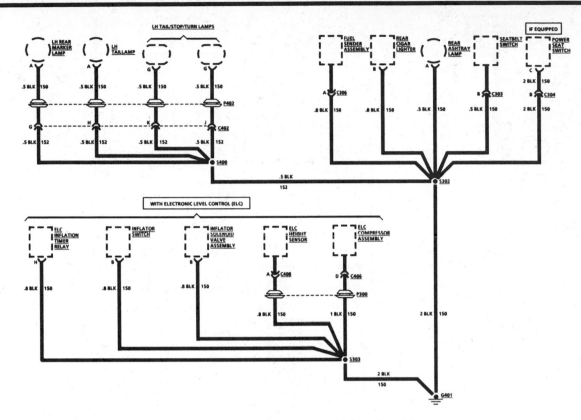

Ground distribution: (G401) — 1990 Lumina APV

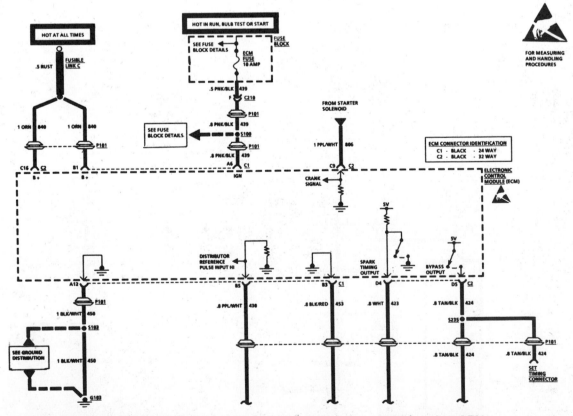

Throttle body injection: (power, ground and ignition) — 1990 Lumina APV

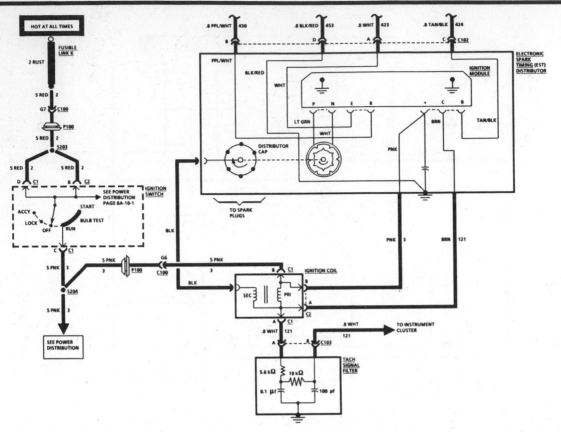

Throttle body Injection: (power, ground and ignition) (Cont.) — 1990 Lumina APV

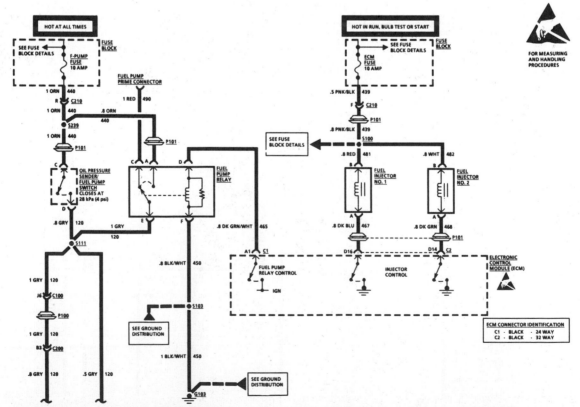

Throttle body Injection: (3.1L V6 fuel control, idle air control) — 1990 Lumina APV

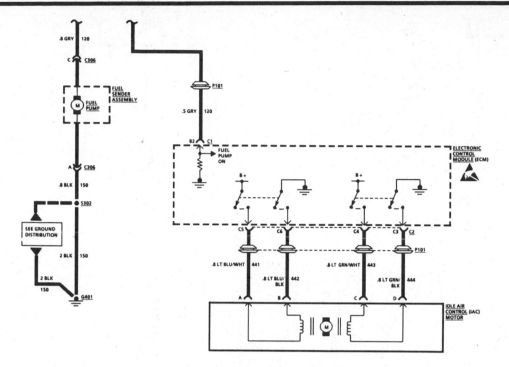

Throttle body injection: (3.1L fuel control, idle air control) (cont.) — 1990 Lumina APV

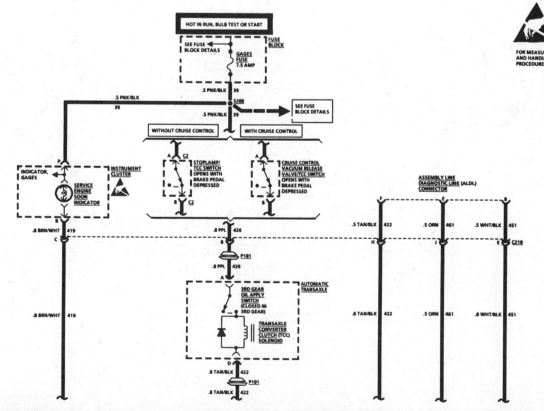

Throttle body injection: (3.1L V6 transaxle converter clutch, service engine soon indicator, transaxle position switch) — 1990 Lumina APV

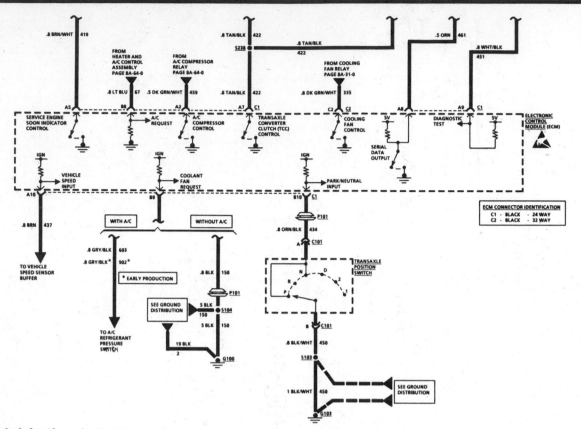

Throttle body injection: (3.1L V6 transaxle converter clutch, service engine soon indicator, transaxle position switch) (cont.) — 1990 Lumina APV

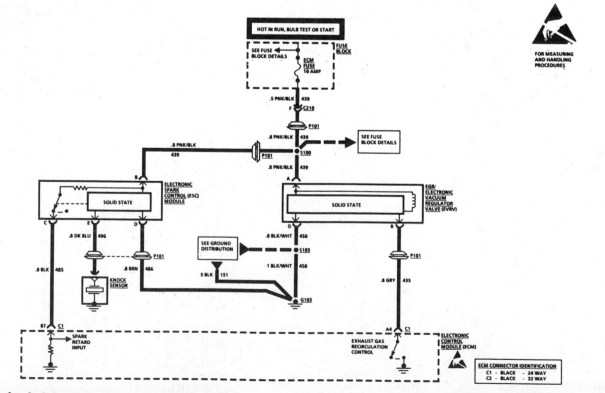

Throttle body injection: (3.1L V6 engine data sensors, spark control, emission control) — 1990 Lumina APV

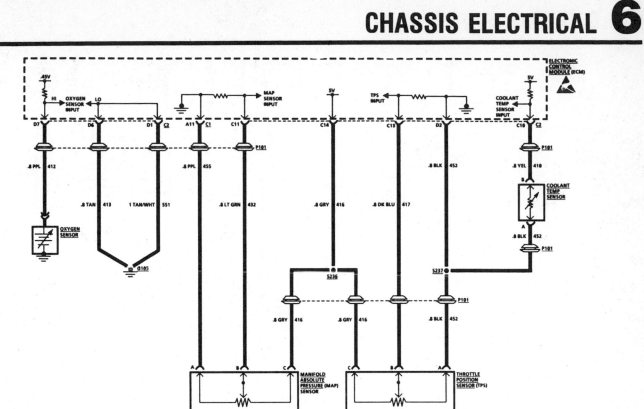

Throttle body injection: (3.1L V6 engine data sensors, spark control, emission control) (cont.) — 1990 Lumina APV

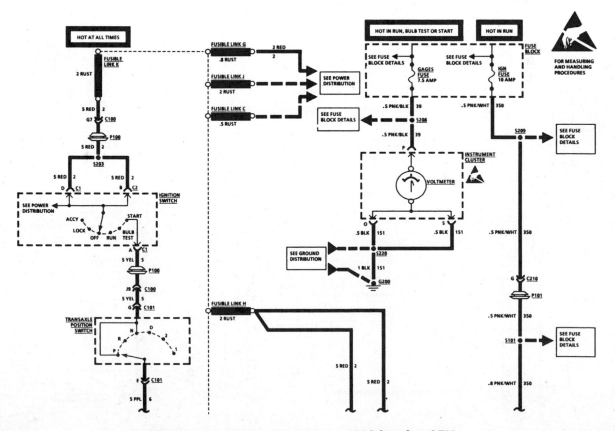

Starter and charging system — 1990 Lumina APV

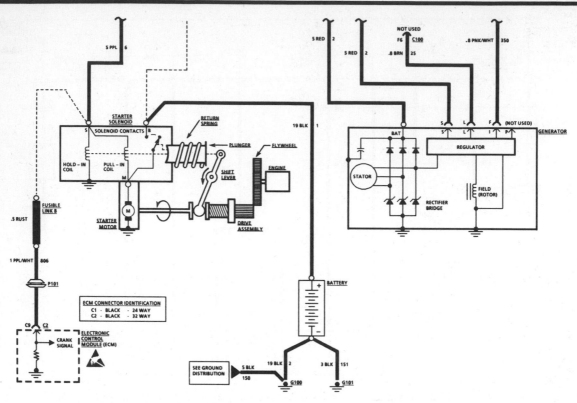

Starter and charging system (cont.) — 1990 Lumina APV

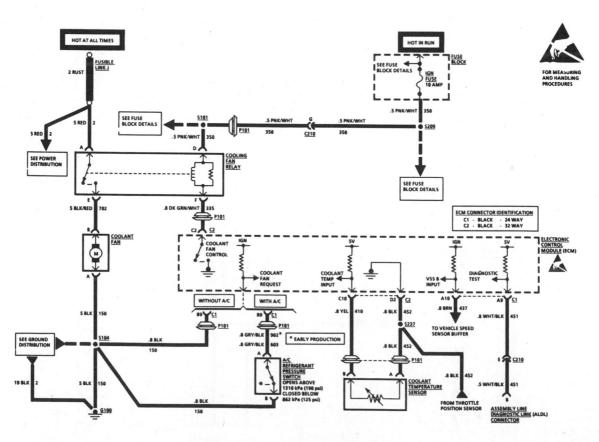

Coolant fan — 1990 Lumina APV

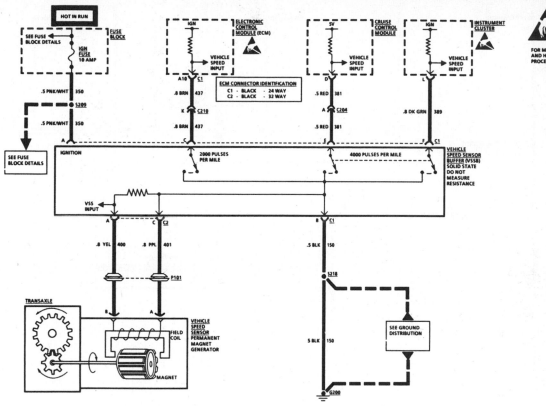

Vehicle speed sensor: (permanent magnet generator) — 1990 Lumina APV

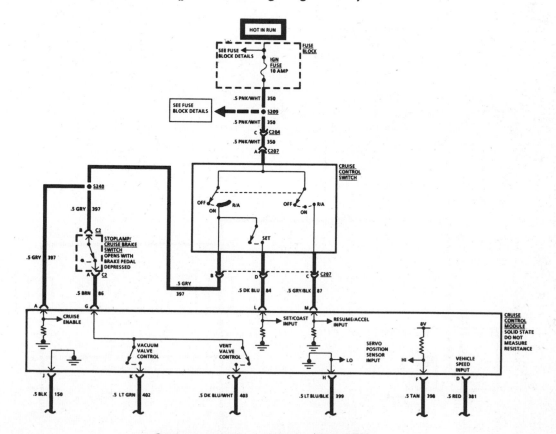

Cruise control — 1990 Lumina APV

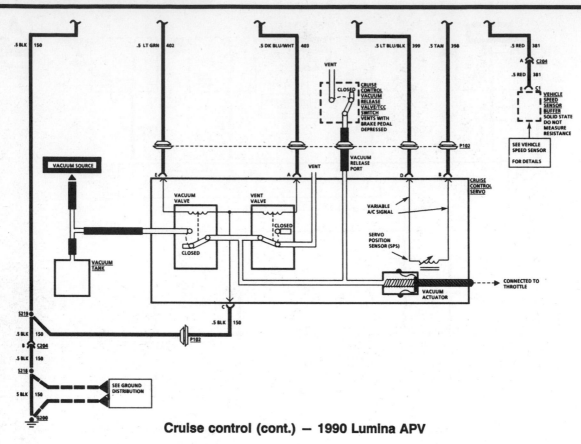

Cruise control (cont.) — 1990 Lumina APV

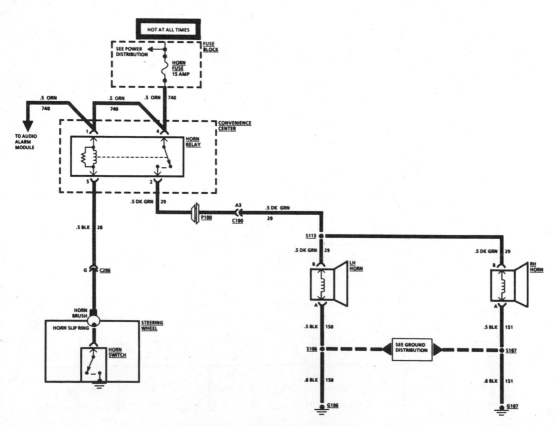

Horns — 1990 Lumina APV

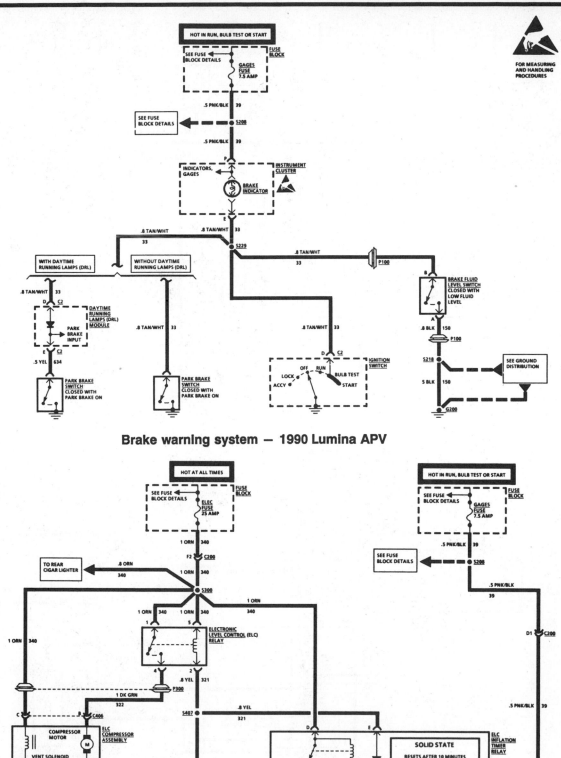

Brake warning system — 1990 Lumina APV

Electronic level control — 1990 Lumina APV

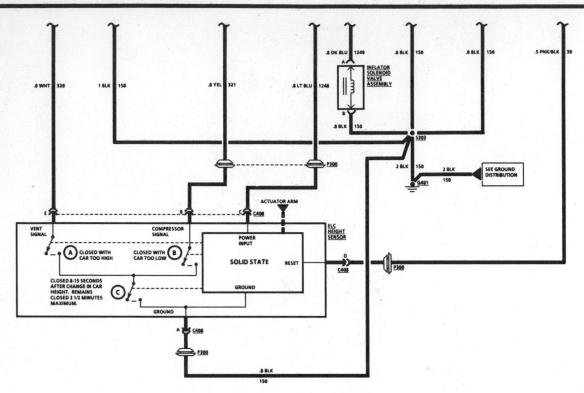

Electronic level control (cont.) — 1990 Lumina APV

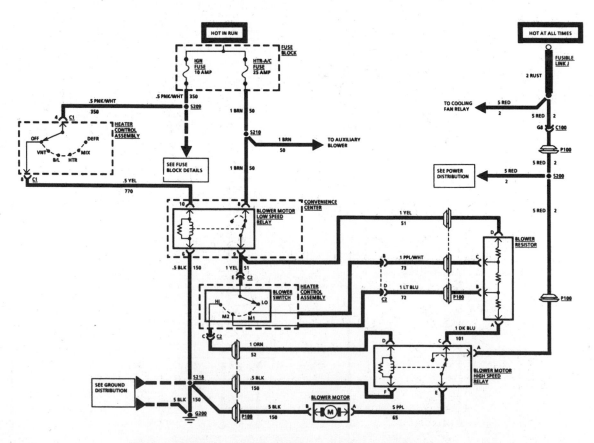

Heater (blower control (C40)) — 1990 Lumina APV

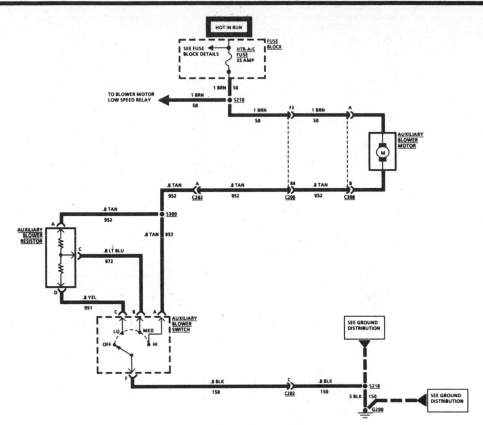

Heater (auxiliary blower control) — 1990 Lumina APV

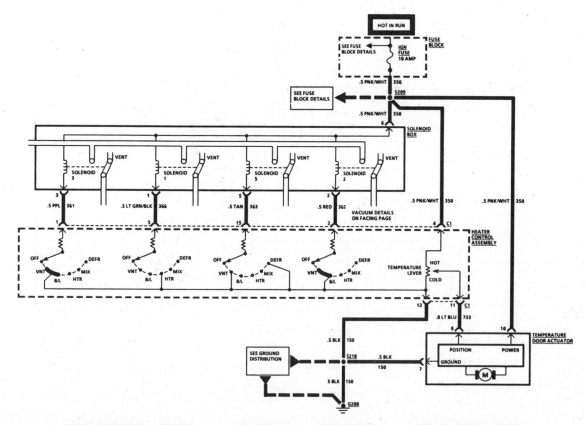

Heater (air delivery and temperature control (c40) — 1990 Lumina APV

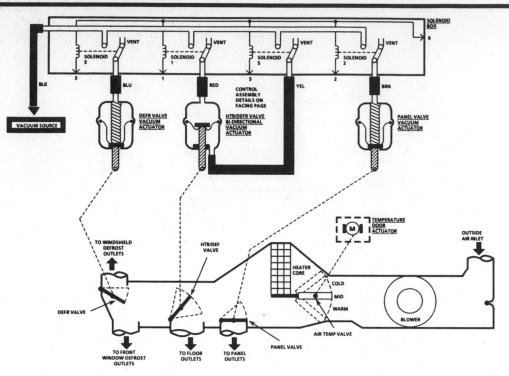

Heater (air delivery and temperature control (c40) — 1990 Lumina APV

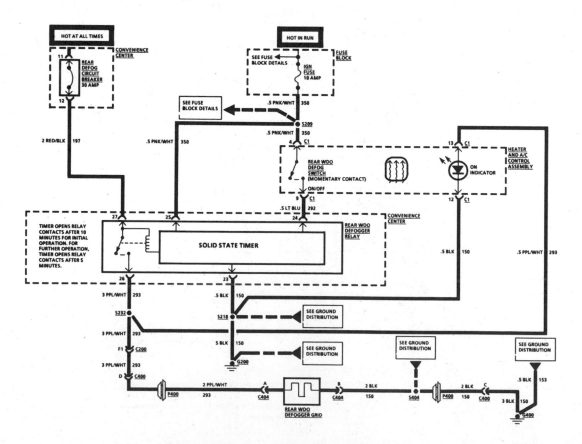

Rear defogger — 1990 Lumina APV

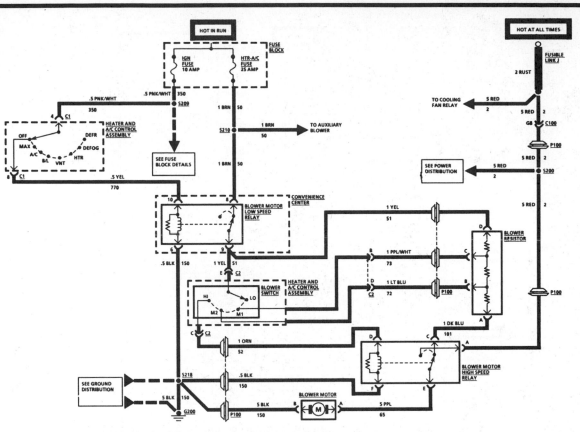

Air conditioning (blower motor control (c67) — 1990 Lumina APV

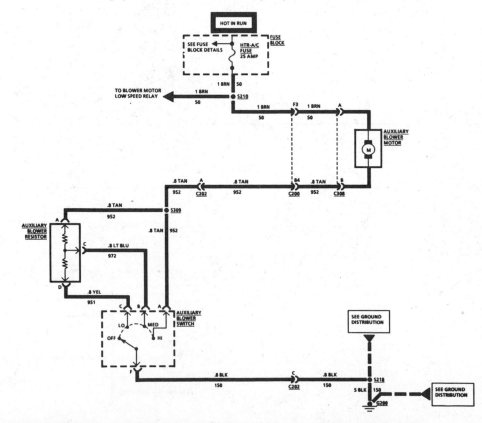

Air conditioning (auxiliary blower motor (c57) — 1990 Lumina APV

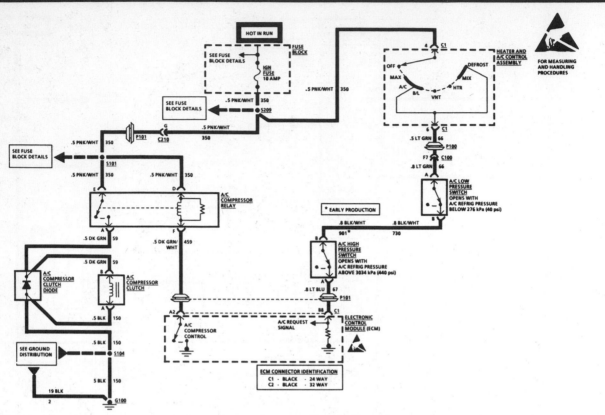

Air conditioning (compressor control (c67) — 1990 Lumina APV

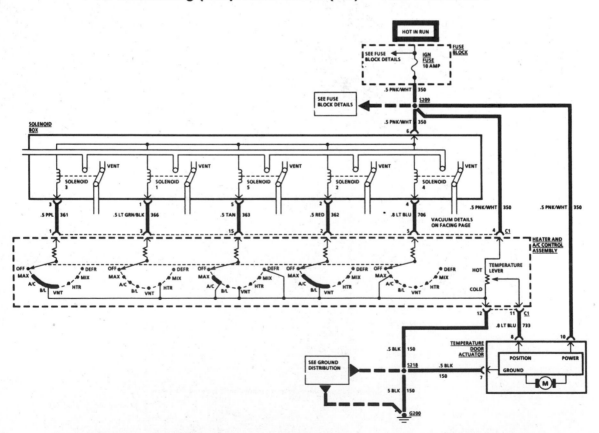

Air conditioning (air delivery and temperature control (c67) — 1990 Lumina APV

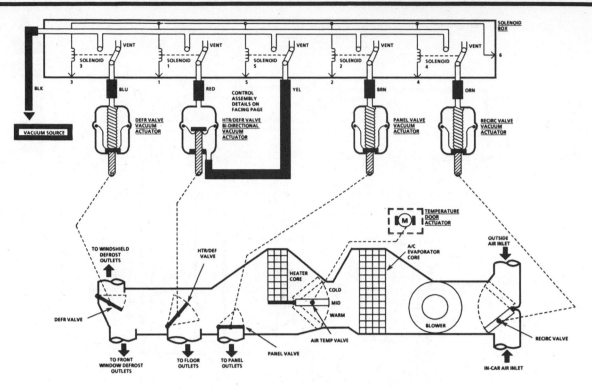

Air conditioning (air delivery and temperature control (c67) — 1990 Lumina APV

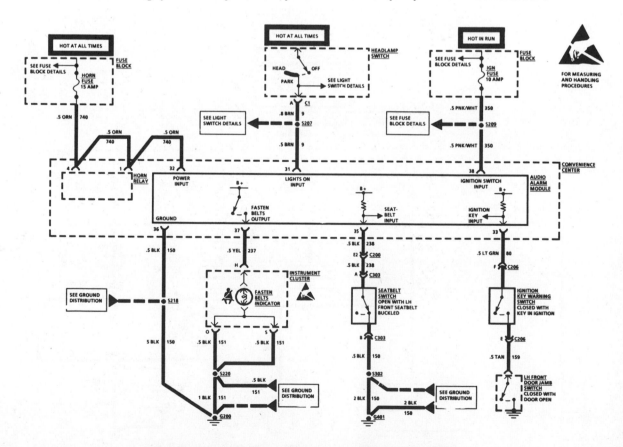

Warnings and alarms: (chime) — 1990 Lumina APV

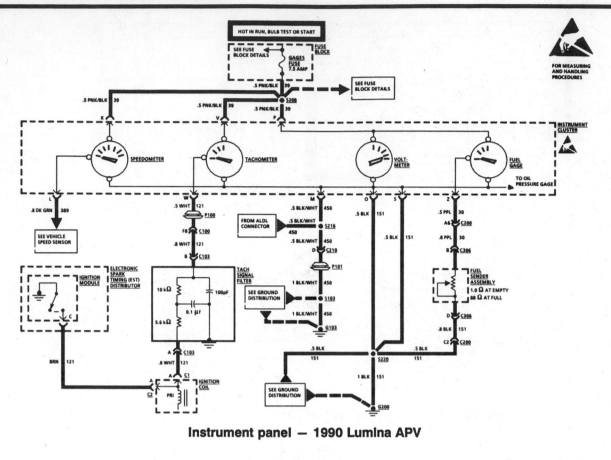

Instrument panel — 1990 Lumina APV

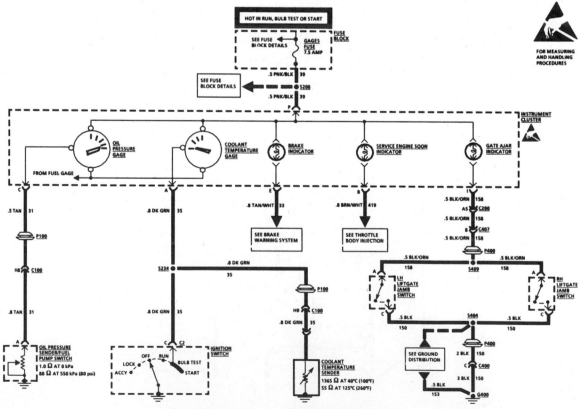

Instrument panel — 1990 Lumina APV

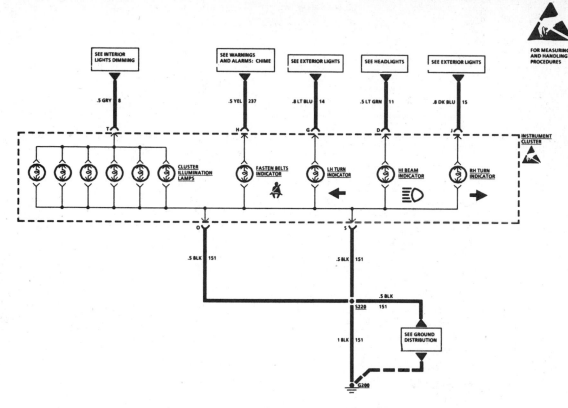

Instrument panel — 1990 Lumina APV

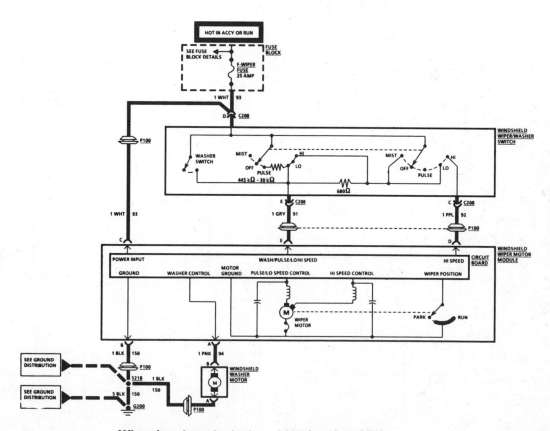

Wiper/washer: (pulse) — 1990 Lumina APV

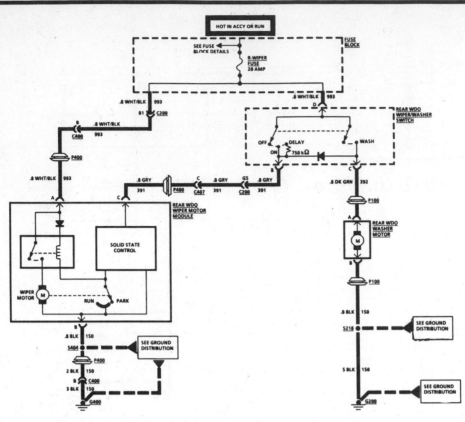

Rear wiper/washer — 1990 Lumina APV

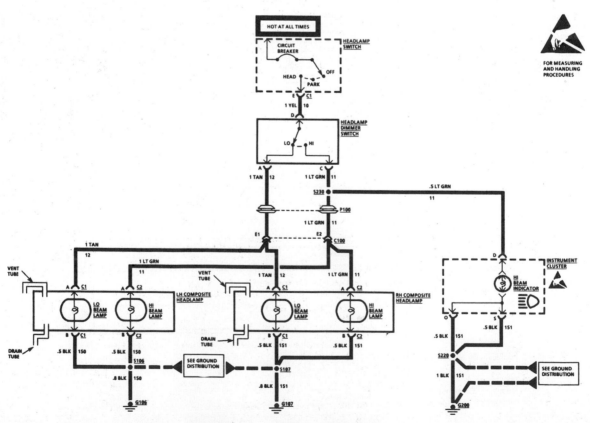

Headlights — 1990 Lumina APV

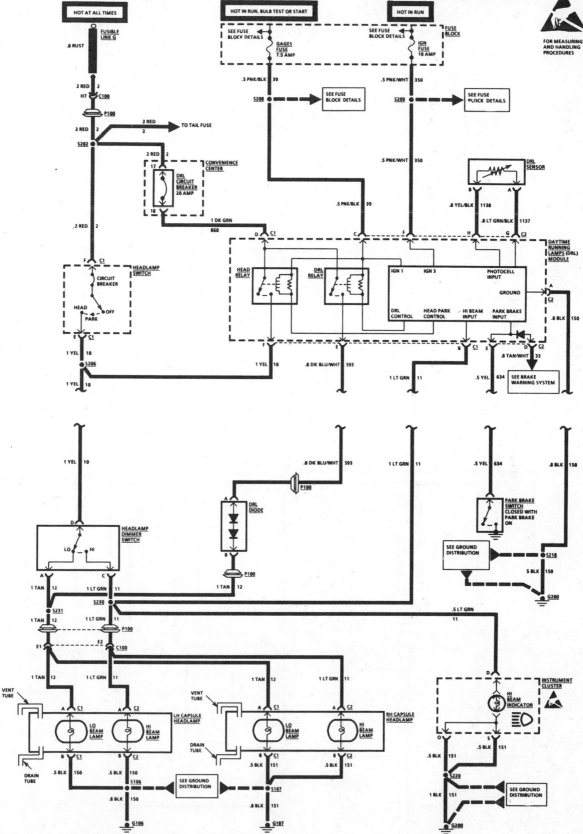

Headlights: (daytime running lamps (drl), T61) — 1990 Lumina APV

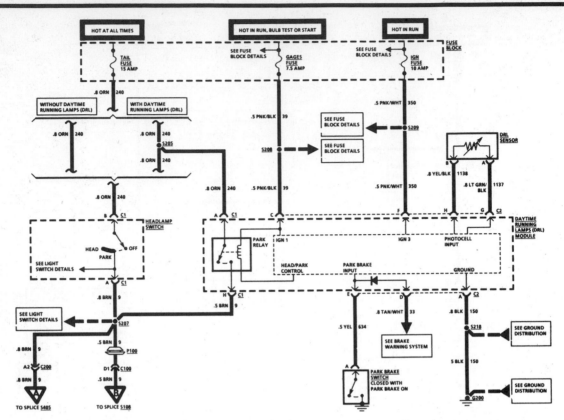

Exterior lights: (turn/hazard/stop/tail/marker/license) — 1990 Lumina APV

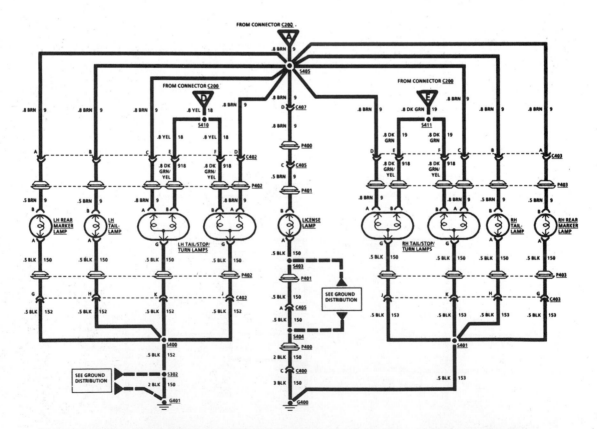

Exterior lights: (turn/hazard/stop/tail/marker/license) (cont.) — 1990 Lumina APV

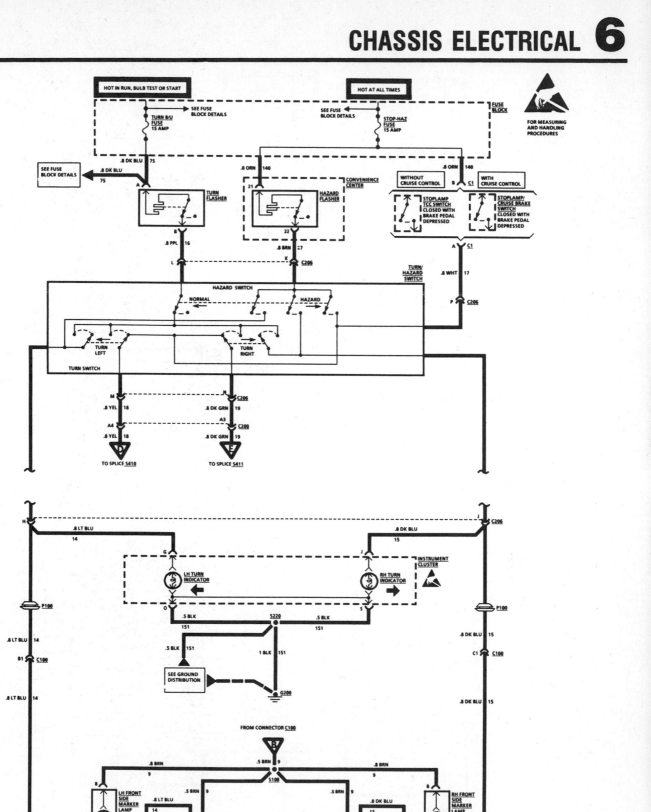

Exterior lights: (turn/hazard/stop/tail/marker/license) (cont.) — 1990 Lumina APV

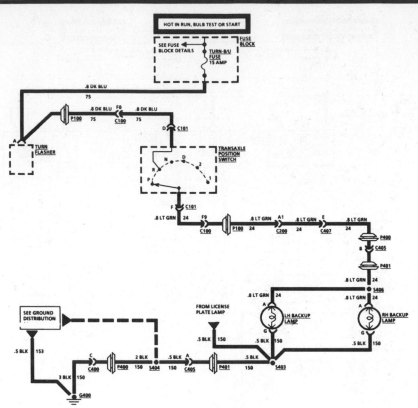

Backup lights — 1990 Lumina APV

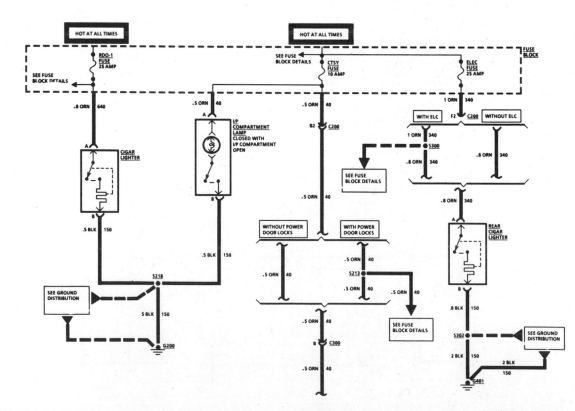

Interior lights (courtesy, dome, I/p compartment, cigar lighter, rear cigar lighter) — 1990 Lumina APV

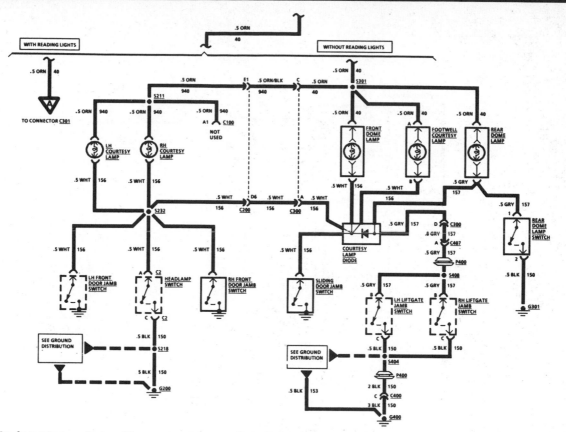

Interior lights (courtesy, dome, i/p compartment, cigar lighter, rear cigar lighter) (cont.) — 1990 Lumina APV

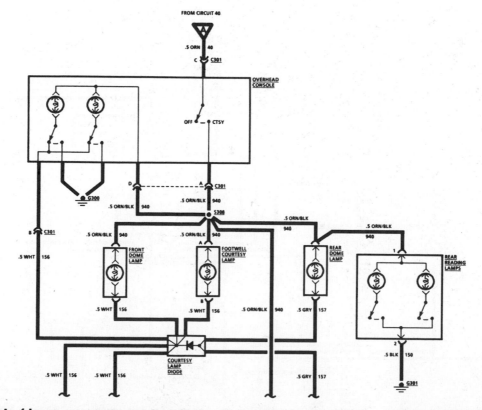

Interior lights (dome, courtesy, reading (tr9) and engine compartment) — 1990 Lumina APV

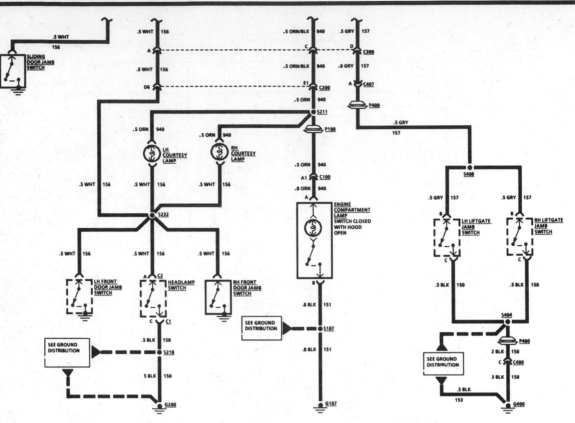

Interior lights (dome, courtesy, reading (tr9) and engine compartment) (cont.) — 1990 Lumina APV

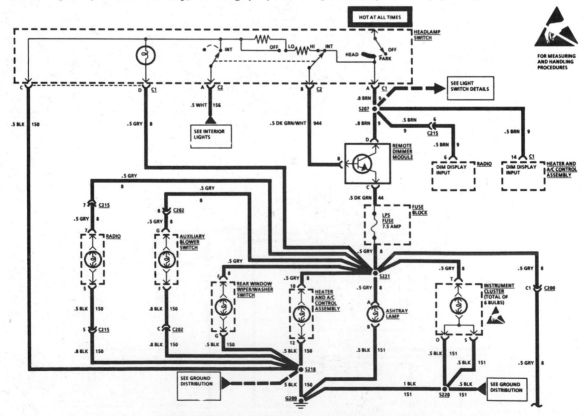

Interior lights dimming — 1990 Lumina APV

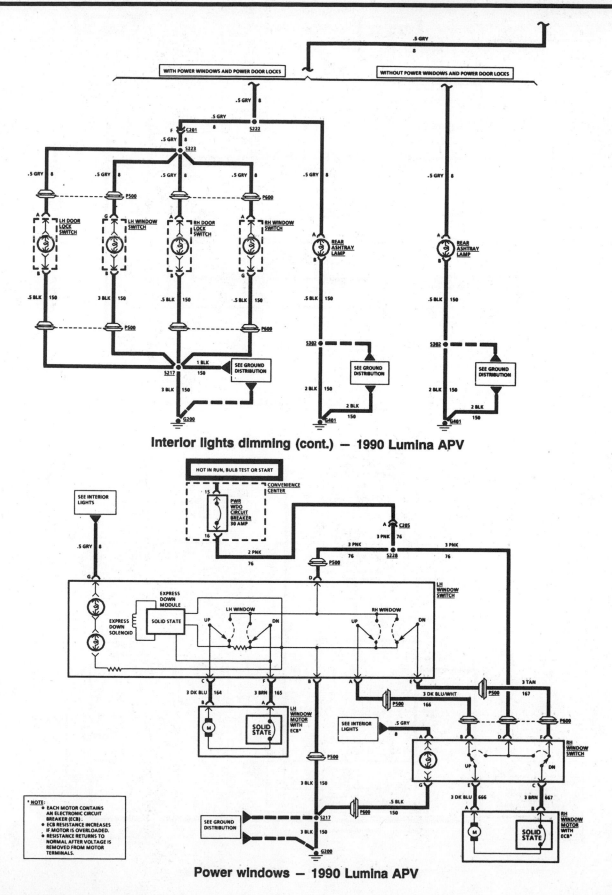

Interior lights dimming (cont.) — 1990 Lumina APV

Power windows — 1990 Lumina APV

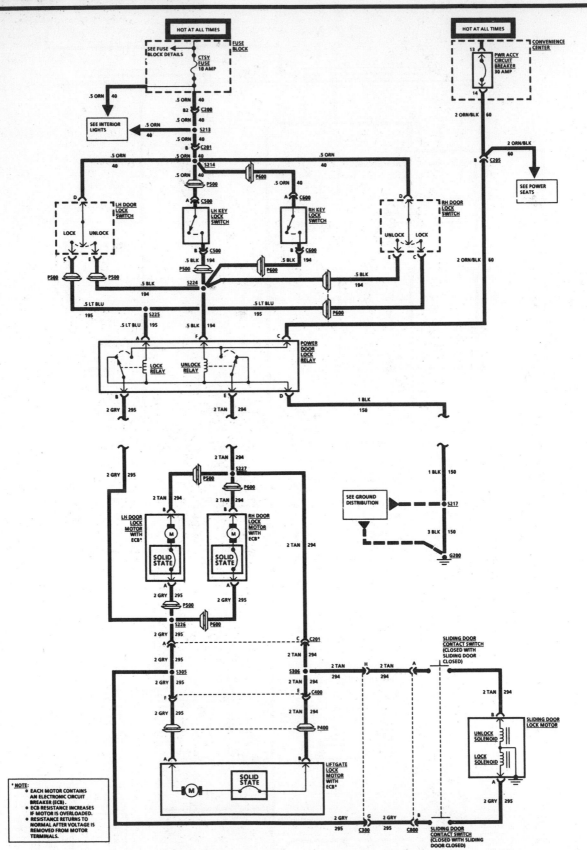

Power door locks — 1990 Lumina APV

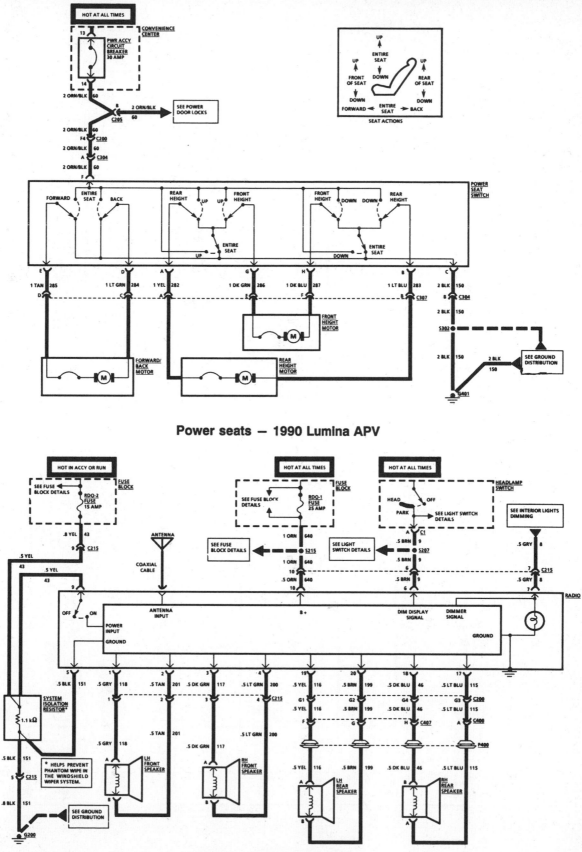

Power seats — 1990 Lumina APV

Radio — 1990 Lumina APV

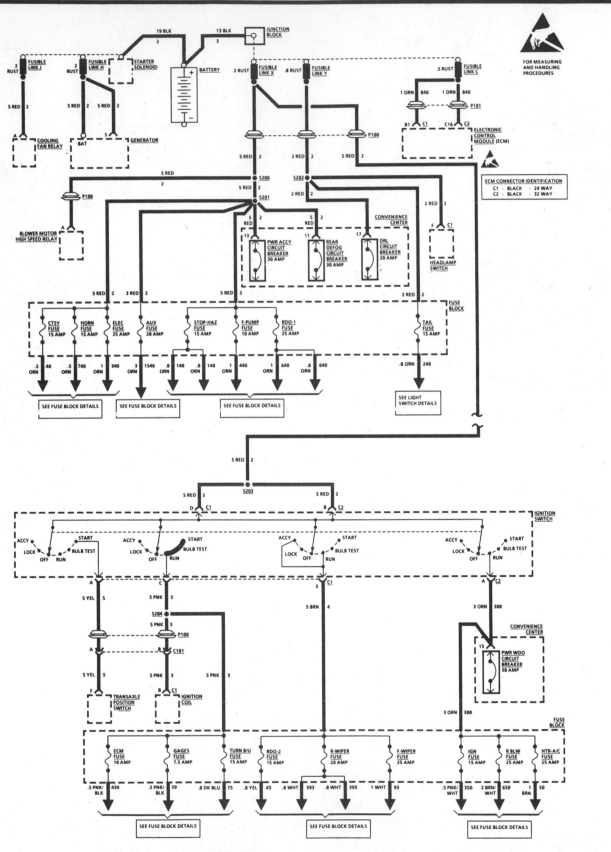

Power distribution — 1991 Lumina APV

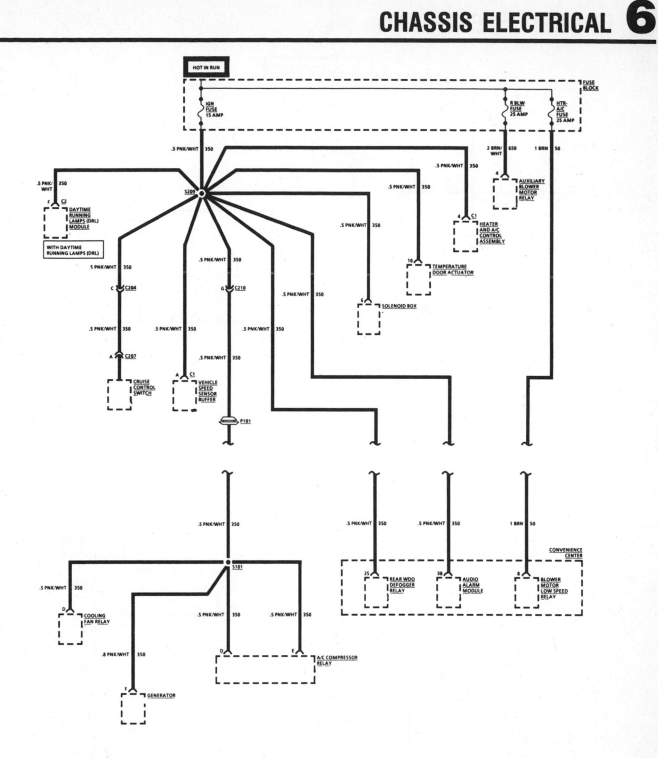

Fuse block details (Ignition fuse, rear blower and heater/a/c fuse) — 1991 Lumina APV

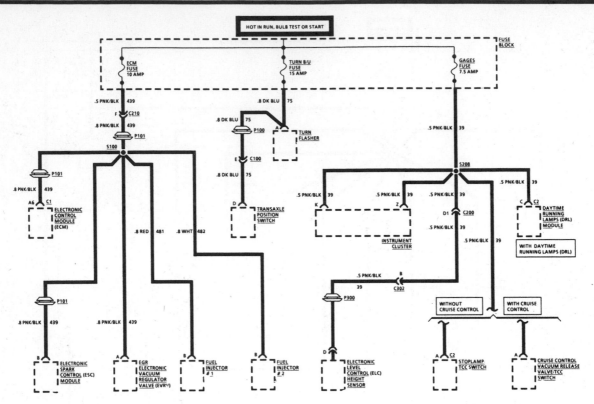

Fuse block details (ECM fuse, turn/back-up fuse and gauges fuse) — 1991 Lumina APV

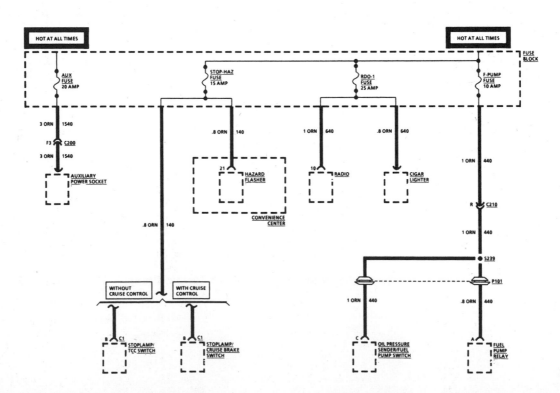

Fuse block details (aux fuse, stop/haz fuse, rdo-1 fuse and fuel pump fuse) — 1991 Lumina APV

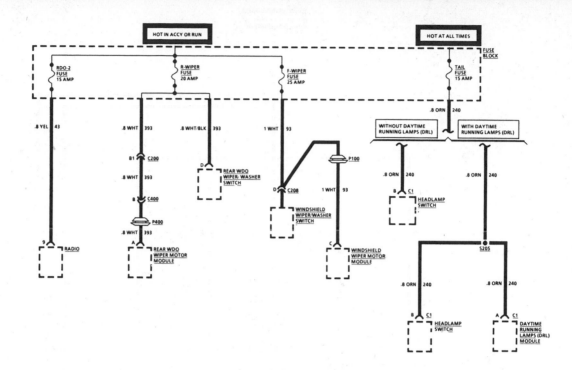

Fuse block details (rdo-2 fuse, front and rear wiper fuses and tail fuse) — 1991 Lumina APV

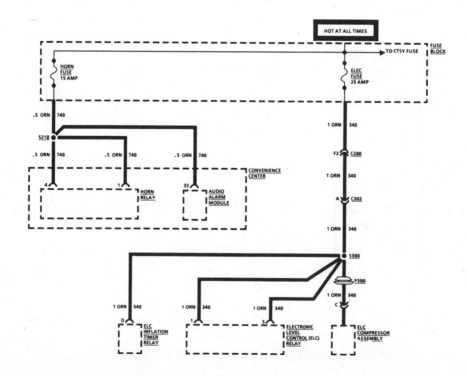

Fuse block details (horn fuse and elec fuse) — 1991 Lumina APV

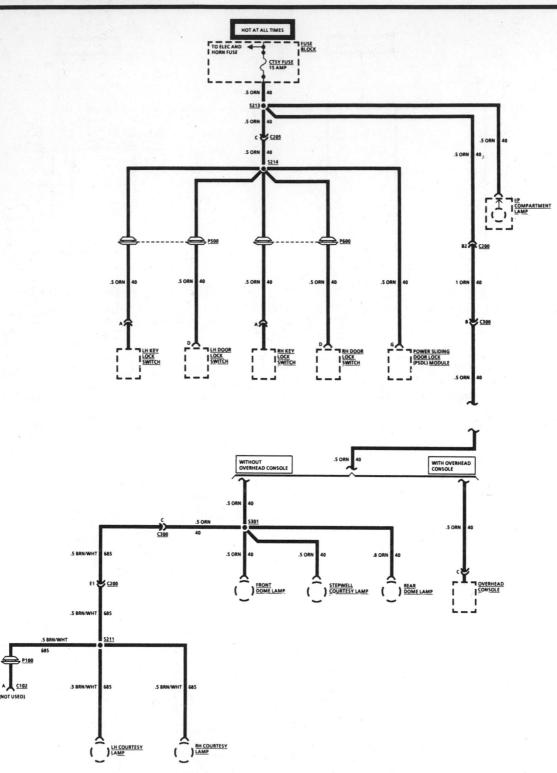

Fuse block details (ctsy fuse) — 1991 Lumina APV

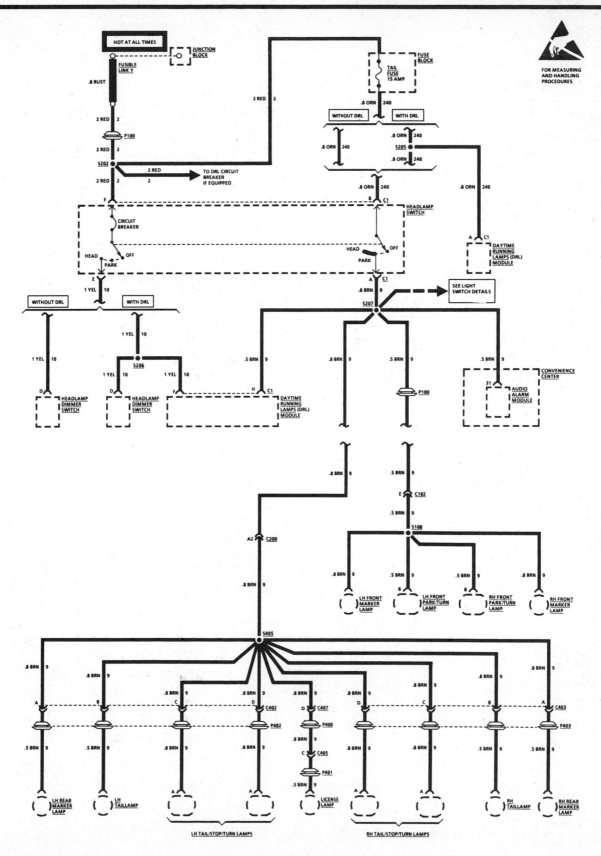

Light switch details — 1991 Lumina APV

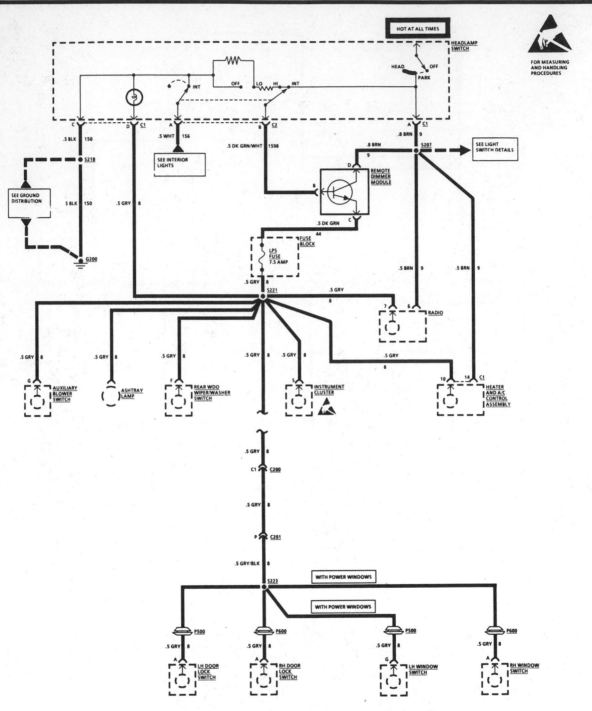

Light switch details (cont.) — 1991 Lumina APV

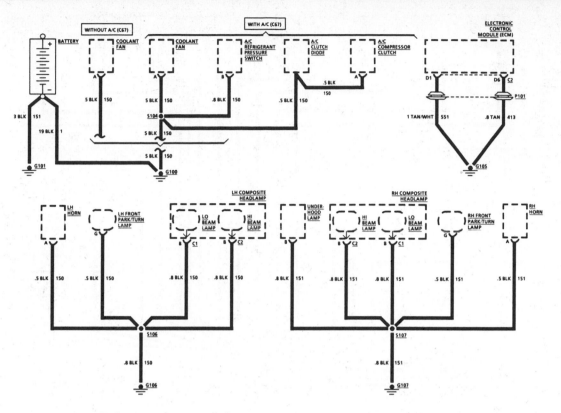

Ground distribution (G100, G101, G105, G106 and G107) — 1991 Lumina APV

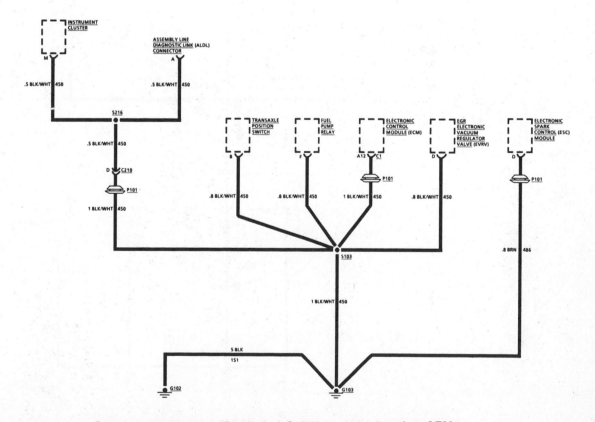

Ground distribution (G102 and G103) — 1991 Lumina APV

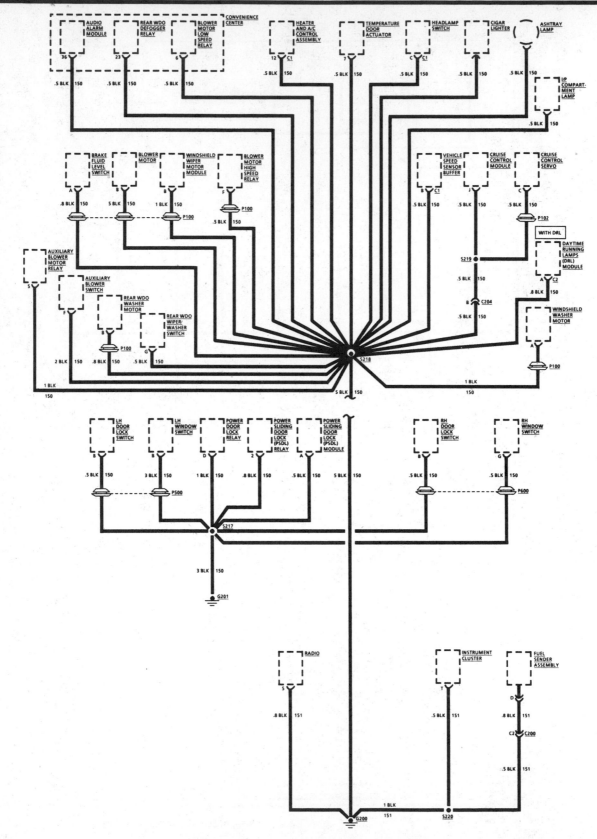

Ground distribution (G200 and G201) — 1991 Lumina APV

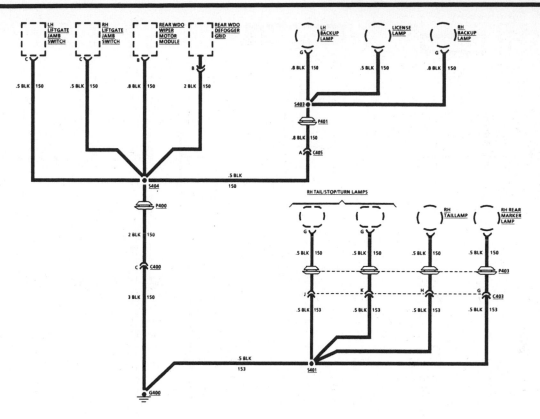

Ground distribution (G400) — 1991 Lumina APV

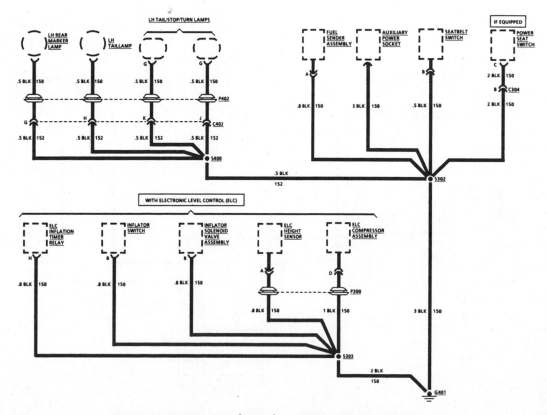

Ground distribution (G401) — 1991 Lumina APV

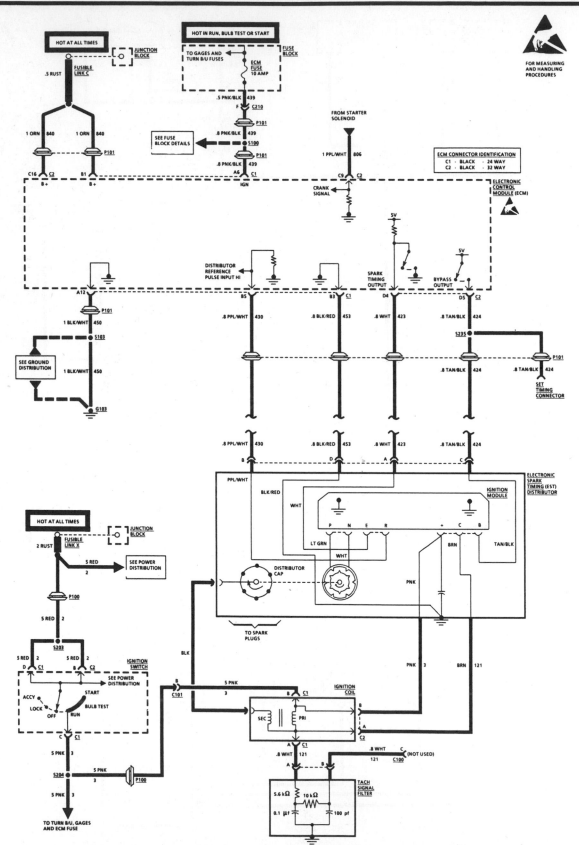

Throttle body injection: (3.1L V6 power, ground and ignition) — 1991 Lumina APV

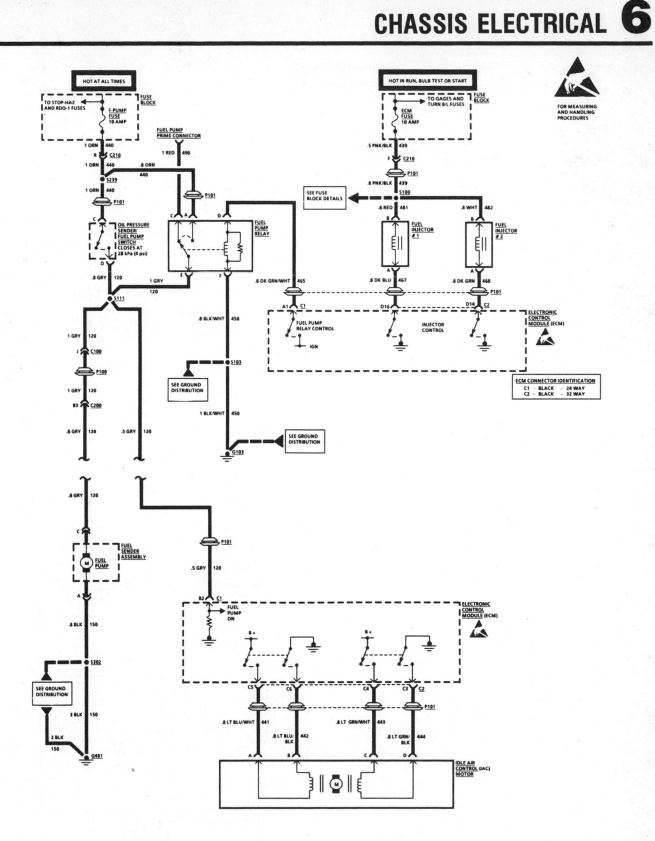

Throttle body injection: (3.1L V6 fuel control, idle air control) — 1991 Lumina APV

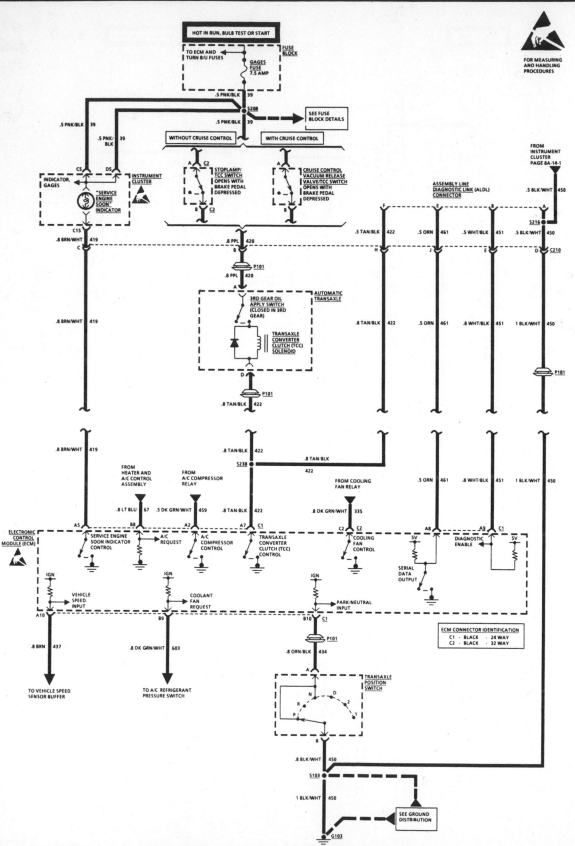

Throttle body injection: (3.1L V6 transaxle converter clutch, "service engine soon" indicator, transaxle position switch) — 1991 Lumina APV

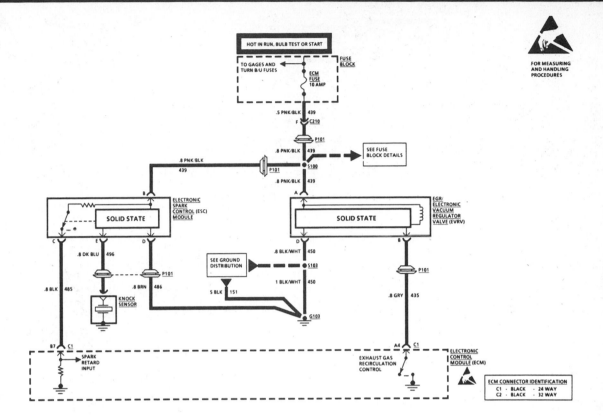

Throttle body injection: (3.1L V6 engine data sensors, spark control, emission control) — 1991 Lumina APV

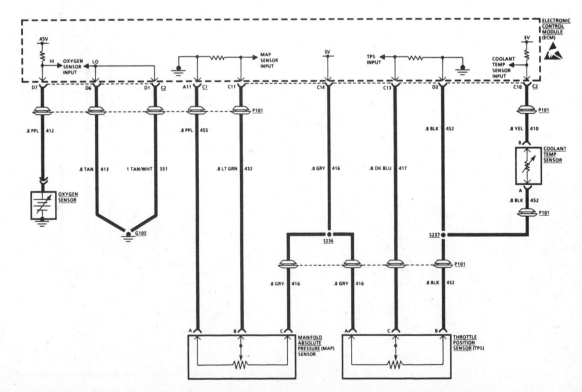

Throttle body injection: (3.1L V6 engine data sensors, spark control, emission control) (cont.) — 1991 Lumina APV

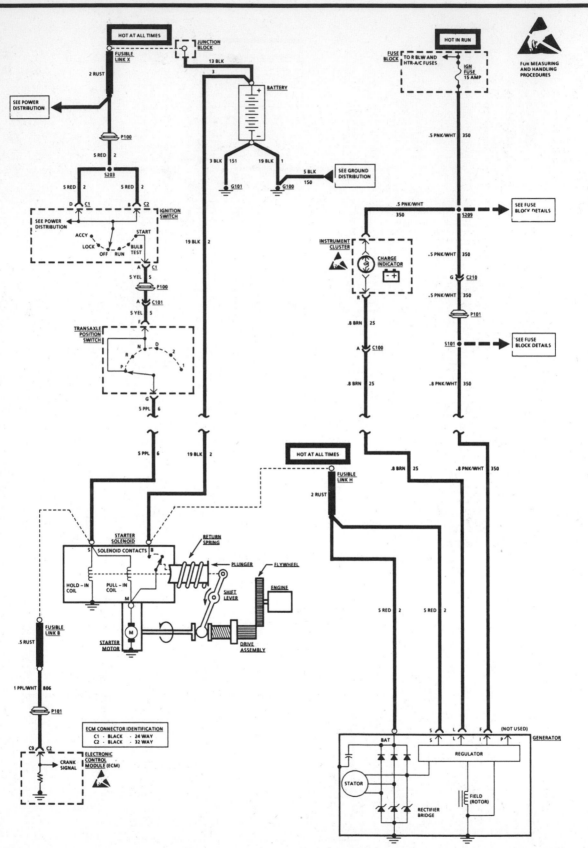

Starter and charging system — 1991 Lumina APV

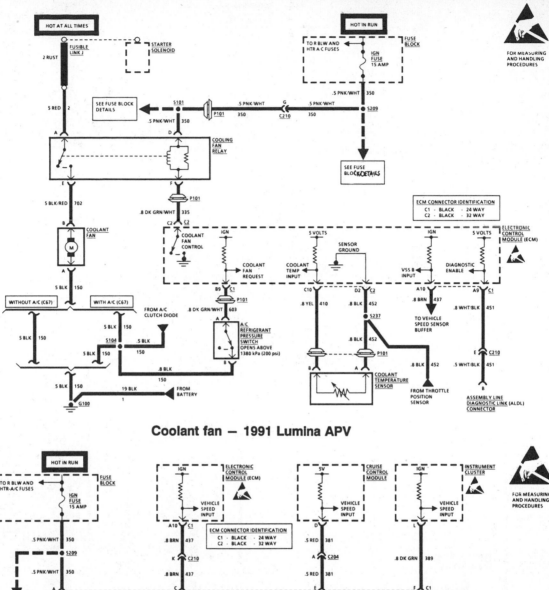

Coolant fan — 1991 Lumina APV

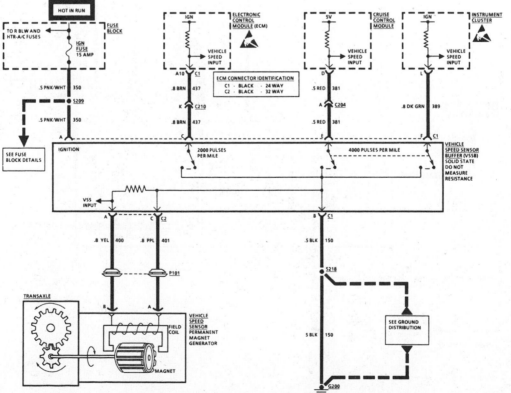

Vehicle speed sensor — 1991 Lumina APV

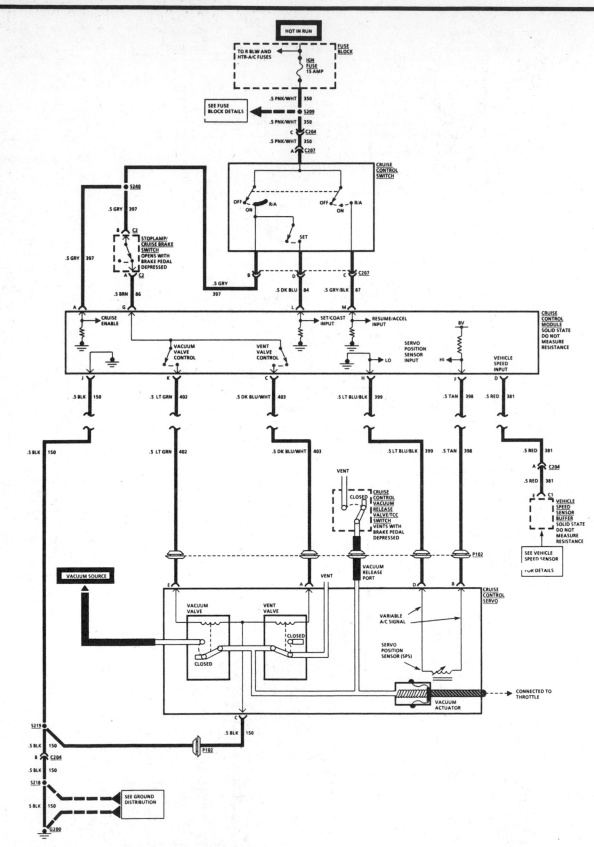

Cruise control — 1991 Lumina APV

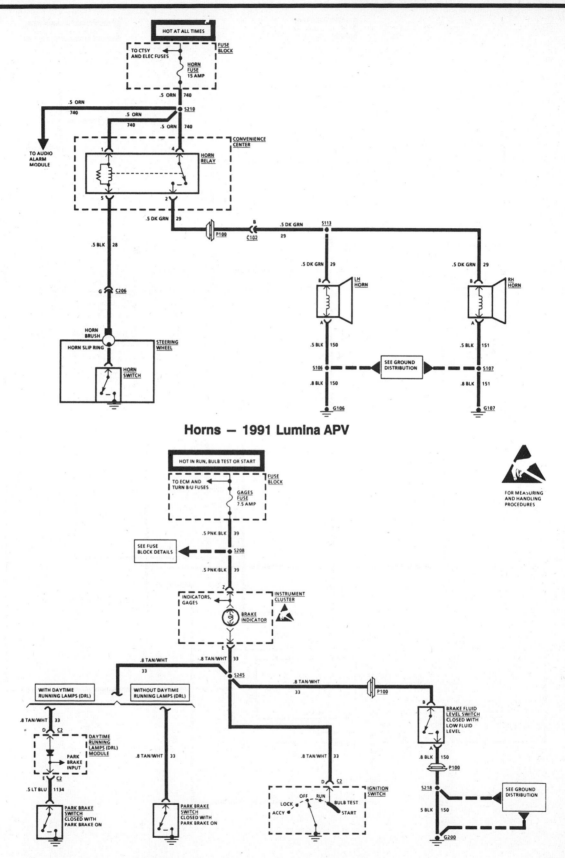

Horns — 1991 Lumina APV

Brake warning system — 1991 Lumina APV

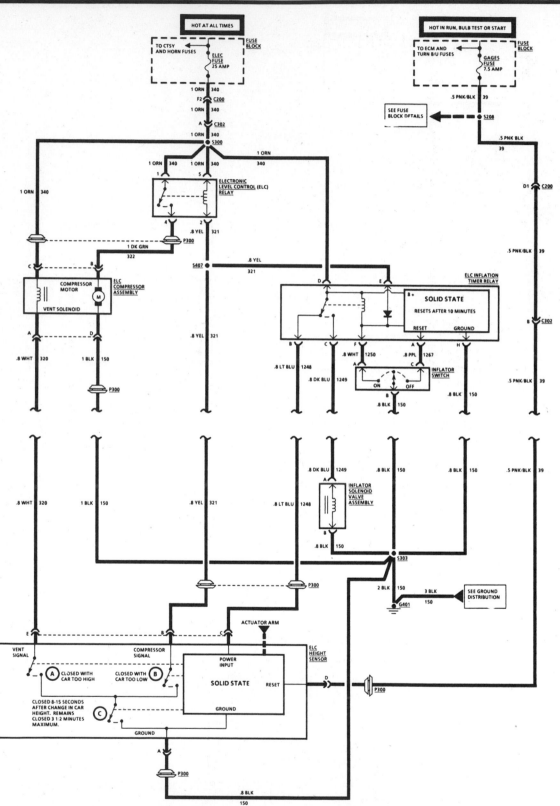

Electronic level control — 1991 Lumina APV

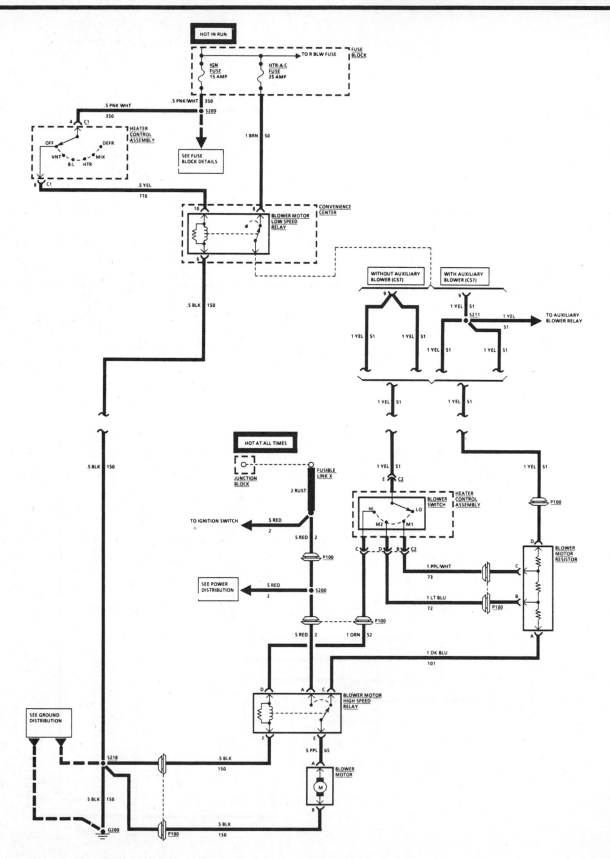

Heater (blower control) — 1991 Lumina APV

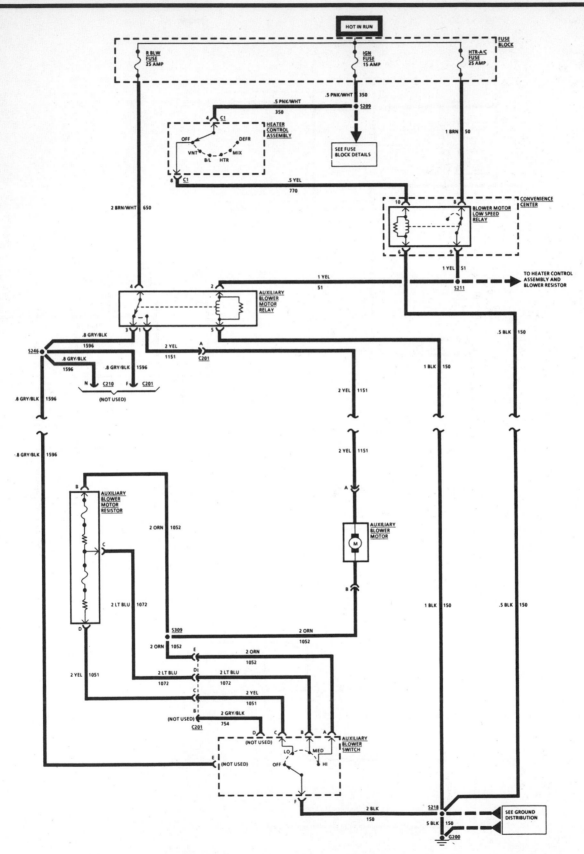

Heater (auxiliary blower control) — 1991 Lumina APV

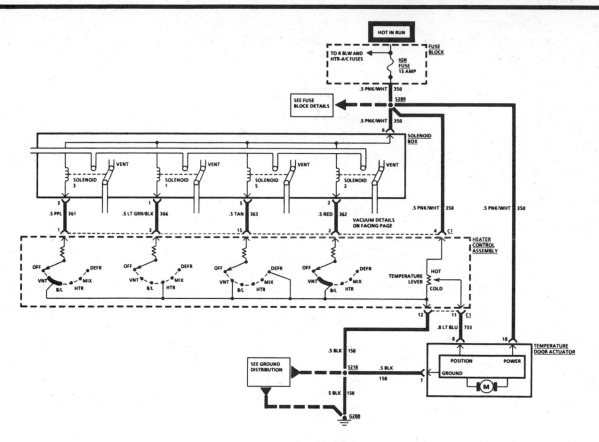

Heater (air delivery and temperature control) — 1991 Lumina APV

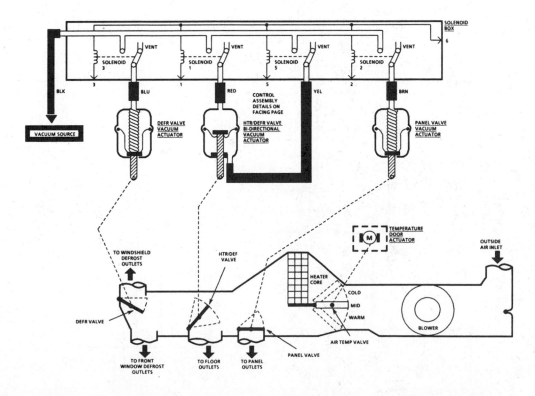

Heater (air delivery and temperature control) (cont.) — 1991 Lumina APV

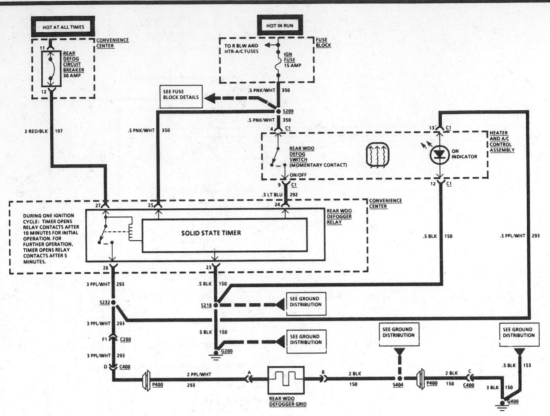

Rear defogger — 1991 Lumina APV

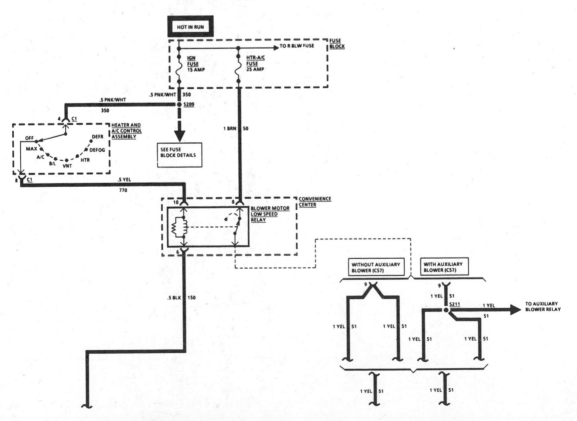

Air conditioning (blower motor control) — 1991 Lumina APV

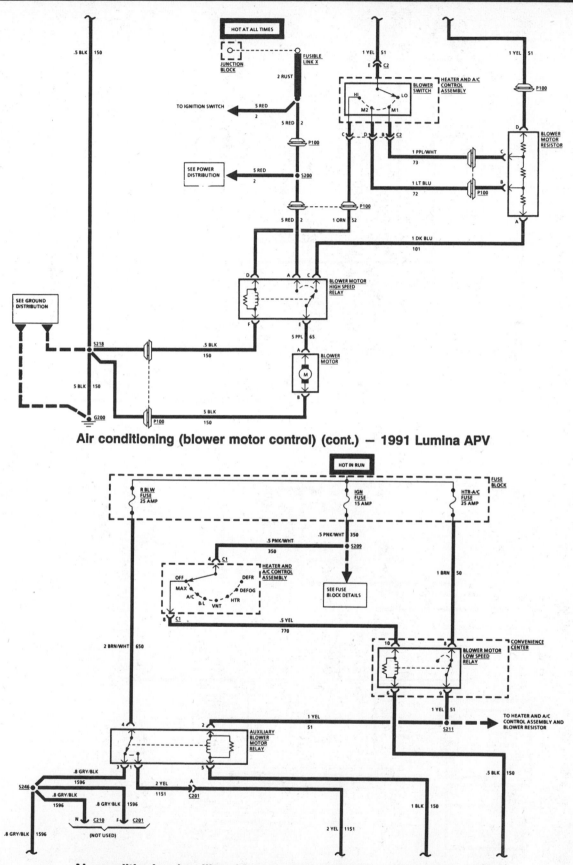

Air conditioning (blower motor control) (cont.) — 1991 Lumina APV

Air conditioning (auxiliary blower motor control) — 1991 Lumina APV

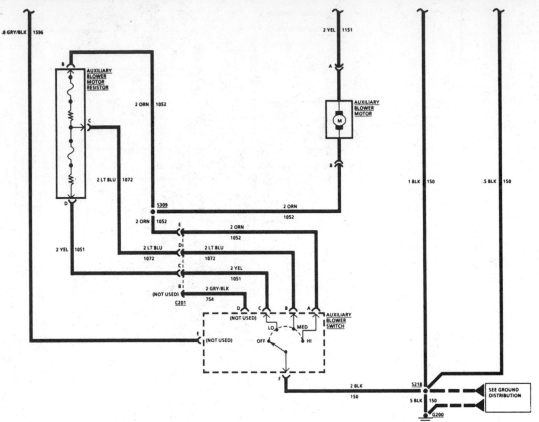

Air conditioning (auxiliary blower motor control) (cont.) — 1991 Lumina APV

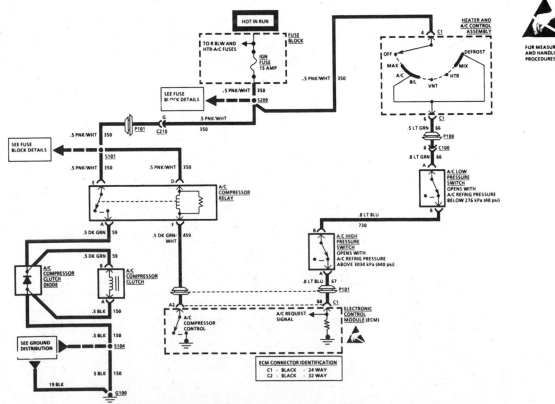

Air conditioning (compressor control) — 1991 Lumina APV

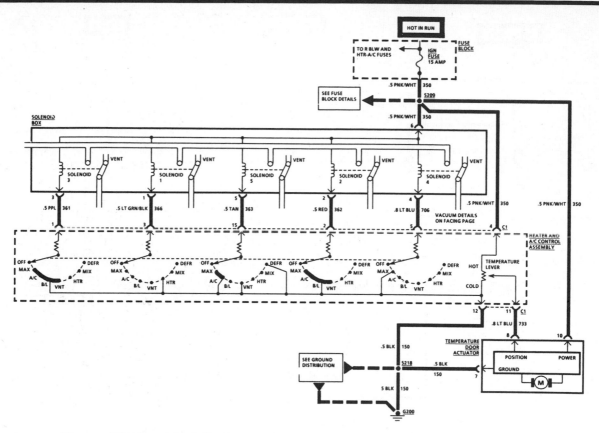

Air conditioning (air delivery and temperature control) — 1991 Lumina APV

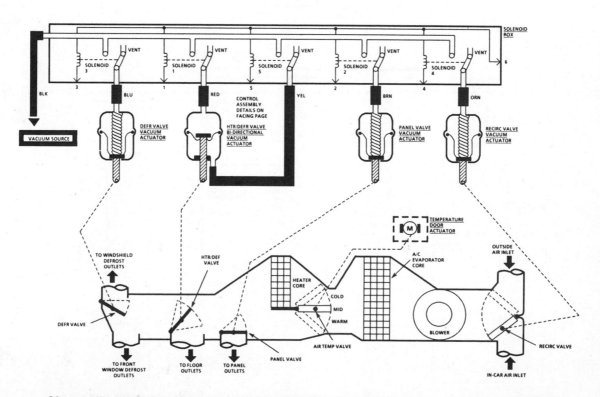

Air conditioning (air delivery and temperature control) (cont.) — 1991 Lumina APV

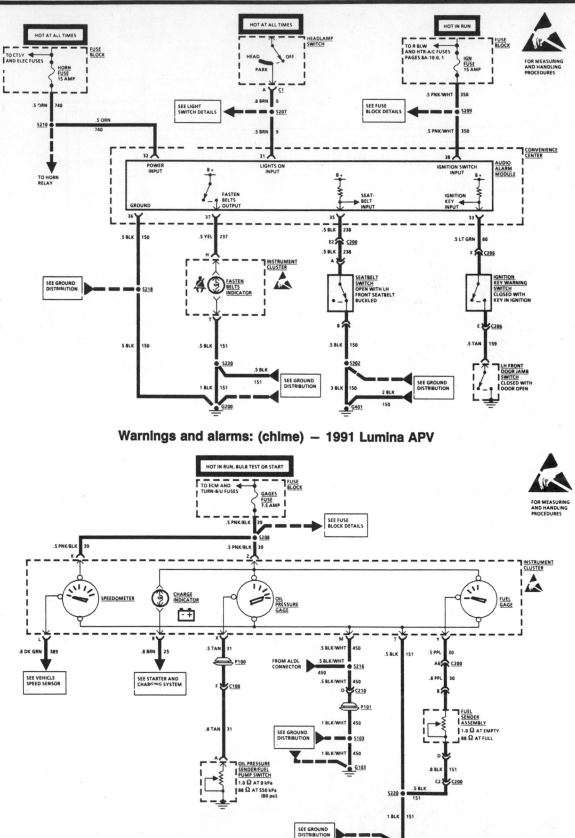

Warnings and alarms: (chime) — 1991 Lumina APV

Instrument panel — 1991 Lumina APV

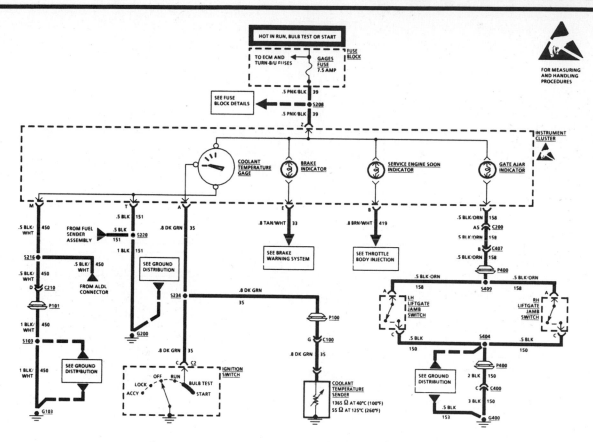

Instrument panel (cont.) — 1991 Lumina APV

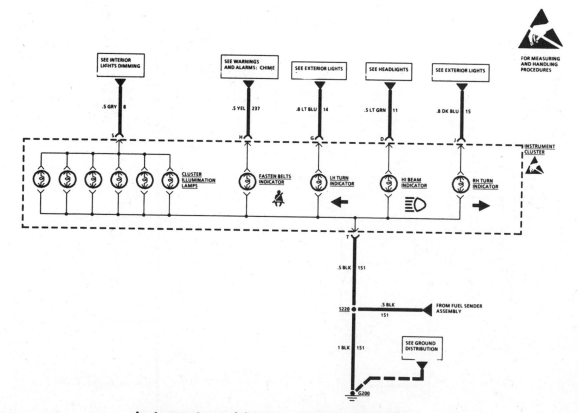

Instrument panel (cont.) — 1991 Lumina APV

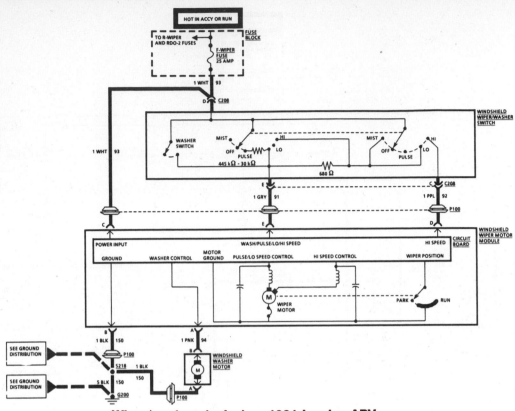

Wiper/washer: (pulse) — 1991 Lumina APV

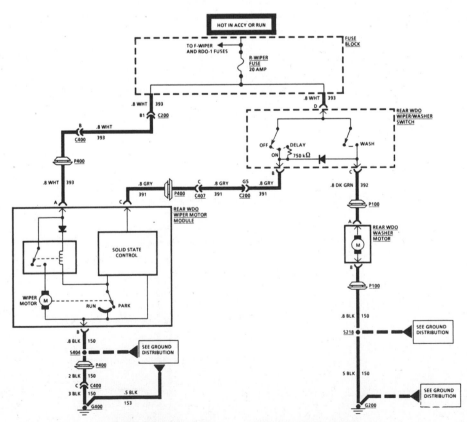

Rear wiper/washer — 1991 Lumina APV

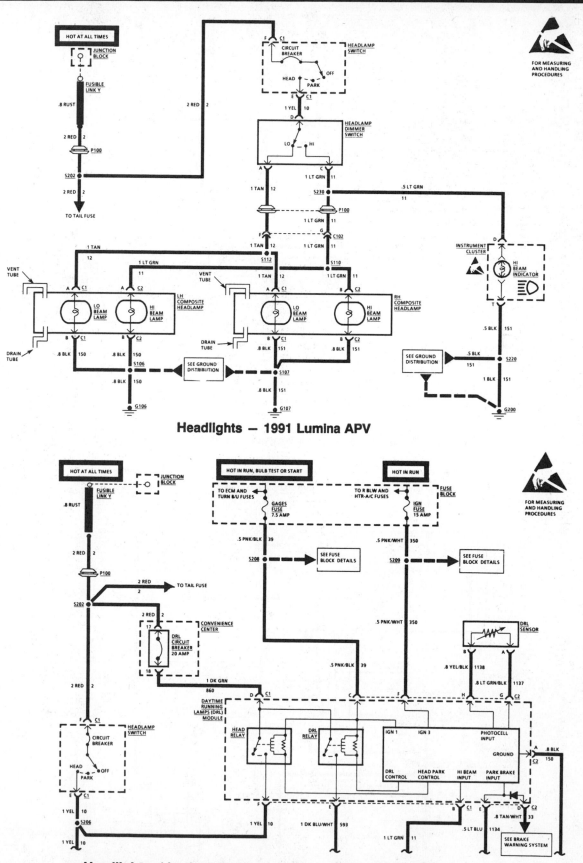

FOR MEASURING
AND HANDLING
PROCEDURES

Headlights – 1991 Lumina APV

FOR MEASURING
AND HANDLING
PROCEDURES

Headlights: (daytime running lamps) – 1991 Lumina APV

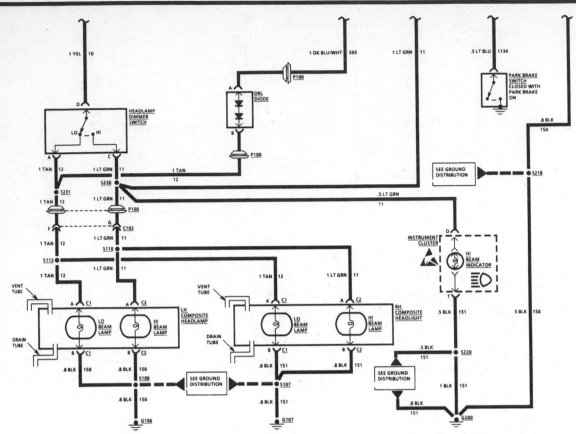

Headlights: (daytime running lamps1) (cont.) — 1991 Lumina APV

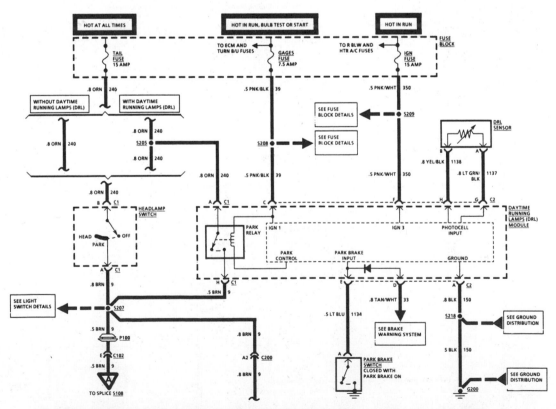

Exterior lights (turn/hazard/stop/tail/marker/license) — 1991 Lumina APV

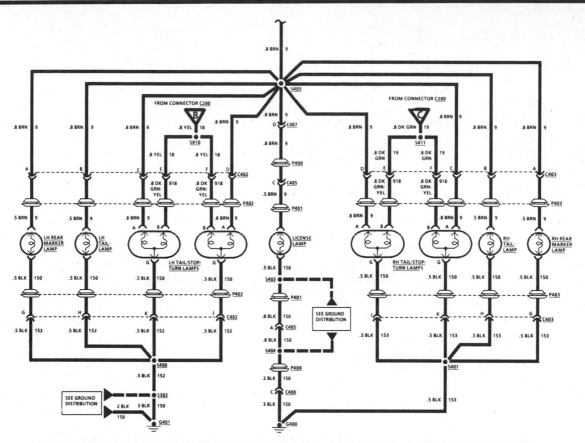

Exterior lights (turn/hazard/stop/tail/marker/license) (cont.) — 1991 Lumina APV

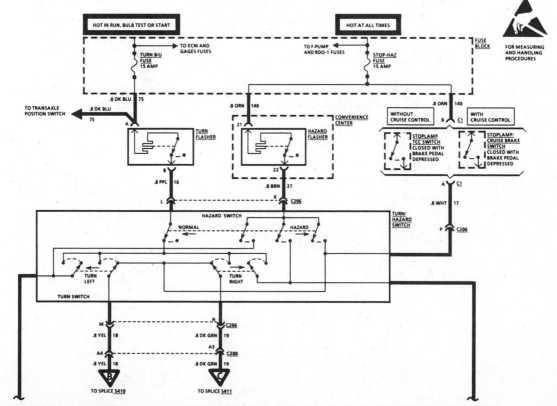

Exterior lights (turn/hazard,stop/tail/marker/license) (cont.) — 1991 Lumina APV

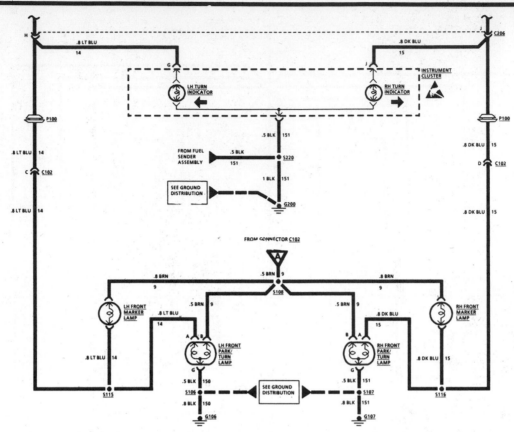

Exterior lights (turn/hazard/stop/tail/marker/license) (cont.) — 1991 Lumina APV

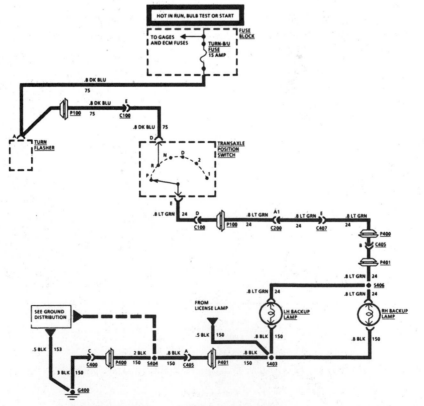

Backup lights — 1991 Lumina APV

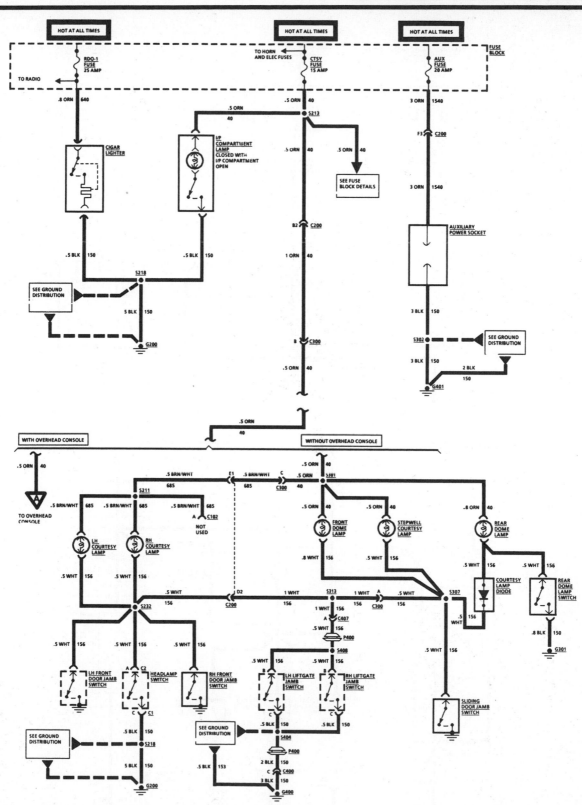

Interior lights (courtesy, dome, I/p compartment, cigar lighter, auxiliary power socket) — 1991 Lumina APV

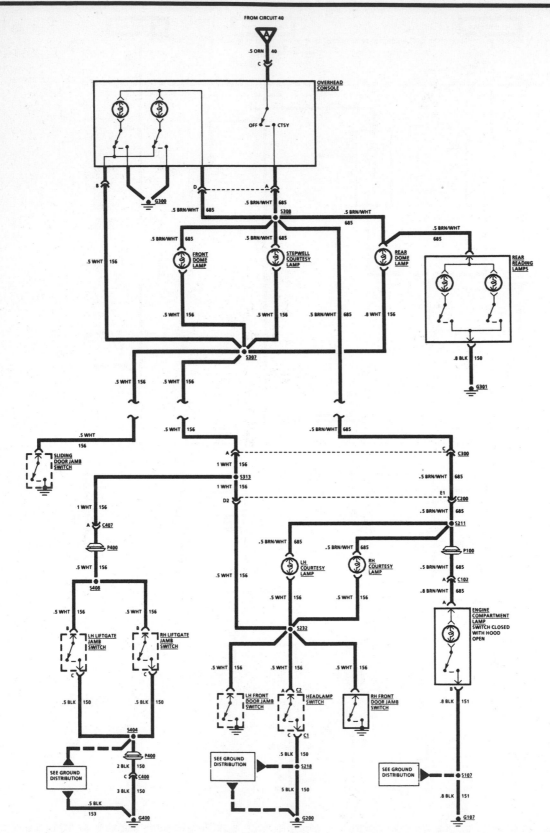

Interior lights (dome, courtesy, reading and engine compartment) — 1991 Lumina APV

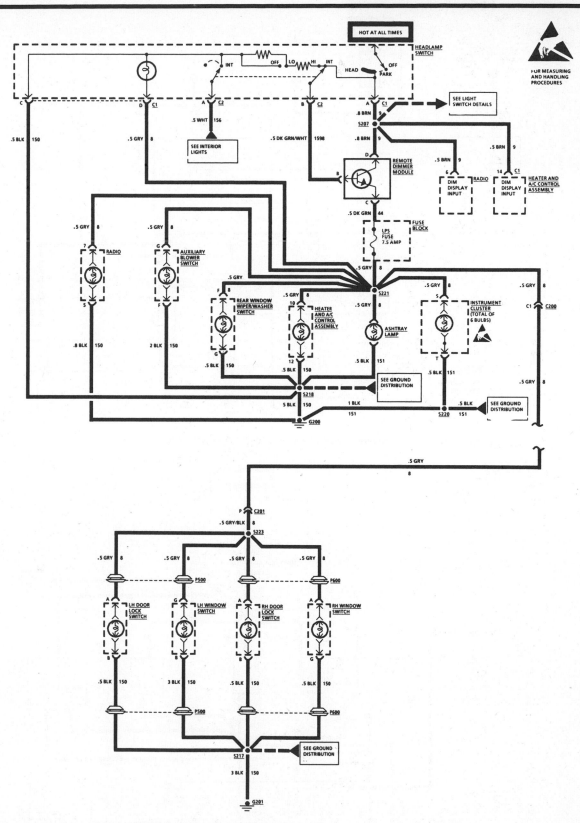

Interior lights dimming — 1991 Lumina APV

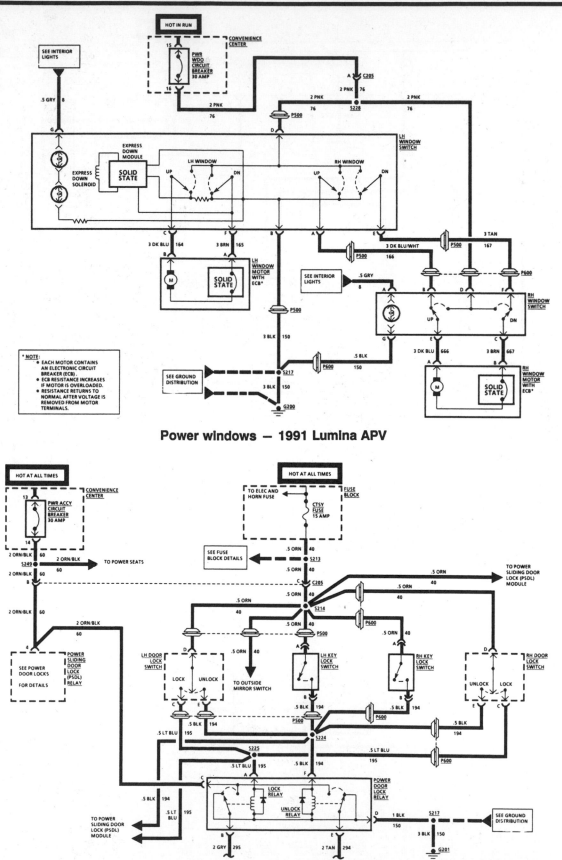

Power windows — 1991 Lumina APV

Power door locks (rh and lh door and liftgate lock motor control) — 1991 Lumina APV

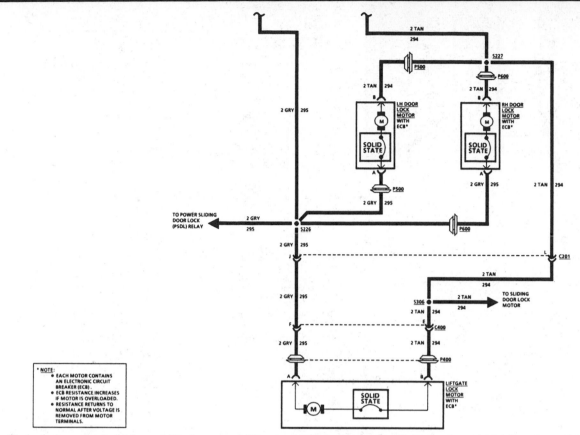

Power door locks (rh and lh door and liftgate lock motor control) (cont.) — 1991 Lumina APV

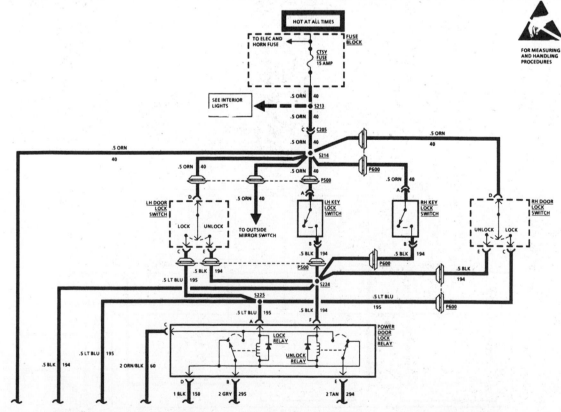

Power door locks (sliding door lock motor control) — 1991 Lumina APV

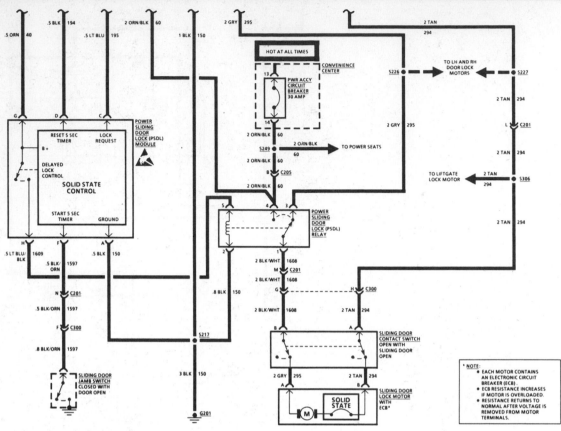

Power door locks (sliding door lock motor control) (cont.) — 1991 Lumina APV

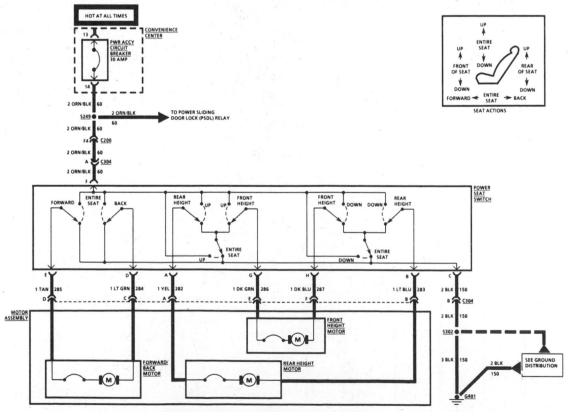

Power seats — 1991 Lumina APV

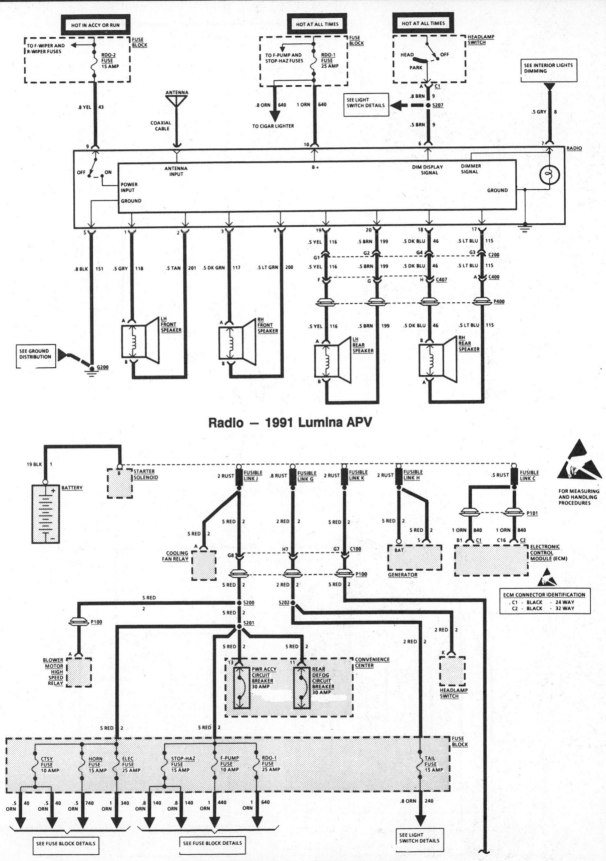

Radio — 1991 Lumina APV

Power distribution — 1990 Silhouette

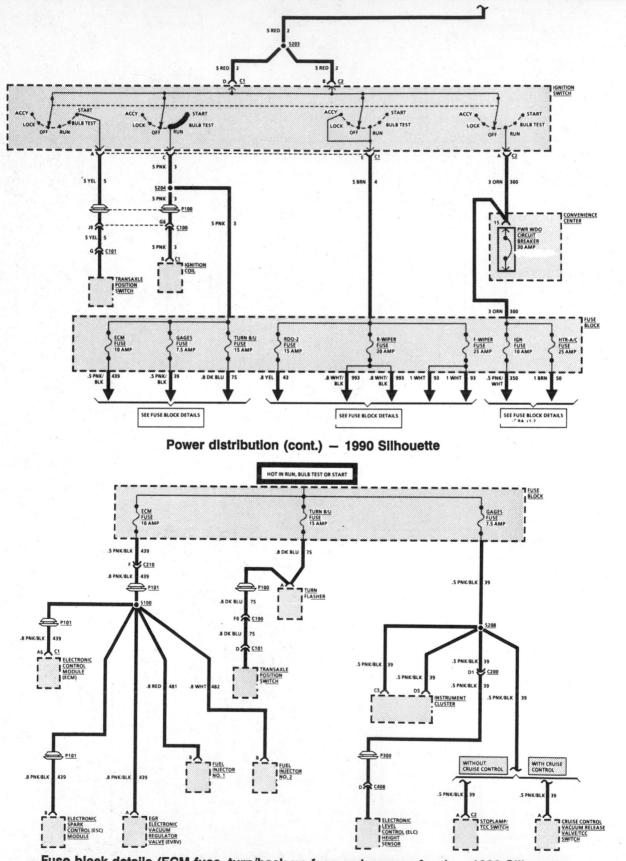

Power distribution (cont.) — 1990 Silhouette

Fuse block details (ECM fuse, turn/back-up fuse and gauges fuse) — 1990 Silhouette

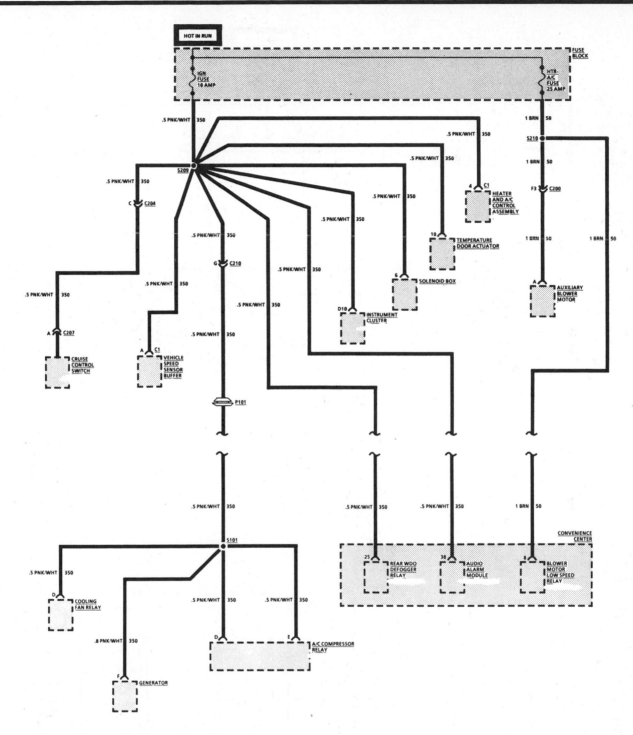

Fuse block details (Ignition fuse and heater/a/c fuse) — 1990 Silhouette

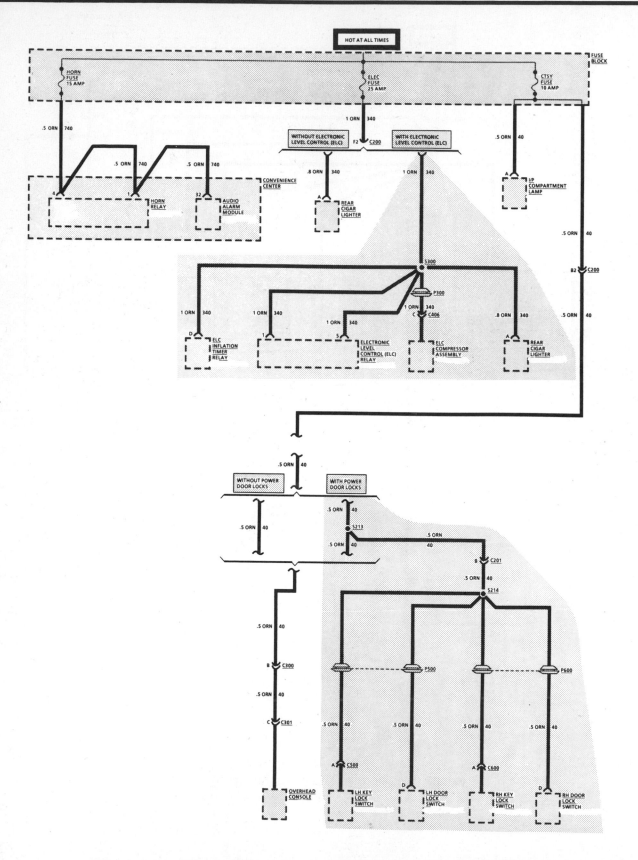

Fuse block details (horn fuse, elec fuse and ctsy fuse) — 1990 Silhouette

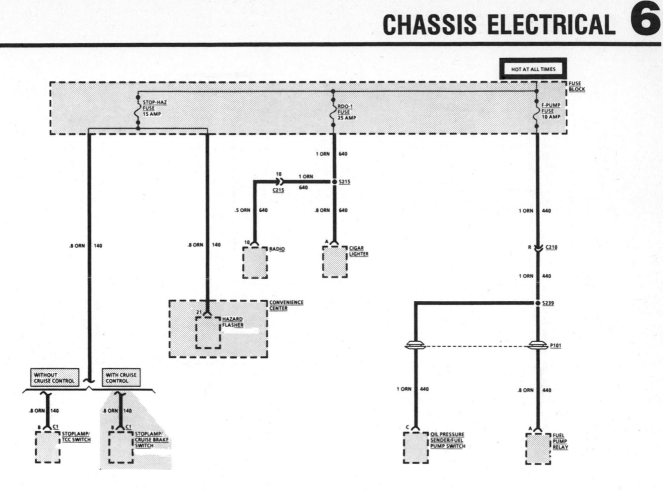

Fuse block details (stop-haz fuse, rdo-1 fuse and f- pump fuse) — 1990 Silhouette

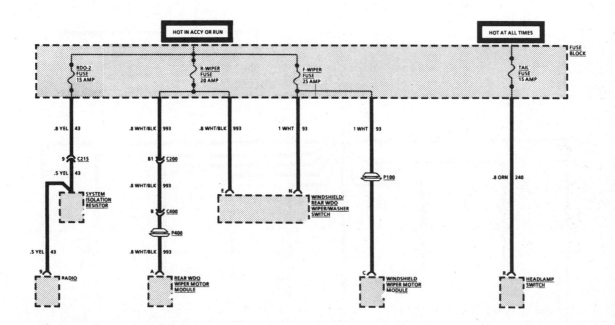

Fuse block details (rdo-2 fuse, r-wiper fuse, f-wiper fuse and tail fuse) — 1990 Silhouette

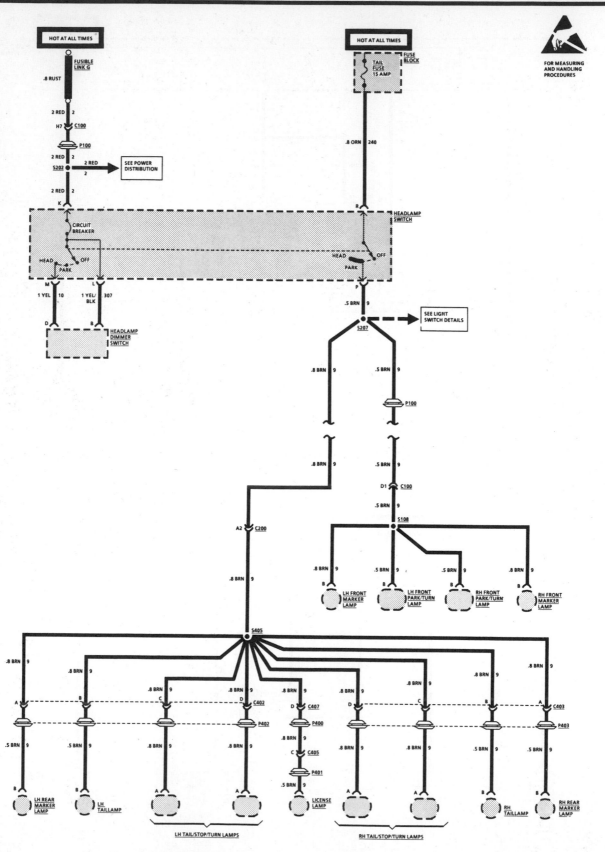

Light switch details — 1990 Silhouette

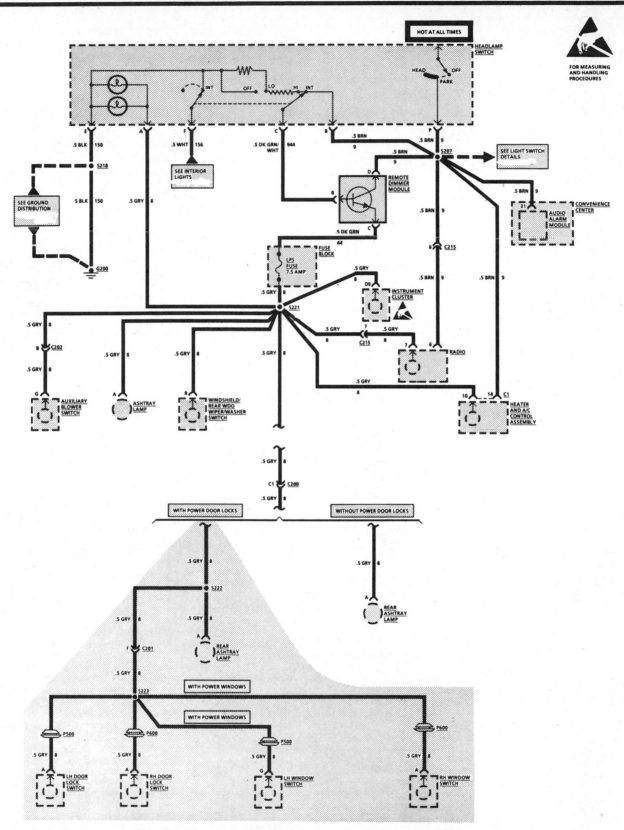

Light switch details (cont.) — 1990 Silhouette

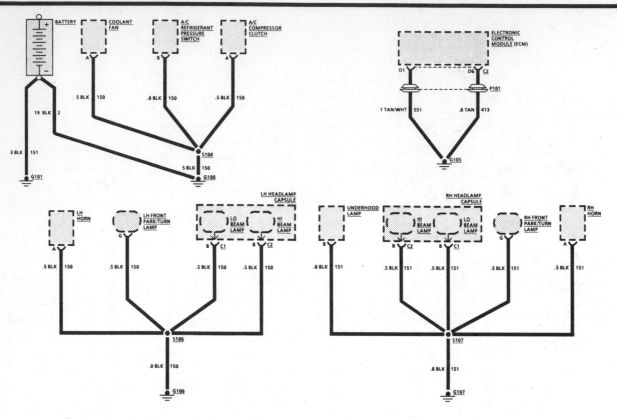

Ground distribution: (G100, G101, G105, G106 and G107) — 1990 Silhouette

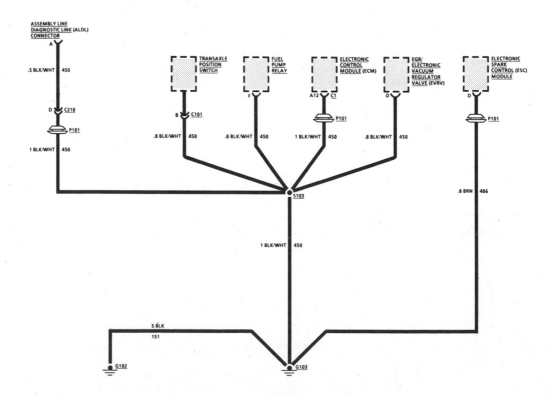

Ground distribution: (G102 and G103) — 1990 Silhouette

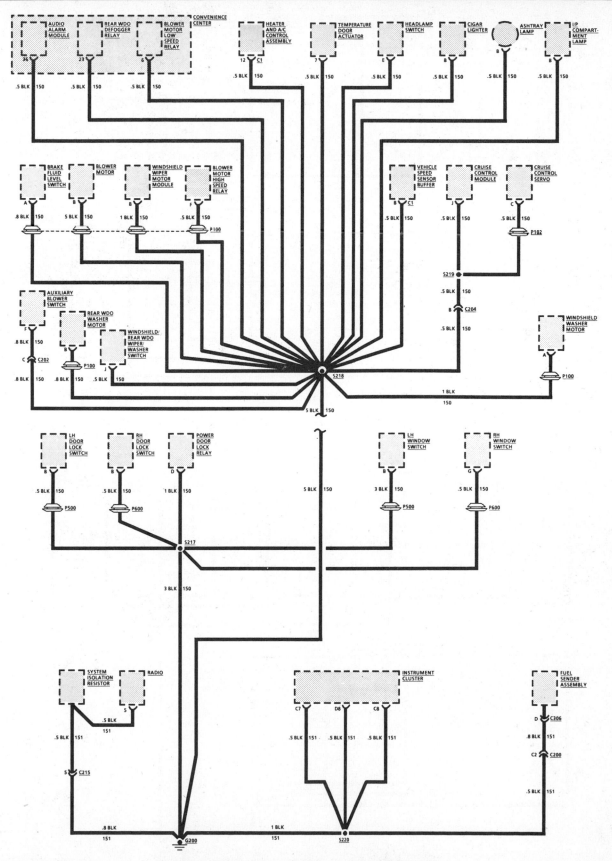

Ground distribution: (G200) — 1990 Silhouette

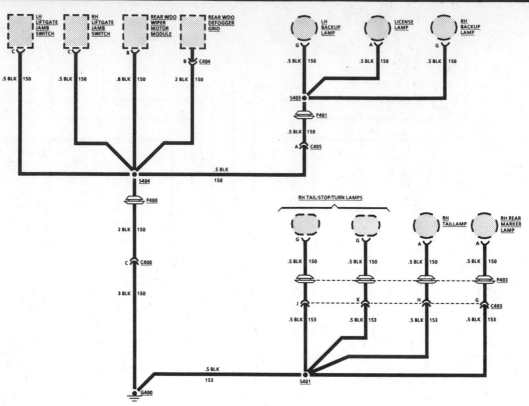

Ground distribution: (G400) — 1990 Silhouette

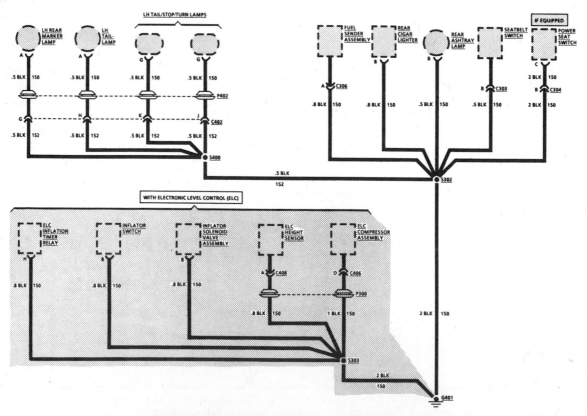

Ground distribution: (G401) — 1990 Silhouette

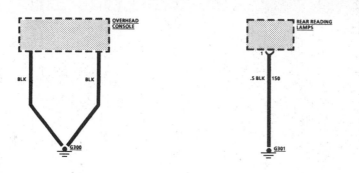

Ground distribution: (G300 and G301) — 1990 Silhouette

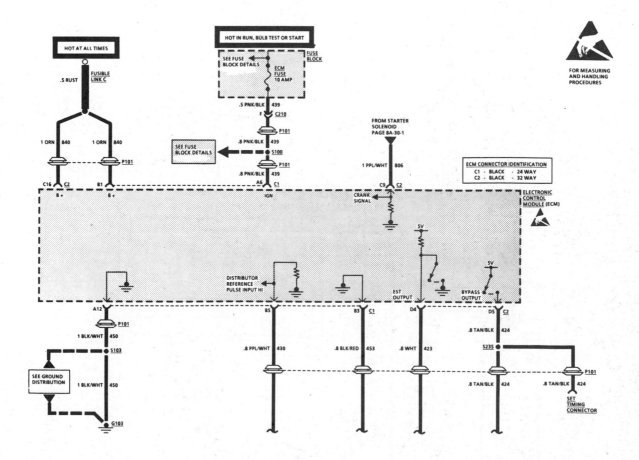

Throttle body Injection: (power, ground and ignition) — 1990 Silhouette

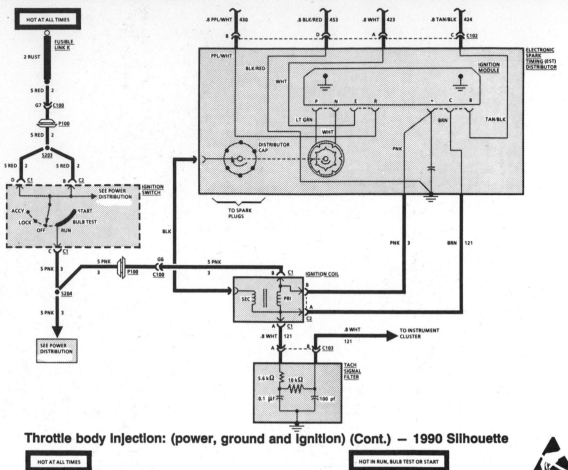

Throttle body injection: (power, ground and ignition) (Cont.) — 1990 Silhouette

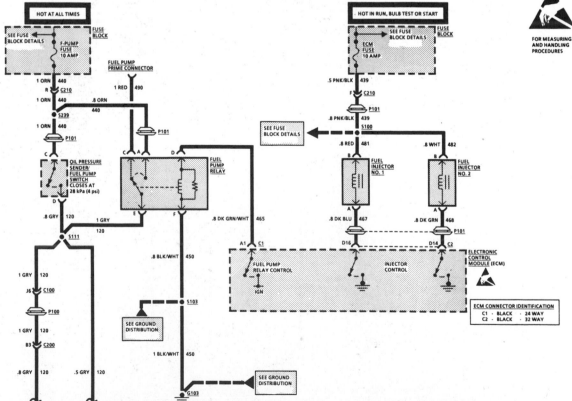

Throttle body injection: (3.1L V6 fuel control, idle air control) — 1990 Silhouette

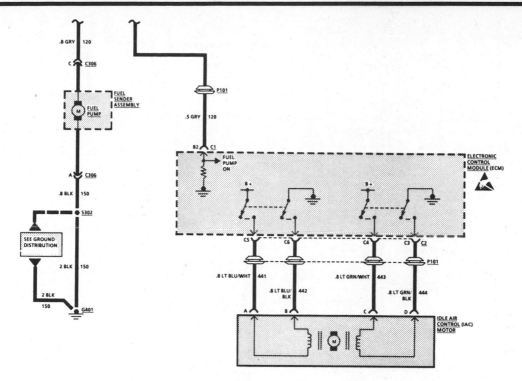

Throttle body injection: (3.1L fuel control, idle air control) (cont.) — 1990 Silhouette

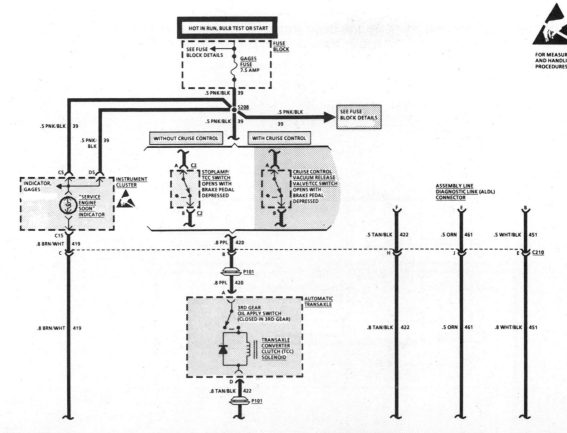

Throttle body injection: (3.1L V6 transaxle converter clutch, service engine soon indicator, transaxle position switch) — 1990 Silhouette

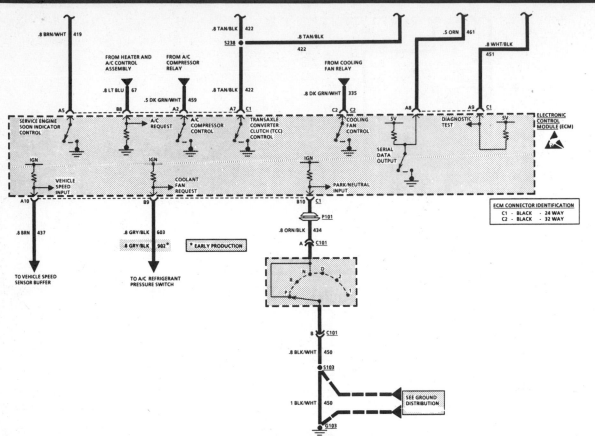

Throttle body injection: (3.1L V6 transaxle converter clutch, service engine soon indicator, transaxle position switch) (cont.) — 1990 Silhouette

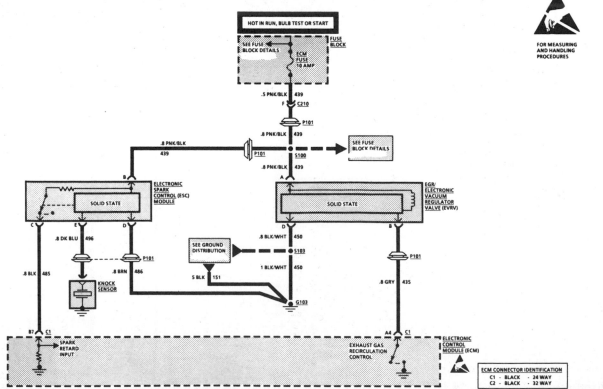

Throttle body injection: (3.1L V6 engine data sensors, spark control, emission control) — 1990 Silhouette

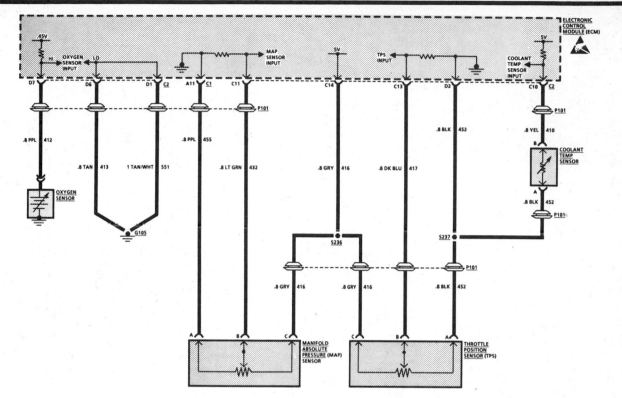

Throttle body injection: (3.1L V6 engine data sensors, spark control, emission control) (cont.) —1990 Silhouette

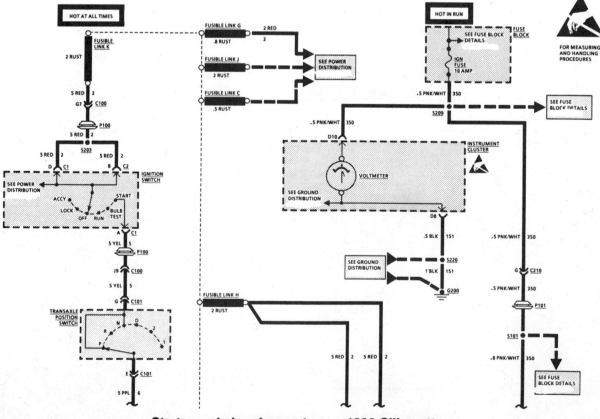

Starter and charging system — 1990 Silhouette

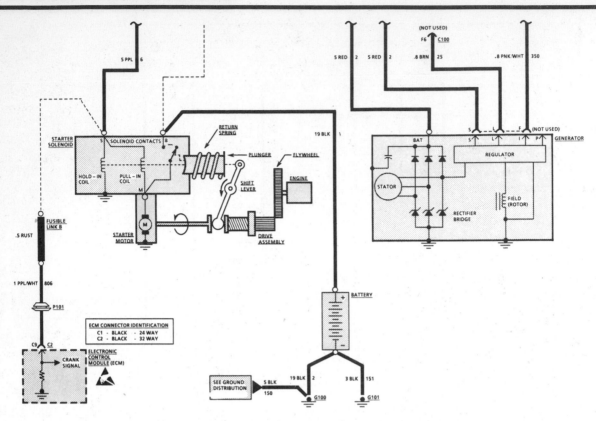

Starter and charging system (cont.) — 1990 Silhouette

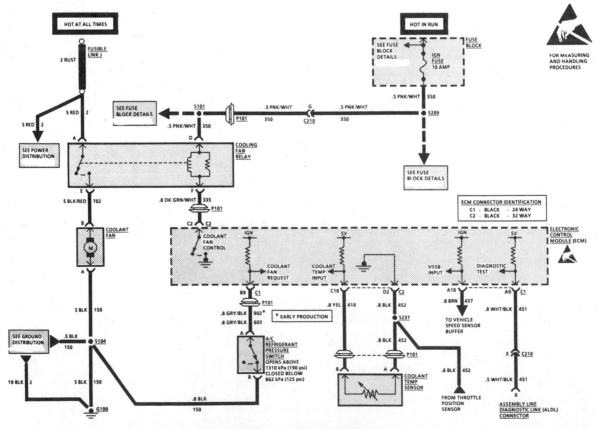

Coolant fan — 1990 Silhouette

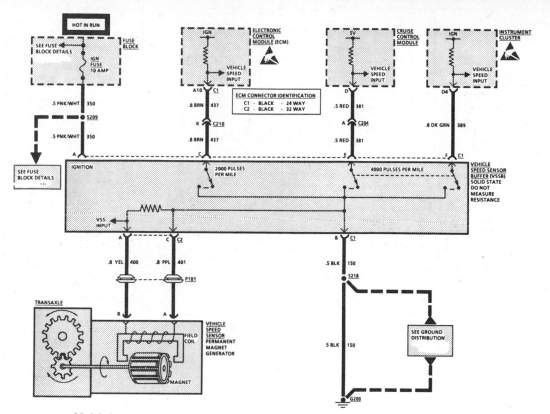

Vehicle speed sensor: (permanent magnet generator) — 1990 Silhouette

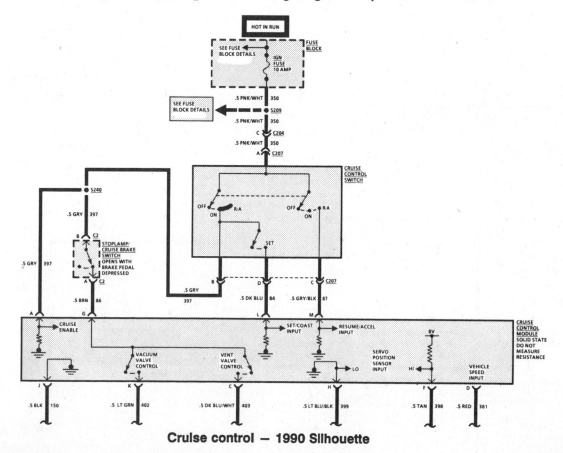

Cruise control — 1990 Silhouette

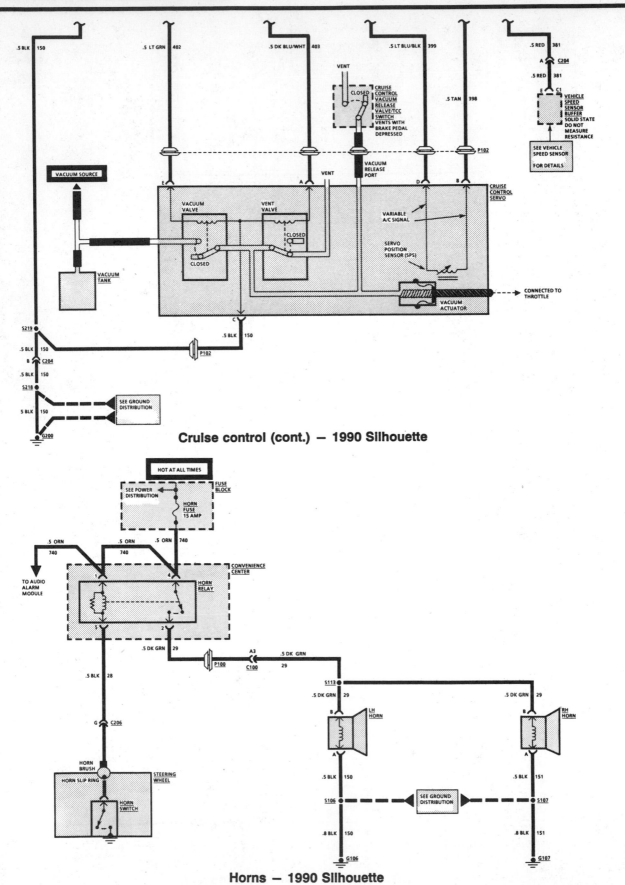

Cruise control (cont.) — 1990 Silhouette

Horns — 1990 Silhouette

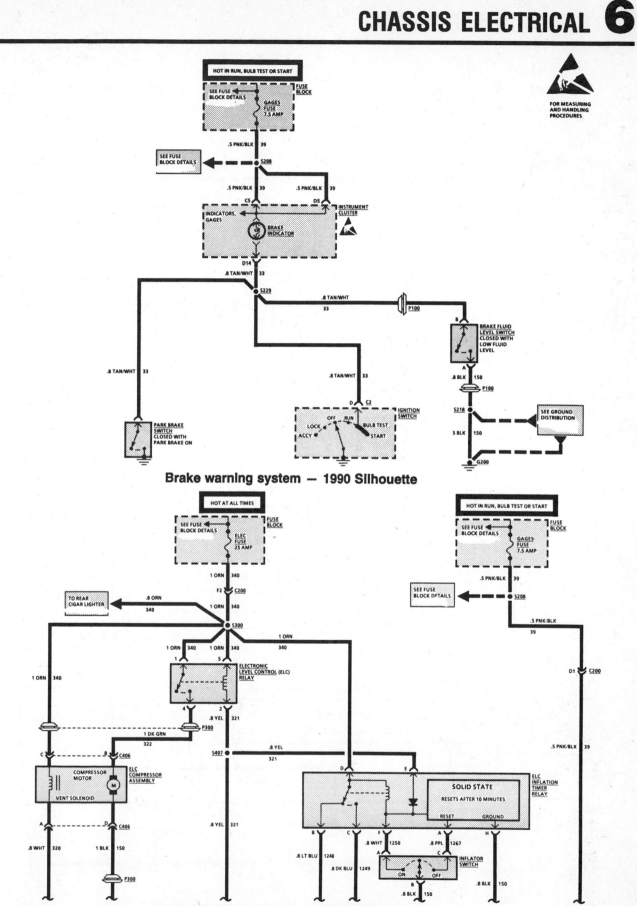

Brake warning system — 1990 Silhouette

Electronic level control — 1990 Silhouette

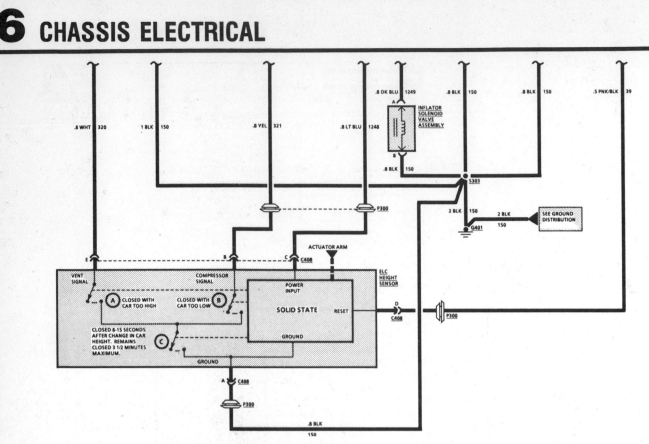

Electronic level control (cont.) — 1990 Silhouette

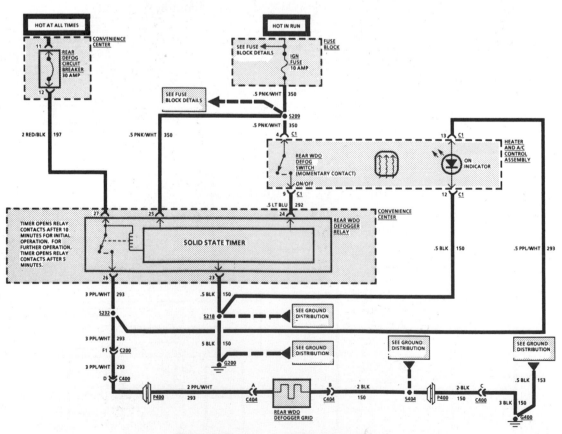

Rear defogger — 1990 Silhouette

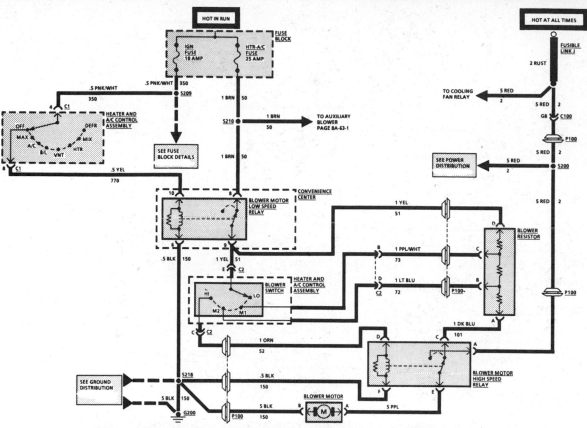

Air conditioning (blower motor control (c67) — 1990 Silhouette

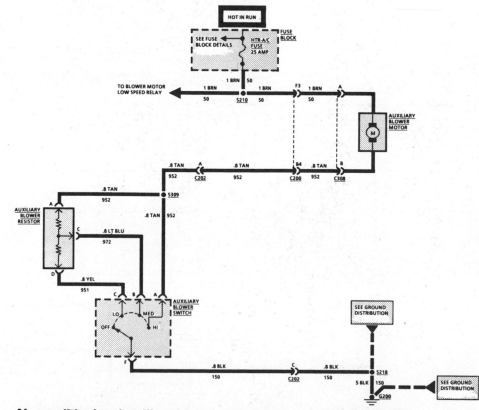

Air conditioning (auxiliary blower motor (c57) — 1990 Silhouette

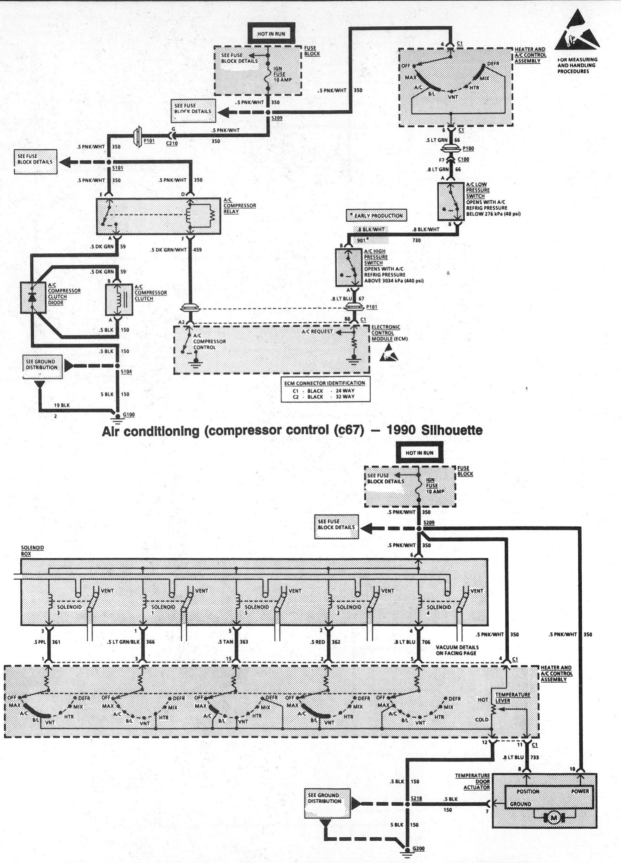

Air conditioning (compressor control (c67) — 1990 Silhouette

Air conditioning (air delivery and temperature control (c67) — 1990 Silhouette

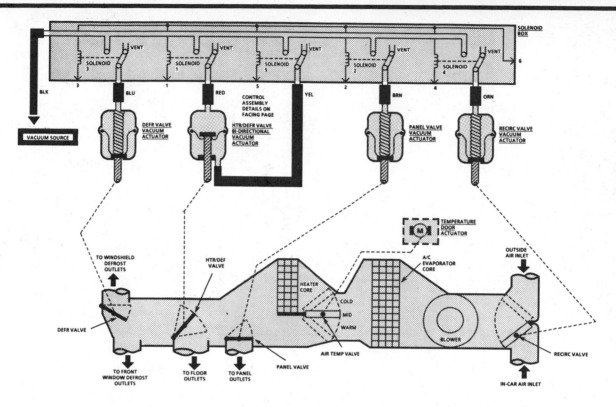

Air conditioning (air delivery and temperature control (c67) — 1990 Silhouette

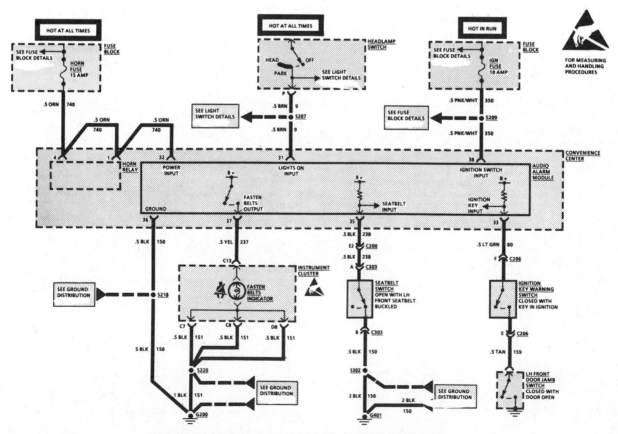

Warnings and alarms: (chime) — 1990 Silhouette

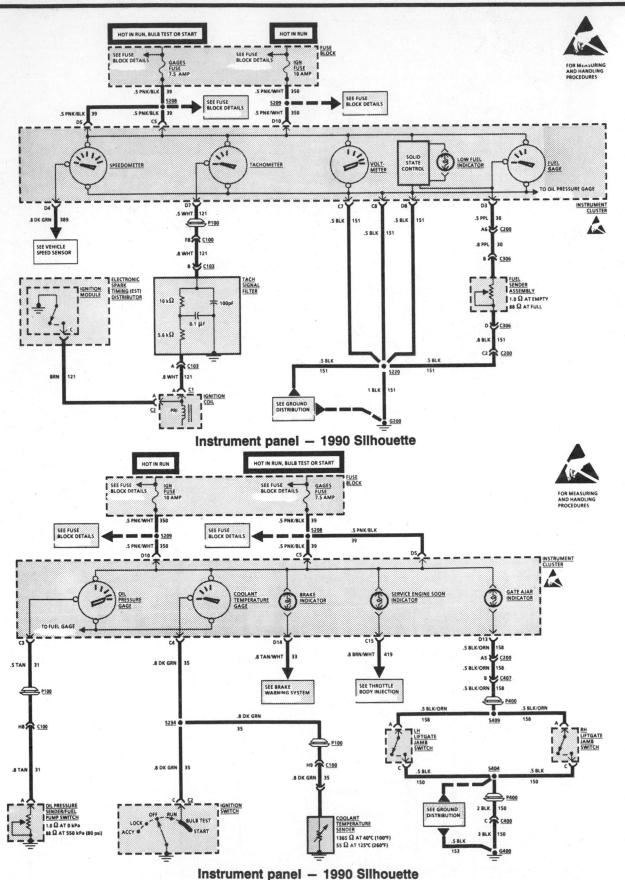

Instrument panel — 1990 Silhouette

Instrument panel — 1990 Silhouette

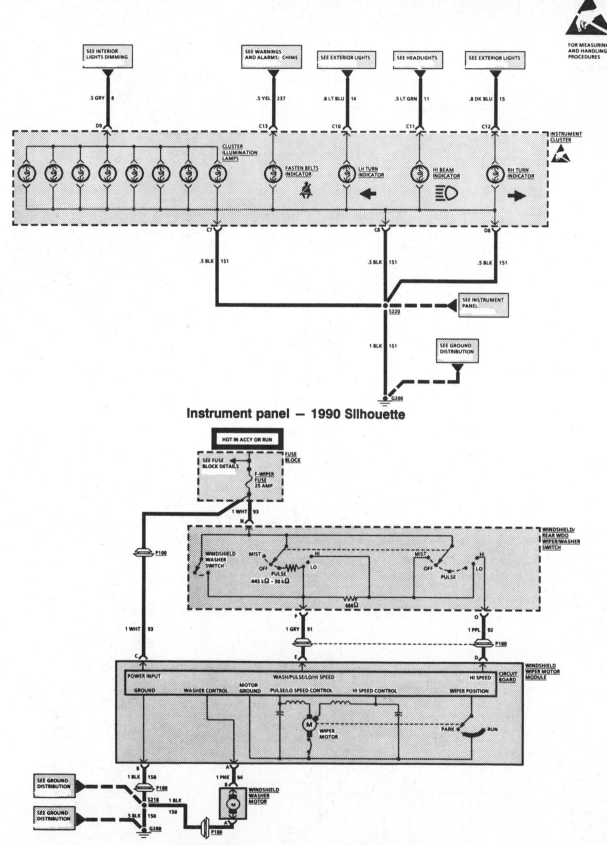

Instrument panel — 1990 Silhouette

FOR MEASURING
AND HANDLING
PROCEDURES

SEE INTERIOR
LIGHTS DIMMING

SEE WARNINGS
AND ALARMS: CHIME

SEE EXTERIOR LIGHTS

SEE HEADLIGHTS

SEE EXTERIOR LIGHTS

.5 GRY 8

.5 YEL 237

.8 LT BLU 14

.5 LT GRN 11

.8 DK BLU 15

D9 C13 C10 C11 C12

INSTRUMENT
CLUSTER

CLUSTER
ILLUMINATION
LAMPS

FASTEN BELTS
INDICATOR

LH TURN
INDICATOR

HI BEAM
INDICATOR

RH TURN
INDICATOR

C7 C8 D8

.5 BLK 151 .5 BLK 151 .5 BLK 151

SEE INSTRUMENT
PANEL

S220

1 BLK 151

SEE GROUND
DISTRIBUTION

G200

HOT IN ACCY OR RUN

FUSE
BLOCK

SEE FUSE
BLOCK DETAILS

F-WIPER
FUSE
25 AMP

1 WHT 93

N

WINDSHIELD/
REAR WDO
WIPER/WASHER
SWITCH

P100

WINDSHIELD
WASHER
SWITCH

MIST

OFF

PULSE

445 kΩ - 30 kΩ

HI

LO

MIST

OFF

PULSE

HI

LO

680Ω

P

P

O

1 WHT 93

1 GRY 91

1 PPL 92

P100

C

E

D

POWER INPUT

WASH/PULSE/LO/HI SPEED

HI SPEED

CIRCUIT
BOARD

WINDSHIELD
WIPER MOTOR
MODULE

GROUND

WASHER CONTROL

MOTOR
GROUND

PULSE/LO SPEED CONTROL

HI SPEED CONTROL

WIPER POSITION

M
WIPER
MOTOR

PARK

RUN

B

A

SEE GROUND
DISTRIBUTION

1 BLK 150

P100

1 PNK 94

B

WINDSHIELD
WASHER
MOTOR

S218

1 BLK
150

SEE GROUND
DISTRIBUTION

5 BLK 150

G200

M

A

P100

Wiper/washer: (pulse) — 1990 Silhouette

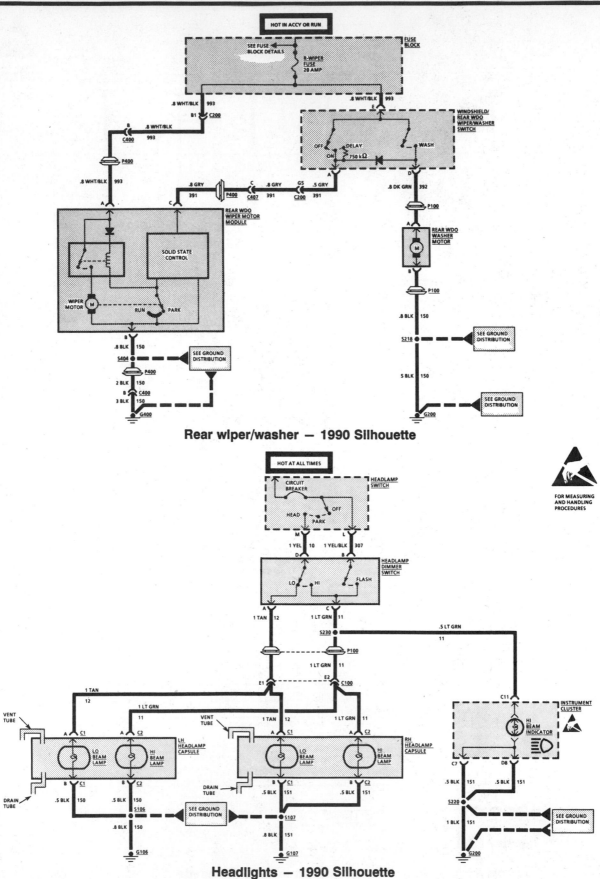

Rear wiper/washer — 1990 Silhouette

Headlights — 1990 Silhouette

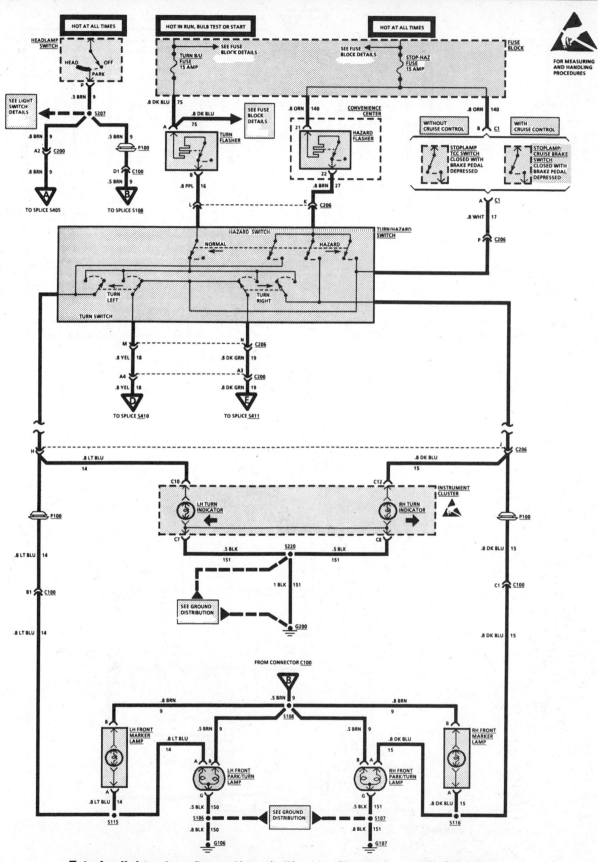

Exterior lights: (turn/hazard/stop/tail/marker/license) — 1990 Silhouette

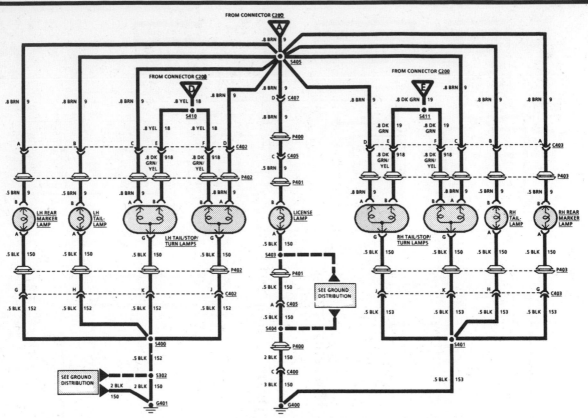

Exterior lights: (turn/hazard/stop/tail/marker/license) (cont.) — 1990 Silhouette

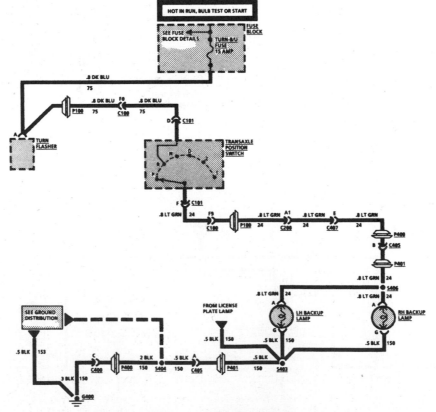

Backup lights — 1990 Silhouette

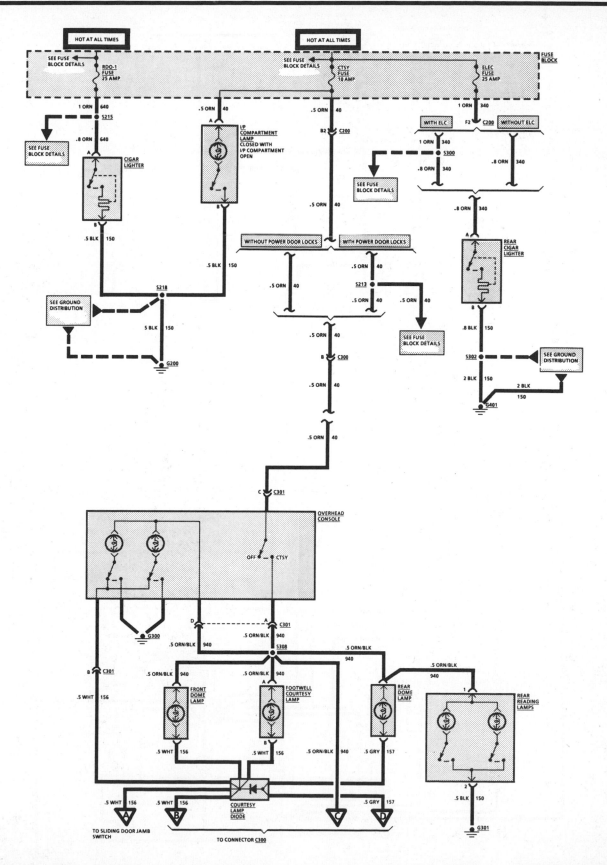

Interior lights (courtesy, dome, I/p compartment, cigar lighter, rear cigar lighter) — 1990 Silhouette

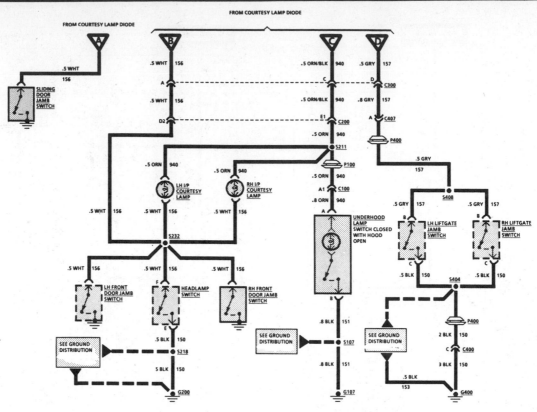

Interior lights (courtesy and engine compartment) — 1990 Silhouette

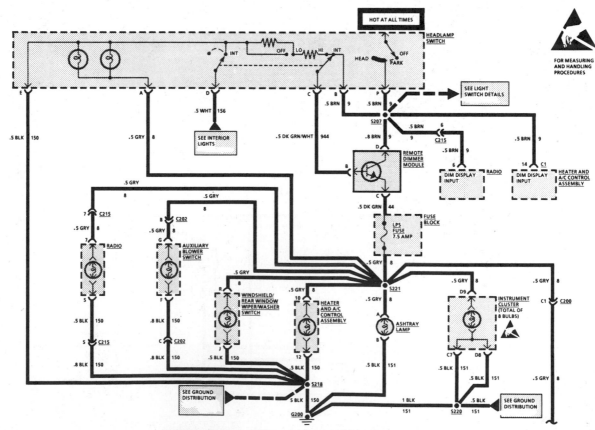

Interior lights (dimming) — 1990 Silhouette

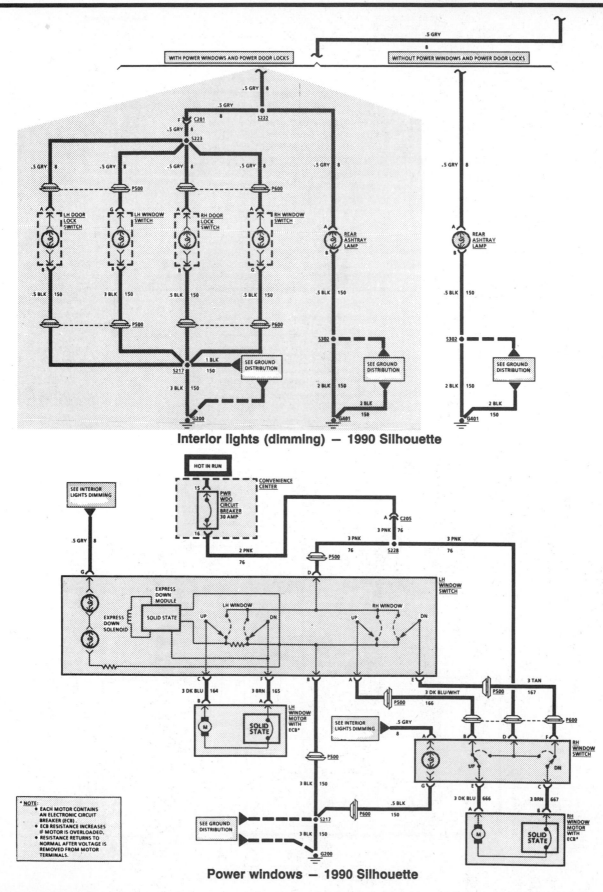

Interior lights (dimming) — 1990 Silhouette

Power windows — 1990 Silhouette

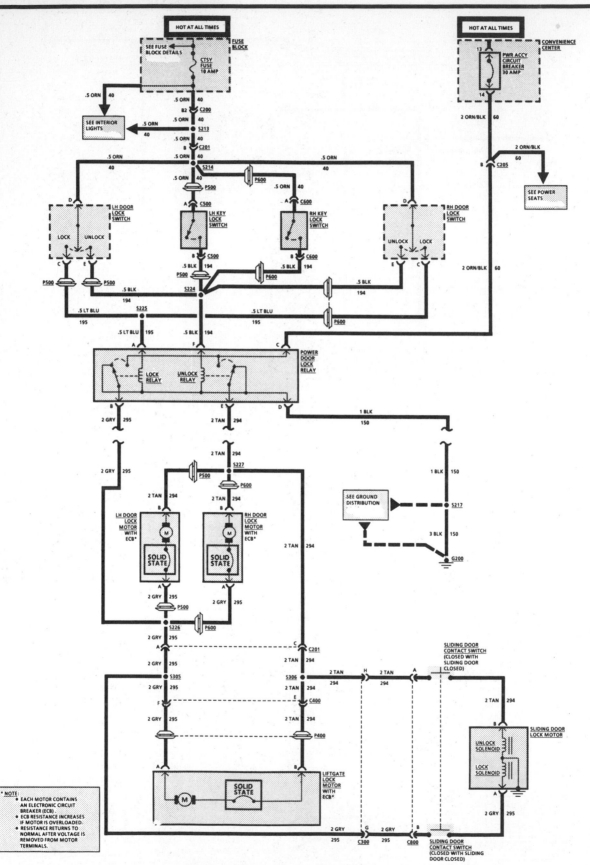

Power door locks — 1990 Silhouette

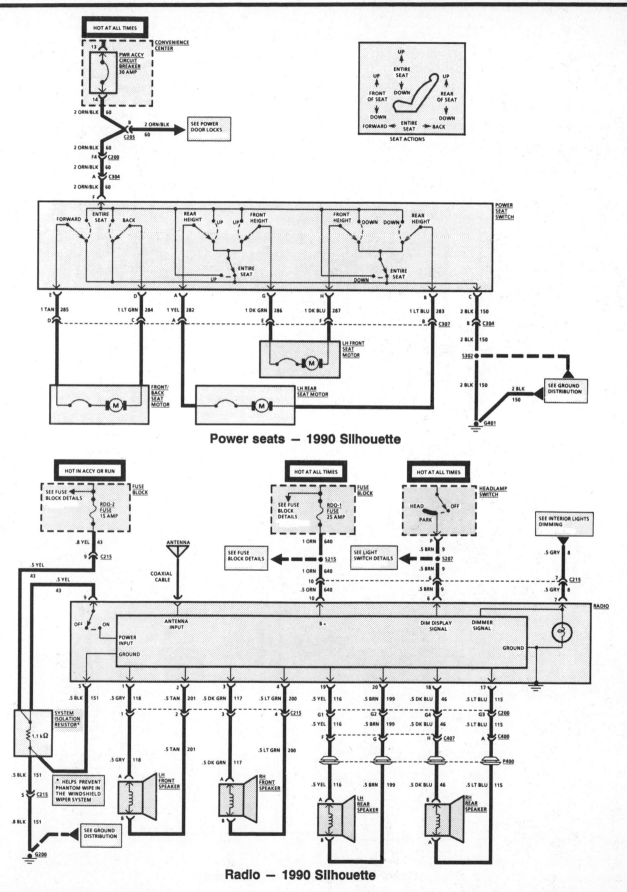

Power seats — 1990 Silhouette

Radio — 1990 Silhouette

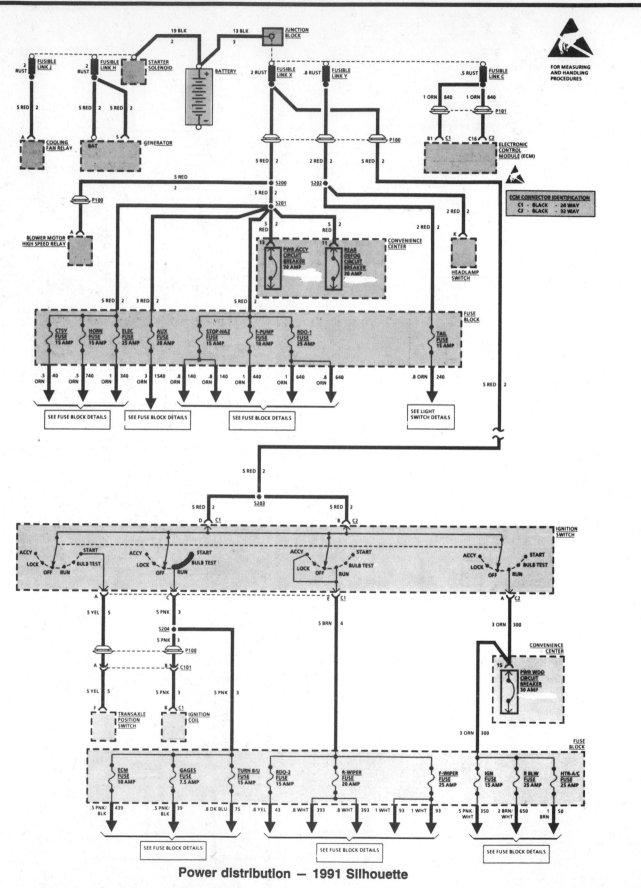

Power distribution — 1991 Silhouette

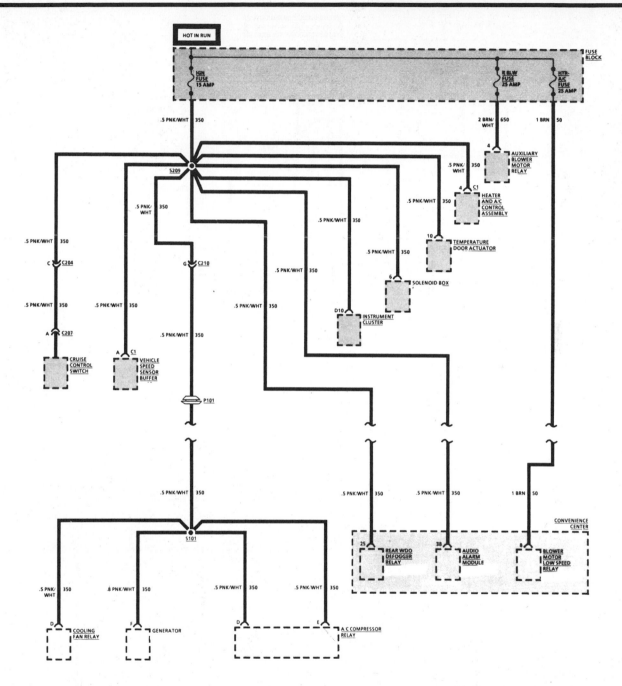

Fuse block details (Ignition fuse, rear blower and heater/a/c fuse) — 1991 Silhouette

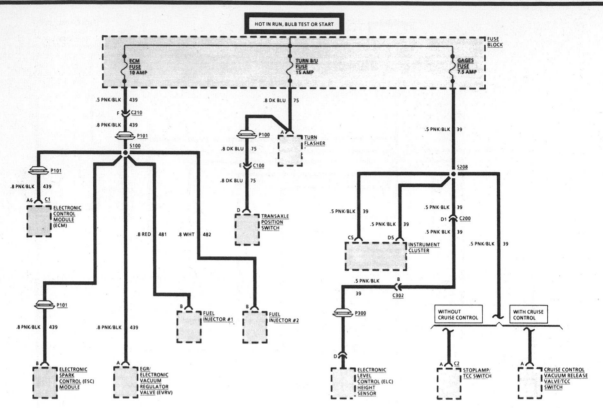

Fuse block details (ECM fuse, turn/back-up fuse and gauges fuse) — 1991 Silhouette

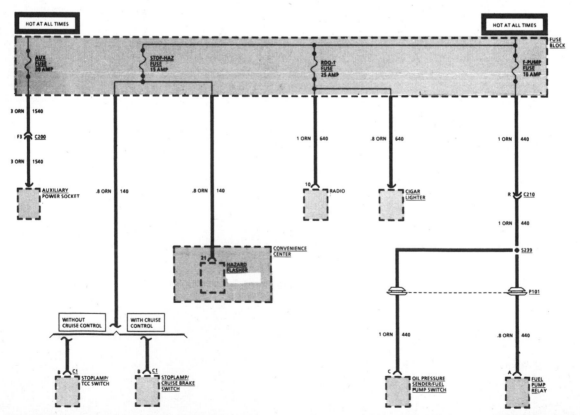

Fuse block details (aux fuse, stop/haz fuse, rdo-1 fuse and fuel pump fuse) — 1991 Silhouette

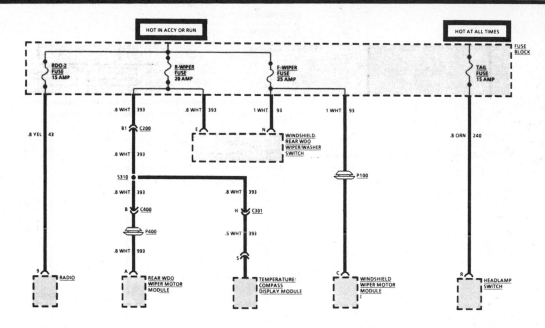

Fuse block details (rdo-2 fuse, front and rear wiper fuses and tail fuse) — 1991 Silhouette

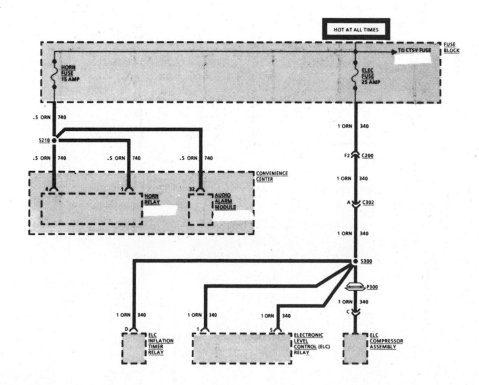

Fuse block details (horn fuse and elec fuse) — 1991 Silhouette

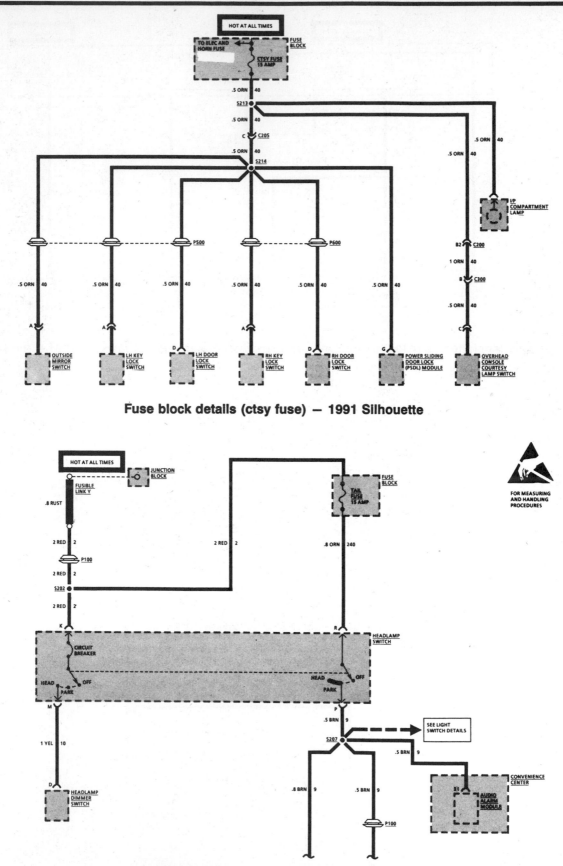

Fuse block details (ctsy fuse) — 1991 Silhouette

Light switch details — 1991 Silhouette

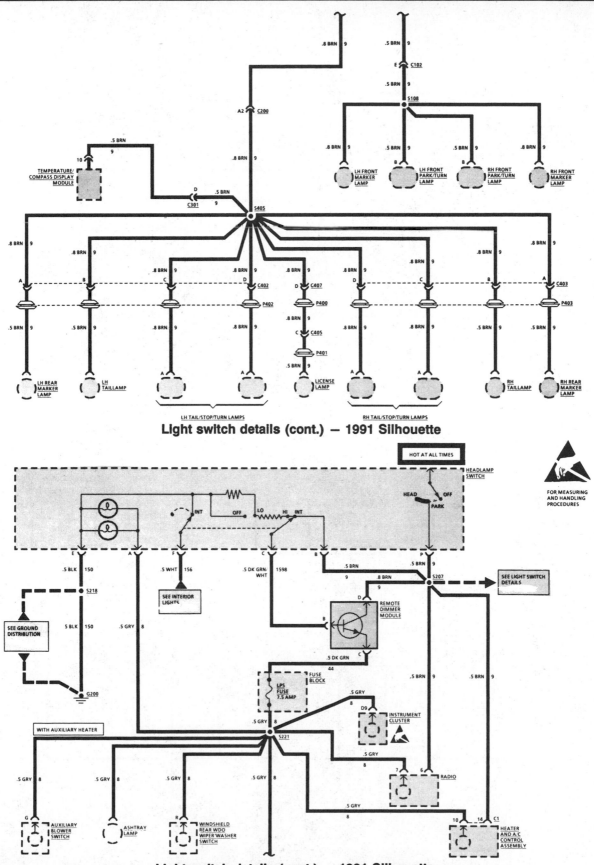

Light switch details (cont.) — 1991 Silhouette

Light switch details (cont.) — 1991 Silhouette

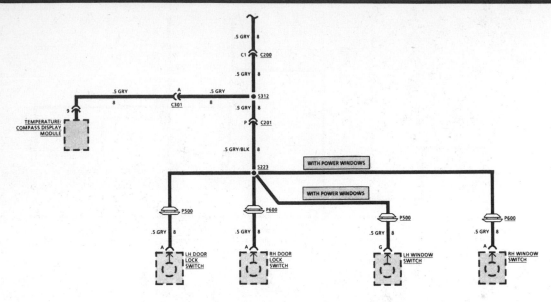

Light switch details (cont.) — 1991 Silhouette

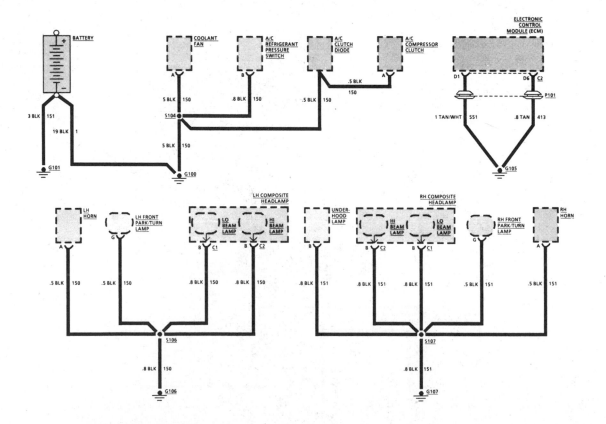

Ground distribution (G100, G101, G105, G106 and G107) — 1991 Silhouette

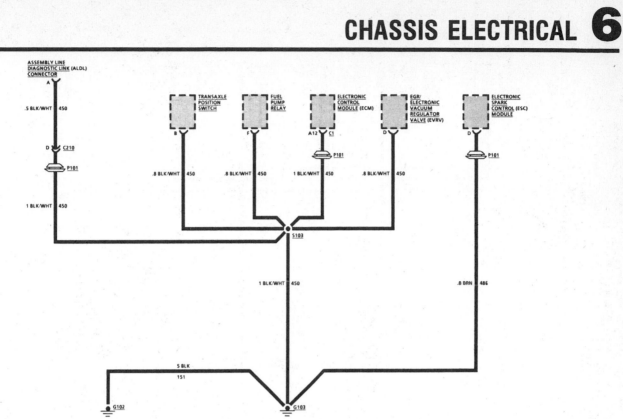

Ground distribution (G102 and G103) — 1991 Silhouette

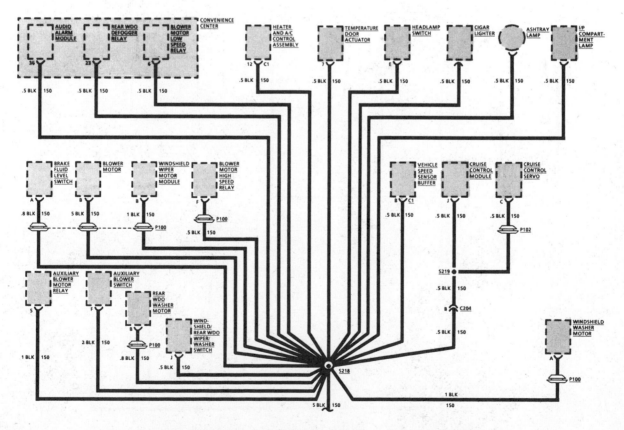

Ground distribution (G200 and G201) — 1991 Silhouette

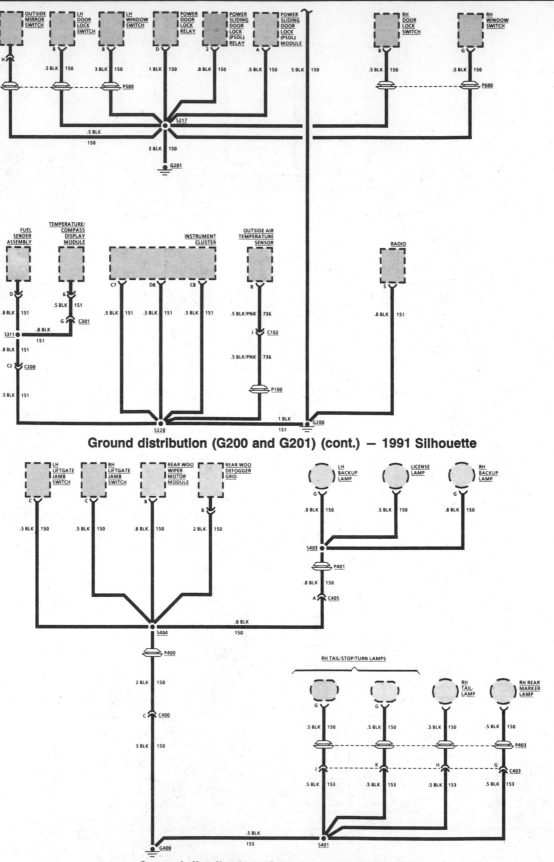

Ground distribution (G200 and G201) (cont.) — 1991 Silhouette

Ground distribution (G400) — 1991 Silhouette

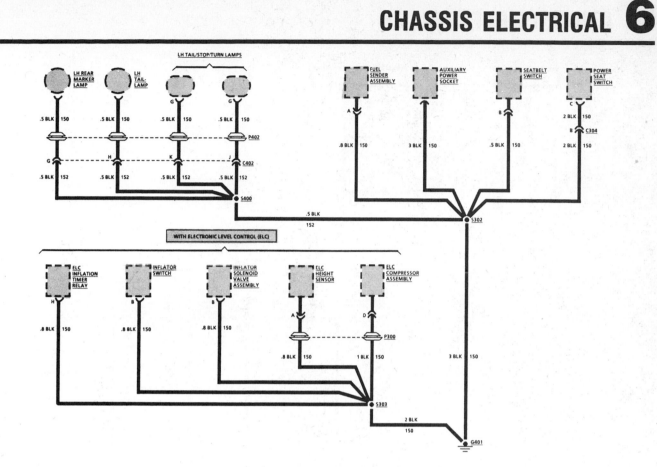

Ground distribution (G401) — 1991 Silhouette

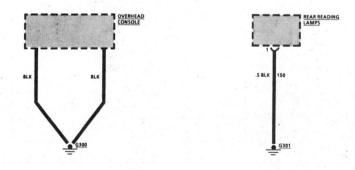

Ground distribution (G300 and G301) — 1991 Silhouette

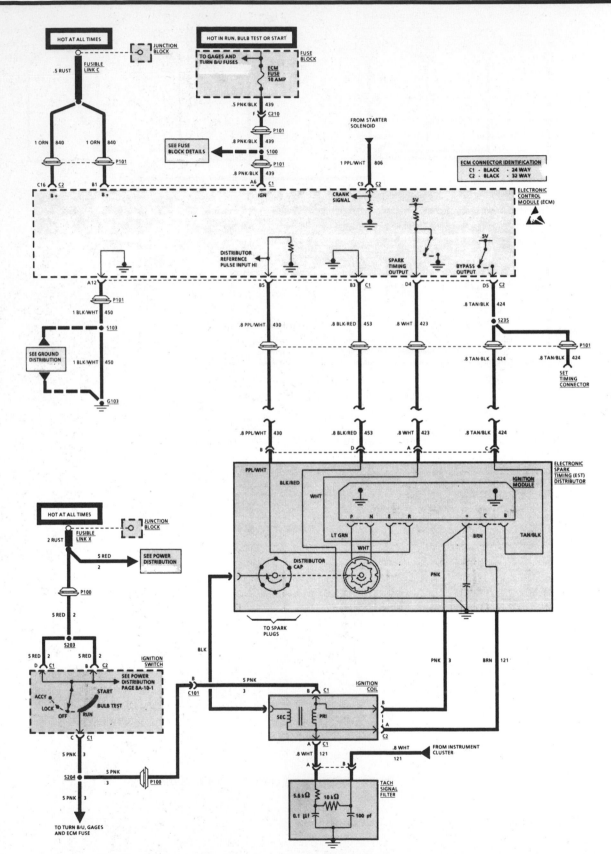

Throttle body Injection: (3.1L V6 power, ground and Ignition) — 1991 Silhouette

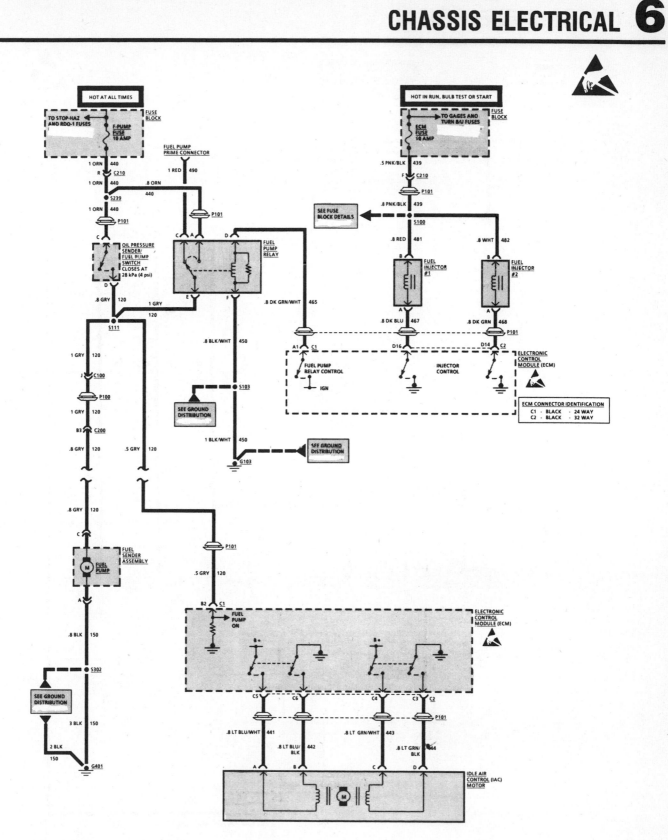

Throttle body Injection: (3.1L V6 fuel control, idle air control) — 1991 Silhouette

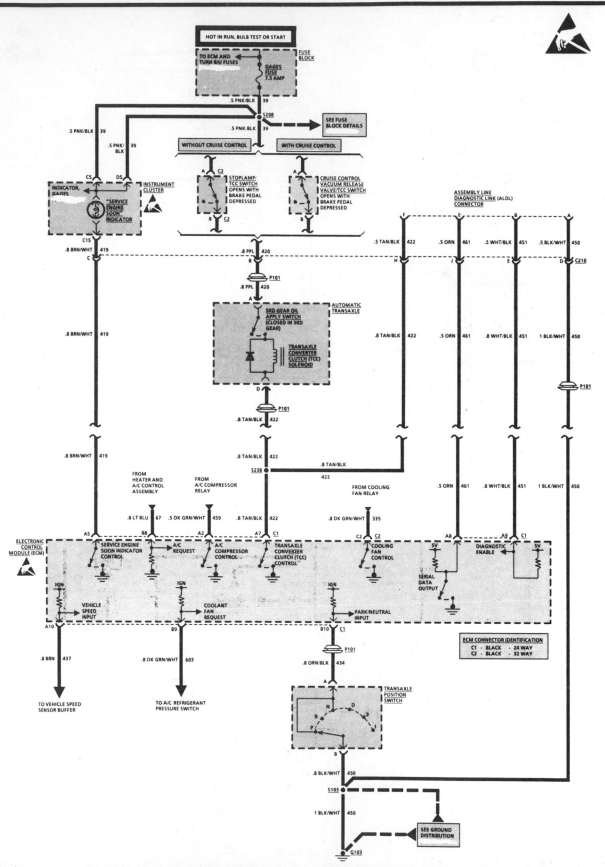

Throttle body injection: (3.1L V6 transaxle converter clutch, "service engine soon" indicator, transaxle position switch) — 1991 Silhouette

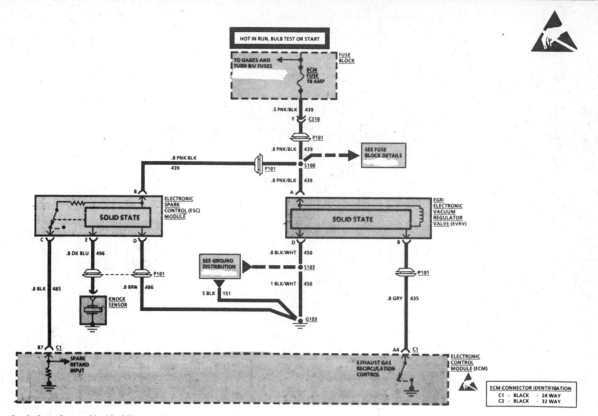

Throttle body injection: (3.1L V6 engine data sensors, spark control, emission control) — 1991 Silhouette

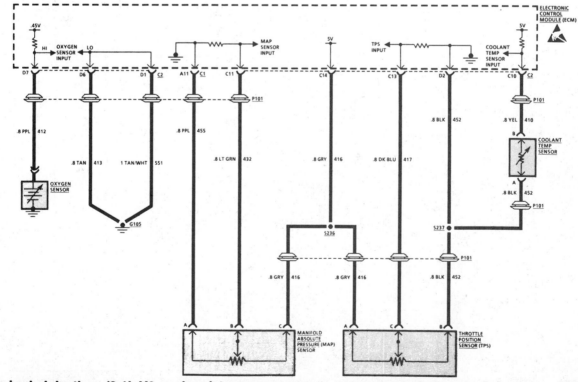

Throttle body injection: (3.1L V6 engine data sensors, spark control, emission control) (cont.) — 1991 Silhouette

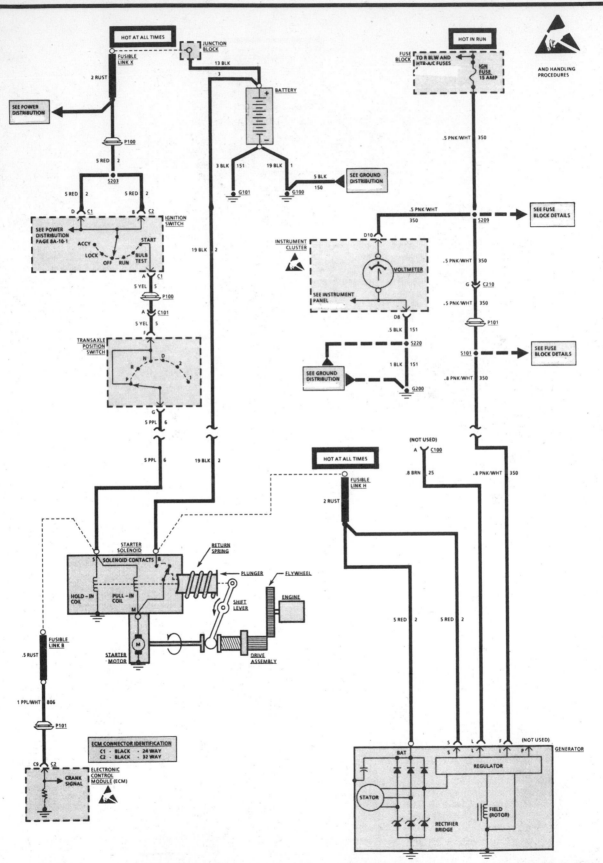

Starter and charging system — 1991 Silhouette

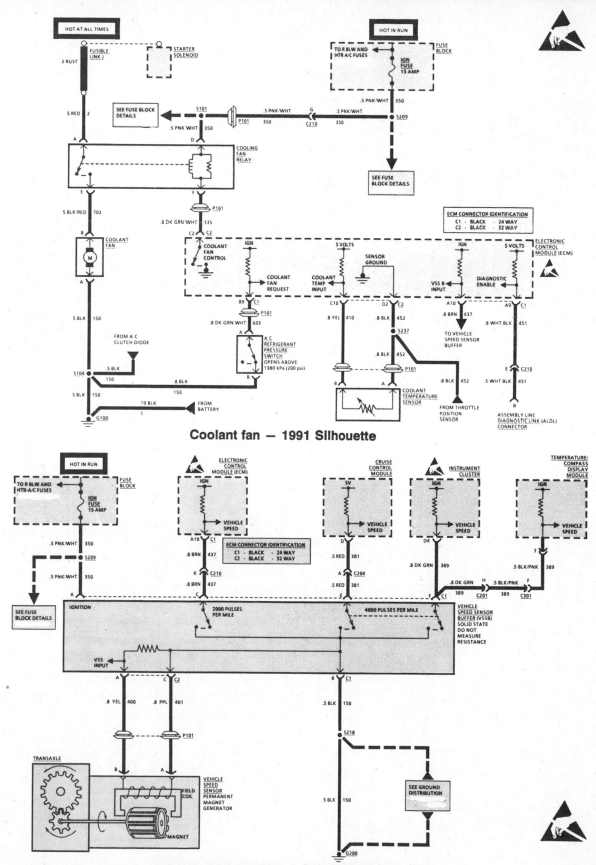

Coolant fan — 1991 Silhouette

Vehicle speed sensor — 1991 Silhouette

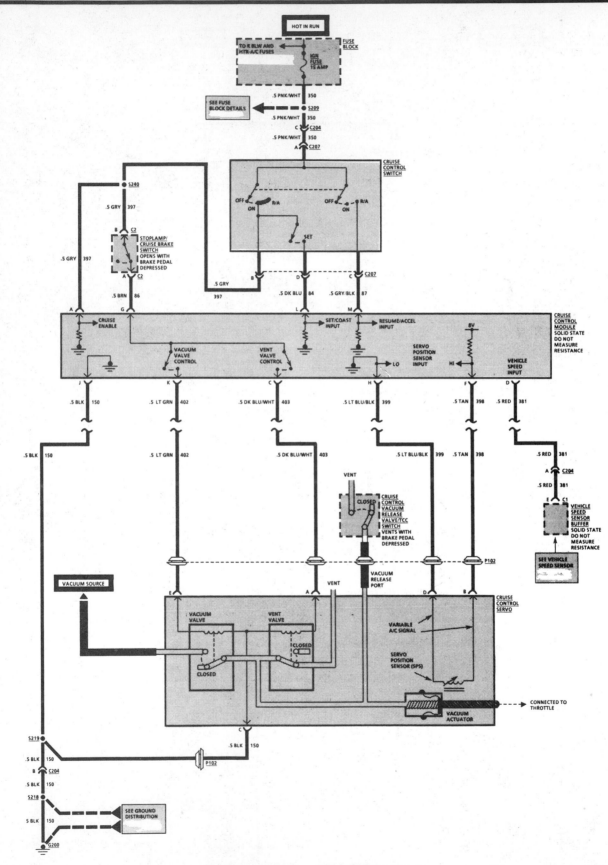

Cruise control — 1991 Silhouette

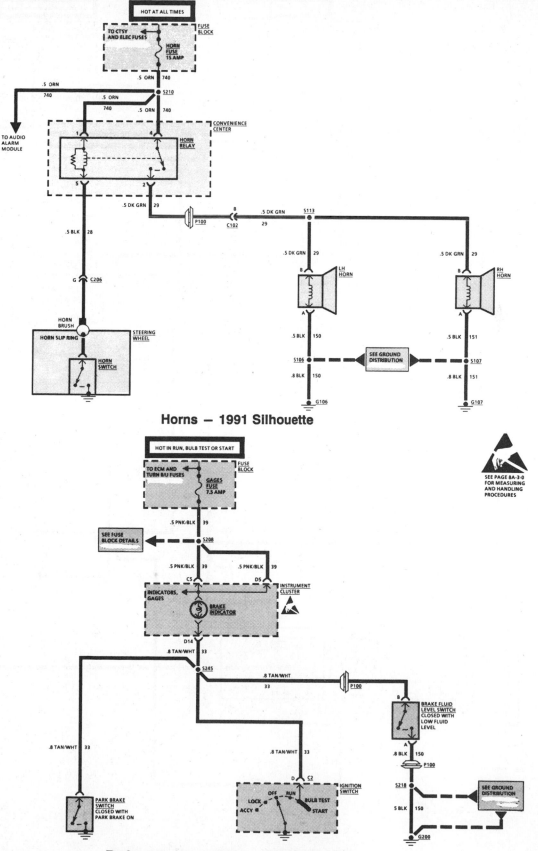

Horns — 1991 Silhouette

Brake warning system — 1991 Silhouette

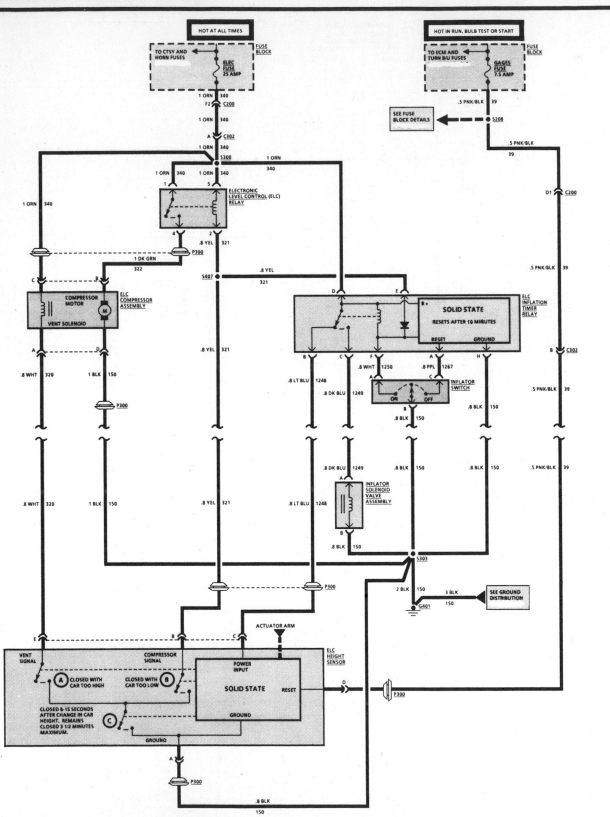

Electronic level control — 1991 Silhouette

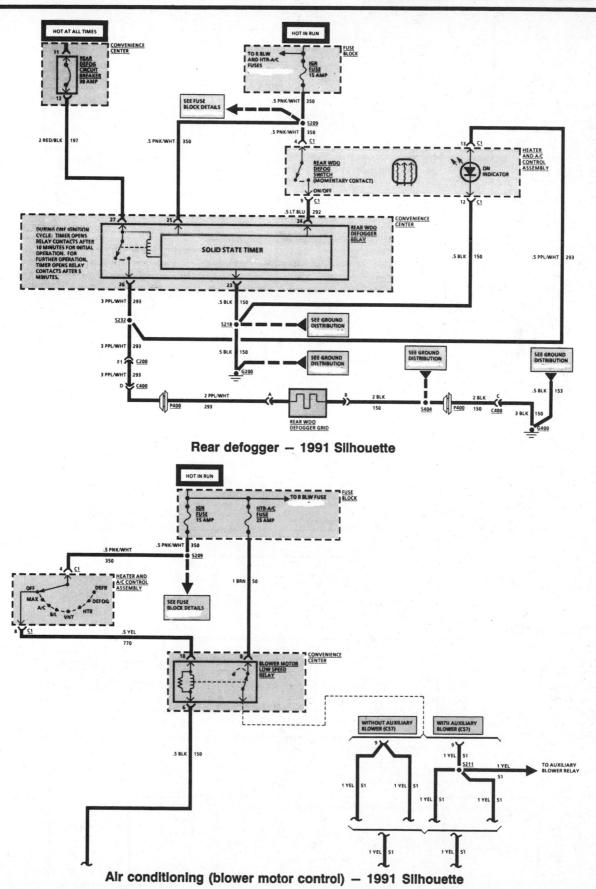

Rear defogger — 1991 Silhouette

Air conditioning (blower motor control) — 1991 Silhouette

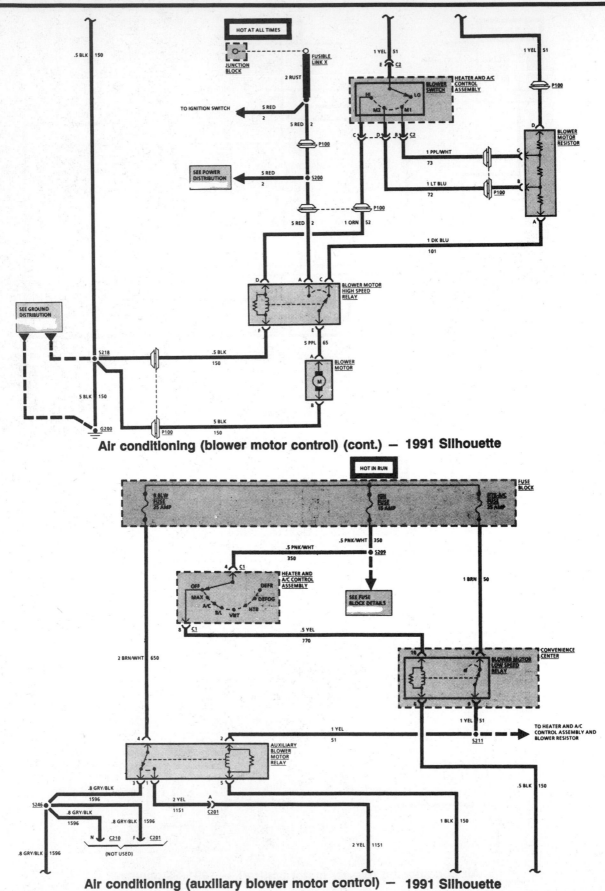

Air conditioning (blower motor control) (cont.) — 1991 Silhouette

Air conditioning (auxiliary blower motor control) — 1991 Silhouette

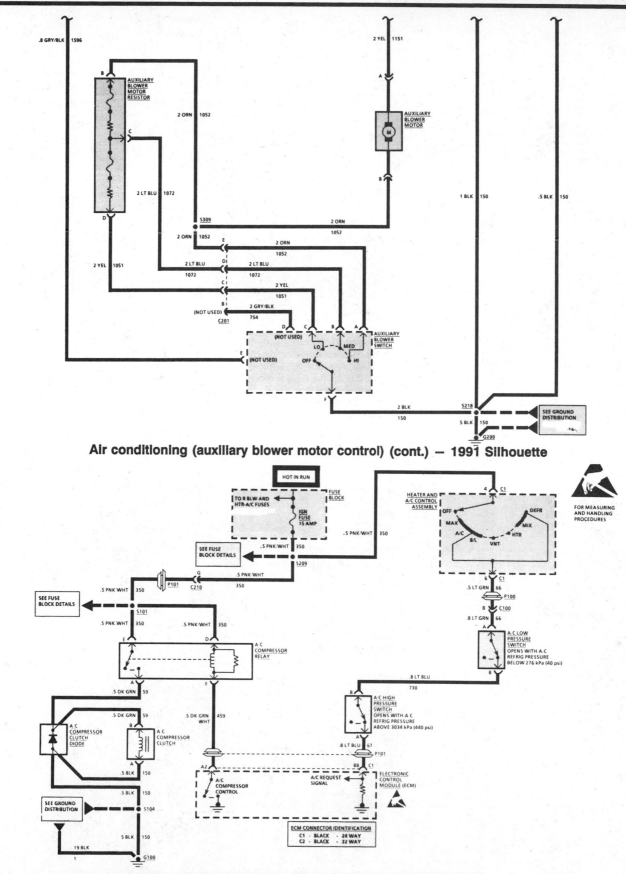

Air conditioning (auxiliary blower motor control) (cont.) — 1991 Silhouette

Air conditioning (compressor control) — 1991 Silhouette

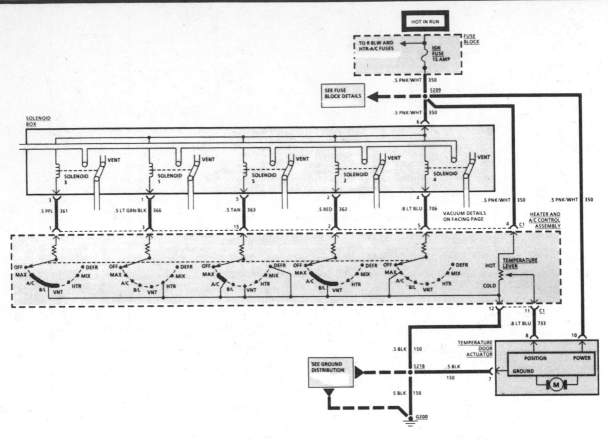

Air conditioning (air delivery and temperature control) — 1991 Silhouette

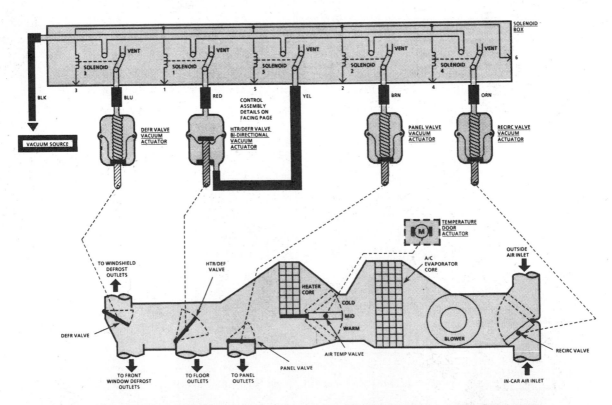

Air conditioning (air delivery and temperature control) (cont.) — 1991 Silhouette

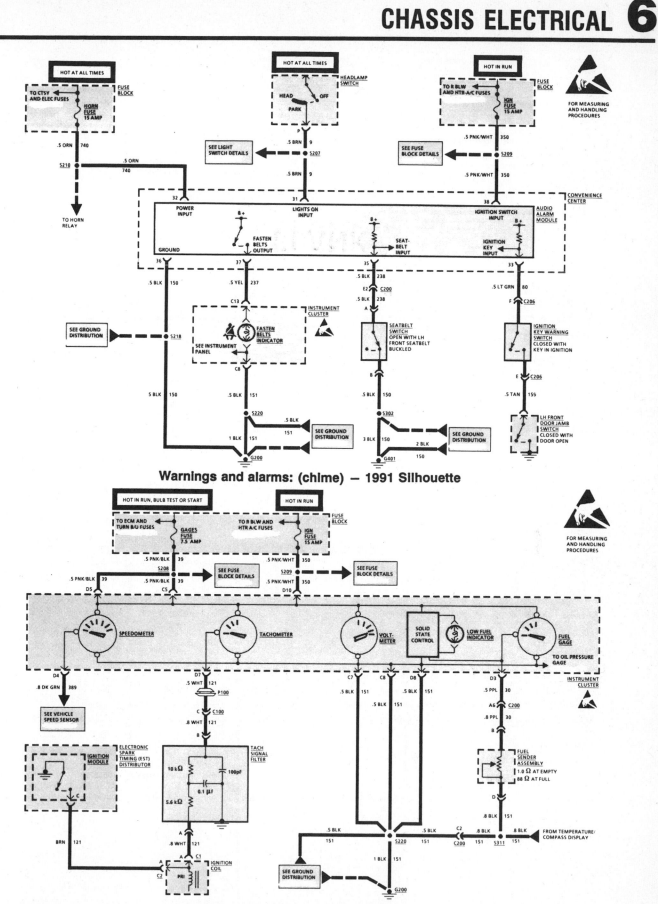

Warnings and alarms: (chime) — 1991 Silhouette

Instrument panel — 1991 Silhouette

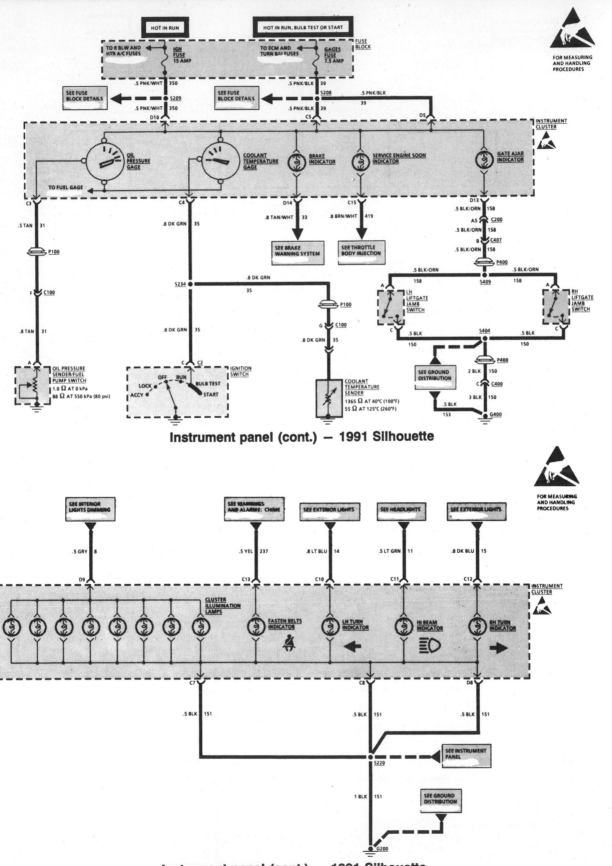

Instrument panel (cont.) — 1991 Silhouette

Instrument panel (cont.) — 1991 Silhouette

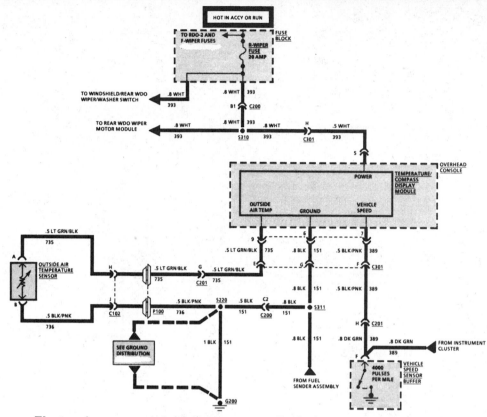

Electronic compass (with temperature display) — 1991 Silhouette

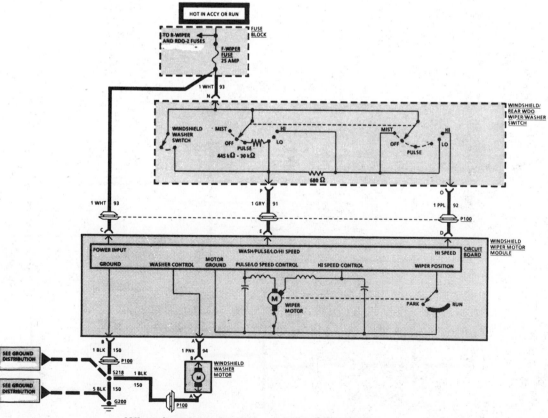

Wiper/washer: (pulse) — 1991 Silhouette

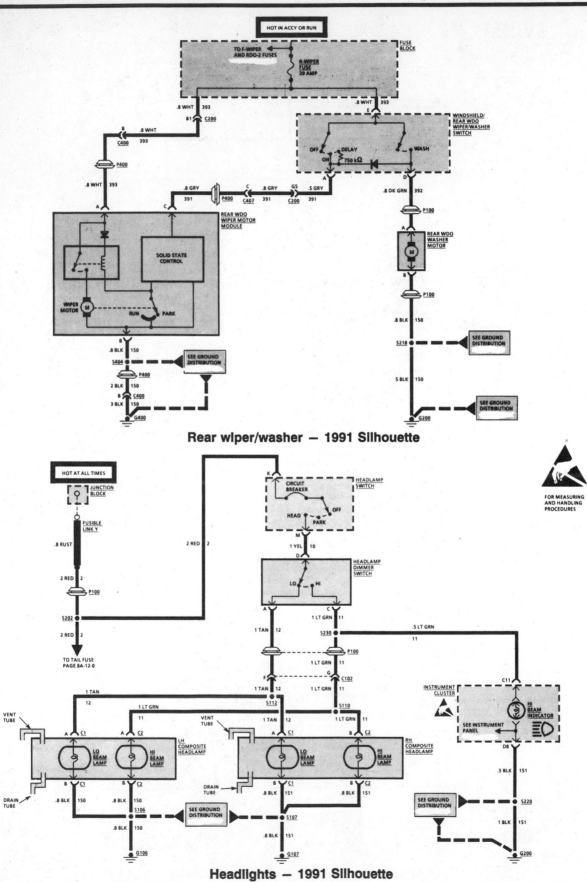

Rear wiper/washer — 1991 Silhouette

Headlights — 1991 Silhouette

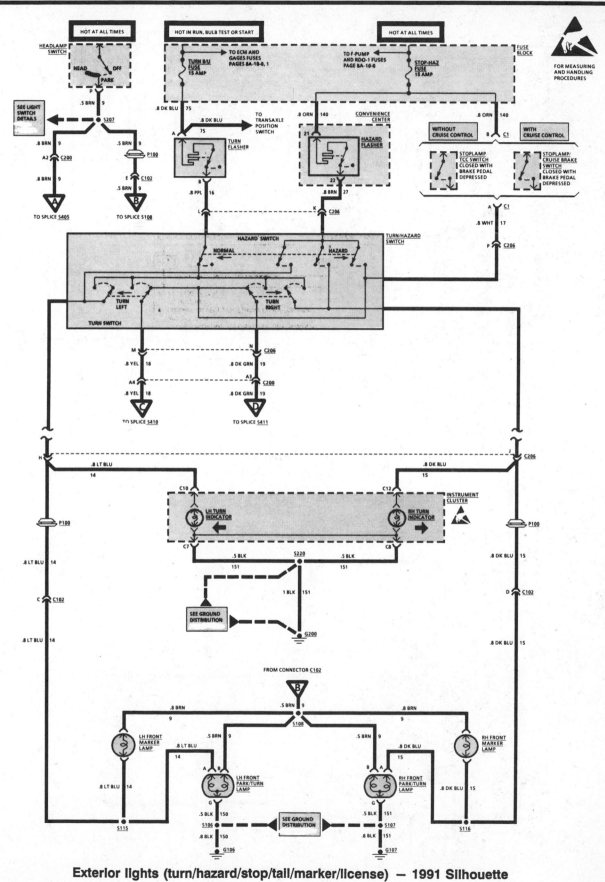

Exterior lights (turn/hazard/stop/tail/marker/license) — 1991 Silhouette

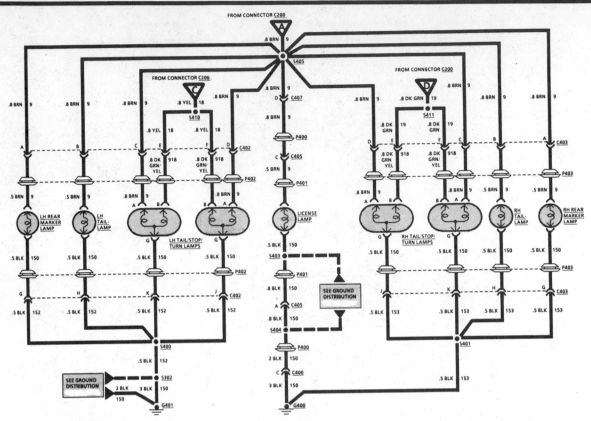

Exterior lights (turn/hazard,stop/tail/marker/license) (cont.) — 1991 Silhouette

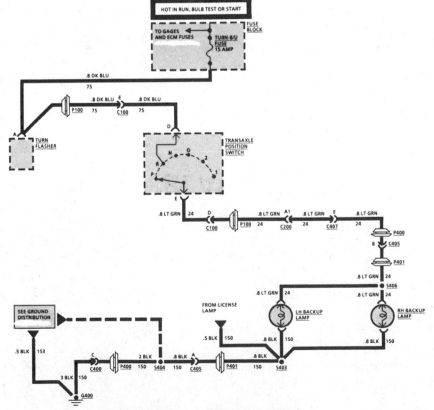

Backup lights — 1991 Silhouette

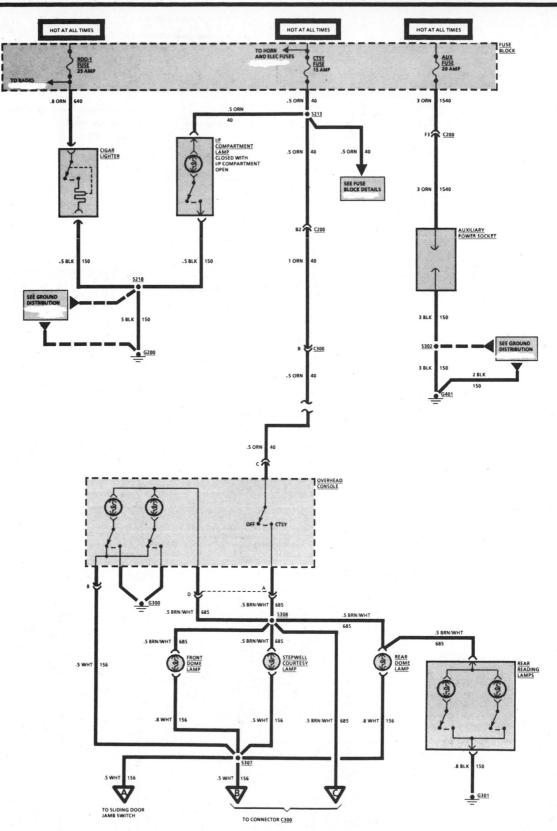

Interior lights (courtesy, dome, I/p compartment, cigar lighter, auxiliary power socket) — 1991 Silhouette

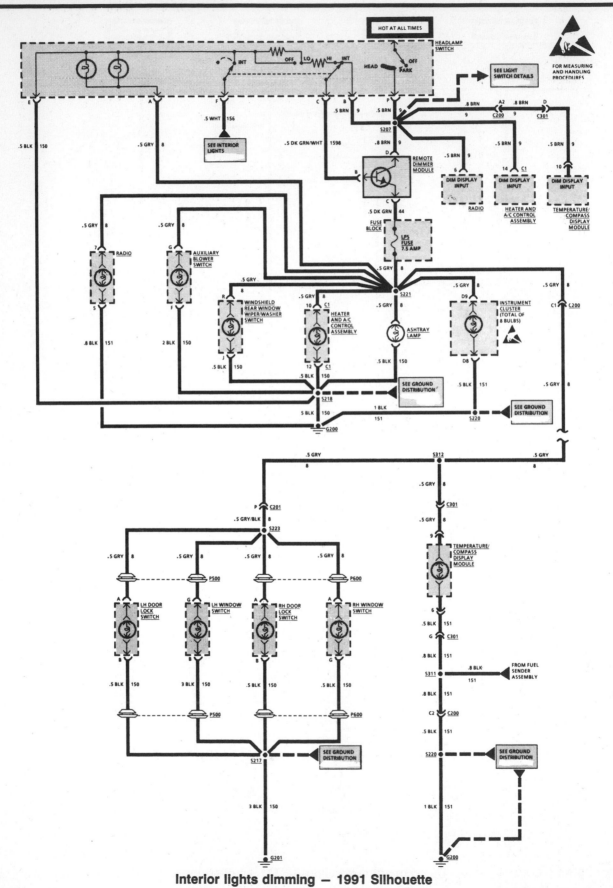

Interior lights dimming – 1991 Silhouette

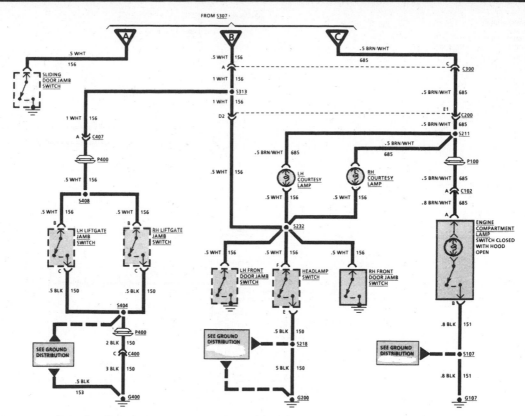

Interior lights (courtesy and engine compartment) — 1991 Silhouette

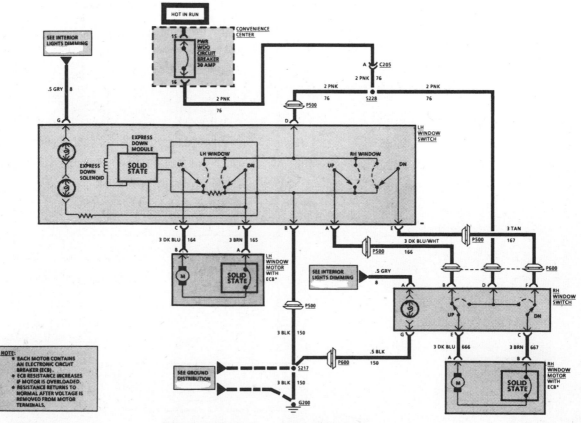

Power windows — 1991 Silhouette

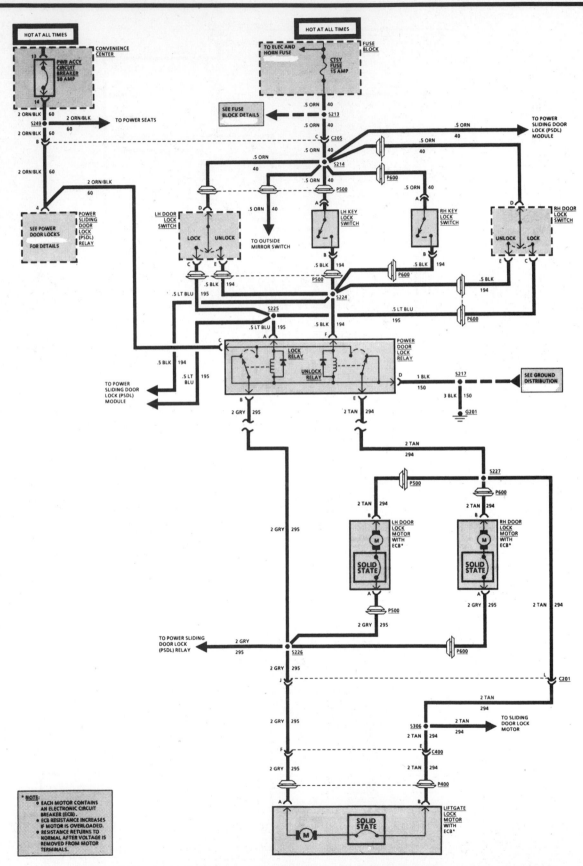

Power door locks (rh and lh door and liftgate lock motor control) — 1991 Silhouette

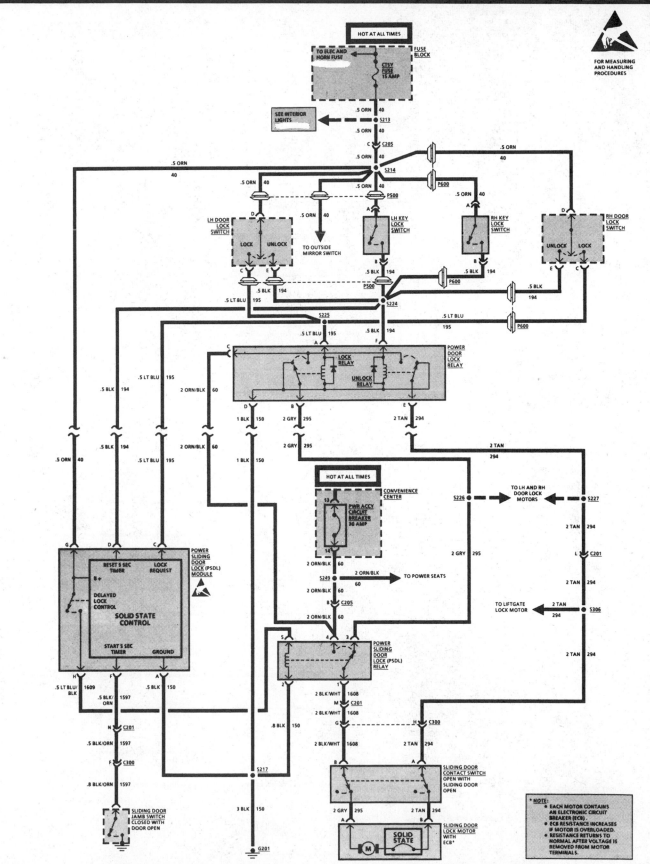

Power door locks (sliding door lock motor control) — 1991 Silhouette

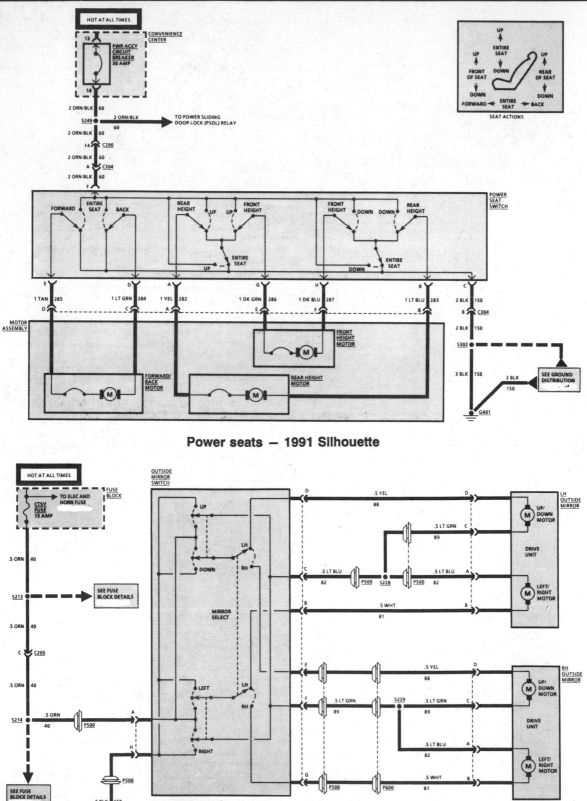

Power seats — 1991 Silhouette

Power mirrors — 1991 Silhouette

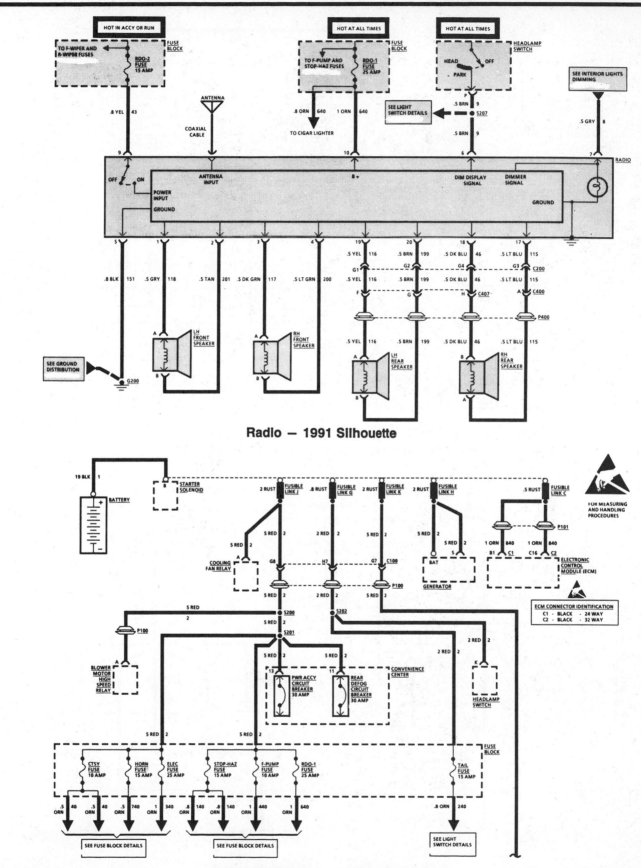

Radio — 1991 Silhouette

Power distribution — 1990 Transport

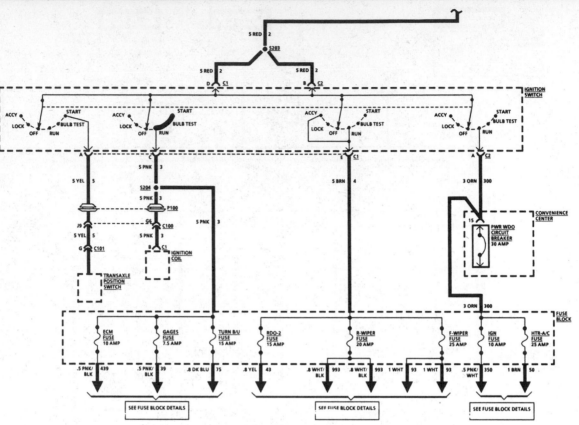

Power distribution (cont.) — 1990 Transport

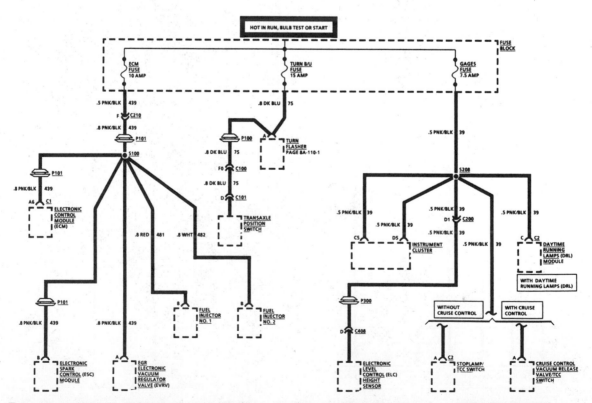

Fuse block details (ECM fuse, turn/back — up fuse and gauges fuse) — 1990 Transport

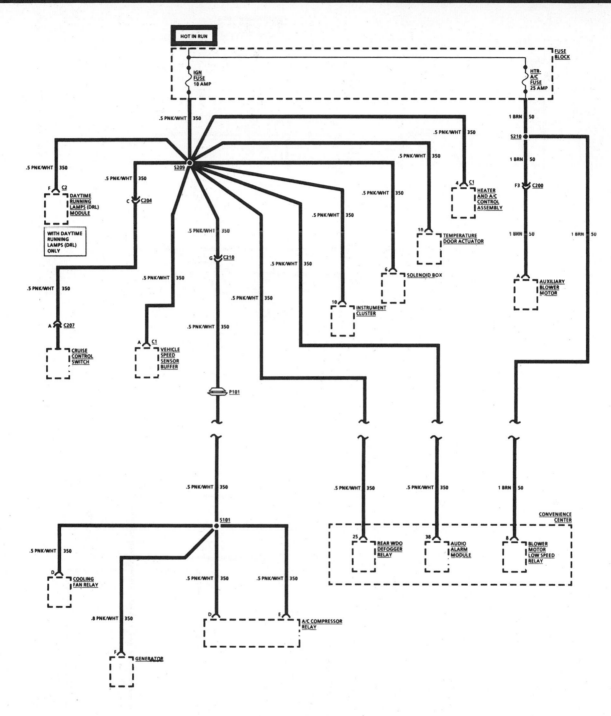

Fuse block details (Ignition fuse and heater/a/c fuse) — 1990 Transport

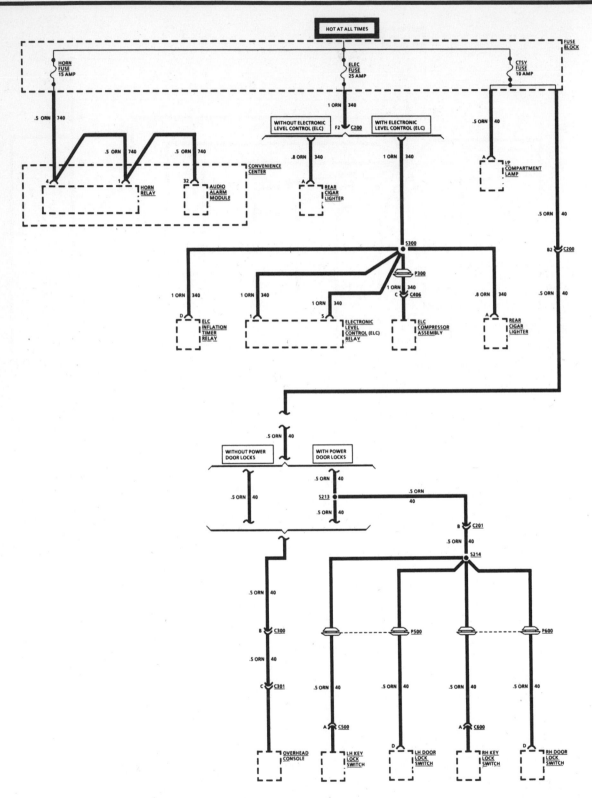

Fuse block details (horn fuse, elec fuse and ctsy fuse) — 1990 Transport

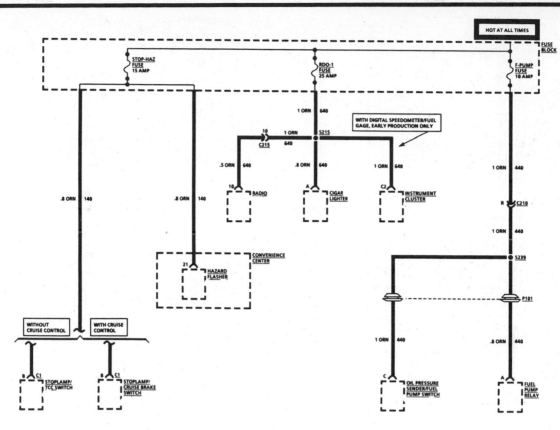

Fuse block details (stop-haz fuse, rdo-1 fuse and f- pump fuse) — 1990 Transport

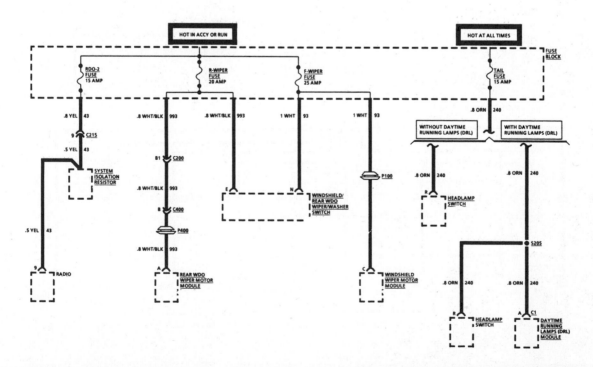

Fuse block details (rdo-2 fuse, r-wiper fuse, f-wiper fuse and tail fuse) — 1990 Transport

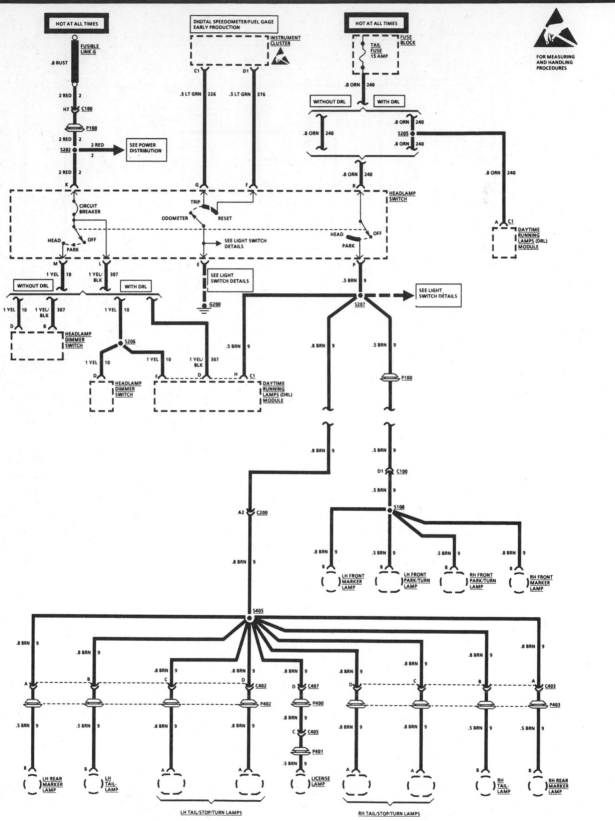

Light switch details — 1990 Transport

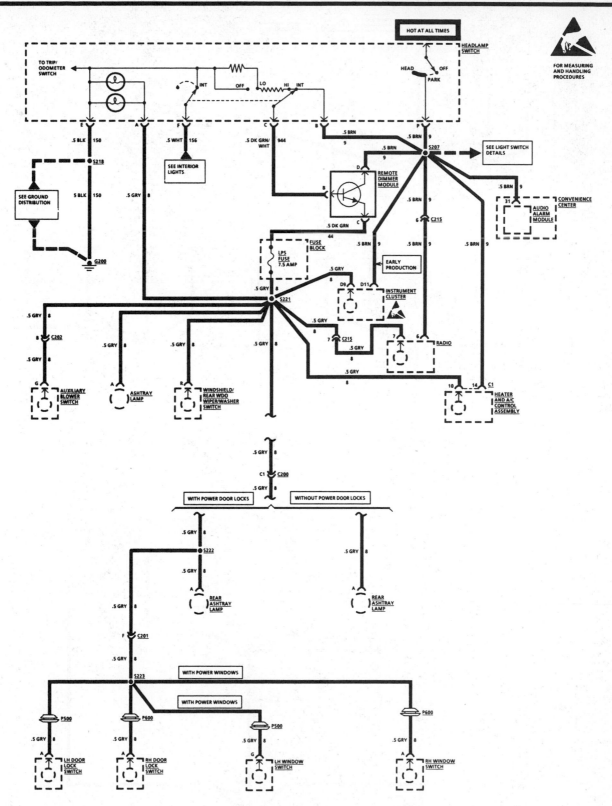

Light switch details (cont.) — 1990 Transport

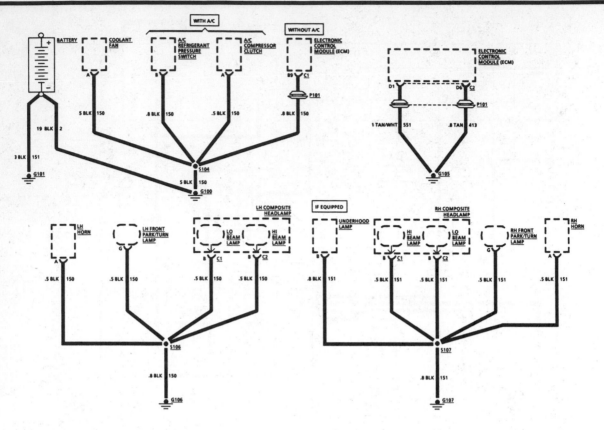

Ground distribution: (G100, G101, G105, G106 and G107) — 1990 Transport

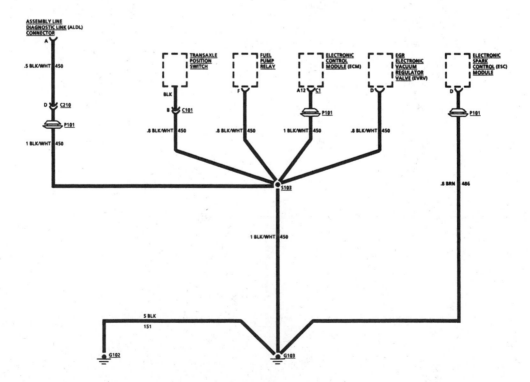

Ground distribution: (G102 and G103) — 1990 Transport

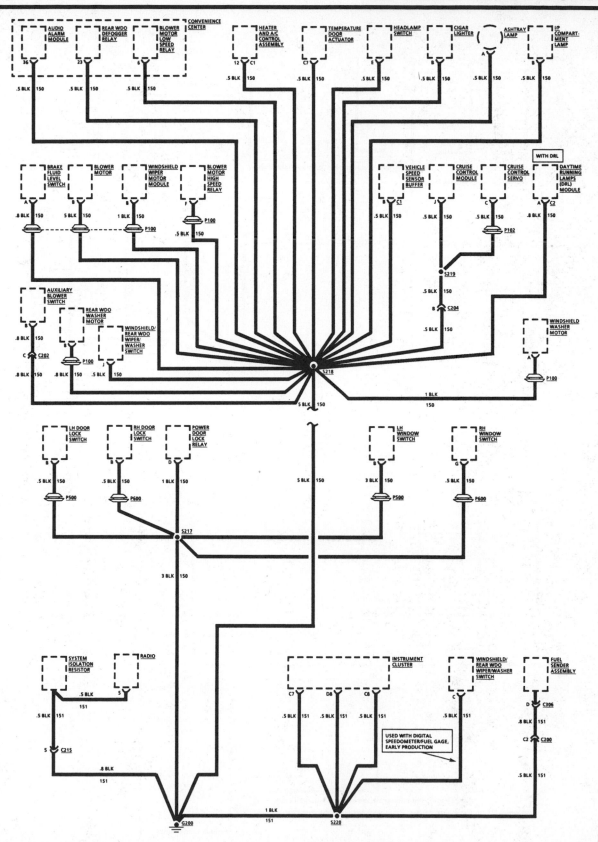

Ground distribution: (G200) — 1990 Transport

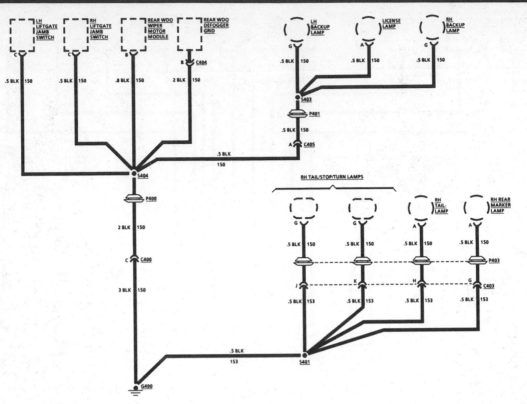

Ground distribution: (G400) — 1990 Transport

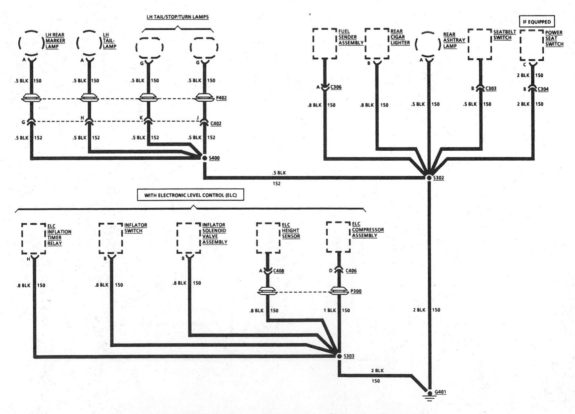

Ground distribution: (G401) — 1990 Transport

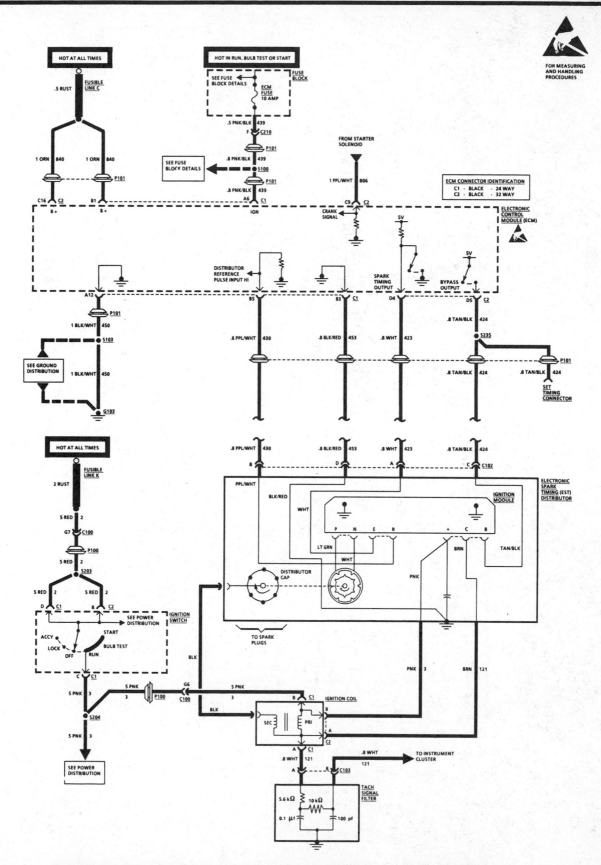

Throttle body Injection: (power, ground and ignition) — 1990 Transport

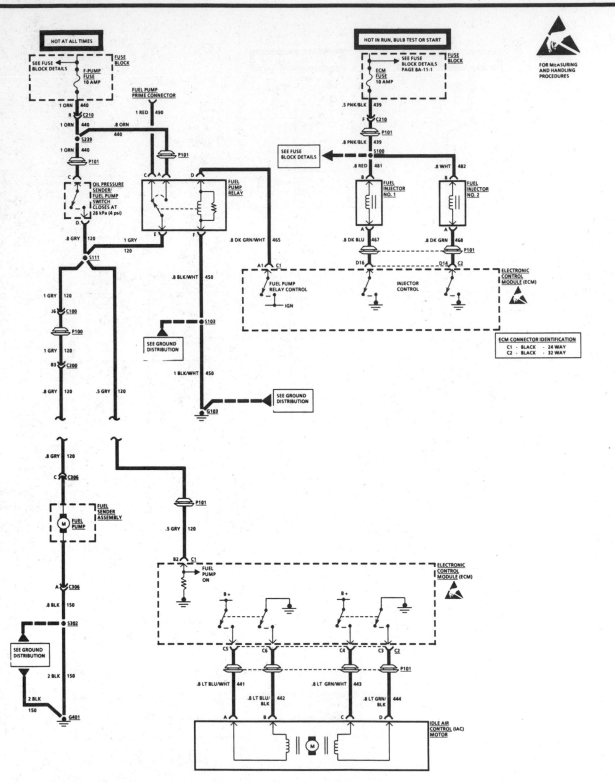

Throttle body injection: (3.1L V6 fuel control, idle air control) — 1990 Transport

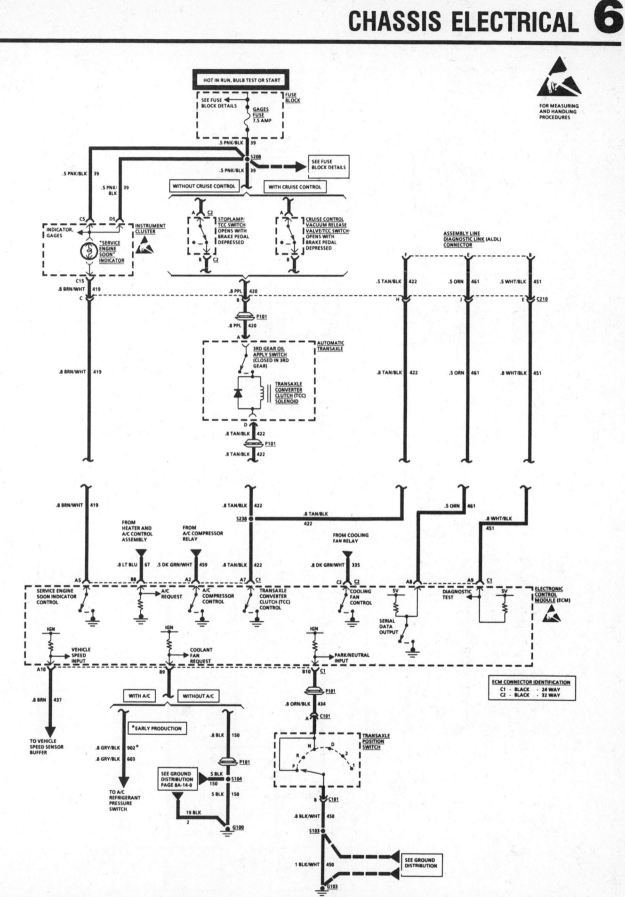

FOR MEASURING AND HANDLING PROCEDURES

Throttle body Injection: (3.1L V6 transaxle converter clutch, service engine soon indicator, transaxle position switch) — 1990 Transport

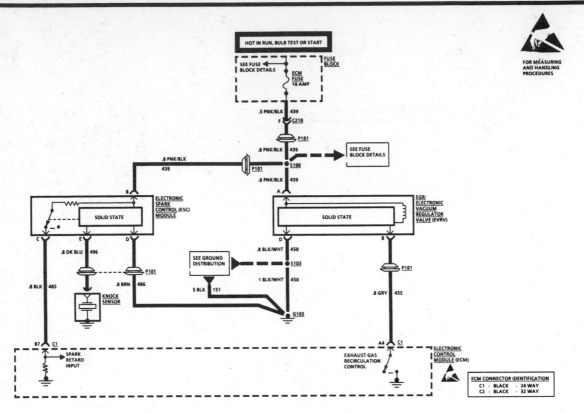

Throttle body injection: (3.1L V6 engine data sensors, spark control, emission control) -- 1990 Transport

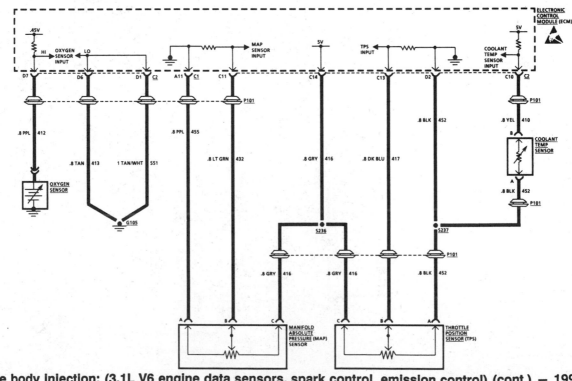

Throttle body injection: (3.1L V6 engine data sensors, spark control, emission control) (cont.) — 1990 Transport

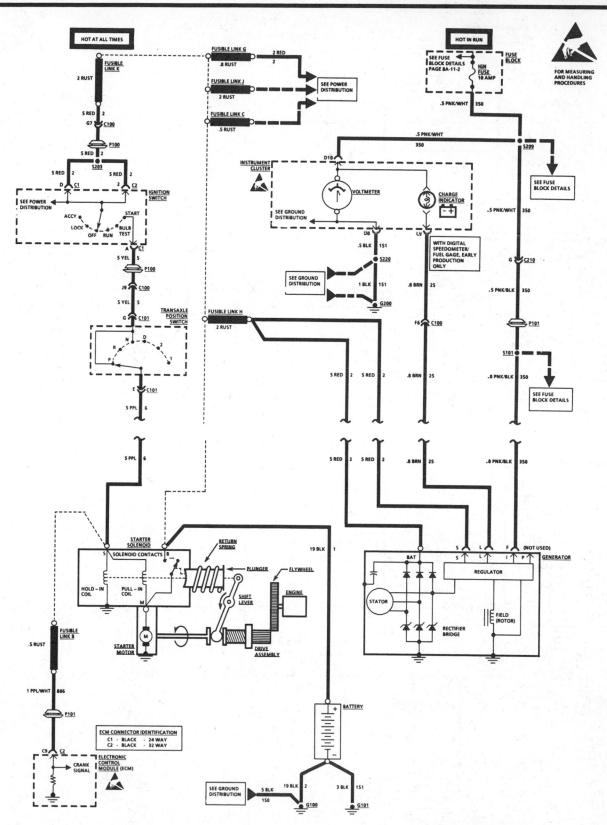

Starter and charging system — 1990 Transport

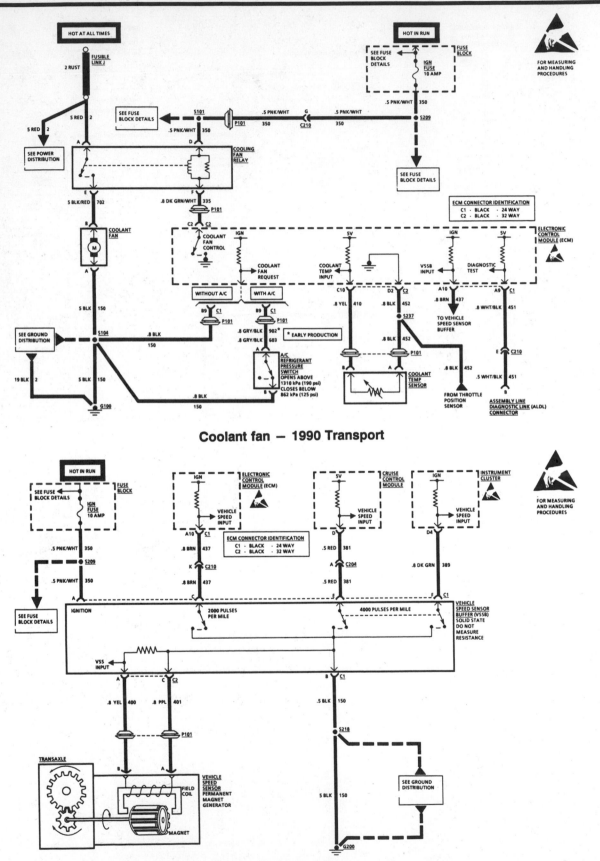

Coolant fan — 1990 Transport

Vehicle speed sensor: (permanent magnet generator) — 1990 Transport

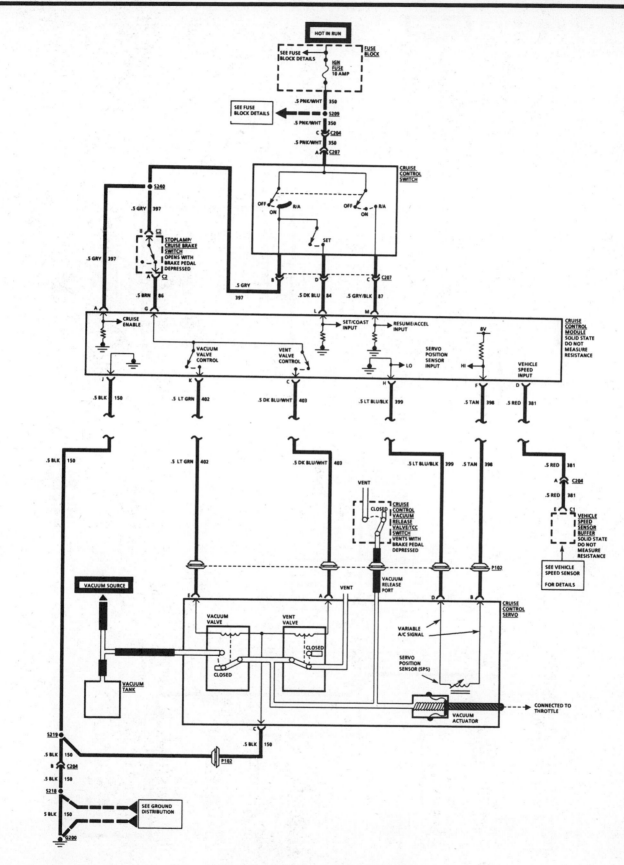

Cruise control — 1990 Transport

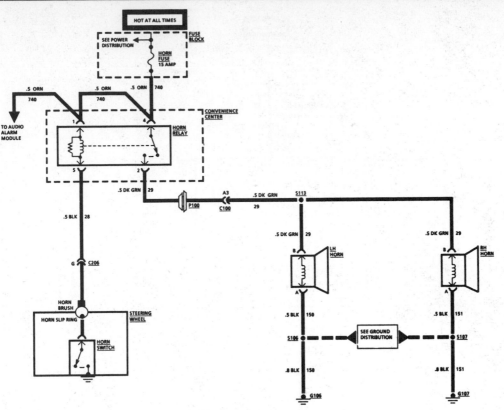

Horns — 1990 Transport

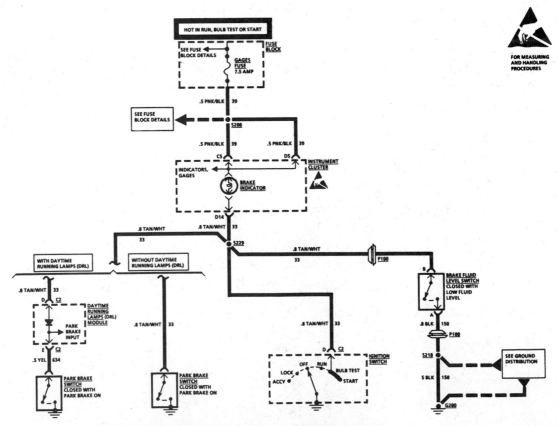

Brake warning system — 1990 Transport

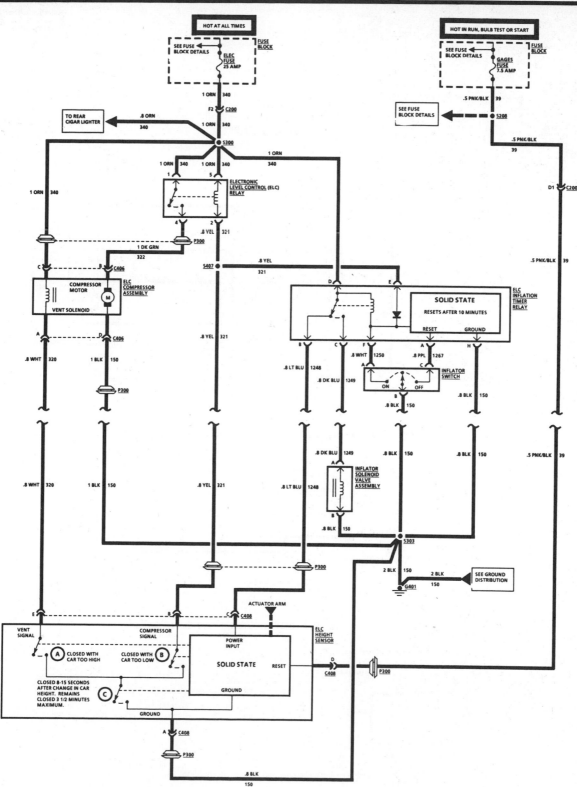

Electronic level control — 1990 Transport

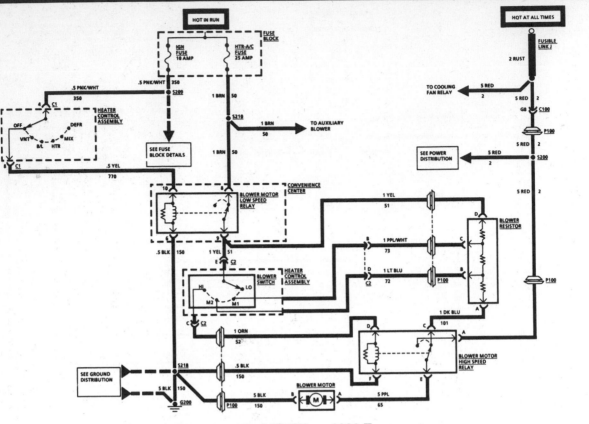

Heater (blower control (C40)) — 1990 Transport

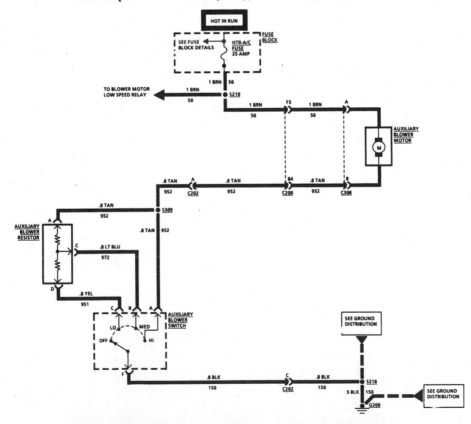

Heater (auxiliary blower control) — 1990 Transport

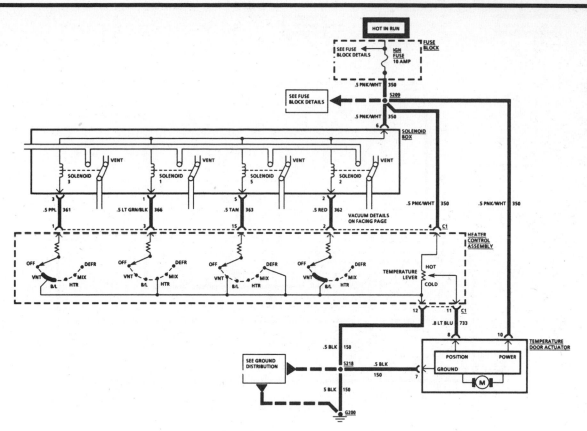

Heater (air delivery and temperature control (C40) — 1990 Transport

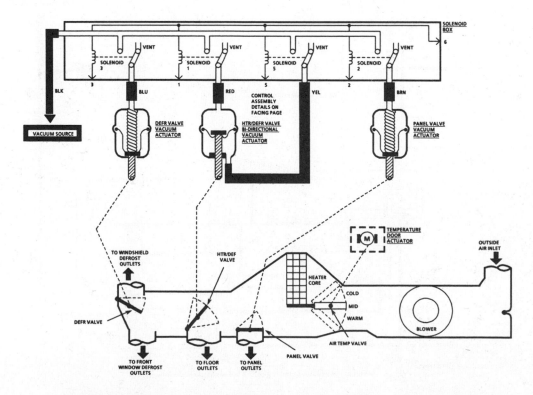

Heater (air delivery and temperature control (C40) — 1990 Transport

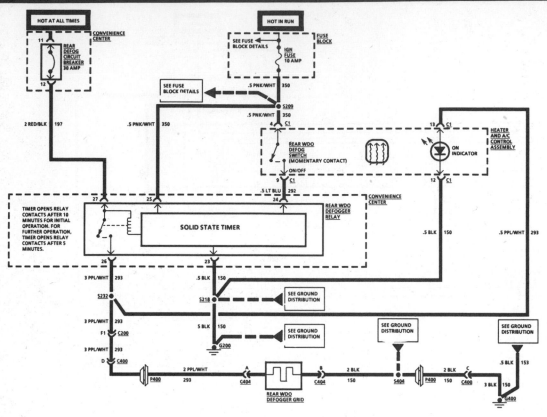

Rear defogger — 1990 Transport

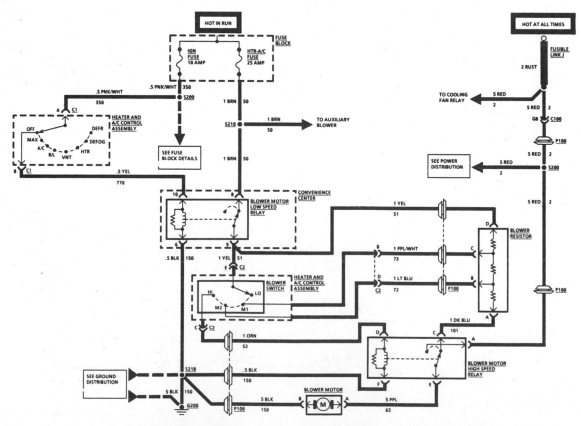

Air conditioning (blower motor control (C67) — 1990 Transport

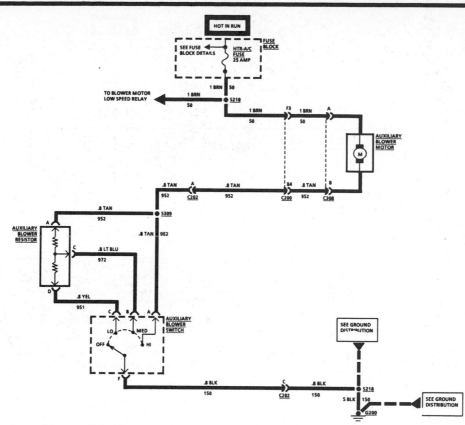

Air conditioning (auxiliary blower motor (C57)) — 1990 Transport

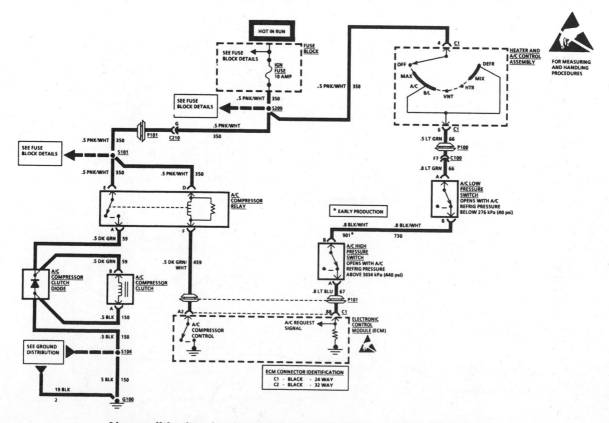

Air conditioning (compressor control (C67)) — 1990 Transport

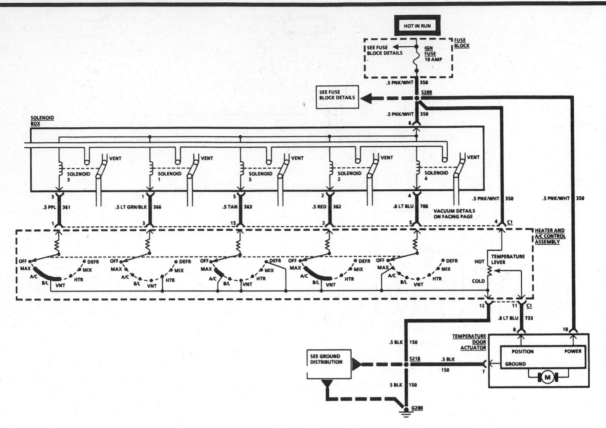

Air conditioning (air delivery and temperature control (C67) — 1990 Transport

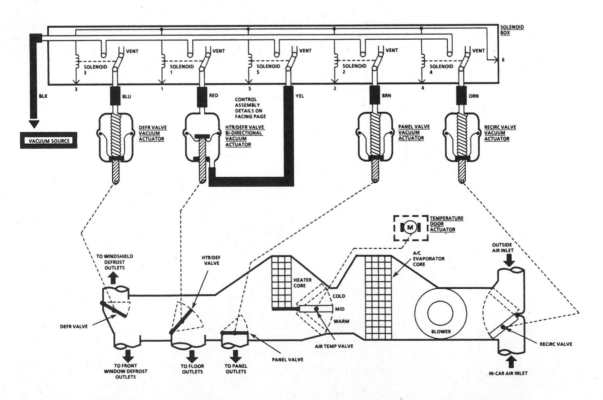

Air conditioning (air delivery and temperature control (C67) — 1990 Transport

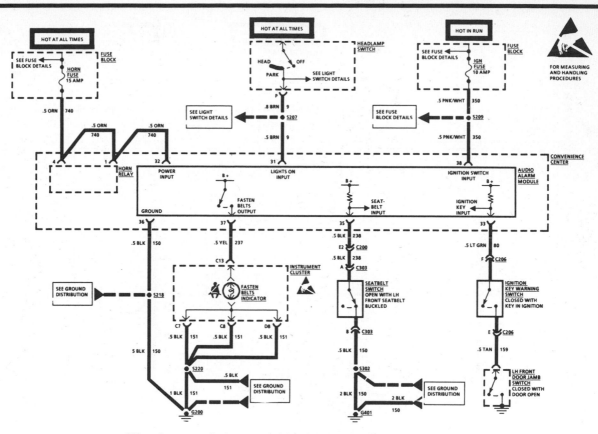

Warnings and alarms: (chime) — 1990 Transport

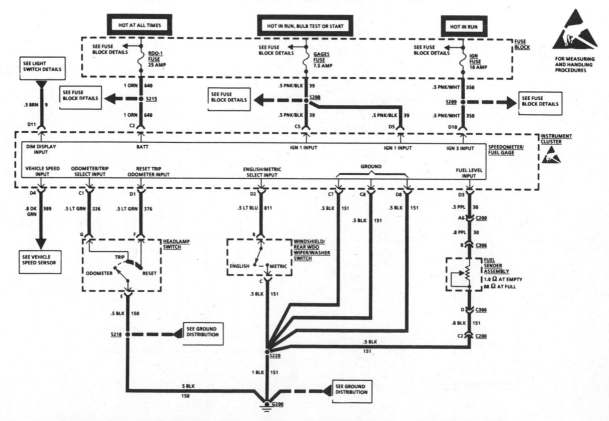

Instrument panel (digital speedometer and fuel gauge — 1990 Transport

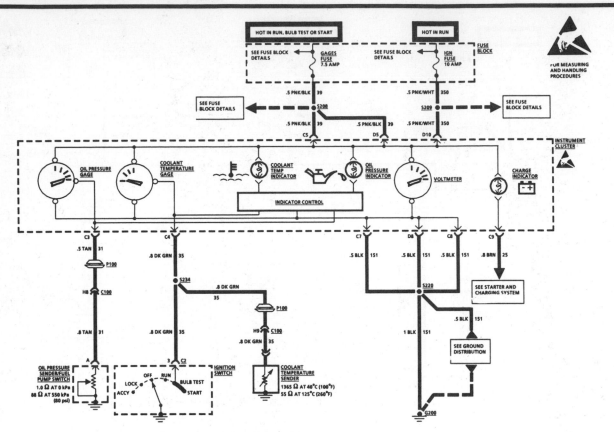

Instrument panel (digital speedometer and fuel gauge — 1990 Transport

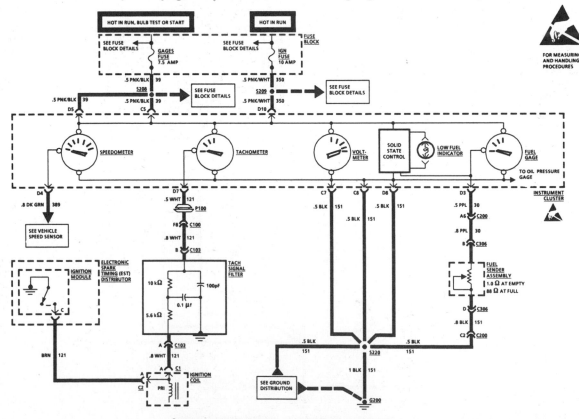

Instrument panel — 1990 Transport

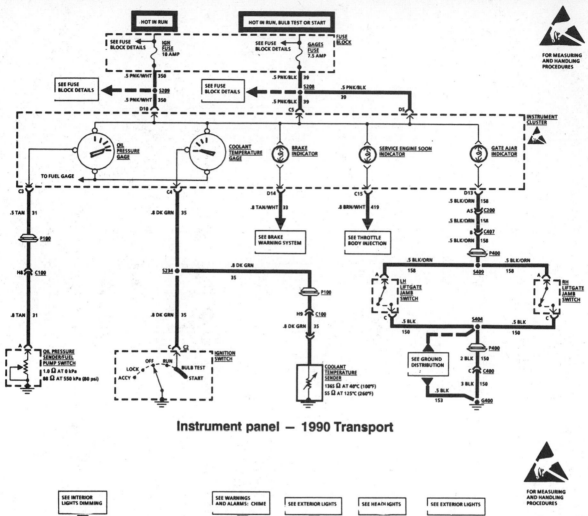

Instrument panel — 1990 Transport

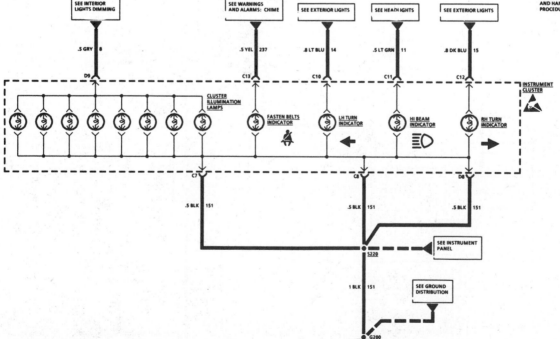

Instrument panel — 1990 Transport

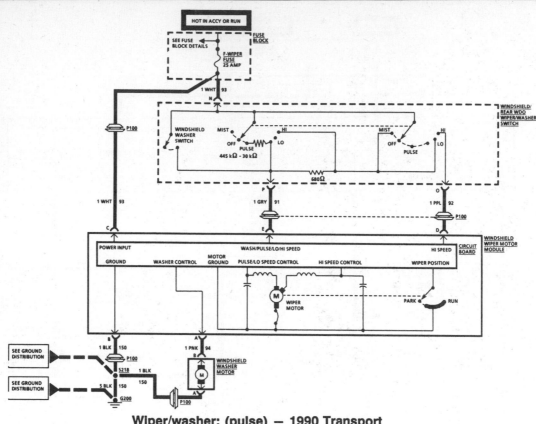

Wiper/washer: (pulse) — 1990 Transport

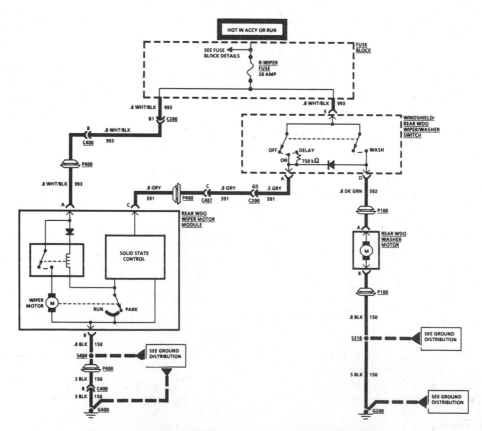

Rear wiper/washer — 1990 Transport

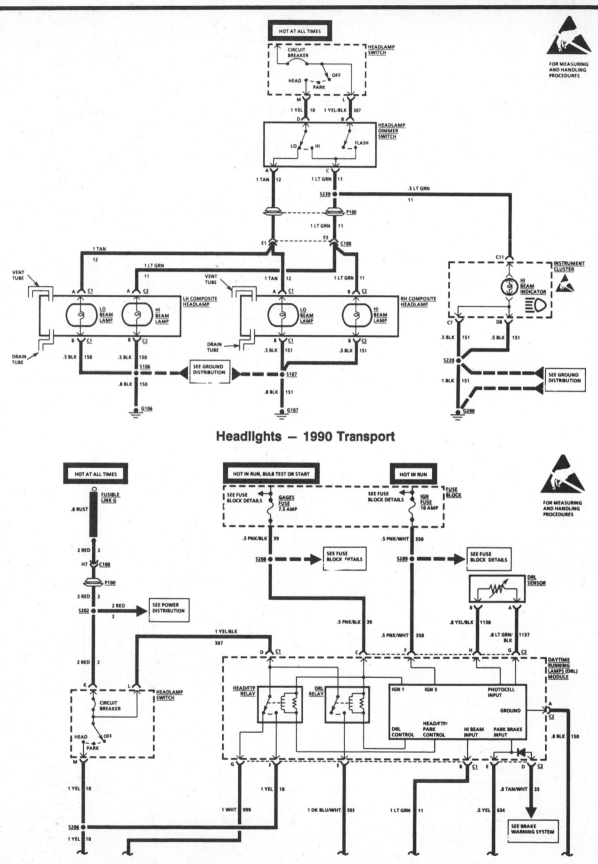

Headlights — 1990 Transport

Headlights: (daytime running lamps (drl), t61) — 1990 Transport

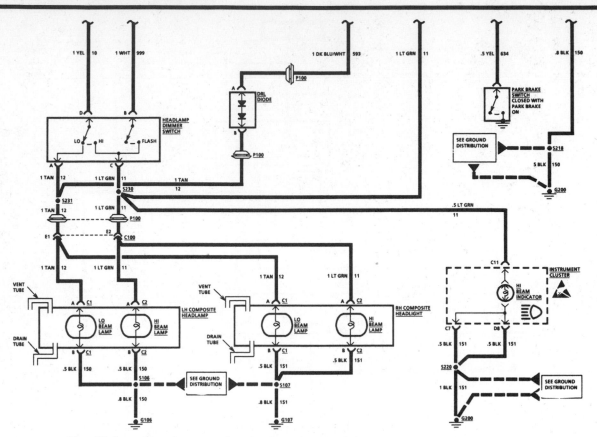

Headlights: (daytime running lamps (drl), t61) (cont.) — 1990 Transport

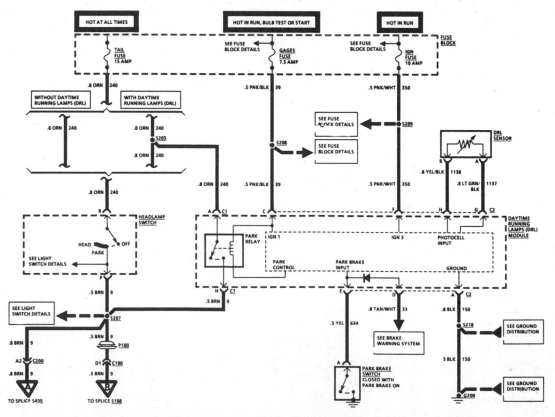

Exterior lights: (turn/hazard/stop/tail/marker/license) — 1990 Transport

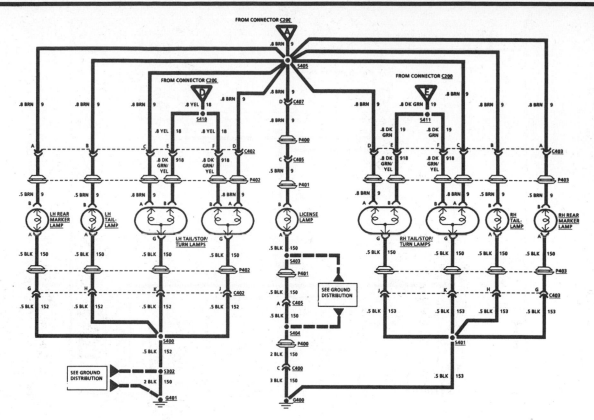

Exterior lights: (turn/hazard/stop/tail/marker/license) (cont.) — 1990 Transport

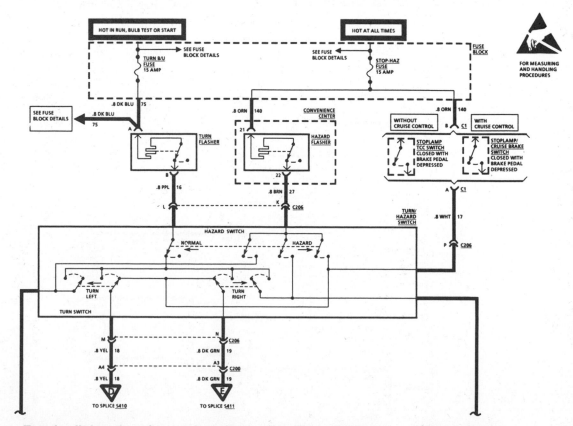

Exterior lights: (turn/hazard/stop/tail/marker/license) (cont.) — 1990 Transport

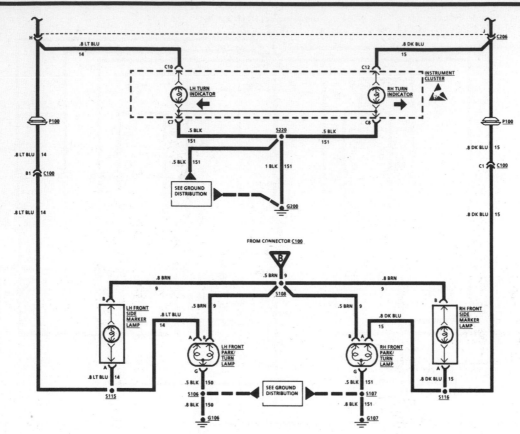

Exterior lights: (turn/hazard/stop/tail/marker/license) (cont.) — 1990 Transport

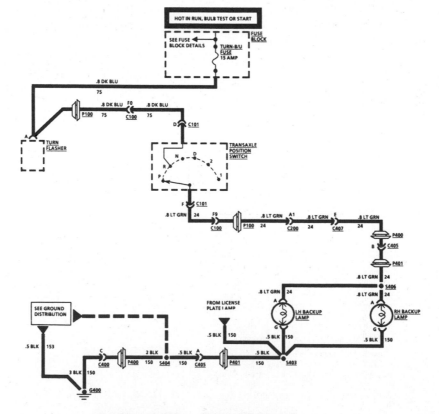

Backup lights — 1990 Transport

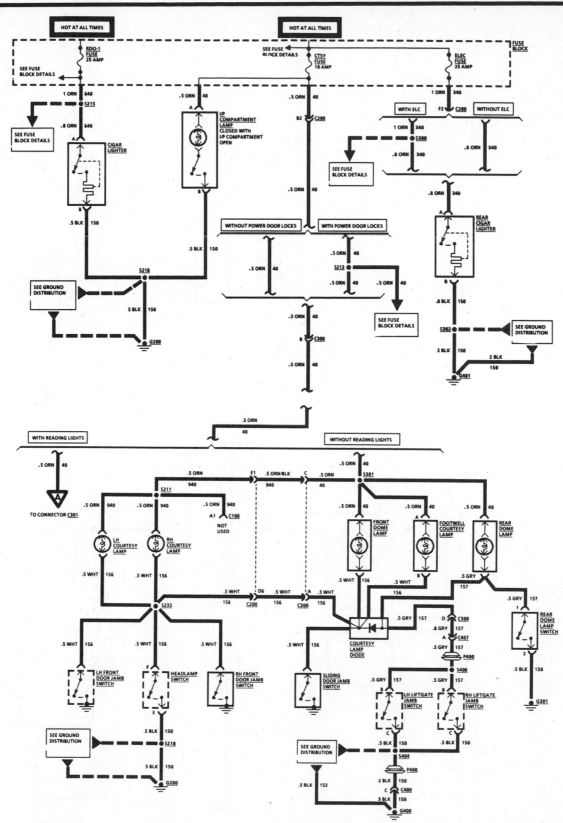

Interior lights (courtesy, dome, I/p compartment, cigar lighter, rear cigar lighter) — 1990 Transport

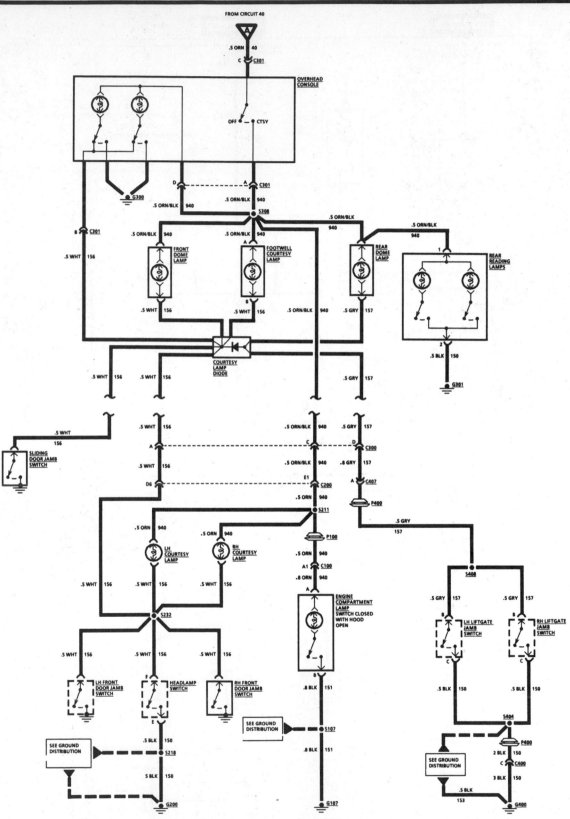

Interior lights (courtesy and engine compartment) — 1990 Transport

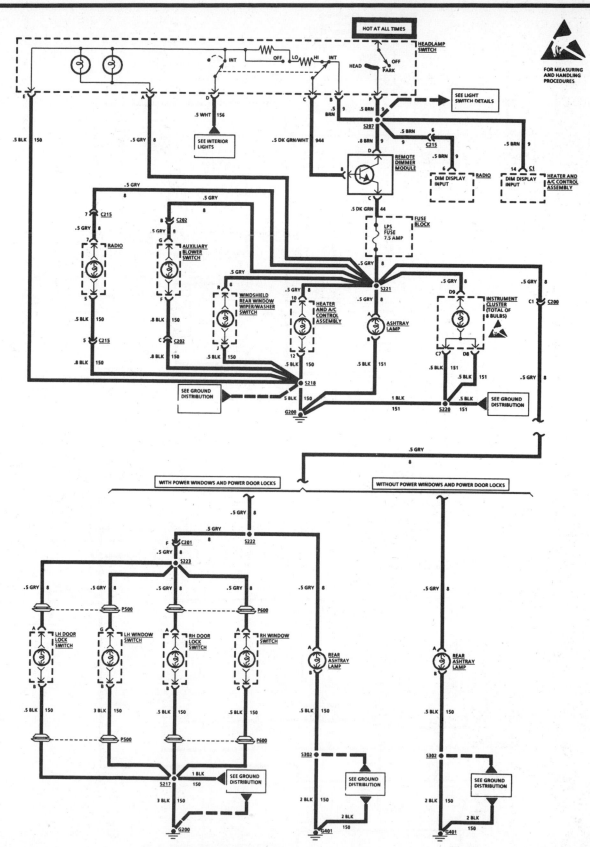

Interior lights (dimming) — 1990 Transport

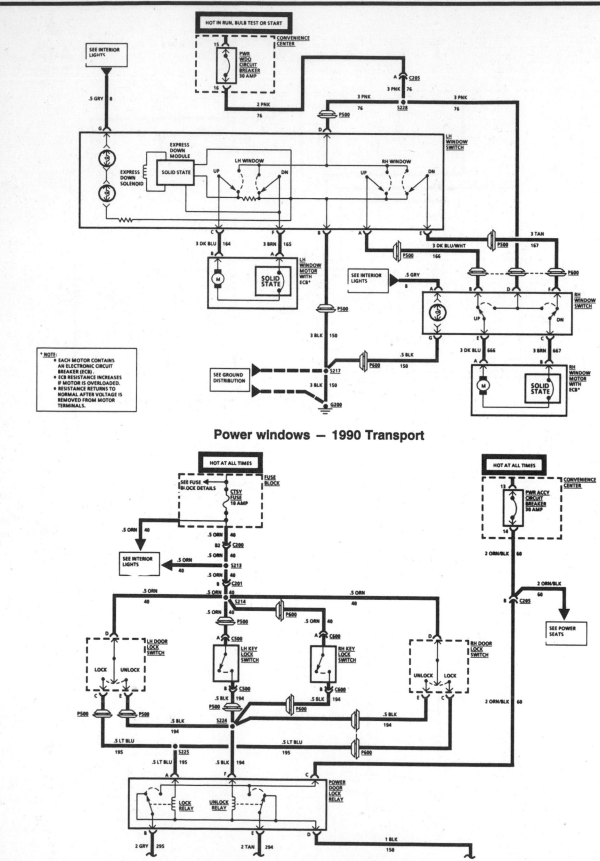

Power windows — 1990 Transport

Power door locks — 1990 Transport

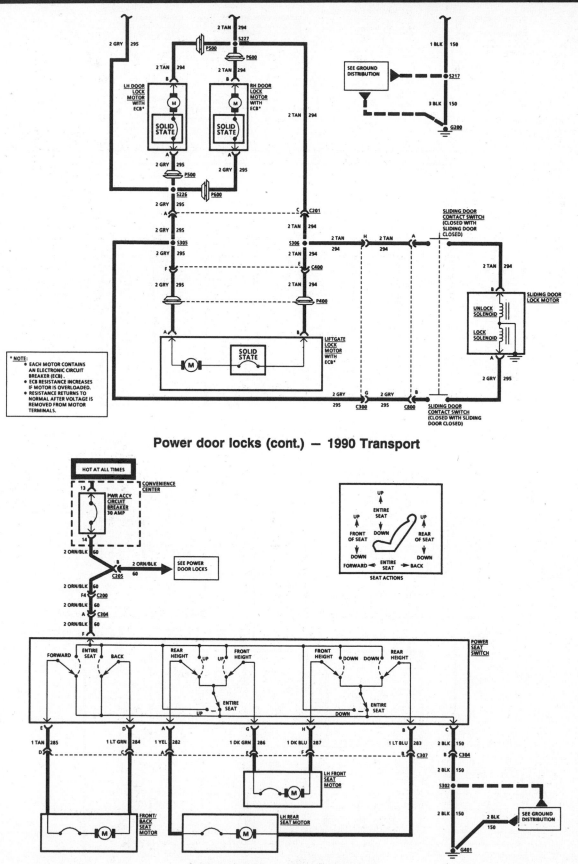

Power door locks (cont.) — 1990 Transport

Power seats — 1990 Transport

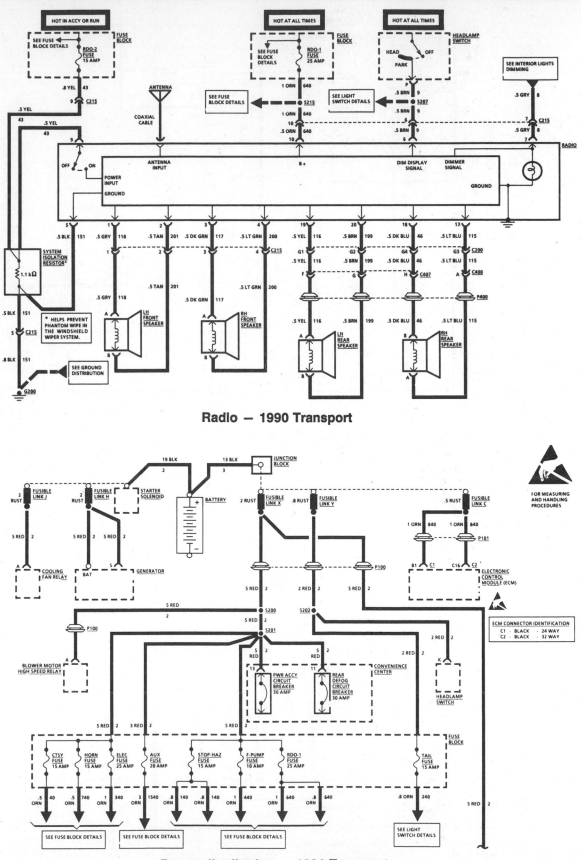

Radio — 1990 Transport

Power distribution — 1991 Transport

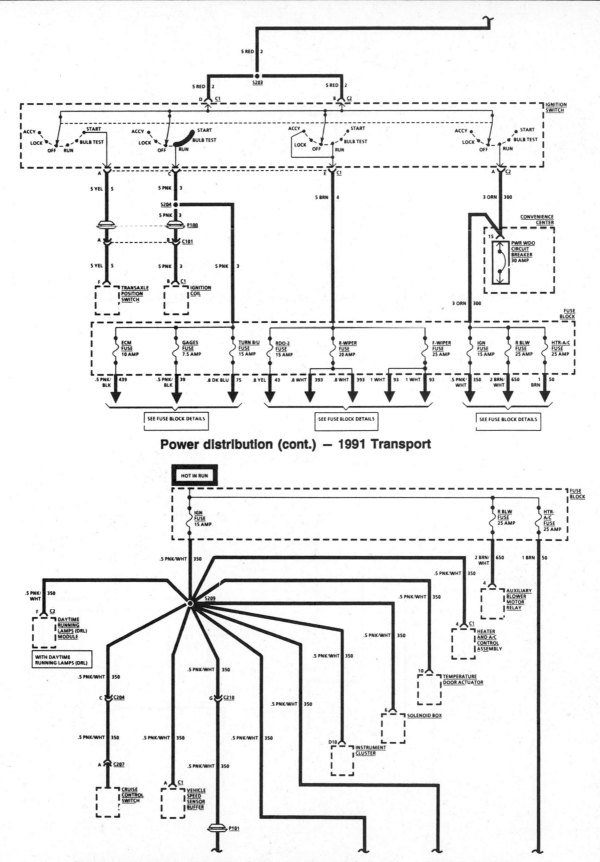

Power distribution (cont.) — 1991 Transport

Fuse block details (Ignition fuse and heater/a/c fuse) — 1991 Transport

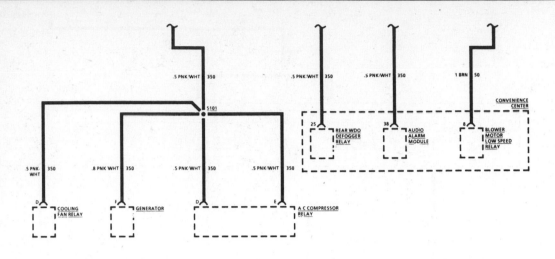

Fuse block details (Ignition fuse and heater/a/c fuse) (cont.) — 1991 Transport

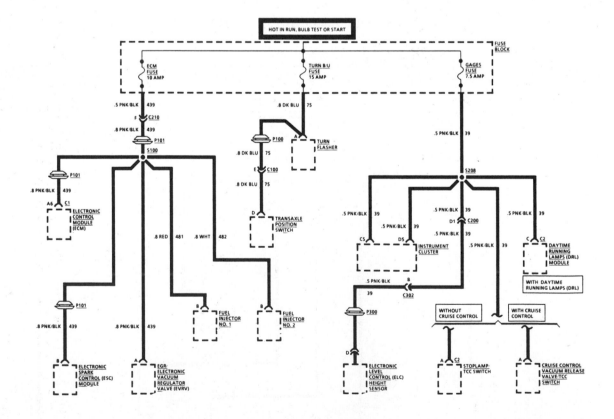

Fuse block details (ECM fuse, turn/back-up fuse and gauges fuse) — 1991 Transport

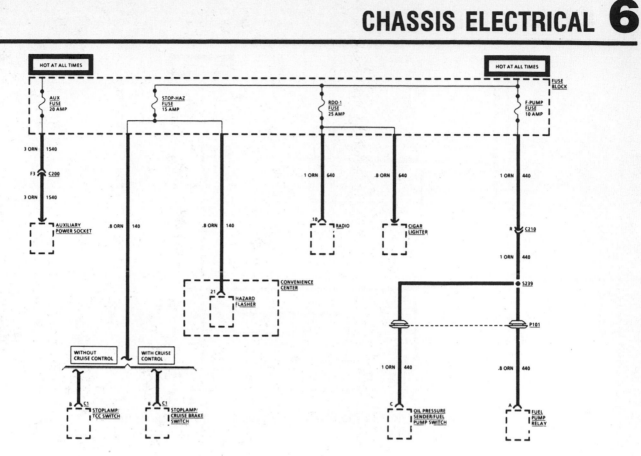

Fuse block details (stop-haz fuse, rdo-1 fuse and f- pump fuse) — 1991 Transport

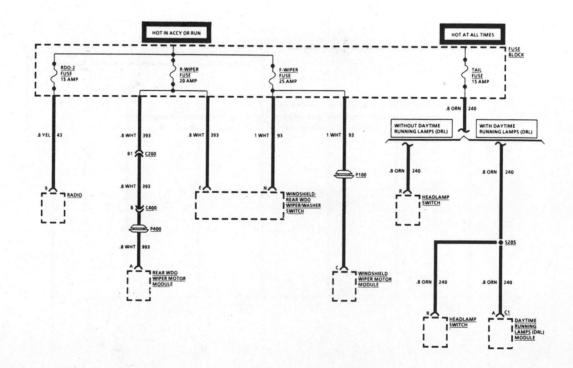

Fuse block details (rdo-2 fuse, r-wiper fuse, f-wiper fuse and tall fuse) — 1991 Transport

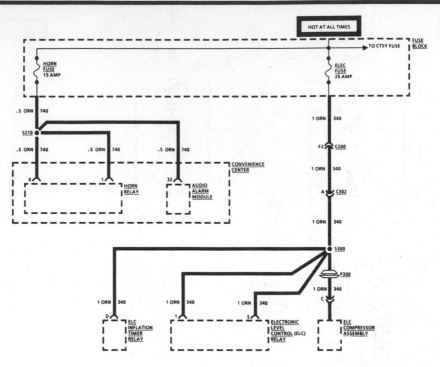

Fuse block details (horn fuse, elec fuse) — 1991 Transport

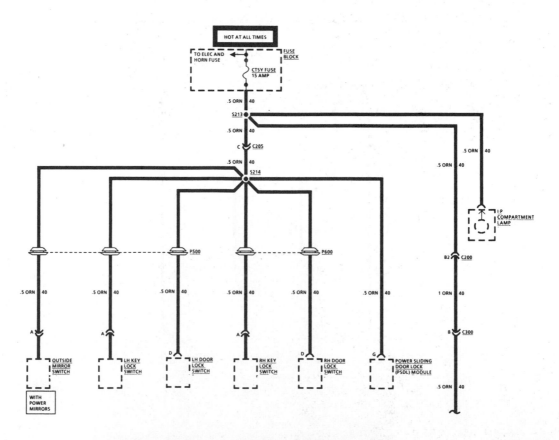

Fuse block details (ctsy fuse) — 1991 Transport

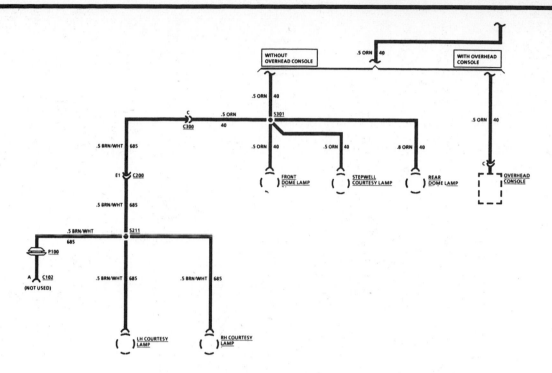

Fuse block details (ctsy fuse) (cont.) — 1991 Transport

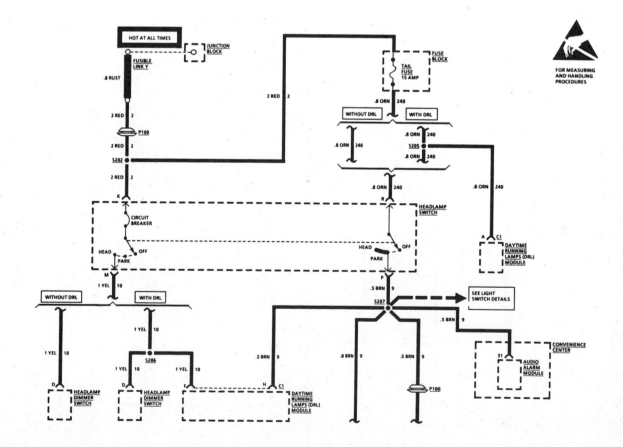

Light switch details — 1991 Transport

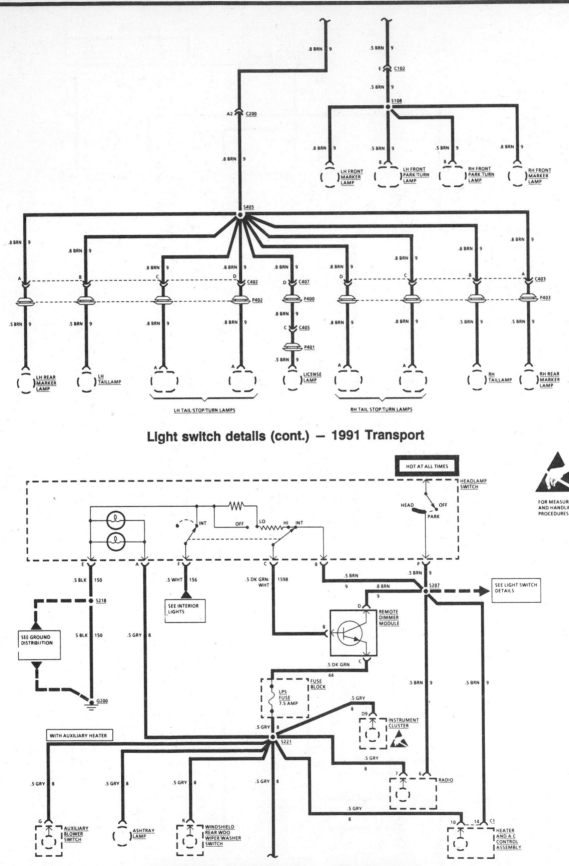

Light switch details (cont.) — 1991 Transport

Light switch details (cont.) — 1991 Transport

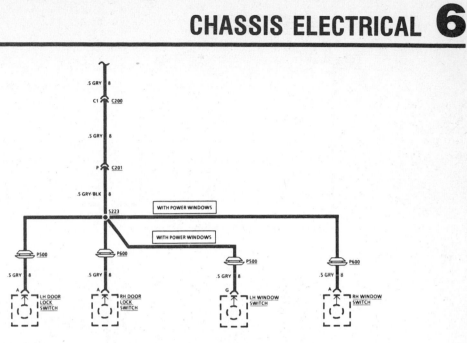

Light switch details (cont.) — 1991 Transport

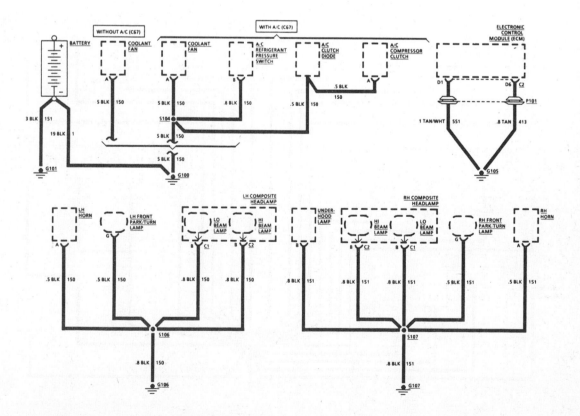

Ground distribution: (G100, G101, G105, G106 and G107) — 1991 Transport

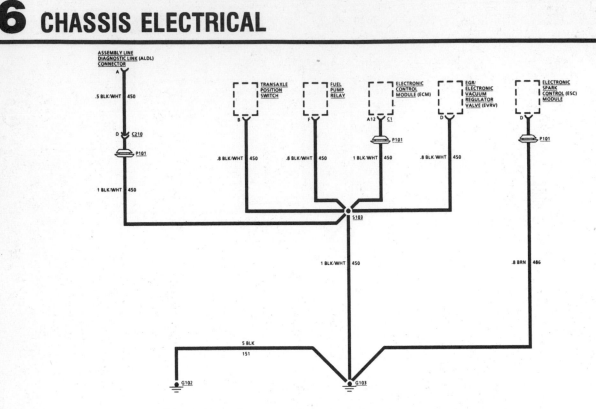

Ground distribution: (G102 and G103) — 1991 Transport

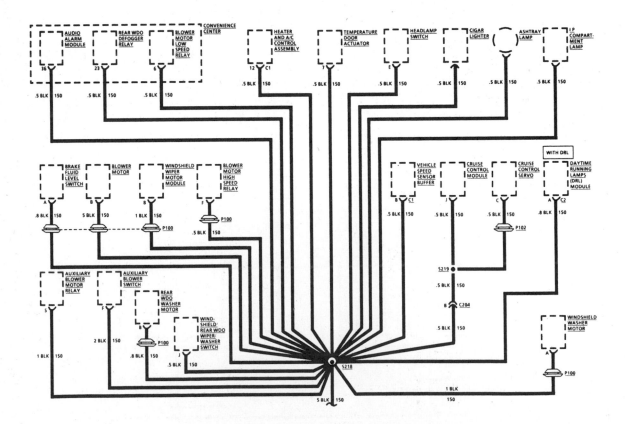

Ground distribution: (G200) — 1991 Transport

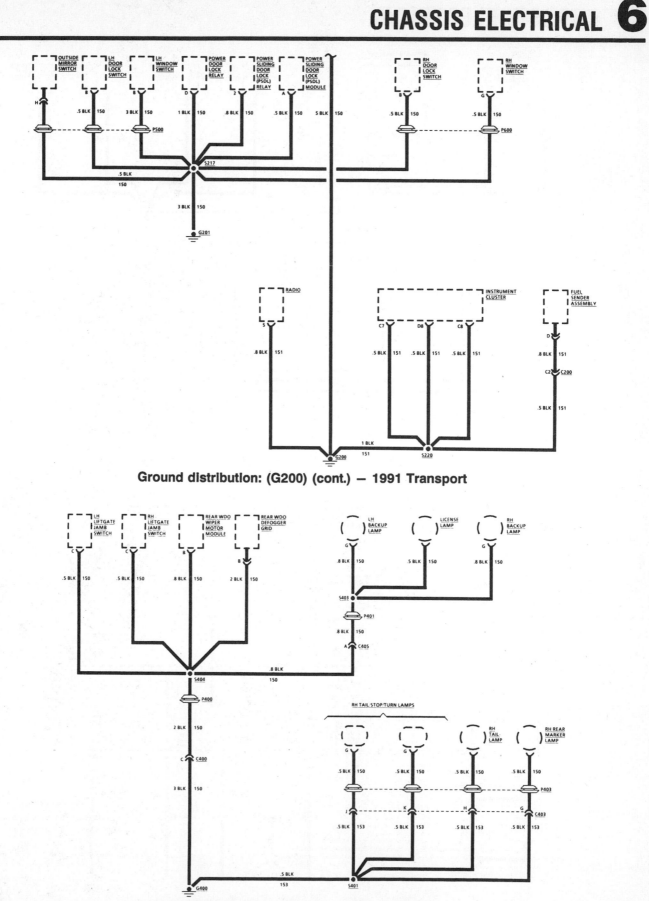

Ground distribution: (G200) (cont.) – 1991 Transport

Ground distribution: (G400) – 1991 Transport

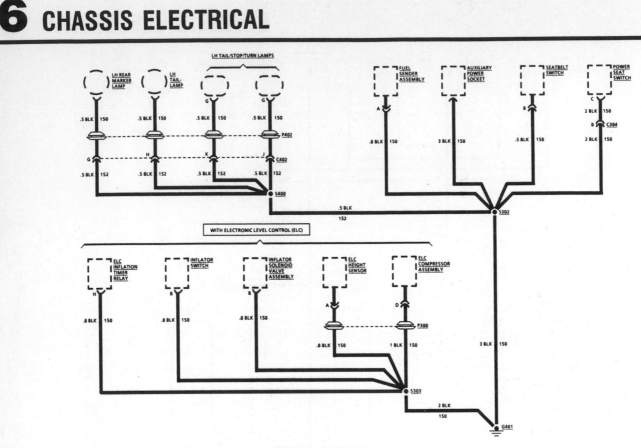

Ground distribution: (G401) — 1991 Transport

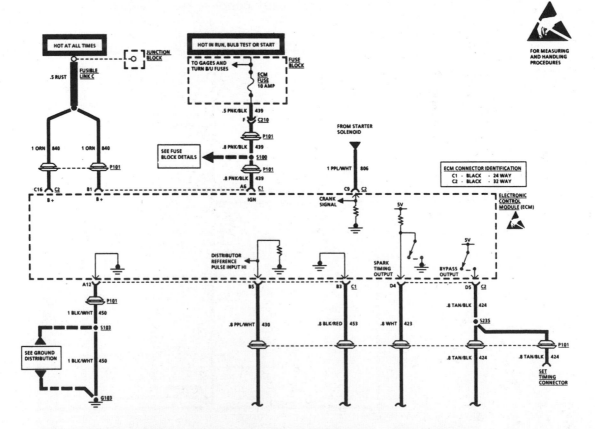

Throttle body injection: (power, ground and ignition) — 1991 Transport

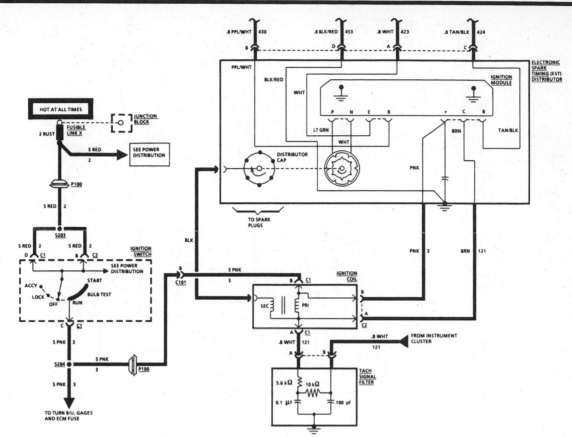

Throttle body Injection: (power, ground and Ignition) (Cont.) — 1991 Transport

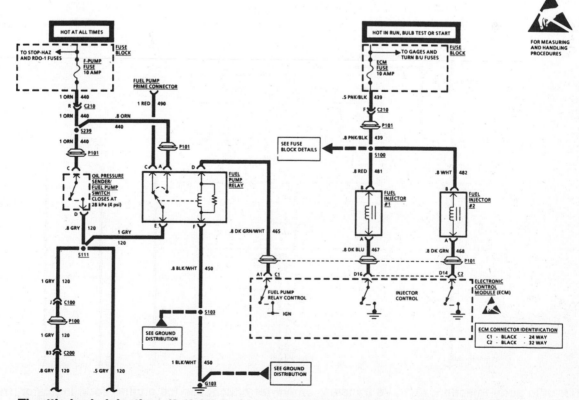

Throttle body Injection: (3.1L V6 fuel control, Idle air control) — 1991 Transport

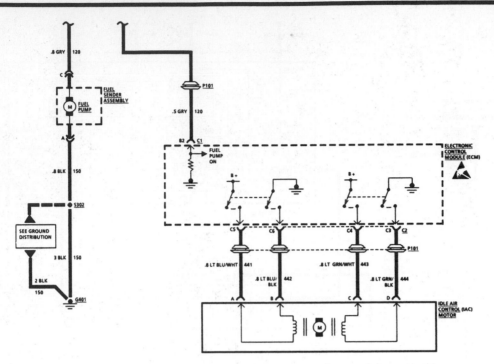

Throttle body injection: (3.1L fuel control, idle air control) (cont.) — 1991 Transport

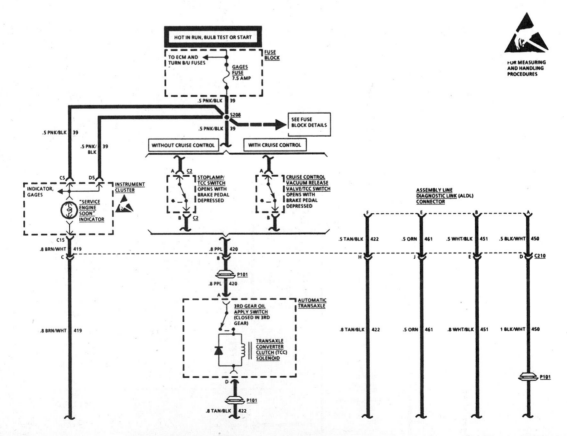

Throttle body injection: (3.1L V6 transaxle converter clutch, service engine soon indicator, transaxle position switch) — 1991 Transport

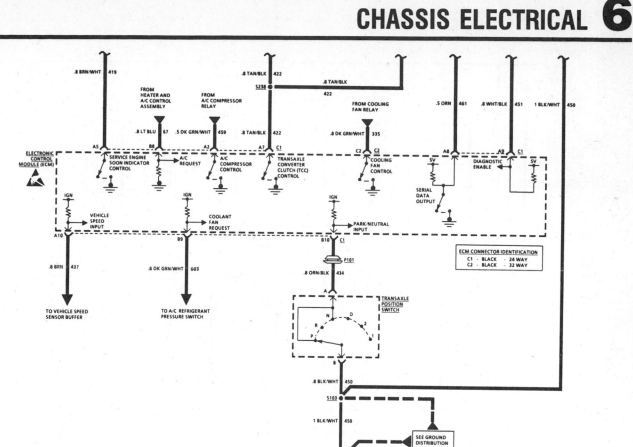

Throttle body Injection: (3.1L V6 transaxle converter clutch, service engine soon indicator, transaxle position switch) (cont.) — 1991 Transport

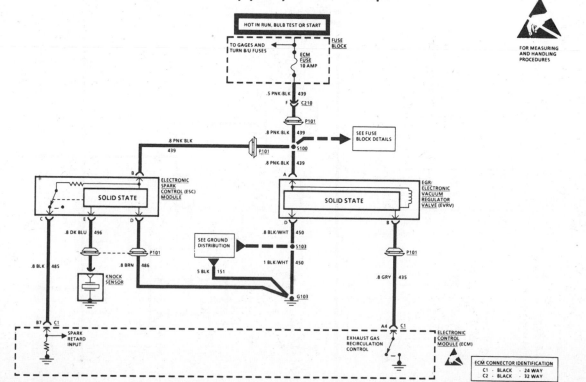

Throttle body Injection: (3.1L V6 engine data sensors, spark control, emission control) — 1991 Transport

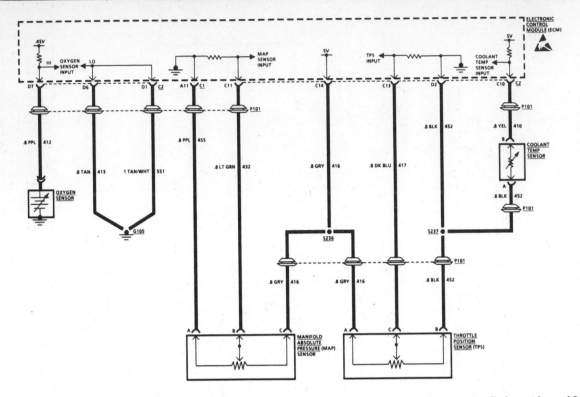

Throttle body injection: (3.1L V6 engine data sensors, spark control, emission control) (cont.) — 1991 Transport

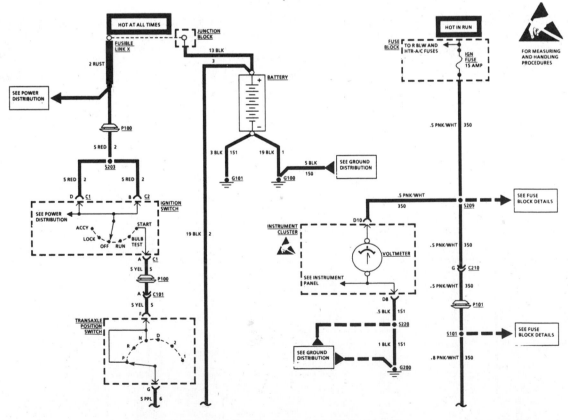

Starter and charging system — 1991 Transport

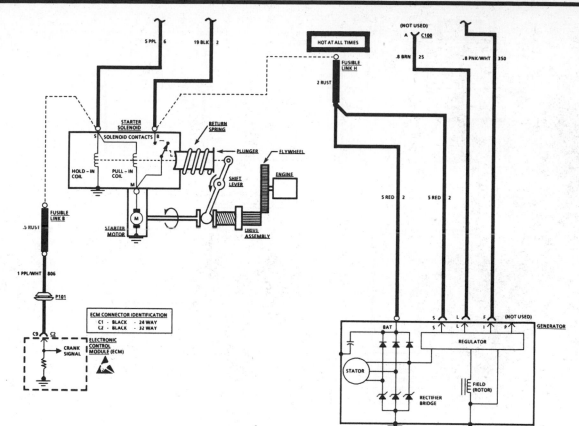

Starter and charging system (cont.) — 1991 Transport

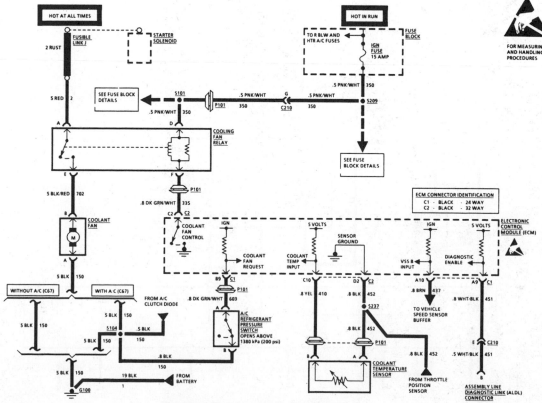

Coolant fan — 1991 Transport

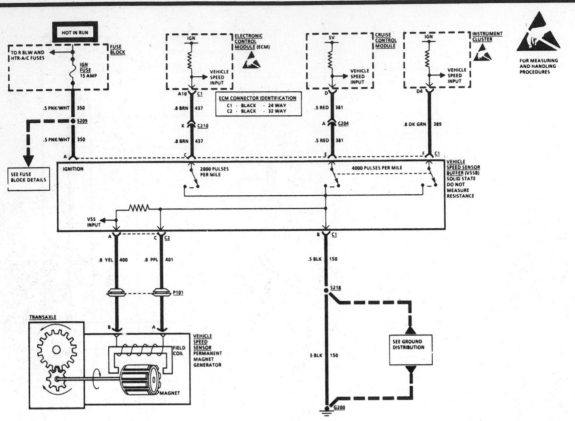

Vehicle speed sensor: (permanent magnet generator) — 1991 Transport

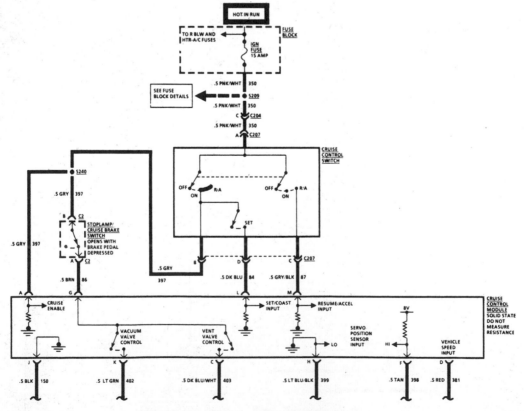

Cruise control — 1991 Transport

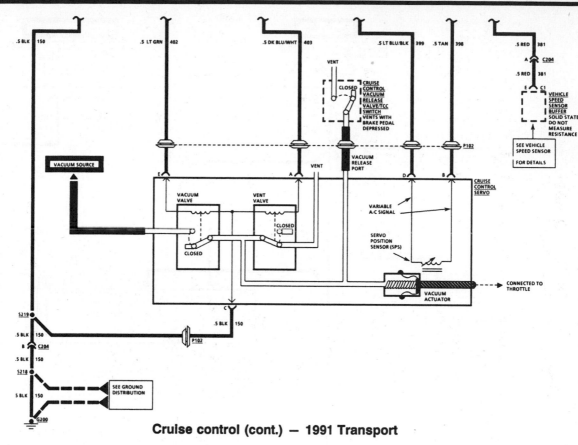

Cruise control (cont.) — 1991 Transport

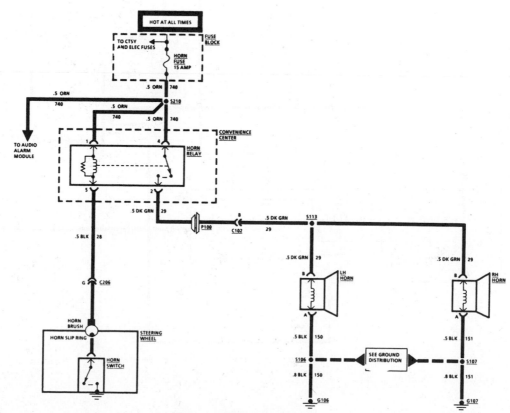

Horns — 1991 Transport

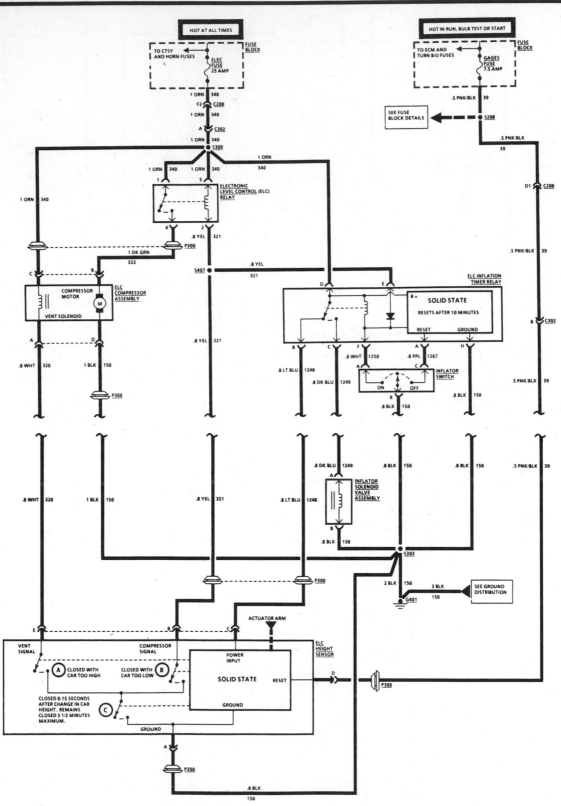

Electronic level control — 1991 Transport

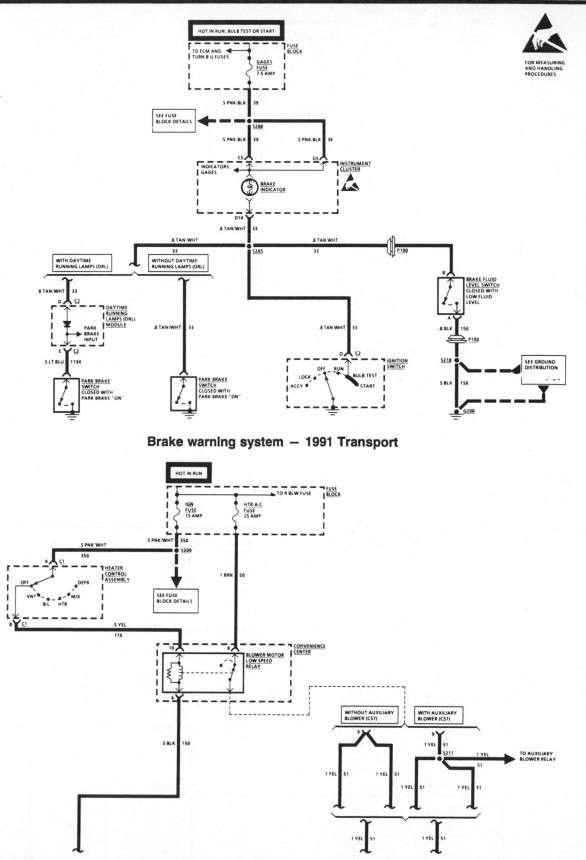

Brake warning system — 1991 Transport

Heater (blower control (C40) — 1991 Transport

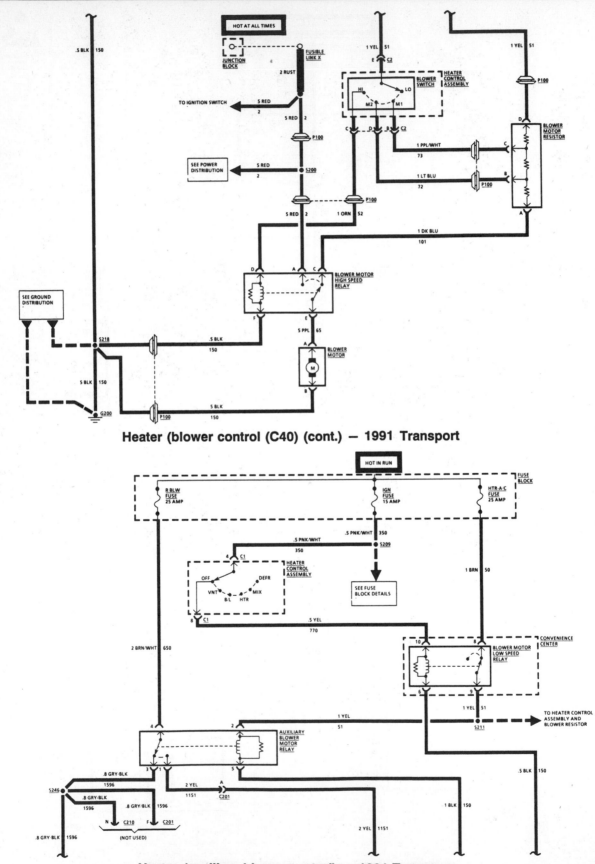

Heater (blower control (C40) (cont.) — 1991 Transport

Heater (auxiliary blower control) — 1991 Transport

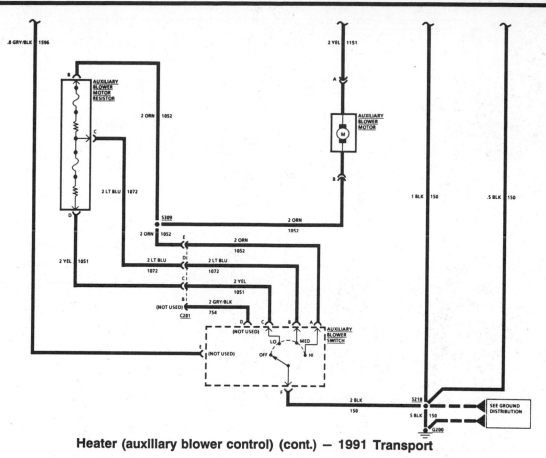

Heater (auxiliary blower control) (cont.) — 1991 Transport

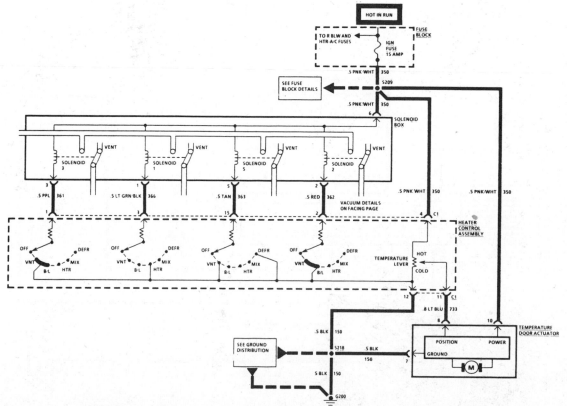

Heater (air delivery and temperature control (C40) — 1991 Transport

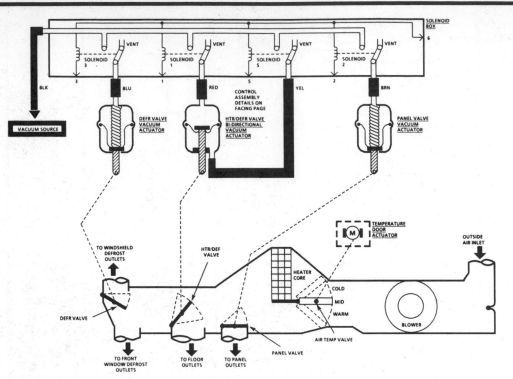

Heater (air delivery and temperature control (C40) — 1991 Transport

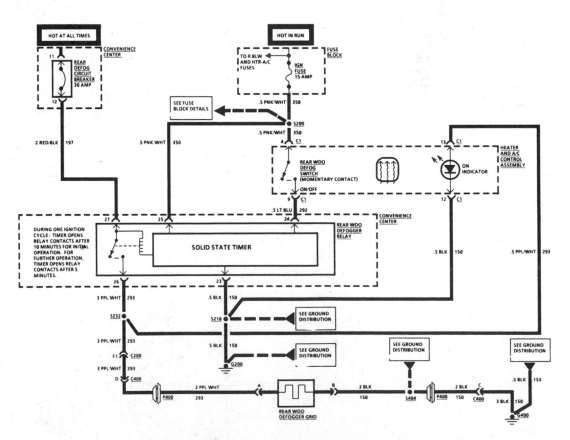

Rear defogger — 1991 Transport

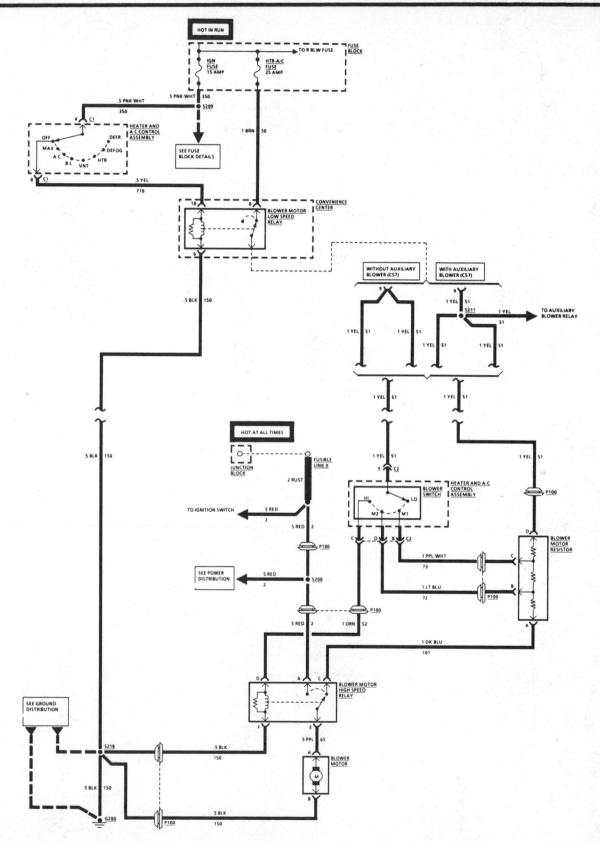

Air conditioning (blower motor control (C67) — 1991 Transport

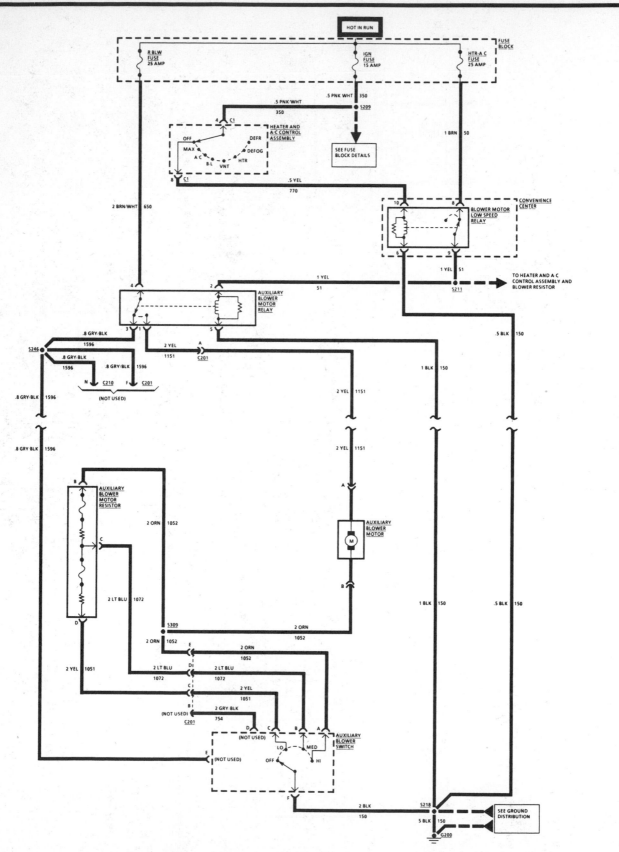

Air conditioning (auxiliary blower motor (C57) — 1991 Transport

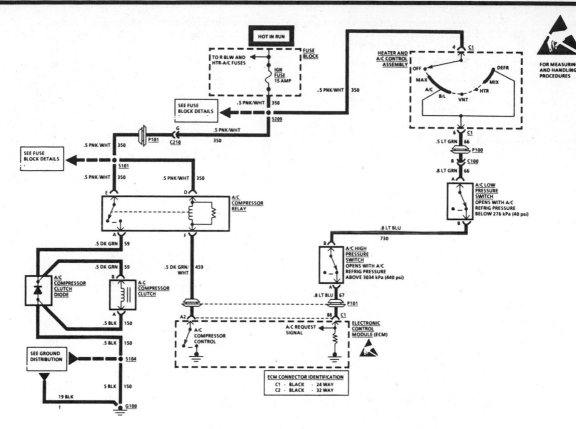

Air conditioning (compressor control (C67) — 1991 Transport

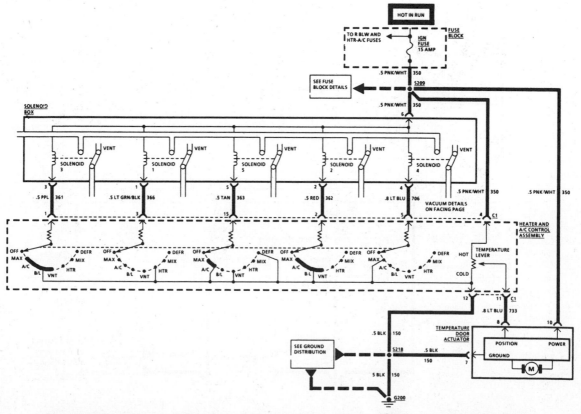

Air conditioning (air delivery and temperature control (C67) — 1991 Transport

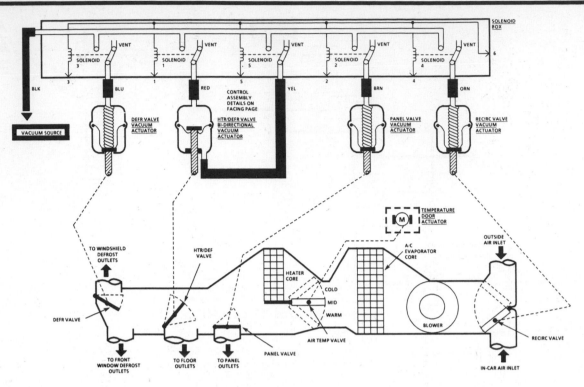

Air conditioning (air delivery and temperature control (C67) — 1991 Transport

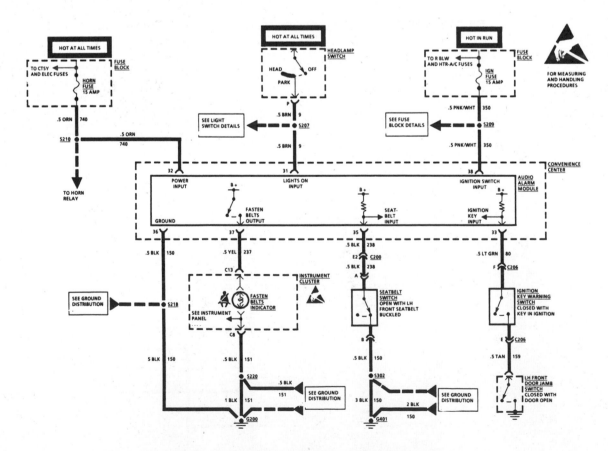

Warnings and alarms: (chime) — 1991 Transport

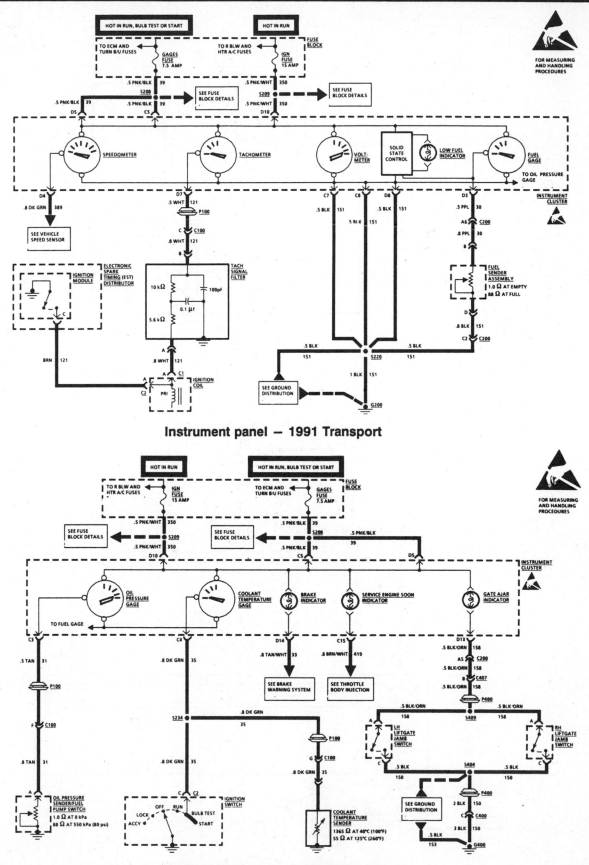

Instrument panel — 1991 Transport

Instrument panel — 1991 Transport

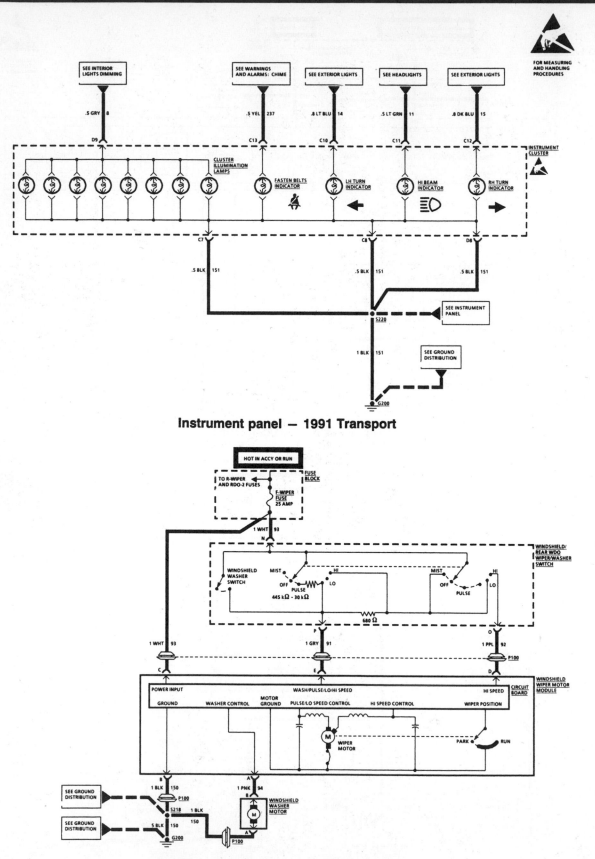

Instrument panel — 1991 Transport

Wiper/washer: (pulse) — 1991 Transport

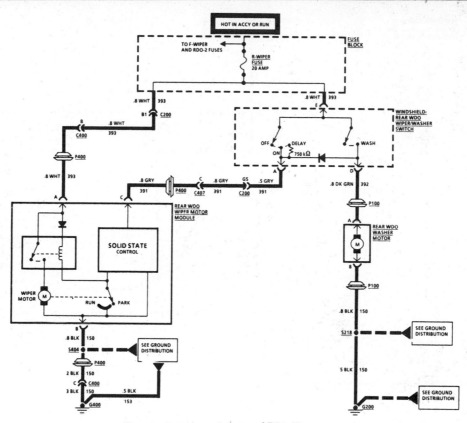

Rear wiper/washer — 1991 Transport

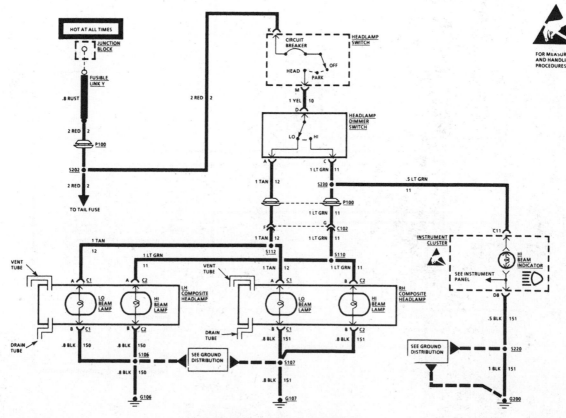

Headlights — 1991 Transport

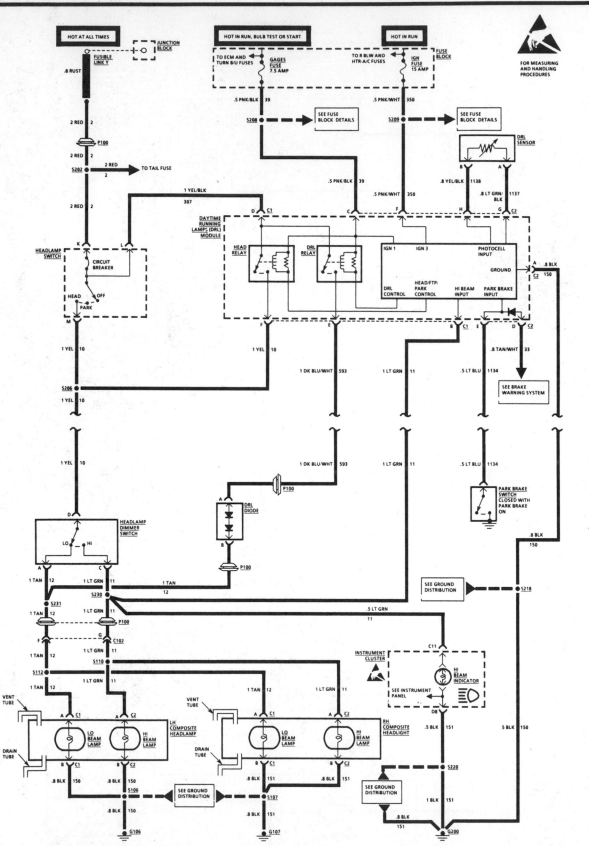

Headlights: (daytime running lamps (drl), T61) — 1991 Transport

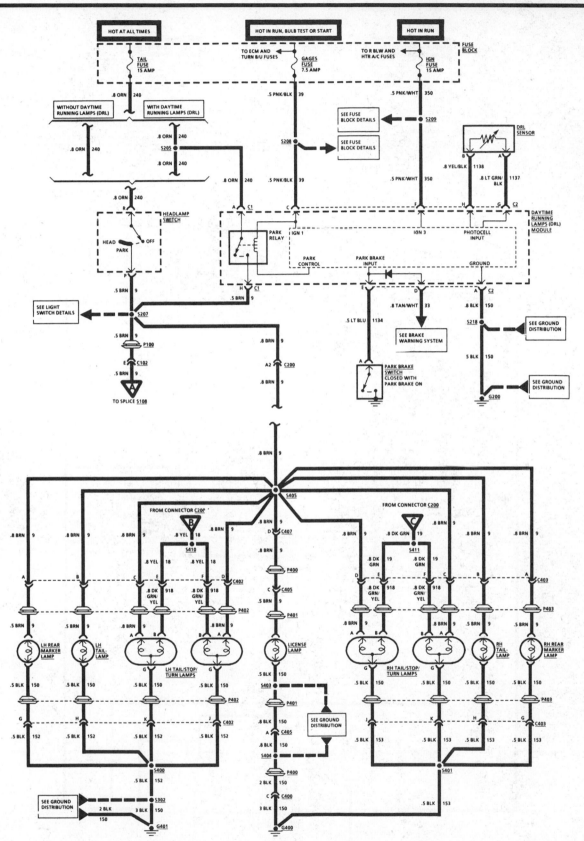

Exterior lights: (turn/hazard/stop/tail/marker/license) — 1991 Transport

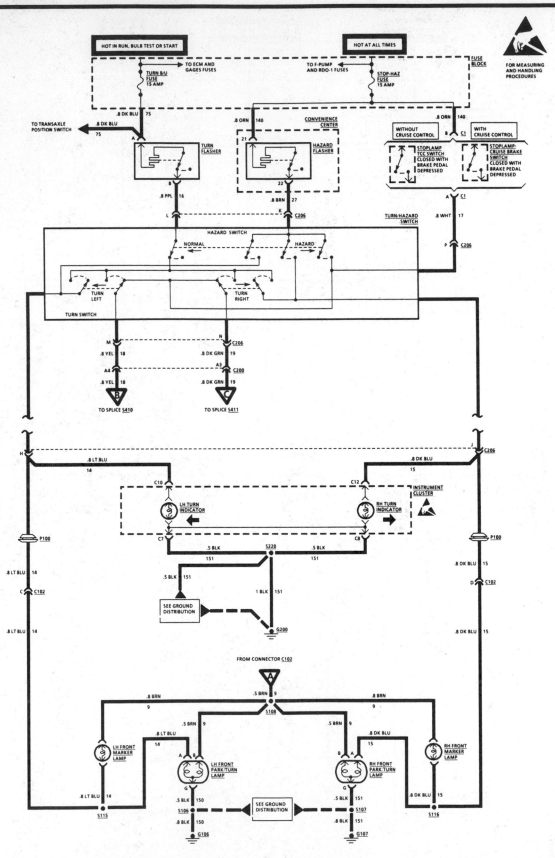

Exterior lights: (turn/hazard/stop/tail/marker/license) (cont.) — 1991 Transport

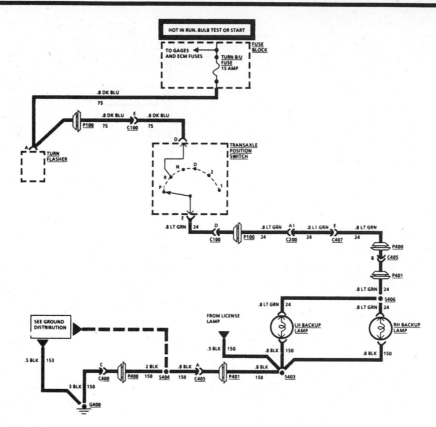

Backup lights — 1991 Transport

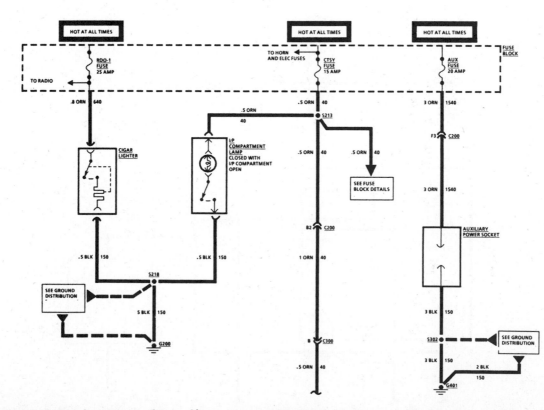

Interior lights (courtesy, dome, i/p compartment, cigar lighter, auxiliary power socket) — 1991 Transport

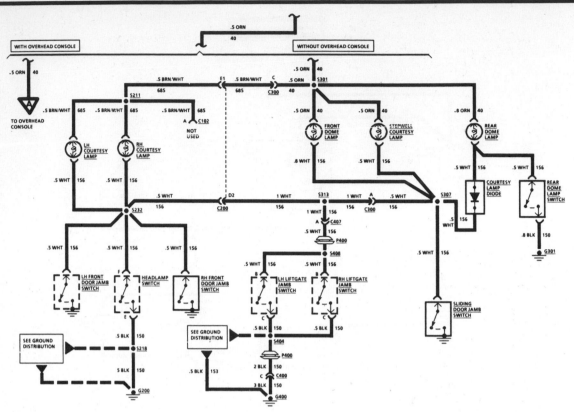

Interior lights (courtesy, dome, I/p compartment, cigar lighter, auxiliary power socket) — 1991 Transport

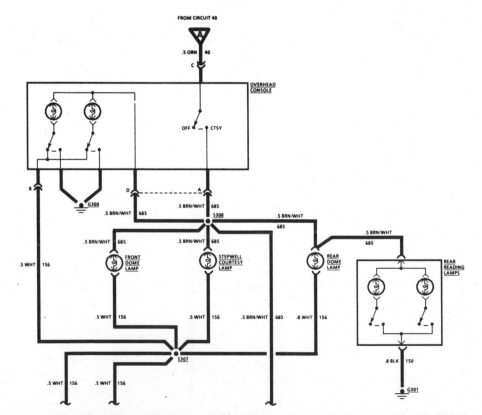

Interior lights (courtesy, dome, reading and engine compartment) — 1991 Transport

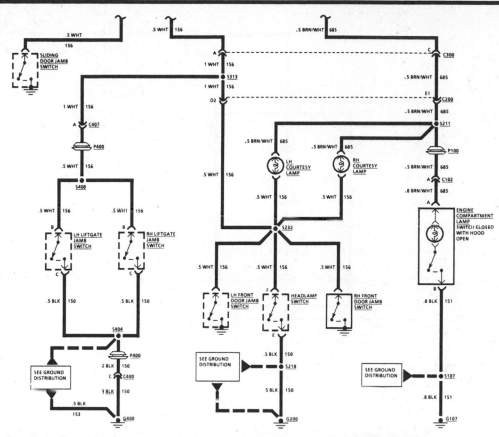

Interior lights (courtesy, dome, reading and engine compartment) (cont.) — 1991 Transport

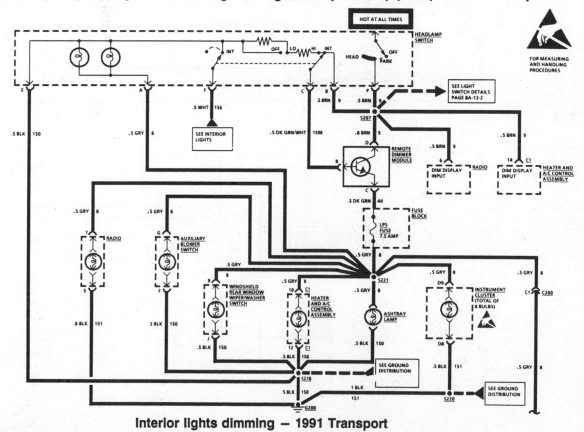

Interior lights dimming — 1991 Transport

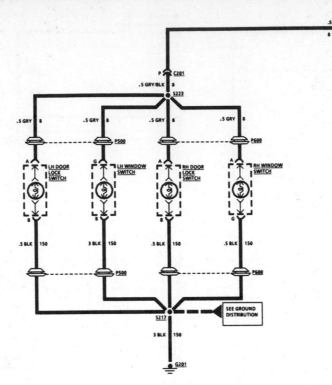

Interior lights dimming — 1991 Transport

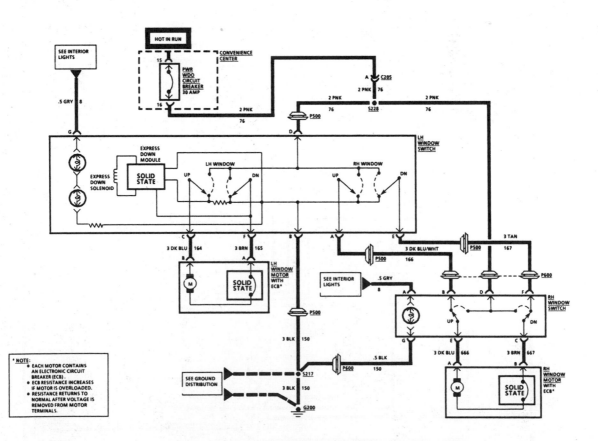

Power windows — 1991 Transport

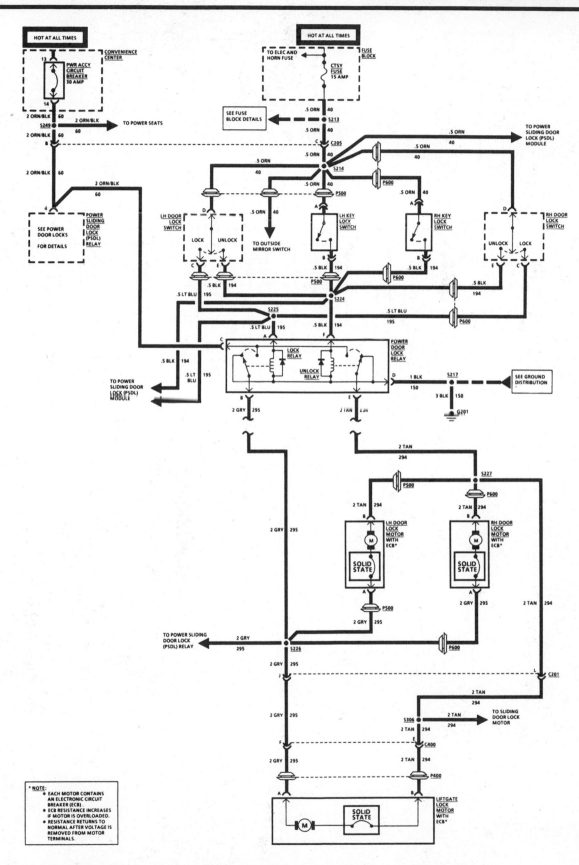

Power door locks (right and left and liftgate lock) — 1991 Transport

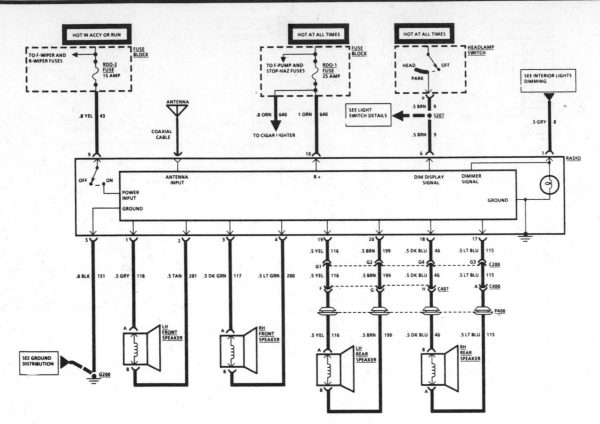

Radio — 1991 Transport

7 Drive Train

QUICK REFERENCE INDEX

GENERAL INDEX

AUTOMATIC TRANSAXLE

Fluid Pan

REMOVAL AND INSTALLATION

1. Raise the vehicle and support it safely.
2. Place a drain pan under the transaxle oil pan.
3. Remove the oil pan bolts from the front and sides only.
4. Loosen the rear oil pan bolts approximately 4 turns.
5. Lightly tap on the oil pan with a rubber mallet to allow the fluid to drain.
6. Remove the remaining oil pan bolts, oil pan and gasket.

To install:
7. Clean the gasket surfaces with solvent and dry air. All traces of gasket material must be removed.
8. Install the oil pan and a new gasket and torque the pan retaining bolts to 15 ft. lbs.
9. Lower the vehicle and fill the transaxle to the proper level with DEXRON® ll fluid.
10. Check the cold fluid level for the initial fill. Do not overfill.
11. Check the fluid level as outlined in Section 1.
12. Check the oil pan for leaks.

FILTER SERVICE

1. Raise the vehicle and support it safely.
2. Place a drain pan under the transaxle oil pan.
3. Remove the oil pan bolts from the front and sides only.
4. Loosen the rear oil pan bolts approximately 4 turns.
5. Lightly tap on the oil pan with a rubber mallet to allow the fluid to drain.
6. Remove the remaining oil pan bolts, oil pan and gasket.
7. Remove the oil filter and O-ring.

NOTE: The oil filter O-ring may be stuck in the case.

To install:
8. Coat the O-ring with a small amount of transgel J-36850, or equivalent.
9. Install the new filter into the case.
10. Clean the gasket surfaces with solvent and dry air. All traces of gasket material must be removed.
11. Install the oil pan and a new gasket and torque the pan retaining bolts to 15 ft. lbs.
12. Lower the vehicle and fill the transaxle to the proper level with DEXRON®II.
13. Check the cold fluid level for the initial fill. Do not overfill.
14. Check the fluid level as outlined in Section 1.
15. Check the oil pan for leaks.

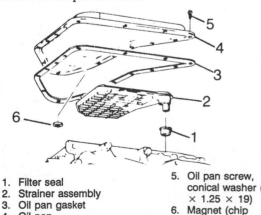

1. Filter seal
2. Strainer assembly
3. Oil pan gasket
4. Oil pan
5. Oil pan screw, conical washer (M8 × 1.25 × 19)
6. Magnet (chip collector)

Transaxle oil pan and filter installation

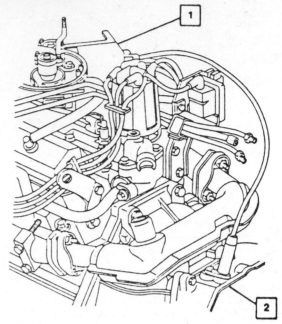

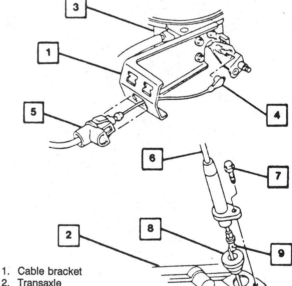

1. Cable bracket
2. Transaxle
3. TBI unit
4. TV cable end to TBI unit
5. TV cable adjuster
6. Cable assembly
7. Bolt (180 inch lbs.)
8. Seal
9. Install the rod through the hole in the cable end

T.V. cable system

Adjustments

T.V. CABLE

1. As required, remove the air cleaner assembly.
2. Depress and hold down the metal readjust tab at the engine end of the throttle valve cable.

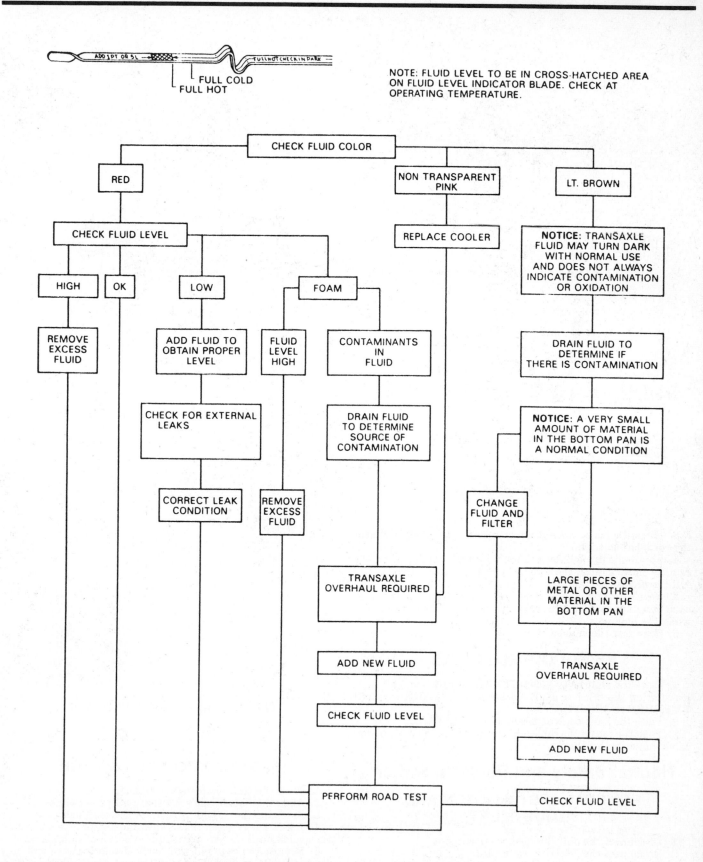

NOTE: FLUID LEVEL TO BE IN CROSS-HATCHED AREA ON FLUID LEVEL INDICATOR BLADE. CHECK AT OPERATING TEMPERATURE.

Checking the fluid level, color and condition

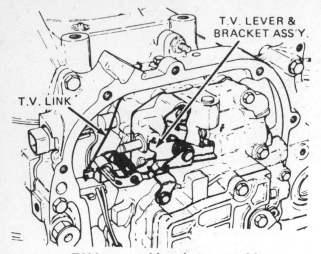

T.V lever and bracket assembly

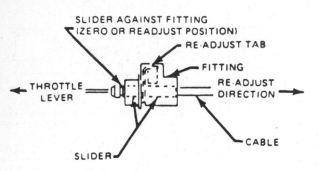

T.V. cable adjustment

1. Shift cable
2. Pin

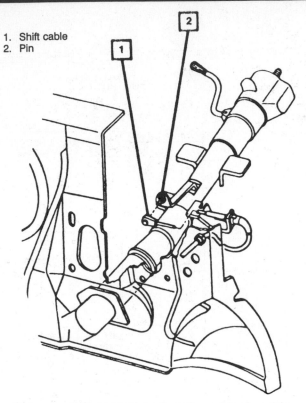

Column shift control and park and lock cable

3. Move the slider until it stops against the fitting. Release the readjustment tab.

4. Rotate the throttle lever to its full travel position. The slider must move toward the lever when the lever is rotated to its full travel position.

5. Check for proper operation. When the engine is cold, the cable may appear to be functioning properly, check the cable when the engine is hot.

6. Road test the vehicle.

SHIFT CONTROL CABLE

1. Place the shift lever in **NEUTRAL**. Neutral can be found by rotating the selector shaft clockwise from **PARK** through **REVERSE** to **NEUTRAL**.

2. Place the shift control assembly in **NEUTRAL**.

3. Push the tab on the cable adjuster to adjust the cable in the cable mounting bracket.

Neutral Safety and Back-Up Switch

REMOVAL, INSTALLATION AND ADJUSTMENT

1. Disconnect the shift linkage, lever and nut.
2. Disconnect the electrical connector.
3. Remove the mounting bolts and remove the switch, cable and nut.

1. Bracket
2. Cable assembly
3. Shift lever
4. Neutral start switch

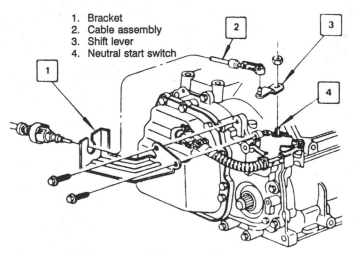

Engine compartment shift control

INSTALLATION-OLD SWITCH

1. Place the shift shaft in **NEUTRAL**.

2. Align the flats of the shift shaft with the switch.

3. Assemble the mounting bolts to the case, loosely.

4. Insert a gage pin in the service adjustment hole and rotate the switch until the pin drops in to a depth of ⅛ in.(3mm).

5. Remove the gage pin and verify that the engine will only start in **PARK** or **NEUTRAL**. If it starts in any other position, readjust the switch.

INSTALLATION-NEW SWITCH

1. Place the shift shaft in **NEUTRAL**.
2. Align the flats of the shift shaft with the switch.
3. Install the mounting bolts and torque to 22 ft. lbs. If the holes do not align with the mounting boss on the transaxle, verify that the shift shaft is in **NEUTRAL** position, do not rotate the switch. The switch is pinned in the **NEUTRAL** position.

NOTE: If the switch has been rotated and the pin broken, the switch can be adjusted using the old switch procedure.

4. Adjust the new switch as follows:
   a. Place the transaxle in the **N** position.
   b. Loosen the switch attaching screws.
   c. Rotate the switch on the shifter assembly to align the service hole in the switch with the hole in the carrier.
   d. Insert a $\frac{3}{32}$ in. (2.4mm) gauge pin into the hole then tighten the mounting bolts.
   e. Remove the gauge pin and check the operation of the switch.
   f. The vehicle should only start in **N** or **P**.

Transaxle Assembly

REMOVAL AND INSTALLATION

The automatic transaxle in the Lumina APV, Silhouette and Trans Sport, can only be removed by removing the engine and transaxle/sub-frame as an assembly.
1. Disconnect the negative battery cable.
2. Drain the cooling system. Disconnect the air flow tube from the air cleaner.
3. Disconnect the electrical connector from the ECM and push it through to the engine compartment. Disconnect the harness from the clips on the body and lay it across the engine.
4. Disconnect the engine harness at the bulkhead connector. Disconnect the throttle and TV cables.
5. Disconnect the fuel lines. Disconnect the transaxle shift linkage.

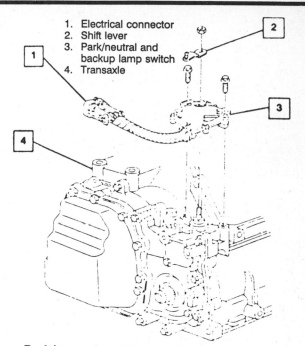

1. Electrical connector
2. Shift lever
3. Park/neutral and backup lamp switch
4. Transaxle

Park/neutral and backup lamp switch

6. Disconnect the cooler lines at the radiator. Disconnect the radiator and heater hoses.
7. Remove the air conditioning compressor from the bracket and support it out of the way. Remove the upper engine support strut.
8. Raise and safely support the vehicle. Remove the front wheel and tire assemblies.
9. Remove the stabilizer bar. Disconnect the tie rod ends and the lower control arm ball joints.
10. Disconnect the halfshafts and support them out of the way. Disconnect the steering shaft pinch bolt.

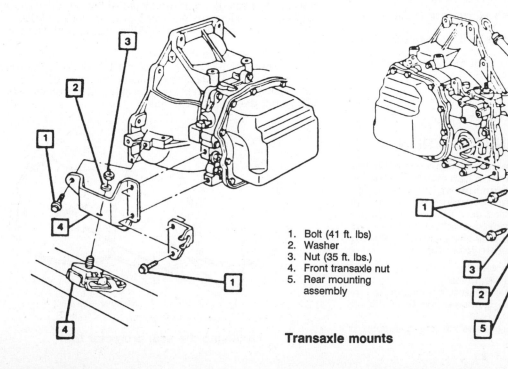

1. Bolt (41 ft. lbs)
2. Washer
3. Nut (35 ft. lbs.)
4. Front transaxle nut
5. Rear mounting assembly

Transaxle mounts

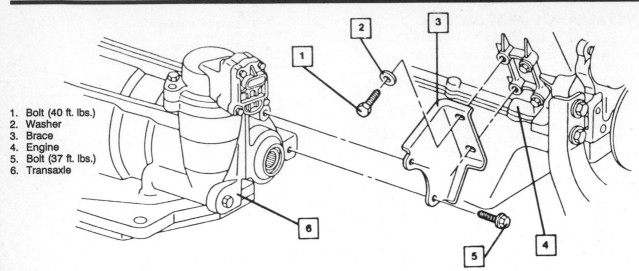

1. Bolt (40 ft. lbs.)
2. Washer
3. Brace
4. Engine
5. Bolt (37 ft. lbs.)
6. Transaxle

Transaxle to engine brace

11. Remove the starter.
12. Disconnect the exhaust pipe at the manifold. Support the engine and sub-frame with a suitable jack.
13. Remove the sub-frame bolts and lower the engine/transaxle and subframe from the vehicle.
To install:
14. Raise the engine assembly into position and install the subframe bolts. Tighten to 35 ft. lbs.
15. Connect the exhaust pipe at the rear manifold. Install the starter.
16. Connect the steering shaft and install the pinch bolt. Connect the halfshafts to the transaxle.
17. Connect the lower control arm ball joints to the steering knuckles.
18. Install the stabilizer bar. Install the upper engine strut.
19. Install the wheel and tire assemblies. Lower the vehicle. Install the radiator and heater hoses.
20. Install the shift linkage. Connect the fuel lines and the throttle and TV cables.
21. Connect the harness to bulkhead connector. Connect the ECM harness to the ECM.
22. Connect the air cleaner hose and the radiator upper support.
23. Fill the cooling system. Install the air conditioning compressor.
24. Connect the negative battery cable.

Halfshaft

REMOVAL AND INSTALLATION

WARNING: Care must be exercised to prevent Tri-Pot joints from being over-extended. When either end of the shaft is disconnected, over-extension of the joint could result in separation of internal components and possible joint failure. Drive axle joint seal protectors should be used any time service is performed on or near the drive axles. Failure to observe this can result in interior joint or seal damage and possible joint failure.

1. Raise and safely support the vehicle.
2. Remove the tire and wheel assemblies.
3. Insert a drift or other suitable tool into the caliper and rotor to prevent the rotor from turning and remove the halfshaft retaining nut and washer.
4. Remove the brake caliper from the rotor and support it aside.

5. Remove the brake rotor from the hub.
6. Disconnect the lower ball joint pinch bolt.
7. Install the drive axle seal protector J-34754 or equivalent, and modify as necessary.

When servicing suspension components in the area in the area of the outer drive axle seal or when removing a drive axle, always install drive axle seal protector J-34754 after modifying it as shown.

8. Remove the ball joint from the steering knuckle.
9. Remove the halfshaft from the hub and bearing assembly using tool J-28733 or equivalent.
10. Remove the halfshaft from the spindle, using tool J-28733 or equivalent.
11. Remove the halfshaft from the transaxle using a suitable tool with a slide hammer attachment.
To install:
12. Install tool J-37292-A or equivalent, to right side of the transaxle in a position so it can be pulled out after drive axle is installed (approximately between 5 and 7 o'clock position).
13. Install axle seal protector J-34754-A or equivalent, to drive axle.
14. Install the axle to transaxle.
15. Remove tool J-37292-A and discard. Make sure that there are no pieces of J-37292-A left inside of the transaxle, if so, repeat necessary steps to remove drive axle and correct condition.
16. Install the axle shaft in hub.

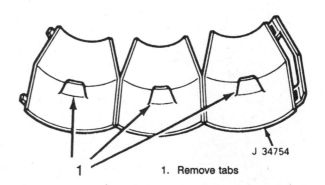

J 34754

1. Remove tabs

Modifying the seal protector tool

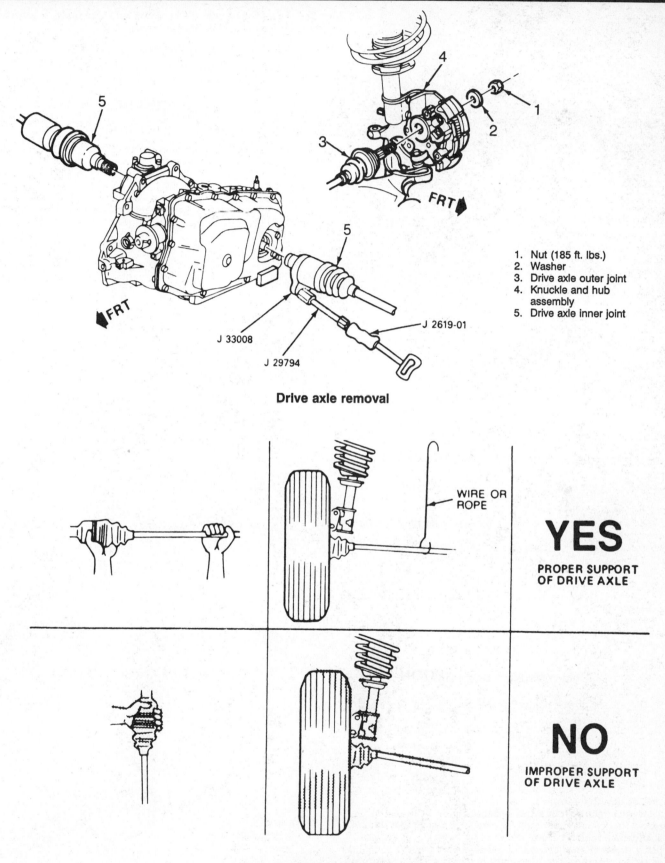

1. Nut (185 ft. lbs.)
2. Washer
3. Drive axle outer joint
4. Knuckle and hub assembly
5. Drive axle inner joint

Drive axle removal

WIRE OR ROPE

YES
PROPER SUPPORT OF DRIVE AXLE

NO
IMPROPER SUPPORT OF DRIVE AXLE

Drive axle handling

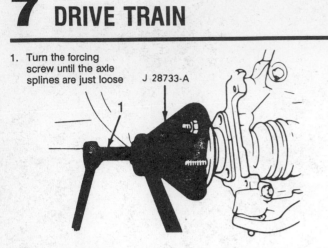

1. Turn the forcing screw until the axle splines are just loose

J 28733-A

Removing the drive axle hub and bearing assembly

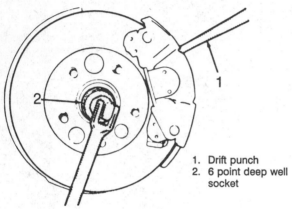

1. Drift punch
2. 6 point deep well socket

Removing and installing the axle shaft nut

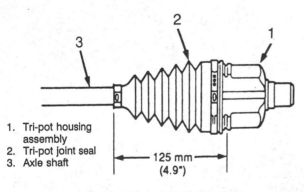

1. Tri-pot housing assembly
2. Tri-pot joint seal
3. Axle shaft

125 mm (4.9")

Seal collapsed dimension

17. Install the lower control arm ball joint to the steering knuckle.
18. Install lower ball joint pinch bolt and tighten ball joint pinch bolt nut to 33 ft. lb. (45 Nm.).
19. Install the brake rotor.
20. Install the brake caliper. Refer to Section 9 as necessary.
21. Install a drift or other suitable tool to the caliper and rotor.
22. Install drive axle washer and new nut and tighten the nut to 185 ft. lb. (260 Nm).
23. Remove the drift or other suitable tool from the caliper and rotor.
24. Remove tool J-34754.
25. Seat the drive axle into the transaxle by placing a suitable tool into the groove on the joint housing and tapping until seated.

26. Verify that drive axle is seated into tranxaxle by grasping on the housing and pulling outboard.

NOTE: Do not grasp and pull on the axle shaft.

27. Install the tire and wheel assembly.
28. Lower the vehicle.

OVERHAUL

Outer Joint Seal

1. Remove the large seal retaining clamp from the CV-joint with a side cutter and discard.
2. Remove the small seal-retaining clamp on the axle shaft with side cutter and discard.
3. Separate the joint seal from the CV-joint race at large diameter and slide the seal away from joint along axle shaft.
4. Wipe grease from face of CV-inner race.

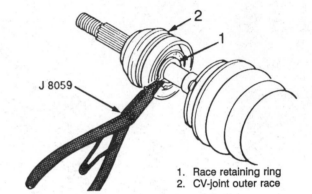

J 8059

1. Race retaining ring
2. CV-joint outer race

CV-joint and axle separation

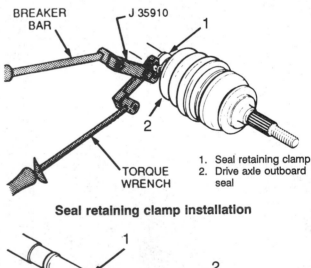

BREAKER BAR

J 35910

TORQUE WRENCH

1. Seal retaining clamp
2. Drive axle outboard seal

Seal retaining clamp installation

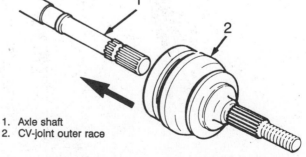

1. Axle shaft
2. CV-joint outer race

CV-joint to axle installation

5. Spread the ears on the race retaining ring with tool J-8059 or equivalent, as shown, and remove CV-joint assembly from the axle shaft.

6. Remove the seal from the axle shaft.

7. Disassemble the joint and flush the grease prior to installing the new seal.

To install:

8. Connect the small seal-retaining clamp on the neck of the new seal. Do not crimp.

9. Slide the seal onto the axle shaft and position the neck of the seal in the seal groove on axle shaft.

10. Crimp the seal-retaining clamp with tool J-35910 or equivalent, to 100 ft. lbs. (136 Nm).

11. Place approximately half of the grease provided inside the seal and pack the CV-joint with the remaining grease.

12. Push the CV-joint onto the axle shaft until the retaining ring is seated in the groove on the axle shaft.

13. Slide the large diameter of seal with the large seal retaining clamp in place over the outside of CV-joint race and locate the seal lip in the groove on the race.

WARNING: The seal must not be dimpled, stretched or out of shape in any way.
If the seal is not shaped correctly, equalize the pressure in the seal and shape the seal properly by hand.

14. Crimp the seal-retaining clamp with tool J-35910 or equivalent, to 130 ft. lbs. (176 Nm).

Outer Joint Assembly

1. Remove the large seal retaining clamp from the CV-joint with a side cutter and discard.

2. Remove the small seal-retaining clamp on the axle shaft with side cutter and discard.

3. Separate the joint seal from the CV-joint race at large diameter and slide the seal away from joint along axle shaft.

4. Wipe grease from face of CV-inner race.

5. Spread the ears on the race retaining ring with tool J-8059 or equivalent, as shown, and remove CV-joint assembly from the axle shaft.

6. Remove the seal from the axle shaft.

7. Disassemble the joint and flush the grease prior to installing the new seal.

8. Use a brass drift and a hammer to gently tap on the CV-joint cage until it is tilted enough to remove the first chrome alloy ball.

9. Tilt the cage in the opposite direction to remove opposing ball.

10. Repeat this process until all 6 balls are removed.

11. Position the cage and the inner race 90° to the center line of the outer race and align the cage windows with the lands of the outer race.

12. Remove the cage and the inner race from the outer race.

13. Rotate the inner race 90° to the center line of the cage with the lands of the inner race aligned with the windows of cage.

14. Pivot the inner race into the cage window and remove the inner race.

To assemble:

15. Put a light coat of the recommended grease on the ball grooves of the inner race and outer race.

16. Install the inner race. Be sure that the retaining ring of the inner race faces the axle shaft.

17. Install all of the 6 chrome alloy balls in the cage.

18. Connect the small seal-retaining clamp on the neck of the new seal. Do not crimp.

19. Slide the seal onto the axle shaft and position the neck of the seal in the seal groove on axle shaft.

20. Crimp the seal-retaining clamp with tool J-35910 or equivalent, to 100 ft. lbs. (136 Nm).

21. Place approximately half of the grease provided inside the seal and pack the CV-joint with the remaining grease.

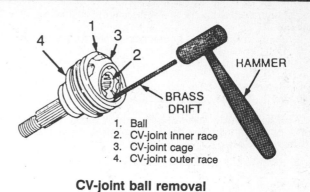

1. Ball
2. CV-joint inner race
3. CV-joint cage
4. CV-joint outer race

CV-joint ball removal

1. Land
2. Windows
3. CV-joint cage
4. CV-joint outer race

Outer race and cage separation

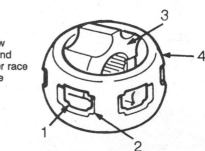

1. Cage window
2. Inner race land
3. CV-joint inner race
4. CV-joint cage

Inner race and cage separation

22. Push the CV-joint onto the axle shaft until the retaining ring is seated in the groove on the axle shaft.

23. Slide the large diameter of seal with the large seal retaining clamp in place over the outside of CV-joint race and locate the seal lip in the groove on the race.

WARNING: The seal must not be dimpled, stretched or out of shape in any way.
If the seal is not shaped correctly, equalize the pressure in the seal and shape the seal properly by hand.

24. Crimp the seal-retaining clamp with tool J-35910 or equivalent, to 130 ft. lbs. (176 Nm).

Inner Tri-Pot Seal

WARNING: Do not cut through the seal and damage the sealing surface of tri-pot outer housing and trilobal bushing.

1. Remove the larger seal retaining clamp from the tri-pot joint with the side cutter and discard.

2. Remove the small seal-retaining clamp from the axle shaft with the side cutter and discard.

3. Separate the seal from the trilobal tri-pot bushing at the

large diameter and slide the seal away from the joint along the axle shaft.

4. Remove the tri-pot housing from the spider and the shaft.

5. Remove the spread spacer ring with tool J-8059 or equivalent, and slide the spacer ring and tri-pot spider back on the axle shaft as shown.

6. Remove the shaft retaining ring from the groove on the axle shaft and slide the spider assembly off of the shaft.

NOTE: Handle the tri-pot spider assembly with care. Tri-pot balls and needle rollers may separate from the spider trunnions.

7. Remove the trilobal tri-pot bushing from tri-pot housing.

8. Remove the spacer ring and the seal from the axle shaft.

9. Flush the grease from tri-pot housing.

To install:

10. Install the seal-retaining clamp on the neck of the seal. Do not crimp.

11. Slide the seal onto the shaft and position the neck of the seal in the seal groove on the axle shaft.

12. Crimp the seal retaining clamp with tool J-35910 to 100 ft. lbs. (136 Nm).

13. Install the spacer ring on the axle shaft and beyond the 2nd groove.

14. Slide the tri-pot spider assembly against the spacer ring on the shaft.

NOTE: Be sure that the counterbored face of the tri-pot spider faces the end of the shaft.

15. Install the shaft retaining ring in the groove of the axle shaft with tool J-8059 or equivalent.

16. Slide the tri-pot spider towards the end of the shaft and re-seat the spacer ring in the groove on the shaft.

17. Place approximately half of the grease provided in the seal and use the remainder to repack the tri-pot housing.

18. Install the trilobal tri-pot bushing to the tri-pot housing

19. Position the larger clamp on the seal.

20. Slide the tri-pot housing over the tri-pot spider assembly on the shaft.

21. Slide the large diameter of the seal, with the larger clamp

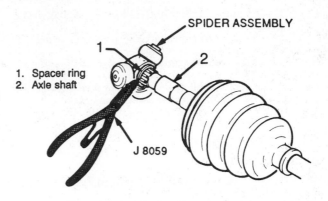

1. Spacer ring
2. Axle shaft

Spider assembly installation

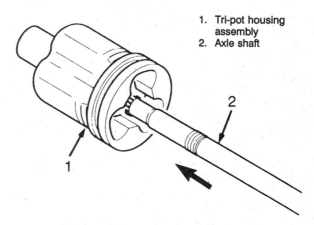

1. Tri-pot housing assembly
2. Axle shaft

Tri-pot to housing installation

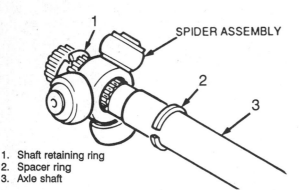

1. Shaft retaining ring
2. Spacer ring
3. Axle shaft

Spider assembly removal

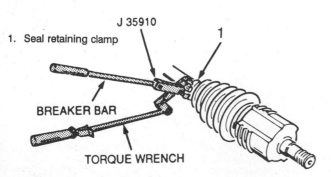

1. Seal retaining clamp

Small seal retaining clamp installation

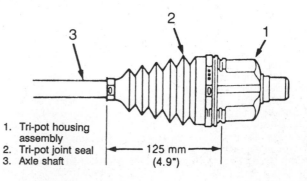

1. Tri-pot housing assembly
2. Tri-pot joint seal
3. Axle shaft

125 mm (4.9")

Tri-pot seal installation measurement

in place, over the outside of trilobal bushing and locate the lip of the seal in bushing groove.

22. Position the tri-pot assembly at the proper vehicle dimension.

WARNING: The seal must not be dimpled, stretched or out of shape in any way. If the seal is not shaped correctly, carefully insert a thin flat blunt tool (no sharp edges) between the large seal opening and the bushing to equalize pressure. Shape the seal properly by hand and remove the tool.

23. Crimp the seal retaining clamp with tool J-35566.

NOTE: Make sure that the seal, housing and the large clamp all remain in alignment while crimping.

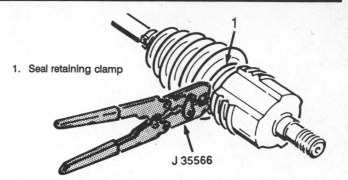

1. Seal retaining clamp

Large seal retaining clamp installation

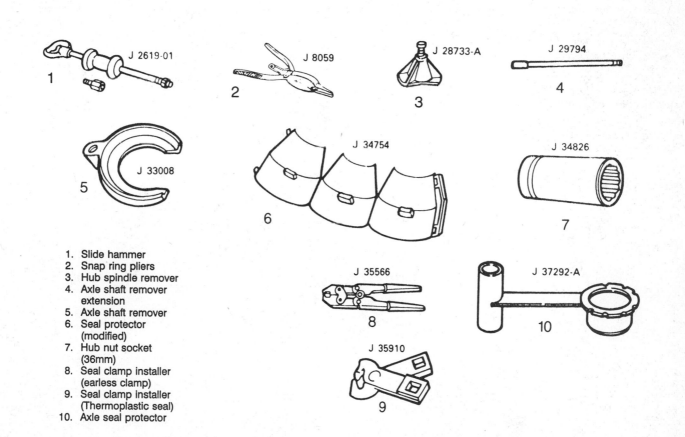

1. Slide hammer
2. Snap ring pliers
3. Hub spindle remover
4. Axle shaft remover extension
5. Axle shaft remover
6. Seal protector (modified)
7. Hub nut socket (36mm)
8. Seal clamp installer (earless clamp)
9. Seal clamp installer (Thermoplastic seal)
10. Axle seal protector

Special tools for axle shaft removal, installation and overhaul

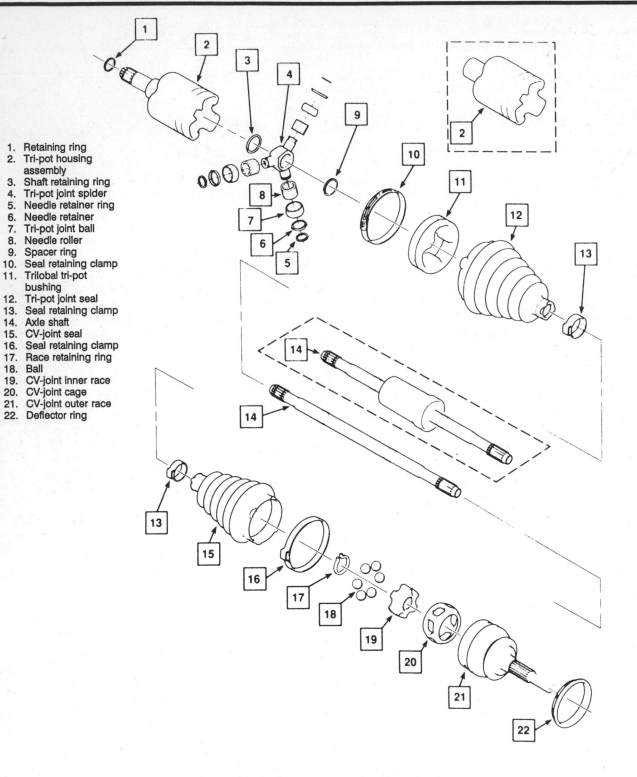

1. Retaining ring
2. Tri-pot housing assembly
3. Shaft retaining ring
4. Tri-pot joint spider
5. Needle retainer ring
6. Needle retainer
7. Tri-pot joint ball
8. Needle roller
9. Spacer ring
10. Seal retaining clamp
11. Trilobal tri-pot bushing
12. Tri-pot joint seal
13. Seal retaining clamp
14. Axle shaft
15. CV-joint seal
16. Seal retaining clamp
17. Race retaining ring
18. Ball
19. CV-joint inner race
20. CV-joint cage
21. CV-joint outer race
22. Deflector ring

Exploded view of the tri-pot design front wheel drive axle

Lockup Torque Converter Service Diagnosis

Problem	Cause	Solution

No lockup	• Faulty oil pump
	• Sticking governor valve
	• Valve body malfunction
	    (a) Stuck switch valve
	    (b) Stuck lockup valve
	    (c) Stuck fail-safe valve
	• Failed locking clutch
	• Leaking turbine hub seal
	• Faulty input shaft or seal ring
		• Replace oil pump
		• Repair or replace as necessary
		• Repair or replace valve body or its internal components as necessary
		
		• Replace torque converter
		• Replace torque converter
		• Repair or replace as necessary

Will not unlock	• Sticking governor valve
	• Valve body malfunction
	    (a) Stuck switch valve
	    (b) Stuck lockup valve
	    (c) Stuck fail-safe valve
		• Repair or replace as necessary
		• Repair or replace valve body or its internal components as necessary

Stays locked up at too low a speed in direct	• Sticking governor valve
	• Valve body malfunction
	    (a) Stuck switch valve
	    (b) Stuck lockup valve
	    (c) Stuck fail-safe valve
		• Repair or replace as necessary
		• Repair or replace valve body or its internal components as necessary

Locks up or drags in low or second	• Faulty oil pump
	• Valve body malfunction
	    (a) Stuck switch valve
	    (b) Stuck fail-safe valve
		• Replace oil pump
		• Repair or replace valve body or its internal components as necessary

Sluggish or stalls in reverse	• Faulty oil pump
	• Plugged cooler, cooler lines or fittings
	• Valve body malfunction
	    (a) Stuck switch valve
	    (b) Faulty input shaft or seal ring
		• Replace oil pump as necessary
		• Flush or replace cooler and flush lines and fittings
		• Repair or replace valve body or its internal components as necessary

Loud chatter during lockup engagement (cold)	• Faulty torque converter • Failed locking clutch • Leaking turbine hub seal	• Replace torque converter • Replace torque converter • Replace torque converter
Vibration or shudder during lockup engagement	• Faulty oil pump • Valve body malfunction • Faulty torque converter • Engine needs tune-up	• Repair or replace oil pump as necessary • Repair or replace valve body or its internal components as necessary • Replace torque converter • Tune engine
Vibration after lockup engagement	• Faulty torque converter • Exhaust system strikes underbody • Engine needs tune-up • Throttle linkage misadjusted	• Replace torque converter • Align exhaust system • Tune engine • Adjust throttle linkage

Lockup Torque Converter Service Diagnosis

Problem	Cause	Solution
Vibration when revved in neutral Overheating: oil blows out of dip stick tube or pump seal	• Torque converter out of balance • Plugged cooler, cooler lines or fittings • Stuck switch valve	• Replace torque converter • Flush or replace cooler and flush lines and fittings • Repair switch valve in valve body or replace valve body
Shudder after lockup engagement	• Faulty oil pump • Plugged cooler, cooler lines or fittings • Valve body malfunction • Faulty torque converter • Fail locking clutch • Exhaust system strikes underbody • Engine needs tune-up • Throttle linkage misadjusted	• Replace oil pump • Flush or replace cooler and flush lines and fittings • Repair or replace valve body or its internal components as necessary • Replace torque converter • Replace torque converter • Align exhaust system • Tune engine • Adjust throttle linkage

Transmission Fluid Indications

The appearance and odor of the transmission fluid can give valuable clues to the overall condition of the transmission. Always note the appearance of the fluid when you check the fluid level or change the fluid. Rub a small amount of fluid between your fingers to feel for grit and smell the fluid on the dipstick.

If the fluid appears:	It indicates:
Clear and red colored	• Normal operation
Discolored (extremely dark red or brownish) or smells burned	• Band or clutch pack failure, usually caused by an overheated transmission. Hauling very heavy loads with insufficient power or failure to change the fluid, often result in overheating. Do not confuse this appearance with newer fluids that have a darker red color and a strong odor (though not a burned odor).
Foamy or aerated (light in color and full of bubbles)	• The level is too high (gear train is churning oil) • An internal air leak (air is mixing with the fluid). Have the transmission checked professionally.
Solid residue in the fluid	• Defective bands, clutch pack or bearings. Bits of band material or metal abrasives are clinging to the dipstick. Have the transmission checked professionally.
Varnish coating on the dipstick	• The transmission fluid is overheating

Troubleshooting Basic Automatic Transmission Problems

Problem	Cause	Solution
Fluid leakage	• Defective pan gasket	• Replace gasket or tighten pan bolts
	• Loose filler tube	• Tighten tube nut
	• Loose extension housing to transmission case	• Tighten bolts
	• Converter housing area leakage	• Have transmission checked professionally
Fluid flows out the oil filler tube	• High fluid level	• Check and correct fluid level
	• Breather vent clogged	• Open breather vent
	• Clogged oil filter or screen	• Replace filter or clean screen (change fluid also)
	• Internal fluid leakage	• Have transmission checked professionally
Transmission overheats (this is usually accompanied by a strong burned odor to the fluid)	• Low fluid level	• Check and correct fluid level
	• Fluid cooler lines clogged	• Drain and refill transmission. If this doesn't cure the problem, have cooler lines cleared or replaced.
	• Heavy pulling or hauling with insufficient cooling	• Install a transmission oil cooler
	• Faulty oil pump, internal slippage	• Have transmission checked professionally
Buzzing or whining noise	• Low fluid level	• Check and correct fluid level
	• Defective torque converter, scored gears	• Have transmission checked professionally
No forward or reverse gears or slippage in one or more gears	• Low fluid level	• Check and correct fluid level
	• Defective vacuum or linkage controls, internal clutch or band failure	• Have unit checked professionally
Delayed or erratic shift	• Low fluid level	• Check and correct fluid level
	• Broken vacuum lines	• Repair or replace lines
	• Internal malfunction	• Have transmission checked professionally

HUB AND BEARING ASSEMBLY DIAGNOSIS

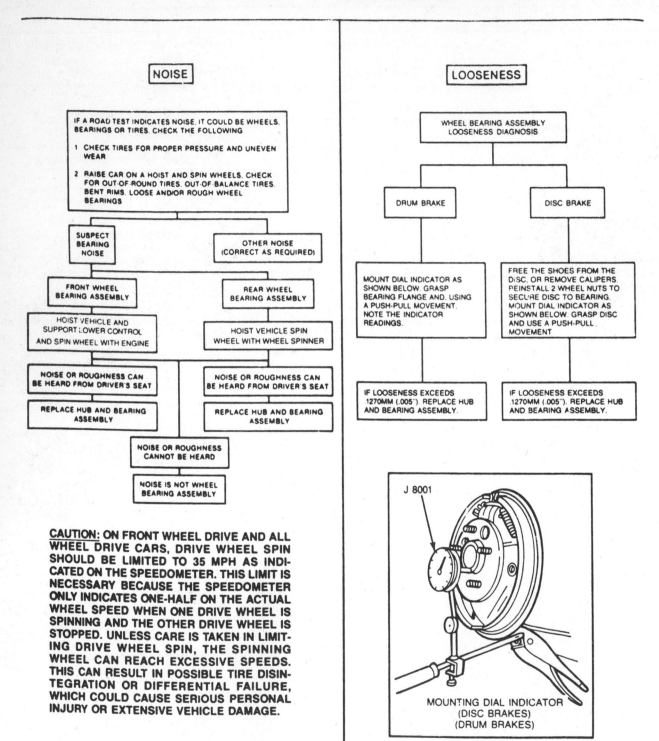

NOISE

IF A ROAD TEST INDICATES NOISE, IT COULD BE WHEELS, BEARINGS OR TIRES. CHECK THE FOLLOWING

1 CHECK TIRES FOR PROPER PRESSURE AND UNEVEN WEAR

2 RAISE CAR ON A HOIST AND SPIN WHEELS. CHECK FOR OUT-OF-ROUND TIRES. OUT-OF-BALANCE TIRES. BENT RIMS. LOOSE AND/OR ROUGH WHEEL BEARINGS

SUSPECT BEARING NOISE

OTHER NOISE (CORRECT AS REQUIRED)

FRONT WHEEL BEARING ASSEMBLY

REAR WHEEL BEARING ASSEMBLY

HOIST VEHICLE AND SUPPORT LOWER CONTROL AND SPIN WHEEL WITH ENGINE

HOIST VEHICLE SPIN WHEEL WITH WHEEL SPINNER

NOISE OR ROUGHNESS CAN BE HEARD FROM DRIVER'S SEAT

NOISE OR ROUGHNESS CAN BE HEARD FROM DRIVER'S SEAT

REPLACE HUB AND BEARING ASSEMBLY

REPLACE HUB AND BEARING ASSEMBLY

NOISE OR ROUGHNESS CANNOT BE HEARD

NOISE IS NOT WHEEL BEARING ASSEMBLY

LOOSENESS

WHEEL BEARING ASSEMBLY LOOSENESS DIAGNOSIS

DRUM BRAKE

DISC BRAKE

MOUNT DIAL INDICATOR AS SHOWN BELOW. GRASP BEARING FLANGE AND. USING A PUSH-PULL MOVEMENT. NOTE THE INDICATOR READINGS.

FREE THE SHOES FROM THE DISC. OR REMOVE CALIPERS. REINSTALL 2 WHEEL NUTS TO SECURE DISC TO BEARING. MOUNT DIAL INDICATOR AS SHOWN BELOW. GRASP DISC AND USE A PUSH-PULL MOVEMENT

IF LOOSENESS EXCEEDS .1270MM (.005"). REPLACE HUB AND BEARING ASSEMBLY.

IF LOOSENESS EXCEEDS .1270MM (.005"). REPLACE HUB AND BEARING ASSEMBLY.

CAUTION: ON FRONT WHEEL DRIVE AND ALL WHEEL DRIVE CARS, DRIVE WHEEL SPIN SHOULD BE LIMITED TO 35 MPH AS INDICATED ON THE SPEEDOMETER. THIS LIMIT IS NECESSARY BECAUSE THE SPEEDOMETER ONLY INDICATES ONE-HALF ON THE ACTUAL WHEEL SPEED WHEN ONE DRIVE WHEEL IS SPINNING AND THE OTHER DRIVE WHEEL IS STOPPED. UNLESS CARE IS TAKEN IN LIMITING DRIVE WHEEL SPIN, THE SPINNING WHEEL CAN REACH EXCESSIVE SPEEDS. THIS CAN RESULT IN POSSIBLE TIRE DISINTEGRATION OR DIFFERENTIAL FAILURE, WHICH COULD CAUSE SERIOUS PERSONAL INJURY OR EXTENSIVE VEHICLE DAMAGE.

J 8001

MOUNTING DIAL INDICATOR
(DISC BRAKES)
(DRUM BRAKES)

Suspension and Steering

QUICK REFERENCE INDEX

GENERAL INDEX

WHEELS

REMOVAL AND INSTALLATION

1. Raise and support the vehicle safely.
2. Remove the wheel cover with the chisel end of a tire tool.
3. If your vehicle has aluminum sport wheels, the plastic protective caps will have to be removed before removing the wheel nuts.
4. Remove the 5 wheel retaining nuts and remove wheel from the vehicle.

NOTE: **Sometimes wheels can be difficult to remove from the vehicle due to foreign material or a tight fit between the wheel center hole and the hub or rotor. These wheel can be removed without damage as follows:**

   a. Tighten all of the wheel nuts on the affected wheel, then loosen each wheel nut 2 turns.
   b. Lower the vehicle onto the floor or ground.
   c. Rock the vehicle from side to side as possible using 1 or more person's body weight to loosen the wheel and/or rock the vehicle from DRIVE to REVERSE allowing the vehicle to move several feet in each direction. Apply quick hard jabs on the brake pedal to loosen the wheel.
   d. Raise the vehicle, remove the wheel nuts and the wheel.

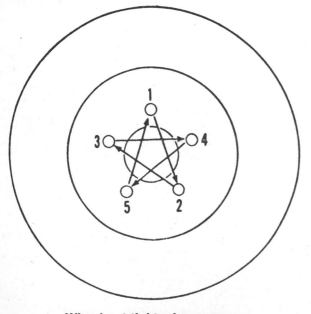

Wheel nut tightening sequence

To install:
5. Before installing the wheels, remove any build up of corrosion on the wheel mounting surface by scraping and wire brushing.
6. Install the wheel into position and screw the wheel nuts onto the studs with the cone shaped ends toward the wheel.
7. Tighten the wheel retaining nuts in sequence to 100 ft. lbs. (140 Nm).

NOTE: **The wheel nuts must be tightened in sequence and to the proper torque to avoid bending the wheel, brake drum or rotor.**

INSPECTION

Wheel must be replaced if they are bent, dented, have excessive lateral or radial runout, leak air through welds, have elongated bolt holes or heavily rusted.

Replacement wheels must be equivalent to the original equipment wheels in load capacity, diameter, rim width, offset and mounting configuration. A wheel of improper size or type may affect wheel and bearing life, brake cooling, speedometer/odometer calibration, vehicle ground clearance, and tire clearance to the body and chassis.

Steel wheels can be identified by a 2 or 3 letter code stamped into the rim near the valve stem. Aluminum wheels have the code, part number and manufacturer ID cast into the back side.

Wheel Stud

REMOVAL AND INSTALLATION

Front

1. Raise and support the vehicle safely.
2. Remove the front tire and wheel assembly.
3. Remove the front wheel hub and bearing as outlined in this section.
4. Using a wheel stud removal tool such as J 6627–A or equivalent, remove the wheel stud from the hub.
To install:
5. Install the washers on the wheel stud and pull into position with the wheel nut.
6. Reinstall the front wheel hub and bearing as outlined in this section.
7. Install the tire and wheel assembly and tighten the lug nuts to 100 ft. lbs.

Rear

1. Raise and support the vehicle safely.

2. Remove the rear tire and wheel assembly.
3. Remove the brake drum as outlined in this section.
4. Using a wheel stud removal tool such as J 6627–A or equivalent, remove the wheel stud from its seat in the hub.
To install:
5. Install the new stud, inserting it from the back side of the hub.

6. Install 4 flat washers on the stud and install the wheel nut with the flat side toward the washers.
7. Tighten the nut until the stud head is properly seated in the hub flange.
8. Install the brake drum and the tire and wheel assembly.
9. Tighten the lug nuts to 100 ft. lbs. and lower the vehicle.

FRONT SUSPENSION

Coil Spring

REMOVAL AND INSTALLATION

1. Remove the strut assembly.
2. Mount strut compressor J 34014 or equivalent, into holding fixture J 3289 20 or equivalent.
3. Mount the strut into the strut compressor. Note that the strut compressor has strut mounting holes drilled for specific car lines.
4. Compress the strut at least ½ its height after initial contact with the top cap.

NOTE: Never bottom the spring or dampener rod.

5. Remove the nut from the strut dampener shaft and place the J 34013 27 guiding rod on top of the dampener shaft. Use this rod to guide the dampener shaft straight down through the bearing cap while decompressing the spring.

Troubleshooting Basic Steering and Suspension Problems

Problem	Cause	Solution
Hard steering (steering wheel is hard to turn)	• Low or uneven tire pressure • Loose power steering pump drive belt • Low or incorrect power steering fluid • Incorrect front end alignment • Defective power steering pump • Bent or poorly lubricated front end parts	• Inflate tires to correct pressure • Adjust belt • Add fluid as necessary • Have front end alignment checked/adjusted • Check pump • Lubricate and/or replace defective parts
Loose steering (too much play in the steering wheel)	• Loose wheel bearings • Loose or worn steering linkage • Faulty shocks • Worn ball joints	• Adjust wheel bearings • Replace worn parts • Replace shocks • Replace ball joints
Car veers or wanders (car pulls to one side with hands off the steering wheel)	• Incorrect tire pressure • Improper front end alignment • Loose wheel bearings • Loose or bent front end components • Faulty shocks	• Inflate tires to correct pressure • Have front end alignment checked/adjusted • Adjust wheel bearings • Replace worn components • Replace shocks

Troubleshooting Basic Steering and Suspension Problems

Problem	Cause	Solution
Wheel oscillation or vibration transmitted through steering wheel	• Improper tire pressures • Tires out of balance • Loose wheel bearings • Improper front end alignment • Worn or bent front end components	• Inflate tires to correct pressure • Have tires balanced • Adjust wheel bearings • Have front end alignment checked/adjusted • Replace worn parts
Uneven tire wear	• Incorrect tire pressure • Front end out of alignment • Tires out of balance	• Inflate tires to correct pressure • Have front end alignment checked/adjusted • Have tires balanced

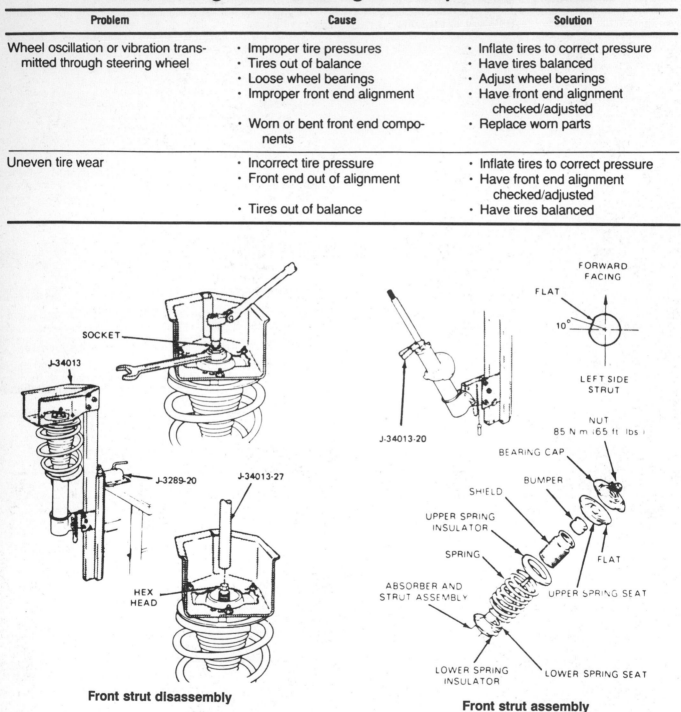

Front strut disassembly

Front strut assembly

6. Remove the components from above the spring and remove the spring from the strut.

NOTE: Care should be taken to avoid chipping or cracking the spring coating when handling the front suspension coil spring.

To install:

7. Install the bearing cap into the strut compressor, if previously removed.

8. Mount the strut into the strut compressor using the bottom locking pin only. Extend the dampener shaft and install the clamp J 34013 20 on the dampener shaft.

9. Install the spring over the dampener and swing the assembly up so the upper locking pin can be installed. Install the upper insulator, shield, bumper and upper spring seat. Be sure the flat on the upper spring seat is facing in the proper direction. The spring seat flat should be 10° forward of the centerline of the strut assembly spindle.

10. Install the guiding rod and turn the forcing screw while the

guiding rod centers the assembly. When the threads on the dampener shaft are visible, remove the guiding rod and install the nut.

11. Torque the nut to 65 ft. lbs. (85 Nm). Use a crowsfoot line wrench while holding the dampener shaft with the socket.

12. Remove the clamp.

MacPherson Strut

REMOVAL AND INSTALLATION

1. Remove the 3 nuts attaching the top of the strut to the body.
2. Raise and safely support the vehicle.
3. Place jack stands under the frame.
4. Lower the vehicle slightly so the weight of the vehicle rests on the jack stands and not on the control arms.
5. Remove the wheel and tire assembly.
6. Place J 34754 (modified) inner drive joint seal protector on the drive axle joints.

NOTE Drive axle joint seal protectors should be used anytime service is performed on or near the drive axles. Failure to observe this could result in joint or seal failure.

7. Remove the brake line bracket from the strut mount.
8. Remove the lower strut to knuckle mounting bolts.

NOTE: The steering knuckle must be supported to prevent axle joint overextension.

9. Remove the strut from the vehicle.
To install:
10. Install the strut assembly and tighten the 3 strut to body attaching nuts to 18 ft. lbs. (25 Nm).
11. Install the steering knuckle to strut assembly bolts to 140 ft. lbs. (190 Nm).
12. Install the brake line bracket to strut bolt to 13 ft. lbs. (17 Nm).
13. Remove the seal protectors.
14. Install the tire and wheel assembly.

15. Raise the vehicle slightly to allow removal of the jack stands and lower the vehicle.

Ball Joint

REMOVAL AND INSTALLATION

1. Raise and safely support the vehicle.
2. Place jack stands under the frame.
3. Lower the vehicle slightly so the weight of the vehicle rests on the jack stands and not on the control arms.
4. Remove the wheel and tire assembly.
5. Place J 34754 (modified) inner drive joint seal protector on the drive axle joints.

NOTE Drive axle joint seal protectors should be used anytime service is performed on or near the drive axles. Failure to observe this could result in joint or seal failure.

6. Remove the pinch bolt from the vehicle.
7. Remove the ball joint from the steering knuckle.
8. Use a ⅛ in. (3mm) drill bit to make a pilot hole through the rivets, then finish drilling the rivets with a ½ in. (13 mm) drill bit.

WARNING: Be careful not to damage the drive axle seals when drilling out the ball joint rivets.

9. Loosen the stabilizer shaft bushing assembly nut.
10. Remove the ball joint from the steering knuckle and control arm.
To install:
11. Install the ball joint in the control arm.
12. Install the 3 ball joint bolts and nuts and tighten to specification as specified in the ball joint kit.
13. Install the ball joint to the knuckle and install a new pinch bolt and nut and tighten to 33 ft. lbs. (45 Nm).
14. Install the stabilizer shaft bushing clamp bolts to 33 ft. lbs. (45 Nm).
15. Remove the seal protectors.
16. Install the tire and wheel assembly.

1. Strut assembly
2. Nut 140 ft. lbs. (190 Nm)
3. Knuckle and hub assembly
4. Lower control arm
5. Frame assembly
6. Bolt/screw
7. Nut 18 ft. lbs. (24 Nm)
8. Bracket (LB6 only)
9. Mount washer
10. Shock tower

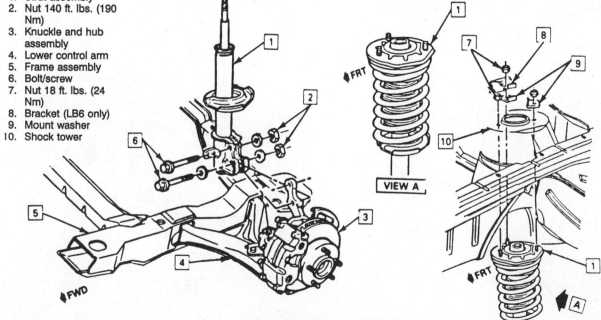

Strut assembly mounting

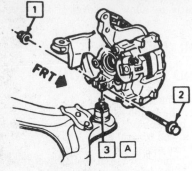

1. 33 ft. lbs. (45 Nm)
2. Pinch bolt
3. Ball joint
A. NOTE: Groove in ball joint stud must be aligned with hole in knuckle before inserting

Removing the ball joint from the knuckle

17. Raise the vehicle slightly to allow removal of the jack stands and lower the vehicle.

Stabilizer Shaft and Bushings

REMOVAL AND INSTALLATION

1. Raise and safely support the front of the vehicle so that the suspension hangs free.
2. Remove the stabilizer shaft insulator clamp and insulator at the control arms; do not remove the studs from the control arms.
3. Remove the plate from each side of the frame.
4. Remove the stabilizer shaft and insulator bushings.

To install:
5. Install the insulator bushings to the stabilizer shaft.
6. Install the stabilizer shaft and insulator bushings to the frame.
7. Install the plate to each side of the frame and tighten the bolts to 40 ft. lbs. (55 Nm).
8. Install the insulator clamp to the control arms and tighten the nuts to 33 ft. lbs. (45 Nm).

Control Arm

REMOVAL AND INSTALLATION

1. Raise and safely support the vehicle.
2. Place jack stands under the frame.

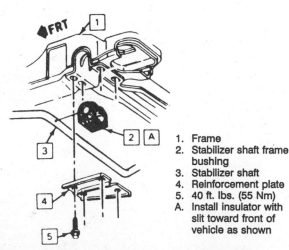

1. Frame
2. Stabilizer shaft frame bushing
3. Stabilizer shaft
4. Reinforcement plate
5. 40 ft. lbs. (55 Nm)
A. Install insulator with slit toward front of vehicle as shown

Front stabilizer shaft and bushing installation

3. Lower the vehicle slightly so the weight of the vehicle rests on the jack stands and not on the control arms.
4. Remove the wheel and tire assembly.
5. Place J 34754 (modified) inner drive joint seal protector on the drive axle joints.

NOTE Drive axle joint seal protectors should be used anytime service is performed on or near the drive axles. Failure to observe this could result in joint or seal failure.

6. Remove the stabilizer shaft to control arm bolt.
7. Remove the pinch bolt and the control arm mounting bolts and remove the control arm from the vehicle.

To install:
8. Install the control arm to the frame and install the mounting bolts but do not tighten at this time.
9. Install the ball joint to the steering knuckle and a NEW pinch bolt and nut and tighten to 33 ft. lbs. (45 Nm).
10. Raise the vehicle slightly so the weight of the vehicle is supported by the control arms.

NOTE: The weight of the vehicle must be supported by the control arms when tightening the control arm mounting bolts.

11. Tighten the stabilizer shaft bushing clamp nuts to 32 ft. lbs. (43 Nm) and the control arm pivot bolt nut to 61 ft. lbs. (83 Nm).
12. Remove the seal protectors.
13. Install the tire and wheel assembly.
14. Raise the vehicle slightly to allow removal of the jack stands and lower the vehicle.

Front Hub and Bearing and Seal

REMOVAL AND INSTALLATION

1. Raise and safely support the vehicle.
2. Place jack stands under the frame.
3. Lower the vehicle slightly so the weight of the vehicle rests on the jack stands and not on the control arms.
4. Remove the wheel and tire assembly.
5. Place J 34754 (modified) inner drive joint seal protector on the drive axle joints.

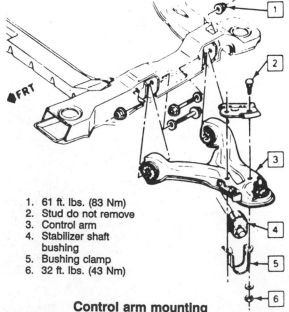

1. 61 ft. lbs. (83 Nm)
2. Stud do not remove
3. Control arm
4. Stabilizer shaft bushing
5. Bushing clamp
6. 32 ft. lbs. (43 Nm)

Control arm mounting

NOTE Drive axle joint seal protectors should be used anytime service is performed on or near the drive axles. Failure to observe this could result in joint or seal failure.

6. Insert a drift punch through the rotor.

NOTE: Clean the drive axle threads of all dirt and lubricant.

7. Remove the hub nut and washer.
8. Remove the caliper bolts and support the caliper.
9. Remove the rotor.
10. Attach tool J 28733 or equivalent, and separate the hub and drive axle.
11. Remove the 3 hub and bearing retaining bolts, shield, hub and bearing assembly and O-ring.
12. To remove the seal, use a punch and tap the seal toward the engine. When the seal is removed from the steering knuckle, cut it off the drive axle using side cutters.

NOTE: The factory seal is installed from the engine side of the steering knuckle. The service replacement seal is installed from the wheel side of the steering knuckle.
To install:
13. Install the new hub and bearing seal in the steering knuckle using the proper installer.
14. Lubricate the hub and bearing seal with grease.
15. Install a new O-ring around the hub and bearing assembly.
16. Install the hub and bearing assembly into the steering knuckle. On vehicles without the heavy duty brakes tighten the hub and bearing retaining bolts to 63 ft. lbs. (85 Nm). On vehi-

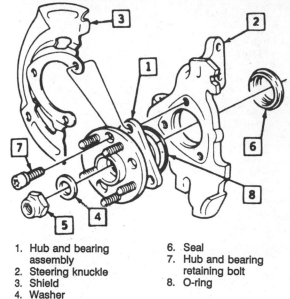

1. Hub and bearing assembly
2. Steering knuckle
3. Shield
4. Washer
5. Hub nut 180 ft. lbs. (245 Nm)
6. Seal
7. Hub and bearing retaining bolt
8. O-ring

Hub and bearing assembly

cles with the heavy duty brakes (option JA2), tighten the hub and bearing retaining bolts to 70 ft. lbs. (95 Nm).
17. Install the rotor and caliper and tighten the caliper retaining bolts to 38 ft. lbs. (51 Nm).
18. Install the hub nut and washer.
19. Insert a drift punch through the rotor and caliper.
20. Tighten the hub nut to 185 ft. lbs. (260 Nm).
21. Remove the seal protectors.
22. Install the tire and wheel assembly.
23. Raise the vehicle slightly to allow removal of the jack stands and lower the vehicle.

Front End Alignment

CASTER

Caster is the forward or rearward tilting of the wheel axis (the center line is an imaginary line that passes through the upper mount and the lower ball joint) from vertical. A rearward tilt (at the top) is positive (+) and a forward tilt is negative (-). Zero caster indicates that the strut is directly above the ball joint. Caster influences directional control of the steering but does not affect tire wear. Weak springs or overloading a vehicle will affect caster. Caster affects the vehicle's directional stability and steering effort. The caster angle is calculated to deliver the best in steering effort, normal wheel-returning forces and wheel-pulling sensitivity.

CAMBER

Camber is an important wheel alignment angle because it is both a tire wear angle and a directional control angle. Camber is the inward or outward tilt of the top of the tires when they are viewed from the front of the vehicle.

Not only will excessive camber result in tire wear, but it will also cause the vehicle to pull or lead to the side with the most positive camber. If there is a difference in camber from one side

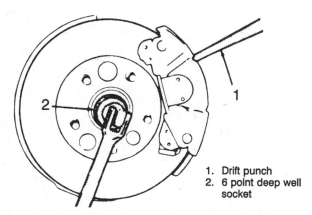

1. Drift punch
2. 6 point deep well socket

Removing and installing the hub nut

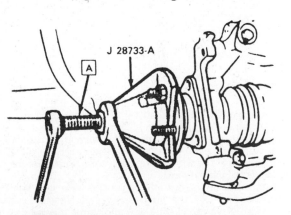

J 28733-A

Separate the drive axle from the hub

1. Front wheel drive shaft kit
2. Strut mounting washer
3. Nut (M8 x 1.25)
4. Nut (M10 x 1.50)
5. Bolt (M16 x 2.00 x 76)
6. Nut (M14 x 2.00)
7. Strut mount
8. Seat, front spring
9. Strut mount
10. Shield
11. Front spring insulator
12. Front coil spring
13. Front shock absorber with strut

15. Upper and lower knuckle bolt washer (M17.0 x 29.0)
16. Steering knuckle
17. Front wheel inner bearing seal
18. Front wheel bearing
19. Brake splash shield
20. Hex bolt (M12 x 1.75 x 40)
21. Bolt, steering knuckle control arm to knuckle
22. Front suspension reinforcement washer
23. Front wheel drive shaft nut
24. Front wheel disc
25. Front wheel mounting bolt
26. Nut (M10 x 1.5)

27. Front disc brake caliper
28. Front brake caliper bolt
29. Front wheel drive shaft kit
30. Lower control arm upper reinforcement and stop
31. Bolt
32. Flat washer (M10 x 20 x 3)
33. Hex bolt (M10 x 1.5 x 85)
34. Front lower control arm stop
35. Control arm ball joint kit
36. Front stabilizer shaft to arm bushing
37. Front stabilizer shaft end bracket
38. Flat washer (10MM)
39. Nut (M10 x 1.5)
40. Lower control arm bushing
41. Front stabilizer shaft insulator
42. Front stabilizer shaft
43. Hex nut
44. Front stabilizer shaft reinforcement
45. Hex bolt

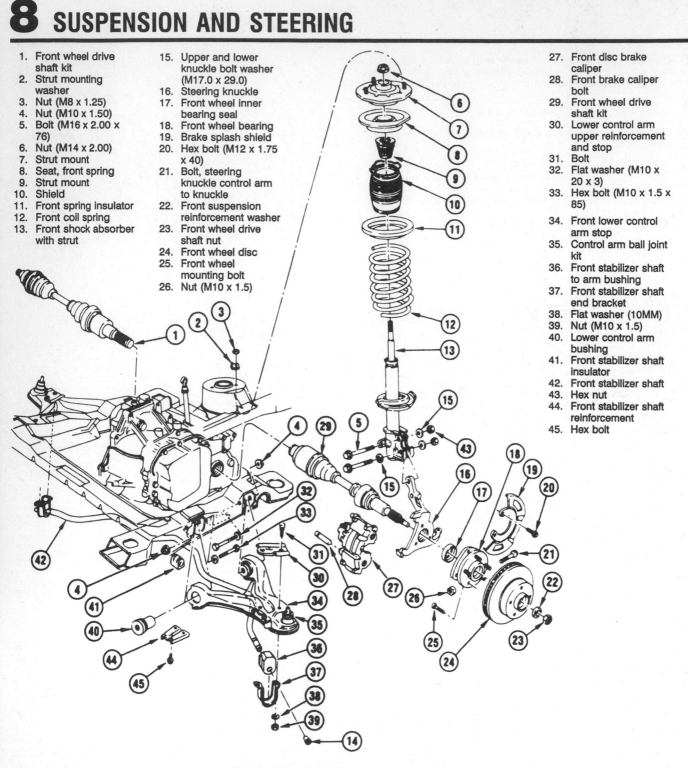

Exploded view of the front suspension

of the vehicle to the other, the vehicle will pull to the side with the most positive camber. To better understand camber's effect on directional control, think of it as a tapered cone that will not roll in a straight line.

TOE

Toe is a measurement of how much the front of the wheels are turned in or out from a straight-ahead position. When the wheels are turned in, toe is "positive" (+). When the wheels are turned out, toe is "negative" (−). The actual amount of toe is normally only a fraction of a degree. The purpose of toe is to ensure that the wheels roll parallel. Toe also serves to offset the small deflections of the wheel support system which occur when the vehicle is rolling forward.

Incorrect toe-in or toe-out will cause tire wear and less than optimum economy. As the suspension and steering systems wear, with extensive vehicle mileage, additional toe will be needed to compensate.

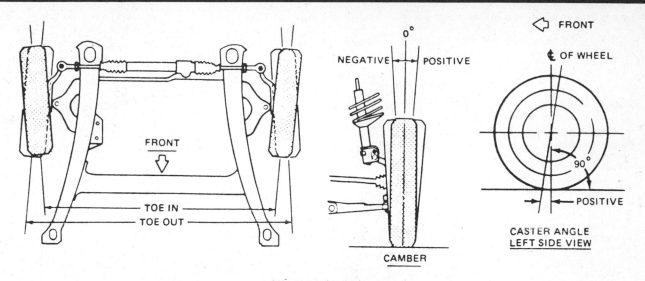

Alignment angles

WHEEL ALIGNMENT SPECIFICATIONS

Years	Models	Caster (deg.)		Camber (deg.)		Toe-in (deg.)
		Range	Pref.	Range	Pref.	
1990	Lumina APV	0.7N–2.7P	1.7P	0.5N–0.5P	0	0
	Silhouette	0.7N–2.7P	1.7P	0.5N–0.5P	0	0
	Transport	0.7N–2.7P	1.7P	0.5N–0.5P	0	0
1991	Lumina APV	0.7N–2.7P	1.7P	0.5N–0.5P	0	0
	Silhouette	0.7N–2.7P	1.7P	0.5N–0.5P	0	0
	Transport	0.7N–2.7P	1.7P	0.5N–0.5P	0	0

REAR SUSPENSION

Coil Springs

REMOVAL AND INSTALLATION

— CAUTION —

When removing the rear springs do not use a twin-post type hoist. The swing arc tendency of the rear axle assembly when certain fasteners are removed may cause it to slip from the hoist which may cause personal injury. Perform operation on floor, if necessary.

NOTE: When reassembling rear axle components, make sure that the bolts attaching the axle to the supports are inserted from inboard to outboard side of chassis, and position the leg of the upper coil on each spring parallel to the axle assembly and towards the side of vehicle within the limits.

1. Support the rear axle and safely raise the vehicle.
2. Remove the right and left brake line bracket attaching screws from the frame. Allow the brake line to hang freely.
3. Disconnect the track bar attaching nut and bolt at the rear axle.
4. Remove the right and left shock absorber lower attaching bolts.

WARNING: Do not suspend the rear axle by the brake hoses or damage to the hoses could result

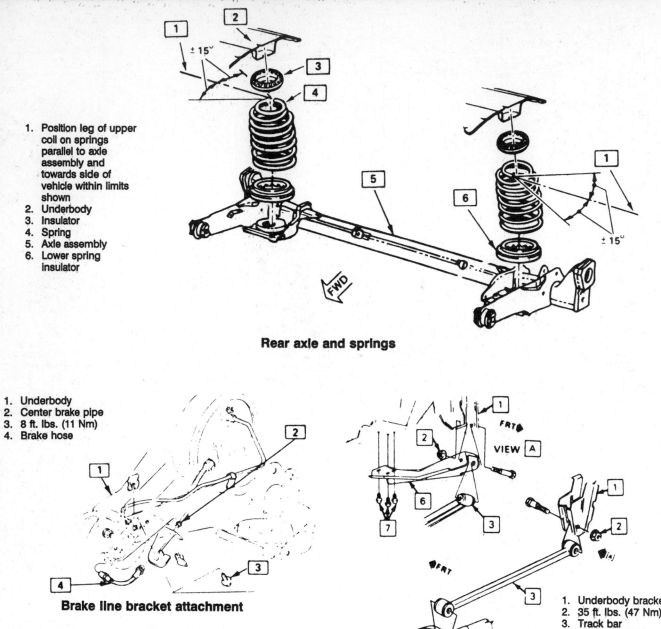

1. Position leg of upper coil on springs parallel to axle assembly and towards side of vehicle within limits shown
2. Underbody
3. Insulator
4. Spring
5. Axle assembly
6. Lower spring insulator

Rear axle and springs

1. Underbody
2. Center brake pipe
3. 8 ft. lbs. (11 Nm)
4. Brake hose

Brake line bracket attachment

1. Underbody bracket
2. 35 ft. lbs. (47 Nm)
3. Track bar
4. Axle assembly
5. 44 ft. lbs. (60 Nm)
6. Track bar brace
7. 35 ft. lbs. (47 Nm)

Track bar attachment

5. Lower the rear axle and remove the springs and insulators.

To install:

6. Position the springs and insulators in the seats and raise the rear axle. The leg of the upper coil on the springs must be parallel to the axle assembly and face outboard within the limits.

7. Install the shocks to the rear axle and tighten the nuts to 44 ft. lbs. (59 Nm).

8. Install the track bar to the rear axle and torque the nut to 44 ft. lbs. (59 Nm).

9. Install the brake line brackets to the frame and torque the screws to 8 ft. lbs. (11 Nm).

10. Remove the rear axle support jack and lower the vehicle.

Track Bar

REMOVAL AND INSTALLATION

1. Support the rear axle and safely raise the vehicle.

2. Remove the nut and bolt at both the rear axle and body attachments and remove the track bar.

To install:

3. Position the track bar at the axle mounting bracket and loosely install the bolt and nut.

4. Place the other end of the track bar in the body reinforcement and install the bolt and nut. Torque the nut at the axle bracket to 44 ft. lbs. (60 Nm). Torque the nut at the underbody reinforcement to 35 ft. lbs. (47 Nm).

5. Remove the rear axle support and lower the vehicle.

Shock Absorbers

REMOVAL AND INSTALLATION

1. Open the lift gate, remove the trim cover and remove the upper shock attaching nut.
2. Support the rear axle and safely raise the vehicle.
3. If equipped with electronic level control, disconnect the air hose.
4. Remove the lower attaching bolt and nut and remove the shock.

To install:

5. Position the shock at the lower attachment and feed the bolt through the holes and loosely install the nut.
6. If equipped with electronic level control, connect the air hose.
7. Lower the vehicle enough to guide the upper stud through the body opening and install the nut loosely.
8. Torque the lower nut to 44 ft. lbs. (59 Nm).
9. Lower the vehicle all the way and torque the upper nut to 16 ft. lbs. (22 Nm).
10. Install the trim cover.

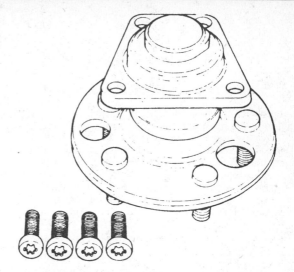

Rear hub and bearing attachment

Rear Wheel Hub and Bearing

REMOVAL AND INSTALLATION

1. Raise and support the vehicle safely.
2. Remove the tire and wheel assembly.
3. Remove the brake drum.

WARNING: Do not hammer on the brake drum or damage to the bearing could result.

4. Remove the attaching bolts and remove the hub and bearing assembly from the axle.

To install:

WARNING: The bolts which attach the hub and bearing assembly also support the brake assembly. When removing these bolts, support the brake assembly with a wire or other means.

5. Install the hub and bearing assembly to the rear axle and tighten the retaining bolts to 45 ft. lbs. (60 Nm).
6. Install the brake drum, tire and wheel assembly and lower the vehicle.

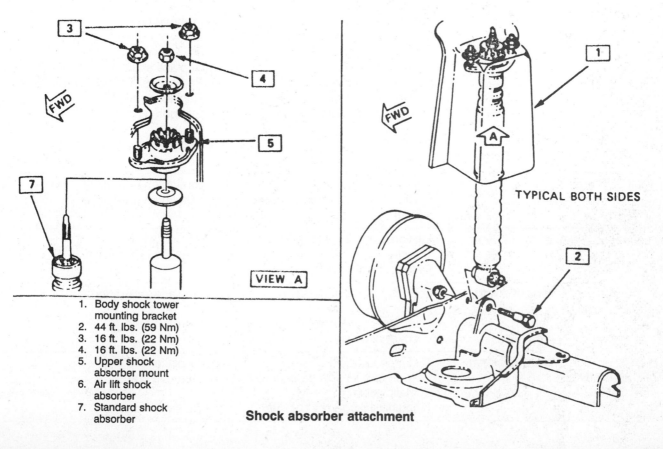

VIEW A

1. Body shock tower mounting bracket
2. 44 ft. lbs. (59 Nm)
3. 16 ft. lbs. (22 Nm)
4. 16 ft. lbs. (22 Nm)
5. Upper shock absorber mount
6. Air lift shock absorber
7. Standard shock absorber

TYPICAL BOTH SIDES

Shock absorber attachment

STEERING

Steering Wheel

REMOVAL AND INSTALLATION

1. Disconnect the negative battery cable.
2. Remove the horn pad by gently prying with a thin bladed tool.
3. Disconnect the horn electrical lead. Push down on the horn lead and turn left, the wire and spring will then come out of the canceling cam tower.
4. Matchmark the steering wheel and the shaft.
5. Remove the steering wheel retainer and nut.
6. Remove the steering wheel, using a suitable puller.

To install:

7. Align the matchmarks made during removal and tighten the steering wheel retaining nut to 30 ft. lbs. (40 Nm).
8. Install the retainer.
9. Install the horn lead electrical connection. Push down on the horn lead and turn right into a lock position.
10. Install the negative battery cable.

Turn Signal Switch

REMOVAL AND INSTALLATION

NOTE: The following special tools will be required for this procedure: Steering wheel puller J 1859-A and lock plate compressor J 23363-C, or their equivalents.

1. Disconnect the negative battery cable.
2. Remove screws from the back of the steering wheel.
3. Remove the horn pad from the steering wheel.
4. Remove the horn contact. Push down on the horn lead and turn left, the wire and spring will then come out of the canceling cam tower.
5. Matchmark the steering wheel and the shaft.
6. Remove the steering wheel retainer and nut.
7. Remove the steering wheel, using a suitable puller.
8. Remove the shaft lock cover.
9. Remove the shaft lock retaining ring using lock plate compressor tool J 23653-C, or equivalent to press down the shaft lock. Dispose of the ring.

Troubleshooting the Steering Column

Problem	Cause	Solution
Will not lock	• Lockbolt spring broken or defective	• Replace lock bolt spring
High effort (required to turn ignition key and lock cylinder)	• Lock cylinder defective	• Replace lock cylinder
	• Ignition switch defective	• Replace ignition switch
	• Rack preload spring broken or deformed	• Replace preload spring
	• Burr on lock sector, lock rack, housing, support or remote rod coupling	• Remove burr
	• Bent sector shaft	• Replace shaft
	• Defective lock rack	• Replace lock rack
	• Remote rod bent, deformed	• Replace rod
	• Ignition switch mounting bracket bent	• Straighten or replace
	• Distorted coupling slot in lock rack (tilt column)	• Replace lock rack
Will stick in "start"	• Remote rod deformed	• Straighten or replace
	• Ignition switch mounting bracket bent	• Straighten or replace
Key cannot be removed in "off-lock"	• Ignition switch is not adjusted correctly	• Adjust switch
	• Defective lock cylinder	• Replace lock cylinder
Lock cylinder can be removed without depressing retainer	• Lock cylinder with defective retainer	• Replace lock cylinder
	• Burr over retainer slot in housing cover or on cylinder retainer	• Remove burr
High effort on lock cylinder between "off" and "off-lock"	• Distorted lock rack	• Replace lock rack
	• Burr on tang of shift gate (automatic column)	• Remove burr
	• Gearshift linkage not adjusted	• Adjust linkage

Troubleshooting the Steering Column (cont.)

Problem	Cause	Solution
Noise in column	• One click when in "off-lock" position and the steering wheel is moved (all except automatic column)	• Normal—lock bolt is seating
	• Coupling bolts not tightened	• Tighten pinch bolts
	• Lack of grease on bearings or bearing surfaces	• Lubricate with chassis grease
	• Upper shaft bearing worn or broken	• Replace bearing assembly
	• Lower shaft bearing worn or broken	• Replace bearing. Check shaft and replace if scored.
	• Column not correctly aligned	• Align column
	• Coupling pulled apart	• Replace coupling
	• Broken coupling lower joint	• Repair or replace joint and align column
	• Steering shaft snap ring not seated	• Replace ring. Check for proper seating in groove.
	• Shroud loose on shift bowl. Housing loose on jacket—will be noticed with ignition in "off-lock" and when torque is applied to steering wheel.	• Position shroud over lugs on shift bowl. Tighten mounting screws.
High steering shaft effort	• Column misaligned	• Align column
	• Defective upper or lower bearing	• Replace as required
	• Tight steering shaft universal joint	• Repair or replace
	• Flash on I.D. of shift tube at plastic joint (tilt column only)	• Replace shift tube
	• Upper or lower bearing seized	• Replace bearings
Lash in mounted column assembly	• Column mounting bracket bolts loose	• Tighten bolts
	• Broken weld nuts on column jacket	• Replace column jacket
	• Column capsule bracket sheared	• Replace bracket assembly
Lash in mounted column assembly (cont.)	• Column bracket to column jacket mounting bolts loose	• Tighten to specified torque
	• Loose lock shoes in housing (tilt column only)	• Replace shoes
	• Loose pivot pins (tilt column only)	• Replace pivot pins and support
	• Loose lock shoe pin (tilt column only)	• Replace pin and housing
	• Loose support screws (tilt column only)	• Tighten screws
Housing loose (tilt column only)	• Excessive clearance between holes in support or housing and pivot pin diameters	• Replace pivot pins and support
	• Housing support-screws loose	• Tighten screws
Steering wheel loose—every other tilt position (tilt column only)	• Loose fit between lock shoe and lock shoe pivot pin	• Replace lock shoes and pivot pin

Troubleshooting the Steering Column (cont.)

Problem	Cause	Solution
Steering column not locking in any tilt position (tilt column only)	• Lock shoe seized on pivot pin • Lock shoe grooves have burrs or are filled with foreign material • Lock shoe springs weak or broken	• Replace lock shoes and pin • Clean or replace lock shoes • Replace springs
Noise when tilting column (tilt column only)	• Upper tilt bumpers worn • Tilt spring rubbing in housing	• Replace tilt bumper • Lubricate with chassis grease
One click when in "off-lock" position and the steering wheel is moved	• Seating of lock bolt	• None. Click is normal characteristic sound produced by lock bolt as it seats.
High shift effort (automatic and tilt column only)	• Column not correctly aligned • Lower bearing not aligned correctly • Lack of grease on seal or lower bearing areas	• Align column • Assemble correctly • Lubricate with chassis grease
Improper transmission shifting— automatic and tilt column only	• Sheared shift tube joint • Improper transmission gearshift linkage adjustment • Loose lower shift lever	• Replace shift tube • Adjust linkage • Replace shift tube

Troubleshooting the Ignition Switch

Problem	Cause	Solution
Ignition switch electrically inoperative	• Loose or defective switch connector • Feed wire open (fusible link) • Defective ignition switch	• Tighten or replace connector • Repair or replace • Replace ignition switch
Engine will not crank	• Ignition switch not adjusted properly	• Adjust switch
Ignition switch wil not actuate mechanically	• Defective ignition switch • Defective lock sector • Defective remote rod	• Replace switch • Replace lock sector • Replace remote rod
Ignition switch cannot be adjusted correctly	• Remote rod deformed	• Repair, straighten or replace

Troubleshooting the Turn Signal Switch

Problem	Cause	Solution
Turn signal will not cancel	• Loose switch mounting screws • Switch or anchor bosses broken • Broken, missing or out of position detent, or cancelling spring	• Tighten screws • Replace switch • Reposition springs or replace switch as required
Turn signal difficult to operate	• Turn signal lever loose • Switch yoke broken or distorted • Loose or misplaced springs • Foreign parts and/or materials in switch • Switch mounted loosely	• Tighten mounting screws • Replace switch • Reposition springs or replace switch • Remove foreign parts and/or material • Tighten mounting screws
Turn signal will not indicate lane change	• Broken lane change pressure pad or spring hanger • Broken, missing or misplaced lane change spring • Jammed wires	• Replace switch • Replace or reposition as required • Loosen mounting screws, reposition wires and retighten screws
Turn signal will not stay in turn position	• Foreign material or loose parts impeding movement of switch yoke • Defective switch	• Remove material and/or parts • Replace switch
Hazard switch cannot be pulled out	• Foreign material between hazard support cancelling leg and yoke	• Remove foreign material. No foreign material impeding function of hazard switch—replace turn signal switch.
No turn signal lights	• Inoperative turn signal flasher • Defective or blown fuse • Loose chassis to column harness connector • Disconnect column to chassis connector. Connect new switch to chassis and operate switch by hand. If vehicle lights now operate normally, signal switch is inoperative • If vehicle lights do not operate, check chassis wiring for opens, grounds, etc.	• Replace turn signal flasher • Replace fuse • Connect securely • Replace signal switch • Repair chassis wiring as required

Troubleshooting the Turn Signal Switch (cont.)

Problem	Cause	Solution
Instrument panel turn indicator lights on but not flashing	• Burned out or damaged front or rear turn signal bulb • If vehicle lights do not operate, check light sockets for high resistance connections, the chassis wiring for opens, grounds, etc. • Inoperative flasher • Loose chassis to column harness connection • Inoperative turn signal switch • To determine if turn signal switch is defective, substitute new switch into circuit and operate switch by hand. If the vehicle's lights operate normally, signal switch is inoperative.	• Replace bulb • Repair chassis wiring as required • Replace flasher • Connect securely • Replace turn signal switch • Replace turn signal switch
Stop light not on when turn indicated	• Loose column to chassis connection • Disconnect column to chassis connector. Connect new switch into system without removing old.	• Connect securely • Replace signal switch
Stop light not on when turn indicated (cont.)	Operate switch by hand. If brake lights work with switch in the turn position, signal switch is defective. • If brake lights do not work, check connector to stop light sockets for grounds, opens, etc.	 • Repair connector to stop light circuits using service manual as guide
Turn indicator panel lights not flashing	• Burned out bulbs • High resistance to ground at bulb socket • Opens, ground in wiring harness from front turn signal bulb socket to indicator lights	• Replace bulbs • Replace socket • Locate and repair as required
Turn signal lights flash very slowly	• High resistance ground at light sockets • Incorrect capacity turn signal flasher or bulb • If flashing rate is still extremely slow, check chassis wiring harness from the connector to light sockets for high resistance • Loose chassis to column harness connection • Disconnect column to chassis connector. Connect new switch into system without removing old. Operate switch by hand. If flashing occurs at normal rate, the signal switch is defective.	• Repair high resistance grounds at light sockets • Replace turn signal flasher or bulb • Locate and repair as required • Connect securely • Replace turn signal switch

Troubleshooting the Turn Signal Switch (cont.)

Problem	Cause	Solution
Hazard signal lights will not flash— turn signal functions normally	• Blow fuse • Inoperative hazard warning flasher • Loose chassis-to-column harness connection • Disconnect column to chassis connector. Connect new switch into system without removing old. Depress the hazard warning lights. If they now work normally, turn signal switch is defective. • If lights do not flash, check wiring harness "K" lead for open between hazard flasher and connector. If open, fuse block is defective	• Replace fuse • Replace hazard warning flasher in fuse panel • Conect securely • Replace turn signal switch • Repair or replace brown wire or connector as required

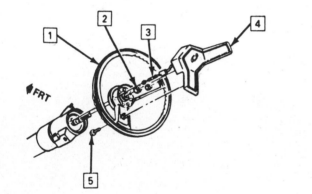

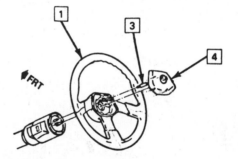

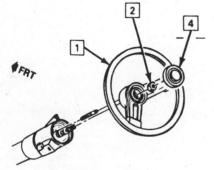

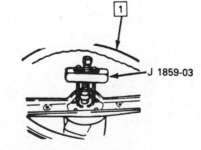

1. Steering wheel
2. 30 ft. lbs. (41 Nm)
3. Horn lead
4. Horn pad
5. 20 inch lbs. (2 Nm)

J 1859-03

Steering wheel removal

10. Remove the shaft lock.
11. Remove the turn signal canceling cam assembly.
12. On vehicles without tilt columns, remove the upper bearing spring and thrust washer.
13. On vehicles with tilt columns, remove the upper bearing spring, inner race seat and inner race.

14. Move the turn signal to **RIGHT TURN**, position up.
15. Remove the multi-function lever.
16. Remove the hazard knob assembly and the turn signal switch arm retaining screw.
17. Remove the turn signal switch screws.
18. Remove the wire protector and gently pull the wire har-

1. Hex locking nut
2. Shaft lock cover
3. Retaining ring
4. Shaft lock
5. Turn signal canceling cam assembly
6. Upper bearing spring
7. Binding head cross recess screw
8. RD wash HD (M4.2x1.41) screw
9. Signal switch arm
10. Turn signal switch assembly
11. Hex washer HD tapping screw
12. Thrust washer
13. Buzzer switch assembly
15. Lock retaining screw

35. Steering column shaft assembly
36. Upper shift lever spring
37. Gearshift lever bowl
38. Gearshift bowl shroud
39. Bowl lower bearing
40. Steering column jacket assembly
41. Dimmer and ignition switch mounting stud
42. Dimmer switch assembly
43. Ignition switch assembly

44. Hexagon (#10-24) nut
45. Washer head (#10-24x.25) screw
47. Dimmer switch rod
48. Shift tube assembly
49. Spring thrust washer
50. Shift tube return spring

51. Adapter and bearing assembly
52. Hex washer head tapping screw
53. Bearing and seal retainer
54. Lower bearing seat
55. Lower bearing spring

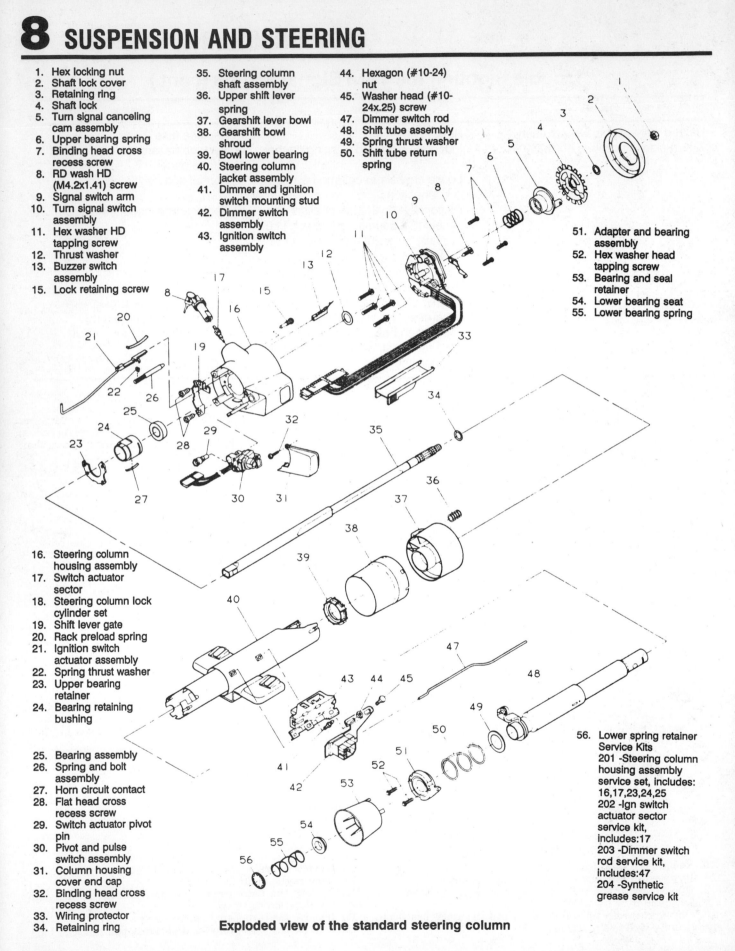

16. Steering column housing assembly
17. Switch actuator sector
18. Steering column lock cylinder set
19. Shift lever gate
20. Rack preload spring
21. Ignition switch actuator assembly
22. Spring thrust washer
23. Upper bearing retainer
24. Bearing retaining bushing

25. Bearing assembly
26. Spring and bolt assembly
27. Horn circuit contact
28. Flat head cross recess screw
29. Switch actuator pivot pin
30. Pivot and pulse switch assembly
31. Column housing cover end cap
32. Binding head cross recess screw
33. Wiring protector
34. Retaining ring

56. Lower spring retainer
Service Kits
201 -Steering column housing assembly service set, includes: 16,17,23,24,25
202 -Ign switch actuator sector service kit, includes:17
203 -Dimmer switch rod service kit, includes:47
204 -Synthetic grease service kit

Exploded view of the standard steering column

ness through the gearshift bowl shroud, gearshift lever bowl, and the steering column housing assembly, and remove the switch assembly.

To install:

19. Feed the turn signal switch wiring harness through the steering column housing assembly, gearshift lever bowl and the gearshift bowl shroud.

20. Install the turn signal switch and retaining screws and tighten to 31 inch lbs. (3.5 Nm).

21. Install the wire protector shield.

22. Install the turn signal switch arm and retaining screw and tighten to 20 inch lbs. (2.3 Nm).

23. Install the hazard knob assembly.

24. Install the multi-function lever.

25. On vehicles without tilt columns, install the upper bearing spring and thrust washer and on vehicles with tilt columns, install the upper bearing spring, inner race seat and inner race.

26. Lubricate with synthetic grease and install the turn signal canceling cam assembly.

27. Install the shaft lock.

28. Install a new shaft lock retaining ring. Align it to the block tooth on the shaft, using lock plate compressor tool J 23653-C, or equivalent to press down the shaft lock.

29. Install the shaft lock cover.

30. Install the steering wheel, aligning the marks on the wheel and the shaft.

32. Install the locking nut and retaining ring.

33. Install the horn contact into the horn tower. Push down on the horn lead and turn right into a lock position.

34. Install the horn pad and the screws in back of the steering wheel.

35. Connect the negative battery cable.

Ignition Switch and Dimmer Switch

REMOVAL AND INSTALLATION

Standard Column

NOTE: The following special tools will be required for this procedure: Steering wheel puller **J 1859-A** and lock plate compressor **J 23363-C**, or their equivalents.

1. Disconnect the negative battery cable.

2. Remove screws from the back of the steering wheel.

3. Remove the horn pad from the steering wheel.

4. Remove the horn contact. Push down on the horn lead and turn left, the wire and spring will then come out of the canceling cam tower.

5. Matchmark the steering wheel and the shaft.

6. Remove the steering wheel retainer and nut.

7. Remove the steering wheel, using a suitable puller.

8. Remove the shaft lock cover.

9. Remove the shaft lock retaining ring using lock plate compressor tool J 23653-C, or equivalent to press down the shaft lock. Dispose of the ring.

10. Remove the shaft lock.

11. Remove the turn signal canceling cam assembly.

12. Remove the upper bearing spring.

13. Remove the thrust washer.

14. Move the turn signal to **RIGHT TURN**, position up.

15. Remove the multi-function lever.

16. Remove the turn signal switch arm retaining screw.

17. Remove the turn signal switch screws and let the switch hang freely.

18. Remove the key from the lock cylinder set.

19. Remove the buzzer switch assembly.

20. Reinsert the key in the lock cylinder.

21. Turn the key to the **LOCK** position.

22. Remove the lock retaining screw and remove the lock cylinder.

24. If equipped with cruise control, Remove the housing cover end cap, unplug the cruise control connector and gently pull through the shroud, bowl, and steering column housing assembly.

25. Remove the washer head screw, the hex nut and dimmer switch.

26. Remove the mounting stud and ignition switch.

To install:

27. If equipped with cruise control, gently pull the connector through the steering column housing assembly, bowl and shroud and connect the plug.

28. Install the housing cover end cap and screw and tighten to 17 inch lbs. (1.9 Mn).

29. Install the ignition switch and mounting stud and tighten the stud to 35 inch lbs.(4.0 Nm). Adjust the ignition switch by moving the switch slider to the extreme left position and then move the slider 1 detent to the right (off lock).

30. Install the dimmer switch hex nut and screw and tighten to 35 inch lbs.(4.0 Nm). Adjust the dimmer switch.

31. To adjust the dimmer switch, depress the switch slightly to allow insertion of a $^3/_{32}$ in. drill bit into the hole above the actuator rod. Force the switch upward then tighten the screw.

32. Install the switch using the original screws. Use of screws that are too long could prevent the column from collapsing on impact.

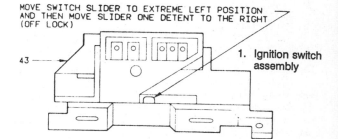

MOVE SWITCH SLIDER TO EXTREME LEFT POSITION AND THEN MOVE SLIDER ONE DETENT TO THE RIGHT (OFF LOCK)

43

1. Ignition switch assembly

Adjusting the ignition switch on the standard column

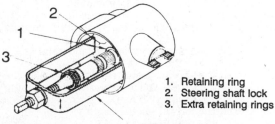

1. Retaining ring
2. Steering shaft lock
3. Extra retaining rings

J 23653-C

Removing the shaft lock retaining ring using the compressor tool

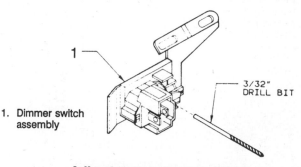

1. Dimmer switch assembly

3/32" DRILL BIT

Adjusting the dimmer switch

33. Install the lock cylinder and retaining screws and tighten to 40 inch lbs. (4.5 Nm).

34. Turn the key to the **RUN** position.

35. Install the buzzer switch assembly.

36. Install the turn signal switch and retaining screws and tighten to 31 inch lbs. (3.5 Nm).

37. Install the wire protector shield.

38. Install the turn signal switch arm and retaining screw and tighten to 29 inch lbs. (2.3 Nm).

39. Install the hazard knob assembly.

40. Install the multi-function lever.

41. Install the thrust washer and upper bearing spring.

42. Lubricate with synthetic grease and install the turn signal canceling cam assembly.

43. Install the shaft lock.

44. Install a new shaft lock retaining ring. Align it to the block tooth on the shaft, using lock plate compressor tool J 23653-C, or equivalent to press down the shaft lock.

44. Install the shaft lock cover.

45. Install the steering wheel, aligning the marks on the wheel and the shaft.

46. Install the locking nut and retaining ring.

47. Install the horn contact into the horn tower. Push down on the horn lead and turn right into a lock position.

48. Install the horn pad and the screws in back of the steering wheel.

49. Connect the negative battery cable.

Tilt Column

NOTE: The following special tools will be required for this procedure: Steering wheel puller J 1859-A, pivot pin removal tool J 21854-01, and lock plate compressor J 23363-C, or their equivalents.

1. Disconnect the negative battery cable.

2. Remove screws from the back of the steering wheel.

3. Remove the horn pad from the steering wheel.

4. Remove the horn contact. Push down on the horn lead and turn left, the wire and spring will then come out of the canceling cam tower.

5. Matchmark the steering wheel and the shaft.

6. Remove the steering wheel retainer and nut.

7. Remove the steering wheel, using a suitable puller.

8. Remove the shaft lock cover.

9. Remove the shaft lock retaining ring using lock plate compressor tool J 23653-C, or equivalent to press down the shaft lock. Dispose of the ring.

10. Remove the shaft lock.

11. Remove the turn signal canceling cam assembly.

12. Remove the upper bearing spring.

13. Remove the inner race seat and inner race.

14. Move the turn signal to **RIGHT TURN**, position up.

15. Remove the multi-function lever.

16. Remove the hazard knob assembly and the turn signal switch arm retaining screw.

17. Remove the turn signal switch screws.

18. Remove the wire protector and gently pull the wire harness through the gearshift bowl shroud, gearshift lever bowl, and the steering column housing assembly, and remove the switch assembly.

19. Remove the screws and remove the lock housing cover assembly.

20. Remove the tilt wheel lever.

21. Remove the cover end cap and the dimmer switch rod actuator.

22. Gently pull the pivot switch wire harness through the bowl assembly and column housing.

23. Remove the tilt wheel spring retainer and spring.

24. Remove the pivot pins, using tool J 21854-01, or equivalent.

25. Reinstall the tilt lever.

26. Pull back on the tilt lever and pull the column housing down and away from the column.

27. Remove the column from the vehicle.

WARNING: Once the column is removed from the vehicle it is extremely susceptible to damage.

28. Remove the bearing and seal retainer.

29. Remove the lower spring retainer and dispose of the retainer.

30. Remove the lower bearing spring and seat.

31. Remove the hex head screws and remove the adapter and bearing assembly.

32. Remove the column shaft assembly and check for accident damage.

NOTE: Mark the upper and lower shaft assembly to ensure proper assembly. Failure to assemble properly will cause the steering wheel to be turned 180°.

33. Disconnect the upper shaft from the lower shaft assembly. Tilt 90° to each other and disengage.

34. Disconnect the centering sphere from the upper shaft assembly. Rotate 90° and slip out.

35. Remove the housing support retaining screws.

36. Remove the column housing support assembly and dimmer switch rod from the steering column jacket assembly.

37. Remove the rod from the column housing support assembly.

38. Remove the 2 screws and remove the shift lever gate from the support assembly.

39. Remove the hex nut and screw and remove the dimmer switch assembly.

40. Remove the mounting stud and remove the ignition switch assembly and actuator rod.

To install:

41. Install the gate to the support assembly and tighten the retaining screws to 33 inch lbs. (3.7 Nm).

42. Install the dimmer switch rod to the support assembly.

43. Install the column housing support assembly and tighten the retaining screws to 78 inch lbs. (8.8 Nm).

44. Install the actuator assembly to the track housing support assembly.

45. Install the joint preload spring to the 2 centering sphere.

46. Install the centering sphere. Lubricate with lithium grease and slip into the upper shaft assembly and rotate 90°.

NOTE: The marks on the upper and lower shaft assembly must line up after assembled. Failure to assemble properly will cause the steering wheel to be turned 180°.

47. Connect the upper shaft to the lower shaft assembly. Line up the marks tilt the assemblies 90° to each other and engage.

48. Lubricate the column shaft assembly with lithium grease and install the jacket assembly.

48. Install the lock cylinder and retaining screws and tighten to 40 inch lbs. (4.5 Nm).

49. Turn the key to the **RUN** position.

50. Install the buzzer switch assembly.

51. Feed the turn signal switch wiring harness through the steering column housing assembly, gearshift lever bowl and the gearshift bowl shroud.

52. Install the turn signal switch and retaining screws and tighten to 31 inch lbs. (3.5 Nm).

53. Install the wire protector shield.

54. Install the turn signal switch arm and retaining screw and tighten to 20 inch lbs. (2.3 Nm).

55. Install the hazard knob assembly.

56. Install the multi-function lever.

57. On vehicles without tilt columns, install the upper bearing spring and thrust washer and on vehicles with tilt columns, install the upper bearing spring, inner race seat and inner race.

1. Hexagon locking nut (M 14x1.5)
2. Shaft lock cover
3. Retaining ring
4. Shaft lock
5. Turn signal canceling cam assembly
6. Upper bearing spring
7. Binding head cross recess screw
8. RD wash HD screw (M4.2x1.41)
9. Signal switch arm
10. Turn signal switch assembly
11. Upper bearing inner race seat
12. Inner race
13. Pan HD 6-lobed soc tap screw
14. Buzzer switch assembly
16. Lock retaining screw
17. Lock housing cover assembly
18. Steering column lock cylinder set
19. Dimmer switch rod actuator
20. Switch actuator pivot pin
21. Pivot and pulse switch assembly
22. Column housing cover end cap
23. Wiring protector
24. Steering column housing assembly
25. Bearing assembly
26. Lock bolt
27. Lock bolt spring
28. Steering wheel lock shoe
29. Steering wheel lock shoe
31. Drive shaft
32. Dowel pin
33. Pivot pin
34. Shoe spring
35. Release lever spring
36. Release lever pin
37. Shoe release lever
38. Switch actuator rack
39. Rack preload spring
40. Steering column housing
41. Switch actuator sector
42. Hex washer head screw
43. Spring guide
44. Wheel tilt spring
45. Spring retainer
46. Steering column shaft assembly
47. Race and upper shaft assembly
48. Centering sphere
49. Joint preload spring
50. Lower steering shaft assembly
51. Support screw

52. Steering column housing support assembly
53. Steering column housing support
54. Oval head cross recess screw
55. Shift lever gate
56. Shift tube retaining ring
57. Thrust washer
58. Lock plate
59. Wave washer
60. Shift lever spring

61. Gearshift lever bowl assembly
62. Steering column jacket assembly
63. Ignition switch actuator assembly
64. Ignition switch assembly
65. Dimmer and ignition switch mounting stud

74. Lower bearing seat
75. Lower bearing spring
76. Lower spring retainer
Service Kits
201-Column sector and rack service kit includes: 12,25,27,38,41,42

66. Dimmer switch assembly
67. Hexagon (#10-24) nut
68. Wash head (#10-24x.25) screw
69. Dimmer switch rod
70. Shift tube assembly
71. Adapter and bearing assembly
72. Hex washer head tapping screw
73. Bearing and seal retainer

202-Pivot and switch assembly service kit includes: 20,21
203-Tilt column spring service kit includes: 11,12,43,44,45
204-Tilt column sphere service kit includes: 48,49
205-Synthetic grease service kit

Exploded view of the tilt steering column

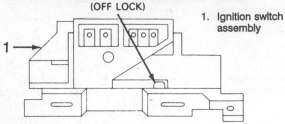

MOVE SWITCH SLIDER TO EXTREME RIGHT POSITION
AND THEN MOVE SLIDER ONE DETENT TO THE LEFT
(OFF LOCK)

1. Ignition switch assembly

Adjusting the ignition switch on the tilt column

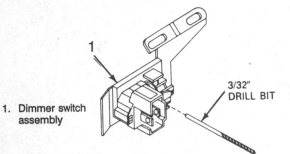

1

3/32"
DRILL BIT

1. Dimmer switch assembly

Adjusting the dimmer switch

58. Lubricate with synthetic grease and install the turn signal canceling cam assembly.
59. Install the shaft lock.
60. Install a new shaft lock retaining ring. Align it to the block tooth on the shaft, using lock plate compressor tool J 23653-C, or equivalent to press down the shaft lock.
61. Install the shaft lock cover.
62. Install the steering wheel, aligning the marks on the wheel and the shaft.
63. Install the locking nut and retaining ring.
64. Install the horn contact into the horn tower. Push down on the horn lead and turn right into a lock position.
65. Install the horn pad and the screws in back of the steering wheel.
66. Coat the inner surface with lithium grease and install the adapter and bearing assembly. Tighten the screws to 30 inch lbs. (3.4 Nm).
67. Install the lower bearing seat and spring. Press the retainer onto the shaft to compress the shaft. Spring height must be 1.0 in. (25.4 mm).
68. Install the bearing and seal retainer.
69. Install the ignition switch and mounting stud and tighten to 35 inch lbs. (4.0 Nm).
70. Install and adjust the dimmer switch and tighten to 35 inch lbs. (4.0 Nm).
71. To adjust the dimmer switch, depress the switch slightly to allow insertion of a 3/32 in. drill bit into the hole above the actuator rod. Force the switch upward then tighten the screw.
72. Install the switch using the original screws. Use of screws that are too long could prevent the column from collapsing on impact.
73. Install the column to the instrument panel.
74. Connect the negative battery cable.

Ignition Lock Cylinder

REMOVAL AND INSTALLATION

NOTE: The following special tools will be required for this procedure: Steering wheel puller J 1859-A and lock plate compressor J 23363-C, or their equivalents.

1. Disconnect the negative battery cable.
2. Remove screws from the back of the steering wheel.
3. Remove the horn pad from the steering wheel.
4. Remove the horn contact. Push down on the horn lead and turn left, the wire and spring will then come out of the canceling cam tower.
5. Matchmark the steering wheel and the shaft.
6. Remove the steering wheel retainer and nut.
7. Remove the steering wheel, using a suitable puller.
8. Remove the shaft lock cover.
9. Remove the shaft lock retaining ring using lock plate compressor tool J 23653-C, or equivalent to press down the shaft lock. Dispose of the ring.
10. Remove the shaft lock.
11. Remove the turn signal canceling cam assembly.
12. On vehicles without tilt columns, remove the upper bearing spring and thrust washer.
13. On vehicles with tilt columns, remove the upper bearing spring, inner race seat and inner race.
14. Move the turn signal to **RIGHT TURN**, position up.
15. Remove the multi-function lever.
16. Remove the turn signal switch arm retaining screw.
17. Remove the turn signal switch screws and let the switch hang freely.
18. Remove the key from the lock cylinder set.
19. Remove the buzzer switch assembly.
20. Reinsert the key in the lock cylinder.
21. Turn the key to the **LOCK** position.
22. Remove the lock retaining screw and remove the lock cylinder.
To install:
23. Install the lock cylinder and retaining screws and tighten to 40 inch lbs. (4.5 Nm).
24. Turn the key to the **RUN** position.
25. Install the buzzer switch assembly.
26. Install the turn signal switch and retaining screws and tighten to 31 inch lbs. (3.5 Nm).
27. Install the wire protector shield.
28. Install the turn signal switch arm and retaining screw and tighten to 29 inch lbs. (2.3 Nm).
30. Install the hazard knob assembly.
31. Install the multi-function lever.
32. On vehicles without tilt columns, install the upper bearing spring and thrust washer and on vehicles with tilt columns, install the upper bearing spring, inner race seat and inner race.
33. Lubricate with synthetic grease and install the turn signal canceling cam assembly.
34. Install the shaft lock.
35. Install a new shaft lock retaining ring. Align it to the block tooth on the shaft, using lock plate compressor tool J 23653-C, or equivalent to press down the shaft lock.
36. Install the shaft lock cover.
37. Install the steering wheel, aligning the marks on the wheel and the shaft.
38. Install the locking nut and retaining ring.
39. Install the horn contact into the horn tower. Push down on the horn lead and turn right into a lock position.
40. Install the horn pad and the screws in back of the steering wheel.
41. Connect the negative battery cable.

Steering Column

REMOVAL AND INSTALLATION

WARNING: Once the column is removed from the vehicle it is extremely susceptible to damage.

1. Disconnect the negative battery cable.
2. Remove the left instrument panel sound insulator.

3. Remove the left instrument panel trim pad and steering column trim collar.

4. Remove the horn contact pad and steering wheel, only if the column is to be disassembled.

5. Remove the steering column to intermediate shaft pinch bolt connection.

6. Remove the column bracket support bolts and bracket support nut.

7. Disconnect the shift indicator cable.

8. Disconnect the electrical connectors.

9. Disconnect the shift cable at the actuator and housing holder.

10. Remove the column assembly from the vehicle.

WARNING: Never support the column by only the lower attachments or damage to the lower retainer will result.

—————————— CAUTION ——————————
If there is a possibility that the steering column may be partially collapsed, check it for accident damage, as illustrated.

To install:

11. Reposition the column in the vehicle.

12. Connect the shift cable at the actuator and housing holder.

13. Connect the electrical connectors.

14. Connect the shift indicator cable.

15. Install column bracket support bolts and bracket support nut and tighten the bolts to 20 ft. lbs. (27 Nm).

16. Install the steering column to intermediate shaft pinch bolt and tighten to 35 ft. lbs. (47 Nm).

17. Install the horn contact pad and steering wheel, if necessary.

18. Install the left instrument panel trim pad and steering column trim collar.

19. Install the left instrument panel sound insulator.

20. Connect the negative battery cable.

Multi-Function Switch Lever
REMOVAL and INSTALLATION

1. Disconnect the negative battery cable.

2. Remove the wiring protector cover underneath the column.

3. Disconnect the multi-function switch.

4. Disconnect the cruise control wire.

5. Remove the switch.

6. Installation is the reverse of removal. Feed the cruise control wire into the column using piano wire or something similar.

Power Steering Rack and Pinion
REMOVAL AND INSTALLATION

1. Disconnect the negative battery cable.

2. Remove the air cleaner assembly.

3. Remove the dust boot from the steering gear.

4. Remove the intermediate shaft lower pinch bolt and disconnect the intermediate shaft from the lower stub shaft.

5. Remove the fluid line retaining clips at the pump and disconnect the lines.

6. Raise and safely support the vehicle.

7. Remove the wheel and tire assemblies. Disconnect the tie rod ends at the steering knuckle.

8. Remove the remaining brackets and clips at the crossmember. Support the body safely with the appropriate equipment, to allow lowering of the subframe.

9. Remove the rear subframe mounting bolts and carefully lower the rear of the subframe approximately 5 in. (127mm).

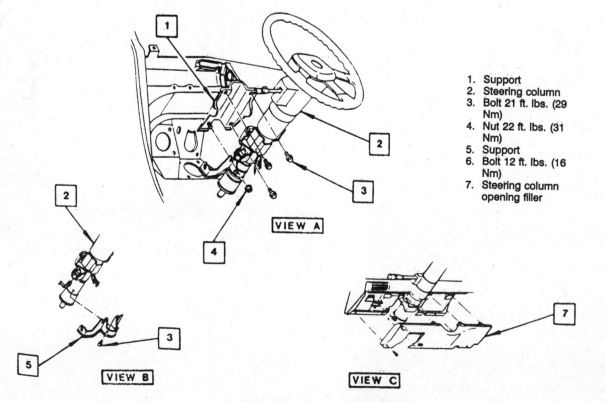

1. Support
2. Steering column
3. Bolt 21 ft. lbs. (29 Nm)
4. Nut 22 ft. lbs. (31 Nm)
5. Support
6. Bolt 12 ft. lbs. (16 Nm)
7. Steering column opening filler

Steering column installation

CHECKING STEERING COLUMN FOR ACCIDENT DAMAGE

NOTICE: Vehicles involved in accidents resulting in frame damage, major body or sheet metal damage, or where the steering column has been impacted, or where supplemental inflatable restraints systems deployed may also have a damaged or misaligned steering column.

CHECKING PROCEDURE

JACKET ASM, STEERING COLUMN

- Check capsules on steering column bracket assembly, all should be within 1.59mm from the bottom of the slots (View A). If not, bracket should be replaced if bracket is bolted to the jacket asm or the jacket asm should be replaced if bracket is welded to jacket asm.
- Check contact surface "A" on capsules (View B). The bolt head must not contact surface "A" or shear load would be increased. If contact is made, replace bracket asm or jacket asm.
- Check for jacket asm collapse by measuring the distance from the lower edge of upper jacket to a defined point on the lower jacket (View E). If measured dimensions are not within specifications, a new jacket must be installed.

SHIFT TUBE ASM

- Visually inspect shift tube for sheared injected plastic (View C). If shift tube shows sheared plastic, a new shift tube must be installed.
- Check operation of shift lever. If you can move lever to "Park" position without raising lever, it is an indication that upper shift tube plastic bearing is broken.

STEERING SHAFT ASM

- Visually inspect steering shaft for sheared injected plastic (View D). If steering shaft shows sheared plastic, a new steering shaft must be installed.
- Any frame damage that could cause a bent steering shaft must have steering shaft runout checked in the following manner. Using a dial indicator at lower end of steering shaft, have steering wheel rotated. Runout must not exceed 1.59mm.

NOTICE: Inflatable restraint coil asm must be removed from steering column and allowed to hang freely before shaft is rotated. Failure to do so could damage coil asm.

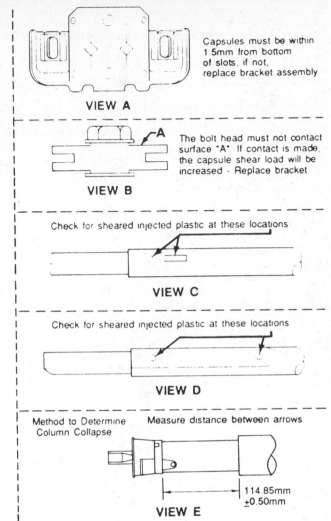

VIEW A — Capsules must be within 1.5mm from bottom of slots, if not, replace bracket assembly

VIEW B — The bolt head must not contact surface "A". If contact is made, the capsule shear load will be increased - Replace bracket

VIEW C — Check for sheared injected plastic at these locations

VIEW D — Check for sheared injected plastic at these locations

VIEW E — Method to Determine Column Collapse. Measure distance between arrows. 114.85mm ±0.50mm

Checking the steering column for accident damage

10. Remove the rack and pinion mounting bolts and remove the rack through the left wheel opening.

To install:

11. Install the rack and pinion through the left wheel opening.
12. Install the rack and pinion mounting nuts, tighten to 70 ft. lbs. (95 Nm).
13. Raise the subframe assembly and install the rear mounting bolts.
14. Remove any supports and install the brackets and clips to the crossmember.
15. Install the wheel and tire assemblies. Lower the vehicle.
16. Connect the fluid lines at the pump and tighten to 18 ft. lbs. (25 Nm).
17. Install the line retaining clips. Connect the intermediate shaft to the stub shaft.
18. Install the dust boot over the steering gear.
19. Install the air cleaner assembly and connect the negative battery cable.
20. Fill and bleed the steering system.

Power Steering Pump

REMOVAL AND INSTALLATION

1. Disconnect the negative battery cable. Disconnect and cap the power steering pump hoses. Remove the accessory drive belt.
2. Remove the power steering pump pulley using a suitable puller tool or equivalent.
3. Remove the pump mounting bolts and remove the pump from the vehicle.
4. Installation is the reverse of the removal procedure. Tighten the pump mounting bolts to 18 ft. lbs (25 Nm).
5. Bleed the power steering system to remove trapped air. Air in the system could cause noise and or damage to the pump.

SYSTEM BLEEDING

1. With the engine off, the wheels off of the ground and

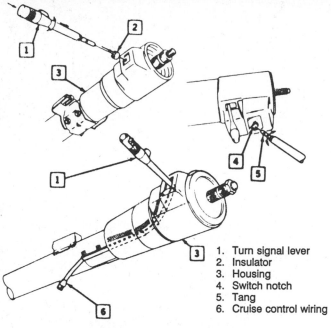

1. Turn signal lever
2. Insulator
3. Housing
4. Switch notch
5. Tang
6. Cruise control wiring

Multi-function turn signal lever

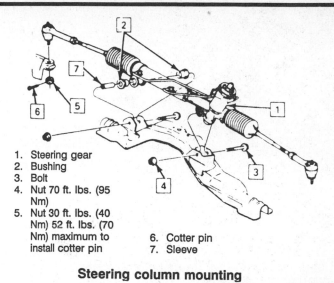

1. Steering gear
2. Bushing
3. Bolt
4. Nut 70 ft. lbs. (95 Nm)
5. Nut 30 ft. lbs. (40 Nm) 52 ft. lbs. (70 Nm) maximum to install cotter pin
6. Cotter pin
7. Sleeve

Steering column mounting

4. Return the wheels to the center position. Lower the front wheels to the ground and continue running the engine for 2 or 3 minutes.

5. Road test the vehicle to make sure the steering functions properly and is free of noises.

Tie Rod Ends

REMOVAL AND INSTALLATION

1. Raise and support the vehicle safely. Remove the tire and wheel assemblies.

2. Remove the cotter pin and castellated nut and using the proper removal tool such as J24319-01 or equivalent, separate the outer tie rod from the steering knuckle.

turned all the way to the left fill the fluid reservoir to the **FULL COLD** mark on the fluid level indicator.

2. Bleed the system by turning the wheels from side to side without hitting the stops. It may be necessary to repeat this several times. Keep the fluid level at the **FULL COLD** mark.

Fluid with air in it has a light tan appearance. This air must be eliminated from the fluid before normal steering action can be obtained.

3. Start the engine and while it is idling, recheck the fluid level and add as necessary to reach the **FULL COLD** mark.

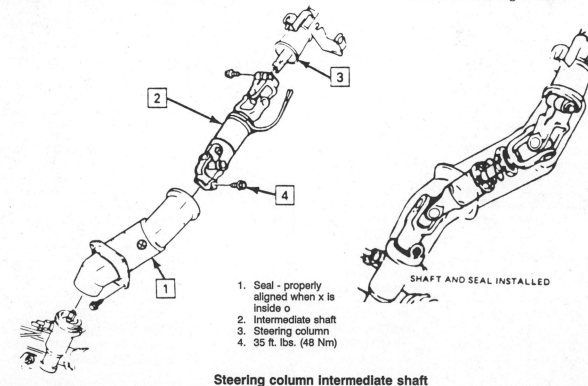

1. Seal - properly aligned when x is inside o
2. Intermediate shaft
3. Steering column
4. 35 ft. lbs. (48 Nm)

SHAFT AND SEAL INSTALLED

Steering column intermediate shaft

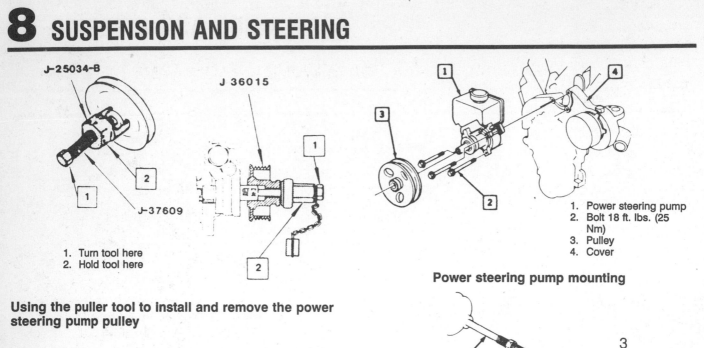

1. Turn tool here
2. Hold tool here

Using the puller tool to install and remove the power steering pump pulley

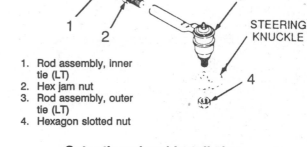

1. Power steering pump
2. Bolt 18 ft. lbs. (25 Nm)
3. Pulley
4. Cover

Power steering pump mounting

3. Loosen the jam hex nut at the inner tie rod and remove the outer tie rod end from the inner tie rod.

4. Installation is the reverse of the removal procedure. Tighten the outer tie rod to knuckle hex slotted nut to 35 ft. lbs. (50 Nm). 45 ft. lbs. (60 Nm) is the maximum permissible torque to align the cotter pin in the slot $\frac{1}{6}$ turn (maximum). The toe is adjusted by turning the inner tie rod then tighten the jam nut to 50 ft. lbs. (70 Nm).

5. Adjust the front end alignment, as required.

STEERING KNUCKLE

1. Rod assembly, inner tie (LT)
2. Hex jam nut
3. Rod assembly, outer tie (LT)
4. Hexagon slotted nut

Outer tie rod end installation

Troubleshooting the Power Steering Pump

Problem	Cause	Solution
Chirp noise in steering pump	• Loose belt	• Adjust belt tension to specification
Belt squeal (particularly noticeable at full wheel travel and stand still parking)	• Loose belt	• Adjust belt tension to specification
Growl noise in steering pump	• Excessive back pressure in hoses or steering gear caused by restriction	• Locate restriction and correct. Replace part if necessary.
Growl noise in steering pump (particularly noticeable at stand still parking)	• Scored pressure plates, thrust plate or rotor • Extreme wear of cam ring	• Replace parts and flush system • Replace parts
Groan noise in steering pump	• Low oil level • Air in the oil. Poor pressure hose connection.	• Fill reservoir to proper level • Tighten connector to specified torque. Bleed system by operating steering from right to left—full turn.

Troubleshooting the Power Steering Pump (cont.)

Problem	Cause	Solution
Rattle noise in steering pump	• Vanes not installed properly • Vanes sticking in rotor slots	• Install properly • Free up by removing burrs, varnish, or dirt
Swish noise in steering pump	• Defective flow control valve	• Replace part
Whine noise in steering pump	• Pump shaft bearing scored	• Replace housing and shaft. Flush system.
Hard steering or lack of assist	• Loose pump belt • Low oil level in reservoir **NOTE:** Low oil level will also result in excessive pump noise • Steering gear to column misalignment • Lower coupling flange rubbing against steering gear adjuster plug • Tires not properly inflated	• Adjust belt tension to specification • Fill to proper level. If excessively low, check all lines and joints for evidence of external leakage. Tighten loose connectors. • Align steering column • Loosen pinch bolt and assemble properly • Inflate to recommended pressure
Foaming milky power steering fluid, low fluid level and possible low pressure	• Air in the fluid, and loss of fluid due to internal pump leakage causing overflow	• Check for leaks and correct. Bleed system. Extremely cold temperatures will cause system aeration should the oil level be low. If oil level is correct and pump still foams, remove pump from vehicle and separate reservoir from body. Check welsh plug and body for cracks. If plug is loose or body is cracked, replace body.
Low pump pressure	• Flow control valve stuck or inoperative • Pressure plate not flat against cam ring	• Remove burrs or dirt or replace. Flush system. • Correct
Momentary increase in effort when turning wheel fast to right or left	• Low oil level in pump • Pump belt slipping • High internal leakage	• Add power steering fluid as required • Tighten or replace belt • Check pump pressure. (See pressure test)
Steering wheel surges or jerks when turning with engine running especially during parking	• Low oil level • Loose pump belt • Steering linkage hitting engine oil pan at full turn • Insufficient pump pressure	• Fill as required • Adjust tension to specification • Correct clearance • Check pump pressure. (See pressure test). Replace flow control valve if defective.

Troubleshooting the Power Steering Pump (cont.)

Problem	Cause	Solution
Steering wheel surges or jerks when turning with engine running especially during parking (cont.)	• Sticking flow control valve	• Inspect for varnish or damage, replace if necessary
Excessive wheel kickback or loose steering	• Air in system	• Add oil to pump reservoir and bleed by operating steering. Check hose connectors for proper torque and adjust as required.
Low pump pressure	• Extreme wear of cam ring • Scored pressure plate, thrust plate, or rotor • Vanes not installed properly • Vanes sticking in rotor slots • Cracked or broken thrust or pressure plate	• Replace parts. Flush system. • Replace parts. Flush system. • Install properly • Freeup by removing burrs, varnish, or dirt • Replace part

9

Brakes

QUICK REFERENCE INDEX

GENERAL INDEX

BRAKE SYSTEM
Troubleshooting the Brake System

Problem	Cause	Solution
Low brake pedal (excessive pedal travel required for braking action.)	• Excessive clearance between rear linings and drums caused by inoperative automatic adjusters	• Make 10 to 15 alternate forward and reverse brake stops to adjust brakes. If brake pedal does not come up, repair or replace adjuster parts as necessary.
	• Worn rear brakelining	• Inspect and replace lining if worn beyond minimum thickness specification
	• Bent, distorted brakeshoes, front or rear	• Replace brakeshoes in axle sets
	• Air in hydraulic system	• Remove air from system. Refer to Brake Bleeding.
Low brake pedal (pedal may go to floor with steady pressure applied.)	• Fluid leak in hydraulic system	• Fill master cylinder to fill line; have helper apply brakes and check calipers, wheel cylinders, differential valve tubes, hoses and fittings for leaks. Repair or replace as necessary.
	• Air in hydraulic system	• Remove air from system. Refer to Brake Bleeding.
	• Incorrect or non-recommended brake fluid (fluid evaporates at below normal temp).	• Flush hydraulic system with clean brake fluid. Refill with correct-type fluid.
	• Master cylinder piston seals worn, or master cylinder bore is scored, worn or corroded	• Repair or replace master cylinder
Low brake pedal (pedal goes to floor on first application—o.k. on subsequent applications.)	• Disc brake pads sticking on abutment surfaces of anchor plate. Caused by a build-up of dirt, rust, or corrosion on abutment surfaces	• Clean abutment surfaces
Fading brake pedal (pedal height decreases with steady pressure applied.)	• Fluid leak in hydraulic system	• Fill master cylinder reservoirs to fill mark, have helper apply brakes, check calipers, wheel cylinders, differential valve, tubes, hoses, and fittings for fluid leaks. Repair or replace parts as necessary.
	• Master cylinder piston seals worn, or master cylinder bore is scored, worn or corroded	• Repair or replace master cylinder
Decreasing brake pedal travel (pedal travel required for braking action decreases and may be accompanied by a hard pedal.)	• Caliper or wheel cylinder pistons sticking or seized	• Repair or replace the calipers, or wheel cylinders
	• Master cylinder compensator ports blocked (preventing fluid return to reservoirs) or pistons sticking or seized in master cylinder bore	• Repair or replace the master cylinder

Troubleshooting the Brake System (cont.)

Problem	Cause	Solution
Decreasing brake pedal travel (pedal travel required for braking action decreases and may be accompanied by a hard pedal.)	• Power brake unit binding internally	• Test unit according to the following procedure: (a) Shift transmission into neutral and start engine (b) Increase engine speed to 1500 rpm, close throttle and fully depress brake pedal (c) Slow release brake pedal and stop engine (d) Have helper remove vacuum check valve and hose from power unit. Observe for backward movement of brake pedal. (e) If the pedal moves backward, the power unit has an internal bind—replace power unit
Grabbing brakes (severe reaction to brake pedal pressure.)	• Brakelining(s) contaminated by grease or brake fluid • Parking brake cables incorrectly adjusted or seized • Incorrect brakelining or lining loose on brakeshoes • Caliper anchor plate bolts loose • Rear brakeshoes binding on support plate ledges • Incorrect or missing power brake reaction disc • Rear brake support plates loose	• Determine and correct cause of contamination and replace brakeshoes in axle sets • Adjust cables. Replace seized cables. • Replace brakeshoes in axle sets • Tighten bolts • Clean and lubricate ledges. Replace support plate(s) if ledges are deeply grooved. Do not attempt to smooth ledges by grinding. • Install correct disc • Tighten mounting bolts
Spongy brake pedal (pedal has abnormally soft, springy, spongy feel when depressed.)	• Air in hydraulic system • Brakeshoes bent or distorted • Brakelining not yet seated with drums and rotors • Rear drum brakes not properly adjusted	• Remove air from system. Refer to Brake Bleeding. • Replace brakeshoes • Burnish brakes • Adjust brakes
Hard brake pedal (excessive pedal pressure required to stop vehicle. May be accompanied by brake fade.)	• Loose or leaking power brake unit vacuum hose • Incorrect or poor quality brakelining • Bent, broken, distorted brakeshoes	• Tighten connections or replace leaking hose • Replace with lining in axle sets • Replace brakeshoes

Troubleshooting the Brake System (cont.)

Problem	Cause	Solution
Hard brake pedal (excessive pedal pressure required to stop vehicle. May be accompanied by brake fade.)	• Calipers binding or dragging on mounting pins. Rear brakeshoes dragging on support plate.	• Replace mounting pins and bushings. Clean rust or burrs from rear brake support plate ledges and lubricate ledges with molydisulfide grease. **NOTE:** If ledges are deeply grooved or scored, do not attempt to sand or grind them smooth—replace support plate.
	• Caliper, wheel cylinder, or master cylinder pistons sticking or seized	• Repair or replace parts as necessary
	• Power brake unit vacuum check valve malfunction	• Test valve according to the following procedure: (a) Start engine, increase engine speed to 1500 rpm, close throttle and immediately stop engine (b) Wait at least 90 seconds then depress brake pedal (c) If brakes are not vacuum assisted for 2 or more applications, check valve is faulty
	• Power brake unit has internal bind	• Test unit according to the following procedure: (a) With engine stopped, apply brakes several times to exhaust all vacuum in system (b) Shift transmission into neutral, depress brake pedal and start engine (c) If pedal height decreases with foot pressure and less pressure is required to hold pedal in applied position, power unit vacuum system is operating normally. Test power unit. If power unit exhibits a bind condition, replace the power unit.
	• Master cylinder compensator ports (at bottom of reservoirs) blocked by dirt, scale, rust, or have small burrs (blocked ports prevent fluid return to reservoirs). • Brake hoses, tubes, fittings clogged or restricted	• Repair or replace master cylinder **CAUTION:** Do not attempt to clean blocked ports with wire, pencils, or similar implements. Use compressed air only. • Use compressed air to check or unclog parts. Replace any damaged parts.
	• Brake fluid contaminated with improper fluids (motor oil, transmission fluid, causing rubber components to swell and stick in bores	• Replace all rubber components, combination valve and hoses. Flush entire brake system with DOT 3 brake fluid or equivalent.
	• Low engine vacuum	• Adjust or repair engine

Troubleshooting the Brake System (cont.)

Problem	Cause	Solution
Dragging brakes (slow or incomplete release of brakes)	• Brake pedal binding at pivot • Power brake unit has internal bind • Parking brake cables incorrrectly adjusted or seized • Rear brakeshoe return springs weak or broken • Automatic adjusters malfunctioning • Caliper, wheel cylinder or master cylinder pistons sticking or seized • Master cylinder compensating ports blocked (fluid does not return to reservoirs).	• Loosen and lubricate • Inspect for internal bind. Replace unit if internal bind exists. • Adjust cables. Replace seized cables. • Replace return springs. Replace brakeshoe if necessary in axle sets. • Repair or replace adjuster parts as required • Repair or replace parts as necessary • Use compressed air to clear ports. Do not use wire, pencils, or similar objects to open blocked ports.
Vehicle moves to one side when brakes are applied	• Incorrect front tire pressure • Worn or damaged wheel bearings • Brakelining on one side contaminated • Brakeshoes on one side bent, distorted, or lining loose on shoe • Support plate bent or loose on one side • Brakelining not yet seated with drums or rotors • Caliper anchor plate loose on one side • Caliper piston sticking or seized • Brakelinings water soaked • Loose suspension component attaching or mounting bolts • Brake combination valve failure	• Inflate to recommended cold (reduced load) inflation pressure • Replace worn or damaged bearings • Determine and correct cause of contamination and replace brakelining in axle sets • Replace brakeshoes in axle sets • Tighten or replace support plate • Burnish brakelining • Tighten anchor plate bolts • Repair or replace caliper • Drive vehicle with brakes lightly applied to dry linings • Tighten suspension bolts. Replace worn suspension components. • Replace combination valve
Chatter or shudder when brakes are applied (pedal pulsation and roughness may also occur.)	• Brakeshoes distorted, bent, contaminated, or worn • Caliper anchor plate or support plate loose • Excessive thickness variation of rotor(s)	• Replace brakeshoes in axle sets • Tighten mounting bolts • Refinish or replace rotors in axle sets
Noisy brakes (squealing, clicking, scraping sound when brakes are applied.)	• Bent, broken, distorted brakeshoes • Excessive rust on outer edge of rotor braking surface	• Replace brakeshoes in axle sets • Remove rust

Troubleshooting the Brake System (cont.)

Problem	Cause	Solution
Noisy brakes (squealing, clicking, scraping sound when brakes are applied.) (cont.)	• Brakelining worn out—shoes contacting drum of rotor	• Replace brakeshoes and lining in axle sets. Refinish or replace drums or rotors.
	• Broken or loose holdown or return springs	• Replace parts as necessary
	• Rough or dry drum brake support plate ledges	• Lubricate support plate ledges
	• Cracked, grooved, or scored rotor(s) or drum(s)	• Replace rotor(s) or drum(s). Replace brakeshoes and lining in axle sets if necessary.
	• Incorrect brakelining and/or shoes (front or rear).	• Install specified shoe and lining assemblies
Pulsating brake pedal	• Out of round drums or excessive lateral runout in disc brake rotor(s)	• Refinish or replace drums, re-index rotors or replace

Adjustments

DRUM BRAKES

Adjustment is automatic when the brakes are applied while the vehicle is moving in reverse.

BRAKE PEDAL TRAVEL

Most low brake pedal problems are caused by air in the hydraulic system. Bleed the system until all air is purged. Other less frequent causes of excessive pedal travel are incorrect push rod length, improperly adjusted parking brake, rear shoe adjusters not operating, linings excessively worn and hydraulic system leakage.

NOTE: In rare cases, too much pedal travel develops if the vehicle is not driven in reverse. The self adjusting mechanisms will only operate when the brakes are applied in reverse.

STOPLAMP SWITCH

With the brake pedal in the fully released position, the Stoplamp switch plunger should be fully depressed against the brake pedal shank.

1. Insert the switch into the tubular clip until the switch body seats on the tube clip.
2. Pull the brake pedal to the rear, against the internal pedal stop. The stoplamp switch will be moved in the tubular clip giving the proper adjustment.

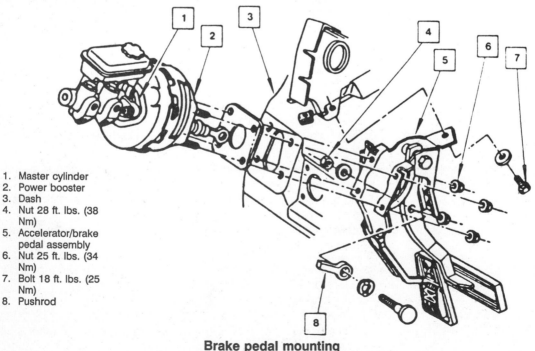

1. Master cylinder
2. Power booster
3. Dash
4. Nut 28 ft. lbs. (38 Nm)
5. Accelerator/brake pedal assembly
6. Nut 25 ft. lbs. (34 Nm)
7. Bolt 18 ft. lbs. (25 Nm)
8. Pushrod

Brake pedal mounting

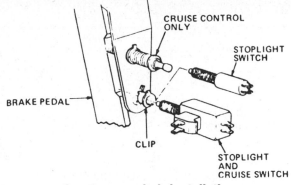

Stoplamp switch installation

NOTE: If no clicks are heard when the pedal is pulled up and the brake lamps do not stay on without the brakes being applied, the switch is properly adjusted.

Master Cylinder

REMOVAL AND INSTALLATION

1. Disconnect the negative battery cable.
2. Disconnect the electrical connection from the fluid sensor.
3. Disconnect and plug the fluid lines.
4. Remove the 2 master cylinder to power booster retaining bolts and remove the master cylinder from the vehicle.
To install:
5. Install the master cylinder in position on the booster. Connect the booster pushrod.
6. Install the master cylinder retaining bolts and tighten to 20 ft. lbs. (27 Nm).
7. Connect the fluid lines to the master cylinder.

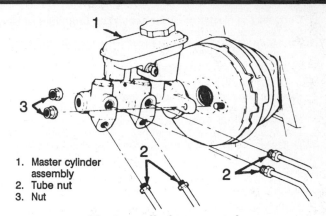

1. Master cylinder assembly
2. Tube nut
3. Nut

Master cylinder removal

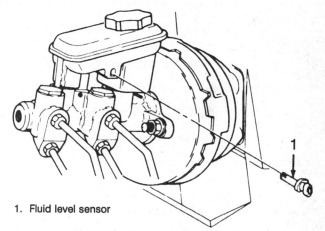

1. Fluid level sensor

Fluid level sensor installation

1. Fluid level sensor
2. Proportioner valve cap assembly
3. O-ring
4. Spring
5. Proportioner valve piston
6. Proportioner valve seal
7. Reservoir cap
8. Diaphragm
9. Spring pin
10. Reservoir assembly
11. O-ring
12. O-ring
13. Retainer
14. Primary piston assembly
15. Secondary seal
16. Spring retainer
17. Primary seal
18. Secondary piston
19. Spring
20. Cylinder body

Disassemble view of the master cylinder

8. Connect the electrical connector to the fluid level sensor.
9. Connect the negative battery cable.
10. Fill the master cylinder and bleed the brake system.

OVERHAUL

1. Remove the master cylinder from the vehicle.
2. Clean, then remove, the reservoir cap and diaphram.
3. Empty the fluid from the reservoir.
4. Remove the fluid sensor and proportioner valve assembly.
5. Depress the primary piston assembly and remove the retainer.

NOTE: Be careful not to damage the piston, bore or retainer groove.

6. Apply low pressure unlubricated compressed air into the upper outlet port at the blind end of the bore and plug all other outlet ports. Remove the primary piston assembly, secondary piston, spring, and spring retainer.
7. Remove the 2 seals and the spring retainer from the secondary piston.

To install:
8. Inspect and clean all parts with denatured alcohol and dry with unlubricated compressed air.
9. Install the 2 brake fluid lubricated seals and the spring retainer onto the secondary piston.
10. Install the spring and the secondary piston assembly into the cylinder bore.
11. Install the lubricated primary piston assembly into the cylinder bore.
12. Depress the primary piston assembly and install the retainer.
13. Install the proportioner valve assemblies and fluid level sensor.
14. Install the diaphragm into the reservoir cap and install on the reservoir.
15. Install the master cylinder.

Power Brake Booster

REMOVAL AND INSTALLATION

1. Disconnect the negative battery cable. Do not disconnect the master cylinder fluid lines, unless there is a clearance problem. Remove the master cylinder and position it to the side.
2. Remove the vacuum booster pushrod. Disconnect the vacuum hose from the booster assembly.
3. From inside the vehicle, remove the mounting studs which secure the vacuum booster to the fire wall.
4. Pull the booster away from the cowl and remove it from the vehicle.

To install:
5. Install the booster and tighten the attaching nuts to 15 ft. lbs. (21 Nm).
6. Install the master cylinder to the booster and tighten the attaching nuts to 20 ft. lbs. (27 Nm).
7. Add fluid to the master cylinder and bleed the system as necessary.

Proportioning Valve

REMOVAL AND INSTALLATION

1. Disconnect the negative battery cable.
2. Remove the electrical connector from the master cylinder.
3. Drain and remove the master cylinder reservoir.
4. Remove the proportioning valve caps from the master cyinder.

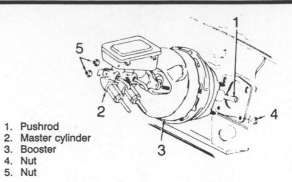

1. Pushrod
2. Master cylinder
3. Booster
4. Nut
5. Nut

Vacuum booster installation

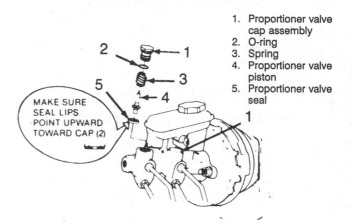

1. Proportioner valve cap assembly
2. O-ring
3. Spring
4. Proportioner valve piston
5. Proportioner valve seal

MAKE SURE SEAL LIPS POINT UPWARD TOWARD CAP (2)

Proportioning valve installation

5. Remove the O-rings, springs and the valve pistons. Use care not to scratch the valves in any way.
6. Remove the valve seals from the valve pistons.
To install:
7. Install new seals on the valve pistons. Lubricate the seals and the pistons with silicone grease.
8. Install the valve pistons and O-rings into the master cylinder.
9. Install the valve cap assemblies and tighten to 20 ft. lbs. (27 Nm).
10. Install the reservoir assembly. Connect the electrical leads.
11. Connect the negative battery cable. Bleed the brake system.

Brake Hoses

REMOVAL AND INSTALLATION

The flexible hydraulic brake hoses should be inspected at least twice a year for road hazard damage, cracks, leaks or blisters. Do not allow brake components to hang from the flexible hoses or let hoses have direct contact with chassis parts or damage to the hoses may occur.

Front

1. Clean the dirt and grease from both ends of the hose fittings.
2. Disconnect the steel pipes from the flexible hose fitting and remove the hose retaining clip bolt.
3. Remove the hose fitting retaining bolt and washers at the caliper.
4. After disconnecting the brake hose from the fittings, be sure to plug the fittings to keep the fluid from discharging and dirt from entering the system.

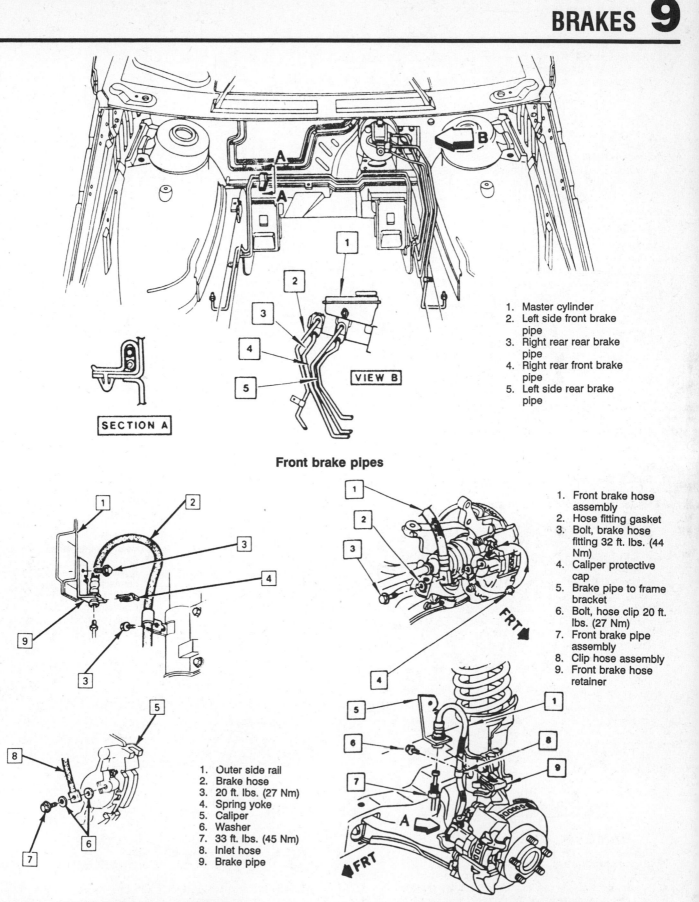

SECTION A

VIEW B

Front brake pipes

1. Master cylinder
2. Left side front brake pipe
3. Right rear rear brake pipe
4. Right rear front brake pipe
5. Left side rear brake pipe

1. Front brake hose assembly
2. Hose fitting gasket
3. Bolt, brake hose fitting 32 ft. lbs. (44 Nm)
4. Caliper protective cap
5. Brake pipe to frame bracket
6. Bolt, hose clip 20 ft. lbs. (27 Nm)
7. Front brake pipe assembly
8. Clip hose assembly
9. Front brake hose retainer

1. Outer side rail
2. Brake hose
3. 20 ft. lbs. (27 Nm)
4. Spring yoke
5. Caliper
6. Washer
7. 33 ft. lbs. (45 Nm)
8. Inlet hose
9. Brake pipe

Front brake hose installation

Front brake hose installation

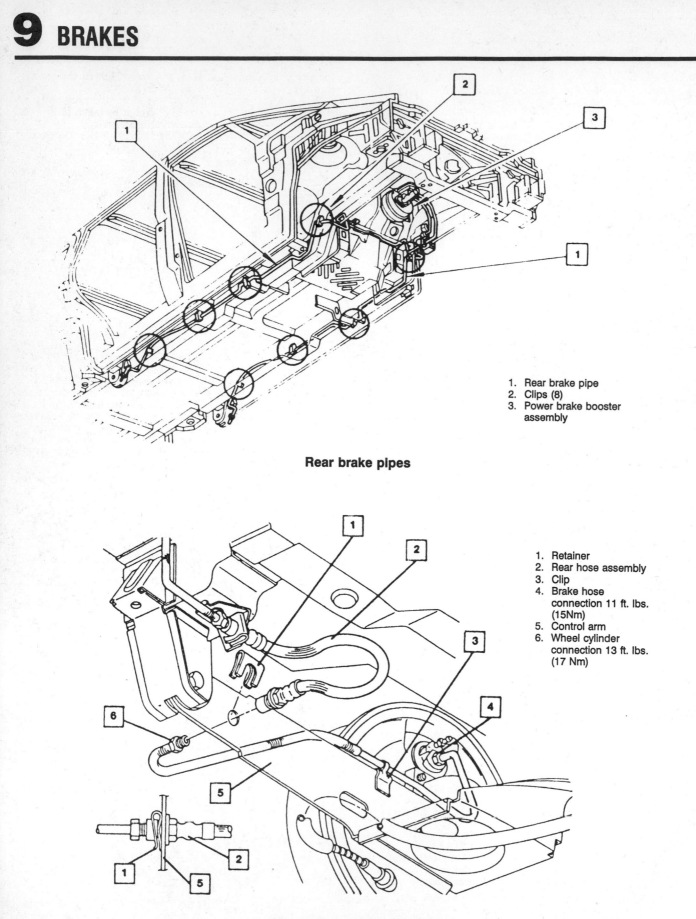

1. Rear brake pipe
2. Clips (8)
3. Power brake booster
   assembly

Rear brake pipes

1. Retainer
2. Rear hose assembly
3. Clip
4. Brake hose
   connection 11 ft. lbs.
   (15Nm)
5. Control arm
6. Wheel cylinder
   connection 13 ft. lbs.
   (17 Nm)

Rear brake pipes and hoses

To install:

5. Install the new hose using new gaskets or washers and tighten the hose fitting to front caliper bolt to 33 ft. lbs. (45 Nm).

6. Make sure that the hoses do not contact any suspension parts and bleed the brake system.

Rear

1. Clean the dirt and grease from both ends of the hose fittings.

2. Disconnect the steel pipes from the flexible hose fittings and remove the hose retaining clips.

3. After disconnecting the brake hose from the fittings, be sure to plug the fittings to keep the fluid from discharging and dirt from entering the system.

4. Installation is the reverse of removal. Bleed the brake system.

Bleeding

A bleeding operation is necessary to remove air when it is introduced into the hydraulic system.

It may be necessary to bleed the hydraulic system at all four brakes if air has been introduced through a low fluid level or by disconnecting brake pipes at the master cylinder. If a brake pipe is disconnected at one wheel, only that wheel cylinder/caliper needs to be bled. If pipes are disconnected at any fitting located between master cylinder and brakes, then the brake system served by the disconnected pipe must be bled.

MANUAL BLEEDING

NOTE: Remove the vacuum reserve by applying the brakes several times with the engine off. The use of a brake bleeder wrench No. J 21472 or equivalent, will be required for this procedure.

1. Fill the master cylinder reservoirs with brake fluid and keep them at least half full of fluid during the bleeding operation.

2. If the master cylinder is known or suspected to have air in the bore, then it must be bled before any wheel cylinder or caliper in the following manner:

a. Disconnect the forward (blind end) brake pipe connection at the master cylinder.

b. Allow brake fluid to fill the master cylinder bore until it begins to flow from the forward pipe connector port.

c. Connect the forward (blind end) brake pipe to the master cylinder and tighten.

d. Depress the brake pedal slowly one time and hold. Loosen the forward (blind end) brake pipe connection at the mas-

ter cylinder to purge air from the bore. Tighten the connection and then release the brake pedal slowly. Wait 15 seconds. Repeat the sequence, including the 15 second wait, until all air is removed from the bore. Care must be taken to prevent brake fluid from contacting any painted surface.

e. After all air has been removed at the forward (blind end) connection, repeat Step **d** and bleed the master cylinder at the rear (cowl) connection.

f. If the calipers and wheel cylinders do not contain any air, it will not be necessary to bleed them.

3. If it is necessary to bleed all the wheel cylinders and calipers, follow this sequence:

a. right rear
b. left front
c. left rear
d. right front

4. Individual wheel cylinders or calipers are bled only after all air is removed from master cylinder.

a. Place a proper size box end wrench, J 21472 or equivalent, over the bleeder valve. Attach a clear tube over bleeder valve and allow tube to hang submerged in a clear container partially filled with brake fluid.

b. Depress the brake pedal slowly one time and hold. Loosen the bleeder valve to purge the air from the cylinder. Tighten bleeder screw and slowly release pedal. Wait 15 seconds. Repeat the sequence, including the 15 second wait until all air is removed. It may be necessary to repeat the sequence ten or more times to remove all the air. Rapid pumping of the brake pedal pushes the master cylinder secondary piston down the bore in a way that makes it difficult to bleed the system.

5. Check the brake pedal for "sponginess". Repeat entire bleeding procedure to correct this condition. Check **BRAKE** warning lamp for indication of low fluid level.

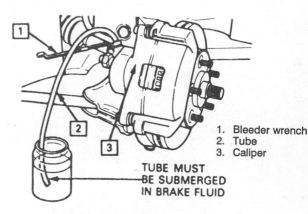

1. Bleeder wrench
2. Tube
3. Caliper

TUBE MUST BE SUBMERGED IN BRAKE FLUID

Bleeding the brake system

FRONT DISC BRAKES

Brake Pads

INSPECTION

With the wheel removed, check the thickness of the lining at both ends of the outer shoe by looking in at each end of the caliper. These are points where the highest rate of wear normally occurs. Look down through the inspection hole in the top of the caliper to view the inner shoe. Whenever the thickness of any lining is worn to within 0.030 in. (0.8mm) of rivet at either end of the shoe, the disc brake shoe and lining assemblies should be replaced. Any time the noise sensor contacts the rotor, the disc brake shoe and lining assemblies must be replaced.

REMOVAL AND INSTALLATION

1. Remove ⅔ of the brake fluid from the master cylinder.
2. Raise and safely support the vehicle.
3. Remove the brake caliper and suspend it from the suspension with a wire hanger.
4. Use a suitable tool and disengage the buttons on the shoe from holes in the caliper housing and remove the outboard shoe and lining.
5. Remove the inboard shoe and lining from the caliper.
6. Remove the sleeves and bushings.

To install:

7. Lubricate the sleeves and bushing with silicone lubricant and install them in the caliper.
8. Position 12 in. (305mm) adjustable pliers over the caliper housing and bottom the piston into the caliper bore.

NOTE: Be careful not to damage the piston or piston boot with the pliers.

9. After bottoming the piston into the caliper bore, fit the inner edge of the boot next to the piston and press out any trapped air. The boot must lay flat.

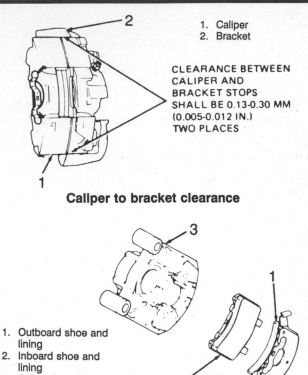

1. Caliper
2. Bracket

CLEARANCE BETWEEN CALIPER AND BRACKET STOPS SHALL BE 0.13-0.30 MM (0.005-0.012 IN.) TWO PLACES

Caliper to bracket clearance

1. Outboard shoe and lining
2. Inboard shoe and lining
3. Caliper housing

Shoe and lining assembly

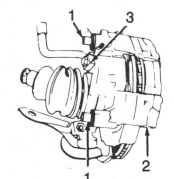

1. Mounting bolt
2. Caliper
3. Inlet fitting

Caliper attachment

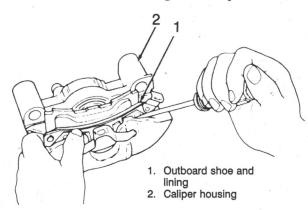

1. Outboard shoe and lining
2. Caliper housing

Removing the outboard shoe and lining

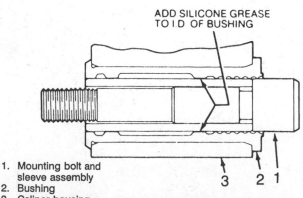

ADD SILICONE GREASE TO I.D OF BUSHING

1. Mounting bolt and sleeve assembly
2. Bushing
3. Caliper housing

Lubricate the caliper cavity using silicone grease

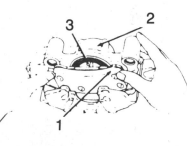

1. Inboard shoe and lining
2. Caliper housing
3. Shoe retainer spring

Installing the inboard shoe and lining

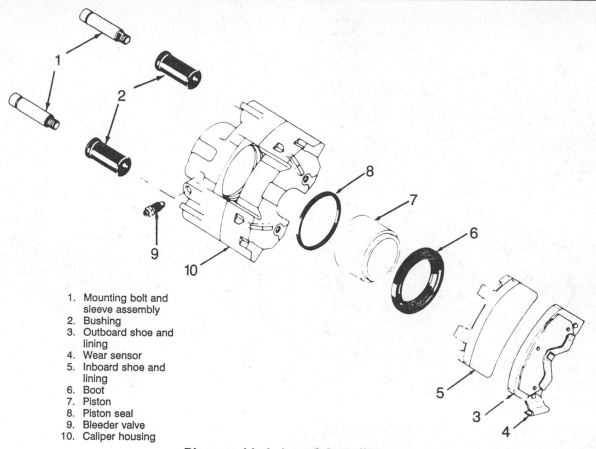

1. Mounting bolt and sleeve assembly
2. Bushing
3. Outboard shoe and lining
4. Wear sensor
5. Inboard shoe and lining
6. Boot
7. Piston
8. Piston seal
9. Bleeder valve
10. Caliper housing

Disassembled view of the caliper

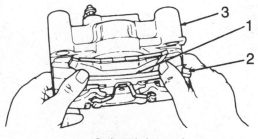

1. Outboard shoe and lining
2. Wear sensor
3. Caliper housing

Installing the outboard shoe and lining

10. Clip the retaining spring onto the inboard pad and install the pad in the caliper. The shoe must lay flat against the caliper.

11. Install the outboard pad into the caliper with the wear sensor at the leading edge of the shoe during forward wheel rotation. The back of the shoe must lay flat against the caliper.

12. Install the caliper in position over the rotor and install the mounting bolts. Apply approximately 175 lbs. of force 3 times to the brake pedal to seat the lining.

13. Install the wheel and tire assemblies.

14. Lower the vehicle and refill the master cylinder to the correct level.

Reinstall 2 wheel nuts to retain the rotor

Remove the bolt from the brake hose retaining clamp to the strut.

Suspend the caliper with a wire hook from the strut

Position 12 in. (305mm) adjustable pliers over the inboard brake shoe tab and the inboard caliper housing and bottom the piston into the caliper bore

Brake caliper mounting bolts

Disengage the buttons on the shoe from holes in the caliper housing to remove the outboard shoe and lining

Clip the retaining spring onto the inboard pad and install the pad in the caliper

Brake Caliper

REMOVAL AND INSTALLATION

1. Remove ⅔ of the brake fluid from the master cylinder reservoir.
2. Raise and support the vehicle safely.
3. Remove the tire and wheel assembly.
4. Reinstall 2 wheel nuts to retain the rotor.
5. Position 12 in. (305mm) adjustable pliers over the inboard brake shoe tab and the inboard caliper housing and bottom the piston into the caliper bore. This is to provide clearance between the linings and rotor.
6. If the caliper is being removed for caliper overhaul, remove the brake hose fitting bolt and plug the opening in the caliper and pipe to prevent fluid loss and contamination.

NOTE: If the caliper is being removed for brake pad replacement, the fluid line do not need to be disconnected.

7. Remove the caliper mounting bolt and sleeve assemblies and remove the caliper from the mounting bracket and sleeve assemblies.

NOTE: If only shoe and linings are to be replaced, suspend the caliper with a wire hook from the strut.

To install:

8. Fill both of the cavities in the caliper housing between the bushings with silicone grease. Install the pads in the caliper.
9. Install the caliper in position over the rotor and install the mounting bolts. Tighten the mounting bolts to 38 ft. lbs. (51 Nm).
10. Connect the fluid lines to the caliper, if disconnected, and tighten to 33 ft. lbs. (45 Nm).
11. Remove the 2 nuts securing the rotor to the hub and install the wheel and tire assembly. Tighten the wheel nuts to 100 ft. lbs.
12. Lower the vehicle and refill the master cylinder to the correct level. Bleed the brake system if the fluid lines were disconnected from the caliper.

OVERHAUL

1. Raise and support the vehicle safely.
2. Remove the caliper from the vehicle.
3. Remove and inspect the bushings for damage and replace as necessary.
4. Use compressed air into the caliper inlet hole and remove the piston.

— CAUTION —
Do not place fingers in front of the piston in an attempt to catch the piston or serious injury may result!

To assemble:

5. Clean all parts with with denatured alcohol and dry with unlubricated compressed air.
6. Install the bleeder valve and torque to 110 inch lbs.
7. Lubricate a new piston seal with clean brake fluid and install it into the caliper bore groove. Make sure the seal is not twisted.
8. Install a lubricated boot onto the piston.
9. Install the piston and boot into the bore of the caliper and push to the bottom of the bore.

1. Bushing
2. Boot
3. Piston
4. Piston seal
5. Bleeder valve
6. Caliper housing
7. Seal groove

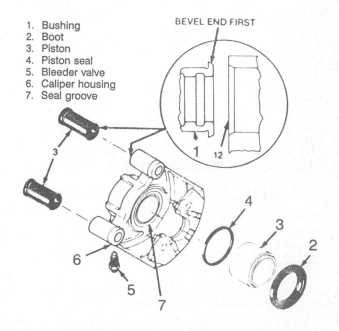

Caliper bushing installation

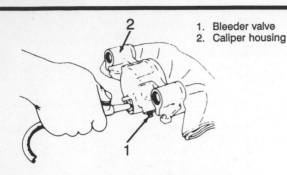

1. Bleeder valve
2. Caliper housing

Removing the piston using compressed air

1. Boot
2. Piston

Installing the piston boot

10. Seat the boot in the caliper housing counterbore, using tool J 26267 or equivalent.
11. Lubricate the beveled end of the of the bushing with silicone grease, pinch the bushing and install the beveled end first through the housing bore.
12. Install the caliper.

1. Caliper housing
2. Tool J26267

Seating the piston into the housing

Brake Rotor

REMOVAL AND INSTALLATION

1. Remove ⅔ of the brake fluid from the master cylinder.
2. Raise and safely support the vehicle.
3. Remove the wheel and tire assemblies.
4. Remove the brake caliper from the rotor and support it aside. Do not disconnect the brake lines.
5. Remove the rotor from the hub.
To install:
6. Install the rotor on the hub. Install the brake caliper.
7. Install the wheel and tire assemblies.
8. Lower the vehicle and refill the master cylinder.

REAR DRUM BRAKES

Brake Drums

REMOVAL AND INSTALLATION

1. Raise and safely support the vehicle.
2. Remove the wheel and tire assembly.
3. Release the parking brake.
4. Use a rubber mallet to tap around the edge of the drum and remove the brake drum from the vehicle.
5. If the drum will not come off, remove the adjusting hole knockout plate from the brake drum and back off the adjusting screw, using a suitable adjusting tool.

NOTE: On some drum designs the knockout plate must be drilled out using a ⁷⁄₁₆ in. (11mm) drill bit then replaced with a rubber hole cover after adjustment.

6. Install the drum on the axle and install the wheel and tire assembly.
7. Lower the vehicle.

Brake Shoes

REMOVAL AND INSTALLATION

1. Raise and safely support the vehicle.
2. Remove the wheel and tire assembly.
3. Remove the brake drum.
4. Remove the return springs from the brake shoes, using a suitable tool.
5. Remove the hold-down springs and pins, using suitable pliers. Remove the actuator lever and pivot.

1. Return spring
2. Return spring
3. Hold down spring
4. Lever pivot
5. Hold down pin
6. Actuator link
7. Actuator lever
8. Lever return spring
9. Parking brake strut
10. Strut spring
11. Primary shoe and lining
12. Secondary shoe and lining
13. Adjusting screw spring
14. Socket
15. Pivot nut
16. Adjusting screw
17. Retaining ring
18. Pin
19. Parking brake lever
20. Bleeder valve
21. Bolt
22. Boot
23. Piston
24. Seal
25. Spring assembly
26. Wheel cylinder
27. Backing plate

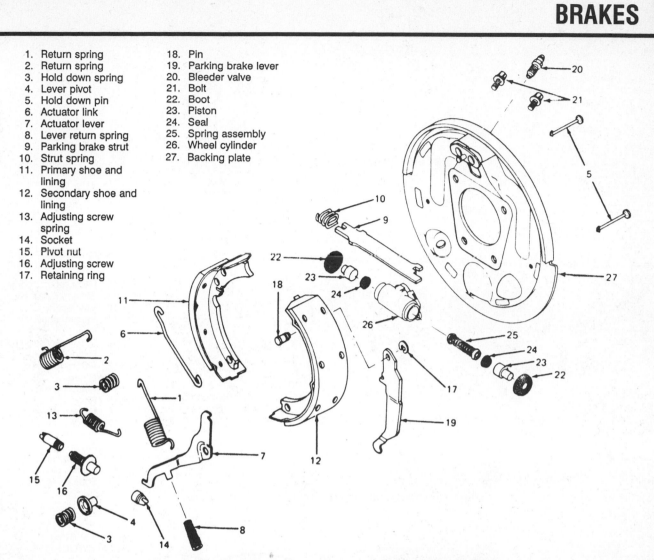

Disassembled view of the rear brake components

6. Remove the actuator link while lifting up on the actuator lever. Remove the actuator lever and lever return spring.
7. Remove the parking brake strut and spring.
8. Remove the brake shoes and the adjuster assembly.

To install:

9. Lubricate the shoe pads and the adjuster with lithium grease.
10. Install the parking brake lever on the secondary shoe with the pin and retaining ring.
11. Install the adjusting screw and spring assembly.
12. Install the shoe assemblies after attaching the parking brake cable.
13. Install the parking brake lever, strut and strut spring by spreading the shoes apart. They must be properly positioned as follows:
    a. The end of the brake strut without the spring should engage the parking brake lever and the secondary shoe and lining.
    b. The end with the spring should engage the primary shoe and lining.
14. Install the actuator lever and lever return spring.
15. Install the hold-down pins, lever pivot and hold-down springs.

16. Install the actuator link on the anchor pin.
17. Install the actuator link into the actuator lever while holding up on the lever.
18. Install the shoe return springs.
19. Install the brake drum in position.
20. Install the wheel and tire assemblies.
21. Check the adjustment of the brakes by turning the star wheel so that the shoe and lining diameter is 0.050 in. (1.3mm) less than inside drum diameter. The brakes should drag just slightly. If the wheel will not turn loosen the adjuster slightly.

Wheel Cylinders

REMOVAL AND INSTALLATION

1. Raise and safely support the vehicle.
2. Remove the wheel and tire assemblies.
3. Remove the brake drum and remove the brake shoes.
4. Disconnect and plug the brake fluid line from the wheel cylinder.
5. Remove the wheel cylinder retaining bolt.

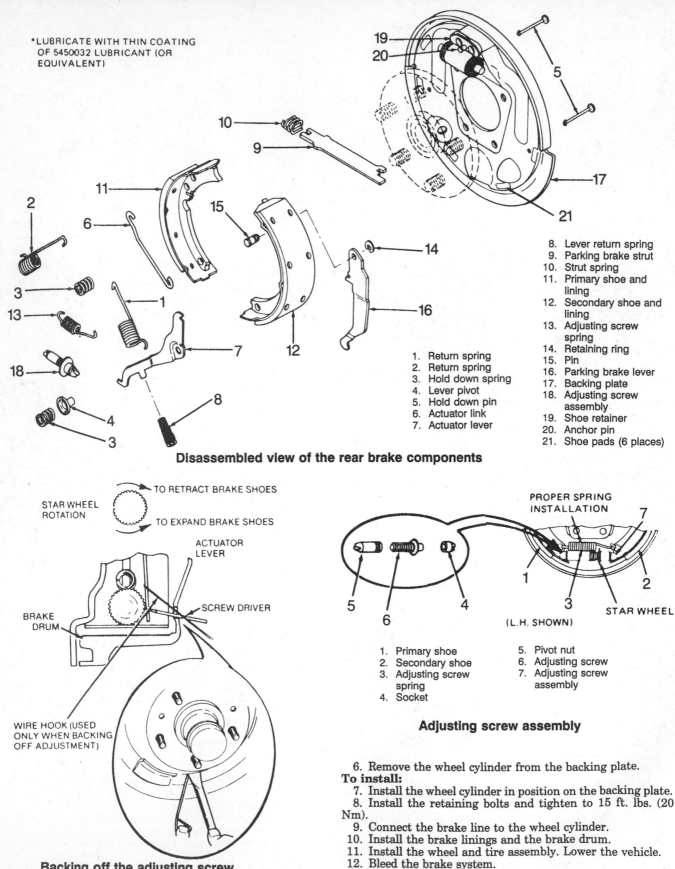

*LUBRICATE WITH THIN COATING
OF 5450032 LUBRICANT (OR
EQUIVALENT)

8. Lever return spring
9. Parking brake strut
10. Strut spring
11. Primary shoe and
    lining
12. Secondary shoe and
    lining
13. Adjusting screw
    spring
14. Retaining ring
15. Pin
16. Parking brake lever
17. Backing plate
18. Adjusting screw
    assembly
19. Shoe retainer
20. Anchor pin
21. Shoe pads (6 places)

1. Return spring
2. Return spring
3. Hold down spring
4. Lever pivot
5. Hold down pin
6. Actuator link
7. Actuator lever

Disassembled view of the rear brake components

STAR WHEEL
ROTATION

TO RETRACT BRAKE SHOES

TO EXPAND BRAKE SHOES

ACTUATOR
LEVER

SCREW DRIVER

BRAKE
DRUM

WIRE HOOK (USED
ONLY WHEN BACKING
OFF ADJUSTMENT)

Backing off the adjusting screw

PROPER SPRING
INSTALLATION

(L.H. SHOWN)

STAR WHEEL

1. Primary shoe
2. Secondary shoe
3. Adjusting screw
   spring
4. Socket

5. Pivot nut
6. Adjusting screw
7. Adjusting screw
   assembly

Adjusting screw assembly

6. Remove the wheel cylinder from the backing plate.
To install:
7. Install the wheel cylinder in position on the backing plate.
8. Install the retaining bolts and tighten to 15 ft. lbs. (20 Nm).
9. Connect the brake line to the wheel cylinder.
10. Install the brake linings and the brake drum.
11. Install the wheel and tire assembly. Lower the vehicle.
12. Bleed the brake system.

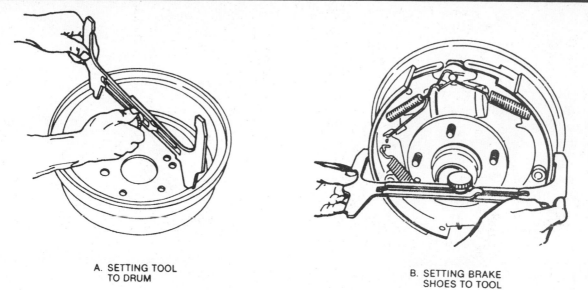

A. SETTING TOOL
TO DRUM

B. SETTING BRAKE
SHOES TO TOOL

Measuring the drum and shoe for adjustment

Remove the return springs from the brake shoes

Location of the hold-down springs and pins

Parking Brake Cable

REMOVAL AND INSTALLATION

Front

1. Raise and support the vehicle safely.

2. Loosen the adjuster nut and disconnect the front cable from the connector.

3. Disconnect the cable from the clip at the frame and the hanger.

4. Lower the vehicle. Remove the 3 screws and 1 nut and lower the driver's side sound insulator panel to gain access to the parking brake pedal assembly.

Removing the hold-down springs and pins, using a suitable tool

Remove the parking brake strut and spring

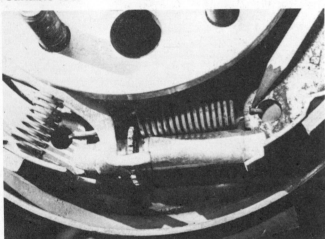

Remove the return springs from the brake shoes

Install the parking brake lever on the secondary shoe with the pin and retaining ring

Remove the actuator link while lifting up on the actuator lever

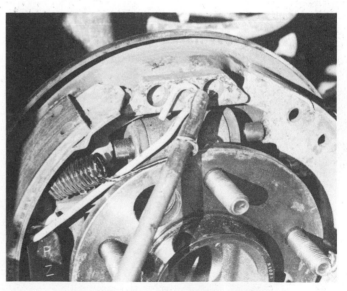

Installing the shoe return springs

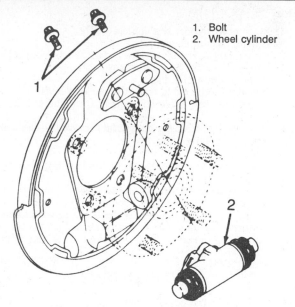

1. Bolt
2. Wheel cylinder

Wheel cylinder installation

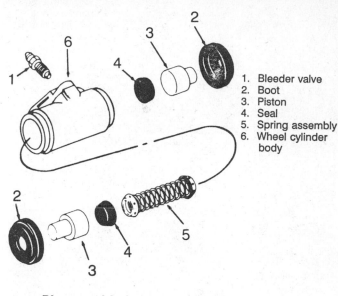

1. Bleeder valve
2. Boot
3. Piston
4. Seal
5. Spring assembly
6. Wheel cylinder body

Disassembled view of the wheel cylinder

5. Remove the carpet finish moulding and lift the carpet.
6. Remove the cable retaining clip at the lever assembly.
7. Disconnect the cable from the parking brake pedal, compress the retainer fingers. Remove the cable from the vehicle.

To install:
8. Insert the cable through the floor pan and grommet and seat the grommet.

9. Install the grommet retainer to the floor pan.
10. Install the cable in the retaining clips.
11. Connect the cable and casing to the control assembly and seat the retaining tangs.
12. Install the cable retaining clip at the lever assembly.
13. Place the carpet in position and install the carpet finish moulding.
14. Install the driver's side insulator panel srcews and nuts.

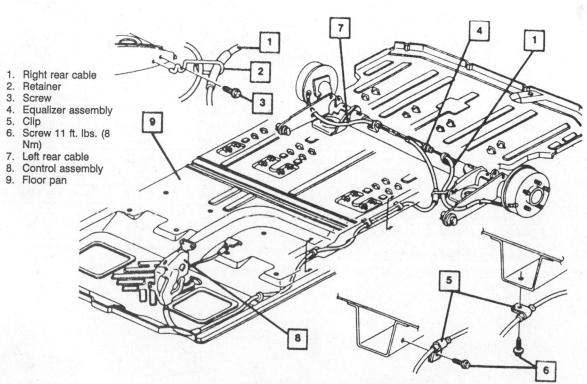

1. Right rear cable
2. Retainer
3. Screw
4. Equalizer assembly
5. Clip
6. Screw 11 ft. lbs. (8 Nm)
7. Left rear cable
8. Control assembly
9. Floor pan

View of the parking brake cables

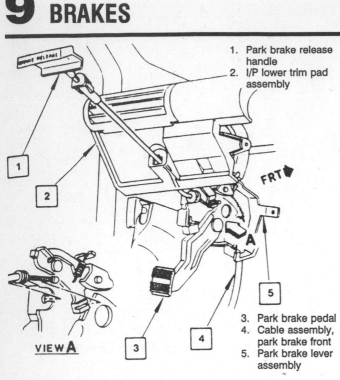

1. Park brake release handle
2. I/P lower trim pad assembly

3. Park brake pedal
4. Cable assembly, park brake front
5. Park brake lever assembly

Parking brake control and release cable assemblies

15. Raise and support the vehicle safely.
16. Install the cable to the hanger and clip at the frame.
17. Connect the cable to the equalizer and connector.
18. Adjust the parking brake cable and lower the vehicle.

Rear

1. Raise and support the vehicle safely.
2. Loosen the equalizer nut.
3. Disconnect the cable at the equalizer and connector.
4. Remove the tire and wheel assembly.
5. Remove the brake drum.
6. Disconnect the cable from the parking brake lever.
7. Disconnect the cable and spring from the bracket at the caliper.
8. Depress the retaining tangs and remove the cable and casing from the backing plate.

To install:

9. Install the cable and casing to the backing plate and seat the retaining tangs.
10. Connect the cable and spring to the bracket at the caliper.
11. Connect the cable at the parking brake lever.
12. Install the brake drum and the tire and wheel assembly.
13. Connect the cable at the equalizer and connector.
14. Adjust the parking brake cable and lower the vehicle.

ADJUSTMENT

1. Set the parking brake pedal 3 clicks.
2. Raise and support the vehicle safely.
3. Lubricate the threaded adjusting rod on both sides of the nut.
4. Tighten the equalizer nut until the right rear wheel can just be turned rearward with 2 hands but cannot be turned forward.
5. Release the parking brake.
6. Rotate the rear wheels in the forward motion. There should be no brake drag.
7. Lower the vehicle.

BRAKE SPECIFICATIONS

All specifications in inches

| Years | Model | Master Cyl. Bore | Brake Disc | | | Brake Drum | | | Wheel Cyl. or Caliper Bore | |
			Original Thickness	Minimum Thickness	Maximum Run-out	Orig. Inside Dia.	Max. Wear Limit	Maximum Machine O/S	Front	Rear
1990	Lumina APV	0.944	1.043	0.957	0.004	8.863	8.909	8.877	NA	0.748
	Silhouette	0.944	1.043	0.957	0.004	8.863	8.909	8.877	NA	0.748
	Transport	0.944	1.043	0.957	0.004	8.863	8.909	8.877	NA	0.748
1991	Lumina APV	0.944	1.043	0.957	0.004	8.863	8.909	8.877	NA	0.748
	Silhouette	0.944	1.043	0.957	0.004	8.863	8.909	8.877	NA	0.748
	Transport	0.944	1.043	0.957	0.004	8.863	8.909	8.877	NA	0.748

NA—Not available

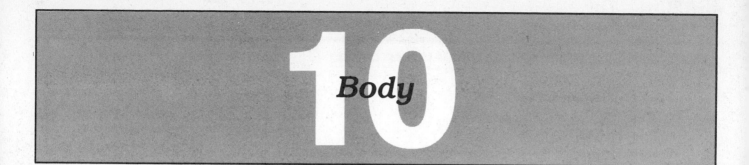

Body

QUICK REFERENCE INDEX

GENERAL INDEX

EXTERIOR

Front Doors

REMOVAL AND INSTALLATION

1. If equipped with power door components, disconnect the negative battery cable.
2. Remove the inner door trim panel.
3. If so equipped, disconnect the electrical connectors from the power door components and remove the electrical harness from the door.

4. Using a suitable tool etch the position of the door, reletive to the hinges, to aid when reinstalling.
5. With an assistant supporting the door, remove the hinge to door bolts and remove the door from the vehicle.

To install:

6. With the aid of an assistant, reposition the door and reinstall the hinge to door bolts.
7. If so equipped, install the electrical harness to the door and connect the electrical connectors to the power door components.
8. Install the door inner trim panel.
9. Connect the negative battery cable.

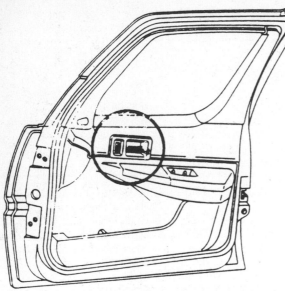

1. Knob assembly
2. Bezel assembly

Door handle bezel installation — Lumina APV and Silhouette

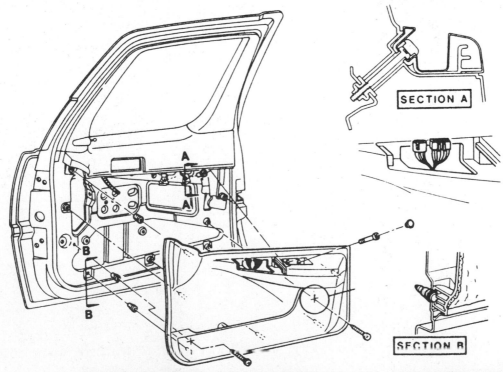

Front door inner trim panel installation — Lumina APV and Silhouette

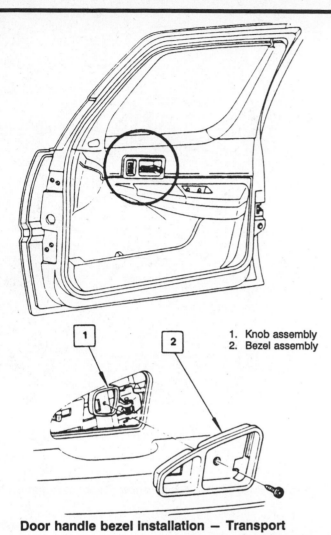

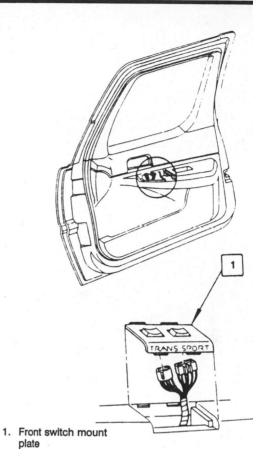

1. Knob assembly
2. Bezel assembly

1. Front switch mount plate

Electric window and door lock switch installation

Door handle bezel installation — Transport

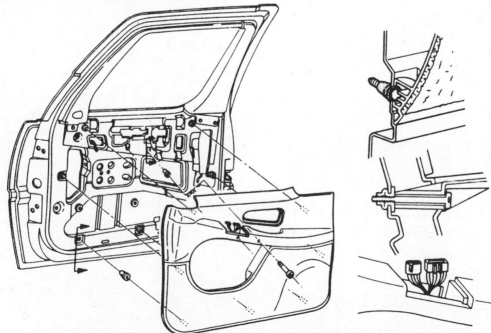

Front door inner trim panel installation — Transport

ADJUSTMENT

1. Adjust the door so that all gaps between the door and body panel are equal and the door closes easily.
2. Make sure the door surface is flush with the body surface.

Front Door Hinges

REMOVAL AND INSTALLATION

1. Remove the front door.
2. Remove the hinge to pillar bolts and remove the hinges.
3. Installation is the reverse of removal. Adjust the door as necessary.

ADJUSTMENT

1. Adjust the door so that all gaps between the door and body panel are equal and the door closes easily.
2. Make sure the door surface is flush with the body surface.

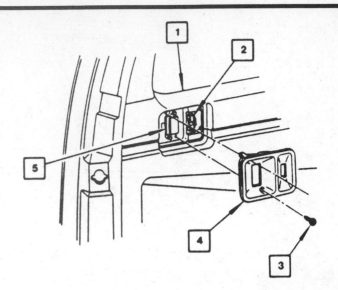

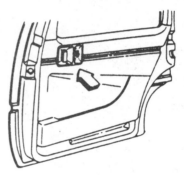

1. Rear side door assembly
2. Lock rod knob assembly
3. Screw
4. Bezel
5. Rear side door inside handle

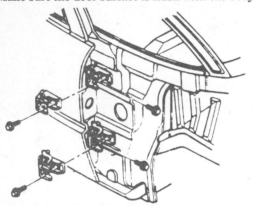

Door hinge installation

Sliding door inside door handle bezel installation

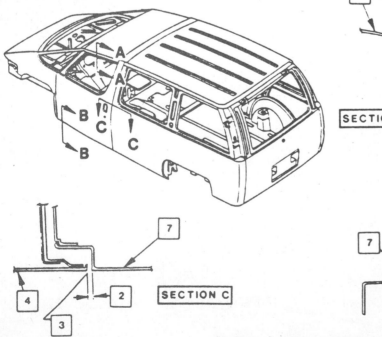

1. Roof panel
2. 6.0mm plus or minus 1.5mm gap
3. Flush plus or minus 1.0mm gap
4. Front side door assembly
5. Flush 4.0 plus or minus 1.0mm gap
6. 5.0 plus or minus 1.5mm gap
7. Body side panel

Front door adjustment specifications

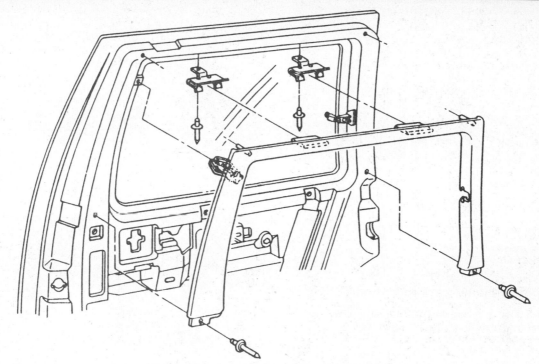

Sliding door garnish molding installation

Sliding Door

REMOVAL AND INSTALLATION

1. Remove the inner door trim panel and the door garnish panel.
2. Remove the center track roller bracket from the door.
3. Remove the upper track roller bracket from the door.
4. Remove the lower track roller bracket from the door and remove the sliding door.

To install:

5. Reposition the sliding door.
6. Install the lower track roller bracket to the door.
7. Install the upper track roller bracket to the door.
8. Install the center roller bracket to the door and align the door as necessary.
9. Install the inner door trim panel and the door garnish panel.

ADJUSTMENT

The ideal sliding door alignment is one where a parallel gap of equal proportion exists along the top and bottom edges of the door.

Adjustments are made by raising or lowering the front or rear of the door. The center roller bracket and the lower roller bracket are used to adjust the height of the rear and the front of the sliding door respectively. To adjust, simply loosen the bracket to door bolts and adjust as necessary.

Roller Brackets

REMOVAL AND INSTALLATION

Center

1. Scribe the location of the existing brackets on the door.

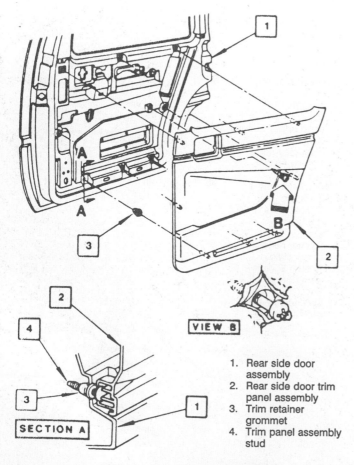

1. Rear side door assembly
2. Rear side door trim panel assembly
3. Trim retainer grommet
4. Trim panel assembly stud

Sliding door inner trim panel

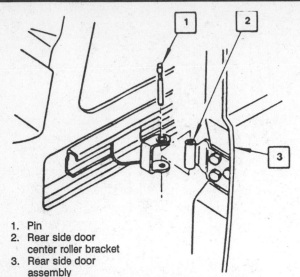

1. Pin
2. Rear side door center roller bracket
3. Rear side door assembly

Sliding door center track roller bracket

2. Support the door and remove the bracket bolts from the door and remove the bracket and roller assembly.
3. Remove the pin from the bracket and roller assembly and remove the bracket.

To install:
4. Install the pin to the bracket and roller assembly.
5. Install the bracket and roller assembly to the track.
6. Install the bracket bolts to the door, adjust the door to properly fit the door frame and tighten the bolts to 20 ft. lbs. (27Nm).

Upper

1. Remove the inner door trim panel and garnish moulding.
2. Support the door and remove the bracket to door screws and remove the bracket.
3. Installation is the reverse of removal.

Lower

1. Remove the door inner trim panel.
2. Scribe the location of the existing bracket on the door.
3. Remove the bracket to door bolts.
4. Disconnect the catch cable from the bracket.
5. Remove the lower striker and remove the lower roller bracket.
6. Installation is the reverse of removal.

Hood Assembly

REMOVAL AND INSTALLATION

1. Raise the hood and place protective coverings over the fenders to protect the paint and mouldings.
2. Mark the position of the hinges on the hood to aid alignment when installing the hood.
3. Remove the hood to hinge retaining bolts and remove the hood.
4. Installation is the reverse of removal.

Rear Liftgate Assembly

The rear liftgate assembly is formed from an inner and outer plastic panel bonded together with structure adhesives. The liftgate has a stationary glass window. The liftgate's hinges are welded to the body spaceframe and bolted to the formed liftgate panels.

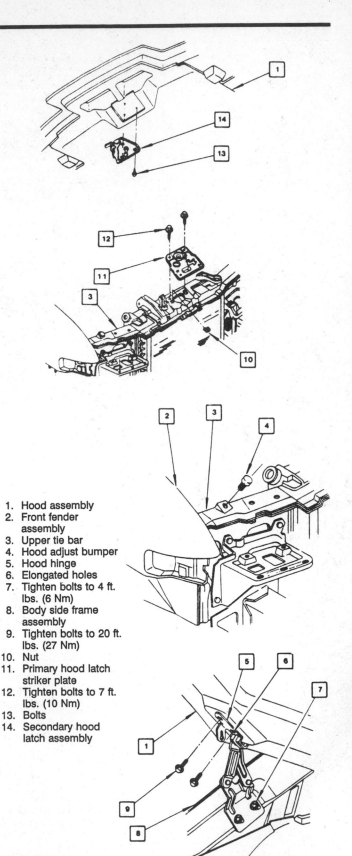

1. Hood assembly
2. Front fender assembly
3. Upper tie bar
4. Hood adjust bumper
5. Hood hinge
6. Elongated holes
7. Tighten bolts to 4 ft. lbs. (6 Nm)
8. Body side frame assembly
9. Tighten bolts to 20 ft. lbs. (27 Nm)
10. Nut
11. Primary hood latch striker plate
12. Tighten bolts to 7 ft. lbs. (10 Nm)
13. Bolts
14. Secondary hood latch assembly

Hood, hood hinges and lock

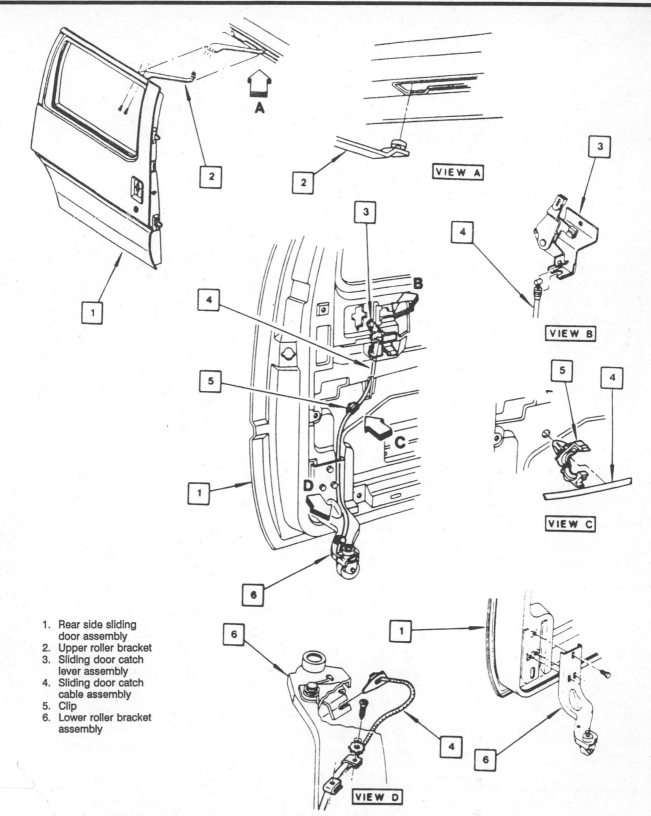

1. Rear side sliding door assembly
2. Upper roller bracket
3. Sliding door catch lever assembly
4. Sliding door catch cable assembly
5. Clip
6. Lower roller bracket assembly

Sliding door catch cable and upper and lower roller brackets

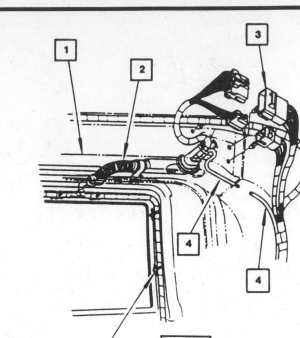

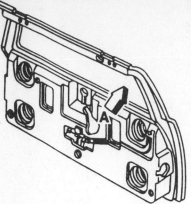

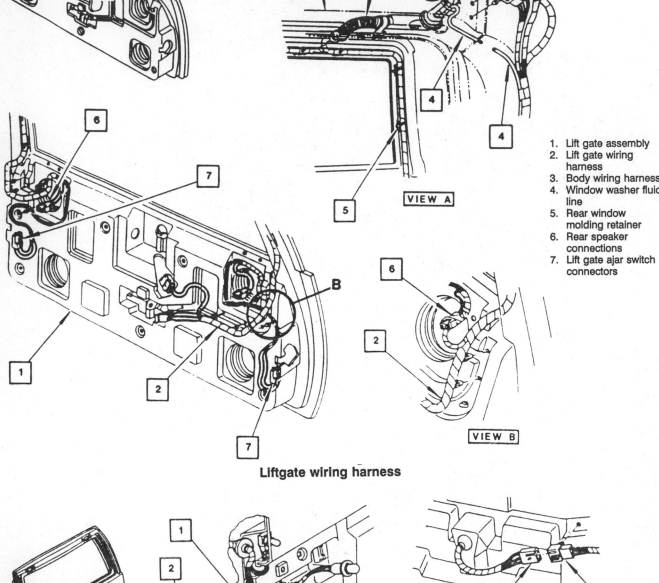

VIEW A

1. Lift gate assembly
2. Lift gate wiring harness
3. Body wiring harness
4. Window washer fluid line
5. Rear window molding retainer
6. Rear speaker connections
7. Lift gate ajar switch connectors

VIEW B

Liftgate wiring harness

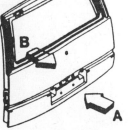

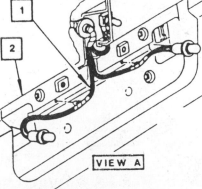

VIEW A

VIEW B

1. License plate-backup lamps harness
2. Lift gate assembly
3. Lift gate wiring harness

License plate and back — up lamps harness

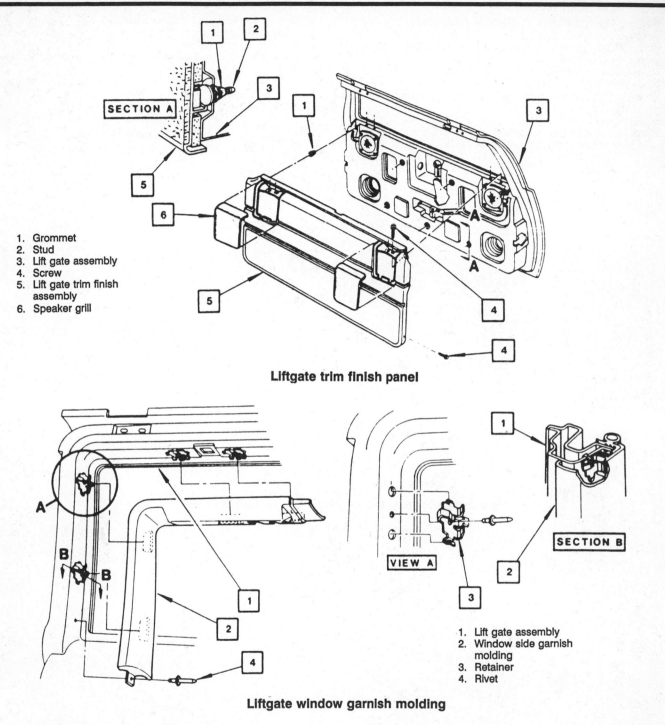

1. Grommet
2. Stud
3. Lift gate assembly
4. Screw
5. Lift gate trim finish
   assembly
6. Speaker grill

Liftgate trim finish panel

1. Lift gate assembly
2. Window side garnish
   molding
3. Retainer
4. Rivet

Liftgate window garnish molding

REMOVAL AND INSTALLATION

1. Disconnect the negative battery cable.
2. Remove the right and left side window garnish mouldings.
3. Remove the liftgate trim finish panel.
4. Disconnect the electrical connectors to the rear speakers, liftagte ajar switch, license plate and back-up lamps and the window release actuator harness connector.
5. With the liftgate open, remove the shoulder bolt securing the upper end of the strut to the strut bracket.

6. With the aid of a helper, remove the liftgate hinge bolts and remove the liftgate assembly.
7. Installation is the reverse of removal.

Bumpers

REMOVAL AND INSTALLATION

Front

1. Remove the right and left wheel well housing.

2. Remove the right and left fascia to fender bolts.

3. Remove the headlights.

4. Remove the right and left headlight frame to fascia fasteners and remove the front fascia.

5. Disconnect the parking lamp connectors.

6. Remove the radiator air flow shields.

7. Remove the bumper to energy absorber bolts and remove the front bumper.

To install:

8. Position the bumper to the vehicle, install the bumper to energy absorber bolts and tighten to 20 ft. lbs. (27 Nm).

9. Install the radiator air flow shields.

10. Connect the parking lamps.

11. Install the front fascia.

12. Install the right and left headlamp frame to fascia fasteners and install the headlamps.

13. Install the right and left fascia to fender bolts and tighten to 53 inch lbs. (6Nm).

14. Install the right and left wheel well housing.

Rear

1. Remove the lower fascia to bumper fasteners.

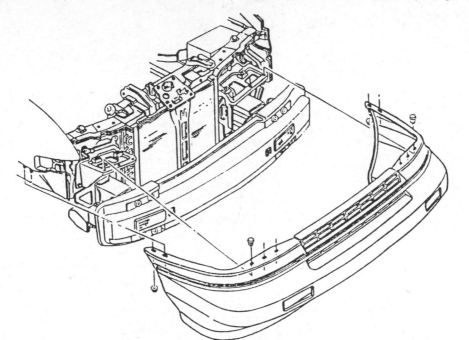

Front bumper and fascia installation — Lumina APV

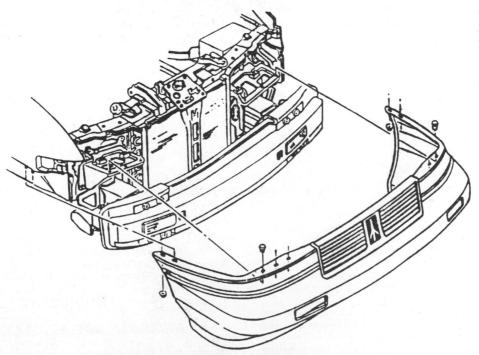

Front bumper and fascia installation — Silhouette

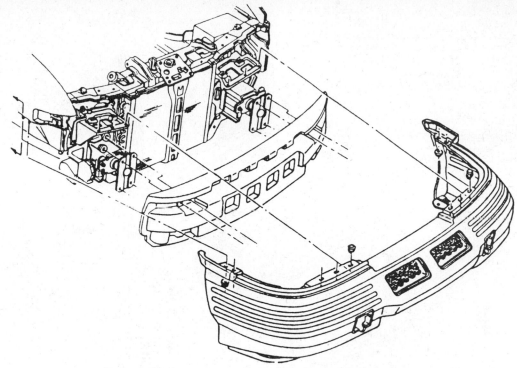

Front bumper and fascia installation — Transport

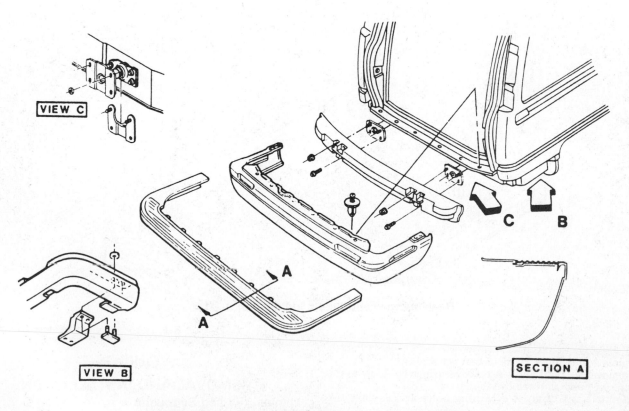

VIEW C

VIEW B

C B

A A

SECTION A

Rear bumper and fascia installation — Lumina APV

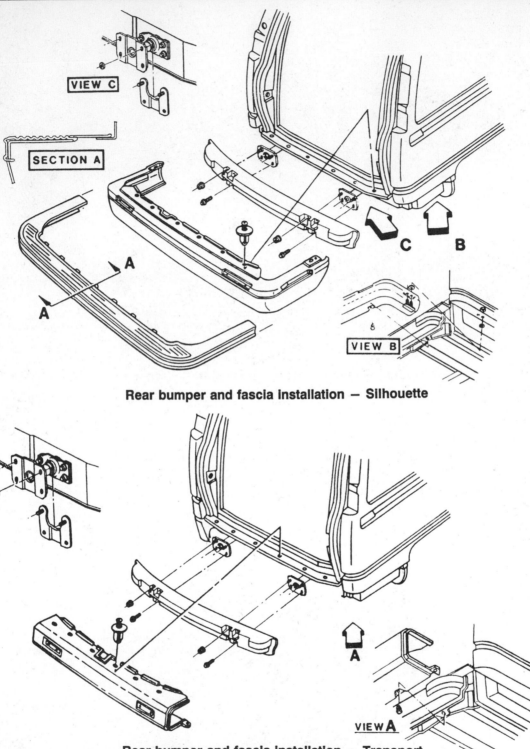

VIEW C

SECTION A

C B

VIEW B

Rear bumper and fascia installation — Silhouette

VIEW A

Rear bumper and fascia installation — Transport

2. Remove the upper fascia to bumper screws.
3. Remove the right and left bolts securing the fascia to the rear quarter panel and remove the fascia.
4. Remove the bumper retaining bolts and remove the bumper.
5. Installation is the reverse of removal.

Grille
REMOVAL AND INSTALLATION
Lumina APV and Silhouette

1. Raise and support the hood.

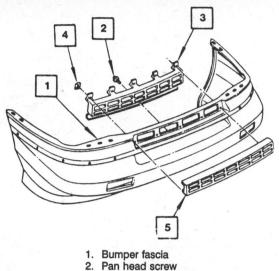

1. Bumper fascia
2. Pan head screw
3. Lower radiator grille
4. Nut-radiator grille
5. Upper radiator grille

Grille Installation — Lumina APV

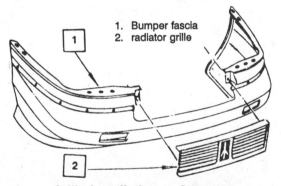

1. Bumper fascia
2. radiator grille

Grille Installation — Silhouette

2. Pop out the upper grille.
3. Remove the lower grille to fascia screws and remove the lower grille.
4. Installation is the reverse of removal.

Transport

1. Remove the right and left wheel well housing.

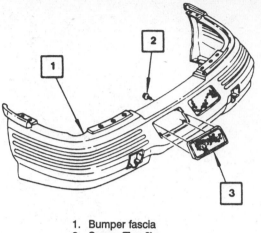

1. Bumper fascia
2. Screw (Torx®)
3. Radiator grille (lower rh)

Grille Installation — Transport

2. Remove the right and left fascia to fender bolts.
3. Remove the headlights.
4. Remove the right and left headlight frame to fascia fasteners and remove the front fascia.
5. Remove the grille to front fascia fasteners and remove the grille.
6. Installation is the reverse of removal.

Fender

REMOVAL AND INSTALLATION

1. Support the hood properly.
2. Disconnect the side marker lamp.
3. Remove the wheel well housing.
4. Remove the fender to bumper fascia bolts.
5. Remove the fender to fascia bolt at the lower door hinge pillar.
6. Remove the fender attaching screws and remove the fender.
To install:
7. Reposition the fender and install the attaching screws.
8. Install the fender to fascia bolt at the lower door hinge pillar.
9. Install the fender to bumper fascia bolts.
10. Install the wheel well housing.
11. Install the side marker lamp assembly.

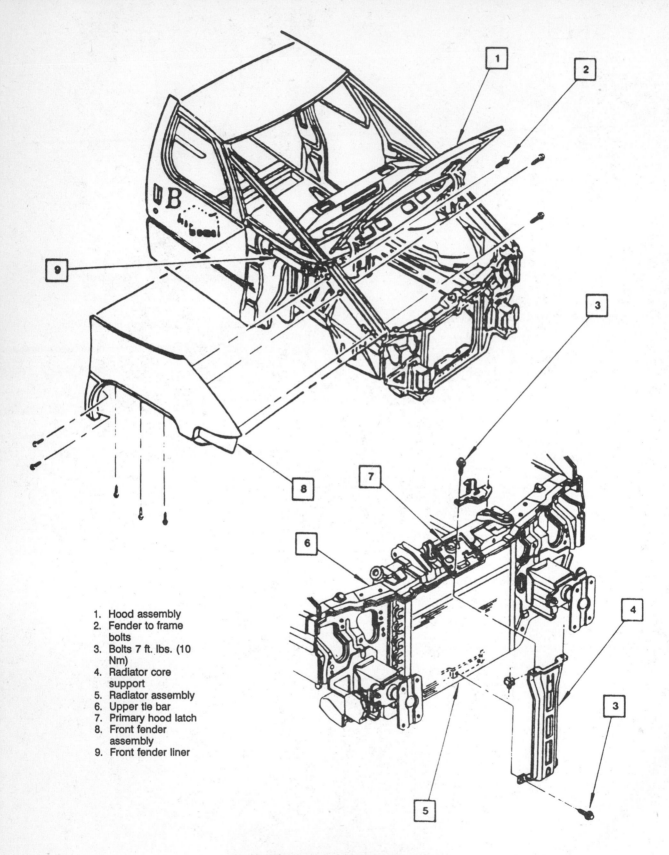

1. Hood assembly
2. Fender to frame bolts
3. Bolts 7 ft. lbs. (10 Nm)
4. Radiator core support
5. Radiator assembly
6. Upper tie bar
7. Primary hood latch
8. Front fender assembly
9. Front fender liner

Front fender and hood latch support

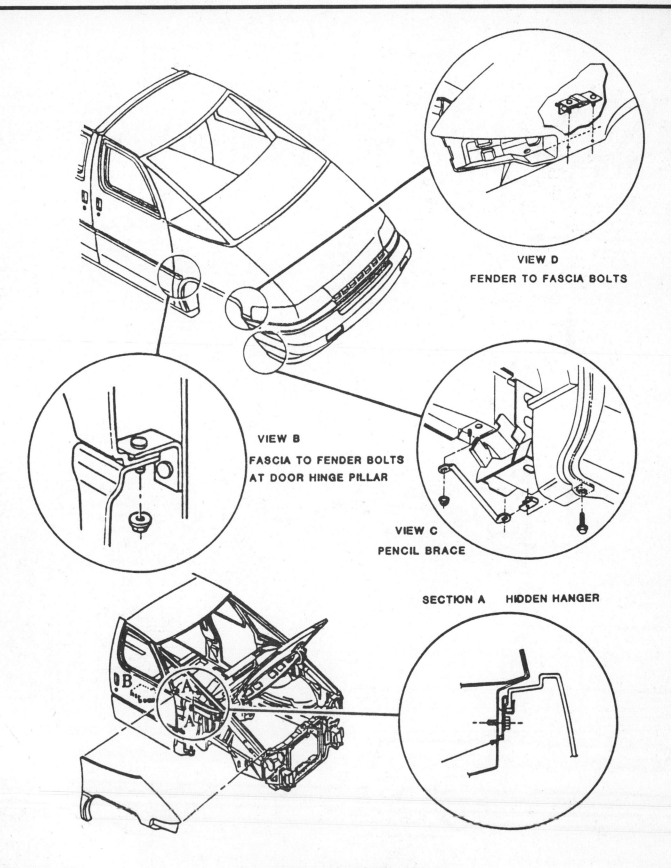

VIEW D
FENDER TO FASCIA BOLTS

VIEW B
FASCIA TO FENDER BOLTS
AT DOOR HINGE PILLAR

VIEW C
PENCIL BRACE

SECTION A   HIDDEN HANGER

Front fender panel hidden hangers

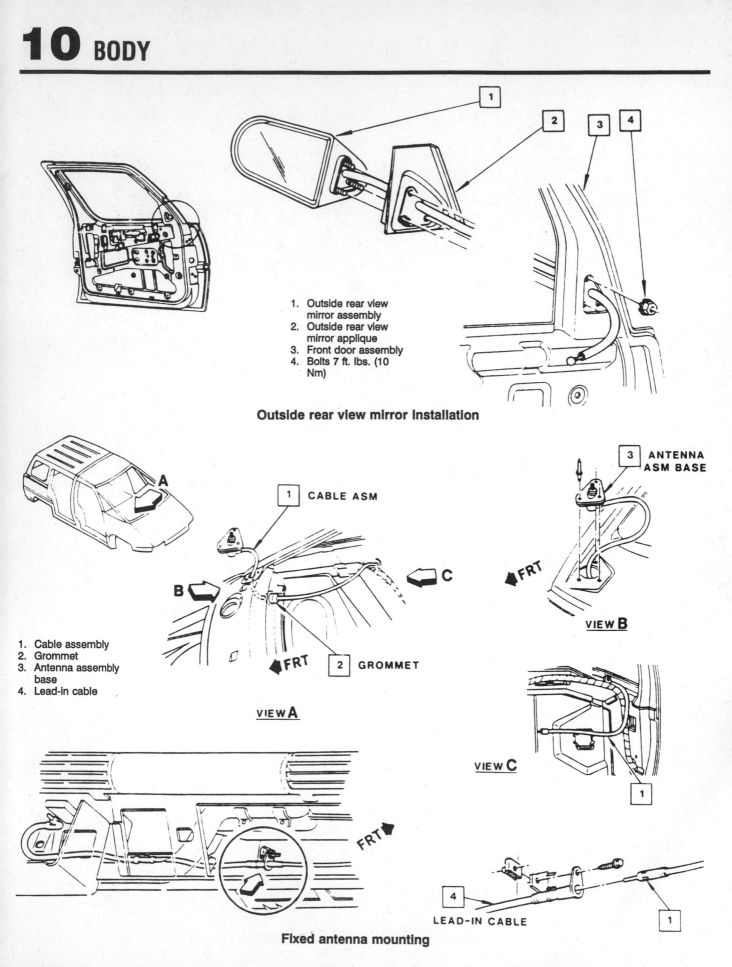

1. Outside rear view mirror assembly
2. Outside rear view mirror applique
3. Front door assembly
4. Bolts 7 ft. lbs. (10 Nm)

Outside rear view mirror installation

1 CABLE ASM

1. Cable assembly
2. Grommet
3. Antenna assembly base
4. Lead-in cable

2 GROMMET

VIEW A

3 ANTENNA ASM BASE

VIEW B

VIEW C

1

FRT

LEAD-IN CABLE

4

1

Fixed antenna mounting

Outside Mirrors

REMOVAL AND INSTALLATION

1. Remove the door inside trim panel.
2. Remove the front garnish mouldings.
3. Remove the nuts securing the mirror to the door.
4. Remove the feed controller and cable through the door and remove the mirror.
5. Installation is the reverse of removal.

Radio Antenna

REMOVAL AND INSTALLATION

1. Disconnect the steel antenna out of the base.
2. Remove the trim from the antenna housing.
3. Remove the 3 antenna mounting screws.
4. Disconnect the antenna lead-in cable and remove from the engine compartment.
5. Remove the antenna base assembly.
6. Installation is the reverse of removal

INTERIOR

Door Panels

REMOVAL AND INSTALLATION

Front

1. Disconnect the negative battery cable, if equipped with power door accessories.
2. Remove the power door lock and window controls, if so equipped.
3. Using a door window handle clip removal tool, remove the clip and handle.
4. Remove the door handle bezel.
5. Remove the fasteners in the armrest and lower panel.
6. Disconnect and feed the electrical connectors through the door panel, if so equipped.
7. Remove the trim panel retainers from the door and pry the trim panel from the door frame at the window seal.
To install:
8. Install the trim panel to the door, placing the window seal portion of the panel over the door frame.
9. Feed the electrical connectors through the door panel, if so equipped.
10. Install the fasteners in the armrest and lower panel.

11. Install the door handle bezel.
12. Install the door window handle.
13. Install the power door lock and window controls, if so equipped.
14. Connect the negative battery cable.

Sliding

1. Remove the inside door handle, bezel to door screws and remove the bezel.
2. Remove the door trim panel fasteners, by prying with tool J 24595-B or equivalent, and remove the trim panel.
To install:
3. Replace any broken retainers and push the door panel with the retainers into the door.
4. Install the door inside handle bezel cover.
5. Install the inside handle and bezel to to door screws.

Tailgate Trim Panel

REMOVAL AND INSTALLATION

1. Open the liftgate and remove the speaker grilles from the

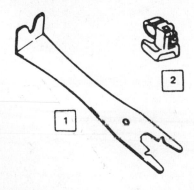
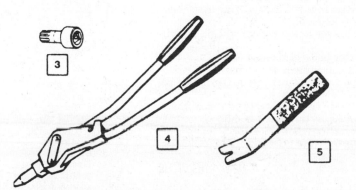

1. J-9886-01 door handle clip remover
2. J-28625 hinge spring tool
3. J-29843-0 door lock striker and safety belt Torx® wrench
4. J-29022-A hand riveter
5. J 24595-B door trim pad and garnish remover

Special door and door trim removal tools.

trim finish panel by carefully releasing the plastic clips at the top of each grille.

2. Remove both speakers.

3. Remove the screws under the grilles retaining the upper end of the trim panel to the lift gate inner panel.

4. Remove the 4 screws along the bottom and the 2 at each end of the trim panel.

5. Remove the pull strap.

6. Disengage the 2 plastic retaining studs from the grommets in the inner panel using a garnish clip removal tool.

7. Installation is the reverse of removal. Align the finish panel retaining studs with rings in the inner panel, then with the palm of hand, tap the retainers into the rings.

Quarter Trim Panels

REMOVAL AND INSTALLATION

Right Side

1. Remove any seats necessary to gain access to the trim panel.

2. Remove the upper and lower E-pillar saftey belt bolts, if so equipped.

3. Remove the back body pillar finishing panel.

4. Remove the quarter trim rear finish moulding assembly.

5. Remove the upper trim assembly.

6. Remove the upper and lower lock pillar safety belt bolts, if so equipped.

7. Remove the rear quarter body lock panel screws.

8. Remove the jack assembly.

9. Remove the lower quarter trim assembly to space frame screws and remove the lower quarter trim assembly.

To install:

10. Install the lower quarter trim assembly and retaining screws to the space frame.

11. Install the jack assembly.

12. Install the rear quarter body lock panel.

13. Install the upper and lower lock pillar safety belt bolts, if so equipped.

14. Install the upper trim assembly.

15. Install the quarter trim rear finish moulding assembly.

16. Install the back body pillar finishing panel.

17. Install the upper and lower E-pillar safety belt bolts, if so equipped.

18. Install the seats as necessary.

Left Side

1. Remove any seats necessary to gain access to the trim panel.

2. Remove the upper and lower E-pillar safety belt bolts, if so equipped.

3. Remove the back body pillar finishing panel.

4. Remove the quarter trim rear finish moulding assembly.

5. Remove the upper trim assembly.

6. Remove the upper and lower lock pillar safety belt bolts, if so equipped.

7. Remove the rear quarter body lock panel screws.

8. Remove the stowage compartment access panel.

9. Remove the Electronic Level Control (**E.L.C**) unit, if so equipped.

10. Remove the lower quarter trim assembly to space frame screws and remove the lower quarter trim assembly.

To install:

11. Install the lower quarter trim assembly and retaining screws to the space frame.

12. Install the Electronic Level Control (**E.L.C**) unit, if so equipped.

13. Remove the stowage compartment access panel.

14. Install the rear quarter body lock panel.

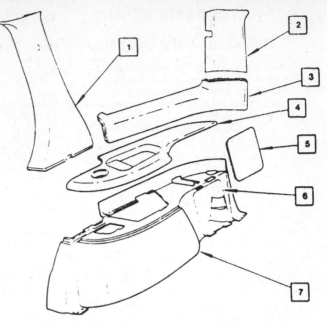

1. Rear quarter body lock panel
2. Back body pillar finishing panel
3. Quarter trim rear finish molding assembly
4. Upper trim assembly
5. Jacking assembly storage door
6. Jacking assembly storage compartment
7. Lower quarter trim assembly

Right side quarter trim panel

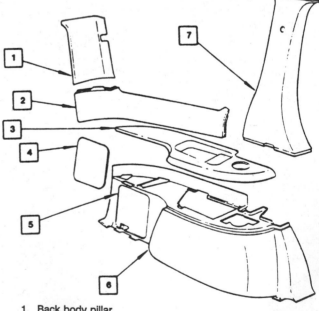

1. Back body pillar finishing panel
2. Quarter trim rear finish molding assembly
3. Upper trim assembly
4. Electronic level control assembly access door
5. Electronic level control assembly compartment
6. Lower quarter trim assembly
7. Rear quarter body lock panel

Left side quarter trim panel

15. Install the upper and lower lock pillar safety belt bolts, if so equipped.
16. Install the upper trim assembly.
17. Install the quarter trim rear finish moulding assembly.
18. Install the back body pillar finishing panel.
19. Install the upper and lower E-pillar saftey belt bolts, if so equipped.
20. Install the seats as necessary.

Left Side Forward

The quarter trim finish panel assembly and the C-pillar trim finish panel assembly are mated at the assembly plant and are collectively referred to as the left side forward quarter trim assembly.

1. Remove any seats necessary to gain access to the trim panel.
2. Remove the upper and lower body lock pillar safety belt bolts, if so equipped.
3. Remove the 2 body lock panel screws and remove the body lock panel.
4. Remove the back body pillar finishing panel.
5. Remove the rear quarter upper trim assembly.
6. Remove the 2 lower quarter trim assembly to space frame screws as necessary to disengage the clips that secure the forward trim assembly to the rear quarter trim assembly.
7. Remove the upper and lower C-pillar safety belt bolts, if so equipped.
8. Remove the C-pillar garnish screws and push the seat belt through the C-pillar garnish.
9. Remove the C-pillar moulding and the forward quarter trim assembly.
To install:
10. Push the seat belt through the C-pillar garnish.
11. Install the C-pillar moulding and the forward quarter trim assembly.
12. Install the 2 C-pillar garnish screws.
13. Install the upper and lower C-pillar safety belt bolts, if so equipped.

14. Reattach the forward trim assembly to the rear trim assembly.
15. Install the 2 quarter trim assembly to space frame screws.
16. Install the rear quarter upper trim assembly.
17. Install the back body pillar finishing panel.
18. Install the body lock panel.
19. Install the upper and lower body lock pillar safety belt bolts, if so equipped.
20. Install any seats removed to gain access to the trim panel.

1. Quarter trim finish panel assembly
2. C-pillar trim finish panel assembly

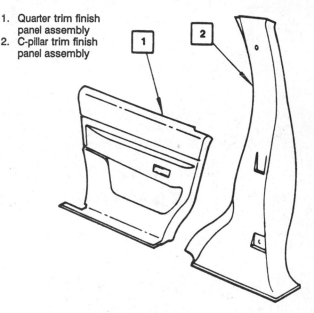

Left side forward quarter trim assembly

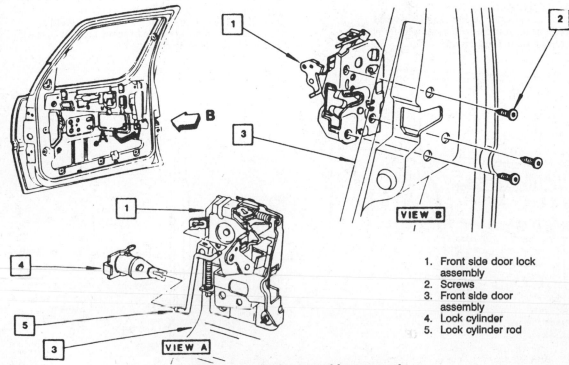

1. Front side door lock assembly
2. Screws
3. Front side door assembly
4. Lock cylinder
5. Lock cylinder rod

Front door lock assembly removal

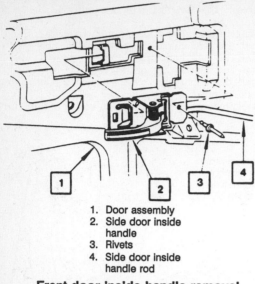

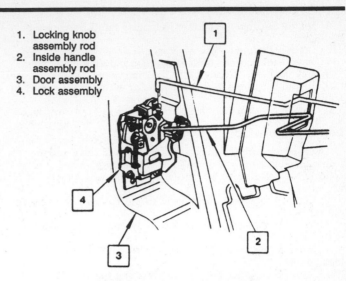

1. Locking knob
   assembly rod
2. Inside handle
   assembly rod
3. Door assembly
4. Lock assembly

1. Door assembly
2. Side door inside
   handle
3. Rivets
4. Side door inside
   handle rod

Front door inside handle removal

Front door lock rod locations

Door Locks

REMOVAL AND INSTALLATION

Front

1. Remove the inside door trim panel.
2. Disconnect the outside handle to lock assembly rod.
3. Disconnect the lock cylinder to lock assembly rod.
4. Disconnect the inside handle to lock assembly rod.
5. Remove the lock assembly screws and remove the lock from the door.

To install:

6. Position the lock assembly to the door and install the retaining screws.
7. Connect the inside handle to lock assembly rod.
8. Connect the lock cylinder to lock assembly rod.
9. Connect the outside handle to lock assembly rod.
10. Install the inside door trim panel.

Sliding

1. Remove the door trim panel
2. Disconnect the control rods from the lock assembly by prying the clip anchor out of the hole and pushing the clip away from the lever.
3. Support the door and remove the center roller bracket to door screws.
4. Using a ¼ in. drill bit, drill out the rod guide to door rivets and remove the rod guide from the door.
5. Remove the lock assembly retaining screws and remove the lock assembly.

To install:

6. Install the lock assembly to the door with the retaining screws.
7. Attach the guide rod to the door using ¼ in. diameter bolts, ½ in. long, with a spring washer and nut.
8. Install the control rods to the lock assembly.
9. Install the center roller bracket to door screws.
10. Install the door trim panel.

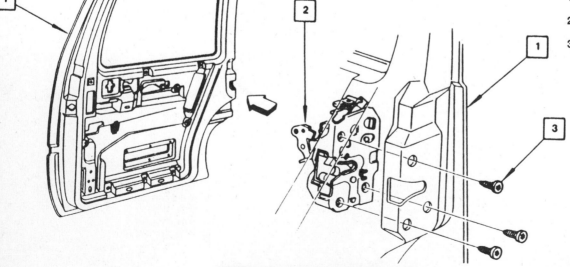

1. Rear side sliding
   door assembly
2. Rear side door lock
   assembly
3. Screws

Sliding door lock assembly replacement

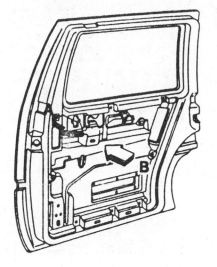

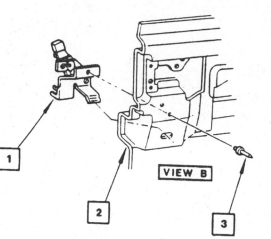

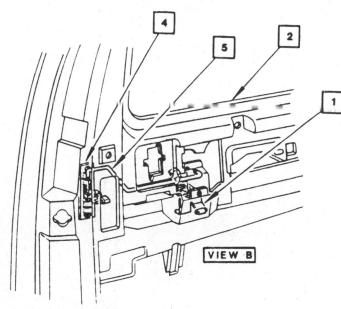

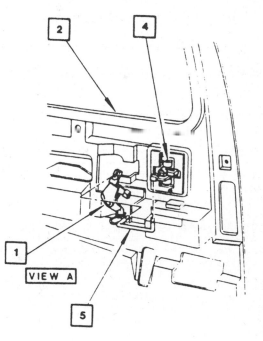

1. Rear side door catch
   lever assembly
2. Door assembly
3. Rivet
4. Rear sliding door
   outside handle
5. Rear sliding door
   catch lever
6. Rear sliding door
   catch lever cable
   assembly

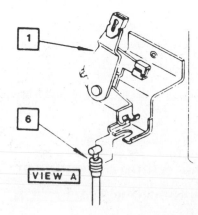

Exploded view of the sliding door catch lever and cable

1. Lift gate assembly
2. Screws
3. Lift gate lock assembly
4. Body harness connector to door ajar switch

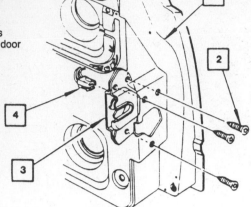

Liftgate lock assembly replacement

Tailgate Lock

REMOVAL AND INSTALLATION

1. Open the liftgate and remove the speaker grilles.
2. Remove the liftgate trim finish panel as outlined in this section.
3. Remove the bolts attaching the lock assembly to the inner door panel and remove the lock assembly through the access hole.
4. Disconnect the electrical connector to the door ajar switch and remove the lock assembly and switch.
5. Installation is the reverse of removal.

Door Glass

REMOVAL AND INSTALLATION

Front

1. Remove the door trim panel.
2. Remove the front and rear garnish mouldings.
3. Remove the lower run channel.
4. Remove the outer window sealing strip.
5. Drill out the rivet and remove the window run channel from the door.
6. Drop the window out of the rear run channel and pull the window up and out of the vehicle.

——————————— CAUTION ———————————

Always wear heavy gloves when handling window glass, to avoid personal injury!

————————————————————————————————————

To install:

7. Install the window to the door frame and bolt or rivet in place.
8. Install the lower run channel.
9. Install the outer window sealing strip.
10. Install the garnish mouldings and the door trim panel.

Manual Window Regulator

REMOVAL AND INSTALLATION

1. Remove the door trim panel.
2. Roll the window up, and apply fabric backed body tape from the window over the top of the door to the other side of the window. This will hold the window in position when the regulator is removed.
3. Using a $\frac{3}{16}$ in. drill bit, drill the rivet heads from the regulator to door rivets.
4. Push the regulator into the door and slide it forward then rearward to remove the regulator arms from the sash and the regulator rail.
5. Fold the regulator arms together and remove the regulator from the door access hole.

To install:

6. Place the regulator into the door through the access hole.
7. Place the regulator arm rollers into the sash and the regulator rail.
8. Push the regulator through the regulator door opening and align the holes in the regulator with the holes in the door.
9. Use $\frac{1}{4}$ in. bolts, about a $\frac{1}{2}$ in. long, with a spring washer and nut to reattach the regulator to the door.
10. Install the trim panel.

Power Window Regulator and Motor

REMOVAL AND INSTALLATION

1. Disconnect the negative battery cable.
2. Remove the door trim panel.
3. Roll the window up, and apply fabric backed body tape from the window over the top of the door to the other side of the window. This will hold the window in position when the regulator is removed.
4. Disconnect the wiring harness from the motor.
5. Use a $\frac{1}{4}$ in. drill bit to drill the rivet heads and remove the regulator from the door.
6. Drill out the motor to regulator rivets and remove the regulator from the motor.

To install:

7. Lubricate the motor drive gear and the regulator sector teeth, check the mesh of the motor to the regulator and rivet the motor to the regulator.
8. Place the regulator through the access opening and position the regulator arm roller into the sash and regulator rail.
9. Push the regulator through the regulator door opening and align the holes in the regulator with the holes in the door.
10. Use $\frac{1}{4}$ in. diameter bolts, $\frac{1}{2}$ in. long, with a nylon inserted nut to reattach the regulator to the door.
11. Install the wiring harness from the regulator to the motor.
12. Install the trim panel and reconnect the battery cable.

Windshield Glass

REMOVAL AND INSTALLATION

To replace a windshield with urethane adhesive requires either partial or complete replacement of the adhesive. Partial replacement of material is referred to as the short method. Complete material replacement is known as the extended method. A windshield pillar modular glass can only be replaced via the extended method.

When replacing a windshield, the short method can be used where original adhesive left on window opening pinch-weld flanges after glass removal can serve as a base for the new glass. This method would apply in cases of cracked windshields that are still intact. The amount of adhesive left in window opening can be controlled during glass removal.

The extended method is to be used when the original adhesive left in window opening after glass removal cannot serve as a base for new glass. This method would be used in cases requiring structural work or paint repair in the opening. In these cases, original material is removed and replaced with new material.

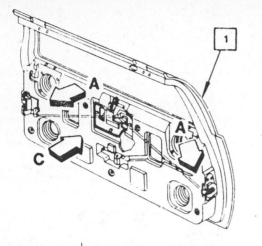

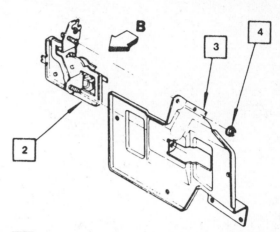

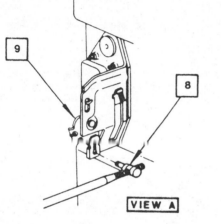

VIEW A

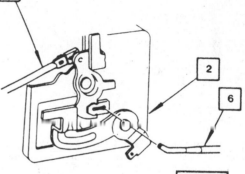

VIEW B

1. Lift gate assembly
2. Lock assembly
3. Lift gate striker
   anchor plate
4. Nut
5. Right hand rod
   assembly
6. Left hand rod
   assembly
7. Bolt
8. Rod adjustment
   screw
9. Latch lock assembly

VIEW C

Liftgate window lock, plate and rod assembly

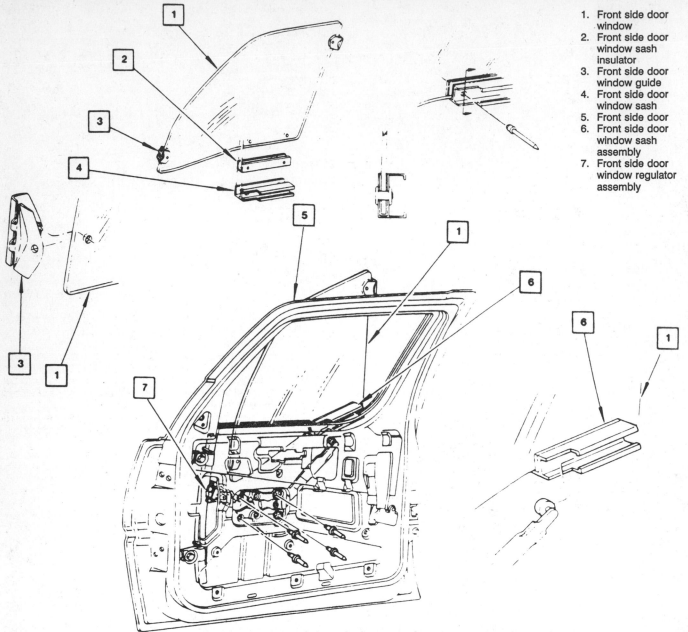

1. Front side door window
2. Front side door window sash insulator
3. Front side door window guide
4. Front side door window sash
5. Front side door
6. Front side door window sash assembly
7. Front side door window regulator assembly

Exploded view of the window regulator components

Adhesive Service Kit

Adhesive Kit No.9636067 (urethane adhesive) or equivalent contains some of the items needed to replace a urethane adhesive installed glass using the short method or any adhesive installed glass using the extended method. Additional items required:

   1. Solvent for cleaning edge of glass (preferably alcohol)
   2. Household cartridge type caulking gun
   3. Commercial type razor knife (for cutting around edge of glass)
   4. Cold knife No.J-24402-A or equivalent
   5. Black weatherstrip adhesive (butyl tape)
   6. Windshield removal knife No.J-38454
   7. Puller No.J-22888-20
   7. Legs No.J-22888-50
   8. Tip No.J-22888-90

The windshield removal method is the same for both the short and extended installation methods with one exception. If the short method is used, more care must be taken during cutout to make certain that an even bead of adhesive remains on the window opening to serve as a base for the new glass.

Short Method

   1. Remove the wiper arms, using puller J-22888-20 or equivalent.
   2. Remove the cowl panel retaining screws and remove the cowl panel.
   3. Lower windshield supports.
   4. Reveal
molding from top of windshield.
   5. Right and left fender garnish moldings.
   6. Right and left A-pillar garnish moldings.

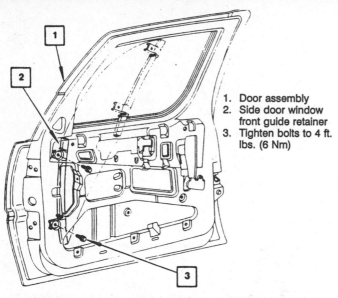

1. Door assembly
2. Side door window front guide retainer
3. Tighten bolts to 4 ft. lbs. (6 Nm)

Window run channel and front guide retainer

7. Mask off area around glass to protect painted surfaces and to aid in cleanup after installation.

8. Using a razor or utility knife, make a preliminary cut around perimeter of glass, staying as close to edge of glass as possible.

9. Using cold knife J-24402-A or equivalent, cut out windshield keeping blade as close to edge of glass as possible, and remove glass.

To install:

10. Clean glass opening of any loose material. If glass is to be reinstalled, all urethane must be removed from glass.

11. Replace glass supports. Position glass in opening, apply a piece of masking tape over each edge of glass and adjacent body pillars. Slit tape vertically at edge of glass. During installation, tape on glass can be aligned with tape on body to guide glass into desired position. Remove glass.

12. Clean the surface of glass to which adhesive will be applied (around edge of inside surface) by wiping with a clean, alcohol dampened cloth. Allow to air dry.

13. Two primers are provided in urethane adhesive kit no. 9636067 or equivalent. The clear primer is used on the glass prior to the black primer. Apply primer around entire perimeter of glass edge and ¼ in. inboard on inner surface. Allow primer to dry five minutes.

14. Apply a smooth continuous bead of adhesive around edge of glass opening on top of what is left of the original bead.

15. With aid of helper, lift glass into window opening. Windshield glass can be positioned without aid of carrying devices. Carry glass with one hand on inside of glass and one hand on outside. At window opening, put the glass in horizontal position. While one person holds the glass in this position, the second person can reach one arm around the body pillar and support the glass while the other person assumes the same position.

16. With glass centered in opening, place glass on supports and use tape guides applied in Step 2 to carefully place glass in proper position.

17. Press glass firmly to wet-out and set adhesive. Use care to avoid excessive squeeze out. Using a small disposable brush or flat-bladed tool, paddle material around edge of glass to ensure watertight seal. If necessary, paddle additional material to fill voids in seal.

18. Water Test vehicle at once using soft spray. Do not direct hard stream of water at fresh adhesive material. If any leaks are found, paddle in extra adhesive at leak point using a small dis-

posable brush or flat-bladed tool. Water applied on top of urethane adhesive, either during water test or as a separate operation, will speed up the cure of the urethane.

19. Install the reveal molding.
20. Install the right and left A-pillar garnish moldings.
21. Install the right and left fender garnish moldings.
22. Install the cowl panel and screws.
23. Install the wiper arms.
24. During windshield installation, the vehicle must remain at normal room temperature for six hours to complete proper cure of adhesive.

Extended Method

It will be necessary to use the extended installation method if urethane material remaining in window opening after window removal is damaged, or must be removed to permit refinishing of window opening.

Using a sharp scraper or chisel, remove the old adhesive material from window opening. It is not necessary that all traces of material be removed, but there should not be any mounds or loose pieces lift.

If refinishing or painting operations are required, or painted surface is exposed during removal of material, black primer should be applied to exposed area.

1. If new glass is being installed, check relationship of glass to adhesive on pinch-weld flange. Gaps in excess of ⅛ in. must be corrected by shimming or by applying more adhesive.

2. With glass in proper position in opening, apply a piece of masking tape over each edge of glass and adjacent body pillar. Slit tape vertically at edge of glass. During installation, tape on glass can be aligned with tape on body to guide glass into desired position. Remove the glass.

3. Clean the surface of glass to which adhesive will be applied (around edge of inside surface) by wiping with a clean, alcohol dampened cloth. Allow to air dry.

4. Two primers are provided in urethane adhesive kit no. 9636067 or equivalent. The clear primer is used on the glass prior to the black primer. Apply primer around entire perimeter of glass edge and ¼ in. inboard on inner surface. Allow primer to dry five minutes.

5. Apply a smooth continuous bead of adhesive around edge of glass opening on top of what is left of the original bead.

6. With aid of helper, lift glass into window opening. Windshield glass can be positioned without aid of carrying devices. Carry glass with one hand on inside of glass and one hand on outside. At window opening, put the glass in horizontal position. While one person holds the glass in this position, the second person can reach one arm around the body pillar and support the glass while the other person assumes the same position.

7. With glass centered in opening, place glass on supports and use tape guides applied in Step 2 to carefully place glass in proper position.

8. Press glass firmly to wet-out and set adhesive. Use care to avoid excessive squeeze out. Using a small disposable brush or flat-bladed tool, paddle material around edge of glass to ensure watertight seal. If necessary, paddle additional material to fill voids in seal.

9. Water Test vehicle at once using soft spray. Do not direct hard stream of water at fresh adhesive material. If any leaks are found, paddle in extra adhesive at leak point using a small disposable brush or flat-bladed tool. Water applied on top of urethane adhesive, either during water test or as a separate operation, will speed up the cure of the urethane.

10. Install the reveal molding.
11. Install the right and left A-pillar garnish moldings.
12. Install the right and left fender garnish moldings.
13. Install the cowl panel and screws.
14. Install the wiper arms.
15. During windshield installation, the vehicle must remain at

normal room temperature for 6 hours to complete proper cure of adhesive.

Windshield Reveal Moulding

REMOVAL AND INSTALLATION

1. With a flat-bladed tool, carefully pry end of molding out about 3 in. (75mm).
2. Grasp with hand and slowly pull molding away from body.
3. If original molding cannot be reused (due to damage, cut short, etc.), discard molding and replace with a new service molding. The service molding has a shorter shank and will not bottom-out when installed. Be sure to prefit service molding by locating on body prior to actual installation.

To install:

4. To reuse original reveal molding, trim off barb (if necessary) and prefit in cavity.
5. Apply clear primer from urethane kit, part No. 9636067 or equivalent, to lower surface of molding.
6. Apply urethane in cavity between body and glass.
7. Start from the center and hand press molding into place. Tape can be applied to keep reveal molding flush with body.
8. Flood the molding with water to speed set-up of adhesive.

Windshield Pillar Modual Glass

REMOVAL AND INSTALLATION

1. Remove the fender garnish molding.
2. Remove the A-pillar garnish molding.

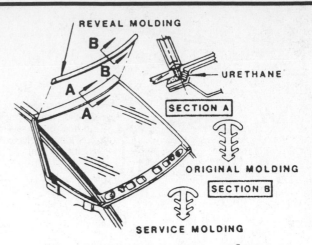

Windshield reveal molding removal

3. With a razor blade or similar tool, cut the urethane along the A-pillar.
4. Heat the blade of tool J 24402-A or equivalent, with a propane torch and cut the urethane along the A-pillar.
5. Slip a windshield removal knife, J-38454 or equivalent, behind the encapsulation and cut the urethane from the bottom to top corners of the glass.
6. Cut the remaining urethane and remove the glass.

To install:

7. Clean the pinchweld surface thoroughly.
8. Prime the pinchweld surface. Two primers are provided in urethane adhesive kit no. 9636067. The clear primer is used prior to the black primer. Apply primer around the perimeter of the window opening along the pinchweld. Allow five minutes to dry.
9. Apply butyl tape to the inside edge of the pinchweld to prevent urethane from squeezing into the vehicle.
10. Apply a smooth, continuous bead of urethane adhesive along the perimeter of the window next to the butyl tape.
11. Position the glass in the opening.
12. Press the glass firmly to wet out and set adhesive. The butyl tape will hold the window in place while the urethane sets.
13. Watertest vehicle at once using soft spray. Do not direct hard stream of water at fresh adhesive material. If a leak is discovered, remove glass immediately and paddle in more urethane.

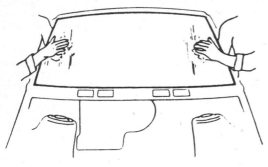

Glass Installation

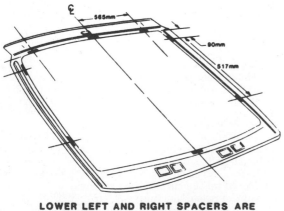

LOWER LEFT AND RIGHT SPACERS ARE TO BE PLACED 2.5mm INBOARD OF INSIDE EDGE OF FLANGE

Glass spacer location

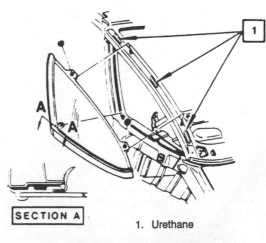

1. Urethane

Modular glass installation

Liftgate Glass

REMOVAL AND INSTALLATION

1. Open the liftgate assembly.
2. Remove the right and left window garnish mouldings.
3. Remove the 2 window bracket assemblies from the liftgate outer panel by drilling out the attaching rivets.
4. Lift the window from the weatherstrip assembly.
5. Remove the 4 bolts and bushings from the window brackets and remove the window.
6. Installation is the reverse of removal.

Inside Rearview Mirror and Arm

REMOVAL AND INSTALLATION

The rearview mirror is attached to a support with a retaining screw. The support is secured to the windshield glass. The support is installed by the glass supplier using a plastic polyvinyl butyl adhesive. To reinstall a mirror support arm to the windshield, follow the instructions included with an inside mirror installation kit, which may be purchased at most auto supply stores.

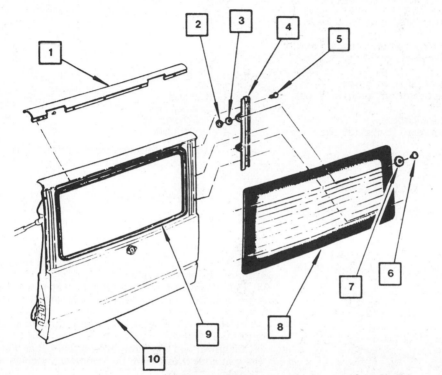

1. Applique (Pontiac only)
2. Nut
3. Washer
4. Window bracket assembly
5. Rivets
6. Bolt
7. Window bushing
8. Lift gate glass
9. Weatherstrip assembly
10. Lift gate outer panel

Liftgate stationary window replacement

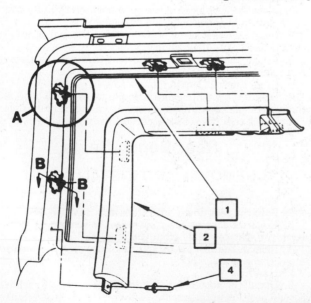

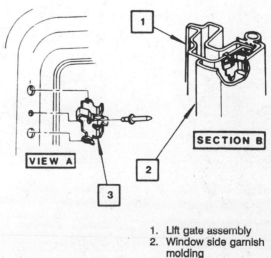

1. Lift gate assembly
2. Window side garnish molding
3. Retainer
4. Rivet

Liftgate window garnish molding removal

Front Bucket Seats

REMOVAL AND INSTALLATION

1. Disconnect the negative battery cable on the driver,s side only, if equipped with power seats.
2. Disconnect the seat belt harness connector to the body wiring harness on the driver's side only.
3. Disconnect the power seat connector from the body wiring harness, if so equipped.
4. Disconnect the fuel filler door release cable, driver's side only.
5. Remove the nuts attaching the seat frame to the seat anchor plate studs on the floor pan.
6. Disconnect the seat belt assembly and remove the seat.

To install:

7. Install the seat belt assembly over the rear inboard seat stud on the right hand side of the driver's seat or on the left hand side of the passenger's seat.
8. Install the power seat connection, if so equipped.
9. Install the seat belt harness connector on the driver's seat only.
10. Install the fuel filler door release cable.
11. Tighten the seat retaining nuts to 20 ft. lbs. (27 Nm)

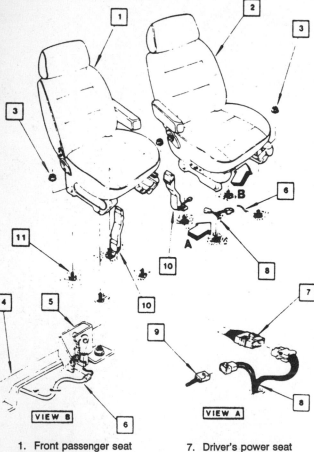

1. Front passenger seat
2. Driver's seat
3. Nut
4. Driver's seat adjuster
5. Fuel filler door release assembly
6. Fuel filler door release cable
7. Driver's power seat connector
8. Body wiring harness
9. Driver's safety belt harness
10. Safety belt assembly
11. Seat anchor plate studs

Front bucket seat installation

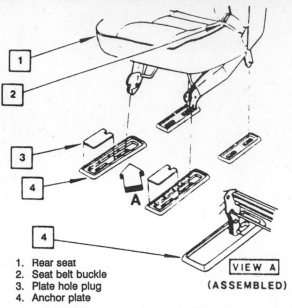

1. Rear seat
2. Seat belt buckle
3. Plate hole plug
4. Anchor plate

Rear bucket seat installation

Rear Bucket Seats

REMOVAL AND INSTALLATION

1. Remove all plugs.
2. Pull up the seat back latch lever and fold the seat back forward onto the seat cushion.
3. Pull up on the rear latch release strap to release the latching bar clamping the rear of the seat assembly to the rear seat anchors.
4. Pivot the rear of the seat assembly upward and toward the front of the vehicle.
5. Pull upward on the front of the latching bar and disconnect the seat riser frame from the front seat anchors and remove the seat.

To install:

6. Place the seat locks in the open position by pulling upward on the strap at the rear of the seat cushion.
7. Install the seat assembly over either the 2nd or 3rd row anchor plates in the floor plan.
8. Install the front legs of the seat through the slots in the front anchor plates and onto the seat anchors.
9. Close the seat locking levers to secure the seat.
10. Install the anchor plate hole plugs, over the open slots in the anchor plates, and snap them down securely into place.
11. Check that the seat is secured firmly to all 4 seat anchors.

Rear Bench Seats

REMOVAL AND INSTALLATION

1. Remove all plugs.
2. Fold the seat down onto the seat's cushion.
3. Press the locking lever between the seat's rear legs to unlatch the seat assembly from the rear seat anchors.
4. Release the front seat legs from the seat anchors and remove the seat assembly.

To install:

5. Install the bench seat aligning the front of the seat over the second position in the anchor plates on the floor pan. Make sure the locks are in the open position.

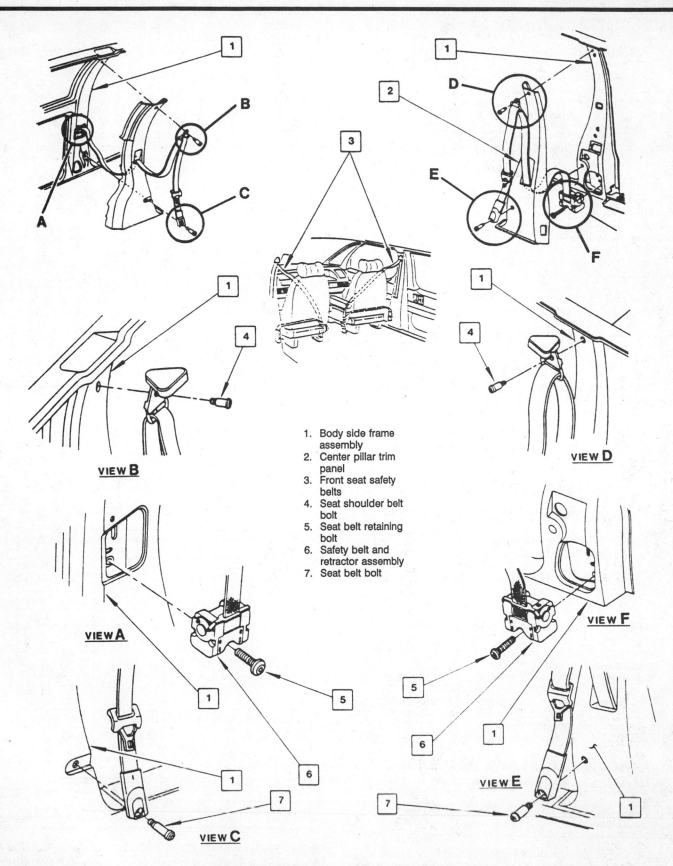

1. Body side frame assembly
2. Center pillar trim panel
3. Front seat safety belts
4. Seat shoulder belt bolt
5. Seat belt retaining bolt
6. Safety belt and retractor assembly
7. Seat belt bolt

VIEW **B**

VIEW **A**

VIEW **C**

VIEW **D**

VIEW **F**

VIEW **E**

Front bucket seat safety belt retention system

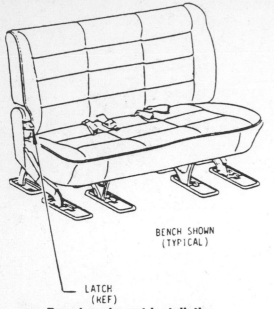

BENCH SHOWN
(TYPICAL)

LATCH
(REF)

Rear bench seat installation

6. Install the front legs of the seat through the slots in the front anchor.

7. Press the rear legs of the seat through the slots in the rear anchor plates and onto the seat anchors.

8. Unfold the seat back to an upright position.

9. Install the anchor plate hole plugs, over the open slots in the anchor plates, and snap them down securely into place.

10. Check that the bench seat is secured firmly to all 8 seat anchors.

Front Seat Belts

REMOVAL AND INSTALLATION

The driver's and front passenger seat belt assemblies are attached to the body side frame locking B-pillars in a similar manner.

1. Remove the center B-pillar trim finish panel assembly from the body side frame.

2. Unsnap the plastic cover off the upper seat belt anchor bracket.

3. Remove the upper seat belt anchor bolt using tool J 29843-9 or equivalent.

4. Remove the lower seat belt anchor bolt using tool J 29843-9 or equivalent and a ratchet wrench.

5. Remove the seat belt retractor mechanism bolt using tool J 29843-9 or equivalent and a ratchet wrench.

6. Remove the seat belt retractor mechanism by feeding the assembly through one opening in the pillar trim finish panel and remove the seat belt retractor assembly.

7. Installation is the reverse of removal.

Shoulder Belt and Retractor Mechanism

REMOVAL AND INSTALLATION

C-Pillar

The right and left side shoulder safety belts for second row bench or bucket seats are attached to the C-pillars in a similar manner.

1. Remove the center C-pillar trim finish panel assembly from the body side frame.

2. Unsnap the plastic cover off the upper seat belt anchor bracket.

3. Remove the upper seat belt anchor bolt using tool J 29843-9 or equivalent.

4. Remove the lower seat belt anchor bolt using tool J 29843-9 or equivalent and a ratchet wrench.

5. Remove the seat belt retractor mechanism bolt using tool J 29843-9 or equivalent and a ratchet wrench.

6. Remove the seat belt retractor mechanism by feeding assembly up through the opening in the pillar trim finish panel and remove the seat belt retractor assembly.

7. Installation is the reverse of removal.

D-Pillar

The right and left side shoulder safety belts for third row bucket seats are attached to the D-pillars in a similar manner.

1. Remove the jack storage compartment cover on the right side or the compressor/inflator rear shock absorber cover on the left side.

2. Remove the seat belt retractor anchor bolt using using Torx Wrench J 29843-9 or equivalent T45 socket.

3. Remove the anchor bolt securing the seat belt to the floor pan.

4. Unsnap the plastic cover off the upper belt anchor bracket at the roof end of the D-pillar.

5. Remove the upper seat belt anchor bolt using tool J 29843-9 or equivalent.

6. Remove the rear wheelhouse upper trim panel assembly.

7. Remove the shoulder belt retractor mechanism.

8. Installation is the reverse of removal.

Power Seat Adjuster and Motor Assembly

REMOVAL AND INSTALLATION

1. Disconnect the negative battery cable.

	PART NAME	METRIC TYPE	THREAD	LENGTH (mm)	TORQUE N·m	TORQUE ft-lbs
	BOLT	1	M12-1.75	36	35-48	26-35
	BOLT	2	M12-1.75	25	35-48	26-35
	BOLT	3	M12-1.75	30	35-48	26-35
	BOLT	4	M8-1.25	20	20-24	15-17
	BOLT	5	M12-1.75	39	35-48	26-35
	BOLT	6	M12-1.75	35	35-48	26-35
	BOLT	7	M12-1.75	43	35-48	26-35
	BOLT	8	M12-1.75	31	35-48	26-35
	BOLT	9	M12-1.75	49	35-48	26-35
	STUD	10	M6-1.00	15	N/A	N/A
	BOLT	11	M12-1.75	53	35-48	26-35
	NUT	12	M12-1.75		35-48	26-35
	NUT	13	M10-1.50		30-40	22-29
	NUT	14	M6-1.00		10-14	7-10
	NUT	15	M8-1.25		18-25	14-19
	STUD	16	M8-1.25	13	N/A	N/A

Always replace safety belt anchor bolts and nuts with the originals or replace with equal size and strength (or stronger)

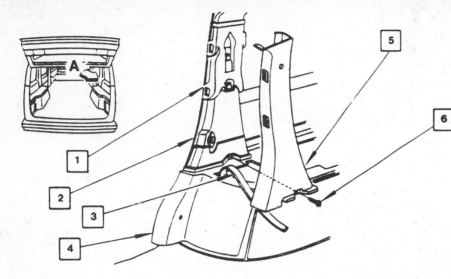

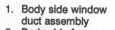

VIEW **A**

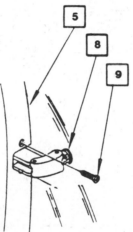

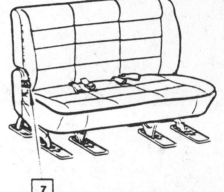

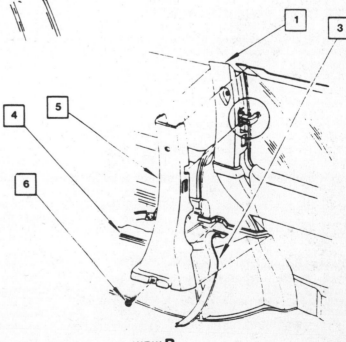

1. Body side window duct assembly
2. Body side frame assembly
3. Safety belt and retractor assembly
4. Wheelhouse lower panel
5. Body lock pillar trim panel
6. Lower pillar trim finish bolt
7. Folding seat back release latch lever
8. Body side window latch
9. Side window latch bolt

VIEW **B**

The right and left side shoulder safety belts for second row bench or bucket seats are attached to the C-pillars

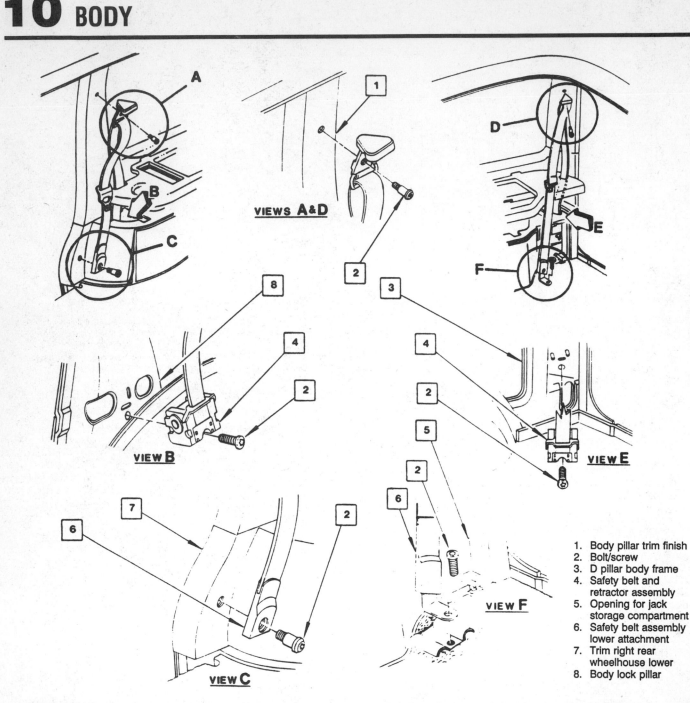

VIEWS A&D

VIEW B

VIEW C

VIEW E

VIEW F

1. Body pillar trim finish
2. Bolt/screw
3. D pillar body frame
4. Safety belt and retractor assembly
5. Opening for jack storage compartment
6. Safety belt assembly lower attachment
7. Trim right rear wheelhouse lower
8. Body lock pillar

The right and left side shoulder safety belts for third row bucket seats are attached to the D-pillars

2. Disconnect the 2 wire connector (power lead) from the floor.

3. Disconnect the fuel door latch cable from the fuel release mechanism.

4. Disconnect the seat adjuster from the floor pan by removing the 4 mounting stud nuts.

5. Remove the 4 mounting studs and separate the seat cushion from the seat adjuster.

6. Loosen the set screw on the fuel release handle and remove the handle.

7. Drill out the 2 rivets from the fuel release assembly and remove the assembly.

8. Remove the inboard and outboard side shields by removing the 2 mounting screws from the top of the shields outward until detached from the seat adjuster.

9. Disconnect the 6 cable connector from the motor and remove the tie wrap from the inboard side shield.

10. Remove the switch module from the inboard side shield.

11. Spread the positive connection prongs, protruding from the rear at the wire harness connector, outward and separate the switch module from the wire harness connector.

12. Using an offset screwdriver, remove the 4 screws securing the motor to the transmission assembly.

13. Disconnect the drive cables from the motor.

To install:

14. Install the 3 drive cables to the motor.

15. Align the drive cables in the motor with the bearing insert on the transmission assembly.

16. Using an offset screwdriver and 4 screws, install the motor to the transmission.

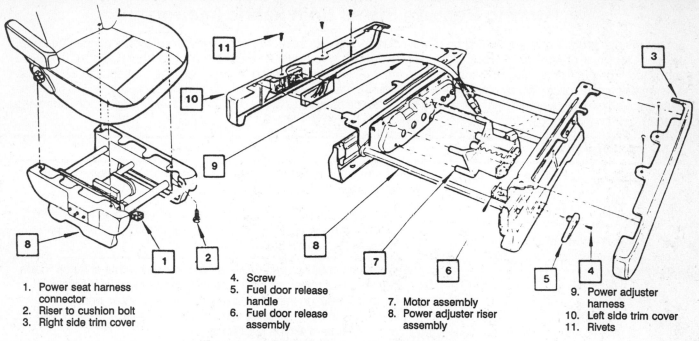

1. Power seat harness connector
2. Riser to cushion bolt
3. Right side trim cover
4. Screw
5. Fuel door release handle
6. Fuel door release assembly
7. Motor assembly
8. Power adjuster riser assembly
9. Power adjuster harness
10. Left side trim cover
11. Rivets

Front seat adjuster and motor replacement

17. Snap the connector on the wire harness assembly into the switch module.
18. Align the switch module with the alignment slots in the inboard side shield and snap the switch module into place.
19. Route the wiring harness over the inboard upper support making certain the harness is situated in the cut out provided in the side shield. Secure the wiring harness to the motor with the tie wrap and reconnect the wiring harness to the motor.
20. Install the inboard and outboard side shields onto the upper supports and insert the mounting screws.
21. Install the fuel release bracket to the inside left hand riser, using 2 rivets.
22. Install the fuel release handle.
23. Install the seat cushion to the adjuster.
24. Install the seat adjuster to the floor pan and tighten the bolts to 32 ft. lbs. (43 Nm).
25. Install the power lead to the connector.
26. Connect the fuel door release cable to the fuel door release lever mechanism.
27. Connect the negative battery cable.

Headliner Panel Assembly

REMOVAL AND INSTALLATION

1. Disconnect the negative battery cable.
2. For ease of removal, remove the rear bench seat assembly, if so equipped.
3. Remove the right and left sun visor support brackets and remove the sun visors.
4. Remove the dome and courtesy light assemblies and body harness connectors.
5. Remove the coat hooks.
6. Remove the shoulder belt retainers and covers.
7. Loosen or remove if necessary, the rear quarter trim panels at the B, C and D-pillars.
8. Remove the rear liftgate headliner upper trim moulding.
9. Remove the headlining from the velcro strips attaching the headliner to the frame and located on both sides and rear liftgate end of the vehicle.

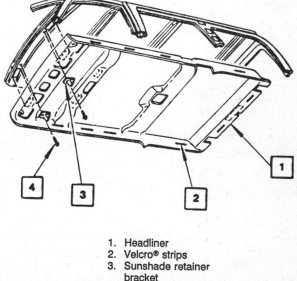

1. Headliner
2. Velcro® strips
3. Sunshade retainer bracket
4. Screws

Headliner panel assembly

10. With the aid of an assistant, remove the headliner through the liftgate opening.
To install:
14. Install the headliner into position with the aid of an assistant.
15. Align the headlining with the cutouts for the sunshades and dome lamps and press into place along the areas with velcro strips. Install the sunshade and dome lamp brackets.
16. Install all other previously removed hardware and interior mouldings.
17. Install the rear bench seat, if so equipped.
18. Install the negative battery cable.

How to Remove Stains from Fabric Interior

For best results, spots and stains should be removed as soon as possible. Never use gasoline, lacquer thinner, acetone, nail polish remover or bleach. Use a 3' x 3" piece of cheesecloth. Squeeze most of the liquid from the fabric and wipe the stained fabric from the outside of the stain toward the center with a lifting motion. Turn the cheesecloth as soon as one side becomes soiled. When using water to remove a stain, be sure to wash the entire section after the spot has been removed to avoid water stains. Encrusted spots can be broken up with a dull knife and vacuumed before removing the stain.

Type of Stain	How to Remove It
Surface spots	Brush the spots out with a small hand brush or use a commercial preparation such as K2R to lift the stain.
Mildew	Clean around the mildew with warm suds. Rinse in cold water and soak the mildew area in a solution of 1 part table salt and 2 parts water. Wash with upholstery cleaner.
Water stains	Water stains in fabric materials can be removed with a solution made from 1 cup of table salt dissolved in 1 quart of water. Vigorously scrub the solution into the stain and rinse with clear water. Water stains in nylon or other synthetic fabrics should be removed with a commercial type spot remover.
Chewing gum, tar, crayons, shoe polish (greasy stains)	Do not use a cleaner that will soften gum or tar. Harden the deposit with an ice cube and scrape away as much as possible with a dull knife. Moisten the remainder with cleaning fluid and scrub clean.
Ice cream, candy	Most candy has a sugar base and can be removed with a cloth wrung out in warm water. Oily candy, after cleaning with warm water, should be cleaned with upholstery cleaner. Rinse with warm water and clean the remainder with cleaning fluid.
Wine, alcohol, egg, milk, soft drink (non-greasy stains)	Do not use soap. Scrub the stain with a cloth wrung out in warm water. Remove the remainder with cleaning fluid.
Grease, oil, lipstick, butter and related stains	Use a spot remover to avoid leaving a ring. Work from the outisde of the stain to the center and dry with a clean cloth when the spot is gone.
Headliners (cloth)	Mix a solution of warm water and foam upholstery cleaner to give thick suds. Use only foam—liquid may streak or spot. Clean the entire headliner in one operation using a circular motion with a natural sponge.
Headliner (vinyl)	Use a vinyl cleaner with a sponge and wipe clean with a dry cloth.
Seats and door panels	Mix 1 pint upholstery cleaner in 1 gallon of water. Do not soak the fabric around the buttons.
Leather or vinyl fabric	Use a multi-purpose cleaner full strength and a stiff brush. Let stand 2 minutes and scrub thoroughly. Wipe with a clean, soft rag.
Nylon or synthetic fabrics	For normal stains, use the same procedures you would for washing cloth upholstery. If the fabric is extremely dirty, use a multi-purpose cleaner full strength with a stiff scrub brush. Scrub thoroughly in all directions and wipe with a cotton towel or soft rag.

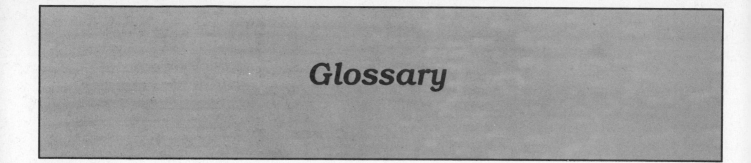
Glossary

AIR/FUEL RATIO: The ratio of air to gasoline by weight in the fuel mixture drawn into the engine.

AIR INJECTION: One method of reducing harmful exhaust emissions by injecting air into each of the exhaust ports of an engine. The fresh air entering the hot exhaust manifold causes any remaining fuel to be burned before it can exit the tailpipe.

ALTERNATOR: A device used for converting mechanical energy into electrical energy.

AMMETER: An instrument, calibrated in amperes, used to measure the flow of an electrical current in a circuit. Ammeters are always connected in series with the circuit being tested.

AMPERE: The rate of flow of electrical current present when one volt of electrical pressure is applied against one ohm of electrical resistance.

ANALOG COMPUTER: Any microprocessor that uses similar (analogous) electrical signals to make its calculations.

ARMATURE: A laminated, soft iron core wrapped by a wire that converts electrical energy to mechanical energy as in a motor or relay. When rotated in a magnetic field, it changes mechanical energy into electrical energy as in a generator.

ATMOSPHERIC PRESSURE: The pressure on the Earth's surface caused by the weight of the air in the atmosphere. At sea level, this pressure is 14.7 psi at 32°F (101 kPa at 0°C).

ATOMIZATION: The breaking down of a liquid into a fine mist that can be suspended in air.

AXIAL PLAY: Movement parallel to a shaft or bearing bore.

BACKFIRE: The sudden combustion of gases in the intake or exhaust system that results in a loud explosion.

BACKLASH: The clearance or play between two parts, such as meshed gears.

BACKPRESSURE: Restrictions in the exhaust system that slow the exit of exhaust gases from the combustion chamber.

BAKELITE: A heat resistant, plastic insulator material commonly used in printed circuit boards and transistorized components.

BALL BEARING: A bearing made up of hardened inner and outer races between which hardened steel balls roll.

BALLAST RESISTOR: A resistor in the primary ignition circuit that lowers voltage after the engine is started to reduce wear on ignition components.

BEARING: A friction reducing, supportive device usually located between a stationary part and a moving part.

BIMETAL TEMPERATURE SENSOR: Any sensor or switch made of two dissimilar types of metal that bend when heated or cooled due to the different expansion rates of the alloys. These types of sensors usually function as an on/off switch.

BLOWBY: Combustion gases, composed of water vapor and unburned fuel, that leak past the piston rings into the crankcase during normal engine operation. These gases are removed by the PCV system to prevent the buildup of harmful acids in the crankcase.

BRAKE PAD: A brake shoe and lining assembly used with disc brakes.

BRAKE SHOE: The backing for the brake lining. The term is, however, usually applied to the assembly of the brake backing and lining.

BUSHING: A liner, usually removable, for a bearing; an anti-friction liner used in place of a bearing.

BYPASS: System used to bypass ballast resistor during engine cranking to increase voltage supplied to the coil.

CALIPER: A hydraulically activated device in a disc brake system, which is mounted straddling the brake rotor (disc). The caliper contains at least one piston and two brake pads. Hydraulic pressure on the piston(s) forces the pads against the rotor.

CAMSHAFT: A shaft in the engine on which are the lobes (cams) which operate the valves. The camshaft is driven by the crankshaft, via a belt, chain or gears, at one half the crankshaft speed.

CAPACITOR: A device which stores an electrical charge.

CARBON MONOXIDE (CO): A colorless, odorless gas given off as a normal byproduct of combustion. It is poisonous and extremely dangerous in confined areas, building up slowly to toxic levels without warning if adequate ventilation is not available.

CARBURETOR: A device, usually mounted on the intake manifold of an engine, which mixes the air and fuel in the proper proportion to allow even combustion.

CATALYTIC CONVERTER: A device installed in the exhaust system, like a muffler, that converts harmful byproducts of combustion into carbon dioxide and water vapor by means of a heat-producing chemical reaction.

CENTRIFUGAL ADVANCE: A mechanical method of advancing the spark timing by using flyweights in the distributor that react to centrifugal force generated by the distributor shaft rotation.

CHECK VALVE: Any one-way valve installed to permit the flow of air, fuel or vacuum in one direction only.

GLOSSARY

CHOKE: A device, usually a moveable valve, placed in the intake path of a carburetor to restrict the flow of air.

CIRCUIT: Any unbroken path through which an electrical current can flow. Also used to describe fuel flow in some instances.

CIRCUIT BREAKER: A switch which protects an electrical circuit from overload by opening the circuit when the current flow exceeds a predetermined level. Some circuit breakers must be reset manually, while most reset automatically

COIL (IGNITION): A transformer in the ignition circuit which steps up the voltage provided to the spark plugs.

COMBINATION MANIFOLD: An assembly which includes both the intake and exhaust manifolds in one casting.

COMBINATION VALVE: A device used in some fuel systems that routes fuel vapors to a charcoal storage canister instead of venting them into the atmosphere. The valve relieves fuel tank pressure and allows fresh air into the tank as the fuel level drops to prevent a vapor lock situation.

COMPRESSION RATIO: The comparison of the total volume of the cylinder and combustion chamber with the piston at BDC and the piston at TDC.

CONDENSER: 1. An electrical device which acts to store an electrical charge, preventing voltage surges.
2. A radiator-like device in the air conditioning system in which refrigerant gas condenses into a liquid, giving off heat.

CONDUCTOR: Any material through which an electrical current can be transmitted easily.

CONTINUITY: Continuous or complete circuit. Can be checked with an ohmmeter.

COUNTERSHAFT: An intermediate shaft which is rotated by a mainshaft and transmits, in turn, that rotation to a working part.

CRANKCASE: The lower part of an engine in which the crankshaft and related parts operate.

CRANKSHAFT: The main driving shaft of an engine which receives reciprocating motion from the pistons and converts it to rotary motion.

CYLINDER: In an engine, the round hole in the engine block in which the piston(s) ride.

CYLINDER BLOCK: The main structural member of an engine in which is found the cylinders, crankshaft and other principal parts.

CYLINDER HEAD: The detachable portion of the engine, fastened, usually, to the top of the cylinder block, containing all or most of the combustion chambers. On overhead valve engines, it contains the valves and their operating parts. On overhead cam engines, it contains the camshaft as well.

DEAD CENTER: The extreme top or bottom of the piston stroke.

DETONATION: An unwanted explosion of the air/fuel mixture in the combustion chamber caused by excess heat and compression, advanced timing, or an overly lean mixture. Also referred to as "ping".

DIAPHRAGM: A thin, flexible wall separating two cavities, such as in a vacuum advance unit.

DIESELING: A condition in which hot spots in the combustion chamber cause the engine to run on after the key is turned off.

DIFFERENTIAL: A geared assembly which allows the transmission of motion between drive axles, giving one axle the ability to turn faster than the other.

DIODE: An electrical device that will allow current to flow in one direction only.

DISC BRAKE: A hydraulic braking assembly consisting of a brake disc, or rotor, mounted on an axle, and a caliper assembly containing, usually two brake pads which are activated by hydraulic pressure. The pads are forced against the sides of the disc, creating friction which slows the vehicle.

DISTRIBUTOR: A mechanically driven device on an engine which is responsible for electrically firing the spark plug at a predetermined point of the piston stroke.

DOWEL PIN: A pin, inserted in mating holes in two different parts allowing those parts to maintain a fixed relationship.

DRUM BRAKE: A braking system which consists of two brake shoes and one or two wheel cylinders, mounted on a fixed backing plate, and a brake drum, mounted on an axle, which revolves around the assembly. Hydraulic action applied to the wheel cylinders forces the shoes outward against the drum, creating friction, slowing the vehicle.

DWELL: The rate, measured in degrees of shaft rotation, at which an electrical circuit cycles on and off.

ELECTRONIC CONTROL UNIT (ECU): Ignition module, module, amplifier or igniter. See Module for definition.

ELECTRONIC IGNITION: A system in which the timing and firing of the spark plugs is controlled by an electronic control unit, usually called a module. These systems have no points or condenser.

ENDPLAY: The measured amount of axial movement in a shaft.

ENGINE: A device that converts heat into mechanical energy.

EXHAUST MANIFOLD: A set of cast passages or pipes which conduct exhaust gases from the engine.

FEELER GAUGE: A blade, usually metal, of precisely predetermined thickness, used to measure the clearance between two parts. These blades usually are available in sets of assorted thicknesses.

F-Head: An engine configuration in which the intake valves are in the cylinder head, while the camshaft and exhaust valves are located in the cylinder block. The camshaft operates the intake valves via lifters and pushrods, while it operates the exhaust valves directly.

FIRING ORDER: The order in which combustion occurs in the cylinders of an engine. Also the order in which spark is distributed to the plugs by the distributor.

FLATHEAD: An engine configuration in which the camshaft and all the valves are located in the cylinder block.

FLOODING: The presence of too much fuel in the intake manifold and combustion chamber which prevents the air/fuel mixture from firing, thereby causing a no-start situation.

FLYWHEEL: A disc shaped part bolted to the rear end of the crankshaft. Around the outer perimeter is affixed the ring gear. The starter drive engages the ring gear, turning the flywheel, which rotates the crankshaft, imparting the initial starting motion to the engine.

FOOT POUND (ft.lb. or sometimes, ft. lbs.): The amount of energy or work needed to raise an item weighing one pound, a distance of one foot.

FUSE: A protective device in a circuit which prevents circuit overload by breaking the circuit when a specific amperage is present. The device is constructed around a strip or wire of a lower amperage rating than the circuit it is designed to protect. When an amperage higher than that stamped on the fuse is present in the circuit, the strip or wire melts, opening the circuit.

GEAR RATIO: The ratio between the number of teeth on meshing gears.

GENERATOR: A device which converts mechanical energy into electrical energy.

HEAT RANGE: The measure of a spark plug's ability to dissipate heat from its firing end. The higher the heat range, the hotter the plug fires.

HUB: The center part of a wheel or gear.

HYDROCARBON (HC): Any chemical compound made up of hydrogen and carbon. A major pollutant formed by the engine as a byproduct of combustion.

HYDROMETER: An instrument used to measure the specific gravity of a solution.

INCH POUND (in.lb. or sometimes, in. lbs.): One twelfth of a foot pound.

INDUCTION: A means of transferring electrical energy in the form of a magnetic field. Principle used in the ignition coil to increase voltage.

INJECTION PUMP: A device, usually mechanically operated, which meters and delivers fuel under pressure to the fuel injector.

INJECTOR: A device which receives metered fuel under relatively low pressure and is activated to inject the fuel into the engine under relatively high pressure at a predetermined time.

INPUT SHAFT: The shaft to which torque is applied, usually carrying the driving gear or gears.

INTAKE MANIFOLD: A casting of passages or pipes used to conduct air or a fuel/air mixture to the cylinders.

JOURNAL: The bearing surface within which a shaft operates.

KEY: A small block usually fitted in a notch between a shaft and a hub to prevent slippage of the two parts.

MANIFOLD: A casting of passages or set of pipes which connect the cylinders to an inlet or outlet source.

MANIFOLD VACUUM: Low pressure in an engine intake manifold formed just below the throttle plates. Manifold vacuum is highest at idle and drops under acceleration.

MASTER CYLINDER: The primary fluid pressurizing device in a hydraulic system. In automotive use, it is found in brake and hydraulic clutch systems and is pedal activated, either directly or, in a power brake system, through the power booster.

MODULE: Electronic control unit, amplifier or igniter of solid state or integrated design which controls the current flow in the ignition primary circuit based on input from the pick-up coil. When the module opens the primary circuit, the high secondary voltage is induced in the coil.

NEEDLE BEARING: A bearing which consists of a number (usually a large number) of long, thin rollers.

OHM: (Ω) The unit used to measure the resistance of conductor to electrical flow. One ohm is the amount of resistance that limits current flow to one ampere in a circuit with one volt of pressure.

OHMMETER: An instrument used for measuring the resistance, in ohms, in an electrical circuit.

OUTPUT SHAFT: The shaft which transmits torque from a device, such as a transmission.

OVERDRIVE: A gear assembly which produces more shaft revolutions than that transmitted to it.

OVERHEAD CAMSHAFT (OHC): An engine configuration in which the camshaft is mounted on top of the cylinder head and operates the valve either directly or by means of rocker arms.

OVERHEAD VALVE (OHV): An engine configuration in which all of the valves are located in the cylinder head and the camshaft is located in the cylinder block. The camshaft operates the valves via lifters and pushrods.

OXIDES OF NITROGEN (NOx): Chemical compounds of nitrogen produced as a byproduct of combustion. They combine with hydrocarbons to produce smog.

OXYGEN SENSOR: Used with the feedback system to sense the presence of oxygen in the exhaust gas and signal the computer which can reference the voltage signal to an air/fuel ratio.

PINION: The smaller of two meshing gears.

PISTON RING: An open ended ring which fits into a groove on the outer diameter of the piston. Its chief function is to form a seal between the piston and cylinder wall. Most automotive pistons have three rings: two for compression sealing; one for oil sealing.

PRELOAD: A predetermined load placed on a bearing during assembly or by adjustment.

PRIMARY CIRCUIT: Is the low voltage side of the ignition system which consists of the ignition switch, ballast resistor or resistance wire, bypass, coil, electronic control unit and pick-up coil as well as the connecting wires and harnesses.

PRESS FIT: The mating of two parts under pressure, due to the inner diameter of one being smaller than the outer diameter of the other, or vice versa; an interference fit.

GLOSSARY

RACE: The surface on the inner or outer ring of a bearing on which the balls, needles or rollers move.

REGULATOR: A device which maintains the amperage and/or voltage levels of a circuit at predetermined values.

RELAY: A switch which automatically opens and/or closes a circuit.

RESISTANCE: The opposition to the flow of current through a circuit or electrical device, and is measured in ohms. Resistance is equal to the voltage divided by the amperage.

RESISTOR: A device, usually made of wire, which offers a preset amount of resistance in an electrical circuit.

RING GEAR: The name given to a ring-shaped gear attached to a differential case, or affixed to a flywheel or as part a planetary gear set.

ROLLER BEARING: A bearing made up of hardened inner and outer races between which hardened steel rollers move.

ROTOR: 1. The disc-shaped part of a disc brake assembly, upon which the brake pads bear; also called, brake disc.
2. The device mounted atop the distributor shaft, which passes current to the distributor cap tower contacts.

SECONDARY CIRCUIT: The high voltage side of the ignition system, usually above 20,000 volts. The secondary includes the ignition coil, coil wire, distributor cap and rotor, spark plug wires and spark plugs.

SENDING UNIT: A mechanical, electrical, hydraulic or electromagnetic device which transmits information to a gauge.

SENSOR: Any device designed to measure engine operating conditions or ambient pressures and temperatures. Usually electronic in nature and designed to send a voltage signal to an on-board computer, some sensors may operate as a simple on/off switch or they may provide a variable voltage signal (like a potentiometer) as conditions or measured parameters change.

SHIM: Spacers of precise, predetermined thickness used between parts to establish a proper working relationship.

SLAVE CYLINDER: In automotive use, a device in the hydraulic clutch system which is activated by hydraulic force, disengaging the clutch.

SOLENOID: A coil used to produce a magnetic field, the effect of which is produce work.

SPARK PLUG: A device screwed into the combustion chamber of a spark ignition engine. The basic construction is a conductive core inside of a ceramic insulator, mounted in an outer conductive base. An electrical charge from the spark plug wire travels along the conductive core and jumps a preset air gap to a grounding point or points at the end of the conductive base. The resultant spark ignites the fuel/air mixture in the combustion chamber.

SPLINES: Ridges machined or cast onto the outer diameter of a shaft or inner diameter of a bore to enable parts to mate without rotation.

TACHOMETER: A device used to measure the rotary speed of an engine, shaft, gear, etc., usually in rotations per minute.

THERMOSTAT: A valve, located in the cooling system of an engine, which is closed when cold and opens gradually in response to engine heating, controlling the temperature of the coolant and rate of coolant flow.

TOP DEAD CENTER (TDC): The point at which the piston reaches the top of its travel on the compression stroke.

TORQUE: The twisting force applied to an object.

TORQUE CONVERTER: A turbine used to transmit power from a driving member to a driven member via hydraulic action, providing changes in drive ratio and torque. In automotive use, it links the driveplate at the rear of the engine to the automatic transmission.

TRANSDUCER: A device used to change a force into an electrical signal.

TRANSISTOR: A semi-conductor component which can be actuated by a small voltage to perform an electrical switching function.

TUNE-UP: A regular maintenance function, usually associated with the replacement and adjustment of parts and components in the electrical and fuel systems of a vehicle for the purpose of attaining optimum performance.

TURBOCHARGER: An exhaust driven pump which compresses intake air and forces it into the combustion chambers at higher than atmospheric pressures. The increased air pressure allows more fuel to be burned and results in increased horsepower being produced.

VACUUM ADVANCE: A device which advances the ignition timing in response to increased engine vacuum.

VACUUM GAUGE: An instrument used to measure the presence of vacuum in a chamber.

VALVE: A device which control the pressure, direction of flow or rate of flow of a liquid or gas.

VALVE CLEARANCE: The measured gap between the end of the valve stem and the rocker arm, cam lobe or follower that activates the valve.

VISCOSITY: The rating of a liquid's internal resistance to flow.

VOLTMETER: An instrument used for measuring electrical force in units called volts. Voltmeters are always connected parallel with the circuit being tested.

WHEEL CYLINDER: Found in the automotive drum brake assembly, it is a device, actuated by hydraulic pressure, which, through internal pistons, pushes the brake shoes outward against the drums.